Blake's Agitation

Blake's Agitation

criticism & the emotions

STEVEN GOLDSMITH

The Johns Hopkins University Press
Baltimore

The Johns Hopkins University Press
2715 North Charles Street
Baltimore, Maryland 21218-4363
www.press.jhu.edu

Library of Congress Cataloging-in-Publication Data

Goldsmith, Steven, 1959–
Blake's agitation : criticism and the emotions / Steven Goldsmith.
    p.   cm.
Includes bibliographical references and index.
ISBN 978-1-4214-0806-4 (hdbk. : alk. paper) — ISBN 1-4214-0806-6 (hdbk. : alk. paper)
1. Blake, William, 1757–1827—Criticism and interpretation. 2. Emotions in literature.
3. Emotions (Philosophy) I. Title.
    PR4147.G65 2013
    821'.7—dc23   2012018228

A catalog record for this book is available from the British Library.

*Special discounts are available for bulk purchases of this book. For more information,
please contact Special Sales at 410-516-6936 or specialsales@press.jhu.edu.*

The Johns Hopkins University Press uses environmentally friendly
book materials, including recycled text paper that is composed of at least
30 percent post-consumer waste, whenever possible.

For Cathy

Contents

Blake's Agitation

The Future of Enthusiasm

Men are admitted into Heaven not because they have <curbed &>
governd their Passions or have No Passions but because they have
Cultivated their Understandings. The Treasures of Heaven are not
Negations of Passion but Realities of Intellect from which All the
Passions Emanate <Uncurbed> in their Eternal Glory
> —William Blake, "A Vision of The Last Judgment"

[F]eeling is no compass (nothing is more deceptive).
> —Sharon Cameron, *Impersonality*

This book begins with an assumption not every reader will share: that it is exciting, even viscerally exciting, to read William Blake. My premise does not deny
Blake's difficulty, a quality obvious to anyone who has ventured beyond his initial
songs. Reading Blake is more often agitating than simply pleasurable, but it is an
exhilarating experience nonetheless. Blake himself had a phrase for the kind of
response, at once intellectual and affective, that he hoped for from his audience:
rather than being passive spectators, they should enter into his work "on the Fiery
Chariot of [their] Contemplative Thought."[1] My interest lies in understanding that
fiery feeling within critical thought, where it comes from and what it is doing
there. For those who disagree with my initial assumption that it *is* there, perhaps it
may suffice if they find their contemplation warmed and mobilized when reading
other difficult authors—such as John Keats, or Herman Melville, or Simone Weil.

This book also begins with a question. Few writers have generated as much enthusiasm in their committed readers as Blake, but is our enthusiasm for Blake to
be trusted? Seeking to explain why such doubt would arise in the first place, I argue
that a question of this kind opens onto a broad consideration of critical agency as
it has been understood and practiced by progressive intellectuals since the Romantic period. On one level, this book is a sustained phenomenology of critical

excitement. I describe as specifically (and sympathetically) as possible the deeply attractive enthusiasm—the particular feeling of engaged, dynamic urgency—that characterizes criticism as a mode of action in Blake's own work, in Blake scholarship, and in recent theoretical writings that identify the heightened affect of critical thought with the potential for genuine historical change. Within each of these horizons, the critical thinker's enthusiasm serves to substantiate his or her agency in the world, supplying immediate, embodied evidence that criticism is not merely another thought-form among others but an action of consequence, accessing or even enabling the conditions of new possibility necessary for historical transformation to occur at all.

Of course this is to move all too quickly from a personal observation about reading Blake to a large, even extravagant, claim about emotion in modern criticism, one that will take the entirety of this book to substantiate, test, and modify. Perhaps the first, most efficient way to give this claim form is to attach it to an example, and one not from Blake. In the final chapter of *Marxism and Form,* where Fredric Jameson models "dialectical thinking in general, as a form in time, as process, as a lived experience of a peculiar and determinate structure,"[2] he does not dwell on the affective dimension of this process. Time and again, however, he resorts to the self-evidence of feeling at crucial junctures of his argument, specifically, whenever he would distinguish genuine critical activity from all the routine thought systems (including bad Marxism) that prevent the mind from approaching what he variously calls "history," the "totality," and "the concrete itself." The characteristic feature of dialectical thought, as Jameson describes it, is its power to reflect on and pressure the limits of its own mediating forms, thus raising thought "to the second power": "This is indeed the most sensitive moment in the dialectical process: that in which an entire complex of thought is hoisted through a kind of inner leverage one floor higher" (307–308). When thought leverages itself upward in this way, calling into question its previously unexamined categories and thus superseding concepts it had mistakenly assumed to be natural, the moment is *literally* "sensitive" (registered as an embodied feeling), for in the next paragraph Jameson describes this discomfiting experience as a kind of intellectual motion sickness:

> There is a breathlessness about this shift from the normal object-oriented activity of the mind to such dialectical self-consciousness—something of the sickening shudder we feel in an elevator's fall or in the sudden dip in an airliner. That recalls us to our bodies much as this recalls us to our mental positions as thinkers and observers. The shock indeed is basic, and constitutive of the dialectic as such: without this transformational moment, without this initial conscious transcendence of an older,

more naïve position, there can be no question of any genuinely dialectical coming to consciousness. (308)

That the awareness of historical contingency enters consciousness through feeling will continue to be a hallmark of Jameson's work: it underlies the idea that "History is what hurts" in *The Political Unconscious,* just as it informs the lament over the "waning of affect" in *Postmodernism, or, the Cultural Logic of Late Capitalism.*³ What makes this passage representative, however, at least for our purpose here, is not just the persistence of such affective appeals across Jameson's career. It is the understanding that the distinctive affective texture of critical thought as it is happening is also evidence of criticism's agency, evidence of its power to participate in and effect transformation. Jameson is not simply drawing an analogy between mind and body, borrowing imagery of the latter to give weight to the former. He is making a stronger claim: that the critical mind is itself embodied, situated, in motion, and receptive to shock—moreover, that its collapse of any Cartesian scheme rigidly separating mental and material processes is central to its innovative potential. In fact the mind in critical action accomplishes the reconciliation between phenomenology and Marxism he establishes as one of his initial goals, for if phenomenology "is precisely the attempt to tell not what a thought is, so much as what it feels like" (*Marxism* 306), then Jameson is attempting to tell us what genuine Marxist thought feels like. And there can be no mistaking the enthusiasm Jameson feels for this moment of affective disturbance in criticism, despite the displeasure (the "sickening shudder") that defines it. The turbulence that occurs when thought is thrown off its routine confirms the moment's effectiveness; it is the guarantee that something *new* is happening. Its absence would indicate the opposite: a thinker too much at ease with a received conceptual framework, too comfortable within the static "realism" of the present moment. Emotion supplies this test whenever Jameson needs a way to distinguish between a criticism that innovates and a criticism that conforms to established paradigms. Its presence or absence, for instance, allows us to tell the difference between the programmatic historical determinism he deplores and the idea of historical necessity he prefers (a difference that is "more a question of a feeling than of a concept" [360]).⁴ Not only is "epistemological shock . . . constitutive of and inseparable from dialectical thinking" as such, its absence is "the telltale symptom of the nondialectical character of much of what passes for Marxist criticism" (375).

At this early stage of our exposition, it is enough to observe the centrality of emotion in Jameson's account of criticism, but before we take leave of this first example, we should note one thing further: the striking tension generated by the rhetorical figures he summons in order to visualize dialectical criticism spatially. On the one hand, critical activity occurs when "an entire complex of thought is hoisted through a kind of inner leverage one floor higher"; on the other, "this initial conscious *transcendence* of an older, more naïve position" involves the *sinking* feeling he mentions: "the sickening shudder we feel in an elevator's fall." Elevator movements would continue to fascinate Jameson. One recalls his description of the saturated hyperspace of the Westin Bonaventure in Los Angeles, with its elevators "rapidly shooting up through the ceiling" and "plummeting back down through the roof to splash down in the lake."[5] Here, however, in Jameson's spatial imaging of critical activity, these contrary motions serve a different purpose: the upward invokes the intellectual activity of rising above the unreflective forms that thought now submits to analysis; the downward reassures us that this new wave of thought is not another empty ascent into abstraction but remains grounded below, always recalling us to material existence. Even the word "hoist" ("thought is hoisted . . . one floor higher") labors rhetorically to incorporate physical strain and mechanical force into the mental act, as if thought were engaging gravity as well as mental error in order to rise. Feeling belongs on the side of this grounding and descent; its "shock indeed is basic," taking place at the level of the base (a term not to be taken lightly in this discourse). But Jameson's confusing figures (are we rising or falling when we think dialectically?) do more than conveniently illustrate aspects of critical thought that for heuristic purposes might be treated separately. In their impossible simultaneity (rising and falling in one motion), these figures jolt the reader into the very state of disorientation Jameson is describing; that is, they are meant *to generate* the feeling of vertigo provoked by the abrupt loss of conceptual bearings. Similar crossings of descriptive and enactive functions occur often in the critical discourses we will be examining. It is rarely enough for an author to describe critical emotions, for these emotions serve most persuasively as evidence of intellectual agency when they are performed, activated, felt.

In Jameson's case, there is a great deal at stake in making this a convincing performance, for the reader's subjective turbulence is the sign of his closer approach to something much larger than his individual or personal embodiment; it indicates his contact with historical dynamism itself, with the fluid medium of temporal and social change that usually remains hidden beneath the culturally generated illusion of a solid, stable reality. Jameson describes dialectical thinking as "a ceaseless generation and dissolution of intellectual categories" (*Marxism* 336), in which thought ultimately "strains to return to that concrete element from which it initially came, to abolish itself as an illusion of autonomy, and to redissolve into history, offering as it does so some momentary glimpse of reality as a concrete whole" (312). Fleetingly and partially, critical feeling accesses this moving "concrete whole" in a way no concept could. (Concepts ordinarily "reify"; they oc-clude this dynamic totality by abstracting aspects of it and giving these limited parts too definite a form.) Thus, by tapping into this dynamic potentiality, the dis-oriented feeling that criticism produces in the present is also an opening onto the future, and Jameson's strongest motive for scrambling the vertical axis of dialecti-cal thought—for confusing rising self-reflection and sinking feeling—is to point the thinking process forward, putting it in contact with new, unthinkable possi-bilities that the present state of "realism" would preclude altogether. In the final sentences of *Marxism and Form*, after lamenting the degree to which "thought as-phyxiates in our culture, with its absolute inability to imagine anything other than what is," Jameson calls upon literary criticism "to keep alive the idea of a concrete future." He finishes with an emotional flourish of his own: "May it prove equal to the task!" (416). Whatever his uncertainty about the extent to which criticism can realize its powers, Jameson sides with enthusiasm against realism—indeed, in an earlier passage he identifies "enthusiasm" with "speculation itself" and the "intellectual transcendence of the empirical present" (367), in other words, with the ability to imagine anything other than what is. The future of criticism depends on this work of emotion. But the stakes are even larger than that, going far beyond the narrow considerations of an academic method or discipline. *Any* future that would be more than a functional extension of present conceptions depends on this forward-moving work of emotion.

These three assumptions—that emotion is the index of an authentic criticism; that this is so because authentic critical thought is a dynamic, materialist action, involving mind, body, and history; and finally that the emotion in criticism acts by impelling thought progressively into the future—are the hallmarks of the mod-ern understanding of criticism addressed in this book. Not every critical practice evinces all of these assumptions, and some do not appear to evince any (one need only recall the anti-affective strain running from Wimsatt and Beardsley to de Man),[6] but if Jameson's case is at all representative, and I believe that it is, then the enthusiasm in criticism, when it does appear, advances large claims indeed. But now we must return to my original question: can the enthusiasm in criticism be trusted? Jameson's is itself a deeply suspicious model of criticism. Dialectical self-consciousness must always be raising its own thought processes to the sec-ond power precisely because thought is ordinarily so one-dimensional, mislead-ing, and unreliable. Yet curiously Jameson never proposes that we hoist *feeling* one floor higher, making *it* the object of skeptical analysis. Instead, he allows feeling to stand—at least in its agitating form—as the inherently trustworthy sign of a historically saturated and forward-moving intellectual agency.

Although we can understand the need for this affective ratification (without it a modern critical thinker would have little confidence that his or her thought is genuinely breaking forward rather than rearranging received ideas and running in place), two parallel problems underlie my own concerns about the self-evidence of affective agency in criticism. *Regarding Blake:* Why did Blake continue to think his work was of *public* importance long after he realized he would never have a wide or capable audience, at least in his lifetime? How did he maintain his conviction that the radical enthusiasm conveyed by his work mattered, even in the absence of readers who would connect him to the "long seventeenth-century" project of corporate intellectual labor that Joanna Picciotto has recently described and that Blake himself envisioned mythically and nationally in the figure of rising Albion?[7] *Regarding us:* On the basis of what evidence could we demonstrate that progressive acts of criticism produce anything like the historical effects we generally desire for them? John Guillory has recently warned that academic critics "tend to indulge in . . . a political fantasy . . . of transforming the world to a degree vastly greater than can reasonably be expected of perhaps any disciplinary practice."[8]

Enthusiasm responds to *this* charge, and thus we can begin to understand the heavy lifting that studies of emotion have been asked to perform in our current academic culture (a workload that has risen exponentially in the forty years since *Marxism and Form*): in the sustained interest in literatures of sentimentalism and sensibility; in the wide attention paid to theories of affect, emotion, and feeling; in the tendency of new formalists to defend aesthetics on the basis of the heightened feeling of agency that form can provoke in a receptive audience. Enthusiasm answers Guillory's charge of fantasy with the substantive effect of powerful feeling: affective disturbance or exhilaration *is* the sign that, rather than making nothing happen, critical thinking makes something real happen. The embodied agitation we call "emotion" stands in as a personal token, in immediate experience and in the body's turmoil, of larger vectors of change already underway and unpredictable changes still to come. But enthusiasm also underscores the doubts raised by Guillory as soon as we try to explain how the dynamism of critical thought opens onto wider, observable effects in the social or political world. "It will be said that it is a very subtle and indirect action which I am thus prescribing for criticism," writes Matthew Arnold, anticipating the defensive maneuvers that writers of all political persuasions will undertake to explain why we should believe that critical thought rises above anything more than personal or ephemeral significance.[9] Starting with Romanticism, modern enthusiasm is always subject to irreconcilable characterizations: either it is the affective engine of history, bearing a volatile, unpredictable energy that is the very condition of future-oriented change (something Derrida calls "teleiopoesis"),[10] or it is a defensive posture intellectuals sometimes adopt to persuade themselves their work matters, even when little empirical evidence arises to support that conclusion.

To state the scope of my inquiry in plain terms, this book examines the work emotion is called upon to perform in the practices and idioms of modern critical engagement: first in Blake himself, who labored within and against his era's new promise of affective agency; then in Blake's reception history, which is structured by tensions found in Blake's own work; and finally in those post-Romantic critics who find they must pass through the intersection of emotion and agency whenever they wish to suggest, following Marx, that criticism might change the world and not just interpret it. To put matters another way, this book pursues three ambitions: (1) to turn the academic study *of* emotion—a topic at the center of scholarly concern for two decades now and across multiple disciplines—into a study of emotion *in* acts of criticism themselves; (2) to situate historically the emergence of emotion as a constitutive element of critical engagement by examining the surprisingly representative case of William Blake; (3) to consider why the work of emotion persists in post-Romantic criticism—and specifically, why it calls for but does not ultimately yield to demystification.

Old and New Enthusiasms

By now it will be clear that my account of enthusiasm in criticism does not adhere to the usual meanings of "enthusiasm." That is, I am following neither the pejorative eighteenth-century usage most famously enshrined in Samuel Johnson's definition of "enthusiasm" ("A vain belief of private revelation; a vain confidence of divine favour or communication"),[11] in which the word functions as a synonym for fanaticism, nor our own popular meaning of passionate excitement of any kind (for orchids, say, or baseball), a usage that carries generally positive connotations even if it is still sometimes hedged with concerns about irrational excess. To begin a discussion of Blake's enthusiasm by pairing it with Jameson's and thus to orient that enthusiasm toward the future of modern critical practices will quickly raise the eyebrows of anyone familiar with the dominant historicist trends in Blake criticism. The best recent work—by Jon Mee, Saree Makdisi, and others—has explicated Blake's enthusiasm by pointing it *backwards* in time, thereby affirming E. P. Thompson's assertion that "The closer we are to 1650 [that is, the closer we are to premodern, antinomian sources], the closer we seem to be to Blake."[12] According to this persuasive and well-established view, we hear Blake's voice most clearly when we set it resonating within a diverse chorus of fellow enthusiasts in the 1790s who revived the earlier voices of seventeenth-century Diggers, Ranters, and other disreputable, radical dissenters. It is hard to believe, then, that the Blake backdated by historicists today was born only 250 years ago; he seems at least a century older, keeping spiritual company with such antediluvians as Gerrard Winstanley and Abiezer Coppe.

By attaching Blake to a residual premodern culture in this way, recent historicists have generally sought to recover the power and integrity of a remote plebeian "enthusiasm" that was diminished but still vital in Blake's era and that continued to act as an underground resource for those, like Blake, resisting incipient modernization. By looking back through the 1790s to the seventeenth century, these scholars have also succeeded in prying "enthusiasm" loose from its subsequent semantic history, redeeming it first from its use as an Enlightenment, regulatory "smear-word"[13] (designating, as in Johnson's definition, a wayward religious intensity against which secular modernity was defining itself) and then from the long-range semantic changes that would eventually transform once "dangerous enthusiasm" into its current innocuous and feel-good form.[14] By 1967, Norman Vincent Peale, the original self-help guru, represented two centuries' worth of cultural and linguistic disarmament when he supplemented his international bestseller *The Power of Positive Thinking* with a new volume urging those competing in the boom corporate economy to understand that, if they wished to get ahead, *Enthusiasm Makes the Difference*.[15] By anchoring Blake in the distant past, the historicist trend has been to detach him from this modernizing future of socially regulated energies and economically self-serving passions, thus firmly establishing his premodernity as a bulwark *against* modernity.

At the same time, there has always been an opposite tendency in Blake criticism: a tendency to read him forward, to see him not as "a very Aged Man" straddling the premodern era but as a figure of "Eternal Youth" whose enthusiasm is a kind of perpetual kindling always ready to be ignited anew, in the present, by the reader's own enthusiastic response.[16] More than twenty-five years ago, when Hazard Adams cautioned fellow Blakeans about the rising tide of poststructuralism in Romantic studies, he too found himself (like Peale, though for different reasons) counseling that enthusiasm makes the difference: "Blake scholarship and criticism ought to be involved in making [Blake's] messages available to a needy world . . . Blake's messages are mainly ones of enthusiasm and good news, and there is no reason for our sense of our various tasks with Blake not to be enthusiastic, too."[17] Given the reputation of seventeenth- and eighteenth-century enthusiasm for contagious volatility and a tendency to overcome containment and spread to others, Adams's call for a mimetic criticism *on* enthusiasm can hardly come as a surprise. According to Pope, Longinus became what he beheld by writing about the Homeric sublime "with a *Poet's Fire*"; something similar might be said of Blake's critics, who often cannot resist expressing the enthusiasm they set out to describe historically and analytically.[18] Caught up in Northrop Frye's "fiery understanding," early reviewers of *Fearful Symmetry* singled out for praise those very qualities in which the critic most fully resembled his subject: his "unflagging energy" and "great enthusiasm."[19] Jon Mee acknowledges that his own recent book on enthusiasm, which culminates in a chapter on Blake, "is also perhaps itself a work of reckless enthusiasm" (1). Any reader of Saree Makdisi's indispensable *William Blake and the Impossible History of the 1790s,* a book this study will return to often, can instantly recognize that the dynamic, materialist "striving" he admires in Blake—"always becoming anew, tracing and retracing different trajectories of actualization, existing in and as and through *striving*" (320)—also describes the exuberant metamorphic cascade of his own fierce rushing prose. Or consider Laura Quinney's preface to *William Blake on Self and Soul,* which begins by declaring, "It has always been clear that William Blake was both a political radical and a radical psychologist," and ends by affirming the critic's decision to mime Blake's affect: "This book is sympathetically and passionately written, not because I share all of Blake's ideas, but because I think that their forcefulness is part of their meaning, and to convey their meaning I had to muster as much of their force as I could."[20]

The point of this brief, selective survey is that Blake's enthusiasm runs backward *and* forward; its power derives from its historical difference (as reconstructed by scholarship) and yet it remains current, vital, and available. Gathering its affective force from sources that are "essentially untranslatable into a modern idiom" (Makdisi 315), this enthusiasm launches itself into an altogether different historical moment (ours), one that would seem to preclude the possibility of its reemergence but somehow does not. It's as if enthusiasm itself were a continuously streaming counterpoint to modernity, a potentiality to be otherwise, a future waiting to be mobilized by an audience whose faculties will have been properly roused to act. The desire to historicize enthusiasm, and thus to identify its difference from our own modernity, is indistinguishable from a desire to activate that difference anew, to put it to work in our still needy world. In Blake criticism, enthusiasm has been every bit as much about enabling the future as it has been about respecting the archive of neglected premodern radicals.[21]

There is more to this recursive relationship between old and new enthusiasms than the idea, longstanding in the rhetoric manuals, that strong emotion can leap the temporal and spatial boundaries between subjects, that "by the contagion of our passions, we catch a fire already kindled in another," as Edmund Burke puts it in the concluding section of his *Philosophical Enquiry,* "How WORDS influence the passions."[22] In modern critical practice, enthusiasm has often served to persuade us that there *is* a future outside or beyond our own dissatisfying modernity, that "impossible history" is not only possible but taking shape right now in the affective experience of reading.[23] This is the task of criticism as Jameson conceives of it: to keep alive the idea of a concrete future as we read and think. The recent interest in enthusiasm among Blake scholars provides us with a convenient starting point, for it allows us to see that even the historicist reconstruction of the past can be driven along by an affective investment in enabling future possibilities, but Blake critics are by no means alone right now in emphasizing the innovative agency of emotion. If "affect too has a history" (1), as Mee suggests, perhaps with Foucault in mind, then this reminder bears just as forcefully on our own affects as it does on the cultural specificity of earlier forms of emotion.[24] The recent Blake scholarship, after all, participates in a much larger academic trend: a sustained, interdisciplinary "surge" in the theoretical, historical, and cognitive study of emotion that has prompted one of its leading contributors, Rei Terada, to "wonder where the attraction to emotion comes from and why it comes just now." [25] Momentarily setting aside the question of what emotion *is*, Terada turns a historicist eye on the present to ask what emotion *does*, and does *now*: what work does our enthusiasm for emotion perform in our own critical practices and our own academic culture?[26] Toward the end of this book, we will consider Terada's important self-reflection more fully. For the moment it is sufficient simply to note the abundance and variety of recent academic work on the emotions, work that forms as crucial (although mostly unrecognized) a context for the recent investigations into Blake's enthusiasm as do seventeenth-century precedents. We can learn a great deal about the motives and assumptions of Blake criticism by considering it alongside works like Terada's *Feeling in Theory* (2001), Martha Nussbaum's *Upheavals of Thought* (2001), William Reddy's *The Navigation of Feeling* (2001), Brian Massumi's *Parables for the Virtual* (2002), Philip Fisher's *The Vehement Passions* (2002), Eve Kosofsky Sedgwick's *Touching Feeling* (2003), Charles Altieri's *The Particulars of Rapture* (2003), Sianne Ngai's *Ugly Feelings* (2005), Denise Riley's *Impersonal Passion* (2005), Thomas Pfau's *Romantic Moods* (2005), Jenefer Robinson's *Deeper Than Reason* (2005), and Daniel Gross's *The Secret History of Emotion* (2006), to mention only a few of the major books on the subject that appeared in the same five-year period as the Blake studies by Mee and Makdisi.[27]

By calling attention to the contemporaneity of our own uses of emotion, I am not claiming that *our* enthusiasm has anachronistically displaced Blake's, as if his remains fundamentally removed from our own present needs. Indeed I am arguing rather the opposite: that Blake's enthusiasm, despite its premodern roots, is already a substantially modern phenomenon and that the current academic enthusiasm for emotion belongs to a continuum that includes Blake as an early practitioner. In this regard, Nicholas Williams is exactly right to see Blake's emphasis on elusive motion and vital energy ("the only life") as a forerunner of Brian Massumi's influential work on "Movement, Affect, Sensation" (the subtitle of his *Parables for the Virtual*). Williams suggests, moreover, that Blake is "perhaps the exemplary instance for thinking more broadly about what a moving criticism, a criticism of energies and intensities, might be."[28] Our critical practices are not so much a departure from Blake's enthusiasm or a falling away but rather a future already held within it. Already in Blake we see the poet turning emotion (pity and wrath, pathos and joy) into an object of critical study, while also insisting that feeling (the *arousal* of the faculties, the *fiery chariot* of contemplative thought) is itself the index of critical agency in action. Already in Blake we see that the affective moment in interpretation—the one Satan's Enlightenment watchfiends cannot find—promises to open onto an unknown future inaccessible to strictly instrumental forms of cognition. And, perhaps most importantly, we already see in Blake's enthusiasm the work many progressive artists and critics will continually ask of emotion for the next two hundred years: that it supply immediate, experiential evidence of a transformative agency whose effects cannot otherwise be measured. Rousing the faculties into action, enthusiasm aims to convince the mobilized reader that critical engagement does not merely interpret a needy world but (as Marx would urge) changes it, widening its possibilities—even when no empirical evidence exists to confirm that outcome.[29]

In all of these ways, Blake anticipates us as much as he revives 1650. By us, I mean not only Blake critics but a wide range of enthusiasts, humanists and posthumanists among them: those who, contesting "Descartes' Error,"[30] would agree with Blake that the body is a portion of the soul and that emotion lies at the origin of transformational energies that are at once intellectual *and* embodied. Blake stands at the early stage of a modern critical legacy that posits the agency of emotion within and against a world that would subordinate the full capabilities of response and action to instrumental reason. Against the old Enlightenment charge that enthusiasm dangerously overleaps the space of reflection and is therefore incompatible with the intellectual distance required by modern critical judgment, against the charge that errant enthusiasm relies instead on experiential immediacy as evidence of its authenticity, this legacy integrates the immediacy of enthusiasm into critical practice, placing charged affect at the vanguard of critique, creativity, and change.

The affective mimesis between Blake and his modern readers will occupy our attention throughout this book, and, as I indicated above, Makdisi's *Impossible History* becomes an especially important touchstone in this regard. As much as any other Blake enthusiast in a long history of such types, including Yeats and Frye, Makdisi mobilizes readerly exhilaration to the point where it promises, by its own affective momentum, to break free from social and ideological constraints that otherwise seem insurmountable. Central to my argument, however, is that enthusiasm is not a rare, specialized occurrence within criticism, limited only to the most extravagant forms of expression, to particular styles or methodologies, or to study of a few select authors. It is far more pervasive and various than that. Consider two less obvious cases. Both are drawn from recent Romantic criticism and both (like much other current criticism) address the topic of emotion explicitly, but they also differ strikingly from one another: one is small, pointed and still within the narrow sphere of Blake studies; the other is vastly ambitious, aiming to do no less than map a structural history of European Romanticism as a series of changes in the collective experience of emotion. Together they might indicate some of the expressive range of modern critical enthusiasm, which can be as loud, bold, and deliberately overheated as Blake himself often chose to be but can also operate in subtler tonalities.

James Chandler's "Blake and the Syntax of Sentiment" is one of three essays in the recent collection *Blake, Nation and Empire* devoted to demonstrating that "Blake's work is implicitly structured in and against the sentimental as a moral and aesthetic mode."[31] Comprehensive study of Blake's involvement with sentimentalism and "middle-class polite culture" (104) is long overdue, and these three essays begin to fill the void. Although each one considers the affective bonds engineered by sentimentalism to be inseparable from the Romantic period's production of national identity, Chandler's essay is particularly noteworthy because its analysis operates at the precise point of mediation between general social structures and Blake's stubborn textual particularity. According to Chandler, Blake recognized that emotions of the kind Adam Smith called "moral sentiments" function like a language, with their own generalizing syntax. Within the program adumbrated in *Theory of Moral Sentiments,* one can only identify sympathetically with other people's suffering when their feelings have been made intelligible; to ask another "What has befallen you?" is to ask her (yes, usually "her") to translate the singularity of actual, painful experience into a form of virtual representation general enough to be shared. Using terms reminiscent of his vocabulary of cases and general categories in *England in 1819,* Chandler suggests that sympathy so conceived requires the "disembodiment" of feeling and its "virtual reembodiment" in a conventional medium accessible to (because shared by) the imaginations of others (107). It is precisely this internal mechanism of generalization, this syntax of emotion turned second nature, that Blake inhabits and jams when he uses "sentimental devices to overturn sentiment" (110). Exposing the scaffolding beneath its illusion of spontaneity, Blake allows us to glimpse that sentiment is "made," and he can do this only by "unmaking" it from within, by exploiting the loose joints of its grammatical construction. Tracking this interior process involves Chandler in a microscopic analysis of representative lyrics from *Songs of Innocence and of Experience,* for the kinds of abrasions that "denaturalize sentiments" (114) turn on the disjunctions of single words or phrases. Consider, for instance, the word "tender" in a line from "The Shepherd": "And he hears the ewes tender reply." Without the expected apostrophe in "ewes," as Chandler notes shrewdly, " 'tender' becomes an economic verb rather than a sentimental adjective" (113). By inviting this small grammatical ambiguity, Blake not only emphasizes "the madeness of the sentiments" but also directs our attention to sentimentalism's underlying economic function—to smooth the social transactions necessary to make commerce seem natural. Time and again in the *Songs,* Blake troubles sentimentalism by ventriloquizing it from within, by making its discursive mechanisms slip even as they speak.

Chandler's understanding of Blake's critique of sentimentalism runs closely parallel to my own, and in the second half of this book we will return to this topic at length when we consider the poem "On Anothers Sorrow" and Blake's other experiments with sympathy. Here, however, I want to point out that Blake's performative critique of emotion and Chandler's account of its intricate grammar each involve an affective texture of their own. It is in fact difficult to separate the two. The syntactical density and complication *within these poems,* as laid bare by Chandler's technical analysis, correspond to an affective disturbance *within the reading experience* of them, and Chandler makes clear that the very moment in which the poem resists the generalizing function of its grammar also involves a charged, conflicted immediacy for the reader. In this sensitive moment of interpretation, the habitual effects of sentimental disembodiment are reversed and the body's difficult particularity is restored to the reader's emotion. "[I]n Blake's songs," he writes, "conflicting emotions are engaged in such a way as to decompose sentiment into passion and sense . . . Blake engages sentiments, in other words, to unmake the sentimental, forcing cogs to turn adversely in his system of wheels within wheels, piercing Apollyon with his own bow" (110). Criticism performs its work not by producing a direct or abstract knowledge of sentimental artifice but by producing a contrary, resistant feeling, by "decompos[ing]" well wrought forms ("sentiments") back into their constitutive, material elements ("passion and sense"), thus recalling the reader to *embodied* feeling much as the "sickening shudder" of the falling elevator, in our earlier example from Jameson, dissolves reified thought systems back into the fluid historical medium from which they had been abstracted. Later we will call this contrary feeling within criticism—this feeling of emotion working against itself—"adverse emotion."[32] And again, as in Jameson, this jolting return from automatic response to agitation creates an opening onto the future. "Blake's aim was to denaturalize the level of habitual reflection and exchange that marks the sentimental. He, by contrast, cast the syntactic joints of his affective production as mind forg'd manacles, links that, having been made by a human being can be so unmade" (116). Blake critiqued his era's sentimental structures in order to unmake and transform them. The little disturbances Chandler identifies are not only cracks in a general structure of emotion that suddenly looks contingent and contrived; they are so many openings onto unfamiliar emotions, onto a future affectivity the poem's critical aesthetics is supposed to enable.

At this point, we can turn from Chandler's account of Blake to Chandler's own critical procedures, for his analysis *enacts* that future affectivity, making it present in the criticism's own subtle but irresistible affects. On a minor scale, the essay mimes the work of critical emotion (the decomposition of readymade feelings into passion and sense) it tracks so diligently in Blake's songs. Every time Chandler guides us through the intellectual struggle of negotiating Blake's strategic grammar, every time he meticulously recreates the twists and turns of this "brilliant piece of syntactical ambiguity" (113) and that "fascinating syntactic interaction" (114), every time he urges us to "heed the call of Blake's poem" and "discover" another instance of its grammatical undoing—this one more striking than the last and that one "most striking of all" (113)—he performs the excitement of critical engagement and reactivates the arousal of faculties in action. Such discoveries are not merely flat and grammatical; "brilliant," "fascinating," and "striking," they resonate experientially. Despite his nearly de Manian emphasis on impersonal linguistic mechanisms and their inevitable structural tensions, despite his insistence on the power of syntax to denaturalize both sentiment and the illusion of inherent human feelings, despite every effort to avoid sentiment himself, Chandler cannot withhold this muted exuberance, this small enthusiasm, which signifies his participation in a critical legacy he has in part inherited from the author he explicates.

As we turn to our other example, Thomas Pfau's *Romantic Moods: Paranoia, Trauma, and Melancholy, 1790–1840,* I must acknowledge that its monumental scope and complexity lie well beyond anything that can be treated justly in this brief engagement. Not only does Pfau make a broad case for understanding European Romanticism in terms of a narrative succession of three historical phases (the "paranoia, trauma, and melancholy" of his subtitle), but he also stakes his project on the idea that "volatile and inscrutable" affects (2), understood as "moods," stand in a privileged relation to historical existence at the moment of its occurrence, prior to any of the post-facto conceptual reconstructions that claim to give history a knowable form. With this understanding, the book contributes mightily to the current Raymond Williams–inflected "structures of feeling" approach to Romantic historicity, a development that began with Kevis Goodman's *Georgic Modernity and British Romanticism: Poetry and the Mediation of History* and extends to the recent

emphasis on Romanticism as a wartime culture, as best represented by Mary Favret's *War at a Distance: Romanticism and the Making of Modern Wartime.*[33] My
focus here is necessarily as narrow as Pfau's vision is grand. Is there any relationship, I want to ask, between Pfau's understanding of emotion as a precognitive
ground or "inherently alien stratum" (7) and his own high-concept style—a style
that, like Chandler's, appears to be as sentiment free as possible?

Pfau's theory of emotion as the effect of history's absent causality (rather than
as personal expression) draws heavily on Lacan, Heidegger, and of course Williams, but his central propositions resemble ideas we have already encountered
in Jameson:

> For the time being, we shall view emotions as signals traceable in the fabric of literary
> and aesthetic form nd i   ersistence of factors or qualities that resist out-
> right assimilation   ical models of discursive thinking. Indeed,
> it is just this pers   ndicates a rupture within the purposive
> logic of rational,   nentous tear in the fabric of quotidian
> knowledge on the   . (33)

> In suspending—   '—the Cartesian axiom of a con-
> scious and auton   on alerts the subject to its having
> been implicated   nable network of antagonistic his-
> torical forces. (31)

Pfau's "moods" a   ging to structural, collective history) and precogn   ous). As the Romantics began to
understand, the value of literature lies in its power to awaken readers to their deep
historicity by taking them back behind their culturally constructed values and concepts to an originary, more authentic experience of "affective and epistemological
bewilderment" (2).

> [I]n dissenting from the vexing determinacy of history . . . , literature does not simply
> imagine some dreamworld but aims to recover a knowledge occluded by the . . . co-
> herence of so-called actual history. From Kant, Godwin, Wordsworth, Schopenhauer,
> and Nietzsche to Freud and Lacan, the basic interpretive figure at issue here posits
> that all empirical experience and culture broadly speaking acquires its formal consis-
> tency and social significance at the expense of another (transcendental, unconscious)
> experience—the real, or "history"—that has necessarily been "missed" . . . Hence
> the language of literature tends to be oriented toward an as yet unknown, perhaps
> unpresentable "openness." (25)

Literature accesses this indeterminate "openness" through affective unease,
thereby discovering a potentiality for history to be something other than the limit-

ing form it currently takes.[34] While thus preserving an experience of history that has been "missed," literature also keeps alive the idea of a concrete future ("*as yet unknown*")—and by invoking this future-oriented "openness," Pfau brings us as close as his rigorous discourse will allow to an outright expression of enthusiasm.

The recovery of historical "openness" does not come easily, however, not least because literature, the vehicle of such recovery, erects obstacles of its own. Foremost among these are the stylized sentiments that a literary culture accumulates in order to stabilize experience and ward off the incursion of historical volatility. Given the stifling force of these cultural and linguistic conventions, it remains unclear whether mood can ever enter into representation without also being deeply compromised. Pfau sees self-awareness of this dilemma at the center of Romantic lyric. Because of "the impossibility of a complete break from social conventions of expression, romantic 'mood' (*Stimmung*) also experiences its transposition into 'voice' (*Stimme*) as intrinsically alienating. It is here, too, that we can locate the origins of romanticism's often vehement reaction against inauthentic or contrived (i.e., purely 'literary') emotions" (32). Romantic poems thus become entangled in the competing functions that Goodman designates "shield" and "aperture": defending against the disturbing effects of history-in-process while also allowing them through in filtered form.[35] In Pfau's version of this idea, lyric form "aims to awaken romantic subjectivity *from* its dormant state and *to* its perilous historical situatedness, all the while sheltering (at least partially) the subject of such awakening from the traumatic impact of the knowledge so produced in the cocoon of aesthetic form" (11). The parenthetical hesitation ("at least partially") indicates that this is indeed a delicate calculus, requiring just enough historicity to awaken a reader but not too much to overwhelm the cocoon that continues to shelter him. Moreover, the fine calibrations needed to measure the authenticity of an aesthetic emotion on this scale (with the more agitating emotions lying closer to genuine historicity) are themselves deeply problematic, especially if we consider them in the light of Pfau's own account of 1790s paranoia. For if the distinction between "mood" and its artificial proxies is a matter of intensity and thus dependent on the evidence of immediate experience, then what happens when the whole realm of immediate experience comes under hermeneutic suspicion and itself seems to be a product of ideological distortion?[36]

The "duplicitous status of emotion" is a problem that escapes resolution: "For the 'mood' in question proves logically anterior to all reflection. Mood appears terminally resistant to conceptual analysis" (32). Even the fact that, in consecutive sentences, "mood" appears first with quotation marks and then without (as "enthusiasm" has in these pages) suggests something of the difficulty that arises when one must validate an emotion by measuring its strength, that is, by one's awareness of having crossed some qualitative threshold of intensity or estrangement. Is Pfau marking a clear distinction between mood (the strong, unfathomable event itself, which "does not belong to the order of signs and reference" [32]) and anything we might *call* "mood," which can only be a weaker, belated sign substitution? Or is he exposing the dubious nature of that distinction in the first place? These questions are symptomatic of a tension between argument and style resonating throughout *Romantic Moods*. If the "persistence of emotion . . . indicates a rupture within the purposive logic of rational, discursive thinking" (33), then what are we to make of Pfau's own critical voice, which never wavers in its densely propositional and declarative authority and, in its largest claims, gives paradigmatic, narrative form to a history of emotions that are supposed, by definition, to be concept resistant? It may be tempting to conclude that Pfau's stylistic choices involve him in a massive performative contradiction, but I prefer to see them as indicating the unusual depth of his convictions. After all, had he attempted to express "mood" rather than to describe it analytically, had he tried to realize it in a form accessible to the reader *as mood*, then the very success of his performance would do little more than compromise or even trivialize the indefinite and intractable quality that is supposed to characterize his privileged term. He would have risked the mistaken impression that mood could be performed, manipulated, and instrumentalized by his own professional discourse. Better to eliminate, to the extent that such elimination is possible, all traces of emotion from one's discourse. Better to ensure the reader that *this* text, *about mood,* is by no means an example *of mood,* thereby allowing the emotion to remain untouched in the purity of its "perhaps unpresentable 'openness'" on the other side of this discourse. Rather than undermining his theory of affective history, the general absence of emotion from Pfau's own language testifies to how deeply he reveres emotion's power. It is the foremost sign of his "enthusiasm" that it must express itself under cover of its absence.

The Future Impersonal: *Milton,* Anonymity, and the Agency of Emotion

Because they are "ontologically anterior" (10) to discursive knowledge, emotions of the kind Pfau calls "moods" are essentially anonymous; they resist a subject's ordinary means of self-identification. Pfau values them because their anonymity poses a severe challenge to the self-protective fictions of identity; in this way he participates in the recent revisionary emphasis on emotion as a source of estrangement rather than as a reassuring indication of familiar humanity. Joining Pfau, one writer calls the feelings "alien influences"; another tells us passion is "impersonal"; still another that, "far from controverting the 'death of the subject,' emotion entails this death."[37] These provocations have their own history, as well as their own basis in ordinary experience; they give theoretical shape to the strange emotional states we often simply describe as feeling "beside" oneself or "not" one-self.[38] As Mary Favret points out, "scholars over the past 15 years have increasingly made visible how affect moves and thrives in a realm independent of individual subjectivity."[39] Blake called the undoing of personal identity "self-annihilation," and he made achievement of that ecstatic state the primary aim of his late prophecies, modeling it on the self-sacrificing Passion of Jesus, but his work nevertheless remains undecided about emotion's relation to the self. The same author who unapologetically professed his enthusiasm in the preface to *Jerusalem* and called on Jesus to "Annihilate the Selfhood in me, be thou all my life!" (5:22, E 147) also recognized the affective basis of ongoing, atomistic selfhood, as in Theotormon's lament in *The Four Zoas*: "I am like an atom / . . . yet I am an identity / I wish & feel & weep & groan Ah terrible terrible" (4:43–45, E 302). By itself, Blake suggests, the presence of emotion provides no sure measure of identity or anonymity, of a self preserved or a self undone.

When the "Self-closd" and "self balanc'd" modern subject (*Urizen* 3:3; 4:18, E 70–72) is considered a constraint to be overcome (as Blake understood it to be), anonymity becomes a goal of critical engagement. The title page of *Milton* famously represents the poem's hero unnaming himself: naked and seen from behind, he steps out from the dull heaven he envisioned in *Paradise Lost* and into the space of a new text (*Milton*), all while shattering his printed name with his open right hand (figure I.1). To step out of heaven is to make oneself vulnerable to revision. As we will see momentarily, *Milton* ties this liberating anonymity to the agency of emotion, but before we turn to Blake's brief epic I want to consider a parallel example of our own continuing enthusiasm for anonymous feelings. Toward the end of his introduction to *Anonymous Life: Romanticism and Dispossession*, Jacques Khalip invokes a modern reading of a Romantic lyric (E. M. Forster's of "Rime of the Ancient Mariner") to exemplify the experience of "unmoored subjectivity" he considers central to Romanticism and persistent ever since.[40] According to Forster, awareness of the author's identity dissolves during the time of reading and "nothing exists but the poem," leading him to conclude "that all literature tends towards a condition of anonymity" (24). Although Khalip worries over prematurely valorizing this "ungrounding" of the subject through literature and frequently warns against naively proclaiming it "a newfound freedom" (5), he in fact consistently promotes the capability activated by such instances of "negative capability." To be anonymous, in his view, is not only to fall outside social categories that require individuation and restrict action to familiar forms of personhood; it is to experience, through estrangement, an expansiveness and empowerment akin to discovering

Figure I.1 Milton a Poem, copy C, title page, Erdman i [I], c. 1804–1811. Rare Books Division, The New York Public Library, Astor, Lenox and Tilden Foundations "new potentialities" (4). Given these terms, who would not want to step forward and shatter his name?

As a culminating statement, the last paragraph of Khalip's introduction touches on many of the virtues that make Romantic anonymity desirable: rather than resulting in disability, the subject's "inscrutability" to itself opens onto new, unexpected forms of agency; "conceiving the self *as* other" involves a "productive power" with political and ethical consequences; reading emerges as the site where this transformative event continually occurs; and by looking back to Coleridge, Forster reactivates the influence of a "romantic aesthetics and ethics" that is always moving forward and "by no means over" yet. If the subject is a product of modernity (or of what Blake would simply call the Fall), then anonymity signals an undercurrent of continually available countermodernity akin to our earlier description of enthusiasm. What makes Khalip's eloquent summation worth quoting at length, however, is not the set of arguments it rehearses in favor of its central term but its last-moment recourse to emotion:

> Questions that address who or what acts or thinks once the subject is no longer asserted as a self-willing agent, or how and why we should conceive nonidentity as politically and ethically viable, open up onto a romanticism that recedes into the "space of literature" where the subject is unmoored from easy solidarities, habits of thoughts, and categorizations. It is in fact this very argument that E. M. Forster was to anticipate in his essay, "Anonymity," where romanticism stands for a particular kind of exemplary reading . . . Forster evokes the subject's confrontation with its own otherness *through* art—a confrontation that defamiliarizes subjectivity from its prosaic conditions in order for it to radically reassess its relation to those conditions themselves. For what is ethically, aesthetically, *and* politically at stake in the concept of anonymity as I have been describing it is the productive power of conceiving the self *as* other . . . By turning us back to the "modernity" of romantic anonymity and the imagination, Forster also moves us forward and helps us see that romantic aesthetics and ethics are by no means over, and that the broadly anti-identificatory strain in romantic thought testifies to the possibility that our inscrutability to ourselves precedes our relationship to others—*something perhaps most deeply felt at the moment when we feel porous and stubbornly unavailable to the rules of evidence.* (23–24, emphasis added to final clause)

Why, in these last words of the introduction, should emotion suddenly make an appearance? Khalip's final clause announces itself as hesitant and provisional, an afterthought introduced by a "perhaps" and appended by a dash, but any hint of disavowal is quickly overmatched by the invocation of a bond of deep feeling shared between author and reader. Apparently, anonymity does not involve relinquishing sensibility (as Khalip's ongoing critique of sentimental sympathy might suggest); it involves a further slide into emotion's depths. Abundant caution notwithstanding, including the idea that the uneasy experience being invoked here is never more than a "possibility," this recourse to feeling is not supplemental to the argument but essential. Anonymity *needs* the reassuring measure of emotion's self-evidence, ratified not conceptually but in the body. Only this disturbing immediacy can substantiate a state of exemption by definition unaccountable to other forms of evidence ("stubbornly unavailable") and therefore outside the rules of demonstration by which a subject functionally produces knowledge of itself and its world. At once fluid (porous), noncompliant (stubborn), and yet still reliable (deep), this feeling endows the critical argument with a truth that is its own testimony, carried alive into the heart by passion. Without it, the critical resistance enabled by anonymity would remain merely hypothetical, a "possibility" rather than something actual, substantial, felt.

The heightened feeling incorporated into Khalip's parting gesture comes as no real surprise. In criticism of all kinds (and especially in its paratexts—in prefaces, introductions, and epilogues), a discursive crescendo often appeals directly to emotion, whether to supplement the preceding rigors of argument or to acknowledge, more or less subtly, that the argument requires more substantiation than its logic and evidence can supply. Even Jameson concluded *Marxism and Form* with an emphatic plea and a rare exclamation point: "May [criticism] prove equal to the task!" Much later we will take up the final words of Susan Wolfson's *Formal Charges: The Shaping of Poetry in British Romanticism*, a seminal text of the new formalism: "Reading the local particularities of events in form, we discover the most complex measures of human art . . . We also feel the charge of an historically persistent, forever various, aesthetic vitality."[41] The more resounding the finish of a critical discourse, the larger its stakes (for Wolfson, nothing less than the persistence of life feeling, "vitality" itself), the greater the implication that the discourse has approached some *charged* ultimate that cannot be known or properly named but only experienced (*Anonymous* Life)—then the more likely it is that emotion will become a means as well as a topic of criticism. These climactic moments are neither personal insertions (tonal signatures, as it were) nor rote exercises of rhetorical convention: they are meant to signal that criticism (like Forster's literature) also aspires to a condition of anonymity. In principle at least, the emotions to which they appeal are not merely personal expressions but evidence of a writing subject undergoing transformation or even leaving itself behind. And because critical feeling of this kind should belong to no one in particular (as indexed by the undefined "we" in both Khalip's and Wolfson's last sentences), it promises inexhaustible latency and unlimited circulation, like a resource of renewable estrangement always ready to dislodge the subject and open onto a future beyond it. As Khalip says of anonymity, its "untapped power keeps it, as it were, always temporally unfinished and suspended, not knowing what it *is*, and what it will *be*" (7). To borrow from the title of his chapter on Shelley, this feeling of anonymity is a "Feeling for the Future" (97).

The ambitions that criticism hitches to anonymous emotion and reveals in its climactic gestures may be outsize, but they do not lie outside the mainstream of current scholarship on emotion. Whether "we feel porous" when we read or "feel the charge . . . of vitality," critical emotion serves the subject as a built-in mechanism of self-supersession, and, in various forms, that is more or less the function most commonly attributed to emotion today. Through emotion, we are told, consciousness redistributes attention to objects and aspects of experience outside the subject's current horizon of awareness, thereby allowing the subject to unsettle, estrange, and even surpass its ruling assumptions.[42] Emotion is an ongoing and unwilled capacity for *self-criticism*. When Khalip writes that anonymity "defamiliarizes subjectivity from its prosaic conditions in order for it to radically reassess its relation to those conditions themselves," he dramatizes a role ordinary emotion is understood to perform all the time. Descartes introduced this theme to modern study when he named wonder the "first of all the passions"; feeling has been closely integrated into learning, defamiliarization, and innovation ever since. In *The Passions of the Soul,* novelty begins as an affective interruption of the closed circle of common, habitual knowledge: "When the first encounter with some object surprises us, and we judge it to be new, or very different from what we knew in the past or what we supposed it was going to be, this makes us wonder and be astonished at it."[43] Following Descartes' belief that wonder "makes learning possible," Philip Fisher describes the pedagogy of emotion in this way: "In wonder we notice against the background of a lawful and familiar world something that strikes us by its novelty and by the pleasure that this surprising new fact brings to us. Each of us has at every stage of our lives a distinct but provisional horizon separating the familiar from the unknown and the unknowable. Any one experience of wonder informs us about the momentary location of this horizon line."[44] Even Sianne Ngai's "ugly feelings"—despite being characterized by an amorphous unease incompatible with Fisher's concentrated, heroic passions—generate curiosity, thus conveying some of the novelty and intrigue promised by Cartesian wonder, though minus the pleasure and the scale. Taking her cue from noir films, Ngai refers to moments of charged inactivity that produce "the inherently ambiguous affect of affective disorientation in general—what we might think of as a state of feeling vaguely 'unsettled' or 'confused,' or, more precisely, a meta-feeling in which one feels confused about *what* one is feeling . . . Despite its marginality to the philosophical canon of emotions, isn't this feeling of confusion *about* what one is feeling an affective state in its own right? And in fact a rather familiar feeling that often heralds the basic affect of 'interest' underwriting all acts of intellectual inquiry?"[45] Within this tradition, Khalip's anonymity lies at the strong end of a continuum in understandings of emotion as a defamiliarizing agent; anonymity radicalizes wonder by making the subject itself the startling object of inquiry. Rather than incrementally adjusting the horizon line that mediates between self and world (what Coleridge and Shelley both called "the film of familiarity"),[46] it punctures the subject's own capacity for self-definition, in the process estranging *everything*.

Common as it is today to affirm the innovative powers of emotion, even its most committed advocates recognize that affective agency encounters resistance continuously, not least from within emotion itself. Theories of emotion tend to be organized by Manichean vocabularies in which one term designates a salutary disruption of the subject (now more often called "shock" or "upheaval" than "wonder")[47] that another term, its conservative counterpart, works steadily to forestall. Pfau's distinction between intensified moods and contrived sentiments is one such example, but pairings of this sort are legion. Fisher contrasts archaic, vehement, and "thorough" *passions* with the "moderate, even reasonable" *emotions* that sustain the modern "prudential self"; Massumi calls upon turbulent *affects*—"regions of swirling potential"—to disrupt the safer *emotions* we experience as mere "subjective content," consciously "owned and recognized"; Terada distinguishes a *discourse of emotion* internally fraught with "self-difference" from an *ideology of emotion* meant to manage and even displace affective unease; Goodman attends to poetry's "affective discomfort [and] cognitive 'noise'" rather than to its shapely, well-wrought emotions, for the former lie closer to "history-on-the-move," as it is happening, prior to higher cognitive shaping.[48] Assimilating the traditional distinction between higher order *emotions* involving sophisticated judgments and primitive, precognitive, or autonomic *affects*, some such version of dichotomization informs most academic discussion.[49] What all of these paired variants share, however, regardless of whether they see emotion working in service of the subject or against it, is an understanding that emotions matter *because* they discomfit (even, or perhaps especially, when the established forms they unsettle are other emotions).[50] My own choice of the word "agitation" participates in this tendency to value dysphoria, while adding a political valence to the notion of subjective disturbance. We are very far from the time when a philosopher might seek to disqualify emotion as blind impulse. Today emotions are more likely to be deemed reliable *because* they disturb; we crave the novelty and authenticity promised by their displeasure. Even Martha Nussbaum, who has worked harder than any recent "cognitive theorist" to fold the emotions into an Enlightenment framework, values them most for the "upheavals" they generate, which revitalize and expand our capacity for judgment. If it appears "counter-intuitive to make . . . emotion itself a function of reason," she contends, that is only because we have failed to recognize how various and "dynamic" a faculty reason can be.[51] Altieri is surely right to complain that Nussbaum represents "in especially clear form the tendency of philosophy to seek control over the emotions" and that her more capacious understanding of reason disguises an "even more ambitious version of philosophical imperialism." But when he urges us to "accept a constant struggle between the clarity reasons bring and the performative qualities enabling individuals to elicit fresh transformations of our normative expectations"—performative or aesthetic qualities that include the "affective turbulence" and "immediate particularity" he favors—he reveals that his disagreement with Nussbaum concerns *how* the emotions access new experience and alter the subject's existing contours, not *whether* they do so.[52]

Before we turn to *Milton* and away from contemporary discourses on emotion, we ought to acknowledge an important dissent to the widely shared notion that anonymous feelings supply the subject with a vital exit from its self-perpetuating routines. Early in *Anonymous Life,* Khalip emphasizes a distinction between "anonymity" and what Sharon Cameron calls "impersonality"; despite the sibling relation between them, he hopes to avoid the paradigmatic asceticism and "disciplined eradication of the personal" her term entails. "Anonymity," as he conceives it, is an "experience of being-in-the-world" (5); it evacuates the subject but still leaves room for sensibility. Indeed, as we have seen, Khalip cannot do without sensibility. What sets Cameron apart from the critical mainstream, then, is her unusual emphasis on authors who refuse to consider emotion as relief from the subject. For austere writers such as Simone Weil or Ralph Waldo Emerson, feelings can never become estranged or unrecognizable enough to detach themselves from personality or point of view. In part, this constraint simply acknowledges the inevitable self-contradiction that results when impersonality becomes a goal "undertaken by persons,"[53] but Cameron goes further, insisting that, for writers who would push off toward the impersonal despite the impossibility of the task, "feeling is no compass (nothing is more deceptive)" (xii–xiii). Consider Cameron's most relevant (and extraordinary) case: Jonathan Edwards's final devotional work, *True Virtue,* in which the former author of *Religious Affections* turns against his earlier enthusiasm. Now, rather than flooding his sensibility ecstatically, he attempts to devise mathematical techniques to void it; as he puts it in "Of Being," his new aim is to render the mind capable of thinking "the same that the sleeping rocks dream of" (21). Thus Edwards refuses altogether the idea of affective self-evidence (inward persuasions, Miltonic rousing motions, intuition), not because he favors rational judgment (as another early skeptic of enthusiasm, John Locke, would do) but because he has come to believe that any feeling whatsoever, no matter how minimal or excessive, still attaches to self. Cameron writes, "This inward sense is missing on principle from Edwards's last work. Although in *True Virtue* 'the heart' is invoked as the object of consideration . . . in instance after instance love to Being in general is just what persons *cannot* know affectively" (33). According to this severe view, which requires acquisition of an *impersonal* heart, anonymity experienced as feeling would be just another version of self-reference in disguise. Any recourse to feeling in order to abandon the self will turn out to be an exercise in self-deception ("nothing is more deceptive"). For Khalip, anonymity is "something perhaps most deeply felt at the moment when we feel porous and stubbornly unavailable to the rules of evidence"; for the Edwards of *True Virtue*, as explicated by Cameron, "such a sense could never be deep enough, and would in fact always be deficient precisely because, notwithstanding any depth, it would be *only* a sense" (40).

By introducing this wedge between a deeply felt anonymity and an impersonality so flat as to be devoid of feeling altogether, I do not mean to force a choice between alternate versions of "self-annihilation"—one with emotion, another without. These two possibilities speak to one another dialectically. The first, currently predominant, identifies emotion (no matter how low key) with dynamism, change, and transformation—in a word, agency. The second identifies emotion with self-deception, especially whenever its presence doubles as a promise of agency. No doubt the modern heir to Jonathan Edwards's turn against enthusiasm would be de Man, who may not have aspired to the empty thoughts of a dreaming stone but nevertheless urged his readers to adopt a sublime "stony gaze": "The dynamics of the sublime mark the moment when the infinite is frozen into the materiality of stone, when no pathos, anxiety, or sympathy is conceivable; it is indeed, the moment of a-pathos, or apathy, as the complete loss of the symbolic."[54] And yet, against *this* view, following Terada's influential reading, we also want to remember that de Man's zero-degree apatheia expresses only a desire to escape personality, not an achievement.[55] The image de Man conjures of stoic self-evacuation leaves behind an affective remainder. After all, even an empty shell of a subject, even an anonymous dreaming stone, would be unable to void the experience Keats called "the feel of not to feel it"[56]—and would still call attention to itself for having achieved that enviable anesthetic state. Terada refers to this "recirculating infinity of feeling living on" as "the *economy of pathos*": "there is no such thing as the absence of emotion" (13, original emphasis). Neither is there any such thing in the economy of criticism: no matter how suspect the promise of emotional agency may be, any attempt to demystify emotion will continue to harbor subtle affects in turn.

In *Milton*, the promise of emotion runs high. Representing literary criticism as an intervention itself worthy of epic narrative, *Milton* ties one poet's reading of another to nothing less than a redemptive transformation of the world. This elevation of critical labor, moreover, is directly related to the modern task Blake believed he shared with Milton: having to sustain the possibility of world transformation (like fire "under ashes")[57] in the aftermath of revolutionary disappointment. The urgent and anonymous emotions of critical engagement come to occupy the place vacated by a discredited revolutionary agency. Inheriting this lesson from Milton and reformulating it for modern critical thought, Blake emphasized the role of anonymity in its transmission. In the poem's memorable allegory of literary reception, Milton falls like a celestial star into Blake's left foot, entering through the tarsus; there he forms an intimate bond with his reader, who (their shared embodiment notwithstanding) fails to recognize him: "I knew not that it was Milton" (21 [23]:8, E 115). The amalgamated agent that results from this anonymous encounter then initiates the poem's transformational forward motion, for only a few lines later the speaker straps on the brightly ornamented sandal of the world "to walk forward thro' Eternity" (21 [23]:14, E 115).[58] In effect, Blake is presenting literary history as an affective transmission that works through persons but without belonging to anyone. Transformed by Milton (one image shows "William" with arms and head thrown back, face out of view, in a pose of bodily convulsion and ecstatic enthusiasm), Blake simultaneously transforms Milton. Mutual incorporation divests both poets of fixed identity. Blake describes their productive nonrecognition not in terms of minds meeting but as corporeal impact, a mingling of moving bodies perceived and felt but not at first susceptible to knowledge or naming.[59] As in Auden's elegy for Yeats, poetry survives, but in this enigmatic scene the words of the dead man are modified in the metatarsals of the living. Here is the passage in full:

> But Milton entering my Foot; I saw in the nether
> Regions of the Imagination; also all men on Earth,
> And all in Heaven, saw in the nether regions of the Imagination
> In Ulro beneath Beulah, the vast breach of Miltons descent.
> But I knew not that it was Milton, for man cannot know
> What passes in his members till periods of Space & Time
> Reveal the secrets of Eternity: for more extensive
> Than any other earthly things, are Mans earthly lineaments.
>
> And all this Vegetable World appeard on my left Foot,
> As a bright sandal formd immortal of precious stones & gold:
> I stooped down & bound it on to walk forward thro' Eternity.   (21 [23]: 4–14, E 115)

For our purposes, the crucial questions raised by these strange lines center on Blake's explanation of his failure to recognize the identity of a figure assimilated into his own body, an explanation that doubles as a reader's confession of his inability to grasp fully what happens to him as he reads: "for man cannot know / What passes in his members till periods of Space & Time / Reveal the secrets of Eternity."

These lines read equally well as lamentation or affirmation. As a complaint, they conform to a traditional eschatology: the "members" or organic components of fallen bodies are so extensive ("more extensive / Than any other earthly things") that full and direct knowledge is reserved only for the end time, when the worldly body will be transcended and Eternity will once and for all reveal its secrets. Now we see as through a glass darkly, and the obfuscating glass that distorts perception of self and other is the biological, "vegetable" body with its five vitiated senses. Turned upside down, however, these same lines reimagine bodily complexity, which no longer appears as an obstacle to apocalypse but as a materialist resource of self-transforming motions, sensations, affects, and energies. According to this understanding, the body comprises a sensorium so subtle and extensive ("more extensive / Than any other earthly things") that it perpetually generates experiences accessible as feeling but beyond the current horizon of knowledge. Eternity so regarded would not designate a final transcendence to be achieved when time runs out but an embodied, affective temporality always happening, manifesting secrets continually—Eternity without end, "in love with the productions of time" (*Marriage* 7:10, E 36).⁶⁰ One walks "thro" this Eternity, not toward it, for it is the medium of ongoing vitality, not a future destination. According to this second reading, which critically undoes the orthodox template that overlays it, the reader's corporate and anonymous body is not a fallen condition to be overcome but a critical resource activated by emotion, an opening onto experiential possibilities the selfhood doesn't already know. Thus the passage also coincides with Blake's aim of cleansing perception by "printing in the infernal method" (*Marriage* 14, E 39), for one of the primary effects of an illuminated book like *Milton* is to restore embodied affectivity to reading, counteracting the dualist illusion, fostered by standardized print, that one can read for information without regard to the medium, as a disembodied eye or mind.

To grasp the full implications of this second, critical reading, I want to parse several of the passage's key words and phrases, starting with the speaker's assertion that he sees "in the nether / Regions of the Imagination." "Nether regions" compresses into one term the double reading sketched above: it designates the cosmologically and psychologically fallen realms of "Ulro beneath Beulah" and (following Milton) hell beneath heaven, but it also refers to an affective underworld essential to the Imagination and deeply integrated with the body.⁶¹ Blake is not simply commenting on the constraints of prophetic vision in a fallen world (as if the poor, bottom-dwelling "I" were *condemned* to see "in the nether / Regions of the

Imagination"); he is extending the roots of Imagination into a substrate of precognitive feelings capable of dilating experience. In this typically Blakean inversion, "nether" is better, just as hell is superior to Miltonic heaven, energy superior to law, and even the body's lowest earthbound point, the foot, is strangely more receptive to poetry than the head. No doubt Wai Chee Dimock is right to claim that Blake's left foot in this scene is "much more than an anatomical locomotive device," a mere organic mechanism; it is his figure for poetry's power to mobilize, not least through the movements of the metric foot.[62] Dimock, however, is much too eager to dismiss biological form as a finite constraint that literary history aspires to leave behind. Blake capitalizes on the foot's base corporeality to exaggerate a point: the work of imagination or poetry cannot be decoupled from its bodily ground.[63] Rather than seeking to transcend biology, Blake is refiguring human being from the bottom up.[64] As Richard Sha acutely observes, he unites "self-annihilation" not with transcendence but with "incarnation."[65]

When Blake adds to his nonrecognition of Milton the general explanation that "man cannot know / What passes in his members," the enjambment helps to clarify what is otherwise a compressed, enigmatic claim: there is significant distance between the plethora of moving sensations we may feel at any given moment—including the current moment of reading—and what we can translate into knowable form. Blake is commenting on the necessarily incomplete knowledge of bodily processes, despite the fact that their interior motions and obscure relations affect the subject continuously and intimately. In this sense, his lines may remind us of Nietzsche's rant—"What do human beings really know about themselves? . . . Does nature not remain silent about almost everything, even about our bodies, banishing and enclosing us within a proud, illusory consciousness, far away from the twists and turns of the bowels, the rapid flow of the blood stream and the complicated tremblings of the nerve-fibres?"[66] But again, rather than serving primarily to decry the subject's alienation from its own living substance, Blake's formulation turns estrangement into a virtue. Limited self-knowledge allows for subjects to be surprised from within, by embodied "secrets" too minute or various or fluctuating to be identified finally and completely. For if one *could* achieve the transparent self-perception invoked by Nietzsche ("just once, stretched out as in an illuminated glass case"),[67] if one could truly *know* what passes in one's members, one could never be more or other than such knowledge would allow. Several plates later in *Milton,* in a passage we will return to at length in chapter 4, Blake locates the origin of all significant change in the body's smallest recurring, somatic event: the pulsation of an artery. Not only does the poet's redemptive labor occur in this moment, but so begin all "Great / Events": "For in this Period the Poets Work is Done: and all the Great / Events of Time start forth & are concievd in such a Period / Within a

Moment: a Pulsation of the Artery" (29 [31]: 1–3, E 127). Rather than mechanically repeating the body's "same dull round" in a way that anatomical science might diagram once and for all,[68] vascular circulation provides a subtle occasion for starting anew with each passing moment. Thus Eternity reveals its secrets affectively and *periodically*—according to the regular, rhythmic intervals of circulation, respiration, and neural pulsation, "periods of Space & Time" all beneath the threshold of knowing self-awareness. These extensive, embodied temporalities solicit the kind of "open feeling" that Gertrude Stein (herself anticipating Gilles Deleuze) describes as "a sense for all the slightest variations in repeating."[69]

As Nicholas Williams reports, a recent wave of criticism has begun to emphasize Blake's "close attention to the body's materiality, to the shape of sensory experience, and to the nature of the processes of bodily life itself."[70] Alert to the body's overlapping and reverberating systems, Blake was every bit as interested as Nietzsche in the "twists and turns of the bowels" and "the complicated tremblings of the nerve-fibres." His attention to affective agency, however, more closely anticipates the materialist enthusiasm soon to arrive in the form of William James's seminal essay, "What Is an Emotion?" In 1884, only a decade after Nietzsche's complaint, James (a former instructor of anatomy and physiology) described the affective body as a bottomless nether region progressively illuminated by the latest research developments but still inexhaustible.

In the earlier books on Expression, written mostly from the artistic point of view, the signs of emotion visible from without were the only ones taken account of. Sir Charles Bell's celebrated *Anatomy of Expression* noticed the respiratory changes; and Bain's and Darwin's treatises went more thoroughly still into the study of the visceral factors involved,—changes in the functioning of glands and muscles, and in that of the circulatory apparatus. But not even a Darwin has exhaustively enumerated *all* the bodily affections . . . More and more, as physiology advances, we begin to discern how almost infinitely numerous and subtle they must be. The researches of Mosso with the plethysmograph have shown that not only the heart, but the entire circulatory system, forms a sort of sounding-board, which every change of our consciousness, however slight, may make reverberate. Hardly a sensation comes to us without sending waves of alternate constriction and dilatation down the arteries of our arms. The blood-vessels of the abdomen act reciprocally with those of the more outward parts. The bladder and bowels, the glands of the mouth, throat, and skin, and the liver, are known to be affected gravely in certain severe emotions, and are unquestionably affected transiently when the emotions are of a lighter sort. That the heart-beats and the rhythm of breathing play a leading part in all emotions whatsoever, is a matter too notorious for proof. And what is really equally prominent, but less likely to be admitted until special attention is drawn to the fact, is the continuous co-operation of the voluntary muscles in our emotional states. Even when no change of outward attitude is produced, their inward tension alters to suit each varying mood, and is felt as a difference of tone or of strain. In depression the flexors tend to prevail; in elation or belligerent excitement the extensors take the lead. And the various permutations and combinations of which these organic activities are susceptible, make it abstractly possible that no shade of emotion, however slight, should be without a bodily reverberation as unique, when taken in its totality, as is the mental mood itself.[71]

More symphonic anthem than catalog, James's survey of dynamic interiority revels in the body as an "almost infinitely" varying field of materialist affects and energies: "More extensive / Than any other earthly things, are Mans earthly lineaments" indeed. Organs and systems until recently neglected (bladder, bowels, glands, mouth, throat, skin, liver) continually modify themselves and signal each adjustment. A century earlier, Voltaire had sought to deflate the pretensions of "enthusiasm" by tracing the word's Greek etymology (incorrectly) to "a convulsion of the entrails."[72] Now the radical empiricist's enthusiasm takes root across the whole field of visceral convulsions, large and small, each minutely tracked and sensitively described.[73] "Change" is James's recurring word of choice, and each of the body's modifications, no matter how infinitesimal, reverberates affectively and immediately, in real time.[74] Whether we realize it or not, these interior changes will be felt; paid attention to, they will "astonish." James is defamiliarizing the self from the materialist inside out. He continues:

> The next thing to be noticed is this, that every one of the bodily changes, whatsoever it be, is *felt*, acutely or obscurely, the moment it occurs. If the reader has never paid attention to this matter, he will be both interested and astonished to learn how many different local bodily feelings he can detect in himself as characteristic of his various emotional moods . . . Our whole cubic capacity is sensibly alive; and each morsel of it contributes its pulsations of feeling, dim or sharp, pleasant, painful, or dubious, to that sense of personality that every one of us unfailingly carries with him. It is surprising what little items give accent to these complexes of sensibility.

The fluid affective substrate that Blake traces back to the exemplary pulsation of an artery, James observes in every one of the body's agitations. And if all of this subterranean commotion serves to prop up the "sense of personality," it also threatens to destabilize and even overwhelm identity. Under this affective microscope, "personality" becomes something much more elusive, complex, and "impersonal," consisting of vast, anonymous processes out of which the subject precipitates but to which it is ordinarily oblivious.[75]

One other feature of James's remarkable survey of visceral feeling warrants attention. Although it is inspired by the latest advances in laboratory technique, innovations that enabled the study of emotion to progress beyond the body's surfaces to its hidden interior, the empirical specificity of his account conveys an impression exactly the opposite of complete mapping. Cumulatively, this discourse lies closer to the sublime than to an anatomy lesson. Because "our whole cubic capacity is sensibly alive," the affective body invites new modes of descriptive particularization; James encourages us to pay finer and finer attention to the slightest corporeal differences. But implied in this process is also an understanding that something unmasterable will remain—something "Unknown, not unpercievd," as the frustrated tyrant-empiricist Bromion says in *Visions of the Daughters of Albion* (4:16, E 48). No matter how advanced or discerning the methods of observation, representation, and taxonomy may become, no matter what new equipment will supplant Mosso's plethysmograph and prosthetically extend perception even further,[76] the nature of affectivity is such that one will still feel more than one can see and name. For James, language itself enhances this disproportion of affectivity to discursive knowledge, for the medium of representation is not a neutral instrument but itself an affective texture of dynamic interior relations almost as "infinitely numerous and subtle" as the body's. "We ought to say a feeling of *and,* a feeling of *if,* a feeling of *but,* and a feeling of *by,* quite as readily as we say a feeling of *blue* or a feeling of *cold,*" James writes in a well-known passage, invoking the bits and "morsels" of a linguistic infrastructure saturated by affectivity all the way down.[77] Calling attention to how a medium's minute particularity multiplies emotion, James reminds us of Blake's own flamboyant assertion that "<as Poetry admits not a Letter that is Insignificant so Painting admits not a Grain of Sand or a Blade of Grass <Insignificant> much less an Insignificant Blur or Mark>"—as well as Blake's corresponding observation that awareness of such particularity can be accessed only by those who enter the medium "on the Fiery Chariot of [their] Contemplative Thought" (E 560).[78]

With James as our guide to Blake's gnomic comments on "what passes in [man's] members" and the extensiveness of his "lineaments," we have been treating affectivity as if it concerned a single isolated body, although a body of almost unlimited internal extension. Although necessary, this approach is clearly insufficient, for the body Blake invokes in *Milton* is also emphatically social (mingling bodies together). In the lines we are examining, this multiplication of relations becomes evident as soon as Blake freely oscillates between individual and plural perspectives: "I saw in the nether / Regions of the Imagination"; "all men . . . saw in the nether regions of the Imagination." It is difficult to tell, then, whether the operative frame of reference is one reader's body (complex enough, as James demonstrates) or the social whole (the aggregate body of "Man"). Do the obscurely interacting *members* that "man cannot know" refer to the organic components of each person's physiology or to fellow participants in a community, the constituents of a corporate body politic? Invoking the relativity of perspective, Blake often describes a sliding scale of corporate unification and dissolution: what appears to be a single body from a distance will reveal the multiplicity of its constituent parts on closer inspection. This is a social as well as an optical phenomenon: "We live as One Man; for contracting our infinite senses / We behold multitude; or expanding: we behold as one, / As One Man all the Universal Family" (*Jerusalem* 34:17–19, E 180). In *Milton*, the slippage between these points of view is crucial, for at the moment Blake receives Milton he is positioning himself at the intersection of two paths away from discrete selfhood, one into the anonymity of the interior (the dissolution of the individual subject into precognitive feelings, of the kind James describes), the other into the anonymity of the public (the participation of the individual subject in a larger collective endeavor). Milton is an apt choice to represent the latter tendency, and not only because of his outspoken involvement in the Puritan revolutionary cause. As Joanna Picciotto has demonstrated, Milton played a significant role in refiguring the medieval *corpus mysticum* into a redemptive image of the modern public as "a corporate body engaged in the labor of truth production," a development that would ultimately feed into Blake's utopian vision of Albion as a giant national body of intellectual exchange. When Picciotto quotes from Milton's defense of Smectymnuus—"I conceav'd my selfe to be now not as mine own person, but as a member incorporate into that truth whereof I was perswaded"—and goes on to assert that "Radical thinkers now praised for their 'rugged individualism' constantly describe their incorporation into a body where 'respect of persons' disappears," her point applies almost as well to Blake as it does to the seventeenth-century experimentalists at the center of her study.[79] By taking Milton into his own body, Blake imagines himself and Milton as self-sacrificing co-workers, members together in the great transhistorical labor of assembling Albion's redeemed body.

At the same time, however, Blake's ideal of self-annihilation also modifies this Miltonic tradition and points in the direction of modern affect theory. Blake insists, first, on the ultimate unknowability of bodies in motion (singularly or en masse), second, on the transformative agency of the affective energies generated by these bodies, and third, on the intersection between these two bodies (individual and collective), such that the internal motions of the one have bearing on the configuration of the other. Central to *Milton* is the idea that the defamiliarizing agitations of personal embodiment will have public consequences. This is a poem deeply invested in the idea that "being moved" is (potentially) a transpersonal event of world-changing proportions. Despite a painful awareness of his relative insignificance to London's public culture (something that would always distinguish him from Milton, regardless of any fantasies of their corporate labor together), Blake never stopped believing that his enthusiasm was a matter of national importance or that his own urgent agitations confirmed the existence of unknowable affects at work in the body politic, potential histories yet to unfold and take shape. In chapter 1, we will see how deeply this belief penetrated into Blake's conception of the public sphere.

Milton ends on the verge of apocalyptic departure, with all living creatures "prepard in all their strength / To go forth to the Great Harvest & Vintage of the Nations" (42 [49]: 39–43 [50]: 1, E 144), and much critical energy has been expended trying to explain why the poem pulls up short on this staging ground.[80] If, as I have been urging, Blake considers Eternity to be a realm of continuous revelation, and affect to be its engine of incompletion, unknowingness, and innovation, then poetry's role is not to bring such movement to completion but to activate the conditions that make motion possible. Rather than asking where the world's living creatures should ultimately go, Blake asks us to consider what enables them "to go forth" at all. Before "emotion" came to signify a distinct state or activity of the psyche, something that did not occur before the early nineteenth century, the word was first synonymous with migration, the transfer of peoples or physical masses from one location to another (*OED*). The Latin *emotionen* literally meant "to move out." Early uses of the word in English made little distinction between turbulent motions of all kinds—in inanimate as well as organic bodies, in populations as well as single persons. "Emotion" signified the whole realm of dynamic transformation (across geographical, physiological, and mental spaces) made possible by embodied parts set in motion.[81]

If nothing on earth is "more extensive" than "Mans earthly lineaments," as our *Milton* passage reports, it is because the body of emotion is always "moving out." Rather than achieving ideal or final form, affectivity continually redraws the individual and collective shape of human being. When it refers to organic forms, "lineaments" combines the formal clarity of boundary and outline with connotations of minute particularity, as in the delicate tracery of insect wings. Blake uses the word often—no surprise from an engraver who prized the sharp "bounding line" (E 550) of traditional English "Drawing on Copper" (E 574) and who devoted his career to rendering variations on the human form, almost the only subject of his art. Blake's vast repertoire of poses is itself testimony to the human body's extension (to say nothing of its flexibility), but at stake in these pliable "lineaments" is a more primary question about what it means to be human in the first place. Blake takes his cue from *Paradise Regain'd,* where Satan puzzles over Jesus being designated "Son of God": "Who this is we must learn, for man he seems / In all his lineaments, though in his face / The glimpses of his Fathers glory shine."[82] What shape would properly fulfill the divine potential of human being? Viewed from Blake's antinomian perspective, Satan is wrong to introduce dualism into the question, as if Jesus' divinity were separable from his humanity and the light emanating through his face were in tension with the merely human lineaments of the rest of his body. Satan hopes that Jesus will turn out to have more creature in him than creator (after all, he reasons, angels and men are also "Sons of God"),[83] not realizing that Jesus will restore paradise by collapsing that distinction, embodying what Blake calls the "Human Form Divine" (*Milton* 32 [35]: 13, E 131). But Satan also inadvertently anticipates Blake's project when he suggests that the character of this Son of God, this pinnacle of human potential, is not immediately apparent but something to be learned over time. "Who this is we must learn," says Satan—to which Blake might respond: only by experiment can we learn what we are capable of becoming. Without fixed origin or outcome, Albion takes shape collectively, in a process of delineation and re-lineation that, like Eternity, will reveal its secrets periodically and endlessly. Like Milton before him—and Foucault after—Blake presents "Man" as an always extendable work in progress.[84] In *Milton*, the spokesman for this program of extension through permanent self-critique is Hillel, whose name is linked to "Lucifer." Appearing only in this work and only on one plate, Hillel advises Milton to "Judge then of thy Own Self: thy Eternal Lineaments explore / What is Eternal & what Changeable? & what Annihilable!" (*M* 32 [35]: 30–31, E 132).[85] These lines are easily deceiving, for they initially appear to support a traditional opposition between the "Eternal Lineaments" of Platonic form and the mutability of a merely mortal body. On closer inspection, however, one realizes that Hillel is proposing a different distinction altogether: between an endless capacity for self-modification (what Blake elsewhere calls energy or imagination) and the concealment of this capacity under forms that masquerade as fixed and permanent but are in fact "Changeable" or even "Annihilable." "To wash off the Not Human" (41 [48]: 1, E 142), as Blake's Milton describes his task, is to remove the incumbency of these stultifying impositions, starting with the monumental name through which Milton breaks on the poem's title page. Beneath these layers of incrustation, then, are not the "Eternal Lineaments" of an a priori form (a prelapsarian soul) but a critical agency, a permanent ability to modify and extend the lineaments of received human being by "exploring" their limits.[86]

Driving these continual shape adjustments are the anonymous events passing unknown (though "not unperceived") through the members of the individual and collective body. These agitations, these large and small convulsions, prevent the knowledge practices available at any one time from circumscribing the subject for all time. They create the friction between the felt and the known that enables critical innovation. Criticism of the kind Blake is both describing and enacting in *Milton* begins with this work of emotion.

In the chapters of *Blake's Agitation* that follow, I try to explain why such enthusiasm for the agency of emotion takes shape in Blake's work at this time. I also try to explain why Blake's work in and on emotion is, from the start, more self-consciously conflicted than the foregoing, "best-case" reading of *Milton* implies. Finally, I try to demonstrate how Blake's ambivalence toward emotion can guide an inquiry into our own critical practices.

Charting the transfer of revolutionary enthusiasm into critical enthusiasm, Part One, "Devils Party," contends that we can understand Blake's aesthetics of "agitation"—political and affective, radical and anxious—only if we consider it alongside his detachment from all regular forms of political participation. From the earliest stages of his career, Blake is characterized by a constitutive doubleness: radical inside the work, inconspicuous outside it. Since the groundbreaking work of Jacob Bronowski, Mark Schorer, and David Erdman in the 1940s and 1950s, politically minded scholars have tended to bring Blake's life in line with the radicalism of his work by emphasizing (and sometimes overreading) a few key events—especially his presence at the Gordon Riots in 1780 and his trial for sedition in 1804—not recognizing that these striking exceptions stand out against a consistent pattern of nonparticipation.[87] Whatever his opinions, Blake mostly stayed out of trouble at a time when staying out of trouble did not come easily to many of his contemporaries. Given the gap between his life and his work, perhaps our sharpest insight into Blake's contradictions comes from an unexpected source, his Prussian contemporary Kant, who in 1795, in an essay that would eventually find its way into *Conflict of the Faculties,* developed his crucial theory of the nonparticipant revolutionary spectator. In the immediate aftermath of The Terror, Kant made the counterintuitive case that the meaning of the French Revolution, indeed its claim to being a world-transforming event, lay not in the actions undertaken in Paris by the revolutionaries themselves but solely in the sympathy and enthusiasm of nonparticipant spectators. In a single decisive move, Kant transfers historical agency to a newly emergent public whose role is to keep watch and exercise critical judgment. From this point on, according to Kant, *only* the genuine enthusiasm of the independent critical thinker, and not the agency of direct action, makes progressive historical change possible. Describing this revolutionary spectator, whose critical engagements take on such urgency as to feel like actions themselves, Kant could have been describing Blake. And if Kant helps us understand why Blake's contradictions are more broadly representative of the modern progressive intellectual than his singular eccentricities might lead us to believe, it is Milton who helps us understand how Blake arrived at this position. What Blake learned from Milton, and especially from *Samson Agonistes,* was how to represent revolutionary violence in a way that sympathetically imagines and sustains its transformative potential while also delaying its enactment, transferring its energies and desires into the patient work of close, critical reading and thinking instead. Following his own political disappointments, Milton transformed himself and his prospective readers into prototypes of the Kantian spectator, endorsing *and* disavowing revolutionary agency, keeping alive in affect a revolutionary impulse he no longer believed in enacting directly.

With Kant supplying the theory, Milton the model, and Blake the practice, Part One of this book emphasizes the compensatory role of emotion at the beginnings of modern critical engagement. Emotion provides a substantive feeling of agency even as criticism begins to disavow any direct course of action; it supplies an immediate feeling of change even as criticism embraces a labor so long, slow, and indeterminate that it resembles nothing so much as inaction. By turning to the self-evidence of emotion, criticism can claim to be "vigorous most" even "when most unactive deem'd" (as Milton's chorus claims of Samson).[88] Part Two, "A Passion for Blake," complicates this account by raising two questions. Even as he came to embody the revolutionary spectator, how did Blake himself understand the promise and limits of the passions as they inflect criticism and agency? And what does Blake's own critique of emotion tell us about the passion modern critics continue to invest in his work and in the transformative role of the emotions more generally? Like others in his sentimental era who were suspicious of Enlightenment abstraction, Blake found the links among emotion, defamiliarization, and innovation deeply attractive, even irresistible. But he also recognized that emotions constrain experience as often as they unsettle and enliven it, and even worse, that it is often difficult to distinguish the liveliness of emotion from the formal mechanisms of social routine. In his investigation of sympathy in a poem like "On Anothers Sorrow" or in his representation of the rhythmic heartbeat in *Milton,* Blake turns sensibility (spontaneity, immediacy, liveliness) into a problem: emotion is the undecidability of mechanism and vitality, not the liberation of the latter from the former. For Blake, there simply is no emotional authenticity that escapes this irresolution, and even the enthusiasm of critical engagement cannot avoid the suspicion that its affective agency may be a type of wishful self-deception, one to which modern cultural critics, who see so little evidence of their influence on the world, may be especially prone. In 1939, Jean-Paul Sartre spoke to the promise and anxiety that have haunted critical enthusiasts from the Romantic period forward. Although he defined emotion as "a transformation of the world," he quickly added that "emotive behavior is not on the same plane as the other behaviors; it is not *effective.*"[89] When is the emotion in criticism transformative? When is it ineffective? Is it possible that emotion could appear to be one but actually be the other? How would one tell these two outcomes apart? These questions do not arise often enough in our own understandings and performances of emotion, but they were already troubling Blake.

"If the Spectator Could Enter into These Images . . . on the Fiery Chariot of His Contemplative Thought"

As Picciotto tells the story in *Labors of Innocence in Early Modern England*, the prehistory of our "modern intellectual ambitions" (16) commences when seventeenth-century experimentalists, motivated by Baconian principles, began to consider critical thinking as a species of action or labor in the world: "The organizing figures of experimentalist labor—the figures through which intellectual life first threw off the dichotomy of action and contemplation and defined itself as productive—have been preserved almost unchanged in the arena of cultural criticism" (27). "Inventing the intellectual as an interventionist spectator," the early experimentalists "tried to link representing the world to acting upon it" (10), and the plausibility of their self-understanding very much depended on the hands-on nature of their work, the proud crafting of laboratory instruments and the physical manipulation of specimens that made their experiments a labor of mind and body both. Although powerfully attractive, and thus of lasting influence on the cultural critic's self-image, this model of intellectual labor from the start "posed an enormous challenge to intellectuals who had only words at their disposal"; indeed, writes Picciotto, it was, "in many ways, a preposterous model for literary authors" (13). Even Milton, who succeeded in turning *Paradise Lost* into a dynamic textual lens analogous to the microscope or the telescope, thereby enlisting his reader as a fellow experimentalist, could not avoid the realization that, "At times, the perfect union of action and contemplation seems achievable only through metaphor, one that obscures the sedentary conditions of reading and writing" (Picciotto 411).

A central argument of this study is that between the critical intellectual's earliest modern attempts at self-definition and the most recent incarnations, the emotions specific to critical labor were summoned to reinforce an association between contemplation and action that was troubled from the start. Whether emotion effectively binds contemplation and action together, turning "Contemplative Thought" into a "Fiery Chariot," or simply obscures more deeply the "sedentary conditions of reading and writing," remains an open question in Blake's critical labors, as it does in our own. Blake, however, presents an especially interesting case in this history.

He is at once exemplary of the new tendency to value the agency of emotion in critical engagement and, because he was a professional engraver, a throwback to earlier models of the intellectual as manual laborer. Picciotto explains that one of the crucial insights leading experimentalists "to imagine the thinker as a worker was their discovery that workers were thinkers" (10); in the seventeenth-century world of collective endeavor, the scientist's innovations were fully integrated with those of craftsmen, artisans, mechanics, and lens grinders. This union of mind and body is something no one needed to explain to Blake, who (as Joseph Viscomi has reconstructed in rich detail) prepared his own plates, inks, waxes, acids, and color washes; owned and operated a large wooden rolling press; and invented a new method of illuminated printing that he believed would make his works less costly to produce and more marketable to the public.[90] The physical exertion and manipulation of materials that were a condition of daily labor for Blake, however, were at best a subject tinged with nostalgia for most Romantic period intellectuals, who indeed "had only words at their disposal" and increasingly became dependent on the evidence of strong emotion to supply a more robust experience of critical thought in action.

Consider, for example, Coleridge's remarkable confession in the *Biographia Literaria* of his appreciation for "Jacob Behmen" (whom Blake of course also admired), "the poor ignorant *shoemaker,* who had dared think for himself."[91] By invoking Kant's "*Sapere aude!*" ("Dare to think!"),[92] Coleridge right away introduces Boehme as an idealized figure in the history of influences he is tracing: his function is to reconcile the practices of modern enlightenment with an older artisanal enthusiasm and if he does not quite fulfill the promise of that role he at least points the way for Coleridge to complete the task. Most importantly, Boehme serves as a reminder that critical thinking can be a whole-body experience, something lost to the subsequent specialization of knowledge and, even worse, actively disdained by the reigning "Literary aristocracy," which has formed "a tacit compact among the learned as a privileged order" (I:140). When Coleridge departs from a methodical defense of occult writings to indulge in his own outburst of sympathetic enthusiasm, one quickly realizes how eager he is to assimilate Boehme's affective power, even as he simultaneously disavows the uneducated man's errors.

> O! it requires deeper feeling, and a stronger imagination, than belong to most of those, to whom reasoning and fluent expression have been as a trade learnt in boyhood, to conceive with what *might,* with what inward *strivings* and *commotion,* the perception of a new and vital TRUTH takes possession of an uneducated man of genius . . . Need we then be surprised, that under an excitement at once so strong and so unusual, the man's body should sympathize with the struggles of his mind; or that

he should at times be so far deluded, as to mistake the tumultuous sensations of his nerves, and the co-existing spectres of his fancy, as parts or symbols of the truths which were opening on him? (I:150–151)

Coleridge takes from Boehme with one hand and pushes away with the other. He yearns to share in the affective convulsion of an overwhelming intellectual discovery but not to the point of delusion, where one might pathologically confuse the body's tumult for insights of the mind (the usual charge against enthusiasm). He wants to recruit Boehme's upheavals as an escape from the self-perpetuating routines that pass for thinking among the formally educated (for "whom reasoning and fluent expression have been as a trade learnt in boyhood"), but only to the extent that they can assist the proper philosopher as an agent of innovation. In essence, what Coleridge wants from Boehme and other working-class enthusiasts is for emotion to renew thought from below, or, as he puts it, "to keep alive the *heart* in the *head*": "For the writings of these mystics acted in no slight degree to prevent my mind from being imprisoned within the outline of any single dogmatic system. They contributed to keep alive the *heart* in the *head*; gave me an indistinct, yet stirring and working presentment, that all the products of the mere *reflective* faculty partook of DEATH, and were as the rattling twigs and sprays in winter, into which a sap was yet to be propelled, from some root to which I had not penetrated, if they were to afford my soul either food or shelter" (I:152). This is no simple case of artisan envy. Mee has described how Coleridge strategically uses Boehme to promote spiritual quietism against the threat of an explosive, collective enthusiasm from below.[93] Still, we should not underestimate how badly Coleridge needs the affective depth he believes Boehme's writings can transmit and the opening onto the future their enthusiasm seems to enable. Although the *Biographia*'s model of organic integration is one where "the whole soul of man" is brought "into activity" (II:15–16), to get there Coleridge must first borrow on the authenticity of working-class embodiment and emotion precisely because he believes they supply a vital sap that the sedentary intellectual laborer now appears to lack.

If this small episode from the *Biographia Literaria* participates in an association between emotion and critical innovation that first became necessary in the Romantic period, it also serves as a cautionary lesson about personifying that association in the figure of the artisan intellectual. Throughout this volume, I have tried to remain cognizant that Blake may play the same role for us that Boehme played for Coleridge.[94] On our side, the professionalization of knowledge production and the specialization of critical practices make it impossible for us not to worry, as Coleridge worried, that intellectuals participate in "a tacit compact among the learned as a privileged order," or that the institutional conditions of our training and our labor make significant innovation increasingly unimaginable, or that our work in words has little demonstrable relation to change in the world. In such circumstances, the work of emotion within criticism takes on charged significance, and Blake—hands dirty from his trade, and self-mythologizing his labor in the heroic figure of Los, equipped with hammer and tongs—becomes a figure of the intellectual worker difficult for those at a desk to resist. Blake's investment in the "Fiery Chariot of . . . Contemplative Thought" is sufficiently modern to reinforce our own conviction that contemplation should itself be a form of action, but he is also sufficiently other (artisanal, self-educated, and antinomian) to ground that possibility in material conditions that can seem, from our vantage point, more vigorous than our own. We desire the visceral movement and excitement and "allusive agility" (as Frye once described it) that "the reading of Blake demands,"[95] much as Coleridge desired the "inward *strivings* and *commotion*" Boehme made available to him. We want to believe that our agitated susceptibility to Blake's work functions as a sign that we are not destined merely to repeat the privileges of our learning and that we too possess the "deeper feeling, and . . . stronger imagination" necessary to conceive what it is like when "a new and vital TRUTH takes possession of an uneducated man of genius." We who have only words at our disposal need the productive estrangement promised by Blake's enthusiasm, perhaps too much so, and for that reason we must always be wary of turning Blake into a personification that answers to our need.

PART ONE

Devil's Party

CHAPTER ONE

Blake's Agitation

Thought works over what is received, it seeks to reflect on it and overcome it. It seeks to determine what has already been thought, written, painted, or socialized in order to determine what hasn't been. We know this process well, it is our daily bread. It is the bread of war, soldier's biscuit. But this agitation, in the noblest sense of the word (agitation is the word Kant gives to the activity of the mind that has judgment and exercises it), this agitation is only possible if something remains to be determined, something that hasn't yet been determined. One can strive to determine this something by setting up a system, a theory, a programme or a project—and indeed one has to, all the while anticipating that something. One can also inquire about the remainder, and allow the indeterminate to appear as a question mark.

—Jean-François Lyotard, "The Sublime and the Avant-Garde"

The moving of (anything) to and fro—shaking. A state or condition of being moved to and fro; commotion, disturbance, perturbation.

—*Oxford English Dictionary* entry for "agitation"

The Agitated Reader: Entering Jerusalem

"Agitation" is a word always moving to and fro among its at least doubled meanings: on one side, an interior, affective state ("to feel agitated"); on the other, a political intervention, often connoting activism, sometimes even criminality ("to agitate").[1] How these paired aspects of "agitation" (active and passive, public and private, political and subjective) converge in the figure of William Blake and what their adhesion tells us about the beginnings of modern critical engagement are the subjects of this chapter. Perhaps our quickest entry into Blake's oppositional aesthetic, however, comes from an obsolete definition of "agitation," which at one time could simply mean "exercise" or "activity." Synonymous with vigorous move-ment or animation, "agitation" is necessary to the health of living organisms, its spirited motion a sign of death-defying vitality.[2] Thus Samuel Johnson illustrated his definition by quoting Francis Bacon: "Putrefaction asketh rest; for the subtle motion which putrefaction requireth, is disturbed by any agitation."[3] To have one's rest disturbed (to be susceptible to agitation) is to be alive. In a late essay on "The Physical Effect of Philosophy," Immanuel Kant quotes Chryssipus to similar effect: "Nature has endowed the pig with a *soul* instead of *salt* so that the pig would not *putrefy.*" This self-agitating soul, which he renames "animal instinct," keeps the pig in motion and prevents it from rotting on its feet.[4] Human beings also require an internal impulse, but because their life depends upon intellectual vitality, Kant recommends critical philosophy as the source of agitation necessary to resist sleep and death (his figures for the *mental* inertia of doctrine or dogma), arguing that the exercise spurred by philosophy will prolong even the life of the body. It was in this spirit of agitation (promoting the mental and bodily health of moving to and fro), though infused with the enthusiasm of dissenting terms like "shaker," "quaker," and "ranter," that Blake undertook his work of "rouz[ing] the faculties to act."[5] Now we know just where to accent a declaration from *Jerusalem*: "I know of no other Christianity and of no other Gospel than the liberty of both body & mind *to exercise the Divine Arts of Imagination*" (77, E 231, emphasis added). As the biblical Book of Daniel suggests, this sort of calisthenic agitation is always the prerequisite of apocalypse: "Many shall run to and fro, and knowledge shall increase" (12:4). Move-ment, exercise, and activity indicate a world not yet settled permanently into place, a world where even death may be subject to change. By means of what Lyotard (after Kant) and Blake (after biblical prophecy) call "judgment," the grave may yet release its corpses into air. In the meantime, the important point is to keep moving to and fro, to keep up the agitation.[6]

Given the significance of vigorous motion or of what Blake continued in his late work to call "energy," it's no wonder that, in the frontispiece to *Jerusalem,* Los looks like he has been caught in an act of transgression (figure 1.1). Sneaking about in the dark, with one foot on either side of a threshold someone doesn't want him to cross, making little effort to conceal an explosive device (his "globe of fire" [45:3, E 194]), Los is on a self-appointed guerrilla mission to agitate. As Morton Paley notes, he is dressed as a London night watchman, but this is surely a disguise, for the activities he undertakes as "the Watchman of Eternity" (*Milton* 24:9, E 119) are purely antinomian.[7] Breaking through the two-dimensional picture plane by stepping forward, using the light of his handheld fire to pierce the confinement of the doorway frame, Los, like a thief in the night, is out to break the law, stir things up, or at least raise hell: "Awake! awake O sleeper of the land of shadows, wake!

Figure 1.1 Jerusalem, copy E, plate 1, frontispiece, 1804-1820. Yale Center for British Art, Paul Mellon Collection

expand!" (4:6, E 146). Even this early on, such hammering exclamations tell us that *Jerusalem* will be a loud poem.[8] In an ongoing act of disturbing the peace, Los will desperately insist that his readers share his insomnia.

And for these reasons, he looks guilty enough to match Blake's melodramatic confession in the poem's dedication "To the Public": "I am perhaps the most sinful of men!" (3, E 145). The frontispiece catches Los in a startled moment, surprised by law, his forward motion into the unregulated suspended as he looks to the right of the picture space. Whether he has literally come under the eye of detection, the

eye of an offstage "watchfiend" (a *real* night watchman) whose voice has hailed
him, or has been suddenly stopped by his own paranoid certainty of invisible,
ubiquitous assassins (Los "saw every Minute Particular of Albion degraded & murderd / But saw not by whom" [45:7–8, E 194]), the image establishes the axis of conflict upon which *Jerusalem* will turn.[9] Forward, moving through the picture plane
and into the book, lies the agitation that is life ("the Divine Mercy / Steps beyond
and Redeems Man" [32:54–55, E 179]); to either side lie the allied cultural forces that
frame, freeze, and in both senses of the term petrify (putrefy?) those who fall under
their scrutiny. These are the agents of moral law; their punishing tactics result in
all those horizontal figures that stretch across *Jerusalem*'s illuminations like so
many sarcophagi blocking the progress of the living (figure 1.2). When Los loses
focus, interrupting his mission to turn his head sharply in profile, he momentarily
succumbs to the single vision he is determined to disrupt, "the deadly sleep of six
thousand years" (96:11, E 255). Much later, in the apocalyptic plate 97, we see only
the back of his head as he strides unhesitantly into Eternity, the dynamite already
detonated and flooding with light a landscape now without boundaries (figure 1.3).

Right at the start of *Jerusalem*, then, the frontispiece aligns truth with intellectual and bodily motion and against the arresting lie of the law: "he who will not defend Truth, may be compelled to defend / A Lie: . . . he might be snared and caught
and snared and taken" (9:29–30, E 152). Blake's lack of readers in a work of public
address notwithstanding, we can see that the frontispiece compels the imagined
viewer to join Los's risky forward momentum; the image enlists the reader in an
act of agitation and thus constructs the moment of reading as itself oppositional.
For all of Blake's warnings about addiction to guilty pleasures (as in the prefatory
poem to *Europe*), we cannot enter *Jerusalem* without the exhilarated feeling that we
are somehow, even if vicariously, sinning. We're behind Los, his silent backers.
Before we even encounter the first word of the poem, we feel agitated, dangerous,
at odds with the powers that be, and we *like* it. And yet, before we get carried away
by this antinomian "visceral vibrato" (to anticipate a term from Lyotard), we need
to ask what it means to become an agitator in this fashion, to have so thoroughly
blurred the affective state and the troublemaking action simultaneously conveyed

Figure 1.2 Jerusalem, copy E, plate 67, 1804–1820, detail. Yale Center for British Art, Paul
Mellon Collection

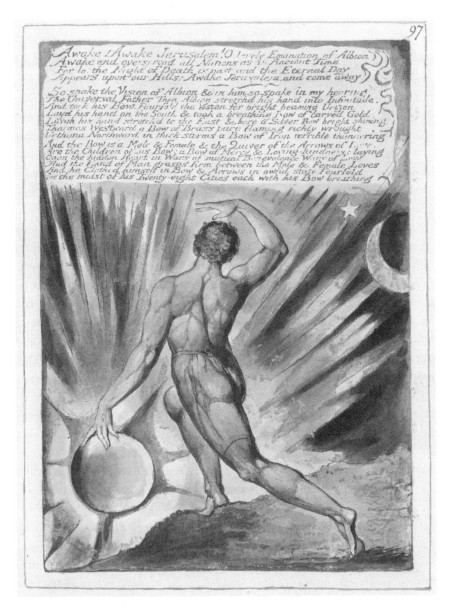

Figure 1.3 Jerusalem, copy E, plate 97, 1804–1820. Yale Center for British Art, Paul Mellon Collection

by the word "agitation." Blake felt strongly that his heightened state of engagement and urgent resistance to social codes, reverberating so loudly in poems that
barely circulated, had public significance: "For Albion's sake / I now am what I
am" (8:17–18, E 151). Presumably the accomplice reader is meant to feel the same.
But this shared conviction raises a question that informs this chapter and the
next: What happens when the troublemaking ways of a critically engaged writer or
reader go almost unnoticed? Blake famously declared that the Milton of *Paradise
Lost* remained a radical despite himself: he was "of the Devils party without knowing it" (*Marriage* 6, E 35). But Blake's agitation allows us to turn this quip upside
down and direct a question to Blake and his readers instead: Is it possible to believe
oneself a revolutionary devil while remaining harmless and inconsequential?

To approach these questions, I want to consider Blake in the context of Kant's
late work. We start with the Kant whose name is a "prologue to postmodernity,"[10]
Lyotard's Kant; then turn to the Kant responsible for theorizing the eighteenth-
century public sphere, as emphasized by Jürgen Habermas; and finally focus on
Kant's response to the French Revolution in *Conflict of the Faculties*. After publishing the Third Critique in 1790, Kant devoted his final works to a set of issues
remarkably similar to those that kept Blake awake at night, namely, how to end
war by promoting "Mental Fight" (*Milton* 1 [i], E 95) instead and why mental fight
requires as its political form a representative republic.[11] At first glance, Kant's
well-known emphasis on "obedience to the laws" would seem to render him an unlikely candidate to illuminate Blake's antinomianism, an incongruity with which
we have to reckon.[12] Blake would have found little appeal in Kant's model of a
rational tribunal to decide cases of conflicting interests; indeed, that model corresponds to his own vision of a police state ("Babylon"), where force secures by
night the hegemony that the law court cannot fully achieve by day: "O Babylon thy
Watchman stands over thee in the night / Thy severe Judge all the day proves thee"
(24:26–27, E 169). To begin, however, I want to join with Lyotard in looking to the
Kant who, like Blake, set the agitation of aesthetic judgment *against* the Enlightenment ideals of self-discipline and rule of law. According to Lyotard, an alternative
mode of judgment emerges in the Kantian sublime, a mode of critical judgment
that bears witness to those unanticipated, not yet expressible conflicts ("differends") the language of the law cannot define and thus cannot logically resolve. In
the sublime moment neither objects nor the subjects engaged in judgment can be
coordinated under a unitary representation. "The appeal to judgment results from
a conflict between faculties. Two phrases from heterogeneous regimes, here, imagination and reason, do not succeed in agreeing about an object that gives rise to
the feeling of the sublime. Their conflict is signaled by a sign, an eloquent silence,
and by a feeling that is always an agitation, that is, an impossible phrase." "Impos-

sible" because no existing linguistic code can articulate it fully without leaving an unspoken remainder, this phrase/feeling creates a commotion difficult to locate, moving as it does across intellectual, linguistic, and physiological sites. Drawing his catalogue from Kant's "Analytic of the Sublime," Lyotard calls this commotion "an alternation, an exchange between two poles, a thrust inhibited by an obstacle, a movement to and fro . . . a visceral vibrato, an excitation of the life force"—in sum, "agitation" or "the syncopated rhythm of health."[13] In short, the subject of sublimity feels moved, and such agitation, always in motion between established modes of representation ("the deafness of established forms"),[14] generates the indeterminate moment that, as Blake puts it, Satan's watchfiends cannot find.[15]

For Lyotard, then, it is the aesthetic component of Kant's philosophy that makes it critical, for affective disturbance indicates thought rubbing against doctrine. Intellectual resistance takes root in the body, invigorates the feeling of life force, and—its personal, interior origin notwithstanding—has public consequences. Triggered by the lack of fit between a given case and the available set of rules, or between singular experience and conceptual norms, judgment's arrhythmia embodies the (paradoxical) health of the agitated and "unfit." As Jerome Christensen points out in his study of Byron, even the word "fit" is characterized by internal agitation, for sometimes it "suggests the synonym of *decorous* or *correspondent*, sometimes the synonym of *convulsion*—the kind of fit, one might say, that is the perfect antithesis of a good fit."[16] One recalls Blake's response to the passage in *The Excursion* where Wordsworth celebrates the exquisite agreement of individual mind and external world: "You shall not bring me down to believe such fitting and fitted I know better" (E 667). In his strangely titled "Announcement of the Near Conclusion of a Treaty for Eternal Peace in Philosophy," Kant recommends the health benefits of such noncorrespondence and disagreement (whether internal, epistemological, or social). Philosophy is inherently contrary and luckily so. "To philosophize" is "to dispute," to dispute is "to bicker," to bicker is "to lead an open war," and this vigorous, belligerent impulse, which is the intellectual counterpart to the pig's animal instinct, averts "the putrefaction of the living body." A primary objective of critical philosophy, Kant argues, is to resist the agreement of the good fit, the kind of unproblematic subject-object correspondence philosophers claim when they want to announce truths, dominate others, and foreclose on dispute.

[Critical] philosophy, which is a perpetually armed state (against those who would perversely confuse appearances with things in themselves) and indeed an armed state that thereby also incessantly accompanies the activity of reason—this philosophy opens the prospect of an eternal peace among philosophers by showing, on the one hand, the impotence of the *theoretical* proof of the opponent and by demonstrating, on the other, the strength of the *practical* reasons for the assumption of its principles. This peace has, in addition, the advantage of always keeping alert the powers of the subject exposed to the apparent danger of attacks, thereby promoting by means of philosophy the intention of nature to enliven the subject continually and to guard against the sleep of death.17

Critical judgment is a mode of perpetual armed resistance, a permanent vigilance against doctrine. If Kant believed that such intellectual resistance directly enhanced the health of the body, he also believed, just as literally, that it corresponded to the health of the body politic. Kant's military metaphor may be jarring, but he did not choose it carelessly. Determined in the 1790s to grasp the intellectual and social conditions by which war would become obsolete, Kant was convinced that the agitation of critical judgment represented not a fanciful but a precise alternative. He seems to have believed quite literally that people who think for themselves will not easily go to war for others. "A constitutional disposition toward conflict," he wrote in reference to both the individual intellect and the enlightened state, "is not yet a war but, instead, should and can keep war at bay."18 By prolonging the war of ideas, critical judgment unfits the subject from the uniform, drumbeat ideology deployed in any military campaign. The strength of the individual's agitation demonstrates the impotence of a warring regime's "theoretical" claim upon its subjects, that is, its strategic effort "to confuse appearances with things in themselves" and make the state's interested representations pass for reality. Kant assesses philosophical positions in terms of "impotence" and "strength" because power is at stake.

More than anything else, this belief that critical judgment guards its enlivened subject against the sleep of a soldier's death, figuratively *and* literarily, marks the point of convergence between Blake and Kant.

> For the Soldier who fights for Truth, calls his enemy his brother:
> They fight & contend for life, & not for eternal death!
> But here the Soldier strikes, & a dead corse falls at his feet   (38:41–43, E 185)

Especially in Blake's later works, written when the campaigns against the French Republic had evolved almost without interruption into the Napoleonic Wars, the objective of agitation, of promoting a "perpetually armed state" of mental fight, was to end actual warfare. Like Kant, Blake considered war a direct consequence of the death of thought by doctrine. One of *Jerusalem*'s most poignant conceits depicts unthinking sailors temporarily asleep in the hold of an English man-of-war; they soon will sleep permanently in a coffin: "Six months they lie embalmed in silent death: warshipped / Carried in Arks of Oak" (21:44–45, E 167). Blake's brilliant, bitter pun, "warshipped," especially when coupled with another on the wooden "ark" carried by ancient Israelites into battle, makes it impossible to separate military service from orthodox belief; the sailor's mind and body have both been conscripted.[19] Hardened by ideology and emptied of its critical resistance, its agitating power, thought is already predisposed to become a sword ("He seizd the bars of condens'd thought to forge them: / Into the swords of war" [9:4–5, E 152]). Amid the hysteria concerning a French invasion under Napoleon—"old Boney" in the press, as Alan Liu has documented—Los watches the Sons of Albion hardening into a single national mind prepared for battle, or as he puts it, "Bonifying into a Scull" (58:8, E 207).[20]

Aware of these consequences of "the sleep of death," the subject of critical judgment keeps himself awake compulsively; he becomes "a sort of insomniac night watchman, a vigilant sentinel who defends himself against the torpor of doctrines by the practice of criticism. Doctrines weave a spell that prefigures death; the spasm is a salutary illness because it shakes us out of the doctrinal torpor."[21] Lyotard's trope of the convulsive, insomniac night watchman describes "the judicious spirit" in Kant,[22] but it could just as easily describe Blake, who announces early in *Jerusalem,* "Trembling I sit day and night, my friends are astonish'd at me . . . I rest not from my great task!" (5:16–17, E 147), and whose mythologically empowered self, Los, "all night watches / The stars rising & setting" (83:80–81, E 242). Insomnia is Lyotard's figure for a resistance to doctrine so tireless and thorough that it contests the very "authority of the idiom in which cases are established and regulated," assuring that language remains "at war with itself" so that warfare might become unnecessary, impossible.[23] In this sense, the right war, the war in which Los is Blake's arsonist-agent, is a war on behalf of "Minute Particulars" against the "Generalizing Gods" (89:17, 30, E 248). Midnight agitation has less to do with violating specific, local prohibitions than with refusing the systematic violence of law per se, the function of which is to subsume radically incommensurate particulars (including people: "& every / Particular is a Man" [91:29–30, E 251]) into a general economy of abstract principles.[24] As Lyotard insists, the vitality of disagreement results not from a competition among preexisting doctrines but from thought's resistance to top-down doctrine altogether. The sleepless, misfit subject of critical judgment "moves between rules and cases," he writes, "not between doctrines. There lies the real war, the right war, the true *differend.*"[25]

In his late prophecies, Blake tells the story of this holy war continuously. Its archetypal scenes are the incarnation (divinity assuming a particular body) and the crucifixion (the divine body judged by law and put to death). Its archetypal antagonists, of course, are Imagination and Reason, the "heterogeneous regimes" that produce irreconcilable phrases and thereby, according to Lyotard, the sublime.

When Reason dominates this antagonism, the many features of Ulro appear: its alliance with state tyranny and the war machine, its repression of eros, its ascetic capitalism, its idolatry of what the deists "call" Natural (52, E 201)—the worship of doxa, the already given. Under Reason, the twin symptoms in Blake's cosmology are rock formation and narcolepsy: objects turn to stone, and subjects fall asleep. Albion lies down upon his "Couch of repose," which in turn rests "Upon the Rock of Ages" (48:4, 6, E 196), where "Every Minute Particular [has] hardend into grains of sand" (45:20, E 194). In the frontispiece to the Fitzwilliam *Jerusalem*, the archway under which Los passes includes this description of Albion: "His Sublime & Pathos become Two Rocks fixd in the Earth" (1, E 144). In Blake's war, the agitator must work to dislodge stone, must set these hardened forms "rocking to and fro" (90:61, E 250). Surrounded by "rocky Spectres" (78:5, E 233), he must transform his readers into subjects of sublimity who can once again feel moved.

Thus Blake's climactic scenes of judgment (apocalyptic, aesthetic, and critical) often feature a recurring set of elements: arousal from numbness, sleep, and death; mobilization of static or inert forms; recovery of the particular from generalization. When Blake and Los join together in *Milton*, for instance, arousal, mobility, and particularity characterize the speech of the revived, inspired prophet: he rises in strength and fury, walks to and fro ("up and down" [22:18, E 117]) in his newly bound sandals, and suddenly sees that "every fabric of Six Thousand Years" (22:20, E 117) has been preserved, every detail of history rescued from oblivion. Because prophecy of this kind is the effect of critical judgment in action, Los's agitation doubles as an idealized description of the empowered reader, who, like Blake, has also merged with Los. If Los moves to and fro across the tapestry of six thousand years without neglecting the significance of a single fabric, hair or particle of dust,[26] then Blake's reader similarly traverses an illuminated text so richly detailed that "not a letter is Insignificant" nor a "Blade of Grass" nor a "Blur or Mark" ("A Vision of the Last Judgment," E 560). Rejecting the monotony of Miltonic blank verse, the introductory note to *Jerusalem* even includes meter among those textual elements so minutely differentiated as to promote (what Lyotard calls) the "syncopated rhythm of health," for the reader must be attuned to "variety in every line, both of cadences & number of syllables" (3, E 146). Blake aims to arouse the reader's faculties in such a way that arousal itself will feel incompatible with generalization. And Blake criticism has eagerly embraced this call to agitation, recognizing strong affect as evidence of opposition. The more vigorously the critical act cartwheels to and fro across the minute particulars of a given text, or even across the entire corpus, tracing an open-ended series of semiotic links, the more convincing the sign that the critic is awake, sharing in the enthusiast's insomnia. Like Los, the reader moves among "the living" (8:35, E 151), resisting putrefaction.[27] And because the exercise of such intra- and intertextual movement can be extended indefinitely, with yet another detail (a passage, an image, a word, a letter, even a blur) available to alter the configuration of meaning, critical activity exceeds any synoptic interpretive strategy brought to bear on Blake's text, disabling the claims of a misguided system criticism. Without recourse to a totalizing composure, critical judgment *is* this activity of agitation, defined by its arousal, particularity, and movement to and fro.

With so much at stake in this initial description of agitation as an affective resistance to generalization and immobility, it may be useful to recall an argument once commonly leveled against poststructuralism, and against deconstruction particularly: although its commitment to radical particularity ("the prosaic materiality of the letter," in de Man's memorable phrase) powerfully undermines theories of organic unity, deconstruction seems to dead-end on the verge of any social or political consequences it promises.[28] As Frances Ferguson puts it, "an infinity of materiality ['the essence of the deconstructive position'] . . . effectively counters the notion that there could be a practical politics."[29] Although he considers Lyotard's joining of aesthetics and politics more promising than de Man's, Martin Jay voices a similar objection: "The sublime may be useful as a warning against violently submitting incommensurable *differends* to the discipline of homogenizing theory, but it doesn't offer much in the way of positive help with the choices that have to be made."[30] If radical particularity is considered incompatible with organizational needs of any sort, then it is indeed hard to understand how such particularity could be translated into a program of positive political action. Why would feeling unfit and agitated ever lead one to agitate? What would one agitate for, and with whom? Reasonable as they may be, these are not quite the right questions to ask of Blake. Despite his extravagant commitment to minute particularity, Blake never argued that such particularity is antithetical to either aesthetic or social formation. In fact, he argued the opposite: "he who wishes to see a Vision; a perfect Whole / Must see it in its Minute Particulars; Organized' (91:20–21, E 251).[31] The challenge with Blake is to understand why he considered minute particularity compatible with collective existence. Addressing that challenge would go far toward reframing a still relevant dispute once waged between John Barrell and Morris Eaves; Barrell emphasized the influence on Blake of eighteenth-century ideas of civic humanism and Eaves Blake's internalization of bourgeois individualism and autonomy.[32] How did Blake manage to merge his private and public commitments? To return to the frontispiece of *Jerusalem*: what social vision allowed Blake to experience his private agitation, his independent acts of resistant critical judgment, as something essential to the health of his nation? ("For Albions sake / I now am what I am.")

And, finally, what if individual affective resistance of the kind I have been describing turns out not to be a form of troublemaking disturbance but a *constitutive* feature of the social order itself?

Agitating in Public

History will show the wonderful Effects of ORATORY . . . Modern
Political Oratory being chiefly performed by the Pen and Press, its
Advantages over the Antient in some Respects are to be shown; as
that its Effects are more extensive, and more lasting.

—Benjamin Franklin, *Proposals Relating to the
Education of Youth in Pennsylvania*

However exclusive the public might be in any given instance, it could
never close itself off entirely and become an isolated clique; for it
was always understood and found itself immersed within a more
inclusive public of all private people, persons who—insofar as they
were propertied and educated—as readers, listeners, and spectators
could avail themselves via the market of the objects that were subject
to discussion. The issues discussed became "general" not merely in
their significance, but also in their accessibility: everyone had to *be
able* to participate.

—Jürgen Habermas, *The Structural Transformation of the Public Sphere*

The keeping of a political or other object constantly before public attention, by appeals, discussion, etc.; public excitement.

—*Oxford English Dictionary* entry for "agitation"

Following Lyotard, we have been emphasizing the internal urgency of critical engagement, but we have not yet recognized the explicitly political history with which "agitation" is also sedimented. Running alongside its association with vigorous affect, another meaning affiliates the word with official governmental processes, leaving it uncertain whether agitation tends toward a notion of personal independence or one of public order and powers of state. From the perspective of the sovereign subject, agitation might describe the healthy commotion generated by different social interests and the multiplicity of individuals exercising critical judgment, a multiplicity best accommodated by decentered, liberal institutions. By the seventeenth century, "agitation" could be used as a nearly technical term for Parliamentary debate, signifying the obligation of representatives to defend positions and allow for open disagreement, thus guarding against arbitrary executive decisions. Not long before he became Latin Secretary to Cromwell's Council of State, Milton could describe Parliament "preparing, discussing, agitating, concluding what is to be done."[33] Traditionally, then, English agitation has been bound up with an ideal of dynamic discourse (Latin, *discurs-us,* running to and fro) in which internal conflict is considered a public good, provoking the exercise of judgment necessary for a healthy body politic. Alternatively, the word has sometimes been taken to express the primacy of a unitary state, with power to make critical judgment a function of its own central administration. The former Soviet Union, for instance, boasted a Department of Propaganda and Agitation as part of the Communist Party's Central Committee. In *Perpetual Peace* (1795), Kant was already worried about a similar tendency in Jacobin democracy, which he considered despotic "because it establishes an executive power in which 'all' decide for or even against one who does not agree; that is, 'all,' who are not quite all, decide."[34] The Jacobin state acted upon the assumption that all the members of a revolutionary polity ("the people") fit.

By the mid-eighteenth century, the British emphasis on healthy controversy had undergone a steady process of generalization, and agitation became broadly synonymous with vigorous discussion itself, as in the phrase "to agitate a question." If the word once referred rather narrowly to an activity *within* Parliament, by the early nineteenth century it could mean (as it can today) an effort to arouse or rally the general public *outside* government and often *in opposition to* official policies. In England, which Habermas takes as his model case, this semantic trajectory parallels the evolution of a bourgeois public sphere independent of and able to criticize the state. According to Habermas, Parliament began to step away from feudal violence when it systematically incorporated conflict into its deliberations, establishing permanent opposition in the form of a minority party out of power. The same principle was subsequently extended when the press won the right to publish parliamentary proceedings so that a reading public could, in principle, be well-enough informed to contest government decisions. The culmination of this struggle encompassed the same half-century as Blake's career, and it informs one of his annotations to Bishop Watson's *Apology for the Bible*: "Nothing can be more contemptible than to suppose Public RECORDS to be true Read them & Judge. if you are not a Fool" (E 617). Blake could urge a skeptical, critical stance only because by 1798 the press published many such records. Journals and newspapers play a central role in Habermas's account of a growing sphere of critical judgment, and he credits the developing strength of the English independent press with making "critical commentary and public opposition against the government part of the normal state of affairs."[35] It is in this "normal state" that agitation came to signify three simultaneous and analogical activities, all joined, we could say, under Blake's banner, "Opposition is true Friendship" (*Marriage* 20, E 42): that of an individual, critical orientation toward received authority; that of government debate, internal but open to view; that of public opinion independent of the state. Alternatively, a nation without agitation was what Blake, in a late letter to Cumberland, ironically called "a happy state," declaring that "since the French Revolution Englishman are all intermeasurable by one another: certainly a happy state of agreement, in which I for one do not agree" (E 783).

In light of the intersection of private and public roles in this period, it is instructive to consider the case of Edmund Burke, whom the *OED* quotes twice to illustrate the meaning of agitation. In his 1774 *Speech on American Taxes,* Burke referred to agitation as a parliamentary activity, lamenting that anti-American sentiment had become inflamed long "before a repeal [of the Stamp Act] was so much as agitated in this house." Some twenty years earlier, in his *Philosophical Enquiry into the Origin of Our Ideas of the Sublime and Beautiful,* Burke had written of "an impassioned countenance, an agitated gesture," phrases that aptly illustrate agitation's heightened sensibility: "Excited, disturbed in mind, having the feelings greatly moved." Although the first of these illustrations refers outwardly to a political activity and the second inwardly to an affective state, agitation in fact continuously slips between the internal and external, not least because it can designate private feelings so animated or perturbed as to be legible on the body's surface (as trembling, or shaking to and fro). It is also noteworthy that *both* citations from Burke refer to oratory; his "impassioned countenance" and "agitated gesture" describe the performance of a public speaker. These phrases appear in the last chapter of the *Enquiry,* "How words Influence the Passions," a brief account of oratory and rhetoric that anticipates the manuals later made popular by Thomas Sheridan, Hugh Blair, and James Burgh, among others; these textbooks, Jay Fliegelman argues, contributed to a wide-ranging and symptomatic "elocutionary revolution" in eighteenth-century Britain and America.[36] Exploiting agitation's inherent doubleness, Burke's "agitated gesture" presents oratory as a way of enacting the private in public, of contributing to the public good by being most genuinely oneself. One agitates most effectively (over American taxes, say) when one feels powerfully agitated. After distinguishing between "clear" and "strong expression" (the latter encompassing the whole arsenal of agitated tones, countenances, and gestures), Burke goes on to argue: "The truth is, all verbal description, merely as naked description, though ever so exact, conveys so poor and insufficient an idea of the thing described, that it could scarcely have the smallest effect, if the speaker did not call to his aid those modes of speech *that mark a strong and lively feeling in himself.* Then, by the contagion of our passions, we catch a fire already kindled in another, which probably might never have been struck out by the object described" (emphasis added).[37] In this account of affective influence the risk of charismatic or theatrical manipulation is manifest, but Fliegelman has demonstrated that the eighteenth-century passion for oratory, especially in the evolution of democratic politics, was primarily concerned with working out the tense relationship between, and competing claims of, privacy and the public good. Oratory involved learning "how to 'be oneself' and to speak in one's own voice without abandoning the conventional forms of a social or civic language" (2).

Combining the public and the private aspects of agitation, Burke's oratory invokes an ideal of social identity in which the particular and the general do not cancel but inform one another, operating as what Blake might call enabling contraries rather than negations. Individualized performance *ought* to insert itself into the arena of political debate. This assumption is crucial to understanding Blake's experience of the public sphere; without it, the emergence of a public founded on Enlightenment disinterestedness and a wide but impersonal print culture would seem by definition to exclude an enthusiast like Blake.[38] As Michael Warner describes it, print culture privileged writing over speech and print over other forms of writing as a way to contain personal influence. It involved three assumptions that, subsuming the particular under the general, could only have alienated Blake: (1) "a negative relation to the hand"; (2) publication, as opposed to "manuscript circulation"; (3) an association with the market and capital.[39] Yet, rather than assuming Blake's uncompromising opposition to these Enlightenment practices, we ought to consider how this public sphere of obligatory self-effacement brought with it, as Fliegelman has shown, the seemingly contradictory mandate of self-assertion. Despite its vigilant opposition to arbitrary power concentrated in privileged persons, the public sphere nevertheless did not require its participants to sacrifice their independent judgments and authentic feelings, a paradox that returns us to the agitation of oratory, and, in the case of Blake, to *Jerusalem*'s dedication "To the Public."

As mentioned earlier, Blake's dedication includes a flamboyant defense of his poem's metrical variety, which he claims to be so minutely differentiated as to resist any generalizing tendencies of blank verse. By no means, however, does Blake detach this principle of incommensurability from social obligation, for he defends it not merely as a prerogative of individual poetic genius but as a broad principle of *public* discourse. Although introducing a visionary epic poem, he presents himself as neither bard nor prophet but as "a true Orator." [40]

When this Verse was first dictated to me I consider'd a Monotonous Cadence like that used by Milton & Shakespeare & all writers of English Blank Verse, derived from the modern bondage of Rhyming; to be a necessary and indispensible part of Verse. But I soon found that in the mouth of a true Orator such monotony was not only awkward but as much a bondage as rhyme itself. I therefore have produced variety in every line, both of cadences & number of syllables. Every word and every letter is studied and put in its fit place. (3, E 145–146)

In his social role as orator, Blake feels compelled to charge "every word and every letter" with rhythmic significance, ensuring that his text's participation in the public sphere will not yield to a homogenizing *mono*tone but be proclaimed by its exaggerated and irreducible tonal specificity, by its unique voice print, as it were. Going so far as to invoke "*the mouth* of a true Orator," Blake insists on the speaker's personal, embodied presence within the text of public address. Given that Blake identifies himself as an orator nowhere else,[41] this passing self-image might be little more than a curiosity did it not directly anticipate the elevated rhapsody on social discourse that, almost 100 plates later, brings *Jerusalem* to its apocalyptic climax. There, agitated oratory becomes virtually the sole activity of the Eternals restored to paradise. When Blake calls the language of these giant figures fully "Human"—and adds that, as they walk and talk to and fro, their discourse varies in "every Word & Every Character"—he clearly means to echo the metrical principles put forth in "To the Public":

And they conversed together in Visionary forms dramatic which bright
Redounded from their Tongues in thunderous majesty, in Visions
In new Expanses, creating exemplars of Memory and of Intellect
Creating Space, Creating Time according to the wonders Divine
of Childhood, Manhood & Old Age[;] & the all tremendous
                                     unfathomable Non Ens
Of Death was seen in regenerations terrific or complacent varying
According to the subject of discourse & every Word & Every Character
Was Human according to the Expansion or Contraction, the
                                     Translucence or
Opakeness of Nervous fibres such was the variation of Time & Space
Which vary according as the Organs of Perception vary & they walked
To & fro in Eternity as One Man reflecting each in each & clearly seen
And seeing: according to fitness & order.   (98:28–40, E 257–258)

An ongoing fascination in *Jerusalem* with the ideals of conversation and mental fight culminates in this passage, which for good reason has been taken to express Blake's "radical social imagination." When the emphasis is placed on oratory, however, with its special function of mediating between the private and the public, these conversations in "Visionary forms dramatic," idealized though they may be, appear to take shape fully within an ideology of the public sphere. That is, they at once manifest the normative as well as the radicalizing tendencies of that ideology's utopian dimensions.[42]

How is "conversation," with its connotations of intimacy, linked to oratory and the idea of exchange in the public sphere? Unlike his famous contemporaries, Blake wrote no "conversation poems"; on the contrary, his polyphonic poetry bears another sound altogether, as if emanating from actors on a public stage (visionary forms *dramatic*). His Giant Forms never talk; they make speeches. Even in nondramatic passages, Blake rarely simulates the tone of personal intimacy that would tempt one to imagine the poet revealing himself to an acquaintance, as if unaware of anonymous eavesdroppers. He seems to have been entirely uninterested in that ruse. While poets such as Wordsworth and Coleridge mastered the art of soft-spoken intimacy, making writing seem like speech in order to mitigate their estrangement from a mass, anonymous audience, Blake *always* wrote as if addressing just such an anonymous public ("Reader! [lover] of books!" [3, E 145])—despite the printing and distribution practices that assured his personal contact with nearly every one of his patrons. Blake's dominant literary mode is not conversation, a man speaking to men as if by the hearth or on a walk, but oratory, a man debating others as if from a podium. This effect involves rhetorical devices every bit as designed as Wordsworth's incorporation of various reader surrogates into his lyrics—it too involves making writing seem like speech, though of a different sort—but it suggests how fully Blake identified with the "dynamics" of public discourse, with its energy born of conflict, but also, especially, with the sheer exhilaration and fullness of its sound. With his ear attuned to language loud and public, even Blake's letters and marginalia, our most intimate records of his voice, tend to slip into an aphoristic, sermonizing, oratorical tone indistinguishable from that of the poems. So ingrained is this pitch that one wonders whether Blake could have written otherwise even if he tried.

As both a pervasive rhetorical texture and a deliberately thematized ideal of subjectivity (simultaneously personal and public), oratory signals Blake's relation to a general print culture empowered by its seemingly unrestricted dissemination but unwilling to sacrifice the individualizing qualities of public speech.[43] Thus Fliegelman takes as his starting point the diacritical marks found in a manuscript of the Declaration of Independence, a text Jefferson apparently wished his readers to receive as if in live performance. In this period, the meaning of "conversation" included communication "by speech or writing or otherwise"; Blake chose the word carefully to modify the values associated with *writing* in the public sphere.

Given his uneasy relation to late eighteenth-century print technology and the book market, it is always tempting to consider Blake antagonistic to the dominant print culture, but as W. J. T. Mitchell has argued, print was also identified with values of democratic inclusiveness and openness Blake clearly found attractive. The term "public" (including the idea of publication) stood in opposition to "mystery" and "secrecy."[44] Blake, moreover, was unwilling to forgo the ideal of an agitated English discourse that could become *national* only through the amplification of print. Thus "conversation" for Blake, like his engraved script, was not so much a rejection of print culture as an attempt to inscribe a personal signature *within* the generalizing tendencies of print—to imagine Albion as at once a national discursive body and an individual man. "Conversation" modifies that body to include multiple participation or dialogue (the presence of others who hear and respond); perpetual event and performance, the forms of which can never be fixed or closed; and the singular, unabstracted voice of an embodied speaker.[45] Redounding from the "tongues" of Blake's Eternals are *visionary* forms dramatic, discourse for the eye and the ear, to be read as if heard. In the climactic passage from *Jerusalem,* Blake struggles to imagine a written performance as individuated as a speech act, "varying / According to the subject of discourse" and marked distinctly in "*every* Word & *Every* Character." Here, exploiting the written medium's materiality, Blake foregrounds print's own capacity for "contraction and expansion" by making the initial "e" of "every" first lower- and then uppercase (two cases without a rule, one might say), as well as by altering its case in variant copies of *Jerusalem.*[46] Rather than being effaced by print, such character distinctions become visible only in print.

Against the impersonal public sphere as set forth by Warner, Blake could insist that "In Great Eternity every particular Form gives forth or Emanates / Its own peculiar Light . . . This is Jerusalem in every Man" (54:1–3, E 203). At the same time, however, and anticipating Warner, Blakean debate would occur not through direct contact, in which personal status might exert influence, but through the mediation among equals of an intellectually charged discourse: "When in Eternity Man converses with Man . . . first their Emanations meet" (88:3–5, E 246)—or earlier, "Man is adjoined to Man by his Emanative portion" (39:38, E 187), by his public contribution toward building Jerusalem. Because this discursive ideal was always a national ideal, its mental fight had to take place over a terrain so wide that it strained any notion of intimacy implied by the word "conversation." Blake's military tropes consist of arrows and spears, effective because of their capacity to traverse distance. Their trajectories map a print distribution field in which those without the literal proximity required by speech, those without any personal relationship whatsoever, could be joined intertextually by the animating force of public debate.

As the giant "body" of mental fight, Albion takes shape through a national network of communication lines ("fibres"), but a network in which identities retain the local differences that an Enlightenment culture can never fully generalize.

> Albion! Our wars are wars of life & wounds of love,
>
> With intellectual spears, & long winged arrows of Thought:
>
> Mutual in one another's love and wrath all renewing
>
> We live as One Man; for contracting our infinite senses
>
> We behold multitude; or expanding; we behold as one,
>
> As One Man all the Universal Family.   (34:14–19, E 180)

The catalogued place-names typical of *Jerusalem* ("Lincolnshire Derbyshire Nottinghamshire Leicestershire . . . Labour within the Furnaces" [16:18–20, E 160]) signify local and national life all at once, rather like the silhouettes listed in *America* who are almost interchangeably representative and yet still identifiable by name: "Washington, Franklin, Paine & Warren, Gates, Hancock & Green / Meet on the coast" (3:4–5, E 52). Apart from his three-year residence in Felpham, Blake was an exclusively mental traveler, and he knew the cities, counties, nations, and continents named in *Jerusalem* as he knew the historical figures of *America*—as print figures.[47] All the sites beyond London are citations, textual phenomena related by their circulation in a public sphere, just as their "community" in the poem is an effect of the catalogue itself, discrete entities organized within the same parallel verse structure. Constituted by exchanges of print, Albion embodies "imagined community" as Benedict Anderson classically described it: "imagined because the members of even the smallest nation will never know most of their fellow-members, meet them, or even hear of them, yet in the minds of each lives the image of their communion."[48] Contracting our infinite senses, we imagine a nation of referential places consisting of empirical individuals like ourselves, multitudes who can be named and listed; expanding them, we see an Albion composed of generic cities giving themselves up to "the clangor of the Arrows of Intellect" (98:7, E 257):

> And [Albion] Clothed himself in Bows & Arrows in awful state Fourfold
>
> In the midst of his Twenty-eight Cities each with his Bow breathing
>
> Then Each an Arrow flaming from his Quiver fitted carefully
>
> They drew the unreprovable String, bending thro the wide Heavens
>
> The horned Bow Fourfold, loud sounding flew the flaming Arrow fourfold
>
>   (97:16–17–98:1–3, E 256–257)

Earlier in *Jerusalem*, a personification of London proclaimed, "My streets are my, Ideas of Imagination" (34:31, E 180). Now the resurrected Albion could say much the same of the mail-coach roads linking his cities, those public avenues of communication figured here as flight paths of intellectual arrows.[49]

In trying to grasp the paradox of Blake's public individual, Morris Eaves has issued a worthy challenge: "What is needed to make better sense of Blake is a notion of self sufficiently enriched to participate in the private-public continuum that romantic writers were attempting, stressfully and not without contradiction, to imagine. Blake conceives a deep individual life connected to a deep collective life: a class, and individual members of a class." Trying to coordinate the Blakean virtues of original genius and self-annihilation has always strained the limits of critical thought, although Eaves points a way forward by focusing on the trope of conversation. Under this rubric, he argues, "Individuality is, as it were, real talking and self-annihilation is real listening."[50] If, as I have suggested, "conversation" is really Blake's name for printed discourse experienced as if it were oratory, then it also represents his own effort to integrate the contradictory functions of his project into a single act. Oratory turns self-assertion (or real talking) and self-annihilation (or real listening) into what Schiller called "reciprocal actions," his term for the cooperation of the formal and the sensuous drive within the paradoxical ideal of beauty. Schiller's aesthetic is an allegory of political relations (or, as Habermas contends, a model of communication); in a passage reminiscent of Blake's persistent commitment to "brotherhood," Schiller describes how "brotherly love" cannot exist among people who divide the functions of listening and talking. Only listening, an individual "will never be himself"; only talking, "he will never be anything else." A footnote to this passage makes explicit the relation between the metaphysical drives and the ideal of a liberal polity: "If we are to become compassionate, helpful, effective human beings, feeling and character must unite, even as wide-open senses must combine with vigour of intellect if we are to acquire experience. How can we, however laudable our precepts, how can we be just, kindly, and human toward others, if we lack the power of receiving into ourselves, faithfully and truly, natures unlike ours, of feeling our way into the situation of others, of making other people's feelings our own?"[51] Blake calls such nonjudgmental acts of social reception "Forgiveness of Sins which is Self Annihilation" (98:23, E 257), superimposing the archetypal sympathy of Jesus onto a liberal principle of tolerance. At the same time, again like Schiller, Blake insists that one can undergo such self-annihilation without losing oneself altogether. Consider, for instance, Blake's lengthiest passage on self-annihilation, in which the eponymous hero of *Milton* announces unhesitantly, without the least fear of contradiction, "*I come in Self-annihilation*" (41:2, E 142, emphasis added). With good reason, Quinney asks: "[W]ho or what is the agent performing the act of self-annihilation?" and "How can Milton know that his assumption of authority does not entail the residual nourishment of selfhood?" Indeed, it may be impossible to "peremptorily denounce ego without seeming hypocritical,"[52] and Milton's audacity should remind us of Sharon Cameron's warning that any ideal of impersonality, "since it is undertaken by persons, could only be contradictory by nature."[53] And yet, within the paradoxical logic we have been tracing, what allows Milton to describe the thrilling event of self-annihilation in his own voice, and for more than thirty lines, is that he is not merely speaking but making a speech, with "terrible majesty" (40:28, E 142). The public character of his performance is conveyed not only by its generalized propositional content ("There is a Negation & there is a Contrary" [40:32, E 142]), but, more importantly, by its stylized tone and rhetoric, including the thundering repetitions that any oratory manual could use to illustrate anaphora: "To cast off Rational Demonstration . . . / To cast off the rotten rags of memory . . . / To cast off Bacon, Locke & Newton" (41:3–5, E 142). Milton is being himself not personally but in public, for a public; by entering into that sphere of discourse for and with others, he annihilates himself in a most particular sense.

As Quinney points out, the disorienting effect of Milton's speech stems from the grand self-confidence with which he preaches self-annihilation, his seizing of the stage to declare, "Obey thou the words of the Inspired Man" (40:29, E 142). Only later in *Jerusalem* will we begin to glimpse the public conversation with other inspired men that Milton is attempting to enter. There, on *that* climactic stage, everyone's words redound from the tongue with Miltonic "thunderous majesty." And yet, these loud, self-important talkers are also listeners, engaging in a "reciprocal action" reminiscent of Schiller's two drives: "the activity of the one both gives rise to, and sets limits to, the activity of the other, [such that] each in itself achieves its highest manifestation precisely by reason of the other being active."[54] When Blake has his Eternals "converse together," he collapses any hierarchy between activity and passivity: "they walked / To & fro in Eternity . . . reflecting each in each & *clearly seen / And seeing*." In public discourse (the to and fro of agitation), every orator is both subject and object, a speaker visible to others who are, at least in principle, potential contributors themselves. The presence of others is already structurally inscribed within any given speech act, the words of which are thus preconditioned by the contingency of response. In this forum, to speak is to agree to hear others, just as listening is understood as a prelude to speech. Mapping the borders of national discourse with his human figure, Albion is thus described as "speaking the Words of Eternity in Human Forms, in direful / Revolutions of Action & Passion" (95:9–10, E 255). In the public state of perpetual agitation, where revolution means not a single decisive act but the ongoing event of conflicted discourse, words are fully human in that they join what can now no longer be divided into the binary components of conversation. Passivity as such no longer exists, having been replaced by "Passion," a term encompassing not only the "agitated gesture" of the Burkean orator ("having the feelings greatly moved"), but also the definitive social act, *the*

Passion: "Offering of Self for Another" (96:21, E 256). Rather than simply contradicting the principle of self-annihilation, then, Milton's "Obey thou the words of the Inspired Man" restores a certain etymological integrity to the word "obey," derived from the Latin *obedire*, "to give ear." His real demand is that others listen in accordance with the values of civic discourse, a demand that already presupposes the possibility of their dissent. In Blakean conversation, "obedience" means no more than listening to others, thinking for oneself, and perhaps responding.[55]

Kant proposed a similar idea under the term "publicity." In an unpublished manuscript with Schiller's name mysteriously scrawled across the top, Kant invokes publicity in order to counteract "a newly raging spirit of domination in philosophy." This abuse has been perpetrated by authors claiming the indisputable authority of revelation, as if their words were unconditioned by the independent judgment of their readers. With no self-irony, their tone declares, "Obey thou the words of the Inspired Man." Kant begins,

> That everyone holds an opinion that he publicly confesses as worthy of being universally dominant already lies in the concept of opinion itself, and completely accords with the freedom to think according to the rule of *audiatur et altera pars* [the other side should also be heard]; that is, not to be beyond the reason of others but, rather, to be by its means a co-proprietor (condominus) of the great store of knowledge that universal human reason offers as a possession . . . The slogan of this employment of reason, which is limited by no preferential right of one despotically peremptory authority over the opinion of another, is contained in the sentence: *audiatur et altera pars*. And even if a voice supposedly heard from heaven were to contradict the voice of human reason, then everyone must freely be able to doubt that it is such a heavenly voice after all.[56]

Like Tom Paine in *The Age of Reason*, Kant never denies the possibility of individual revelation; he does, however, deny that any *published* revelation can transcend the judgment of others and demand rather than solicit agreement.[57] Because of the nature of public opinion, the potentially dissenting views of others are already inscribed in any discourse that claims to be of general significance. Virtually synonymous here with judgment, "opinion" is hardly the degraded term we know today, and in the annotations to Watson, Blake seems to have employed the word similarly: "Every honest man is a Prophet he utters his opinion both of private & public matters . . . a Prophet is not an Arbitrary Dictator" (E 617). Because the "general public" ought to consist of prophets so defined—intellectually enlivened individuals, armed with critical judgment—the public sphere should never come under the arbitrary imposition of a would-be Milton who thinks his opinion "universally dominant," demanding assent rather than real listening.

Kantian publicity, then, returns us to the insomniac night watchman. Indeed, the one would be meaningless without the other, and perhaps together they name a single idea—publicity from the general perspective, the night watchman from the particular. Especially as it is theorized in Kant's late work, from which both Habermas and Lyotard claim to derive their competing projects, the public sphere promises a social formation in which it becomes almost impossible to distinguish between acts of communing with and resisting others.[58] Accordingly, agitation involves both independent judgments (critical, aesthetic) and dynamic social relations (discussion, debate, public excitement). With its idealization of social and discursive conflict, publicity becomes Kant's key organizational concept after the Third Critique, and Habermas can justifiably assert, "The idea of the bourgeois public sphere attained its theoretically fully developed form with Kant's elaboration of the principle of publicity."[59] As we have seen already, judgment is the individual's armed state against doctrine. In *The Conflict of the Faculties,* Kant in turn models academic freedom on the principles of public service and useful disagreement, with the "lower" philosophy faculty serving a role analogous to that of the permanent opposition party in Parliament: "But in as free a system of government as must exist when it is a question of truth, there must also be an opposition party (the left side), and this is the philosophy faculty's bench."[60] Even the venerated domain of law must be, in its own way, subject to the oppositional criterion of publicity. In *Perpetual Peace,* Kant explains that if one were to subtract the specific content of all existing public laws, what would remain would be "only the *form* of publicity," which leads him to propose a "transcendental formula of public law: 'All actions relating to the right of other men are unjust if their maxim is not consistent with publicity.' "[61] Just as a philosophical claim to universal dominance already lies within a framework of opinion, so political action (including legislation) is preconditioned by a larger social principle—a principle defined not according to the a priori unity of "the people" but according to the values of reasoned conflict, opposition, difference. One recalls Kant's critique of the Jacobin state, in which " 'all,' who are not quite all, decide." In order to be just, Kant's legislators must not only act in such a way as would withstand general scrutiny, they must take disagreement into account in advance, strengthening their laws by considering possible objections. Without in any way subordinating the state to individual opinion—which in Kant's view would amount to lawlessness—legislators cannot presuppose an identity between individual subjects and the state.[62]

Unlike a monarch, then, when the republican state says, "Obey," it invokes a principle of debate that, having preceded legislation, may afterward continue into the public sphere. Like a monarch, however, the state also continues to enforce obedience in the more familiar sense of the term—the sense that Kant understood when, in 1784, he celebrated the benevolence of Frederick the Great: "Only one ruler in the world says: *Argue* as much as you like, about what you like, *but obey.*"[63] Given Kant's unwavering insistence on obedience, the "transcendental formula" equating publicity with justice can appear somewhat insubstantial. He could be remarkably candid in calculating the general benefits of obedience that result when a republican constitution respects the freedoms of intellectual fight in an independent public sphere: "The problem of organizing a state, however hard it may seem, can be solved even for a race of devils, if only they are intelligent. The problem is: 'Given a multitude of rational beings requiring universal laws for their preservation, but each of which is secretly inclined to exempt himself from them, to establish a constitution in such a way that, although their private intentions conflict, they check each other, with the result that their public conduct is the same as if they had no such intentions.'"[64] One may feel agitated; and one may agitate publicly as much as one likes, about whatever one likes—as long as one obeys.[65] By all means, consider yourself a member of the devil's party—but obey. Kant seems to assume that all people are by nature closet antinomians, and that the challenge of organizing a state is to honor that impulse while maintaining law and order. Resistance to the generalizing function of the law must somehow be made coincident with good citizenship: "thus a state of [restless] peace is established in which laws have force."[66] We will not take up Blake's characteristic union of impulse and caution until the next chapter, but even now we can see how Kant's cagey pragmatism bears on the situation of a poet, who—despite a fervent, lifelong commitment to republican antinomianism—was never convicted of breaking any law and whose name has yet to turn up in any spy report from the extensive government archive. Would Blake's "public conduct" have differed significantly if he had never felt himself internally radical, if agitation had never kept him awake? Blake was inclined to consider himself an agitator exempt from the law, and yet, for the most part, he obeyed.

"A Wishful Participation That Borders Closely on Enthusiasm"

> For enlightenment of this kind, all that is needed is *freedom*. And the freedom in question is the most innocuous form of all—freedom to make *public use* of one's reason in all matters.
>
> —Immanuel Kant, "An Answer to the Question: 'What Is Enlightenment?'"

> The mental tossing of a matter to and fro; consideration, debate, discussion.
>
> —*Oxford English Dictionary* entry for "agitation"

Regarding *Jerusalem*'s strained combination of public address and defiant obscurity, Jon Mee has asked whether Blake's enthusiasm is "so dangerous as to be incapable of sustaining a conversation[.] Is his idea of 'Mental Fight' too arduous and extreme to allow any kind of exchange in the public sphere?"[67] Such questions imply an explanation for Blake's isolation from his social world: his views and practices were simply too radical, a point Saree Makdisi amplifies dramatically. According to Makdisi, Blake's "radical antinomian enthusiasm" made him "an outsider, an other" to the bourgeois liberal hegemony then establishing itself, placing him more comfortably alongside the plebeian public sphere notoriously neglected by Habermas, that underworld of "other radicalisms—more extreme, more subversive, more dangerous."[68] Without denying the good reasons for these arguments, I want to ask a different question: What did Blake mean by continuing to think of himself as a public figure despite his nonparticipation in *any* public sphere, middle or low, bourgeois or plebeian?

We can begin to explore this conundrum by returning once more to "agitation" and the *OED*. If "debate" and "discussion" are activities obviously connected to the public sphere, the elision at the heart of "agitation" surfaces again in its synonym "consideration," for that type of "mental tossing of a matter to and fro" can occur either collectively or in isolation. We are accustomed to seeing Blake's Zoas as both the dynamic, internal principles of a single psyche (a conflict of the faculties) and the social agents of a wider, interactive community, but we have not really considered how such a nondifferentiation of mental and social states inflects Blake's understanding of the term "public." One could argue, as Kant does, that these states must be reciprocally constituted: an invigorating culture of open, ongoing debate depends upon the participation of independent, intellectually enlivened individuals who can really talk and really listen because of their ability to "consider [a matter] on all sides" and "revolve [it] in the mind"— another definition of "agitation." This is the work of the insomniac night watchman, who, for the public good, remains attentive to the disturbing conversation in his head; rather than resolving a matter of importance into a comfortable, static idiom, he continues to *revolve* it, recognizing that his internal, conflicted discourse already includes multiple voices clamoring to be heard. The watchman thus enacts internally a version of those social exchanges that on a monumental scale constitute the public sphere; he understands that the mind's interior monologue is always already dialogic. If he is capable of conversing with himself (Latin, *conversare*, "to turn about, to turn with, to move to and fro"), he is already publicly engaged—for genuine thinking is an inherently public activity.

Blakean "conversation" embodies this notion of a porous boundary between the private and the public, while also complicating it. Kant's vision of discursive traffic flowing in both directions, with the critical thinker's consideration of public matters returning to the public sphere through speech or publication, does not always clearly or fully apply to Blake. In "A Vision of the Last Judgment," where Blake represents "Paradise with its Inhabitants walking up & down in Conversations concerning Mental Delights" (E 562), his utopian space could equally well describe uninhibited social interaction or intellectual self-sufficiency, a state without any real need for others once vigorous mental activity is underway. Edenic conversation of this latter, extreme sort would be a decidedly solitary affair; one recalls a report of Catherine complaining that Blake spent too much of his time in paradise.[69] Blake's eccentric conversations with himself sometimes posed a problem for his earliest biographers, who wished to acknowledge the "difficult subject" of his talking visions, but in such a way as to contain embarrassment.[70] J. T. Smith, for instance, described this recurrent phenomenon sympathetically but also cautiously, almost clinically: "Blake was supereminently endowed with the power of disuniting all other thoughts from his mind, whenever he wished to indulge in thinking of any particular subject; and so firmly did he believe, by this abstracting power, that the objects of his compositions were before him in his mind's eye, that he frequently believed them to be speaking to him."[71] And Frederick Tatham once reported on these visionary episodes in terms that echo *Jerusalem*'s oratorical ideal: "[Blake] said that he was the companion of spirits, who taught, rebuked, argued & advised, with all the familiarity of personal intercourse."[72] Such spirited conversation, a sort of internal debating society, short-circuits what Kant called "thinking in community with others" ("to whom we *communicate* our thoughts and who communicate their thoughts to us").[73] It inverts what Habermas, following Kant, calls "thinking aloud," for conversation of this kind is more a matter of thinking loudly, or oratorically.[74]

Setting aside occult explanations and clinical diagnoses, we can see that even in its most solipsistic forms Blake's prophetic mode internalized the "mental fight" of the public sphere, absorbing it into the very textures of his thought without requiring him to contribute fully to that sphere in turn. We have long recognized the discrepancy between the interior volume of Blake's voice(s) and his virtual silence in public (or his silencing: therein lies the crux.)[75] But we still don't understand why Blake, long after he must have realized that his voice would never be heard in the public sphere, continued to write in a public voice, continued to address a general public on matters of public urgency, and continued to simulate in his illuminated books the public agitation of intellectual warfare—*as if* whatever took place on the internal stage of his mental fight did in fact participate in the public sphere. Blake was forty-seven years old when he introduced *Jerusalem* by announcing, "I again display my Giant forms to the Public" (3, E 145); he was still printing the book at age sixty-nine. Blake would conclude his last address to a public in *Jerusalem* ("To the Christians") by urging, "Let every Christian as much as in him lies engage himself openly & publicly before all the World in some Mental pursuit for the Building up of Jerusalem" (77, E 232). Even with the hedging ("as much as in him lies," "some *Mental* pursuit"), the statement astonishes. What Blake called "public" somehow managed to elide the difference between mental pursuit and public engagement such that an essentially private experience could be felt as if on the order of a public action. Somehow, the antinomian could participate in the public work of building Jerusalem without fully disclosing his activity "openly & publicly before all the World." How was it that a little known engraver, albeit an uncompromising critic of national affairs, continued to believe that his combative engagement with his culture (and with his own internalization of that culture, his "Spectre") amounted to an action of public significance when his audience was limited, in Erdman's stinging words, to "a few uncritical or even uncomprehending friends"?[76]

Although it is fraught with idiosyncrasies, we can begin to approach Blake's case by setting it within a broader trend: the merging of active and passive roles encouraged by the one activity considered indispensable to the health of the eighteenth-century public sphere: *reading*. Accounts of the developing public sphere often emphasize the role played by letters to the editor in the various eighteenth-century print media.[77] Kant's "Answer to the Question: 'What Is Enlightenment?' " (published in the *Berlinische Monatsschrift*) is only the most famous instance. By including their readers' responses, newspapers and journals not only made their print space analogous to the meeting places (salons, clubs, coffeehouses, taverns) where people of unequal social status could, in principle, debate as equals, but they also encouraged the idea that reading and writing—at least for a small, educated audience—are "reciprocal actions." According to Clifford Siskin and William Warner, the proliferation of periodicals changed the experience of reading, leading readers "to behave as writers."[78] Thus real listening was always potentially real talking, and such exchanges fostered a cherished narrative of the public sphere as a product of expanded literacy. As the public gradually assumed its mature role as "critical judge" (Habermas's term) or adversary to arbitrary authority, reading was redefined as an act of supervision. It thus became, in Michael Warner's words, "the paradigmatic public action"[79]—the work of a civic-minded daytime watchman. Echoing other historians, Warner points to the significance of the publication that helped launch the Anglo-American public sphere: the *Spectator*, the title of which acquired a republican inflection unanticipated by Addison and Steele.[80] In the republican context, to read or to observe with a critical eye is itself an act of public importance—a duty no less, regardless of whether one exercises the writing potential latent in such spectatorship. Merging activity and passivity, print culture elevated reading into a public passion, leaving only words of "Action and Passion." If this early tendency already risked exaggerating the reader's significance, its image of an engaged public became even more problematic with the increase of mass periodicals toward the end of the century, an expansion recently documented by William St Clair.[81] As Jon Klancher has argued, these periodicals simulated the ideal of public-sphere exchange for readers who, given the dramatic growth in audiences and the consequently shrinking proportion of published writers, would likely never become writers themselves. By 1790, the public sphere that existed for most people only through the mediation of the mass market "had itself become an image to be consumed by readers who did not frequent it."[82]

In cultivating this idea of reciprocity between reading and writing, eighteenth-century print culture helped to enable a new experience in which public identity took shape through the passion and independence felt in the act of reading. In *Jerusalem,* the giant Eternals "converse in Visionary forms dramatic," talking and listening in turn, but when Blake introduces himself into this monumental public scene, reinserting his "I" into the poem's final line, he does so *as a listener* at the margins: "And I heard the Name of their Emanations and they are named Jerusalem" (99:5, E 259). Whatever Blake hoped and intended for his printed work, its publication was not the basis of his claims to "publicity," for the public character of that work was measured less by its negligible circulation than by the vastness and vigor of its critical response to national and international events, events that he gleaned as a reader in and of the public sphere. Blake aggressively interrogated a whole world of signs made newly available to him by his print culture, and in this role as vigilant critic, his agitated faculties were aroused so acutely as to make arousal itself feel like action—the necessary, daring duty of a watchman to his sleeping country.[83]

In a curious way, then, Blake's marginalia—that extensive, combative dialogue at the fringes of printed discourse—might be taken to represent his work generally. Tatham marveled at how thoroughly this autodidact possessed his books, marking them as his own through repeated use; volumes in Latin, Greek, Hebrew, French, and Italian were all "well thumbed and dirtied by his graving hands."[84] In the Reynolds marginalia, Blake describes his habitual practice of annotation as an ongoing, antagonistic debate with famous authors, but he also symptomatically elides the distinction between (their) published and (his) unpublished words:

> I read Burke's Treatise when very Young at the same time I read Locke on Human Understanding & Bacons Advancement of Learning on Every one of these Books I wrote my Opinions & on looking them over find that my Notes on Reynolds in this Book are exactly Similar. I felt the Same Contempt & Abhorrence then; that I do now.

They mock Inspiration & Vision Inspiration & Vision was then & now is & I hope will always Remain my Element my Eternal Dwelling place. how can I then hear it Contemned without returning Scorn for Scorn. (E 660–661)

Taking up Kant's rule of publicity (the other side should also be heard), Blake feels obliged to respond yet unobliged to publish, as if debating, by oneself, in the reader's unprinted margins, fulfilled that obligation and sufficiently returned scorn for scorn. In her study of Romantic period marginalia, H. J. Jackson has demonstrated that Blake's practices were more or less mainstream: "He talked back to his books and, like certain other readers, he took steps to disseminate his opinion in a form of manuscript publication," a term general enough to include circulating an annotated book among acquaintances.[85] Commonplace as it may have been, the elision of scale between printed and unpublished opinion takes on dramatic proportions in Blake, especially in his telling response to Watson's *Apology for the Bible*. In this case, Blake seems to have prepared his comments for publication, forming them into a sociopolitical critique breathtaking in scope. As Makdisi puts it, Blake's notes amount to a systematic "denunciation of the power of authoritarian discipline and behavioral codes *in any form*" (original emphasis).[86] Moreover, Blake's annotated copy of *An Apology for the Bible* perfectly models the polyphony of mental fight in the public sphere, for it inscribes three distinct voices tossing about matters of public urgency—Blake's, Watson's, and (since Watson was responding point by point to *The Age of Reason*) Paine's. In eerie miniature, this artifact captures the 1790s pamphlet culture—"eerie" only because Blake decided not to publish his contribution after all, mysteriously claiming he was "commanded from Hell' (E 611) not to do so.

The Watson annotations demonstrate how thoroughly confused agitation has become—"the mental tossing of a matter to and fro: *consideration,* debate, discussion." In the last sentences written on the back of Watson's title page, leading ultimately to the announcement (for whom?) that he will not print his critique, Blake uses "consideration" three times, first linking it unequivocally with the patriotic imperative to act, even if action is dangerous. Blake has been explaining that in the current repressive climate, no one is willing to defend the real Bible: "But to him who sees this mortal pilgrimage in the light that I see it. Duty to [my] <his> country is the first consideration & safety the last" (E 611). The second and third instances of "consideration" advance the same logic, but they also begin subtly to modify the idea of public action, oddly preparing for the decision to withdraw. If "consideration" involves the self-annihilating act of putting others first, of being radically considerate, even altruistic, it also turns out to mean reading and exercising critical judgment. Thus it is unclear whether duty obligates one to enter the discursive fray as an orator-author (speaking up, offering ideas for others to consider) or simply as a reader (considering the ideas of others): "Read patiently take not up this Book in an idle hour the consideration of these things is the [entire] whole duty of man & the affairs of life & death trifles sports of time <But> these considerations business of Eternity" (E 611). Take not up *what* book in an idle hour? Consideration of *which* things is the whole duty of man? Is Blake asking an imagined reader to take up the pamphlet he will have published or does he anticipate passing Watson's book to someone he hopes will read it as carefully as he has? Or is he now conversing with himself, urging himself on in his own act of reading, just as the last line, announcing that he will not print his annotations, seems addressed only to himself? In such agitation, I would suggest, the engaged reader begins to feel that independent acts of judgment meet one's duty to the nation, to others, that the antinomian integrity of thinking for oneself is tantamount to a public good. The logic of the Watson annotations is to downplay the significance of their publication while augmenting the significance of what, for lack of a ready phrase, we might call thinking publicly.

Before we too quickly reduce Blake's maneuver in the Watson annotations to a failure of courage—an act of almost conscious rationalization with implications that extend well beyond the small decision to closet that piece—we should return one last time to Kant. In *The Conflict of the Faculties,* Kant posits a new type of readerly agitator, emerging at the margins of the French Revolution, who bears an uncanny resemblance to Blake. In Kant's most sustained meditation on the Revolution, the strange paradoxes we have observed in Blake—the idea that critical thought can be public yet undisclosed; the idea of an affective state so powerful as to make one feel engaged in history without having to participate publicly—become not the anomalous signs of eccentricity or pathology but the general attributes of a new political subjectivity and, beyond that, the very sign of a progressive, bourgeois culture constituted by such subjects. The second essay of *The Conflict of the Faculties* takes up "An Old Question Raised Again: Is The Human Race Constantly Progressing?" In Section 6, "Concerning an Event of Our Time Which Demonstrates this Moral Tendency of the Human Race," Kant answers this question with a startling affirmation. The exemplary event, it turns out, is not technically an event at all, or at least not the main event, for it lies outside the Revolution itself. This event involves a special kind of *reading* of the Revolution by nonparticipant spectators:

> This event consists neither in momentous deeds nor crimes committed by men
> whereby what was great among men is made small or what was small is made great,
> nor in ancient splendid political structures which vanish as if by magic while others

come forth in their place as if from the depths of the earth. No, nothing of the sort. It is simply the mode of thinking of the spectators which reveals itself publicly in this great game of revolutions, and manifests such a universal yet disinterested sympathy for the players on one side against those on the other, even at the risk that this partiality could become very disadvantageous for them if discovered . . .

The revolution of a gifted people which we have seen unfolding in our day may succeed or miscarry; it may be filled with misery and atrocities to the point that a sensible man, were he boldly to hope to execute it successfully the second time, would never resolve to make the experiment at such cost—this revolution, I say, nonetheless finds in the hearts of all spectators (who are not engaged in this game themselves) a wishful participation that borders closely on enthusiasm, the very expression of which is fraught with danger; this sympathy, therefore, can have no other cause than a moral predisposition in the human race.[87]

This remarkable passage has drawn the attention of a wide range of modern political theorists—Lyotard and Habermas among them, but also Arendt, Foucault, and Žižek—and we will return to it again toward the end of the next chapter.[88] In this context, however, I want to focus on two of its leading paradoxes: (1) that the spectatorial "mode of thinking" "reveals itself publicly" and yet remains, at least for now, undiscovered; and (2) that this "mode of *thinking*" is characterized as an aesthetic *feeling* aroused "in the *hearts* of all spectators."

The first paradox is easily overlooked. Habermas, for instance, briskly summarizes how Kant found his historical sign of moral progress "not in the French Revolution itself but, rather, in the openly expressed enthusiasm with which a broad public had fearlessly greeted these events as an attempt at a realization of principles of natural law."[89] Given his emphasis on the open expression of sympathy, Habermas's spectators are presumably also writers or public speakers; their mode of thought is thinking aloud. Kant's argument for a "universal" moral predisposition would seem to hinge largely on the idea that people without anything to gain from a neighboring country's revolution, without any immediate self-interest, will nevertheless express their solidarity despite potential repercussions from their own repressive regimes.[90] Such people would indeed be fearless, but they are not exactly the people Kant describes; they don't take their spectatorial role quite literally enough. Kant's subjects are observers who feel moved in a particular way, an audience defined not so much by its expression of solidarity as by its unspoken experience of solidarity, which agitates its members precisely because they fear the consequences of its exposure: it "could become very disadvantageous for them if discovered." Some such spectators may publish their opinions, exercising at great risk the reader's writing potential, but Kant chooses to make representative the anonymous majority who do not. As far as danger is concerned, then, what matters is not that the spectator be at risk but that the spectator, concealing a thrilling privacy, feel at risk—and by virtue of selflessly identifying with unrelated, even unknown, others. When Kant concludes this section by exclaiming, "With what exaltation the uninvolved public looking on sympathized then without the least intention of assisting," thus clearly distancing this mode of thinking from revolutionary action on a foreign stage, he has also succeeded in separating it even from the act of publication at home.[91] What, then, could it possibly mean to say that this mode of thinking, confined to the hearts of spectators, "reveals itself publicly"?

Unlike Habermas, Lyotard acknowledges the paradox that this crucial feeling remains unpublished, that it is public only by virtue of the unrealized possibility that it might someday be communicated: the spectator's enthusiasm is "certainly not 'said,' but publicly expressed as a feeling in principle able to be shared."[92] According to this view, the restraint on communication stems not from any immediate fear of repression but from the limitations of language: no available phrasing can express the powerful experience these spectators share. Their enthusiasm remains an unspoken *feeling* because, for now, it escapes the range of what can be spoken; it is a shared, radical, unrepresentable privacy struggling to become public. Lyotard's spectators, in other words, would be fearless Habermasian writers if they could be, if language could accommodate the content of their agitated hearts, but that impossibility does not erase them from history. Rather, their "eloquent silence," consisting of exclamatory feelings pressing against the limits of existing discourse, places them at history's vanguard; this unspoken affect points toward a future whose idioms remain to be discovered.[93] Lyotard's Kant has transformed historical agency from a matter of revolution into a matter of reading. As an actual historical event, a revolution is necessarily limited by the available stock of interests, idioms, and actions that shape its course. It belongs to the discourse of the currently conceivable. But those who read revolution as a "sign of history," as a figure for an "as if referent,"[94] experience the profound gap between a revolution's unspeakable possibilities and its present realization; such readings thus point toward a future that the event has not yet encompassed, no matter what achievements may be claimed by revolutionary leaders. With the agitated reader lies history's undetermined future.

By identifying the "sign of history" with these spectators, Kant has begun to decenter history, locating its dynamism in the interpretive struggle undertaken by unspecified, uncelebrated observers at the periphery, rather than in the high profile actions of a few great men.[95] Thus we can begin to understand why Kant, the earliest theoretician of publicity, might claim that the spectator's unprecedented mode of thinking "reveals itself publicly." If the revelatory event is that the Revolution can be read, and that historical progress is driven along by acts of reading, then this new form of engagement can emerge (reveal itself) only through the precondition of publicity. Kant is trumpeting the primary innovation of his century, the development of a print culture. There can be no general response to a distant revolution without the mass media to represent it and an infrastructure for its broad and various dissemination. History must already be a print event for such spectators to observe it. Their responses are public, then, because they share this experience of mediation; separate though they may be from the event and from each other, they collectively become "the uninvolved public looking on." As Kant speculates on the future anticipated by the sympathy of these spectators, he can confidently declare that the human race is surely progressing, pointing to a monumental cultural change that has already taken place.

Now if the sign of history is a print event (a mode of reading enabled by the mediation of a public sphere), it is also clearly an aesthetic event. Kant's rhetoric of spectators, games, and players, along with his collapsing of thought and feeling, already underscores the point, but the aesthetic experience of this event takes a specific form, one closely resembling the sublime as theorized in the Third Critique. There Kant explains that only a nonparticipant spectator can experience sublimity, for one must be secure from whatever threatening object it is that both attracts and repulses. We can experience the sublime only "as if" we were at risk: "The sight . . . becomes all the more attractive the more fearful it is, as long as we find ourselves in safety."[96] For anyone on the stage of such dangerous forces, which Kant describes in terms of natural disasters, the aesthetic effect achieved by distance is immediately lost; as far as the participant is concerned, there is no "stage," and the only perspective is that of self-interest, namely, self-preservation. By a similar logic, Kant disqualifies the revolutionaries engaged directly in the game of history from experiencing sublimity; for them there is no game. With so much immediately, personally at stake, the players lose the ability to separate principles from self-interest; they cannot experience the spectatorial state Kant calls "genuine [i.e., disinterested] enthusiasm." Having described the revolutionary idea that has so moved the international audience—the right to popular sovereignty manifested in a republican constitution—Kant explains, "This, then, plus the passionate participation in the good, i.e., enthusiasm (although not to be wholly esteemed, since passion as such deserves censure), provide through this history the occasion for the following remark which is important for anthropology: genuine enthusiasm always moves only toward what is ideal and, indeed, to what is purely moral, such as the concept of right, and it cannot be grafted onto self-interest."[97] Enthusiasm is an aesthetic response; it signals the tendency toward the ideal within history, and thus Lyotard links it to the mixed mode of the sublime. Enthusiasm names "an extreme mode of the sublime," an "extremely painful joy . . . an *Affekt,* a strong affection,"[98] for while the spectators are repulsed by what Kant calls the Revolution's "misery and atrocities," they are also passionately attracted to its unrealized principles. The sublime disjunction between imagination and reason becomes the historical disjunction between the event as perceived in the present and a future possibility that can only be inarticulately anticipated: "Enthusiasm is a modality of the feeling of the sublime. The Imagination tries to supply a direct, sensible presentation for an Idea of reason . . . It does not succeed and it thereby feels its impotence, but at the same time, it discovers its destination, which is to bring itself into harmony with the Ideas of reason through an appropriate presentation. The result of this obstructed relation is that instead of experiencing a feeling for the object, we experience, on the occasion of that object, a feeling 'for the Idea of humanity in our subject.' "[99] Against the revolutionary's arrogant belief that his declarations and actions fulfill the promise of history, the spectators' enthusiasm restlessly drives history forward; "as a pure aesthetic feeling," their enthusiasm "is a sentimental anticipation of the republic" that has not yet arrived.[100] These internally conflicted readers move history forward by feeling moved.[101]

As theorized by Kant and glossed by Lyotard, these spectators provide the earliest model of the future-oriented, critical enthusiasm we considered at length in the introduction. In 1795, a year of revolutionary disappointment, Kant proposes that critical engagement is the real engine of history and that evidence of such agency is immediately available in the critic's powerful feeling. But if this spectatorial enthusiasm is "a kind of agitation in place," as Lyotard aptly calls it, then where exactly does such agitation *take place*?[102] In the mind and the heart, certainly, or rather in language, where the heart's inarticulate feeling collides with the mind's ready and inadequate phrases, but also, more prosaically, in the place where a critical reader sits, "uninvolved . . . without the least intention of assisting": a chair, a desk, a study. We must be careful not to allow the dynamic language of enthusiasm to "obscure the sedentary conditions of reading and writing," to recall the phrase Joanna Picciotto usefully applies to Milton's metaphorical "union of action and contemplation."[103] In Hannah Arendt's words, Kant's domestic spectators, "as it were, made the event at home in the history of mankind."[104] Lyotard is right, then, to privilege the relation between enthusiasm and the sublime by which Kant tips the balance of history toward the reader, toward the critical-aesthetic thinker; carried along by his own enthusiasm, however, he tends to underemphasize Kant's careful qualification of the term. Something about enthusiasm worries Kant, for he calls the spectator's mode of thinking "a wishful participation that *borders closely* on enthusiasm." If Kant defines full-strength enthusiasm as "the *passionate* participation in the good," then what seems to distinguish the spectator's mode from enthusiasm per se is its *"wishful* participation," its imaginative (sympathetic) and imaginary (unrealized) quality. This modified enthusiasm never crosses the border between thought and act, although it hugs that border so closely, agitating thought so fully, that the result is an experience that feels *like* participation in the stimulating object from which it is by definition detached. Kant divides enthusiasm or passionate participation into two types, wishful and actual, which is why he must introduce the new category of *"genuine* enthusiasm." Ordinary enthusiasm can never be wholly esteemed because its misguided passion might tempt the enthusiast to translate ideas directly into history, an effort that, whatever motivates it, entangles one in self-interest.[105] Genuine enthusiasm "always moves only toward what is ideal." Moving vigorously and vertically, detached from the horizontal axis of error-prone action, it is "a kind of agitation in place."[106] Schematically, enthusiasm is passionate thought mistakenly translated into historical act; genuine enthusiasm is thought so passionate as to feel like historical act.

Identifying contemplation with action, Lyotard never fully grasps the wariness in Kant's spectatorial enthusiasm, the caution that places his account within the history of "enthusiasm and regulation" that Mee has traced. Kant describes as a new historical phenomenon (new because the public sphere submits an event of world-historical importance to general, critical response) the spectators he also strives to influence, channeling their revolutionary inclinations into a form of critical-aesthetic judgment not incompatible with their obedience. Here and elsewhere, Kant makes it clear that he is opposed not only to the French Revolution, with its troubling mix of sordid and heroic motives, but to revolution in principle.[107] The moral progress he claims to predict by observing the modern phenomenon of revolutionary spectatorship is moral progress of a kind he himself wishes to promote by constructing this particular type of spectator. Section 9 of *The Conflict of the Faculties* asks, "What Profit Will Progress Toward the Better Yield Humanity?" The answer: "Not an ever-growing quantity of morality with regard to intention, but an increase of the products of legality in dutiful actions whatever their motives . . . Gradually violence on the part of the powers will diminish and obedience to the laws will increase."[108] Poised on the border of revolutionary, antinomian desire and lawful obedience, genuine enthusiasm is the perfect harbinger of such progress. Its ideological function is to blur the difference between judgment and act, making it nearly impossible to distinguish between an arousal of the faculties and the more direct type of historical participation that arousal simulates.

Thus Lyotard's insomniac night watchman is the worthy heir to Kant's sublime spectator. He acts by listening, by tuning his critical judgment to such a fine pitch of agitation that he might just hear conflicts that cannot yet be spoken in the entrenched idioms of the present. He agitates by "bearing witness," by reading the state of language with "the hope of permitting other phrases, perhaps heterogeneous."[109] He believes his reading of the present makes the future possible, so he stays up all night selflessly reading, talking back to his books, perhaps recording his response. And by no means is his insomnia, his agitation, inherently incompatible with the smooth operation of the social order, for it may constitute a public intervention so inaudible as to seem nonexistent.

Given this profile, which can double as a profile of Blake, perhaps we should modify the idea of enthusiasm presented in the introduction to this book. In *Jerusalem,* when Blake chose to record his opposition to Enlightenment culture by reclaiming the "smear-word" Johnson and others had stigmatized—"I labour day and night . . . That Enthusiasm and Life may not cease" (9:26, 31, E 152)—he was honoring both the new examples of faith flourishing among Methodist followers of Wesley and Whitefield and the whole antinomian legacy extending back to the seventeenth century, with its deep revolutionary roots. But Blake did not live in the seventeenth century, and one difference made by his modernity was the enormous expansion of the public sphere and the kinds of enthusiasm its mediation made possible. One would be hard-pressed to find a more apt description of Blake's relation to his revolutionary era than Kant's "wishful participation that borders closely on enthusiasm." Kant's theory of the revolutionary spectator allows us to recognize a distinctly modern, nonactivist Blake whose orientation to the world was both public and radically aesthetic—not in terms of a retreat into fantasy but in terms of a critical engagement with history intense enough to have felt like participation in history.

CHAPTER TWO

Blake's Virtue

The misfortunes of the human race speak urgently to the man of
feeling; its degradations more urgently still; enthusiasm is kindled,
and in vigorous souls ardent longing drives impatiently on toward
action. But did he ever ask himself whether those disorders in the
moral world offend his reason, or whether they do not rather wound
his self-love? If he does not yet know the answer, he will detect it by
the zeal with which he insists upon specific and prompt results. The
pure moral impulse is directed towards the Absolute . . . Impart to
the world you would influence a Direction towards the good, and the
quiet rhythm of time will bring it to fulfillment.

    —Friedrich Schiller, *Letters on the Aesthetic Education of Man* (1795)

Hyacinth had now known [the bookbinder Poupin and his wife] long
enough not to be surprised at the way they combined the socialistic
passion, a red-hot impatience for the general rectification, with an
extraordinary decency of life and a worship of proper work. The
Frenchman spoke, habitually, as if the great swindle practiced upon
the people were too impudent to be endured another moment longer,
and yet he found patience for the most exquisite "tooling," and took
a book in hand with the deliberation of one who should believe that
everything was immutably constituted.

    —Henry James, *The Princess Casamassima* (1886)

A critical analysis . . . usually meets with reproach: "Do you mean we
should do *nothing*? Just sit and wait?" One should gather the courage
to answer: "YES, precisely that!" There are situations when the only
truly "practical" thing to do is to resist the temptation to engage
immediately and to "wait and see" by means of a patient, critical
analysis.

    —Slavoj Žižek, on resisting "fake urgency," *On Violence* (2008)

The Double Life of "Albion rose"

"I am really sorry to see my Countrymen trouble themselves about Politics . . .
Princes appear to me to be Fools Houses of Commons & Houses of Lords appear
to me to be fools they seem to me to be something Else besides Human Life."
On the evidence of this notebook passage, one might reasonably agree with Peter
Ackroyd that Blake "displays not the slightest interest in any particular political or
social philosophy."[1] Calling it his "most elaborate statement about organized or
doctrinal politics" and a "wholesale rejection" (160), Blake's popular recent biographer quotes this passage twice, first to finish off a discussion of Blake's politics
in the 1790s, and then again some 150 pages later to arrive at the same conclusion
regarding Blake's attitude toward the agitation and repression of the 1810s. In the
earlier period, Blake is supposed to have quickly withdrawn his brief identification
with Jacobinism (removing the bonnet rouge) after the September massacres of
1792. "Now," writes Ackroyd of the older Blake, "when the same pattern of events
was restored within the city, we have only one extant remark" (306). Then follows
the notebook passage equating politics with fools' play and alienated life. Repeated
in this way, at such a wide interval, the statement provides a framework for Ackroyd's consistently apolitical *Blake*.

Since the groundbreaking work of Jacob Bronowski, Mark Schorer, David Erdman, and A. L. Morton over fifty years ago, politically minded critics have chafed at
this kind of depoliticization of Blake. Indeed, with half a century of training behind
us, it would be easy to chip away at the assumptions that allow Ackroyd to diminish Blake's politics so unapologetically. First, although he acknowledges the rough
edges of Blake's London-inflected radicalism, Ackroyd considers it little more
than an insurmountable local accent, "a natural and almost instinctive stance"
(73), a defiant tone of voice. Given his time and place, of course Blake spoke that
way. Then Ackroyd delays introducing the French Revolution until nearly halfway
through the biography, well after he has begun to discuss poems from the 1790s.
Subordinated and compartmentalized, politics invariably follows art, religion, and
psychology as an explanatory resource. When the 1790s finally require a sustained
political discussion, Ackroyd's treatment essentially follows that of his Victorian
predecessor Alexander Gilchrist (to whom we owe the story of the bonnet rouge);
both biographers dissociate Blake from any real intimacy with the circle of radical publisher Joseph Johnson.[2] It is as if Ackroyd has been all along preparing his
reader to accept Blake's disavowal of politics as his motto, though he never explains
why a notebook comment written around 1811 for possible inclusion in the *Public
Address* to the Calcographic Society is relevant to Blake's response to the turbulent
early years of the French Revolution. The return of the same quotation to describe

Blake at the end of the 1810s is similarly perplexing, since Ackroyd deploys a statement made early in the decade to comment on political turmoil that culminated years later in the Seditious Meetings and Habeas Corpus Suspension Acts of 1817. Precise timing seems less important to Ackroyd than the appeal of a thematic rhyme; the echo of similar political circumstances calls for a repetition of Blake's political disavowal: "*Now* . . . we have only one extant remark." Only by stretching this "now" to cover an entire decade can Ackroyd make this remark contemporaneous with political events he suggests mattered little to Blake anyway: "Now the events of the world simply passed over his head" (306).

It would take little more than reflex, in other words, to show that Blake's bias against politics is in fact Ackroyd's own in an otherwise sensitive and accomplished biography. And yet it is exactly this reflexive privileging of the political that I wish to qualify. In his own way, in the biographer's way, Ackroyd is right. If we recoil at his confidence that a single notebook passage might be elevated into Blake's "most elaborate statement" and made to stand for his politics generally (as if *Jerusalem* were not a rather more elaborate political statement)—or at his certainty that this notebook passage can speak for itself unequivocally, without our even having to ask whether Blake means to reject politics altogether or *existing*, parliamentary politics only—we nevertheless cannot easily rebut the biographer's apolitical construction by turning to the evidence of Blake's obviously engaged texts—even though, as Mee accurately observes, "Radical discourse . . . informs Blake's language at almost every level."[3] Critics may disagree about whether Blake's political orientation is best described as antinomian or liberal; they may further disagree about the extent to which his political commitments turn increasingly private, mythical, and recessive with each passing stage of his career. But for most critics the content and formal strategies of his aesthetic production still point to one conclusion: "It has always been clear that William Blake was . . . a political radical."[4] To Blake's biographers, however, this conclusion has not always seemed obvious. Beginning with his own contemporaries' insistence on his harmlessness, biographers like Ackroyd have tended to minimize the significance of Blake's politics not because they are uncomfortable with such radicalism but because Blake left almost no trace of anything we can justifiably call political activity.[5] Surrounded by the volatile culture of London's underworld, acquainted with some of its figures, Blake neither joined any radical group nor participated informally in radical activities. So compatible are Blake's situation and views with the opportunities afforded by London's political activism that his nonparticipation sometimes strikes admirers as bordering on the inexplicable. After noting, for instance, how "many of the radical and revolutionary movements of Blake's day were founded and run by other artisans," and after reciting the personal circumstances that should have made

Blake a likely leader or recruit—"his worsening financial situation, his involvement in the Gordon Riots, and later on his trial on a charge of treason" (we take
up all three momentarily)—Makdisi concedes that Blake "seems not to have been
actively involved in any organized radical movements."[6]

Broadly speaking, Blake criticism has compensated for the absence of actual
political activity in the Blake record in two ways. Working primarily by contiguity
and association, historicists have inserted Blake into a thoroughly politicized world
of dissenting sects, engaged artisans, and underground or bourgeois activists. At
the same time, formalist critics have found in Blake's literary and artistic production a thoroughgoing critique of his era's ideology that emphasizes the potential
of textual and aesthetic forms to act upon an audience in transformative and liberating ways.[7] One could argue with this hasty schematization, especially with its
division into camps, but it is important to see how these approaches prop up one
another. In order to fit Blake into a radical world they describe in ever increasing
detail, historicists benefit from an engaged Blake who exercises the kind of agency
Susan Wolfson has called "activist formalism."[8] In this sense of activism, Blake's
oppositional aesthetic strategies can be considered "a literary counterpart to the
various radical working-class movements of the time."[9] At the same time, textually
oriented critics rely on their historicist counterparts to tether Blake's formal experiments to a substantive world, and to provide historical ground for the hypothetical readers invoked whenever they raise reader response (rousing the faculties to
act) to the level of a vanguard political activity. Thus, formalist methods provide
agency in a world provided by historicism, and the *Cambridge Companion to William Blake* can include as consecutive chapters "The Political Aesthetic of Blake's
Images" and "Blake's Politics in History."[10] If at one time the colossal formalism
of Northrop Frye and the uncompromising historicism of David Erdman seemed
to divide the realm between them, the two enterprises have now fully merged, with
the most generative scholarship moving reciprocally and complexly between the
two modes.[11] A thoroughly contextualized Blake seems perfectly situated for the
historically informed close reading that currently goes under the name of "new
formalism." Although dissenters to this view have begun to emerge, the general
result has been a Blake with solid political credentials because he lived in a politically saturated world and created his works as if they were momentous public acts
determined to transform and liberate a general audience.

From the perspective of this joint construction it seems ludicrous, prima facie,
to claim that Blake "displays not the slightest interest in any particular political
or social philosophy." Yet Ackroyd can make that claim precisely because Blake's
politics—whatever his sympathies and urgencies—never exceeded the smallest
circle of expression. Across the more than forty years of his literary production,

he never adopted a mode of public participation shared by or even recognized as such by others. Blake's earliest, pious biographers may not have understood their subject well, but when they glossed over his politics there is little reason to doubt that they accurately reflected the relatively small role it appeared to play in a life visibly consumed by art, professional craft, and spiritual concerns. The initial challenge I propose for this chapter, then, is to hold in view a double vision of Blake, to see simultaneously the activist Blake of criticism (formalist *and* historicist) and the nonparticipant Blake of biography. How can Blake's critics and biographers both be right? And rather than "locat[ing] different aspects of his work within plural and apparently incompatible spheres," as some critics skeptical of the radical Blake have begun to do, I want to consider why Blake's political and apolitical tendencies are knitted together within the most characteristic practices of his art and verse, rather than being parceled out among different texts, different times, and different influences.[12] Once again this will become a question of emotion: If Blake's critical engagement and nonparticipation were mutually constitutive, then what kind of affective experience allowed him to hold these strands together?

The touchstone for this chapter is the untitled image Gilchrist disarmingly called "Glad Day" and Erdman defiantly restored to political meaning by insisting it be called "The Dance of Albion" or "Albion rose." Erdman was not the first to prefer this title, derived from an inscription Blake added to the print many years after its initial design and earliest etching. However, he was the first to argue that the image is a "terrific social utterance" aligned with revolutionary energy.[13] Erdman's reading of "Albion rose" launches the polemical mission of *Prophet Against Empire*; it provides our first instruction in how not to read Blake (ahistorically and apolitically), and, anticipating a favorite strategy of next-generation historicists, it expertly deploys a seemingly incidental date provided by the inscription ("WB inv 1780") to retrieve the image's original and occluded political context. Because Blake initially designed the image in 1780 and returned to it with new productions over roughly a twenty-five year period, it comes to represent for Erdman Blake's abiding commitment to democratic revolution, from which he (unlike Gilchrist) supposes Blake never to have retreated. In that sense, we might consider his "Albion rose" the antitype of the notebook passage Ackroyd lifts out of context in order to generalize the relative insignificance of Blake's politics, an attitude Ackroyd implies remained fairly consistent across Blake's career. In other words, both writers reject the still common thesis that Blake's revolutionary enthusiasm modulated into quietism and retreated into private mythology after the Terror, but they do so for opposite reasons—Erdman to sustain Blake's radical commitments, Ackroyd to deny they ever amounted to much. This chapter aims to explain how they might both be right, and to see in "Albion rose" an image at once politically oriented and inoperative, public but also private and intransitive, an image that blurs activity and passivity to the point where one no longer can sustain a meaningful distinction between those terms. This image will return us to the alleged scene of Blake's earliest and formative political experience (the Gordon Riots), while also—because of its close relation to *Samson Agonistes*—prompting us to reconsider Blake's understanding of Milton, his primary influence on questions of literature, revolution, and violence. If "Albion rose" signifies any consistency across Blake's career, it is the consistency of his particular type of agitation.

"Albion rose"

"Albion rose" is "perhaps Blake's most famous separate plate,"[14] finding its way onto calendars, posters, and screensavers almost as frequently as his "Ancient of Days." The design mattered enough to Blake that he revisited it several times over many years, and despite some caution over dating, there is a general consensus about the image's career. Lightly sketching the figure first in 1780, Blake had engraved his exuberant, naked youth with arms thrown wide by 1793, though he did not include it in the prospectus of designs he advertised that year. By 1796, he had color-printed the image (figure 2.1) following the technique he experimented with at the time, applying paint directly to the copper plate before printing, and he incorporated it into the *Large Book of Designs* commissioned that year by Ozias Humphry. Finally, sometime after 1800, and probably around 1804, he altered the original plate (figure 2.2), adding a few iconographic details (a bat-winged moth and a worm), his initials, a date ("WB inv 1780"), and an inscription: "Albion rose from where he labourd at the Mill with Slaves / Giving himself for the Nations he danc'd the dance of Eternal Death."[15]

Any narrative one observes in this sequence can arise solely on the basis of internal evidence and the allusions provided by the images themselves; Blake offered no independent comment on this design (not even a title), and he does not seem to have privileged it over other images he similarly reworked over long periods. In criticism after Erdman, however, "Albion rose" has become an indispensable key to political readings of Blake. There are several reasons for this, not least the brilliance of Erdman's groundbreaking reading in *Prophet Against Empire*. Even without the later version's date and inscription, the youth's resemblance to Orc in *America* would have made the image's political associations unavoidable, but with them, Erdman was able to look back to Blake's earliest productions and forward to the initial stages of his late, epic prophecies to indicate a Blake whose revolutionary commitments were so primary as to be unswerving. By recalling the original design of the image in 1780, Blake's dating invited a contextual link between "Al-

Figure 2.1 Albion rose, color-printed engraving finished with pen and ink and watercolor, c. 1790 / c. 1796. Courtesy of the Huntington Art Collections, San Marino, California

Albion rose from where he labourd at the Mill with Slaves.
Giving himself for the Nations he danc'd the dance of Eternal Death

Figure 2.2 The Dance of Albion (Glad Day), c. 1803/1810. Rosenwald Collection. Photo courtesy of the National Gallery of Art, Washington, D.C.

bion rose" and the explosive energies of the Gordon Riots, which Erdman argued were less an outbreak of vulgar, anarchic, and anti-Catholic street violence than an expression of frustration with English tyranny and a mass protest against the injustices of the American war.[16] And by inscribing his image with lines on Albion's heroic self-sacrifice in a "dance of Eternal Death," Blake affirmed his continuing opposition to the Burkean counterrevolution. In 1796, as Erdman explained, Edmund Burke also looked back to the Gordon Riots and lamented how closely England then verged on "the death-dance of democratic revolution" that a decade later swept over France. With his references to Burke and the Gordon Riots in place, it was easy for Erdman also to secure a political meaning for the unadorned image of 1793. "On a mountain top, arms in a gesture of tremendous energy and confidence" (9), Blake's youth illustrated in giant, singular form the defiant "naked multitude" described in *America* (also printed in 1793), the united crowd of Englishmen who cast away their arms and refused to support their government's campaign against the colonies. Erdman's reading was so startling, so forceful, that others either followed his lead in emphasizing the radical content of the image or risked having their own interpretations look embarrassingly evasive.[17]

After Erdman, then, one would think that a biographer wishing to minimize Blake's political interests would do well to avoid "Albion rose" altogether. There is no returning to the Blake of Gilchrist's "Glad Day." Even Ackroyd considers the early-1790s version a figure of "energy and revolt," which along with its companion pieces, "Our End Is Come" and "Lucifer and the Pope in Hell," resembles "political cartoons of a familiar late eighteenth-century kind, wrought to a pitch of intensity beyond the reach of anyone but Gillray" (168). As such, these separate plates were too controversial—too topical and too engaged—to risk publishing in 1793. But that's the *only* concession Ackroyd makes, and it is a strategic one, meant *to contain* the image's political reference by attaching it to a moment of passing enthusiasm. Rather than allowing the politics of the 1793 image to govern other variants in the series, Ackroyd turns it into an aberration, the exception that proves the rule, framed historically on either end (1780 and 1804) by first and last instances he boldly dissociates from political reference altogether. Flaming into political significance only briefly, "Albion rose" provides Ackroyd with a story of deviation and return (as we see in more detail momentarily). In short, the untitled engraving of the early 1790s is Blake's artistic equivalent of the bonnet rouge, put on in a moment of revolutionary enthusiasm but quickly removed and without much struggle. By virtue of a few strategic concessions, the very image that seemed to shatter the illusion of Gilchrist's apolitical Blake instead paves the way for his reintroduction. If Ackroyd's reading of "Albion rose" is ultimately dissatisfying, as I argue it is, it is sufficiently plausible to render Erdman's reading incomplete as well. At the least, it forces us to recognize how *insistently* Blake criticism has pressed the case for his political engagement—and to ask why that case should need such advocacy in the first place.

"Involuntary Participation" (1780)

For the past sixty years, discussion of "Albion rose" has been inseparable from discussion of the Gordon Riots. This eighteenth-century London uprising provided a spectacle of mass, sectarian violence so disturbing that Edward Gibbon likened the volatile crowd to a resurrection of "forty thousand Puritans such as they might be in the time of Cromwell."[18] It also provides the single moment in Blake's career when he can be placed at the scene of urban political action. Occurring when Blake was only twenty-two years old, it has taken on the proportions of an irresistible primal scene in the criticism. "[W]ho can say how deeply the event burned itself into his consciousness . . . ?" Schorer asked in 1946.[19] The answer he implied ("Deeply!") has become widely accepted. Here is Stanley Gardner: "The rioters were opening the prisons; they were against the war, against the king, against the government. It all must have spoken Blake's mind."[20] Such confidence began when Erdman identified "Albion rose" as the utterance that indeed spoke Blake's mind at the time.

In rehearsing this consensus, however, we must face an irony: the political reading of "Albion rose" depends upon an anecdote with only a single source, the biographer Gilchrist, who told the story because he wished to absolve Blake from any direct involvement in the rioting. Attributing his account to Blake's own reminiscence, but without indicating how this reminiscence came into his hands (it receives no mention from the earliest biographers who knew Blake personally), Gilchrist tells of the young artisan swept up in rioting that rolled through the central neighborhoods of London.[21]

> In this outburst of anarchy, Blake long remembered an involuntary participation of his own. On the third day, Tuesday, 6th of June . . . the rioters, flushed with gin and victory, were turning their attention to grander schemes of devastation. That evening, the artist happened to be walking in a route chosen by one of the mobs at large . . . Suddenly, he encountered the advancing wave of triumphant Blackguardism, and was forced (for from such a great surging mob there is no disentanglement) to go along in the very front rank, and witness the storm and burning of the fortress-like prison [Newgate], and release of its three hundred inmates. This was a peculiar experience for a spiritual poet; not without peril, had a drunken soldier chanced to have identified him during the after weeks of indiscriminate vengeance: those black weeks

when strings of boys under fourteen were hung up in a row to vindicate the offended majesty of the Law. (35)

Although biographers still sometimes quote this account without comment, as if it were fact, most Blake scholars have turned to "Albion rose" to dispute Gilchrist's straining effort to extricate Blake from any but the most involuntary and accidental participation, but also to corroborate that some such episode indeed occurred.[22] If "Albion rose" is the companion piece of Gilchrist's anecdote, then it offers the indirect record of Blake's experience of the Gordon Riots, invaluable because unmediated by Gilchrist's antirevolutionary bias. If it is not, however, then there is no other record to corroborate Blake's presence at the scene, for none of Blake's writings or images explicitly refers to the event, and in the eyewitness accounts of his contemporaries, his presence receives no mention. George Cumberland, who only weeks earlier in the *Morning Chronicle* gave special notice to a picture of Blake's on exhibit at the Royal Academy, recounted the rioting but not his associate's involvement.[23] "Albion rose" has thus been summoned to fill a gap; it supplies Blake with a voice, a commentary on a crucial event, which would otherwise be lacking. With the evidence hanging by a thread—a date (1780) added twenty-four years later to an image not obviously related to the event—the scene has taken on a surprising clarity in the criticism, despite the extent to which it is underwritten by conjecture. "Who *can* say how deeply the event burned itself into his consciousness?" (Schorer 157).

Strangely, then, Blake is a vague presence at what would be his own primal political scene. He leaves barely a trace at or of the very event that would best throw him into relief. This is not the last time he will disappear at the moment his political identity seems ready to precipitate into a specific historical profile. In 1780 and 1804, the same years we attach to the first and last incarnations of "Albion rose," Blake was personally involved in two significant political events, sharing with other contemporary radicals the experience of being detained as a spy and brought to trial for sedition. In Blake's case, however, these two familiar incidents serve primarily to foreground his *absence* from organized radical activity. In the same year as the Gordon Riots, Blake and Thomas Stothard were held under suspicion of spying during a drawing expedition undertaken along the River Medway. Stothard left a sketch of the scene; unlike "Albion rose," it requires no speculative reconstruction to be linked to its source event. Detained only by mistake, the young artists were released within hours, and without consequences. There is simply no reason to believe that Blake's activities ever brought him to the systematic attention of government agents (police operations investigated extensively by David Worrall and others), as did the activities of many of his contemporaries and some of his associates.[24] In 1804, in an event of far greater personal import, Blake was brought to trial for sedition by John Scofield, the soldier he had forced from his garden in Felpham. Here, too, the allegations seem empty; Blake does not appear to have used the inflammatory language against the king that formed the basis of Scofield's charges. In a trial lasting only an hour, his attorney, Samuel Rose, made a case convincing enough to have his client acquitted, calling him "as loyal a subject as any man in this court . . . , [a subject who] feels as much indignation at the idea of exposing to contempt or injury the sacred person of his sovereign as any man."[25] We imagine Blake bristling with silent indignation upon hearing such misrepresentations, but we should also remember that only a few years later Blake was elaborately dedicating his edition of *The Grave* to the queen, a tribute that could only be published by royal permission.[26] With its complex negotiations of private outrage and practiced concession, Blake's relation to political authority was rather more complicated than any caricature of militancy or submission would allow. Contrast, for instance, Blake's 1804 trial with the earlier, more famous prosecution of Thomas Hardy—shoemaker, rights-of-man enthusiast, and co-founder of the London Corresponding Society. In 1792, Hardy's judge acknowledged the defendant's religious virtues but lectured the court on the dangers of enthusiasm: "if a man is an enthusiast, his being a moral and religious man is at least a neutral circumstance, because a moral, religious man, if he chooses to let his enthusiasm carry him beyond his judgement, is exposed to be drawn into the circumstances in which the prisoner now stands."[27] Blake's enthusiasm contributed to all kinds of urgencies, eccentricities, and aesthetic productivity, all conducted with little regard for the model of prudent self-control promoted by Hardy's magistrate. Yet in political matters it almost never carried him "beyond his judgement" and therefore never drew him into activities as risky as Hardy's. However heated his passions could become, there was a line Blake would not cross, certainly not in the radical 1790s and later—even in the Scofield episode—only in an instance of isolated, personal altercation.

What remains consistent across the otherwise unrelated incidents of 1780 and 1804 is Blake's apparent insignificance whenever his political identity might draw public notice. No one seems to have paid him much attention. Blake feared recognition, perhaps because he believed (as Gilchrist reported) that his republican tendencies could be read openly on his face, putting him at risk no matter how carefully he guarded his sympathies. But every time Blake found himself entangled in a political incident, he managed to escape consequences by going unrecognized. In 1780, as Ackroyd puts it, Blake "was fortunate . . . in not being recognized by any of the soldiery" who put down the Gordon Riots and brutally made examples of the rioters (75). Twenty-four years later, he was fortunate to appear at trial as a stranger unknown to the law, without any reputation for disturbance that might prejudice the magistrate against him. Upon being congratulated for acquitting an excellent man, the Duke of Richmond could only reply, "I know nothing of him."[28] The same Blake who lamented his anonymity as an artist ("I am hid")[29] depended on it to shelter himself politically. He escaped recognition by habitually occupying the margins and remaining uninvolved.[30] In the eyes of the law, he was "as loyal a subject as any man."[31]

If not exactly a primal scene, then, the Gordon Riots do provide our first glimpse into Blake's elusive half-presence at the scene of political activity—that is, if we can assume Gilchrist's anecdote is credible enough to place him there at all. From its beginning in 1863, when this scene first enters the record, Gilchrist is already taking advantage of its central indeterminacy (What did Blake do? What did he think?) to install a Blake politically engaged against his will, a Blake substantiated in the scene by his elusive passivity. Other, mostly dissenting, installations have followed. If Blake was "in the very front rank" of rioters, it could not have been because his participation was coerced; surely he could have escaped into streets he had known since childhood. It seems unlikely anyone could be forced a mile and a half against his will, and others on the scene managed to disentangle themselves from the crowd and move about freely.[32] In the Erdman tradition, the thrust of such common sense is to make Blake's participation in the Gordon Riots willing and therefore compatible with the impulsive exuberance of "Albion rose." Reading against the grain, we observe a Blake aligning himself deliberately with the street politics Gilchrist disparaged as "Blackguardism," a Blake who might well idealize the scene as a naked youth exulting in his own liberated energies.

Accordingly, the one phrase that seems to goad modern readers of Gilchrist is "involuntary participation." Curiously, however, even those who object most vehemently to this manufactured notion have found it necessary to substitute a variant of their own, for without the immunity Gilchrist's phrase affords him, it is possible to credit Blake with a revolutionary participation too voluntary for comfort. By taking the reversal of Gilchrist to its logical and disturbing conclusion, William Keach, for instance, identifies the Gordon Riots as the formative moment of Blake's persistent "attraction to physical force": "Blake knew directly what it meant to participate in mass violence."[33] Given the evidence of "Albion rose," he apparently liked it rather too well. Addressing those critics who have devoted themselves to rescuing Blake's street-wise impulse from Gilchrist's moralizing caution, Keach raises the opposite question: Who can save Blake from himself? Although his reconstruction of the scene is no less conjectural than the others, Keach points out that readers of Blake risk glorifying violence whenever they would overturn Gilchrist entirely—which, I would add, is exactly why they almost never do so. Although there are a few notable exceptions, Makdisi foremost among them, we generally find readers restoring "involuntary participation" in modified form, as they struggle to explain how Blake could have participated and not participated at the same time, retaining just enough passivity to escape the charge of criminal violence, while remaining sufficiently active to avoid any suggestion of political indifference.[34]

Here Ackroyd is especially instructive. Recognizing Gilchrist's prejudice, but with little interest in monumentalizing Blake's political commitments, he specu- lates, "It is much more likely that [Blake] went along with the mob willingly, per- haps impulsively, and, when he saw the fire and heard the screaming, he stayed out of sheer panic or overwhelming curiosity" (75). "Willingly" slides through "impul- sively" until it lands on "overwhelming curiosity": Blake can no more disentangle himself from internal compulsion than he could escape Gilchrist's surging mob. Here Blake experiences all the immediacy of the scene but not out of any affirma- tive political judgment or agency. He is the fascinated but involuntary observer of others' actions. Acknowledging Blake's political will only to evacuate it and then substitute a passive, even panicked curiosity, Ackroyd prepares the way for the next step of his argument—to uncouple the riots from the drawing of liberated exuberance Blake executed sometime the same year. In this light, " 'Albion rose' looks more like a study connected with his work in the Academy Schools . . . It may even be related to his new sense of freedom after completing his apprenticeship, or to a general youthful exuberance, or to the recognition of his own great powers" (75–76). In other words, it may be related to anything but political enthusiasm. Subordinating politics to art, and then subordinating political to personal freedom, Ackroyd envisions a drawing that in 1780 could not anticipate the association with revolutionary Orc Blake provided for it some thirteen years later. And because the image expresses personal and artistic freedom initially, Ackroyd describes Blake's final return to it in 1804 as a return to original impulses. Having renewed his com- mitment to religious art after his spiritual reawakening in the Truchsessian Gallery that autumn, Blake reworked and inscribed the image (see figure 2.2) to convey his private ambition to rise above the common mill of laboring commercial engrav- ers. Without mentioning Blake's newly added reference to *Samson Agonistes,* and thus avoiding the complex politics raised by that allusion, Ackroyd suggests that in 1804 we can best gloss "Albion rose" not by remembering the Gordon Riots but by turning to Blake's painting *The Resurrection* and other contemporary images of religious transcendence.[35]

Oddly enough, however, the same strategy that helps Ackroyd deliver a mini- mally political Blake from his entanglement in plebeian violence recurs in those reconstructions of the scene that aim at just the opposite result. Schorer objected to treating the episode as little more than a colorful anecdote, but he also resisted

those who crudely imply "Blake 'rioted with the rest.'" The compromise he proposed posits an intensity of trancelike *visual* participation: "the spectacle of three
hundred prisoners of law and darkness freed suddenly, against the background of
fire, to the open air . . . [H]ere was an experience that combined . . . the revolutionary idea with the revolutionary image." Blake was receptive to the scene, which
"burned itself into his consciousness," without seeking to contribute his own
warm energy to its fires (157–158). Gardner likewise imagines a Blake more acted
upon than acting, suggesting the mob "drew Blake . . . hypnotically" (21). Although
he is more insistent than other early commentators on Blake's active engagement
in protest, even Erdman begrudgingly concedes, "we may let [Gilchrist's] 'involuntary' stand," at least "for any physical participation" (8). From the start, then,
political critics have managed to restore Blake's participation in this scene only by
subdividing his agency. So long as it is internal and affective, a matter of "idea" and
"image," his solidarity with the crowd must have been as voluntary as it was ardent, but any enactment of his enthusiasm in direct participation must have been
strictly involuntary. "[C]aught in the tumult," writes Gardner, "his understanding
was with the rioters, his regret with the rioting" (23). Engaged but inactive at the
scene of the Gordon Riots, Blake satisfies the needs of critic and biographer alike,
straddling a border of partial agency that nullifies any clean differentiation of activity and passivity. Already installed at the center of Blake's primal political scene,
a scene largely invented by criticism, is a figure closely resembling the Kantian
spectator we examined in the previous chapter. Blake's wishful participation in
the revolutionary moment borders closely on enthusiasm, but he has no intention
of involving himself in the action. On the edge of violent urban revolt, he is at no
real risk of letting "his enthusiasm carry him beyond his judgement," to recall the
anxious words of Hardy's magistrate. "Albion rose" could indeed be the companion piece of *this* scene, for the isolated figure's kinetic vitality is also an intransitive
vitality, detached from any referential world in which and upon which it might act,
detached from any other agents it might join with collectively. The energy of this
naked youth explodes *without consequence.*

It bears repeating that we have no reliable knowledge about Blake's involvement in the Gordon Riots, about what took place on the street or in his mind.
The rewriting of Gilchrist's "involuntary participation" has always involved replacing one fantasia with another, and so these reconstructed scenes inevitably tell us
more about the needs of criticism than they do about Blake, not least about criticism's need for some founding moment of Blake's political engagement. Ackroyd
skillfully constructs a barely political Blake and then reads that construction back
into an originary scene, not unlike those priestly redactors of the Bible who supported their own Sabbath laws by establishing a seven-day creation myth. Blake's

political critics have done no less. Into the Gordon Riots, as glossed by "Albion rose," they backload a Blake whose fierce political commitments will always coincide with the absence of direct political participation. By valorizing that ambiguous political stance suspended between body and spirit, engagement and detachment, and by joining to it the image of youthful vigor in "Albion rose," such criticism may be writing the origin myth of its own wishful self-image—seeking to validate the political significance of its own uncertain activity—as if the scholarly vindication of a politically committed Blake were somehow itself a politically consequential act in *our* world.

"Unobserv'd & at liberty" (1804)

Paradoxically, Blake's final version of "Albion rose" historicizes the image and, at the same time, detaches it from historical reference. That is, the changes he introduces historicize the *original* design by supplying a specific date (1780) and perhaps a crucial referent (the Gordon Riots), but they provide no such information for the *final* design. The result is that an image now historically anchored at its beginning floats free from specific reference at its end. The year 1804 is a current best guess for the final state of the copper plate, based on textual evidence (Blake did not introduce "Albion" as a mythic character until 1800) and graphic technique (no image with the extensive burnishing employed here can be dated prior to 1804)—but there exists no clear connection between the image and the context of its production.[36] This absence of topical reference has made it possible to accent either the personal or the political meanings of "Albion rose," a design that shuttles between the most intimate gestures of self-portraiture and the broadest possible national allegory. If Blake's return to the design coincides with his spiritual and artistic renewal upon returning to London from Felpham (as Ackroyd and Essick prefer), then the pertinent context would be his letters exulting in the restoration of a visionary ecstasy he had not experienced since his youth. If instead it coincides with the massive mobilization for war against France that horrified Blake upon his return to London, then the logical reference points would include Blake's memory of wartime protest in 1780 and any number of scenes in his poetry where defiance takes the form of rebellious, youthful (and sometimes naked) uprising.[37]

In fact, the image is so generalized (a single naked figure dominating a vague landscape) and the added inscription so elusive that they cannot be reduced to any of the particular references they invite us to entertain. Erdman was so confident that Albion's affirmative "dance of death" responded to the "death-dance of revolution" in Burke's *Letter to a Noble Lord* that he dated the image to reflect this correspondence (circa 1796). The association weakened somewhat when new evidence demanded a later date.[38] More immediate associations prove no less difficult to pin down. With Albion rising "from where he labourd at the Mill with Slaves" and rising to an act of self-sacrifice for the nations, the inscription refers unequivocally to the opening of *Samson Agonistes,* where we find Milton's hero "Eyeless in *Gaza* at the Mill with slaves."[39] The relationship between "Albion rose" and Milton's Samson has a long, complex history in the criticism, and we will return to the topic of Blake's response to Milton later in this chapter. For now, however, I simply want to sketch a few of the options this intertextual relation makes available, starting with the one that has seemed obvious to most commentators, its confirmation of the image's revolutionary content.

When Christopher Hill described *Samson Agonistes* as Milton's "call of hope to the [politically] defeated," urging "potential Samsons . . . enslaved at the mill" to "be ready to act when the time comes," he was so sure Blake heard this call that he turned to "Albion rose" to confirm its revolutionary message.[40] Hill's chapter on *Samson Agonistes* in *Milton and the English Revolution* begins with an epigraph from *A Defense of the English People* signaling Milton's faith in the justice of revolutionary violence: "The heroic Samson . . . thought it not impious but pious to kill those masters who were tyrants over his country" (428). It ends: "Blake picked up the image of Samson as 'a gigantic national hero, who fights against foreign tyrants.' He saw him as a sun-figure, and—picking up *Areopagitica*'s image—as Albion rising 'from where he laboured at the mill with slaves,' like a strong man after sleep shaking his invincible locks" (448). In the penultimate speech of Milton's drama, Manoa proposes to build a monument so inspiring that memory of his son's final deed—the destruction of the Philistine temple that cost him his life—will "inflame [the] breasts" of future youths "To matchless valour and adventures high" (ll. 1739–1740). For Hill, Blake is that future youth and *Samson Agonistes* the monument he turns to in order to rekindle revolutionary memory. Unapologetic about the necessity of violence, Hill found it impossible to reconcile Milton (and by implication, Blake) with a modern, liberal Christianity: "Milton believed that the war against Antichrist continued, and that it was the duty of God's people to hit back when they could" (442). It is not hard to imagine Hill's Blake saying the exact words Scofield alleged when he brought Blake to trial for sedition, that "he was *a strong Man* and [would] certainly begin to cut throats" if Napoleon made good on his threat to invade England.[41]

A powerful (if controversial) strand of criticism continues to identify Milton and Blake as radical antinomians openly attracted to revolutionary enthusiasm and the promise of transformational violence—and therefore badly served when readers misconstrue them as "soft liberals." Stanley Fish has championed this view among Miltonists, Makdisi among Blakeans.[42] Occasionally, one still observes a Miltonist repeating Hill's gesture of summoning Blake to support an argument in favor of Samson's violence. Describing *Samson Agonistes* as "a work of harsh and uncompromising violence, indeed, a work that exults in violence," Michael Lieb is one of the few critics to consider even Fish too soft on the question of Milton's enthusiasm for violence. Invoking *The Marriage of Heaven and Hell* at the end of a recent essay, he leaves little doubt about where he believes Blake would stand in current debate: "The choice is ours to make, but be prepared to join the devil's party if you hook up with Lieb."[43] Questions surrounding Milton's view of religiously motivated violence have taken on amplified urgency since September 11, 2001, and especially since the John Carey–Stanley Fish controversy that erupted soon after. It has now become impossible to discuss Samson at the pillars without also debating whether his killing of three thousand Philistines resembles contemporary acts of terrorism and whether Milton approves of the holy war Samson undertakes.[44] Such controversy has yet to engulf Blake, but it is worth noting that, when Simon and Schuster rushed to reissue Robin Morgan's *The Demon Lover: The Roots of Terrorism* in 2001, they thought fit to adorn the cover with an image from *America* of Orc rising in flames.[45]

Because Samson so fully dramatizes the consequences of voluntary participation in revolutionary violence, his presence in "Albion rose" reinforces all the uneasiness surrounding Blake's involvement in the Gordon Riots. The date and the Miltonic allusion of "Albion rose" make for an inflammatory combination. Perhaps it should not surprise us, then, to hear an echo of Samuel Johnson's complaint against Milton—"his predominant desire was to destroy rather than establish[;] . . . he felt not so much the love of liberty, as repugnance to authority"[46]—in Keach's against Blake: his imaginative investment in revolutionary violence expresses a "vengeful and retaliatory fury against the ruling order" (144). Both assessments recall an old judgment against Samson, summed up in Andrew Marvell's poem on *Paradise Lost*: Samson "groap'd the Temples Posts in spight / The World o'erwhelming to revenge his Sight."[47] Yet despite Hill's certainty that Blake followed Milton in affirming Samson's heroism and thereby expressed a similar willingness to endorse divinely inspired violence in the cause of political justice, the evidence is far from clear. Erdman noted that, after his acquittal at trial, Blake was painting ecstatic works like *Samson Bursting his Bonds,* but he neglected to mention that Blake completed his sequence with *Samson Subdued,* a complementary image of dismal, self-induced failure (figures 2.3 and 2.4).[48] According to Joseph Wittreich, Blake was drawn to *Samson Agonistes* by Milton's ambivalence, not by his zealotry. There he would find Milton "embrac[ing] the revolutionary but not the revolution," just as Blake, at the Gordon Riots, had understood the rioters but regretted the rioting.[49] Wittreich's Blake is the son of a Milton turned circum-

Figure 2.3 Samson Breaking His Bonds, 1805. Courtesy of the Morgan Library and Museum

spect with hindsight, and "Albion rose" is his *Samson Agonistes,* a cautionary lesson about the attraction of "false apocalypse," "less a celebration of revolution than a critique of it."[50] Finally, if it is possible to see in Blake's reference to Milton either a commitment to or a hesitancy before revolutionary action, it has also been possible to empty the reference of political content altogether. Those who interpret "Albion rose" as a statement of personal and artistic renewal favor a letter, also from 1804, in which Blake bends the language of *Samson Agonistes* into a figure of professional drudgery, the copy work he wished to transcend: "I was a slave bound in a mill among beasts and devils."[51]

When we return to Samson, we will consider why such mutually exclusive read-

Figure 2.4 Samson Subdued, ink and watercolor over traces of graphite on paper, c. 1800. Sheet: 15⅜ × 13⅞ inches (39.1 × 35.2 cm.). Philadelphia Museum of Art, Gift of Mrs. William Thomas Tonner, 1964

ings as Hill's and Wittreich's remain plausible, and why neither can stand alone. As Blake represents him, Samson becomes a figure who inspires action and inaction all at once, joining impulse and hesitancy so completely as to redefine the nature of action altogether. Samson is the object of attraction *and* repulsion, and Blake's identification with him resembles the paradoxical states we have been calling (after Gilchrist) "involuntary participation" or (after Kant) "wishful participation." That is, Blake identifies with Samson's strength without claiming a share in his violence; he straddles the border between strength held in reserve and strength enacted, as if by proximity he could borrow upon the figure's tangible potency to enhance his own less conspicuous agency, which is the agency of criticism or "mental fight." Like Milton before him, Blake attempts to manage this delicate negotiation by transforming *reading* itself into an action, one that would assimilate Samson's transformative strength while also disavowing his dangerous will to act.

Let us conclude here with some questions about "Albion rose" in 1804. If Blake's last version of this print is indeed a political and even a revolutionary image, then why does its protest remain so obscure, relying on oblique historical and literary references beyond the certain grasp of any reader other than Blake himself? If, on the other hand, it is an autobiographical image of spiritual renewal, then why would Blake include such volatile political inferences at all? In the final version of "Albion rose," Blake has heightened the design's political content while rendering that content dormant, perhaps even inaccessible. Modern political readings of the image depend upon an inscription and a date that seem to have had little audience, and certainly no public, in Blake's lifetime. Like all public statements, "Albion rose" is addressed to no one in particular, but in this case, Blake seems to have addressed his gesture to no one at all. In 1804, "Albion rose" resembles the Bishop Watson annotations we considered earlier: a defiant act intervening in public affairs but preserved within an opaque intimacy, circulating, if at all, to a few acquaintances least likely to understand its private code. An even closer analogy might be *Jerusalem*'s address "To the Public," etched perhaps in the same year and sharing a similar tendency to conflate private and public acts, as if the engraver's individual critical engagement were itself a matter of national importance.

In 1803, when Blake was preparing to return from Felpham to London, he was confident he could achieve commercial independence there, explaining to his brother James, "I know that the Public are my friends & love my works" (E 727). Everything at the time—from his preparation of *Vala* in publishable form to his decision to write epic, the most public of genres—indicates that Blake saw his return from rural life as a return to public participation. Yet given the marginality and obscurity he tended to cultivate for himself, his statement to James seems inexplicable. A few months later, still in Felpham, Blake was writing a letter to Thomas Butts that may serve as a gloss. Due to the stifling intimacy and scrutiny of Hayley's small domestic circle, it is not surprising that Blake would seek relief from Felpham in London's public world. It is surprising, however, to hear him associate London with increased privacy. "I can alone carry on my visionary studies in London unannoyd, & . . . [there] I may converse with my friends in Eternity. See Visions, Dream Dreams & prophecy & speak Parables" (E 728). In London, Blake can resume his role of visionary prophet, "utter[ing] his opinion both of private & public matters" (E 617), because in that setting he remains *"unobserv'd & at liberty from the Doubts of other Mortals"* (emphasis added, E 728). Only in the metropolis can Blake be among the crowd and left alone, engaged and apart. The liberating privacy-in-public he experienced there, which he would eventually represent in the

exhilarating, utopian conversations of *Jerusalem*, was perhaps always the precondition of his work. If this does not explain his conviction that the public loved his
work, it does help explain why he continued to love the public—despite, perhaps
even because of, its neglect.

Where is Blake? An Interlude on Blake's Residences

"Where is Blake among these slogans?" (158), wonders Ackroyd, after citing several
of the republican demands ("No King!") written on palace walls in 1792. The question is rhetorical, given away by "slogans." Ackroyd's Blake will never be located
by cultural formula, least of all by the formula of programmatic politics. What
Blake shares with others in his world (opposition to kings, for instance) does not
prevent him from remaining apart: "he never joined any particular group or society" (73). If this practiced detachment separated Blake from friends who joined
the Society for Constitutional Information (William Sharp, George Cumberland,
Thomas Stothard), "suggest[ing] that his was, from the beginning, an internal
politics both self-willed and self-created" (73), it serves Ackroyd as an organizing
principle of wider consequence. As with others in the genre, a dominant trope of
this biography is the "social circle." By passing through one round of local relations
after another, Blake accrues a circumstantial specificity that nevertheless leaves his
autonomy uncompromised. Each circle—starting with his immediate family ("He
remained profoundly uncomfortable" with anyone but Robert; "he might almost
have been self-created" [20]) and continuing on through the "little club" of artists,
"all committed political radicals" (71–72); the circle of Reverend Mathew and his
wife, Harriet; the Joseph Johnson circle; and even the New Jerusalem Church that
Blake joined briefly—tells us only where we won't find Blake.[52]

Ackroyd has been justly praised for immersing Blake in the London of his time,
but the contexts he expertly evokes paradoxically isolate the unique talent of his
subject, an individual enhanced but ultimately undefined by place. We recognize
the convention: Wordsworth virtually invented it in his verse autobiography. Structured by the series of residential spaces through which Wordsworth passes, *The
Prelude* enables the poet, as Celeste Langan has shown, to present himself as "an
infinitely mobile subject," whose home is "with infinitude, and only there."[53] Geography sets off the wished-for autonomy of spiritual *biography*; no determinate local condition can arrest the elusive interior life of a perpetual "*transient*." "Walking,
the poet . . . is neither here nor there," writes Langan.[54] In Ackroyd's biography, the
solitary walker similarly becomes a device of Blake's self-representation—in his
often engraved pilgrim, for instance, or in his recurring passages on the "states"
through which "Man . . . passes . . . like a traveller."[55] Describing the late engrav-

ing of "Colinet's Journey" for R. J. Thornton's *Pastorals of Virgil* (1821), Ackroyd writes: "a traveller, with staff and broad-brimmed hat, walks away from a distant gleaming city; in his solitary journey there emerges once more an image of Blake himself as he pursues his own lonely course through the world" (334). According to the mile-marker in the foreground, the traveler is sixty-seven miles from London, about the distance to Felpham. As Ackroyd describes it, this scene resembles nothing so much as the "Glad Preamble" of *The Prelude,* with the poet "Now free," "escaped / From the vast City,"[56] though it is difficult to tell if Blake's use of the solitary walker trope indeed resembles Wordsworth's or whether Ackroyd's biography of Blake has fallen under the spell of romantic autonomy that Wordsworth, though not without trouble, was among the first to cast.[57]

Among historicists inclined to privilege Blake's working-class radicalism, the alternative to the biographer's outdated coupling of individual genius and free mobility is "bricolage," a concept that assumes a more permeable relation between subject and world. Rather than expressing the uncompromised originality of a unique, impenetrable self, the bricoleur finds himself immersed in a local world, assembling whatever materials lie at hand. For Blake, that world consisted of London's diverse radical subcultures. Unlike his liberal and conservative peers anxious to preserve their individual autonomy, "Blake seems to have been much more open to the currents of dangerous secular and religious enthusiasms swirling around the London of his time."[58] Levi-Strauss famously opposed the contingent bricoleur to the self-creating engineer, who, in Derrida's words, "would be the absolute origin of his own discourse and supposedly would construct it 'out of nothing.' "[59] If "genius" is shorthand for the subject's distinction from social space, "bricolage" would be shorthand for its constitutive immersion, for a collective subject built upon the discourse of others. Guided by this notion, Iain McCalman discusses Blake in exactly the terms Ackroyd avoids, blurring the line between self and context, between Blake and others of his "underworld" class: "Bricoleurs like Blake fashioned their explosive art and cosmology from the rich diversity of signs, symbols and discourses available to their milieu."[60] Internalizing a social and discursive world he shared with Richard Brothers, Thomas Spence, Robert Wedderburn, William Sharp, Richard Lee, Thomas Bentley, and "many others who drew to a greater or lesser extent on the antinomian heresies of the seventeenth century" (this list of usual suspects courtesy of Makdisi), Blake the bricoleur produced work "steeped in political significances."[61] Moreover, as a counterpoint to inflated concepts of individual genius, bricolage bears the additional advantage of tying intellectual labor to a working-class, artisanal figure; it represents words and ideas as physical materials, writing as manual labor, and the subject as a porous, materialist entity defined by its outward orientation.

Despite these advantages in representing the relationship between agents and social space, however, bricolage still preserves elements of the genius model it disavows, for in these accounts the bricoleur maintains an ability to manipulate pieces of his world *more or less freely*. The same bricolage celebrated by historicists becomes for Ackroyd an index of Blake's genius: "he picked up separate ideas, or fragments of knowledge, as he needed them. He was a synthesiser and a systematiser, like so many of his generation, but it was *his own* synthesis designed to establish *his own* system of belief. He was likely to adopt an item he had read in a periodical or a pamphlet with the same frequency that he borrowed notions from Swedenborg or Paracelsus" (90, emphasis added). With every new bit of world the historicist discovers in and around Blake's work (this periodical, that pamphlet), the biographer heightens the distinctive genius with which Blake made it "his own." Where is Blake? In the world, but not exactly of it, occupying two spaces simultaneously—the vast social and discursive space of London that supplied his materials, and the stand-alone space of his transformative genius.

Trying to grasp the proper ratio of self to social and linguistic space, Blake's contextualizing scholars sometimes resort to a vocabulary of "both complicity with and resistance to," leaving open the question of just how far one should lean toward one side or the other when grappling with the problem of Blake's agency.[62] In this interlude, I want to approach that question from another angle, one that doesn't lend itself automatically to constructions of Blake as either artistic genius or radical bricoleur. If we consider the ordinary spaces Blake literally occupied in London and Sussex—his residences in Broad Street, Lambeth, Felpham, and South Molton Street—we can observe a relationship between self and social space characterized by persistent bourgeois aspirations and a slow, uneven, but mostly upward mobility. By no means does such an emphasis cancel the radical antinomianism of Blake's fiery prophetic works; rather, it prompts us to ask how an inconspicuous daily life more or less conforming to mainstream values can coexist with and underwrite the most heretical attitudes.

On facing pages of Ackroyd's *Blake* are three consecutive pictures, all commonly reproduced: a 1950s photograph of No. 28 Broad Street, where Blake first lived with his family and where he moved next door in 1784; an engraving by Frederick Adcock of Blake's Lambeth residence, No. 13 Hercules Buildings, where he lived from 1790 to 1800; and Herbert H. Gilchrist's studied, melancholy sketch of Blake's cottage in Felpham. These images (figures 2.5–2.7) span the first forty-seven years of Blake's life, that is, until the reversal of fortune he experienced upon returning from Felpham. Juxtaposed in this way, they chart a general upward mobility, with each residence surpassing the previous one in size, expense, or privacy, and sometimes all three. Blake had already improved upon his family origins when

Figure 2.5 No. 28 Broad Street, Golden Square. Photo courtesy of the Victoria University Library (Toronto)

he and Catherine moved from Broad Street to nearby and more fashionable Poland Street in 1785, but it is the house in Lambeth that best indicates an elevated status or at least a desire to attain new signs of distinction. Scholars tend to emphasize two things about "Lambeth Marsh": it was a place of "tough factories and seedy pleasure," and it was "a place of ultra-radical activity throughout the period."[63] They also tend to anticipate prematurely the nineteenth-century urban slum it would start to become by the time Blake left it for Felpham. When Blake came to Lambeth, which was changing but still largely rural, the "comfortable middle-class homes" of Hercules Buildings, as Michael Phillips calls them, were relatively new (built around 1770).[64] Blake rented one of the most expensive of the development's

BLAKE
23 HERCULES ROAD
F·A

Figure 2.6 No. 23 Hercules Buildings (formerly No. 13), Frederick Adcock, illustrator.
A. St. John Adcock, *Famous Houses and Literary Shrines of London* (London: Dent and Sons, 1912)

Figure 2.7 Blake's Cottage at Felpham, illustration by Herbert H. Gilchrist, in *Life of William Blake, with selections from his poems and other writings,* by Alexander Gilchrist (London: Macmillan and Co., 1880). Courtesy of the Bancroft Library, University of California, Berkeley, PR4146 .G5 1880

twenty-six terraced houses. It consisted of nine or ten rooms and was set off from street and neighbors by fenced-in gardens, front and back.[65]

On Broad Street, in a commercial London neighborhood, Blake's family lived above his father's hosiery shop in a row house whose facade, contiguous with the street, differentiated minimally between domestic and mercantile spaces. Blake would resume this type of living arrangement on South Molton Street when he returned from Felpham in a precarious financial state and could afford no better. In 1790, however, he separated himself from the commercial center of London by moving across the river, where he occupied a home with a gated front garden that, small as it was, symbolically distanced the house from the street's public space. Behind was a much larger garden, and when Blake set up his painting room, he chose to face the garden rather than the street. At the end of the eighteenth century, Hercules Buildings was already appealing to the architectural values of privacy and detachment that would soon become the hallmarks of an anti-urban Victorian domestic ideology. As Sharon Marcus has documented, because the terraced row houses common in London contradicted the British ideal of "a free-standing structure designed for one family," modeled on the rural cottage, architects devised numerous ways to highlight the singularity and privacy of individual homes, almost all of which are evident in Adcock's rendering of No. 13 Hercules Buildings. They added gated and locked gardens; they demarcated each property with iron railings; they interrupted the row's continuous façade by framing individual entrances; they emphasized a verdant screen (ivy, for instance) between house and street. In their renderings, they employed chiaroscuro to create the illusion of a three-dimensional space housing an unseen interior life, and they tried to make each home stand separately, as if it were surrounded by open space rather than by the neighboring houses with which it in fact shared walls on either side.[66] In Adcock's nostalgic illustration, Blake's residence precipitates into existence through an abundance of graphic detail as the neighboring structures fade to white, empty space.[67]

At times, Blake sharply criticized bourgeois domesticity for its divisiveness and self-involvement: "we cover [Man]," an Eternal declaims in Night the Ninth of *The Four Zoas*, "& with walls / And hearths protect the Selfish terror till divided all / In families we see our shadows born" (133:19–21, E 401–402). But Blake also willingly participated in that domesticity, and like many other London renters, he internalized the desire that, according to Marcus, "linked all Englishmen" of the next generation: "the desire to own and occupy a self-contained house" (86). One of the most rhapsodic passages in *Milton*, indeed in all of Blake, culminates in the uninterrupted survey available to the visionary eye of a man "standing *on his own* roof" (29 [31]: 6, E 127, emphasis added). The lines reflect the poet's three-year tenure at the cottage in Felpham, the only residence he would ever occupy that was freestanding. Blake incorporated a charming sketch of this cottage into *Milton* (figure 2.8); it not only becomes the scene of Ololon's descent and the poem's climactic events but also provides an opportunity, on the same plate, to repeat the phrase "my garden" or "my cottage" six times, as well as to supply a caption: "Blakes Cottage at Felpham" (36 [40], E 136–137). Surely this proprietary pride factored into Blake's impulsive decision to force Scofield from *his* garden. Throughout his life, the single-occupant house would return as a figure of autonomy; it signified the self-possession of "The Mind in which every one is King & Priest *in his*

Figure 2.8 *Milton a Poem*, copy C, Erdman plate 36 [40], c. 1804–1811, detail. Rare Books Division, The New York Public Library, Astor, Lenox and Tilden Foundations

own House" (E 784, emphasis added). Morris Eaves has suggested we should stop hoping to resolve "the baffling union of individualism and communalism at the heart of [Blake's] thinking"; it is an irreducible paradox that cannot be explained away, not even by recourse to Blake's fascination with antinomian traditions of radical collectivity.[68] And this paradox is not solely a question of the consistency of Blake's thought; it is also a matter of acknowledging the bourgeois aspirations and conventional practices that, from the start, and especially in Lambeth, quietly accompanied Blake's trenchant social critique. If there is any truth to the story that Blake shocked the visitor who found him and Catherine naked in their garden behind No. 13 Hercules Buildings, reading aloud Book IV of *Paradise Lost,* then we ought to remember that he engaged in such unconventional behavior only because he could afford the privacy that sheltered it.[69] Blake's acts of prophetic audacity at home differ from, even as they mimic, Isaiah walking "naked and barefoot three years" (*Marriage* 13, E 39) or Abiezer Coppe preaching naked in the street. Lambeth may not have provided the home he imagined for himself when, as an apprentice, he signed his copy of Winckelmann's *Reflections on the Painting and the Sculpture of the Greeks,* "William Blake, Lincolns Inn," or when he signed "Gentleman" on his marriage bond. But here he would briefly employ a servant, here he would own property worth stealing, and here, in the relative security of a quasi-suburban seclusion, he would invent a new form of public engagement in the furious political prophecies he finished while facing his garden.

The modest upward mobility of a move to Lambeth should not lead us to exaggerate Blake's actual success as a professional engraver; his disappointments are well documented. But neither should we exaggerate his failings and read the relative poverty of later times (he was never destitute) back into those years that carried him well into middle age. It seems unlikely, for instance, that Blake's removal from Lambeth to Felpham was a financial necessity brought on by commercial failure, as Ackroyd implies: "better to work in the country than starve in the city" (215). In a letter to Hayley, John Flaxman wrote of Blake's prospects in Felpham, "I see no reason why he should not make *as good a livelihood* there as in London, if he engraves & teaches drawing."[70] The fact that Blake continued to pay the same rent in Felpham that he paid in Lambeth (£20) suggests that his earnings, though not on the rise, were not falling either.[71] Blake felt the sting of watching inferior artists pass him by, and it is possible that Felpham allowed him, at least early on, to maintain a fantasy of renewed gentrification. Developments such as the Hercules Buildings attempted to assimilate elements of a rural cottage ideal into urban living, and as Lambeth began to urbanize and deteriorate, a buffering garden may have lost some of its power to connote privacy and solitude. Felpham was the real thing, with rising property values to show it. "Why here are several cottages," exclaimed Blake's landlord, Mr. Grinder, "that might have been let heretofore for four or five pounds a year that [are] being now furbished up and whitewashed, with a little furniture and staircase carpets put into them."[72] It is at this time that Jane Austen's crass Robert Ferrars could "advise every body who is going to build, to build a cottage,"[73] thus already expressing the genteel sentimentalization of rural dwelling we see fully blown in Gilchrist's romantic sketch of the Felpham cottage (see figure 2.7). The trend might have enhanced the cottage's value in the eyes of a middle-aged but still aspiring craftsman. Blake's effusion upon his arrival at Felpham shows him matching in imagination what the landlord had already achieved with whitewash and staircase carpets: "furbishing up." As he wrote to his far more successful friend, Flaxman (the same fellow engraver who felt free to remark on Blake's earning potential to Hayley):

> We are safe arrived at our Cottage which is more beautiful than I thought it. & more convenient. It is a perfect Model for Cottages & I think for Palaces of Magnificence only Enlarging not altering its proportions & adding ornaments & not principals. Nothing can be more Grand than its Simplicity & Usefulness. Simple without Intricacy it seems to be the Spontaneous Effusion of Humanity congenial to the wants of Man. No other formed House can ever please me so well nor shall I ever be perswaded I believe that it can be improved either in Beauty or Use. (E 710)

When a freestanding, single-family house seems not to have been designed, constructed, and rented but to have sprung spontaneously from human nature, we glimpse the roots of a domestic ideology that will flourish fully later in the century.

This cottage "congenial to the wants of Man" reflects the ideology of a particular man universalizing his own middle-class needs. And when Blake explains the perfect features of this model—neither too large nor too small, balancing beauty and utility—we understand him to be describing the space he wishes to occupy in the world, above his dependent, artisan station, but beneath the aristocratic excesses he scorns—though curiously, only in terms of scale, not proportions or principals.[74]

If Felpham is the extension of a bourgeois model already evident in Lambeth, then we can join Eaves in locating Blake's social status in the middle, rather than on the radical side of a clear, uncompromised divide, despite Makdisi's forceful case for positioning him there.[75] By emphasizing Blake's preference for mental over physical labor and his disdain for ignorant journeymen who labor thoughtlessly, Eaves has argued, not without controversy, that the *Public Address* is "an exercise in middle-class self-construction." It strives "to make economic room for autonomous middle-class artist-heroes who see the possibility of combining in themselves the aesthetic judgment of an elite and the technical skills of a working class" (169–170). In the next generation, artisans like Francis Place and engravers like John Pye would embrace such middle-class self-construction in order to distance themselves from an earlier, now disreputable association between artisans and Jacobins. Privileging their enterprising "commercial spirit" and downplaying the political threat embodied in their class, they emphasized the developing virtues of respectability: discipline, education, self-improvement, and upward mobility.[76] About the same time, Frederick Tatham was eulogizing the recently deceased Blake in identical terms, celebrating in particular "the never failing industry of the active man . . . whose energy is gain."[77] For Tatham, "energy" involved neither Orc's revolutionary activity nor Los's prophetic vision; it meant productivity, profitability, and the cultural capital that came with both.

Of course, Blake critiqued every one of the respectable virtues Tatham claimed to observe in him, and it is customary to judge Tatham as one of Blake's least reliable biographers, retroactively installing moral standards of the 1820s and 1830s.[78] But the Blake Tatham knew, quite apart from the Blake whose radicalism was as "conspiratorially secretive" as it was extreme,[79] also anticipated some of the changes in social code that would eventually produce figures such as Place and Pye. As early as 1790, residing at No. 13 Hercules Buildings, Blake was invested in maintaining the respectable virtues he would vigorously interrogate in writings either unknown to Tatham or cryptic beyond his biographer's understanding. Even at his poorest, when he and Catherine shared two rooms above a shop on South Molton Street, Blake still earned more than a typical journeyman engraver (according to Ackroyd, 265); that his income slipped dangerously close to plebeian status may account for the vehemence with which he wished to differentiate between his artistry and their mechanical craftsmanship. Some forty years earlier, when Blake was apprenticed to James Basire, the middle station he would later defend and idealize was already inscribed in the cost of his apprenticeship. At the same ceremony where James Blake indentured his son for £52, two boys were bound at twice the price (£100 each, one to a haberdasher, the other to a stationer) and nine others bound to a print seller, a stationer, three printers, a mathematical instrument maker, and an ironmonger at no fee at all.[80] Perhaps it should not surprise us, then, that we later find Blake at home in the houses of Lambeth or Felpham, and not in the Jacobin clubs—certainly not with other activist artisans on the street. The most radical artisans, as McCalman has shown, were those who had the least investment in respectability because they had the least to lose: shoemakers, tailors, and weavers. They "belonged to trades that were not greatly esteemed within the artisan world because of their paucity of skill, cleverness, strength or capital, their lax apprenticeship requirements and their vulnerability to competition from unskilled or sweated workers."[81] Our notion of the skilled, proud, humanist worker who was also *militant* has led Jacques Rancière to write of "the myth of the artisan."[82] In a sense, Blake did combine aspects of the skilled and the radical artisan, but he achieved this union through a division of spheres, sheltering his radicalism under the cover of privacy. He protected himself by circulating impenetrable social critiques in fairly expensive editions of small number—and he did so in part because he had something to lose.[83]

Jon Mee has put forth another version of Blake suspended in the middle, caught between the upward aspirations he associated with the middle-class intellectuals of the Johnson circle and his vulgar enthusiasm, which would have made "the newly politicized lower classes" his proper audience, if only he had sought them.[84] Mee's argument is reminiscent of Crabb Robinson's comment in 1811 that Blake's enthusiasm "has more than anything else injured his reputation" and Benjamin Heath Malkin's earlier contention that Blake was "stigmatised" and thus "kept from public notice" by the class of rationalist gentlemen above him.[85] The earlier accounts emphasize the religious eccentricities that ostracized Blake. Mee adds that the same middle-class intellectuals who shared Blake's democratic politics excluded him from participating in their circle because his radicalism was inseparable from popular forms of religion they found offensive. The class bias of Blake's social superiors prevented his participation in the new public sphere they were in the process of creating.

Persuasive as it generally is, Mee's argument tends to underestimate what Erdman long ago called Blake's "self-censorship" (383). Blake was not only a victim of class stigma, unstable markets and audiences, and his own "over-confidence in the power of the truth to find its way" (Mee, *Dangerous Enthusiasm*, 224); his absence from the public sphere also resulted from his unvarying practice of nonparticipation. Mee chastises critics who are "ever eager to read political quietism in Blake's texts as early in the 1790s as possible" (209), in part because he wants to keep Blake's radicalism alive as late into the 1790s as possible. But Blake's was always a muted radicalism. When *should* we date the advent of Blake's self-censorship? From 1804 and the trauma of his sedition trial? From 1798, when he decided not to publish his response to Bishop Watson's attack on Paine? From 1795, when the incarceration of millenarian prophet Richard Brothers coincided with Blake ceasing to produce new illuminated books? From 1793, when topical reference first gave way to an increasingly private mythology in his work? From 1790, when *The French Revolution* was not published, for reasons that might never be clear? Or from the very beginning, when Blake's characteristic impulse to withdraw led him to avoid joining "any particular group or society" (Ackroyd 73)? If the first indication of Blake's self-censorship was his "nervous fear" of participation, then the radicalism Mee wishes to preserve—though no doubt real—was only ever half there.

Explaining why late eighteenth-century antinomianism was perceived as a significant threat despite the small number of nonconformists actually practicing such beliefs, Makdisi has shown that antinomianism challenged the very notion of obedience right at the moment when modernizing, industrializing systems increasingly emphasized the need for submissive virtues. "For any disciplinary system," he writes, "whether political, religious, or economic, virtue is primarily understood in terms of obedience" (119). In these circumstances, he goes on to argue, antinomianism moved beyond religion to assume powerful political implications, for it involved "a disregard for any kind of moral or disciplinary authority" and was in fact "incompatible with any form of authoritarianism." For that reason, "antinomianism was repeatedly denounced as a threat to the law, and even to duty of any kind" (120). Like Mee's, Makdisi's arguments are convincing, as is his identification of Blake (who never stopped denouncing Moral Virtue) among the antinomians. They falter only by assuming a strict boundary between law-abiding virtue and radical antinomianism. Blake was every bit as passionate and oppositional as Makdisi describes, but his habitual practices were sufficiently ambiguous to allow for Ackroyd's apolitical emphasis or Eaves's middle-class construction as well. We need a better way to describe the puzzling double life of an image like "Albion rose," which has underwritten an array of interpretations as plausible as they are mutually exclusive. How is it that a single image can identify with revolution, critique revolution, and serve as a personal expression having nothing to do with revolution? Perhaps Makdisi points us in the right direction when he comments, "Blake can hardly be seen as merely a casual observer of the so-called Revolution controversy" (53). Although this statement suggests that Blake took sides (which he did), it also implies that Blake involved himself actively in the politics of his day (which he did and did not). By no means a *casual* observer of events, Blake was an observer nonetheless—an enthusiastic, *critical* observer. If this stance involved a compact between his work's intensity of engagement and his life of "little external incident,"[86] then this tension also found its way into the very texture of his work, as a simultaneous demand for urgency, energy, and *patience*. For Blake, the activity that promised to hold together such contrary elements was critical reading, and that tense union is perhaps nowhere better seen than in his response to Milton's *Samson Agonistes*.

Neither to Act nor to Desist: Blake, Milton, and the Virtue of Criticism

[G]ive us wisedome to know when to goe forward and when to stand
still . . . [so] that by making hast we may not strengthen the hand of
the enemy, nor by standing still neglect the opportunity he puts into
our hands, but that, being on our Watch Tower, and living by faith,
we may see our duty so plainly, that when the Lord's tyme is come we
may up and be doing.

     —Edmund Ludlow, "A Voyce from the Watch Tower" (1660)

he stood, as one who pray'd,
Or some great matter in his mind revolv'd.

     —John Milton, *Samson Agonistes*

But when I was on the *other side*, I received no instructions. Guide
pressed me, and when I was about to enter a trance I would pray to be
given an order to give [the church], so they could take action. I wanted
this so much, and I prayed as I went into a trance, and it was all quite
painful and trying. In the end when I returned, completely spent,
the message that Guide heard from me and reworked into ordinary
language told them *neither to take action nor to desist*.

     —Patron, in Kenzaburo Oe's *Somersault*
     (1999, trans. 2003, second emphasis added)

"Vigorous most / When most unactive deem'd"

When Samuel Johnson complained that *Samson Agonistes* lacks a narrative middle ("nothing passes between the first act and the last, that either hastens or delays the death of Sampson" [sic]),[87] he raised a question that has always troubled readers of Milton's drama: what is the source of Samson's restoration from abject passivity (grinding "at the Mill with slaves" [l. 41]) to a one-man military power capable of unleashing colossal force upon his enemies? What causes Samson's "fierie vertue" to rouse "From under ashes into sudden flame" (ll. 1690–1691)? Disinclined to acknowledge the possibility of direct divine influence, Johnson saw a play structured by weakness at one end and tragic power at the other, but with no clear explanation of the passage from one state to the other. When we first see Samson, he belongs among the living dead—a blind, "moving Grave" (l. 102) unable to take even a few feeble steps without the support of a "guiding hand" (l. 1). He is an emblem of emasculated lethargy: "see how he lies at random, carelessly diffus'd, / With languish't head unprop" (ll. 118–119), "to visitants a gaze / Or pitied object" (ll. 567–568). These images of extreme passivity and objectification play off of the reader's foreknowledge of the climactic events soon to come at the Philistine theater, when Samson's masculine vigor will revive with devastating consequences. The ledger between passivity and activity could not be drawn more starkly: on one side, the weak and sleeping self, lost "in the lascivious lap" of Dalila and shorn "Like a tame Weather" (ll. 536–538)—the very image of Blake's "Samson Subdued" (see figure 2.4); on the other, the strong self waking to decisive action, like the Samson figure of *Areopagitica*, "rousing . . . like a strong man after sleep, and shaking [his] invincible locks"—the very image of Blake's "Samson Breaking his Bonds" (see figure 2.3). This set of oppositions—between weakness and action, sleep and arousal, night and day, feminine and masculine—lies deep within the story Milton inherited from the Book of Judges, where Samson's fate is intimately associated with the diurnal rising and setting of the sun.[88]

If Milton exploited such clear-cut oppositions to heighten the drama of Samson's mysterious reversal—in the process provoking readers like Johnson—he also systematically upended them. Even as it invites us to recognize an archetypal schema, *Samson Agonistes* involves no clear ledger of passivity and activity. As Stanley Fish points out, the drama pivots on the moment when Samson recovers agency by paradoxically choosing to evacuate his will. When he allows himself to be led to the Philistine theater for no reason his limited understanding (or ours) can discern, Samson relinquishes any designs of his own upon the events unfolding. He arrives upon the scene of action only by abandoning himself to passivity. Writes Fish:

[W]hen Samson declares, "I with this Messenger will go along" (1384) . . . he offers himself up to a future that will mark him in ways that he cannot know in advance; he moves forward into a story that, as far as he can tell, has yet to be written; he leaves the fortress (or is it the illusion?) of a centered, settled self and embarks on a journey (going out not knowing whither he went) in the course of which the self will be endlessly revised by forces it cannot control. In short, he ceases to *be* a self—in the masculine sense of an entity already saturated with meaning—and becomes instead a text, a pliable feminized medium.[89]

After the event, an exultant semichorus likens Samson to a phoenix rising from the ashes (a sacrificial, feminine image Johnson thought oddly out of place among the more aggressive figures that precede it).[90] It further describes Samson in terms of a chiasmus that challenges the very distinction between vigor and inactivity: in the end, Samson proved himself to be "vigorous most / When most unactive deem'd" (ll. 1704–1705). The phrase echoes one of Milton's favorite scriptural verses, 2 Corinthians 12:9, "my strength is made perfect in my weakness," which resonated for him politically as well as personally. We will return to Milton's suggestion that the spirit of revolution survives even in the ashes of political defeat, and we must also take up his implication that Samson's violence, brutal as it may be, is nevertheless a passive violence—"passive" because he seems to believe that his agency expresses God's will, not his own. For the moment, however, the point is that Milton's Samson complicates the relationship between strength and weakness in ways that correspond with Blake's own thinking on the subject when he chose to invoke *Samson Agonistes* in the inscription he added to the final version of "Albion rose."

Shortly before 1804, as he prepared to leave Felpham, Blake wrote to Thomas Butts that "none can know the Spiritual Acts of my three years Slumber on the banks of the Ocean unless he has seen them in the Spirit or unless he should read My long Poem descriptive of those Acts" (E 728). This long poem is probably the *Four Zoas*, but several years later, while preparing the *Public Address*, Blake would echo and alter the same language to describe *Milton* as "a Poem concern[in]g my Three years <Herculean> Labours at Felpham" (E 572). In both descriptions, the time frame remains the same ("three years"), as does the location ("on the banks of the Ocean" / "at Felpham"), but what took place then and there seems to involve mutually exclusive constructions. Was it "three years *Slumber*" or "Three years <*Herculean*> *Labours*"? The remarkable substitution of one phrase for the other confounds not only a conventional logic of opposition (sleep/work, passivity/activity, weakness/strength) but also any sequence in which the seemingly positive term would follow the seemingly negative one in a narrative of transformation, "like a strong man *after* sleep." Slumber and labor converge upon what Blake calls "spiritual Acts"—actions inconsequential to the empirical eye (like dreams, say) but actions that nonetheless perform a labor heroic enough to warrant Blake's addition, "<Herculean>." Is it possible to perform the work of a national liberator, of a *"Herculean Samson"* (to borrow the language of *Paradise Lost*), *while* remaining dormant in the semiretirement of an inconspicuous Sussex village?[91] Is it possible to be a strong man *while* sleeping? In the work of this period, Blake would test this paradox in a number of ways: he cast his first attempt at national, epic statement in a series of "nights"; he claimed that his epic prophecies were written in a passive state of unpremeditated trance—dictated to him by spiritual agents without the participation of his voluntary will; he explored, in *Milton*, the figure of a hero simultaneously at rest and in action, who from one angle appears to be "sleeping on a couch / Of gold" (15 [17]: 12–13, E 109), while from another he engages in the hand-to-hand struggle with Urizen upon which the hopes for general liberation depend. One of Blake's sources for the conundrum of strength in apparent weakness was *Samson Agonistes*, and in its engagement of Milton's play, "Albion rose" belongs with Blake's other explorations of active passivity at the time.

As readers have long understood, *Samson Agonistes* involves a series of intractable ambiguities. Does Samson act on his own initiative or under divine influence? Does he think or pray when standing between the pillars? Does Milton endorse his tragic hero's aggression or recoil from it?[92] "[W]e are unsure," writes Victoria Kahn, "as Milton certainly intended us to be, whether Samson's political act is an expression of divine authority or of merely human violence." Dramatizing "the equivocal nature of human attempts to act justly in the absence of authoritative knowledge," the poem's epistemological anxieties also extend to the reader's act of interpretation.[93] Samson's earliest lament of his blindness harbors a readerly desire to transcend the disability of embodiment altogether. If only the body were all eyes, he complains, and vision—no longer localized in such tiny, fragile organs—were "through all parts diffus'd / That she might look at will through every pore" (ll. 96–97). Whether the enthusiast's desire for total transparency, for a body fully illuminated, is realized by the "inward" illumination attributed to Samson at the play's climax remains unanswerable, not least because that fantasy lies beyond the achievement of any reader who must grapple with the opacities of a textual medium that does not (cannot) fully reveal the meaning of the actions it represents. And although this dilemma could describe the reading of any narrative text, the stakes are heightened here both by the extreme violence of Samson's actions and by their historical reference, for Milton clearly places Samson in an allegorical relation to the recently defeated English Revolution. It can hardly be coincidental that in the corrected text (incorporating lines from the 1671 *Omissa*) the stanza describing Samson's self-destructive heroics ("He tugg'd, he shook, till down [the pillars] came" [l. 1650]) begins at line 1640, the year of the "Long Parliament," and ends at 1659, the year before Charles II resumed the throne. Milton knits recent historical memory into the poem's formal dimensions: to assess the events reported in those twenty lines is to assess the events of those twenty years.

Because that historical judgment entails the irreducible ambiguities Fish, Kahn, and others have described so effectively, *Samson Agonistes* always leaves open the possibility that the revolution, including its regicidal violence, may indeed have been divinely justified, though evidence for such a case will necessarily remain inconclusive. Consider, for example, the moment of Samson's transformation, when his despair gives way to prophetic intuition, as manifested in his sudden compliance with the Philistine command to perform at the festival honoring their god Dagon:

> Be of good courage, I begin to feel
> Some rouzing motions in me which dispose
> To something extraordinary my thoughts.
> I with this Messenger will go along,
> Nothing to do, be sure, that may dishonour
> Our Law, or stain my vow of *Nazarite*.
> If there be aught of presage in the mind,
> This day will be remarkable in my life
> By some great act, or of my days the last.   (ll. 1381–1389)

The vagueness of Samson's language ("some rouzing motions," "something extraordinary," "some great act") signifies the antinomian potential of the moment and thus the potential authenticity of Samson's revolutionary enthusiasm. Whether he misinterprets his inner persuasion or not, Samson speaks as if he were suddenly an agent emptied of clear intention, acting without specific aim because he responds to an influence unconfined by his own volition, beyond his capacity to conceive or articulate. His passivity—really a receptivity—becomes an aperture, opening history to the influence of an apocalyptic agency that the exercise of his own natural will would preclude. The contrast is evident moments earlier, when Samson *volunteers* his strength, threatening the Philistine strong man, Harapha. Blind though he may be, he pictures the blows he might inflict in exquisite detail (ll. 1123 ff.), suggesting that, even at this late point in the drama, he still conceives of the future only in the limited forms he knows from past experience. History has become a programmatic succession of blind, arbitrary force (with Israelite and Philistine warriors cyclically exchanging positions of dominance), and its chain can be broken only when Samson releases the future from his own premeditation and instead becomes the recipient of inward illumination. By incorporating this possibility into the drama, Milton maintains the notion that human beings may indeed be the revolutionary agents of divine justice, but paradoxically only if they empty their actions of specific intentions, goals, and desires, "Happ'n what may" (l. 1423).

For readers eager to dissociate Samson from the contemporary suicide bombers to whom he is now so often compared, the vagueness of his intentions and the improvisation of his actions are a decisive rejoinder, for they bear little resemblance to the meticulous planning, preparation, and execution of, say, Muhammad Atta and his 9/11 accomplices.[94] The point is valid but hardly comforting. Samson's willingness to accompany the Philistine messenger may involve him in a future "he cannot know in advance" and may precipitate "a story that, as far as he can tell, has yet to be written," as Fish puts it. But the story's outcome, as every reader of *Samson Agonistes* does know in advance, is irreversible and no less disturbing: three thousand dead. Scholars looking for evidence of Milton's militant antinomianism often turn to a passage from *A Treatise of Civil Power,* where Milton expresses a commitment (Fish calls it his "general rule") firm enough and broad enough to countenance the transgression of legal protections against violence: "I here mean by conscience or religion, that full perswasion whereby we are assur'd that our beleef and practise, as far as we are able to apprehend and probably make appeer, is according to the will of God & his Holy Spirit within us, which we ought to follow much rather than any law of man." Milton was not naïve about the potential danger of this creed.[95] That Samson describes the enthusiasm leading him to the pillars ("some rouzing motions") in language similar to that he previously used for his marriage to the woman of Timnah ("they knew not / That what I motion'd was of God; I knew / From intimate impulse" [ll. 221–223]) signals the difficulty of disentangling base and divine influences when both are routed through the "intimate impulse" of embodied feelings. The impossibility of discerning Samson's motives—which may be divinely inspired, or mistaken for divine inspiration, or simply blind and vindictive—is also the impossibility of arriving at a final judgment regarding the revolutionary violence he enacts. In *Samson Agonistes,* such violence remains attractive even as it is suspicious and fundamentally appalling.

Milton's equivocal representation of violence entered deeply into Blake's work in the revolutionary 1790s in ways not always under his artistic control and extending well beyond his eventual citation of *Samson Agonistes* in "Albion rose." In 1804, as we will see, "Albion rose" borrows on Samson's revolutionary strength while also suspending it, transferring its heroic labor to the urgent but hesitant agency involved in critical engagement. As Blake conceives it, critical reading becomes a type of action irreducible to an opposition between vigor and passivity. But to understand Blake's final revisions of his print, and the kind of reading for which it calls, we must first consider several of his other responses to Samson at the pillars, for Milton's scene of violence haunted Blake, even though it recurs only indirectly and obscurely in his discourse and images.

"Cracked Across": Samson Agonistes and the Noise of History

Given Blake's enduring passion for Milton, which led him to illustrate every other major poem of Milton's except "Lycidas," it is remarkable that he never illustrated *Samson Agonistes*.[96] This omission becomes even more puzzling when we consider that Blake executed several paintings on the Samson cycle from the Book of Judges (see figures 2.3 and 2.4), including a *Samson Pulling Down the Temple*, mentioned by William Rossetti and now regrettably lost.[97] On the rare occasions when Blake links a visual image to *Samson Agonistes*, he does so obliquely. As we have seen, the relationship between image and source text in the inscription of "Albion rose" is sufficiently opaque to have generated strikingly different interpretations. The figure that lies closest to Milton's Samson at the pillars is not "Albion rose" but the last of the 537 watercolors Blake prepared for an illustrated version of Edward Young's *Night Thoughts* (figure 2.9), where his representation of an open-eyed Samson directly contradicts the biblical narrative and instead echoes Milton's description of a Samson "with inward eyes illuminated" (l. 1689). But despite this secondary allusion to *Samson Agonistes*, the picture primarily refers to the final, apocalyptic lines of *Young*'s poem: "like Him of *Gaza* in his Wrath, / Plucking the Pillars that support the World."[98] *Samson Agonistes* sneaks in under cover, leaving us still to wonder why Blake never illustrated it directly.

This absence of direct visual representation by no means indicates the relative unimportance of Milton's tragedy to Blake—I believe it indicates the opposite. Blake returned to Samson at the pillars almost obsessively, and if he never represents that scene directly it is because he *cannot*. That is, he cannot form that moment into a unified image or series that would achieve a comprehensive interpretation of the dramatic poem, in the same way that his other illustrations of Milton's poetry brashly attempt to do. Despite Manoa's concluding promise to build his son a monument, *Samson Agonistes* leaves its reader with a heap of ruins, a tangled wreckage of bodies and building, and the poem likewise enters into Blake's work *in collapse*, as a multitude of fragments we can view only serially and collectively, in pieces, but never unified into a single whole. Blake felt this dis-integration powerfully. In a way never fully in his command, fragments of *Samson Agonistes* enter into Blake's vocabulary as so many verbal bits and pieces, broken words and phrases like shards scattered from an explosive event that cannot be reconstructed and was without knowable structure or meaning in the first

Figure 2.9 Night IX, page 119, illustration to Young's *Night Thoughts*. Samson bringing down the temple, c. 1795–1797. Pen and grey ink, with grey wash and watercolor. © Trustees of the British Museum

place. What Blake returns to most obsessively in *Samson Agonistes* is its sound, the sound of fracture, its noise. This fracture passes through his work like an irregular sound path, an inconsistent crack in the textual grain that corresponds to the inconsistent movement of violence through history and to Blake's unresolved ambivalence toward that violence. Referring to "the noise of history" in this way, I wish to recall Kevis Goodman's discussion of the ways history comes to be felt as disturbance in eighteenth-century Georgic poetry, a model I touched on briefly in the introduction to this book. Adapting Raymond Williams's concept of "structures of feeling," and especially his late elaborations in his *New Left Review* interviews, Goodman describes how "cognitive 'noise'" and "affective . . . dissonance" enter into the period's poetry as the "records of an otherwise unknowable history," occurring whenever cognitive and discursive "categories cannot accommodate the flux or the excess of events."[99] One source for the noise of history in Blake's work is *Samson Agonistes*; it is a poem he continuously hears but can neither visualize nor interpret fully.

In the following sections, I consider three windows onto Blake's engagement with *Samson Agonistes*, each belonging to a fractured series that ultimately includes "Albion rose." We begin by tracking the dispersal of Milton's climactic scene at the pillars into powerful phrase-fragments that continue to sound through Blake's poetry of the 1790s. We end by returning to Blake's visualization of Samson in the *Night Thoughts* illustration, an image he cannot let stand alone and instead routes through a network of self-qualifying signs, as if he were perpetually testing this figure by resetting it in alternate picture spaces. My larger aim, however, is to reconsider Blake's debt to Milton by focusing on the problem of revolutionary violence, itself a problem that each poet found inseparable from the question of religiously motivated violence. For Blake and Milton both, such violence becomes the occasion for developing the alternative virtues of criticism, but as we will also see, this strategy cannot be reduced to a simple expression of quietism, aestheticism, or even modern liberalism, for it stubbornly preserves the transformational potential of divine violence even as it puts up every possible hedge against the error of believing one might act as the historical agent of such violence. The noise first transmitted by Milton's drama and then picked up by Blake supplies no authority for violence, but it also resolutely refuses to rule against it.

"O WHAT NOISE"

Of the various words and phrases from *Samson Agonistes* that move brokenly through Blake's discourse, the most commonly recognized is the one describing Samson's initial subjection to tyranny: "Eyeless in *Gaza* at the Mill with slaves" (l. 41). Blake first quotes the second half of this line in 1793 in a crucial plate of

America: A Prophecy (Copy H, 8:6), long before he again incorporates it into the 1804 inscription of "Albion rose." The sound of *Samson Agonistes,* however, extends further and penetrates more deeply. Referring either to the sky or the upper limit of a solid enclosure, Blake uses a variant of the phrase "cracked across" in four of his books, with two instances appearing widely apart in *The Four Zoas.* By itself, the phrase is hardly surprising in an apocalyptic poet. "The crack of doom" had long since become a convention of last judgment discourse; Blake could have taken his resounding "crack" from any number of sources—Lear on the heath, for instance: "Blow, winds, and crack your cheeks! . . . And thou, all-shaking thunder, / Strike flat the thick rotundity o' th' world! / Crack nature's moulds."[100] He could have, but he didn't. This particular noise came from Milton, though the source has remained somewhat obscured by the fact that the first instance of this cracking pattern, the one that ties it most closely to *Samson Agonistes,* occurs in a canceled plate that Blake excluded from his final printing of *America* (figure 2.10).

No one knows with certainty why Blake canceled what we now call "plate b" of *America.* The most common explanation—that with new laws against seditious publication passed in 1793, he feared to print a text openly referring to Albion's Angel as "George the third" (l. 9)—does not explain why he would consider his final version so much less risky, referring openly as *it* does to "the King of England" (6:12).[101] Perhaps Blake was more worried about the canceled plate's echo of Milton. If not, he should have been, for the plate's last lines imagine the collapse of Parliament in language that amounts to a free variation on Samson pulling down the Philistine theater. Blake's structure-to-be-destroyed is a "house" (l. 12) and a "hall of counsel" (l. 2) where "Lords & Commons meet" (l. 9); Milton's a "Theatre" (l. 1605) holding "Lords" and "Councellors" (l. 1653) among others. Each likens the moment of wreckage to a seismic event: in Milton, "Mountains tremble" (l. 1648); in Blake, "the valley mov'd beneath" (l. 23). But perhaps the best way to demonstrate the tightly woven correspondence is simply to set the two core passages beside one another, noting the images that pass from one to the other in bold:

Samson Agonistes:

He tugg'd, he shook, till **down they came** and drew

[they: "those **two massie Pillars**"   (l. 1648)]

The **whole roof** after them, with **burst of thunder**

Upon the heads of **all who sate beneath,**

Lords, Ladies, Captains, Councellors, or Priests . . .   (ll. 1650–1653)

America, cancelled plate b:

So still the terrors rent . . .

. . . so the dark house was rent

Figure 2.10 (left) America: A Prophecy, cancelled plate b. *(right) America: A Prophecy,* copy E, plate 6. Lessing J. Rosenwald Collection, Library of Congress. Copyright © 2011 the William Blake Archive. Used with permission.

> The valley mov'd beneath; its **shining pillars** split in twain,
>
> And its **roofs crack across down falling** on th'Angelic seats.   (ll. 20–24)

In the printed version substituted for this text, Blake depicts the rise of revolutionary agency rather than its destructive effects: "in the red clouds rose a Wonder o'er the Atlantic sea" (Copy H, 6:7). A few plates later, this at first unnamed figure will be identified as Orc, the "terror" who aims to stamp the "stony law . . . to dust" (8:1–5), thus assimilating the pillar-splitting terrors of the original canceled plate.

At the same time, the Samson allusion suppressed in *America* will resurface in *Europe,* the book's sequel, where it now carries forward the story of Albion's oppressive plague cloud rebounding upon England in the form of revolutionary violence:

> In council gather the smitten Angels of Albion
> The cloud bears hard upon the council house; down rushing
> On the heads of Albions Angels. (9:12–14, E 63)

In this highly compressed rendition of the scene, one begins to see how *Samson Agonistes* continues to reverberate in Blake's ear. For at the very moment that the source has become almost unrecognizable, including the elimination of its noisy "burst of thunder," Blake draws into his verse a new Miltonic phrase fragment absent from his first, more extensive treatment: now the council house falls "*On the heads* of Albions Angels," just as Milton's roof had fallen "*Upon the heads* of all who sate beneath."

It is the missing "burst of thunder," however, that concerns us here, the phrase Blake translates into "crack across" and then disperses across several of his texts. If *Samson Agonistes* first enters into Blake's work as recurring sound fragments, why would Blake, who at times echoes Milton quite closely, so substantially alter *this* phrase, the signifier of noise, replacing it with a word ("crack") Milton himself never used in verse? Here we need to consider Milton's own handling of sound, for in the climactic account of Samson's violence, the words "burst of thunder" are both crucial and expendable: crucial in that they refer to the primary sound event; expendable in that they have already displaced the noise to which they refer, the noise that Blake's "cracked across" would set sharply resonating again. "Burst of thunder" is spoken by the witness-messenger in *Samson Agonistes* who reconstructs events for those who were not present at the scene; it compresses into a three-word phrase, a cliché really, a disruptive violence that the play's characters first experience as a prolonged, unaccountable noise. "O what noise!" (l. 1508) Manoa exclaims, when it first breaks in upon the poem; eight lines later, he is still saying, "Oh it continues" (l. 1516). Across these lines the speakers repeat the word "noise" five times, but we are made to understand that even this minimal signifier misrepresents the apocalyptic sound-event: "Noise *call you it* or universal groan / As if the whole inhabitation perish'd" (ll. 1512–13, emphasis added).[102] Milton contrasts this noise with the derisive shouts that forty lines earlier greeted Samson upon entering the Philistine theater, shouts loud enough to "[tear] the Skie" and thus anticipate the event to come, but also easily explained by anyone hearing them from a distance: "Doubtless the people shouting to behold / Thir once great dread, captive & blind before them" (ll. 1472–1474). The second wave of sound is categorically different, unrecognizable, doubt*ful*: "Horribly loud," says Manoa, "unlike the former shout" (l. 1510). This noise has "Ruin" in it "at the utmost point" (l. 1514), and the first thing it ruins is the structure of discourse. Tearing more than sky, it bursts in upon Manoa midsentence, exploding every formal continuity that the conversation then taking place is supposed to represent: continuities of syntax, community, and history. Manoa is affirming the good will of his fellow tribesmen, who have encouraged his expectations of ransoming his son, as if history were a medium reasonably conformable to prediction and effort: "I know your friendly minds and—O what noise!" (l. 1508). The Philistine Lords Manoa had solicited—including the few "generous . . . and civil" ones "who confess'd / They had anough reveng'd" (ll. 1467–1468), figures who stand for the possibility of détente—are by now also among the dead. The noise that breaks in precisely at this moment has nothing to do with ransom. Outside of communicability and therefore outside of the promise and the compromises of civil communities, this noise retains an impenetrable moral blankness; it is an impersonal, rigorously neutral force inaccessible to a common language of law and negotiation. It would be impossible to determine whether this noise lies beneath or beyond the threshold of civil discourse. Is it the expression of a blind, savage violence or of a sublime agency whose revolutionary work begins by exceeding the limits of representation?

"Neutral," I admit, is a provocative word to describe a noise with "Blood, death, and deathful deeds" (l. 1513) in it, but if we are to maintain a commitment to *Samson Agonistes'* ambiguities, I think we must insist on it. After 9/11, when John Carey contrasted the Israelites' jubilation over Samson's "triumph" with the messenger's first, horrified response to the violence he witnessed firsthand, he suggested that by juxtaposing these responses Milton was demonstrating "the enormous gulf between theory and practice, belief and action, words and reality." He further concluded that "the lesson Milton's drama teaches is that if you suppose you have private access to God's mind, and act on the supposition, it can have hideous consequences."[103] Yet Carey neglected the fact that his own moral argument, admirable and well reasoned as it may be, is every bit as much an after-the-fact interpretive construction as the monument Manoa proposes to build in honor of his son's military prowess or the choral sonnet that concludes *Samson Agonistes* with such composure and restraint. No formal construction (starting with the messenger's own ever more articulate account) answers satisfactorily to the meaning-resistant noise that cracks across Milton's text. Carey's premise suggests that the ambiguity enshrouding Samson's act is sufficient to turn a moral reader against him, but if Samson's act is truly ambiguous, then it must also allow for the possibility that the reader will identify with him, and not simply in a way we learn to discard as error. Against the possibility of an instrumental ambiguity in service of a clear didactic message, the noise of *Samson Agonistes* preserves an austere indeterminacy. Like all readers of *Samson Agonistes,* Blake also struggled with Milton's "lesson," but it is the play's noise that strikes him first and foremost, and it is this noise (rather than some lesson) that he in turn conveys.

Appended to this book are all the variants on "cracked across" that appear in Blake's poetry. As Leslie Tannenbaum was the first to recognize, the closest of these to *Samson Agonistes* and also the most despairing occurs in *The Book of Los,* where Los finds himself "Bound in . . . A vast solid without fluctuation," like Samson between stone pillars (4:7–9, E 91).[104] With a burst of prophetic rage, Los shatters the structure that confines him: "the vast solid / With a crash from immense to immense / Crack'd across into numberless fragments" (4:16–18, E 92). Los's impatience (a word Blake emphasizes) neither liberates him from his fallen world nor results in him being buried in the rubble like Samson; it leads only to further, endless falling. Los falls right alongside the fragments his violence has created, bits and pieces of breakage that include bits and pieces of a language in ruins, sound-words carrying the noise of history: "crash," "Crack'd," "crumbling," "bursting." In this mythic narrative, set prior to the creation of the sun in Genesis, Blake attributes the creation of time itself to the "incessant whirls" of Los' continuously falling, continuously "revolving" body, as he tumbles head over heels into the void (4:35–37, E 92). It is as if his impatient violence marks the beginning of fallen history, of a cyclical destruction potentially without end. To render this scene, Blake employs a suffocating, tautological language. Hardly a word appears that is not repeated, suggesting we have entered a long, dark era of repetition without any hint of redemptive difference: "Falling, falling! Los fell & fell / Sunk precipitant heavy down down / Times on times, night on night, day on day" (4:27–29, E 92). As Wittreich has powerfully argued, this is the same blind history Milton's Samson might also be taken to embody.[105] Starting with the hero's wrenching lament—"O dark, dark, dark, . . . / Irrecoverably dark" (ll. 80–81)—*Samson Agonistes* is similarly organized by a tautological discourse that shadows and competes with its expressions of enthusiasm. Samson is a hero "still watching to oppress / *Israel*'s oppressours" (ll. 232–233), who thinks single combat with Harapha will "decide whose god is God" (l. 1176), who believes "force with force / Is well ejected when the Conquer'd can" (ll. 1206–1207). Manoa takes comfort in the restoration of ferocious strength that allows Samson to finish his career in the very same way it began—"*Samson* hath quit himself / Like *Samson*" (ll. 1709–1710)—but the echo chamber of his words also allows for a darker reading, one that Mary Ann Radzinowicz (despite her own disagreement with such a reading) has caricatured so well: "[Samson] despairs, he talks, he no longer despairs, he acts, blind throughout."[106] According to this view, Samson undergoes no transformation, and whether he is victim or agent, the unvarying constant of his world is violence.

If *The Book of Los* entertains the same bleak assessment, other extensions of Blake's sound-cracks are more difficult to read, not least because they form no consistent pattern. As Roland Barthes would say, they are not isotropic.[107] The apocalyptic opening of Night the Ninth of *The Four Zoas*, in which Sun and Moon come down like Samson's pillars, explodes with the noise of *Samson Agonistes*.

Los his vegetable hands
Outstretchd his right hand branching out in fibrous Strength

> Siezd the Sun. His left hand like dark roots coverd the Moon
>
> And tore them down *cracking the heavens across from immense to immense*
>
> (117:6–9, E 386, emphasis added)[108]

Into this scene of monumental and potentially transformative violence, more of Milton's language enters than ever before, though, as always, noisy, shattered, and rearranged. The instances are too numerous to catalogue fully here. Samson "tugg'd" and "shook" those "two massie Pillars / With horrible convulsion to and fro," "till down they came . . . with burst of thunder." Now Blake's "heavens are shaken" with "thunderous noise & dreadful shakings rocking to & fro" (117:15–16, E 387). Like Milton's, these apocalyptic noises remain unreadable; they lie beyond the reach of easy moralizing. Although Blake provides enough ambiguity to slow even the most enthusiastic reader—starting with the "vegetable hands," "fibrous Strength," and "dark roots" that call Los's agency into question—it is also impossible to deny the energies of identification Blake directs toward the hallucinatory fantasy of apocalyptic inversion and revenge unfolding here:

> The poor smite their opressors they awake up to the harvest
>
> The naked warriors rush together down to the sea shore
>
> Trembling before the multitude of slaves now set at liberty
>
> They are become like wintry flocks like forests stripd of leaves
>
> The opressed pursue like the wind there is no room for escape   (117:19–23, E 387)

Blake inverts the Exodus narrative; it is the Egyptian oppressors who now find themselves pinned against the sea, the liberated slaves who pin them there. If Blake intends a subtle warning about the dangers of cyclical, retaliatory violence—along the lines of Beatrice's remark in *The Cenci*: "what a world we make, / The oppressor and the oppressed"[109]—he does so at the risk of allowing vengeful desires free play, under cover of the idea that violence can be purgative. "The blood pours down incessant," he writes, adding, "Kings in their palaces lie drownd" (119:7–8, E 388).

Amid this affective dissonance, with all its attendant moral and cognitive noise, I want to call attention to one other phrase fragment that found its way to Blake from *Samson Agonistes*. Blake uses it only here, and repeats it twice, each time in lines describing the resurrection of the dead at the last judgment.

> And all the while the trumpet sounds from the clotted gore & from the hollow den
>
> Start forth the trembling millions into flames of mental fire
>
> Bathing their limbs in the bright visions of Eternity . . .   (118:17–19, E 387)[110]

Blake specifically lifts the words "clotted gore" and much of the image generally straight from Milton, and their role in *Samson Agonistes* significantly complicates their presence here. Once Manoa concludes that Samson has "heroicly . . .

finish'd / A life Heroic" (ll. 1711–1712), he next determines to recover and preserve his son's body:

> Let us go find the body where it lies
> Sok't in his enemies blood, and from the stream
> With lavers pure and cleansing herbs wash off
> The clotted gore.   (ll. 1725–1728)[111]

Much depends upon the success of separating Samson's body from the "clotted gore" in which he became entangled—"immixt, inevitably" (ll. 1657), as the messenger puts it; "tangl'd in the fold, . . . conjoin'd . . . with [his] slaughter'd foes" (ll. 1665–1667), adds the chorus. The biblical Samson, we remember, was born to be a "nazarite"; in ancient Hebrew the word means "one separated." Now at his death, however, the only way to "separate" Samson from his Philistine enemies and thus remove him from a history of reciprocal violence that blurs the moral distinction between hostile parties is to find and clean his body. Identifying it among the general wreckage, disentangling it from the other bodies, washing off the blood it has shed—all these become the first necessary steps toward honoring the dead warrior and airbrushing him into an image of unambiguous national heroism. Just before Manoa proposes his search and recovery mission, he has already begun the work of "separating" Samson in discourse, distilling a message of noble triumph from any lingering suspicions or lamentations:

> Nothing is here for tears, nothing to wail
> Or knock the breast, no weakness, no contempt,
> Dispraise, or blame, nothing but well and fair,
> And what *may quiet us* in a death so noble.   (ll. 1721–1724, emphasis added)

Shifting between visual and auditory registers, Milton invites us to consider an analogy: cleansing Samson's body of its messy violence is like quieting the noises that would disturb the moral satisfaction accompanying victory. Of course the aim of Milton's language is precisely to disquiet, by reminding us that Samson in fact lies dead, "sok't in his enemies blood," crusted in "clotted gore" like the others.

What is Blake doing, then, with this dissonant image? His whole apocalyptic scene is also concerned with the logic of "separation." It begins with Jesus standing beside Los and Enitharmon, "separating / Their Spirit from their body" (117:4–5, E 386). At the moment of universal and indiscriminate ruin, the bodies of Los and Enitharmon lie "buried in the ruins of the Universe / Mingled with the confusion" (118:5–6, E 387), like Samson's "immixt" and "tangl'd in the fold." And when the dead begin to rise from this "clotted gore" into "mental fire," "Bathing their Limbs in the bright visions of Eternity," they directly invoke the wishful image of Samson's body fresh from the stream, newly washed with "lavers pure and cleansing herbs." Like Manoa, then, is Blake resurrecting a purely heroic Samson from the dead, identifying him now with a longstanding tradition that sees his action at the pillars as a typological anticipation of the last judgment itself? Or is Blake correcting Manoa's *bad* judgment? If Manoa delights to think that a purified Samson image will "inflame [the] breasts" of future "youth" (ll. 1738–1739), then perhaps Blake, in counterpoint, is redefining heroism by detaching intellectual acts of "mental fire" from the grim history of physical force and "clotted gore." Perhaps he means for his internalized apocalyptic scene to stand in direct contrast to the devastation Samson brought about and Manoa intends to celebrate. Or does Blake mean for the corrosive irony surrounding Manoa's triumphal fantasies to extend even into his own apocalyptic tableau, where it becomes so difficult for a reader to separate the revenge fantasy being played out there from the purely *mental* fight that is supposed to transcend such violent impulses? At the very least, Night the Ninth of the *Four Zoas* leaves open the question of how—or even whether—mental fight *could* cleanly separate itself from a history of "clotted gore." How, in other words, *would* a post-apocalyptic world "[b]athing . . . in the bright visions of Eternity" emerge from a history of violence so thoroughly fallen? Each of the possibilities I have mentioned remains active in this scene, and each is set resonating by the noise Blake inherited from *Samson Agonistes*.

"HE WHO STANDS DOUBTING"

In 1798, not long after he had finished illustrating *Night Thoughts* and while he was first working on the manuscript that would become *The Four Zoas*, Blake was defending Tom Paine from the attack by Bishop Richard Watson of Llandaff, writing his long, furious annotations in the margins of Watson's *Apology for the Bible*. As we observed in chapter 1, Blake ultimately declined to publish his commentary. In a calm, friendly, and (to Blake) maddening tone, Watson tried to put Paine firmly in his place by demonstrating that *The Age of Reason*, despite its rationalist posture, is in fact less reasonable than the divine justice and biblical revelation Paine's deist analysis wished to discredit. Watson's critique begins by raising questions about Paine's "conscience." As evidence of the firmness of his convictions, Paine claimed that his unorthodox principles had managed to survive the trial of a nearly fatal fever, with no eleventh hour conversion needed. Conceding Paine's sincerity, Watson instead attacks his overconfidence: yes, one can be sure of one's opinions—one can even firmly believe one is obeying the dictates of conscience—and yet still be terribly wrong. "What is conscience?" Watson asks. "Is it, as has been thought, an internal monitor implanted in us by the Supreme Being, and dictating to us, on all occasions what is right, or wrong? Or is it merely our own judgment of the moral rectitude or turpitude of our own actions?"[112] At stake in this opening question is whether individual conscience is a reliable indicator of the divine will. Can one be confident that one's own moral persuasion is aligned with God's? Can one act on that basis? Without the least intention of doing so, Watson has raised the question of Samson at the pillars: "he stood, as one who pray'd, / Or some great matter in his mind revolv'd" (ll. 1637–1638). In turn, Blake's point-by-point rebuttal of Watson becomes a remarkable, if also subtextual, commentary on *Samson Agonistes*.

On the central question of conscience and inner persuasion, Watson aligns himself with John Locke (whom he names) and thus with a century-old critique of enthusiasm. His position stands directly opposite the argument that would make Stanley Fish's reading of *Samson Agonistes* seem so inflammatory after 9/11. "In the end," Fish writes, "the only value we can put on Samson's action is the value he gives it in context. Within the situation, it is an expression, however provisional, of his reading of the divine will; and insofar as it represents his desire to conform to that will, it is a virtuous action."[113] Samson is virtuous because he acts conscientiously, in good faith, whether he gets the divine will right or wrong. When Carey responds—"why should we not expect a moral being to question and assess the instructions he thinks he is getting from a supernatural agency?"[114]—he, like Bishop Watson before him, is resuming an argument Locke first articulated in a chapter on enthusiasm added to the *Essay Concerning Human Understanding* in 1700: "The strength of our Persuasions are no Evidence at all of their own rectitude . . . He . . . that will not give himself up to all the Extravagancies of Delusion and Error must bring this Guide of his *Light within* [that is, his moral feeling] to the Tryal. God when he makes the Prophet does not unmake the Man. He leaves all his Faculties in their natural State, to enable him to judge of his Inspirations, whether they be of divine Original or no . . . *Reason must be our last Judge and Guide in every Thing*."[115] It is exactly this Lockean call to perpetual self-examination that Watson invokes as a necessary safeguard against the violence that can result from moral overconfidence. Among the "thousand" well-meaning "perpetrators of different crimes" invoked by Watson, criminals convinced they were following "the dictates of conscience," he names only one specifically: "Robespierre, who massacre[d] innocent and harmless women" (6–7). A firm persuasion of the good is no proof of anyone's virtue, and it offers no acceptable justification for violence.[116]

Where Blake positions himself in the Paine-Watson debate comes as no surprise: with immediate inspiration, against deliberation and prolonged moral calculation; with Paine, against Watson, Locke, and (by implication) Carey; with poet-prophets confident that "a firm perswasion that a thing is so, make[s] it so," as Isaiah and Ezekiel affirm in *The Marriage of Heaven and Hell,* and against those self-doubting moderns "not capable of a firm perswasion of any thing" (12, E 38–39). With a twist

of delicious irony, Blake defends Paine as "an Inspired man" and turns the Anglican Bishop into a mere reasoner, neither hot nor cold (E 613). On the subject of
conscience and virtue, Blake could not be more emphatic: "Virtue is not Opinion";
"Conscience in those that have it is unequivocal, it is the voice of God" (E 613). He
insists it is impossible to follow conscience and be wrong: "Virtue & honesty or the
dictates of Conscience are of no doubtful Signification to any one" (E 613). According to Blake's logic, Samson could not err if he was indeed "perswaded inwardly
that [his inspiration] was from God" (*Riverside Milton* 800), as Milton puts it in
"The Argument" to his play. When it strikes, divine inspiration strikes unambigu-
ously; it is "of no doubtful Signification to any one." And yet, as they touch on
Samson at the pillars, Blake's comments *do* allow room for the equivocation that
conscience is supposed by definition to preclude. To say that "Conscience *in those
that have it* is unequivocal, it is the voice of God," is not necessarily to affirm that
Samson has it. This point comes home in an annotation so striking it cannot but
call to mind the figure of Milton's Samson standing at the pillars: "The truth &
certainty of Virtue & Honesty i.e. Inspiration needs no one to prove it it is Evident
as the Sun & Moon *He who stands doubting of what he intends* whether it is Virtuous
or Vicious knows not what Virtue means. No man can do a Vicious action & think
it to be Virtuous. no man can take darkness for light" (E 614, emphasis added). In
the long debate over whether Samson is divinely or selfishly motivated, Blake's
comment leans toward the latter, but it does so for reasons exactly opposite those
proposed by figures like Carey or Bishop Watson in the Lockean tradition against
enthusiasm. Blake faults his Samson figure not for failing to deliberate, not for acting on an impulse he mistakenly takes to be divine in origin, but for deliberating
too long, "revolving some great matter in his mind," as if it were possible to arrive
at a well-reasoned decision in favor of slaughter. In a way that is more disturbing
than Carey's reading—in which endless deliberation over "doubtful significations"
might serve as a preventative against violence—Blake continues to allow for the
possibility of a genuinely inspired, genuinely impulsive agent of divine justice, but
he suggests that Samson is *not* that agent.

Blake's ambivalence toward Samson is further underscored when Watson
turns to defending biblical violence and "God's moral justice." Paine had complained that the mass extermination of Canaanites by the Israelites under Joshua
makes a mockery of any belief in the Bible as the word of God. Watson responds
by calmly and rationally justifying holy war. "As to the Canaanites," he writes,
"it is needless to enter into any proof of the depraved state of their morals." God
"made the Israelites the executors of his vengeance" because these "idolaters" were
"immersed in the filthiness of all manner of vice" (13). Assuming it is self-evident
that the Canaanites deserved to die, Watson, again inadvertently, echoes a chorus

in *Samson Agonistes* describing the Philistines as "Drunk with Idolatry" (l. 1670) and thus responsible for their own mass destruction—foolish enough "[a]s thir own ruin on themselves to invite" (l. 1684).[117] These arguments produce palpable outrage in Blake's annotations. There is no defense, he states, for "murdering so many thousands *under pretence of a command from God*"; "God never makes one man murder another nor one nation" (E 614, emphasis added). In these comments and others, Blake's condemnation of Old Testament violence is so sweeping—he calls it "an Example of . . . Human Beastliness in all its branches" (E 614), exactly the savagery Christ came to abolish—that Samson's massacre of three thousand Philistine men and women could hardly be exempt.

At the same time, nothing in Blake's arguments, or in the subtextual reservations about Samson they express, would declare him a simple pacifist. That God does not condone genocide and that he never commands murder provide little guidance with more difficult cases, such as the one Walter Benjamin would discuss under the category of "the revolutionary killing of the oppressor" in his "Critique of Violence." Benjamin dismisses outright the first premise of the pacifists, that the "sanctity of life" by itself turns the commandment against murder into a universal commandment against killing. He insists that one must defend a just life, not mere life.[118] Like Blake, and perhaps even like Milton (for whom, Fish conjectures, "there are worse things than death"),[119] Benjamin insists on retaining the theoretical possibility of what he calls "divine violence," a "pure immediate violence" genuinely free of self-interest and error, even as he remains skeptical about every actual case and makes it nearly impossible to imagine the circumstances in which one might conclude such violence is justifiable in human hands.[120] In principle at least, another Samson at other pillars *could* hear "the voice of God" and get it right, whether Milton's Samson did or not.

"HIS FIERIE VERTUE ROUZ'D"

Perhaps that other, genuinely virtuous Samson is the figure Blake meant to illustrate on the last page of Edward Young's *Night Thoughts* (see figure 2.9). Because Samson is in fact "eyeless," the open eye Blake features so prominently recalls a semichorus in *Samson Agonistes*: "With inward eyes illuminated / His fierie vertue rouz'd / From under ashes into sudden flame" (ll. 1690–1692). Most commentators on this image—Wittreich is an exception here—have emphasized Blake's identification with Samson's visionary energy.[121] And why not? If "[h]e who stands doubting of what he intends . . . knows not what Virtue means," then *this* Samson, past any doubt and fully in action, has earned his claim to "fierie vertue." Like Jesus, as an antinomian devil praises him in *The Marriage of Heaven and Hell*, he is "all virtue," having acted "from impulse: not from rules" (23–24, E 43). Concentrating on the isolated heroic figure in his moment of decisive action, Blake risks the kind of direct visual identification with violence that Milton himself avoided, first by following the protocols of Greek tragedy and setting the main action offstage and then by indicating that his drama was never meant to be staged at all. And yet, Blake's image of irreversible action still gives us reason to pause over Samson's "virtue," once again opening a space of "doubtful signification." Directly across from Samson's illuminated eye, in the second line of Young's text and italicized in a way that redirects *the reader's* eye, the word "*Virtue*" appears, described by Young in negative terms directly opposite the "fierie" and heroic associations of Milton's semichorus: "*Virtue* abounds in Flatterers, and Foes; / 'Tis Pride, to praise her; Penance to perform" (Night IX, p. 119).[122] Without entering into even a minimal interpretation of Young's moralizing lines or trying to determine how Blake structures the relationship between Young's virtue and Milton's, we can see that, at the very moment Samson has pulled down his pillars, Blake has placed us between two more. While Samson is beyond the point of hesitation, we are still procrastinating, pausing to read. Blake's *Night Thoughts* page is not about the immediacy of enthusiasm—either Samson's for divinely motivated violence or ours for Samson—but about delay. Rather than dangerously "hurrying the Will in Pursuit of an Object,"[123] as one eighteenth-century author defines enthusiasm, Blake deflects his object (Samson at the pillars) into a network of words and images that require closer and further reading, thus redirecting the concentrated urgency of Samson's action into the lateral, slower motion of reading.

Emphasizing Blake's subtle visual associations and the patient interpretation they require will inevitably risk reopening an old quarrel between politics and close reading; that is, it invites the charge that we are rerouting an urgent political message, indeed a call to action, into an insular aesthetic activity.[124] Derrida addressed this charge on numerous occasions, but nowhere more directly than in his *Politics of Friendship*. Careful, attentive reading, he explains there, will always risk appearing "too philological, micrological, *readerly*—complacent, too, with the time it allows itself when matters are urgent, at just the moment when one should no longer wait. At a moment when our world is delivered over to new forms of violence . . . the political and historical urgency of what is befalling us should, one will say, tolerate less patience, fewer detours and less bibliographic discretion. Less esoteric rarity." The slogan of Samson at the pillars might well be the words Derrida expected from those impatient with criticism: "This is no longer the time to take one's time."[125] Having prayed or revolved the matter in his mind, Samson "*At last*"—how long we are not told—"cryed aloud" (l. 1639), made his final speech, and pulled the pillars down. Yet even though a similar sense of "political and historical urgency" would continually lead Blake back to this scene, whenever he represents

Samson his subject is also the detour and delay of reading, and this practice of tak-ing time he need only to have learned from Milton.[126]

Regardless of whether we consider Samson a figure for the ruined world left behind (as Young describes him) or for revolutionary transformation (as various Blake and Milton critics suggest), the *Night Thoughts* Samson is clearly a figure of last judgment, the last thing encountered on a long poem's final page. Appearing in the final lines of Night IX as a figure for the end time, Young's Samson ("Him of Gaza in his wrath") gathers up and draws to a close the book's persistent apocalyp-tic imagery. Alert to this tendency, Blake anticipated the climactic Samson image more than a hundred pages earlier, choosing to illustrate lines describing the "*final* Fate," with "All *Nature*, like an Earthquake, trembling round" (Night IX, p. 14). The scene he depicted there—a crowd buried beneath the fragments of a collapsed building—significantly complicates our understanding of Samson tugging and shaking the pillars, for even though it precedes Samson's act in page sequence, it presents an image that could *follow* it in narrative sequence. In other words, Blake scrambles time and invites us to read backwards, to run the hallucinatory film of his illustrations in reverse, and so return to an earlier moment that gathers new interpretive potential only *after* we have passed beyond the book's last page. The time of reading thus extends beyond the stand-alone Samson image, the very im-age that associates apocalyptic finality with decisive action and is supposed to bring both time and reading to a close. Restoring these images to narrative sequence (figure 2.11), moreover, involves the reader in a dizzying exchange of perspectives— from Samson's act to its consequences, from the agent of divine violence to his victims.[127] At the bottom center of the earlier page Blake dangles a body disjointed and broken by a world turned upside down. By subordinating this figure's empty eyes to the wide, expressive void of her mouth—features echoed in the less detailed figure to the left—he also introduces an auditory resonance into his design, an effect reinforced by the Ionic column tumbling at the upper right whose spiral capital invokes Blake's persistent emblem of the ear.[128] Within the constraints of visual representation, this picture displaces the eye in favor of mouth and ear, drawing attention to the event's blind, piercing sound and once again setting the "noise" of history in stark, unresolved tension with the single-minded determina-tion that emboldens Samson and inwardly illuminates his vision. Faced with this aftereffect, the reader cannot unambivalently identify with Samson's open eye.

Even to the extent that Blake does attach this visionary Samson to Milton's, he also subtly departs from his predecessor in a way that opens onto other complicat-ing images. Milton's semichorus exults in the illumination of Samson's "inward *eyes,*" but by presenting Samson almost completely in profile, Blake makes only *one* eye visible. This detail would seem too trivial to notice did it not lead us to ask whether Samson is a figure for the *narrowness* of perception Blake called "single vision," perhaps even for "Newtons sleep" (E 722). In Martin Butlin's view, Blake "exaggerates [Samson's] open eye to suggest the moral victory of energy destroying matter,"[129] but even setting aside the problem that the matter destroyed here includes other people, we can see how difficult it is to distinguish Samson's visionary "energy" from the "matter" it would destroy. With a hyperbolic strength almost too heavy to bear, Samson's muscular limbs are as round and massive as the pillars he brings down; Blake emphasizes the continuity between them by repeating the deepening shadows of the falling columns in the shading of Samson's braced and bending legs.[130] Blake's whole design is organized by a syntax of descending triangles, first in the inverted V of the columns above Samson's head, then in the upward gaze of his one-eyed profile, and finally in the thick legs joined at the apex of his phallus. Structuring both the hero's body and the architecture collapsing upon it, these triangles recall the geometry of Newton's compass in one of Blake's most famous recurring designs. Blake had this very image in mind while executing *Night Thoughts*, for he included a version of it on an earlier page of Night IX to illustrate Young's reference to "*Newtonian* . . . Angels" (Night IX, p. 91) (figure 2.12).[131] In one sense, Samson reverses Newton's narrow earthbound preoccupation by staring upward, and yet all the motor force he exerts pulls downward and inward nonetheless. He can do nothing but contribute his own muscle to the work of gravity that defines his action, for whatever rebellious energy he releases contributes only to further falling.

And if the massive, angled pillars above Samson's head rhyme visually with Newton's modest compass, we may further identify those pillars with the enormous, world-forming instrument in "The Ancient of Days" (figure 2.13), an association assisted by Milton. In *Samson Agonistes*, Milton erects the Philistine theater on "two massie pillars," a phrase he repeats. In turn Blake enlists the word "massy" in *The Book of Urizen* to catalogue the measuring devices formed by Urizen to create the Newtonian universe, compass included:

> 7. He form'd a line & a plummet
> To divide the Abyss beneath.
> He form'd a dividing rule:
> 8. He formed scales to weigh;
> He formed *massy* weights;
> He formed a brazen quadrant;
> He formed golden compasses . . .   (20:33–39, E 80–81, emphasis added)

Gazing upward, Samson stares straight into the world formed by the Urizenic God himself, and whatever mass and force he directs toward undoing that world ironi-

> [119]
>
> Of *Fancy*, when our *Hearts* remain below?
> *Virtue* abounds in Flatterers, and Foes;
> 'Tis Pride, to praise her; Penance to perform:
> To more than Words, to more than Worth of Tongue,
> LORENZO! rise, at this auspicious Hour;
> An Hour, when Heaven's most intimate with Man;
> When, like a falling Star, the Ray Divine
> Glides swift into the Bosom of the Just;
> And Just are All, *determin'd* to reclaim;
> Which sets their Title high, within thy Reach.
> Awake, then: Thy PHILANDER calls: Awake!
> Thou, who shalt wake, when the Creation sleeps;
> When, like a Taper, all these Suns expire;
> When TIME, like Him of *Gaza* in his Wrath,
> Plucking the Pillars that support the World,]
> In NATURE's ample Ruins lies entomb'd;
> And MIDNIGHT, *Universal* Midnight! reigns.
>
> *End of the Night-thoughts*

Figure 2.11 (*left*) Night IX, page 119, illustration to Young's *Night Thoughts*, c. 1795–1797. Samson bringing down the temple. Pen and grey ink, with grey wash and watercolor. © Trustees of the British Museum (*right*) Night IX, page 14, illustration to Young's *Night Thoughts*, c. 1795–1797. Pen and grey ink, with grey wash and watercolor. © Trustees of the British Museum

cally ends up repeating it, instantiating its fallen laws and materials. Samson at the pillars does not command force at will but submits to it. Tugging and pulling, he is like the misguided warriors in Simone Weil's sobering reading of the *Iliad*, not as much an agent of violence as its instrument: "The true hero, the true subject matter, the center of the *Iliad* is force. The force that men wield, the force that subdues men, in the face of which human flesh shrinks back. The human soul seems ever

[14]

O Day of Confummation! Mark fupreme
(If Men are wife) of human Thought! nor leaft,
Or in the Sight of Angels, or their KING!
Angels, whofe radiant Circles, Height o'er Height,
Order o'er Order, rifing, Blaze o'er Blaze,
As in a Theatre, furround This Scene,
Intent on Man, and anxious for his Fate.
Angels look out for Thee: For Thee, their LORD,
To vindicate His Glory, and for Thee,
Creation univerfal calls aloud,
To dif-involve the *moral* World, and give
To *Nature*'s Renovation brighter Charms.

SHALL Man alone, whofe Fate, whofe *final* Fate,
Hangs on That Hour, exclude it from his Thought?
I think of nothing elfe; I fee! I feel it!
All *Nature*, like an Earthquake, trembling round!
All *Deities*, like Summer's Swarms, on Wing!
All bafking in the full Meridian Blaze!
I fee the JUDGE inthron'd! The flaming Guard!
The Volume open'd! Open'd every Heart!
A Sun-Beam pointing out each fecret Thought!

No

conditioned by its ties with force, swept away, blinded by the force it believes it can control, *bowed under the constraint of the force it submits to.*"[132]

In strictly visual terms, Blake's Samson also bears a striking resemblance to plate 21 of *The Marriage of Heaven and Hell*, copy D (figure 2.14), where another naked figure with a one-eyed upward gaze finds his body encompassed by a massive descending angle. Even before Blake introduced the background pyramids that would align this composition with the Samson design of *Night Thoughts* (circa

Figure 2.12 (left) Newton, 1795 / c. 1805, color print finished in ink and watercolor on paper. Tate Gallery London *(right) Night IX*, page 91, illustration to Young's *Night Thoughts*, c. 1795–1797. Pen and grey ink, with grey wash and watercolor. © Trustees of the British Museum

1795, and only in copy D),[133] this naked youth already bore a strong general association with revolution and a specific one with Samson. Rising literally from the grave and figuratively from subjection, the same figure also appears atop plate 8 of *America* (figure 2.15). This boldly apocalyptic text likens revolution to resurrection ("The grave is burst" [8:2]) and—with direct reference to Milton's Samson—to a final exodus from slavery ("Let the slave grinding at the mill, run into the field: / Let him look up into the heavens & laugh in the bright air" [8:6–7]). To complete the transition from slavery to freedom for which he stands, to be a strong man rising after sleep, to become the ascendant sun and "fresher morning" (8:13) of "Albion rose," all this man need do is stand, and in every other version of this oft-repeated design, nothing impedes him. Either he looks up into the heavens, ready to laugh in bright air (*Marriage*, copy I) or he finds himself released altogether from surrounding constraints into the uninscribed space of an open textual margin (*Marriage*, copy K) (figure 2.16). Only in copy D of *The Marriage* does the foregone conclusion of his capacity to rise become a problem for interpretation (see figure 2.14).

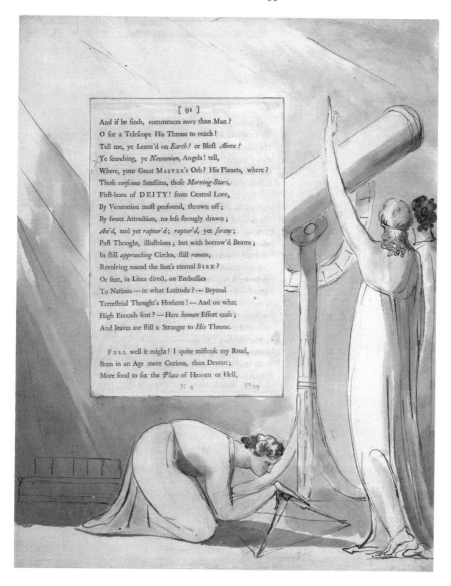

[91]

And if he finds, commences *more* than Man?
O for a Telescope His Throne to reach!
Tell me, ye Learn'd on *Earth!* or Bleſt *Above!*
Ye ſearching, ye *Newtonian*, Angels! tell,
Where, your Great MASTER's Orb? His Planets, where?
Thoſe *conſcious* Satellites, thoſe *Morning-Stars*,
Firſt-born of DEITY! from Central Love,
By Veneration moſt profound, thrown off;
By ſweet Attraction, no leſs ſtrongly drawn;
Aw'd, and yet *raptur'd*; *raptur'd*, yet *ſerene*;
Paſt Thought, illuſtrious; but with borrow'd Beams;
In ſtill *approaching* Circles, ſtill *remote*,
Revolving round the Sun's eternal SIRE?
Or ſent, in Lines direct, on Embaſſies
To Nations — in what Latitude? — Beyond
Terreſtrial Thought's Horizon! — And on what
High Errands ſent? — Here *human* Effort ends;
And leaves me ſtill a Stranger to *His* Throne.

FULL well it might! I quite miſtook my Road,
Born in an Age more Curious, than Devout;
More fond to fix the *Place* of Heaven or Hell,

N 2   Than

In a design newly dominated by pyramids, this problem is appropriately one of angles: a tension between points of view. From the figure's own perspective within the picture space, the pyramids to his back could be emblematic of past constraints left behind (death or slavery). Because he is *outside* them as he is *above* the grave, they do not interfere with his now unmediated gaze "into the heavens." From our frontal perspective, however, as readers of the plate, the figure appears painfully constricted by the composition's geometric design; he remains entombed within the pyramid's rigid outline. One would no more expect him to rise within

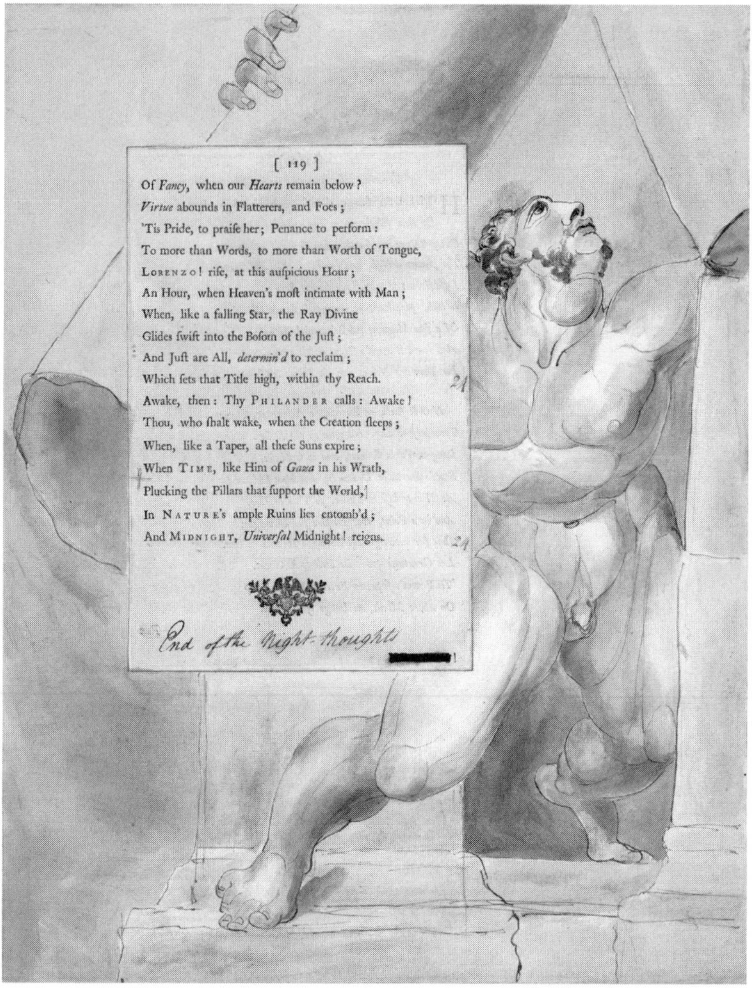

[119]

Of *Fancy*, when our *Hearts* remain below?
Virtue abounds in Flatterers, and Foes;
'Tis Pride, to praife her; Penance to perform:
To more than Words, to more than Worth of Tongue,
LORENZO! rife, at this aufpicious Hour;
An Hour, when Heaven's moft intimate with Man;
When, like a falling Star, the Ray Divine
Glides fwift into the Bofom of the Juft;
And Juft are All, *determin'd* to reclaim;
Which fets that Title high, within thy Reach.
Awake, then: Thy PHILANDER calls: Awake!
Thou, who fhalt wake, when the Creation fleeps;
When, like a Taper, all thefe Suns expire;
When TIME, like Him of *Gaza* in his Wrath,
Plucking the Pillars that fupport the World,
In NATURE's ample Ruins lies entomb'd;
And MIDNIGHT, *Univerfal* Midnight! reigns.

End of the Night-thoughts

Figure 2.13 (*left*) Night IX, page 119, illustration to Young's *Night Thoughts*, c. 1795–1797.
Samson bringing down the temple. Pen and grey ink, with grey wash and watercolor.
© Trustees of the British Museum (*right*) *Europe*, copy E, frontispiece. Lessing J. Rosenwald
Collection, Library of Congress. Copyright © 2011 the William Blake Archive. Used with
permission.

this cramped, Newtonian space than one would expect Urizen to stand within the
circle of his own making in "The Ancient of Days." The questions that surround
this figure, then, are the same questions surrounding Samson's "rouzing" virtue.
Is he about to rise, phoenix-like, overcoming the ashes of past defeats? Or is he an
enthusiast whose would-be apocalyptic agency conforms to a structural paradigm
of which he may not even be aware? Perhaps he thinks he sees without boundaries

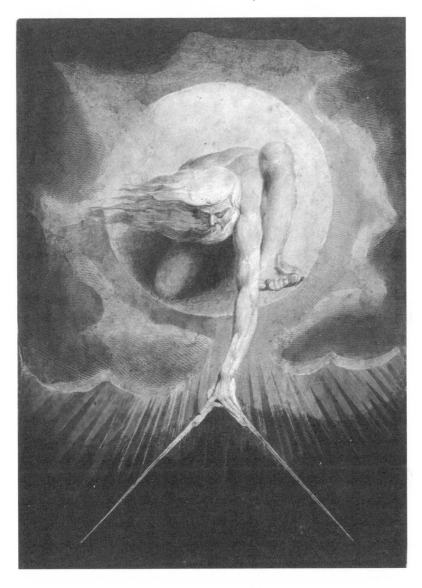

into heaven, with all the force of a transparent, unmediated revelation, but we see the confining framework that indicates otherwise.

Ambiguity is further irritated by the prose text of plate 21. Here the topic is overconfidence, the same charge Watson would level against Paine and that Blake now levels against the "vanity" of Angels who fail to recognize that their authority, "sprouting from systematic reasoning," corresponds to their narrow angle of vision. Blake underscores the association between arrogant angels and narrow an-

[119]

Of *Fancy*, when our *Hearts* remain below?
Virtue abounds in Flatterers, and Foes;
'Tis Pride, to praife her; Penance to perform:
To more than Words, to more than Worth of Tongue,
LORENZO! rife, at this aufpicious Hour;
An Hour, when Heaven's moft intimate with Man;
When, like a falling Star, the Ray Divine
Glides fwift into the Bofom of the Juft;
And Juft are All, *determin'd* to reclaim;
Which fets that Title high, within thy Reach.
Awake, then: Thy PHILANDER calls: Awake!
Thou, who fhalt wake, when the Creation fleeps;
When, like a Taper, all thefe Suns expire;
When TIME, like Him of *Gaza* in his Wrath,
Plucking the Pillars that fupport the World,]
In NATURE's ample Ruins lies entomb'd;
And MIDNIGHT, *Univerfal* Midnight! reigns.

End of the Night-thoughts

Figure 2.14 (*left*) Night IX, page 119, illustration to Young's *Night Thoughts*, c. 1795-1797. Samson bringing down the temple. Pen and grey ink, with grey wash and watercolor. © Trustees of the British Museum (*right*) *The Marriage of Heaven and Hell,* copy D, plate 21. Lessing J. Rosenwald Collection, Library of Congress. Copyright © 2011 the William Blake Archive. Used with permission.

gles with a playful visual-verbal pun: the large capital A of "Angels" in the first line of text mirrors the large closed "angle" of the pyramid almost directly above it in the image (see figure 2.14). The text specifically targets one such self-deceived angel, the false prophet Emanuel Swedenborg, whose promise of apocalyptic innovation amounts to nothing more than plagiarism and repetition: "Thus Swedenborg boasts that what he writes is new; tho' it is only the Contents or Index of already

I have always found that Angels have the vanity to speak of themselves as the only wise; this they
do with a confident insolence sprouting from systematic reasoning;

Thus Swedenborg boasts that what he writes is
new: tho' it is only the Contents or Index of already
publish'd books

A man carried a monkey about for a shew, & because he was a little wiser than the monkey, grew
vain, and conciev'd himself as much wiser than seven men. It is so with Swedenborg; he shews the
folly of churches & exposes hypocrites, till he imagines that all are religious. & himself the single

                                            one

The morning comes, the night decays, the watchmen leave
their stations;
The grave is burst, the spices shed, the linen wrapped up;
The bones of death, the cov'ring clay, the sinews shrunk & dry'd.
Reviving shake, inspiring move, breathing! awakening!
Spring like redeemed captives when their bonds & bars are burst;
Let the slave grinding at the mill, run out into the field:
Let him look up into the heavens & laugh in the bright air;
Let the inchained soul shut up in darkness and in sighing,
Whose face has never seen a smile in thirty weary years;
Rise and look out, his chains are loose, his dungeon doors are open
And let his wife and children return from the opressors scourge;
They look behind at every step & believe it is a dream.
Singing. The Sun has left his blackness, & has found a fresher morning
And the fair Moon rejoices in the clear & cloudless night;
For Empire is no more, and now the Lion & Wolf shall cease.

Figure 2.15 *America: A Prophecy,* copy E, plate 8. Lessing J. Rosenwald Collection, Library of
Congress. Copyright © 2011 the William Blake Archive. Used with permission.

publish'd books." Contents or Index: Swedenborg is the alpha and omega of the already known. In earlier and later versions of this plate, the design's apocalyptic and Samson-related youth would seem to be an authentic counterpoint to the deadening repetition of Swedenborg's writings, which he would leave behind in his naked ascent like so much linen at an empty tomb. But here, the naked figure might himself be *another* Swedenborg, another angel convinced he sees an unrefracted truth and ready to stand upon his vision with authority, but in fact unable to rise above the limits that precondition his knowledge and agency unawares. The skepticism Blake directs so effectively toward Swedenborg is devastating and general: if any act with pretense to apocalyptic inspiration ("inward illumination") may be programmed in advance by subtle, unrecognized constraints, then how would an agent ever know whether he is transforming his world or reproducing its fallen conditions? Once again Blake returns us to the problem rendered in shorthand by Samson at the pillars (see figure 2.9).

"Urgent: Slow Down"

There is probably no end to the texts and images we might bring to bear on the *Night Thoughts* Samson, for Blake has routed this figure of "fierie vertue" into a diffuse network of mutually qualifying signs.[134] In *Samson Agonistes,* the "rouzing motions" (l. 1382) that lead Samson to the pillars initiate an irreversible sequence that can only end one way: with pillars falling. Across Blake's open-ended network of signs, however, the reader's centrifugal, incomplete, and even retrograde movements leave those pillars still in air, perhaps never to fall. That Blake learned this slow readerly motion from Milton might best be conveyed by invoking Joanna Picciotto's recent account of Milton's difficult syntax, for her rendering of the reading experience provoked by Milton could pass almost verbatim as a description of effects produced by Blake:

> [A]mbiguities proliferate through double syntax . . . , while delayed exposure to crucial information creates the conditions for surprise "discoveries" that demand repeated acts of re-reading and re-seeing, literally retarding our movement down the page . . . [L]ong blocks of steeply enjambed lines provide a sense of headlong forward momentum while staving off a complete representation of what is happening. This paradoxical progress . . . combin[es] the copious accumulation of experimental results with a modest deferral of certainty about their meaning. The autoinquisition forced by Milton's repeated invitations to perceptual self-consciousness intensifies the sense of retarded movement, prompting us to hesitate, to reexamine, like victims of a checking compulsion.[135]

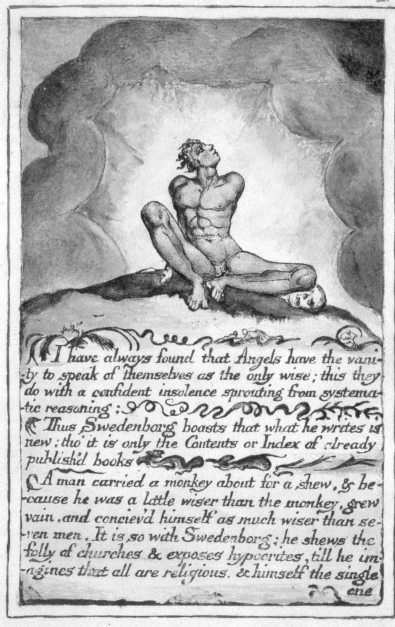

I have always found that Angels have the vanity to speak of themselves as the only wise; this they
do with a confident insolence sprouting from systematic reasoning:

Thus Swedenborg boasts that what he writes is
new; tho' it is only the Contents or Index of already
publish'd books

A man carried a monkey about for a shew, & because he was a little wiser than the monkey, grew
vain, and conciev'd himself as much wiser than seven men. It is so with Swedenborg; he shews the
folly of churches & exposes hypocrites, till he imagines that all are religious. & himself the single
one

Figure 2.16 (A and B) (left) The Marriage of Heaven and Hell, copy I, plate 21. © Fitzwilliam Museum, Cambridge (right) The Marriage of Heaven and Hell, copy K, plate 21. © Fitzwilliam Museum, Cambridge

I have always found that Angels have the vanity to speak of themselves as the only wise; this they
do with a confident insolence sprouting from systematic reasoning;
Thus Swedenborg boasts that what he writes is
new; tho' it is only the Contents or Index of already
publish'd books

A man carried a monkey about for a shew, & because he was a little wiser than the monkey, grew
vain, and conciev'd himself as much wiser than seven men. It is so with Swedenborg; he shews the
folly of churches & exposes hypocrites, till he imagines that all are religious. & himself the single
one

Although Picciotto is describing the halting, incremental adjustments that *Paradise Lost* requires of its readers, her insight gathers additional force when brought to bear on the climax of *Samson Agonistes*. There Milton's thick figuration detaches Samson's "fierie vertue" from the immediacy and transparency allegedly characteristic of enthusiasm ("because [enthusiasm] overleaps the space of reflection"),[136] submitting it instead to the reader's self-checking experimentalist response. This downshift from revelation becomes evident as soon as Milton's semichorus attempts to clarify Samson's virtue by resorting to three avian similes: "as an ev'ning Dragon" (l. 1692); "as an Eagle" (l. 1695); "Like that self-begott'n bird" (i.e., the phoenix, l. 1699). Rather than rendering the revolutionary moment transparent, as if it formed "a single action so dazzling in its clarity and force that the moral structure of the universe comes clearly into view," this sequence of figures makes critical reading both inevitable and inconclusive.[137] To mention only a few disorienting elements Milton's reader must negotiate:

—Spatially, both dragon and eagle *descend,* while the phoenix *rises* from the ashes.

—An *"ev'ning* Dragon" both *levels* and *darkens.* That is, this twilight image invokes the revolutionary virtue of flattening hierarchies while also contradicting the idea that Samson acts the part of a rising, liberating sun. An evening dragon brings "years of mourning" (l. 1712), not a fresher morning.

—Typologically, the resurrected phoenix associates Samson with Christ, while the dragon recalls the *Anti*christian powers of the Book of Revelation and even the name of the Philistine god Samson opposes. Alternatively, as Picciotto points out, the missing "r" in "Dagon" may make all the difference between blind idolatry and proper worship, given the etymological root of "dragon": "the seeing one."[138]

We could continue in this vein, but for our purpose the point is sufficiently clear. For Blake and Milton both, Samson's decisive, irreversible action becomes suspended in a field of polyvalent representations. Without entirely nullifying the force (and appeal) of his revolutionary violence, this complex mediation transfers its energies to the alternate rhythms, motions, and temporality of critical reading instead. The chiasmic effect of this transference is captured perfectly by Blake's *Night Thoughts* image. At the very moment when Samson, the figure of action, becomes immobilized in a still image, the sedentary reader, in a posture of apparent inaction, begins to move among words and images, embarking on the tentative but nevertheless exhilarating work of interpretation. While Samson's moment of judgment has passed, the reader dilates the interval prior to making a judgment of his or her own. Gathering strength, the *reader* becomes "vigorous most / When most inactive deem'd."

At stake in the scene of Samson at the pillars, then, is a relationship between critical thought and action that associates Blake with Milton's example while also pointing forward to subsequent critical models. On one side modifying the antinomian tendency to value unpremeditated action (the still attractive belief that one should act on impulse, not rules), while also, on the other, resisting any tendency to oppose thought to action altogether (as if contemplation were a corrective to action), Milton and Blake initiate a mode of critical judgment in which thought would become dynamic enough *to feel like* action. Samson provides a figure for this critical labor—as well as an object for it to work upon. In the early stages of his career, the biblical Samson was famous for a zero-time coincidence between inspiration and violent act: "the Spirit of the Lord came mightily upon him, and he rent [the lion] as he would have rent a kid" (Judg. 14:6); "the Spirit of the Lord came upon him, and he went down to Ashkelon, and slew thirty men" (Judg. 14:19). Although designated a "judge," Samson acts with a reckless immediacy we ordinarily associate with poor impulse control and lack of judgment.[139] With its long redaction history, the Book of Judges already toggles between an ancient folkloric admiration of Samson's irresistible powers and a more skeptical editorial overlay that views them as anarchic forces incompatible with civil order and social life. At that time, the final sentence of Judges intones, "every man did *that which was* right in his own eyes" (21:25).[140] In this way, Samson's hyperbolic immediacy anticipates the kind of activity that Freud, continuing an ironic use of the term, would also call "judging." Although in Freud's view "judging" is still a cognitive activity, it is minimally contemplative; he distinguishes it altogether from deliberation. "Judging" occurs at the exact interface where consciousness (however motivated) meets the physiology of motor force and decision becomes act. Freud describes it in terms of a nearly deterministic causal chain, as a step within a mechanical sequence reminiscent of dominos (or pillars) falling; it is "the intellectual action which decides the choice of motor action, which puts an end to the postponement due to thought and which leads over from thinking to acting."[141] Whatever Milton's Samson was doing between the pillars (thinking or praying), Freudian "judging" was uninvolved right until the moment he began to tug and pull—that is, right until the moment Blake represents in *Night Thoughts*. Crucially, Freud opposes thought to judging; if the latter acts, the former "postpones"; its special power is the power of procrastination. Only "[b]y interposing the process of thinking," Freud tells us in *The Ego and the Id*, can the subject "secur[e] a postponement of motor discharges."[142] By forestalling the entry into embodied action, thoughtful hesitation becomes a subtle but vigorous exercise of agency; what Picciotto calls the experimentalist's "checking compulsion" offers the subject a reprieve from the strict linear causality and irreversible outcomes that otherwise entangle it. For that reason, Freud distinguishes thought from mere inaction and passivity, calling it "experimental action" instead—that is, an action without immediate consequences but also free of predetermined results.

In the experiments of Benjamin Libet, recent cognitive science has found some empirical support for Freud's model.[143] Libet studied the electrophysiological "readiness potential" (539) that precedes seemingly voluntary acts (subjects were asked to flex a finger at intervals of their choosing), discovering that "the brain 'decides' to initiate or, at least, to prepare to initiate the act" (536) before consciousness ever becomes aware it has made a decision to act. Rather than concluding that we are all materialist Samsons, fated to enact the intimate neuronal impulses that descend upon us, Libet instead attempted to salvage free will in the split-second delay he measured between initial brain activity and final enactment. That interval, however brief, meant that "conscious control of the actual motor performance of voluntary acts definitely remains possible" (538), if also unguaranteed. Providing an experimental basis for "the postponement due to thought" described by Freud, Libet speculated that, even though consciousness cannot initiate actions freely or spontaneously, it retains "trigger" and "veto" power (538), the capacity to permit an impulse to proceed or to block its enactment. Libet tentatively suggested that this capacity "not to act in certain ways," what we ordinarily call "self-control," is consistent with "certain religious and humanistic views of ethical behavior and individual responsibility" (539)—views enshrined in the negative formulations of seven of the Ten Commandments Moses received at Sinai.[144]

With its reference to biblical law, Libet's conclusion directly collides with Blake's antinomianism, and there can be little doubt that Blake, rejecting any equivalence between thought and negative self-discipline, would find "Thou shalt not" writ over Libet's door. And yet, as we saw in the Watson annotations, Blake's antinomian faith in immediate inspiration never precluded him from incorporating "doubtful signification" into his texts and images, equivocations serving precisely to cultivate an interval between impulse and action. In fact, the tight braiding of experimental action and delay within critical engagement lies close to the central dynamic of Blake's work; with its precedent in Milton, it also becomes an important principle for post-humanist thinkers such as Derrida, Foucault, and Žižek, all considerably less invested in defending moral tradition than Libet.[145] Within this modern trajectory, critical thought defers the narrow, compulsive modes of enactment available at any given moment to an overdetermined biological and historical subject, thus slowing the automatic passage from thinking to acting and expanding the range of possible actions when action is ready. The more pressing the matter, the more patiently thought must proceed—though without sacrificing any of the urgency that demands action. In *Paradise Regained*, Milton models this method of "active restraint" in Jesus' messianic refusal to enter any of the action pathways presented to him by Satan, including the revolutionary one of overthrowing Roman rule by force. As Gordon Teskey has argued, referring to the climactic balancing act upon the pinnacle, the hero's "perfect sense of timing in action . . . is manifested precisely in . . . his refusal to move."[146] In *Politics of Friendship*, the same text in which he defends the slow time of critical reading against the political imperative of immediate action, Derrida incorporates a similar emphasis into his celebrated notion of the "passive decision"—the pause for deliberation that slows judgment and forces any would-be Samson to pass through an interval of indeterminacy: "It must be difficult to judge and to decide. A decision worthy of the name—that is, a critical and reflective decision—could not possibly be rapid or easy."[147] A slower, reflective Samson—blocking some impulses in order to experience others—could not finish his career just as he began, unchanged, still blindly impulsive, "quit[ting] himself / Like Samson." For Derrida, although no decision is made freely, the conditions of possibility to which any decision responds—what "has not yet been thought through"[148]—can be widened or narrowed, like bandwidth. Just as no reader invents the textual materials to which he responds, so no subject can initiate the impulses upon which it acts. But by stalling the inclination to seize upon some stimuli and act prematurely, and by augmenting the "passive" or receptive capacity involved in delay, the subject allows itself to be surprised by impulses and materials it may otherwise have neglected. A decision "worthy of the name" (that is, neither calculating nor mechanical) requires time to reflect and more material to reflect upon.

Inherent in this notion of experimental action or generative delay, however, is the problem of timing emphasized by Teskey. If the goal is readiness, as Milton's fellow republican Edmund Ludlow wrote from exile in Switzerland, so "that when the Lord's tyme is come we may up and be doing," then in practice it becomes impossible to know whether action arrives too soon or too late.[149] With so much critical attention directed to the question of whether Samson thinks or prays between the pillars, it is easy to miss the weight Milton loads onto the two small words that immediately follow: "At last . . ." (l. 1639). They are among the most poignant in the drama. As an imperfect agent in exigent circumstances, Samson lacks the gift (or luxury) of that flawless "sense of timing" necessary "for the transcendental politics of saving the world," a quality belonging only to Jesus.[150] Milton provides no measure for the interval between thought (or prayer) and act. However long Samson revolves the matter in his mind, his decision—like any decision—still risks being hasty. Anticipating the criticism that his experiments measured only the most minimal of spontaneous, "voluntary" actions (flexing fingers), and therefore could not account for the effects of more complex and patient planning, Libet argued that, in the end, the length of preparatory deliberation was irrelevant. Whenever it arrived (after seconds, minutes, weeks, or even years), the moment of judgment and act would "still be initiated unconsciously, regardless of the preceding kinds of deliberative processes."[151] When "at last" agency was exercised, it would still consist of "trigger" and "veto" power only. No matter how far one extends the benefits of Freudian procrastination, one can never escape being an impulsive Samson in the end. Arriving at a similar conclusion, Derrida asserted the inherent madness of every decision.[152] Even Foucault, who argued that critical analysis must be put to the patient test of experimental practice, acknowledged that the most modest efforts at self-transformation might still be rash. "[D]o we not run the risk," he asks, framing the problem of progressive agency in the idiom of haste, "of letting ourselves be determined by more general structures of which we may well not be conscious, and over which we may have no control?"[153] Concerned more about ideological determinants than physiological ones, Foucault's question recalls Blake's naked youth in *The Marriage of Heaven and Hell*, copy D, the figure who at last finds himself ready to stand and act freely but may still be constrained by "more general structures" (the background pyramids) of which he is unaware. Even though precipitance remains a serious danger in all of these considerations of timing, infinite delay is no less problematic; reflection can be so distended as to become a permanent state, a "checking compulsion" and nothing more. "The question," writes Derrida, "is not only the one which brings on semantic vertigo [and thus delay], but the one which asks 'what is to be done?': What is to be done today, politically, with this vertigo and its necessity?"[154]

Dilemmas of this kind, I believe, are deeply embedded in the Samson figure as Milton and Blake understood him; they also underlie the heightened significance of affectivity in Blake's critical practices. Driven by an unresolved ambivalence toward revolutionary violence, Blake's fractured, inconsistent representations of Samson rehearse a variety of responses, ranging from direct identification with spontaneous, explosive force to revulsion at its devastating effects. For Blake, moreover, this irresolution was never simply a matter of being unable to work out a conscious attitude toward revolution or arrive at a consistent political philosophy. The complex relays among impulse and delay, thought and act, became integrated into the daily, practical tension between Blake's uneventful life and the urgency within his work—between the restraint, patience, nonparticipation, and spectatorship of the one, and the passionate, headlong dynamism of the other. Under these various pressures, Blake's style acquired its signature affect: "Contemplative Thought" took on the reckless force and prophetic feeling of a "Fiery Chariot" (E 560). For Blake, like Foucault after him, thought itself sustains a promise of liberating forward motion despite the paralysis that the dilemma of structure and agency or impulse and act might induce. According to Foucault, thought performs

its work by transforming action itself into an object of contemplation, thus bringing its conditions and contingencies to light. "Thought is not what inhabits a certain conduct and gives it its meaning; rather it is what allows one to step back
from this way of acting or reacting, to present it to oneself as an object of thought
and question it as to its meaning, its conditions, and its goals. Thought is freedom
in relation to what one does, the motion by which one detaches oneself from it,
establishes it as an object, and reflects on it as a problem."[155]

Contemplative, but not static, critical thought is neither fully active nor passive
here. It acts by *not acting,* by decelerating action to the point where the actor's instinctive, habitual blur might acquire focus. As Foucault writes elsewhere, critical
practice becomes "a patient labor giving form to our impatience for liberty."[156] "Patient," but perhaps also "<Herculean>," thought allows the subject to observe the
way it enacts its unfreedom, as if in slow motion. Here we are very close to Blake's
strategy on the last page of *Night Thoughts*—slowing action to a standstill in order
to render it problematic. Samson's "impatience for liberty" remains palpable but in
a state of suspended animation, sustained indirectly now in the active passivity of
the reader's scrutiny. And despite its slower, back-step motion, the reader's critical
thought takes on enough of Samson's urgency and strength to feel consequential
in its own right. Whether negotiating the tension between Milton's "vertue" and
Young's "virtue" or tracing the play of Newton's compass across any number of
Blake's designs (or following the lead of some equally plausible series of associations), the reader can always procrastinate, postponing the Freudian moment that
"leads over from thinking to acting"—while, in the meantime, continuing *to do
something* that feels compelling, restless, even heated. Blake's challenge was never
really to slow himself down in the face of historical and political exigency; impulsive outrage and patient disengagement seem to have been his habitual response
in every instance except his confrontation with Scofield. Turbulent as it was, his
enthusiasm rarely risked carrying him beyond his judgment into dangerous action. Blake's challenge was rather to merge his caution and his passion, a challenge he met by assimilating the affective qualities of inspired action into critical
thought itself.

Perhaps we are "at last" in better position to grasp the final changes that, around
1804, would place "Albion rose" within the fractured sequence of Blake's Samson
figures (see figure 2.2). In the mid-1790s, this design (see figure 2.1) was characterized by its stunning immediacy, a burst of color and figure upon the sensory
eye, uninterrupted by even so much as the artist's signature. Bearing all the self-
evidence of sun and moon, and "of no doubtful Signification to anyone" (E 613),
this figure's radiance is as unequivocal as virtue itself, as Blake describes virtue in
the Watson annotations. Now, years later, Blake has slowed his viewer by assigning

him much more reading, first in the inscription that alludes both to his own *America* and to Milton's *Samson Agonistes,* and then in every other new detail: the artist's initials, the date of invention, the bat-winged moth, and the reticulated worm or chrysalis at Albion's feet. The latter are clearly icons within a sign-system we are invited to decipher, but—like the figures for virtue in *Samson Agonistes* (dragon, eagle, phoenix)—they provoke a reading process we cannot hope to resolve.[157] Even the elimination of color serves to promote reading rather than the self-evidence of seeing. Reducing the immediacy of visual pleasure, the line engraving converts Albion into a dark-on-light figure continuous with the newly added print of the inscription; now he too is a figure inked for reading. With his open, athletic posture unchanged, the naked youth stands poised between the exuberance expressed in his earliest incarnation (1780) and the signifying apparatus within which he is now reconstituted, an apparatus that delays the reader's judgment *and* substantiates the figure's energy in the critical vitality required to interpret it. Like the figure itself, the reader must now direct his or her energies outward, centrifugally, taking into account a network of complementary and competing significations beyond the boundaries of this single image. Although prompted at first by the image's own immediate echoes and allusions (to Milton, to Blake's previous work, to other Samson images), this movement across significations ultimately extends without end.

Finally, in a single deft move, Blake heightens and postpones the figure's association with revolution, adding the date that will irrevocably link the picture to the Gordon Riots—but not until the image acquires a reader passionate enough and patient enough to discover this open secret, which would elude viewers for nearly a century and a half. Joining political commitment to scholarly care, Erdman could hardly contain the excitement of his discovery, which in turn became the cornerstone of an entire way of reading Blake. In the early pages of *Prophet Against Empire,* when Erdman announces with well-earned drama that "Albion rose" is "a terrific social utterance,"[158] he not only restores the image's original passion and revolutionary commitment—still warm after all these years, like "fierie vertue" hidden "under ashes"—he also assimilates a portion of that dormant energy into his own critical utterance. That is, his passionate tone expresses a conviction that criticism also matters in *his* world of social utterance. In 1954 (this tone insists), a scrupulous, time-consuming reading of "Albion rose"—more attentive than any the image had previously received—is not some neutral or self-indulgent academic exercise but a meaningful act of political engagement in its own right. Nurtured by the critic's urgency, Blake's impatience for liberty remains affectively alive even as it downshifts skillfully to the slow time of the critic's infinitely patient labor, a work characterized by actions so "subtle and indirect," so "slow and obscure" (as Matthew Arnold called the work of criticism), that they will always risk looking like a species of inaction.[159] And this process is hardly a matter of Erdman illegitimately aggrandizing his own professional activity at the expense of Blake's original political gesture, for Erdman only does with Blake what Blake had already done with Milton and Samson—transfer political energies into criticism.

Still, although our emphasis has been on the integration of political urgency into the slow time of criticism, it would be a mistake to conclude that either Blake or Milton before him was willing to relinquish the impulsive Samson altogether. Even as they hedge this figure round with every possible caution that an incremental, self-correcting interpretive process might provide, the reading activity they initiate through Samson never fully displaces the enthusiasm he continues to represent, even at the risk of sustaining its potential for violence. If Blake or Milton meant for their "doubting significations" to disable any identification with Samson, they surely adopted a dangerous strategy. For even as the reader's negotiation of ambiguity slows and perhaps even supplants any tendency toward revolutionary haste, it never fully eliminates the possibility of revolutionary justice Samson *might* represent, keeping that possibility alive not only conceptually but affectively, as an object still working on the reader's desire. Rather than raising and purging enthusiasm in a zero-sum game of catharsis, resulting in "calm of mind all passion spent" (l. 1758), these Samson figures never fully cancel the enthusiasm they arouse.[160] That is, they continue to fuel the very same impatience they aim to keep in check. At a moment in *Samson Agonistes* when events are still in doubt, the chorus tells Samson that two outcomes remain open to him: restored strength or saintly patience—"Either of these is in thy lot" (l. 1292). If Samson must alternate between force and patience, or play them out in sequence, it becomes the reader's lot to hold them together simultaneously, to experience reading as an activity that carries a passion for revolutionary justice into the future—still warm, like "fierie vertue . . . under ashes"—even while exercising the patience necessary to resist imitating those who violently act on their enthusiasm as if it were divinely authorized. Reading Samson performs this dual function by transferring the hero's sublime strength to the critical act of assessing the hero's validity. By making Samson's virtue undecidable, Blake and Milton would make a virtue of criticism. To revert to the language of Kenzaburo Oe's novel *Somersault,* cited as an epigraph at the beginning of this section, reading would be the space where it becomes possible "neither to take action *nor to desist*."[161]

Finally, it is worth mentioning that Foucault recognized precisely this paradox—of acting by *not* acting—in Kant's account of the revolutionary spectator. What fascinated Foucault was how the critical hesitation that immobilized the spectator before the scene of actual revolution served only to heighten his affective identification with the principles of revolutionary justice. Kant wrote that the "miseries and atrocities" of the event were such that "a sensible man, were he boldly to hope to execute it successfully the second time, would never resolve to make the experiment at such cost."[162] Foucault, acknowledging the risk of precipitance inherent in political action, comments in turn, "the Revolution will always run the risk of falling back into the old rut." "[B]ut," Foucault continues, "as an event whose very content is unimportant, its existence attests to a permanent potentiality that cannot be forgotten: for future history it is the guarantee of the very continuity of progress."[163] The mixed fortunes of the event itself matter less than the collective memory the event initiates. The revolution leaves behind an affective remainder, an excess of enthusiasm that carries into the future, continuing to demand recognition. Thus the question raised by the Kantian spectator, according to Foucault, is "What is to be done with the will to revolution?"[164] This will (which Foucault sometimes calls a "desire") persists despite the repugnant violence of events like Samson at the pillars, the Jacobin Terror, or, in the twentieth century, "the programs for a new man" implemented by "the worst political systems."[165] Responsibility for this will to revolution, this permanent potentiality, this continuity of progress despite the evidence of defeat, now belongs to the critical labor of spectators who neither act on their enthusiasm nor desist.

The Virtue of Hayley's Milton

"There was much in Milton with which [Blake] was closely in sympathy" (310). It is symptomatic of Ackroyd's *Blake: A Biography* that the affinities he catalogues—from their comparable understanding of "sacred vision" to "an element of London hardness in their nature" (310)—does not include their republicanism. Ackroyd cites a poem Blake sent in a letter to Flaxman, "Milton lovd me in childhood & shewd me his face," but he neglects to mention that only three lines later Blake's recitation of influences includes the "mighty & awful change" that began with the American and continued with the French Revolution (E 707–708). The continuity of literary and political influences in the letter becomes, in the biography, the erasure of one by the other. Reviewing the same evidence, one can of course arrive at an altogether different lineage. Christopher Hill, for instance, sees Blake inheriting a revolutionary Milton who "had the springs of action too deeply embedded in him to have doubts about the duty of action . . . His problem was rather . . . to grasp the psychology of those who did not feel his compulsion to act."[166] As we saw in the case of "Albion rose," these divergent emphases are each rooted in Blake's own practices, for Blake half hid his revolutionary passions and references, leaving them to rouse the faculties of a politically sympathetic reader but also chancing that they might be missed altogether. From the start, the politics of Blake's critical engagement were both radical and inconspicuous. Works such as "Albion rose" will always have their Hills and their Erdmans as well as their Ackroyds. Each tells a mutually correcting truth about Blake's "spiritual Acts," which never retreated to the spirit world altogether but never quite entered into action either.

In this last section, I want briefly to consider a biography, almost certainly read by Blake, that champions Milton himself as a figure capable of holding together the contradictory imperatives of waiting and acting. First published in 1794, with an expanded edition in 1796, William Hayley's *Life of Milton* was almost exactly contemporary with Kant's *Conflict of the Faculties* (published in 1798, but probably written in 1795). By aligning Milton's passionate dissent with late eighteenth-century liberal virtues, Hayley represents the master poet as a cooler, slower Samson, able to maintain the force of republican feeling while suspending it in inaction. In Hayley's treatment, Milton becomes the model of "enthusiasm" for a new audience of revolutionary spectators.

Hayley is among literary history's easiest targets, and we need to qualify our customary aversion in order to grasp the significance of his Milton for an understanding of Blake. Almost alone among Blake critics, Wittreich has taken up Hayley's cause, arguing that, despite their obvious incompatibility, he and Blake shared similar attitudes toward Milton.[167] Thus Blake's *Milton* "elaborates and extends" what he learned first from Hayley's *Essay on Epic Poetry* (1782) and then from the *Life*.[168] Wittreich is right, I believe, though his insertion of Blake and Milton into a triangle that includes Hayley will inevitably dissatisfy any reader tracing Blake's antinomianism back to Milton. After all, Hayley was exactly the kind of "modern liberal Christian" that Hill declares Milton was not, and his *Life of Milton* is partly responsible for a Whig tradition of interpretation Hill is determined to reverse.[169] "Liberal" is a word found everywhere in Hayley's biography, from its emphasis on "the liberal mind of Milton" to its acknowledgement of Joseph Warton (brother of Thomas Warton and author of "The Enthusiast") as a "liberal friend to the freedom of literary discussion."[170] Following the example set by Shaftesbury earlier in the century, Hayley turned civility and tolerance into his guiding, self-conscious principles. "[N]ot fond of literary strife" (xvii), he campaigned against a pervasive culture of scholarly antagonism. Including a new dedication to Warton in his second edition (the one Blake likely read at Felpham), he wrote that criticism "should humanize," not add to "the field of cruelty"; "O that the spleen-correcting powers of mild and friendly ridicule could annihilate such hostilities!" (xviii). Hayley especially wished to annihilate the politically motivated hostilities Samuel Johnson had directed at Milton, and he set out to do so by numbing his opponents with mildness. His was a generous spirit that would never tell its wrath but rather "deligh[t] to honour the excellencies of an illustrious antagonist" (x). No "political rancour" (214), he hoped, could survive such kindness. In sum, there is much in this biography to support Byron's judgment of Hayley—"For ever feeble and forever tame"[171]—as well as Blake's own: "Genteel Ignorance & Polite Disapprobation" (E 730). "Liberal," in Hayley's parlance, means "no fighting." It is a word Blake almost never used.

What prevents *Life of Milton* from becoming yet another triumph of Hayley's mild temper, and more fodder for his vilification in Blake criticism, is its incomplete assimilation of Milton into its ostensible program of moderation. Hayley expends equal energy preserving and defusing Milton's revolutionary republicanism, attempting to render it safe for intellectual consumption in the volatile 1790s. Strangely, this biography is bold *and* tame, and it is difficult to determine which quality ultimately serves the other. Dwelling at length on Milton's controversial prose, Hayley may be assimilating revolutionary memory into a triumphant liberal context that would neutralize its threat, much as, in an example supplied by his dedication, the generous Romans allowed "a statue of Hannibal to be raised and admired within the walls of the very city, which it was the ambition of his life to distress and destroy" (x). Blake understood well the hazards of such absorbent generosity: "You know Satans mildness and his self-imposition," says Palamabron, contributing to *Milton*'s covert portrait of Hayley, "seeming a brother, being a tyrant, even thinking himself a brother" (7:21–22, E 100). At the same time, however, under cover of liberal kindness, Hayley's biography was reintroducing English audiences to the republican Milton at the very moment when writers like Gibbon considered the danger of Milton's political example self-evident.[172] At the height of political "panic" (viii)—Hayley completed and first published *Life of Milton* during the Terror—Hayley never apologizes for Milton's motives, only for his occasional "intemperance of zeal, which defeats its own purpose" (68). The republican poet remains "[o]ur constant advocate for freedom, in every department of life" (88). Remarkably, nearly half of this biography concerns Milton's political career and the polemical tracts he wrote to justify his participation in revolution. For that reason, Hayley's publishers (Boydell and Nicol) omitted a number of passages referring to Milton's republicanism, passages Hayley restored in the 1796 edition.

The audacity of Hayley's attention to politics exceeds even his own attempt to contain it, no matter how extravagant his efforts. In the first edition, containment begins to take shape in an argument Hayley would elaborate upon in the second: that the Glorious Revolution of 1688 had rendered Milton's political grievances obsolete. Had the poet lived to see that event, Hayley was convinced, "he would probably have exulted as warmly as the staunchest friend of our present constitution can exult, in that temperate and happy reformation of monarchical enormities" (215). At the very moment when the revolution controversy pivoted upon debate over the constitution, and some radical pamphleteers even looked to Milton for a "rational and satisfactory answer to the splendid sophistries of Edmund Burke," Hayley removes the stigma attached to Milton's political voice by making him the unlikely ally of Burke, not Paine.[173] In 1794, who else would qualify as "the staunchest friend of our present constitution"? Two years later, the newly added dedication is even more emphatic. If Milton's "impassioned yet disinterested ardour for reformation was excited by those gross abuses of power, which that new settlement of the state very happily corrected," then there is no reason now to fear the consequences of his prose, or to make "the mistake of regarding it as having a tendency to subvert our existing government" (vi–vii). Because he wrote in specific circumstances long ago superseded, Milton's political "arguments, if they could by any means be pointed against our existing government, are surely . . . incapable of inflicting a wound, . . . completely dead for all the purposes of hostility" (vii). By sheathing Milton's sharp hostilities in the safety of a distant past, Hayley could instead emphasize the continuing relevance of his "mild energy" (69).[174]

Blake may well have been aware that Hayley understood his own oppositional energies in similarly disarming, neutralizing terms.[175] Determined to defend Milton against Johnson's accusation that his personal "repugnance to authority" led him into reckless militancy, Hayley insisted on the poet's accommodating, liberal virtues: "No human spirit could be more sincerely a lover of just and beneficent authority; for no man delighted more in peace and order" (214). Under Hayley's patronage, Blake would soon find himself facing similar political charges, and, as we have seen, hear himself successfully defended in similar terms—by an attorney Hayley probably procured for him. How could Blake have told Scofield he was a strong man, ready to cut throats for Napoleon, when he was "as loyal a subject as any man in this court"? Finding nothing contradictory in reconciling Milton's enthusiasm with his own liberalism, Hayley surely believed Blake's enthusiasm would only benefit from his friendship as well.

And why not? Hayley knew little (and understood less) of the cryptic illuminated books in which Blake both expressed and buried his political indignation. Like other contemporaries who misunderstood Blake, he would have found the engraver's *life* exactly as Bataille would later describe it: "almost banal," "regular and unadventurous."[176] With his radical inclinations covered over by the apparent virtue of his nonparticipation, Blake had already completed half the work of moderation for Hayley. We would be mistaken to charge Hayley with simply misunderstanding the *real* Blake, the antinomian Blake with whom his own liberalism was deeply, inevitably incompatible. Demeaning, irreconcilable differences in social status and temperament led to Blake's angry departure from Felpham and to a stream of notebook couplets reviling his benefactor, but these antipathies did not extend in any obvious way to their politics. On the contrary, more than a year after his return to London, Blake was soliciting Hayley's partnership in a new literary and political magazine to be "calld a Defence of Literature." Blake's proposal introduced one of his new associates (bookseller Richard Phillips) to Hayley as a comrade "spiritually adjoind with us" (E 746), which is to say, generally in line with their republican views. Hayley agreed to become editor, though the magazine never materialized.[177] There was enough of Hayley's liberalism in Blake's enthusiasm (and perhaps enough of Blake's enthusiasm in Hayley's liberalism) to seal a sufficient if imperfect bond, and one point of contact between them was Milton.

It will always remain tempting to see Hayley's Milton as the opposite of Blake's. The one is "Unhappy tho in heav'n" (*Milton* 2:18, E 96) and must descend in order to redeem the authentically prophetic portion of his work, which might still be turned apocalyptically against the current establishment. The other looks down upon late eighteenth-century England and, liking the political arrangement he sees well enough, finds no further reason to agitate. If Milton still belonged to the devil's party inadvertently, Hayley seems not to have known it any more than Milton himself. Nevertheless, the quietism of Hayley's *Life* is never simple, for this biography stubbornly refuses to empty *all* the fight out of Milton. Hayley disarms the republican poet, rendering him ineligible for immediate Jacobin purposes, while also insisting that we remember, even admire, the example of his activism. Even if "Liberal spirits" disapprove of Milton's opinions, as Hayley himself sometimes disapproves, they should never forget what matters most: "the patriotic benevolence, the industry, and the courage, with which Milton endeavoured to promote what he sincerely and fervently regarded as the true interest of his country" (52).[178]

The consistent message of *Life of Milton* is that we can follow the admirable example of Milton's revolutionary passion without having to follow it into action. Writing with the "asperity of a man in wrath" (76), Milton's one mistake was sometimes to act incautiously. He could never completely balance the paradoxical ideal Hayley would have him exemplify, one that would maintain a passion for justice *and* the "spirit of self-command" (220) Milton represented best in *Paradise Regained,* where Jesus demonstrates a new form of heroism by resisting every temptation to act. As if it were a corrective addressed to those same "valiant youth" who might find their breasts inflamed by Manoa's monument in *Samson Agonistes,* Hayley particularly recommends *Paradise Regained* "to ardent and ingenuous youth" (220). But the "triumph of christianity" (220) he sees in Milton's Jesus does not require readers to neglect Milton's Samson altogether. Offset properly, they can be bundled together. Hayley's discussion of Milton's politics serves a single, overarching purpose, which he summarizes thus: to "impress a just and candid estimate of his merits and mistakes on the temperate mind of his country"

(159). The passion that carried Milton into political action was both his merit and his mistake. By purging its strident excess ("intemperance of zeal") while preserving its essential affective core (sincere and fervent regard for his country), the "temperate" reader of Hayley's *Life* can achieve the vigorous inactivity that partially eluded Milton's own best self.

In Milton, then, Hayley was constructing a figure who might answer a question not unlike the one Kant answered by proposing his theory of the revolutionary spectator: How can the passion for liberty be upheld and deferred simultaneously? Or as Foucault formulated the question of the spectator: "[W]hat is to be done with that will to revolution, that 'enthusiasm' for the Revolution, which is quite different from the revolutionary enterprise itself"?[179] Hayley's Milton gestures toward a subjective economy in which undiminished political passion might be uncoupled from the impulse to act, which henceforth will always appear hasty, compulsive, and insufficiently reflective. The term for this subjective economy—in Kant, in Foucault, and in Hayley—is "enthusiasm." Against Johnson's assumption that religious enthusiasm was responsible for the political disasters of the previous century, Hayley would invent a liberal enthusiasm that retains the arousal of revolutionary aspirations while strictly avoiding the detrimental consequences of their enactment. His *Life* therefore slides fluidly between descriptions of Milton's liberalism and his enthusiasm, for Hayley believes these qualities are continuous rather than contradictory. Milton may have had a "liberal mind," but "Enthusiasm was the characteristic of his mind" as well (208). By tempering his ardor, liberalism rescues Milton from Johnson's accusation ("his predominant desire was to destroy rather than establish");[180] at the same time, enthusiasm allows him to retain as much heat as is safe. "I trust," he writes at the conclusion of his long foray into Milton's political career, "the probity of *a very ardent but uncorrupted enthusiast* is in some measure vindicated in the course of these pages" (159, emphasis added). The alternating attraction and repulsion of the phrase I have emphasized surfaces whenever Hayley would describe Milton's "impassioned yet disinterested ardour for reformation." Enthusiasm carries the affective intensity of the "uncorrupted enthusiast" right to a dangerous threshold it nevertheless resists crossing. The Miltonic ideal is to sustain a subjective engagement of political matters at the highest possible pitch—to be very, but not too, ardent. It is to burn slowly and self-sufficiently with a hard, gemlike flame.

Even prior to *Conflict of the Faculties*, Kant was considering a similar solution to enthusiasm, though the rapid turns of his own discussion suggest that he could not settle his ambivalence to the same degree of satisfaction achieved by Hayley. In *Critique of Judgment,* the difficulty lies in determining whether enthusiasm is genuinely sublime or only imperfectly so, a challenge to interpretation not unlike the one presented by Samson's strength in *Samson Agonistes*. Kant's uneasy answer is to parcel enthusiasm into legitimate and illegitimate modes of expression. Thus he disables enthusiasm *ethically*, disallowing it as a rational ground of action, only to rehabilitate it *aesthetically*. "The idea of the good conjoined with [strong] affection is called *enthusiasm*," he begins, the bracketed revision already symptomatic of his struggle to determine just how much affection would be too much affection. "This state of mind seems to be sublime" but is not, because "every affection is blind," making it "impossible to exercise a free deliberation . . . Nevertheless, aesthetically, enthusiasm is sublime, because it is a tension of forces produced by ideas."[181] Such ideas act more powerfully on the mind than anything we can observe in actual experience. Enthusiasm describes the combustible space where ideas meet passions, and Kant's dilemma is to determine just the right ratio that will lead passion toward ideas rather than involve ideas in regrettable acts of passion. Lyotard's commentary rightly identifies the tension between pathology and norm on which this passage turns. Although it "is to be condemned ethically as pathological," bordering even on dementia, "the pathos of enthusiasm . . . retains an aesthetic validity."[182] In order to maintain a distinction between enthusiasm and *schwärmerei*, its unacceptable double, the variable to be measured is excess. At what point, precisely, does aesthetic feeling become so excessive as to risk triggering a misguided impulse to act on one's ideas? At what point does an inspired pathos become a reckless pathology? Here one might join Blake in proclaiming, "Enough! or Too much" (*Marriage* 10, E 38). As this final proverb of Hell suggests, it is impossible to limit experience in advance by means of such formal calculations. Who can tell until after the event? Lyotard was convinced that Kant (a member of the devil's party without knowing it?) had inadvertently let loose the enthusiasm he struggled to police through binary definition, creating a dangerous, destabilizing contact zone between intellect and embodied passion, the very terms he wished to keep rigorously apart.

Blake of course did not read Kant on enthusiasm, but by reading Hayley on Milton he would have encountered the irresolution that results from attempting to siphon off aesthetic response from political enthusiasm: "Enthusiasm was the characteristic of his [Milton's] mind; in politics, it made him sometimes too generously credulous, and sometimes too rigorously decisive; but in poetry it exalted him to such a degree of excellence as no man has hitherto surpassed" (208). Like Kant, and like Shaftesbury before Kant, Hayley's strategic answer to "dangerous enthusiasm" is to reduce the danger rather than eliminate the enthusiasm, preserving the latter by channeling it into aesthetic expression.[183] His mild pathologization of Milton's political judgment ("too rigorously decisive") serves not to repress Milton's ardor but to select among its modes of expression. Crucial to Hayley's parallel syntax, however, is the idea that enthusiasm, originary and irreducible, *precedes* its manifestation in either political or aesthetic expression. Hayley prefers the merit of Milton's poetry to the mistake of his political haste, but before his sentence branches in those opposite directions, a single, undifferentiated enthusiasm lies at the root of either outcome. Still stored within the poetry, then—like solar energy within kindling, like a virtue that might rise from under ashes—is the original enthusiasm that once led Milton into revolution. Whether he means to or not, Hayley keeps alive (and attractive) the same urgent energies that he also insists are now "completely dead for all the purposes of hostility" (vii), too confident, perhaps, in his own ability to manage the uncertain measurement of "Enough! or Too much." Modifying an already well-established tendency to divide Milton's poetry from his politics, Hayley's strategy would continue to prevail—Coleridge adopts it wholesale in the *Biographia*.[184] But as Jon Mee has demonstrated, the literary containment of enthusiasm, though a powerful cultural mechanism of lasting influence, was never entirely successful. For while "the dangerous energies of enthusiasm could be regulated into aesthetic form, it was also potentially a treacherous inlet for 'the combustible matters' that 'lie prepared and within ready to take fire at a spark.'"[185]

As we saw at the end of chapter 1, Kant's anxiety over enthusiasm, his desire to validate it only as it belongs to the spectator's attitude, mandates a series of increasingly fine distinctions. "*[G]enuine* enthusiasm," we remember from *Conflict of the Faculties*, "always moves only toward what is ideal." In contradistinction, Kant defines the compromised enthusiasm of the revolutionary actor as "the passionate participation in the good," which cannot "be wholly esteemed, since passion as such deserves censure." Kant's axiomatic separation of enthusiasm into acceptable and unacceptable forms—one for contemplation, the other for action—clearly lands the spectator on the side of political quietism ("revolution . . . is always unjust," he argues).[186] This bias against action will take its most familiar form (at least for students of English literature) in Matthew Arnold, whose essay, "The Function of Criticism at the Present Time" (1864), promotes the virtues of Kantian "disinterestedness" and declares unequivocally: "There is the world of ideas and there is the world of practice." Arnold's topic, like Kant's, is the pathology of revolutionary haste. The "grand error of the French Revolution" was its "*mania* for giving an immediate political and practical application to all these fine ideas of the reason," thereby "quitting the intellectual sphere and *rushing furiously* into the political sphere" (emphasis added).[187] Whatever lingering admiration he retained for the Revolution's achievements (France is "the country in Europe where *the people* is most alive"), Arnold loathed the form of radical, collective action Blake called "fierce rushing" (*America* 14:12, E 56).[188]

But even as it anticipates Arnold, Kant's polarization of thought and act carries within it the slippage that has been this chapter's ongoing subject. His spectator bears the burden of preserving a revolutionary passion for justice, even though it would undermine his integrity were he to act uncritically upon that passion. Kant answers this double obligation, for and against enthusiasm, by relocating it to an experimental space of imaginative or intellectual engagement, neither active nor altogether passive, where the spectators can experience a vicarious dynamism, as if their nonparticipation were somehow itself already in action. These spectators experience "a wishful participation that borders closely on enthusiasm."[189] No doubt Arnold would find even a wishful participation too ardent, too risky, for it continues to harbor an impatience akin to urgency and action.[190] Even if Kant's spectators are "condemned" to what Arnold calls "a slow and obscure work, . . . the only proper work of criticism"—a work that "may perhaps one day make its benefits felt," though perhaps not—they continue to experience the slow time of their nonparticipation as if in fast forward, charged with the affective immediacy and velocity of an action making something happen now.[191] Indeed, Kant argued that the spectator's enthusiasm—*by virtue of doing nothing*—was already a sign, the only genuine sign, of historical progress taking place, for it demonstrated the inspired subject's freedom from a history of predetermined, compulsive actions.

It is tempting (perhaps irresistible) to say that Kant's theory of the critical spectator serves primarily to justify the author's own detached inactivity, soothing an old anxiety that philosophy, even critical philosophy, makes nothing happen. But who could say with certainty whether criticism is ineffective? Yes, critical enthusiasm risks the apotheosis of its own attractive passivity. Borrowing the affect of action without any certainty of consequence, it risks mistaking its own inactivity for the keenest of agencies, and thus it risks reconciling the critic to the world he mistakenly believes he is changing. Insight into the exaggerations of critical agency led de Man to suspect the temptations of enthusiasm and preach instead the Kantian virtue of apatheia. At the same time, by preserving the affect of action, enthusiasm occupies an indeterminate zone between waiting and acting, where latent political desires (the impatience for freedom, the will to revolution) may precipitate unexpectedly, where they may be working even now. Insight into the unpredictable potentiality of critical thought led Lyotard to preach the Kantian virtue of agitation. Because it is "Vigorous most / When most unactive deem'd," criticism will always be susceptible to dueling accounts—one emphasizing the transformative vigor at work beneath its appearance of inactivity, the other emphasizing the absence of demonstrable impact accompanying its inflated claims to significance. Angels virtuous in appearance may actually be devils in disguise, but disruptive devils may also turn out to be more compliant than they wish to admit. For progressive critics after Kant, the uncertainty of party affiliation has become an integral aspect of their labor.

Coda

"[G]reat promises and small performance." So Johnson scolded Milton, who returns from the continent "because his countrymen are contending for their liberty, and, when he reaches the scene of action, vapours away his patriotism in a private boarding-school."[192] More than any other passage in Johnson's *Milton*, this one aroused Hayley's indignation. How dare Johnson render "Milton ridiculous for having preferred the pen to the sword" or "merely for having thought that he might serve his country more essentially by the rare and highly cultivated faculties of his mind, than by the ordinary service of a soldier" (60)? Hayley let Milton speak in his own defense, quoting at length from the *Second Defense of the English People*:

> [T]hough I can claim no personal share [in the just rebellion], yet I can easily defend myself from a charge of timidity or indolence, should any such be alledged against me; for I have avoided the toil and danger of military life only to render my country assistance more useful, and not less to my own peril, exerting a mind never dejected in adversity, never influenced by unworthy terrors of detraction or of death . . . I devoted myself to that kind of service for which I had the greatest ability . . . [so] I might add all the weight I could to the pleas of my country and to this most excellent cause. (60–61)

Participating in the revolution as a writer, Milton understood he might be charged with avoiding the real scene of action, but his confidence in his revolutionary credentials derived in no small part from his certainty that his words were deeds, reaching and influencing an audience. If Blake knew the entire paragraph that Hayley's *Life* quotes in part, perhaps he recalled these additional words: "I seem now to have embarked on a journey and to be surveying from on high far-flung regions and territories across the sea, faces numberless and unknown, sentiments in complete agreement with mine . . . Wherever liberal sentiment, wherever freedom, or wherever magnanimity either prudently conceals or openly proclaims itself, there some in silence approve, others openly cast their votes, some make haste to applaud, others, conquered at last by the truth, acknowledge themselves my captives."[193] Milton wrote for an elite European audience, but by addressing even that small, anonymous public he also anticipated the arrival of Kant's cosmopolitan spectators. He believed that an international audience personally unknown to him would share his enthusiasm for the justice of the English Revolution. Moreover, at least at the time of the *Second Defense*, Milton was sure he shared the historical stage with his fellow revolutionary actors; unlike many of the spectators he addressed, he had made his choice to proclaim rather than prudently conceal his sympathies, identifying himself unequivocally as a revolutionary participant and thus putting himself at risk.

When Blake read this page in Hayley's *Life of Milton*, what would have troubled him more, Johnson's criticism or Milton's proleptic self-defense? Blake certainly included himself among those "men who have *written or acted* in the service of liberty" (emphasis added, 214), as Hayley described Milton's honorable company, just as he certainly believed that "mental fight" served the cause of liberty better than the sword. Writing indefatigably "for Albions sake" (*Jerusalem* 8:17, E 151), he could rebut anyone willing to charge him with indolence—but he could not so easily escape the charge of timidity. Nor could he claim that, like a Samson at the pillars, he had leaned with all his weight into the cause of his country. If, as Wittreich suggests, Blake read *Life of Milton* at Felpham, did he remember his own Miltonic bravado from only a few years earlier? "Duty to [my] <his> country is the first consideration & safety the last" (E 611), he declared in the Watson annotations. There he also insisted on the vast political agency of print, boasting that Paine overthrew "all the armies of Europe with a small pamphlet" (E 617). And there, on the back of the title page, he announced his decision not to publish his own fiery political commentary but rather to burn slowly with an indignation upon which he would never fully act. Now, reading Johnson's attack and Milton's justification of his revolutionary writing, did he worry that he was vaporing away his own patriotic duty in what Flaxman called his "rural retreat"?[194] And earlier, during the first, inflammatory stages of the revolutionary conflict, before the option of participation had been effectively closed by government repression, had he vapored away in Lambeth while some among his countrymen were contending for liberty? In the passage that so infuriated Hayley, Johnson describes the incongruity of Milton removing himself from the scene of revolutionary action that occasioned his return to London: "Finding his rooms too little, he took a house and garden in Aldersgate-street . . . and chose his dwelling at the upper end of a passage, that he might avoid the noise of the street."[195] At the peak moment of political urgency, Blake also adopted a semi-detached position, improving his own privacy with a house and garden removed from the noise of the street. There he too engaged the revolution as a writer and an artist, though he could not quite share in Milton's defense of his public service. In Ackroyd's memorable words, "it is as if [Blake] were another Milton raging in a darkened room" (163).

This hypothetical scene of reading, with its troubled drama of self-recognition, probably never took place, even if Blake did read *Life of Milton* where and when we surmise—for rather than worrying about his nonparticipation, Blake seems to have experienced critical engagement as participation enough, as itself a significant action substantiated by its affective urgency. The *Second Defense* assumes a clear division between revolutionary actor and spectator that was already blurring by the time Blake encountered it. In *Samson Agonistes,* after the defeat of the English Revolution, Milton was already relocating revolutionary agency to the critical reader, investing reading with a dynamism Blake would in turn valorize in "Albion rose." In Hayley's *Life,* Milton would retain all the revolutionary vigor of his earlier self-defense *and still* back away from the intemperate violence that made Samson a figure of such sublime ambivalence, thereby legitimating Blake's own characteristic urgency and hesitation. Blake's "republican passion" would soon become a given feature of the poet's lore: Swinburne accepted that Blake's political commitments were immediately legible to anyone, as if written in bold across his forehead. It did not require an expert phrenologist to observe in Blake's romantic countenance the "[i]nfinite impatience" accompanying his pursuit of "an idea of justice not wholly attainable," for Blake had "the look of one who can do all things but hesitate."[196] Blake's readers still respond to the "unrelenting sense of urgency and crisis" immediately evident in his work.[197] But Blake was also by profession an engraver, and as Hogarth noted, "fine engraving which requires cheifly [*sic*] vast patience care and great practice is scarcely ever attain but by men of a quiet turn of mind."[198] Who could possibly join such urgency to such quiet patience? Hayley himself recognized something of this strange convergence in Blake: "Engraving, of all human Works, appears to require the largest Portion of patience, and [Blake] happily possesses more of that inestimable Virtue, than I ever saw united before to an Imagination so lively & so prolific!"[199]

I want to conclude with another portrait of an impassioned social critic, one drawn with a good deal more acuity than Hayley's representation of Blake but with no less a sense of amazement. Almost two hundred years after Hayley's *Life of Milton* and his failed experiment with Blake, Habermas would eulogize Foucault in terms of his "stubborn energy" and ardent patience. Like many others, Habermas was surprised (though pleased) by Foucault's late turn to Kant, and he chose to commemorate his sometimes rival by discussing Foucault's "Lecture on Kant's *What Is Enlightenment?*"—which in the version he knew also included a commentary on the Kantian spectator. Whether or not he does so deliberately I cannot say, but Habermas begins by remembering Foucault as if he instantiated that very spectator. Habermas confesses to being baffled by Foucault, who managed to participate in the present historical moment with an enthusiasm that somehow also left him detached and uninvolved. The portrait he draws is by no means a perfect match for Blake, especially in terms of his emphasis on the historian's aspiration to objectivity, but the merger of urgency and patience that he observes in Foucault indicates an intellectual type we can recognize clearly enough in Blake, but probably not before.

> And yet in him the stoic attitude of keeping an overly precise distance, the attitude of the observer obsessed with objectivity, was peculiarly entwined with the opposite element of passionate, self-consuming participation in the contemporary relevance of the historical moment. I met Foucault only in 1983, and perhaps I did not understand him well. I can only relate what impressed me: the tension, one that eludes familiar categories, between the almost serene scientific reserve of the scholar striving for objectivity on the one hand, and the political vitality of the vulnerable, subjectively excitable, morally sensitive intellectual on the other.[200]

Borrowing Hayley's language for Milton, perhaps we could call Foucault a "very ardent but uncorrupted enthusiast," one who understood the critical task as (in his own words) "a patient labor giving form to our impatience for liberty."[201]

A Passion for Blake

Introduction: Critique of Emotional Intelligence

Barnett and Ratner . . . proposed a new word for what we do when we think-feel: "cogmotion," a term better able than words currently in use to represent "the interactive and inseparable nature of cognition and emotion."

—William M. Reddy, *The Navigation of Feeling*

The Eastern Gate, fourfold: terrible & deadly its ornaments:
Taking their forms from the Wheels of Albions sons; as cogs
Are formd in a wheel, to fit the cogs of the adverse wheel.

—*Jerusalem* 13:12–14, E 156

"Cogmotion": a neologism so awkward one would wish to avoid it, were it not irresistible to place it alongside Blake's image of cogs in motion, and force applied in one direction to move a wheel in another. Invented words are meant to signal the rusty inadequacy of an established lexicon, and "cogmotion" is no exception. Douglas Barnett and Hillary Ratner are child development scholars who hope to "move [their] field forward" by introducing a new term.[1] These authors, however, have managed to rename something so widely accepted today that few would seriously challenge it. "Emotional intelligence" is a better-known term for two current trends that underwrite what amounts to a new age of sensibility: the widespread rejection of dualism (*Descartes' Error,* according to the title of a popular book) and the corresponding turn to the affects as a cognitive resource necessary to agency while remaining irreducible to either mind or body.[2] We are today swept along by a sentimental revival so deep and so wide that both humanists and post-humanists, in fields as diverse as anthropology, philosophy, neuroscience, economics, and literature, agree: without emotions we could neither acquire new knowledge nor act upon it. Mainstream liberals and radical materialists meet now over terms like "rational passion" or "the embodied mind,"[3] even if they can't agree whether the hybrid tilts right or left. Today, when a philosopher explains that "[r]eason . . . becomes ever more corporeal; . . . the body becomes increasingly intellectual. Affect and knowledge . . . recompose themselves in the body and in opposition to all transcendental divisions," it is hard to know whether that philosopher might be Martha Nussbaum or Antonio Negri.[4] Emotional intelligence invites strange traveling companions.

Let's begin by considering some representative pairings from the current era of emotion studies, starting with the cover designs of two books, William M. Reddy's *The Navigation of Feeling* and Eve Kosofsky Sedgwick's *Touching Feeling* (figure II I.1). Every detail of Sedgwick's stagy cover—its tactile emphasis, its disturbance of subject-object boundaries, even the straddling of its title and subtitle across the borderlines of design—works to disrupt the balanced subject position that Reddy's visual confidence would maintain with equanimity. As Reddy's title indicates, "feeling" is both the navigating subject and the object being navigated, forming a circuit of lucid agency. Like the deep, soothing green that harmonizes his cover tonally, matching painting to background, "feeling" joins the object and the framework of analysis within a single, coherent field, confirming the mind's capacity to form meaningful frames in the first place. Indeed, one of the book's major arguments is that the disaggregated subject of postmodernity can be reconciled with a cogent account of intellectual agency. Supported by the confident language of social science (he is an anthropologist), Reddy's extraordinary ambition is to map a comprehensive theory of emotion by systematically defining key terms, and thus to explain not only the historical variability of emotion but also the nature of historical change enabled by emotion. With classical ruins on the left delicately balancing mercantile ships to the right, the cover's eighteenth-century *Italian Harbor Scene* holds the ancient past and the early modern present together, reassuring us of our ability to make sense of the transition from past to present. Whatever the dynamic, history-making work of feeling, it takes off, like ships in a painting, from the safe harbor of intelligibility.

Sedgwick's cover is less panoramic and more disorienting. Here the scene of feeling (or is it touching?) swells so emphatically that it upends any comfortable balance between print and image, squeezing the words that would frame the scene into upper and lower margins. Together, the neither-nouns-nor-verbs of Sedgwick's title (*Touching Feeling*) and the mere parataxis of her subtitle (*Affect, Pedagogy, Performativity*) indicate the strain language must undergo to leave abstraction behind and to approach embodied experience. Nondualistic thought, she writes in her introduction, is "likeliest to occur near the boundary of what a writer can't figure out to say readily."[5] In this border zone, words turn porous; "touching" and "feeling" dissolve into one another. Indeterminacy is an attribute of language and perception both, for "the sense of touch makes nonsense out of any dualistic understanding of agency and passivity" (14). Ultimately, the relational instability actively solicited by this cover targets the reader too; it means to put her autonomy at risk: "For me, to experience a subject-object distance from this image is no more plausible than to envision such a relation between ['outsider artist' Joan] Scott and her work" (22). The irrelevance of subject-object boundaries *within* the image overtakes the viewer *of* the image. If Reddy's design, then, is all about securing cogent frameworks (folding emotion into the work of intelligence), Sedgwick's is all about collapsing them (dissolving intelligence into the work of emotion). Each author disavows the stale Cartesian dualism, but Sedgwick's disavowal leads her to explore the effects of nonsense, while Reddy's would revise our understanding of what it means to make sense, first of all by turning feeling into the very instrument of sense-making (its sextant, as it were).

No wonder, then, that neither work mentions the other, although they were published only two years apart, by authors who at the time were colleagues at the same university (Duke). Yet, despite their obvious differences, these projects share a common ground; they each identify a mutually constitutive relationship between emotion and (broadly speaking) "criticism." Both authors explore the role "critical thinking" plays in enabling change—personal, social, and historical; both consider affect a necessary condition of this agency; both understand the work of affect to involve a particular kind of performativity, specifically the capacity of feeling to inflect and transform linguistic performance. For all their apparent incompatibility, Reddy sets out to explain conceptually what Sedgwick tries to make happen rhetorically. He defines his key term—"emotional liberty"—as "the freedom to change goals in response to bewildering, ambivalent thought activations that exceed the capacity of attention and challenge the reign of high-level goals currently guiding emotional management."[6] Such arid words may choke on their own performative contradiction, but they strive to articulate the same object of desire conveyed by Sedgwick's brilliant experiments with style: the agency born of emotional intelligence. For these authors, emotion loosens the constraints on subjectivity, allowing it to think otherwise and change direction. It is the very medium of critical agency.

Let's turn to a second pair of emotion theorists, whose striking differences again mask a shared, underlying investment in the feelings they each wish to describe more accurately. According to Philip Fisher, the "vehement passions" provide "the most potent experience of our own individual reality"; in the subjective immediacy of fear, rage, or grief we experience the unified state of undistracted intensity he calls "thoroughness."[7] In such states, we are ourselves all the way down. Yet according to Rei Terada, strong emotion evacuates the self and even "requires the

Figure II I.1 (left) Cover, William Reddy, *The Navigation of Feeling: A Framework for the History of Emotions* (2001). By permission of Cambridge University Press (*right*) Cover, Eve Kosofsky Sedgwick, *Touching Feeling: Affect, Pedagogy, Performativity* (2003). By permission of Duke University Press and photographer Leon Borensztein

death of the subject": "we feel not to the extent that experience seems immediate, but to the extent that it doesn't."[8] Because Fisher's passions are affective nodes of sudden, concentrated unity, they stand "at the farthest remove from irony . . . and all forms of double-consciousness" (44); they tell us we are not really the dual, self-monitoring, prudential subjects of ordinary experience. Terada's emotions, on the other hand, *are* a form of double-consciousness; they are constituted by the persis-

tent experience of "self-difference within cognition" (3). They tell us that, whatever we are, we are not subjects at all.

We could continue back and forth in this way, but doing so would overlook a motivating principle underlying each of these approaches. Fisher and Terada value emotion for its revelatory power, for its agency in disclosing what ordinarily remains hidden from experience, though in each case emotion reveals something antithetical about subjectivity. For both of them, in other words, emotion serves what we might call a pedagogical function; it startles the subject with unexpected knowledge (or, antithetically, with nonknowledge). Emotion marks the transition from familiar, habitual thought to critical thought, the moment when something new enters into experience, interrupts routine, and makes itself known—or at least makes known the limits of the settled, ruling concepts it exceeds. As we saw earlier, the model for Fisher's "vehement passions" is wonder.[9] Although Terada might prefer the less uplifting term "aporia," and though her account of feeling involves a higher ratio of struggle to pleasure, her assertion that "the first emotion *is* cognitive difficulty" accords well with Fisher's argument, borrowed from Descartes, that "wonder [is] the first of the passions" because it "makes learning possible" (1). The kind of learning enabled by emotion involves the unlearning of comfort: emotions defamiliarize. Affect—or the *Upheavals of Thought,* as Nussbaum's title puts it—would disrupt cognitive inertia and rewrite the horizon line of the knowable Blake designated by the name Urizen. Blake tells us what happens to "[t]he man who never alters his opinion" ("like standing water, [he] breeds reptiles of the mind") (*Marriage* 19, E 42). Theories of emotional intelligence would tell us how opinions get altered.

In our new age of sensibility, we cannot agree on what emotion is (witness the terminological disputes over emotions, passions, feelings, affects, moods, and desires featured in every discussion of the topic), but we seem able to agree that emotion enables the cognitive rubbing-against-the-grain required for critical thought.[10] Emotion would be the cog of the cognitive machine, supplying the adverse pressure necessary to move an otherwise stationary cognitive wheel.[11] Although cognitive theorists like Reddy tell us that emotional intelligence is a critical resource available to all activities—reorienting attention and opening onto the possibility of "thinking otherwise" in any circumstance—it also bears special significance for the practice of literary criticism. It is no accident that three of the four writers we have featured thus far began their venturesome careers as literary critics, while another mentioned in passing (Nussbaum) relies heavily on the evidence of literature to support her own philosophy of emotion. Fisher writes, "In wonder we notice against the background of a lawful and familiar world something that strikes us by its novelty"; later he adds, "we do not choose the objects we end up thinking about. Something, as we put it, catches our attention." Describing emotion, he is also describing the redistribution of attention involved in reading, what we might call the affective precondition of literary criticism, without which interpretation could only repeat the same dull round of inherited frameworks for generating meaning.[12] Fisher's "wonder" and Terada's "cognitive difficulty" have deep roots in eighteenth-century aesthetics, but their proximate models are the events of noticing that de Man simply called "reading texts closely as texts." Honoring the Harvard professors who taught him how to expand his field of attention, de Man recalled how they would "start out from the bafflement that such singular turns of tone, phrase, and figure were bound to produce in readers attentive enough to notice them and honest enough not to hide their non-understanding behind the screen of received ideas."[13] Felt but not understood, poised at the juncture between textual singularities and interpretive norms, "bafflement" is criticism's way of recognizing the limitless redistribution of attention that a single text can provoke.

At the same time, emotional intelligence also helps explain why the literary objects critics end up thinking about, the ones that catch their attention, are not confined to the striking novelties of tone, phrase, and figure within potentially inexhaustible single works (formerly the "classics"). When readers began to complain that deconstruction merely propped up the canon it made such a show of treating irreverently, they were seeking to widen the discursive field within which attention might wander and thus surprise itself with the discovery (or rediscovery) of neglected bodies of work, altering large contours of literary history in the process. The relevant example here is the collective scholarly attention recently directed toward eighteenth- and nineteenth-century sentimental literatures, a shift in literary historical noticing roughly coincident with the death of de Man and the professionalization of feminist criticism. In this revival of interest, one observes the powerfully reciprocal relation between emotion and criticism that currently prevails, guiding what we read and how. Consider a representative case: the recovery project Jerome McGann undertakes in *The Poetics of Sensibility*. McGann argues that reading earlier sentimental literature (as opposed to "pre-reading" it or judging it dismissively in advance) requires an against-the-grain intervention that would rescue such texts from the modernist judgment ("embarrassment") that relegated them to obscurity.[14] At the same time, the earlier literature (as McGann sees it) was enacting a paradigm shift of its own. It introduced "a momentous cultural shift," a "revolution," whose "new thoughts . . . assume that no human action of any consequence is possible—including 'mental' action—that is not led and driven by feeling, affect, emotion." By returning to the poetics of sensibility, scholarship discovers for our era the critical work of emotional intelligence that an earlier era—Blake's—was in the process of discovering for itself. Moreover, changes in what we read (canon reform) cannot be divorced from changes in how we read: "Poetry . . . forces one to attend to 'the word as such.' It foregrounds the physique of lexical and grammatical fields . . . Consequently, studying the poetries of sensibility and sentiment gives one a specially clear view of how a language of affective meanings—of how language *as* affective thought—functions." McGann's hope is that by returning attention to the forgotten poetry of feeling we will in turn revive the minutely attentive, historically informed reading skills he feels we have recently lost. Remarkably, this critical project on sensibility is so thoroughly informed *by* sensibility that feeling becomes virtually synonymous with the practice of criticism itself, with its origins and ends, its objects and its methods. A single word ("sensibility") characterizes three mutually constitutive elements: the critical act (the capacity to think otherwise—minutely, with feeling, against modernist bias); the neglected literature that comes into focus when one thinks critically in this way; and, finally, the materialist medium that makes these transformations possible, the domain of (dare we say) "cogmotion" that McGann, with his own version of anti-Cartesianism, refers to as "language as affective thought."[15]

Eventually, and in chapter 5 most directly, I will return to the argument I first broached in this book's introduction—that this kind of faith in the transformative potential of affect-driven reading has become a perennial feature of modern critical sensibility. The extent to which criticism and emotion have become indispensable to each other is especially evident in studies of Romanticism (and Blake studies in particular), but it also characterizes a wide and various swath of contemporary criticism. For now, however, I want to frame this inquiry in terms of a general question about the relation between emotion and criticism, one that shadows our own investment in emotional intelligence just as it shadowed the eighteenth-century culture of sensibility. If "[f]rom the very beginning of life feelings are worked on, and passions shaped, by a symbolic order," as Geoffrey Hartman puts it, then how can one know when the emotional intelligence enacted by criticism successfully cuts against the grain of established intelligence?[16] That is, how can one distinguish the emotions that genuinely startle because they access something new from those that merely result from training and therefore confirm the status quo? How can one tell agitation from conditioned response? Even worse, what if agitation *is* a conditioned response? "The history of the study of feelings," writes Adela Pinch, "consists of a constant oscillation between recognizing feeling as form, and seeing feeling as the animation of form."[17] "Feeling," in other words, names both the formal mechanisms of social routine (including linguistic convention) *and* the innovative pulse that would animate the machine, alter it, make it live. In her analysis of the Preface to *Lyrical Ballads* and its supplements, Barbara Johnson identifies Wordsworth's inability to differentiate between passion and mechanism as "the problem in any modern theory of poetic language": "the problem of articulating authenticity with conventionality."[18] Blake's attempt to reimagine the human form entangles him in a similar problem. Albion's "machines are woven with his life," we learn in *Jerusalem* (40:25, E 188); the phrase suggests that the mechanical and the animate are from the start so thoroughly integrated (interwoven) that it would be naïve to deplore the mechanical as if it were simply the imposition of industrial forms on some a priori form of human life. In such circumstances, when it becomes difficult to distinguish the influences that deaden from those that enliven, what *is* an emotion?

The oscillation described by Pinch and Johnson raises a particular concern for literary criticism: What if the disturbing or joyful bafflement readers associate with a freedom from convention takes its shape within a horizon of expectations defined by received ideas? Recent advocates of formalism and aesthetics generally pin their theories of critical agency on the moment when the singularity of a text startles the reader into a response of unfamiliar affect (Fisher's "wonder," Terada's "cognitive difficulty," or, to add another, Charles Altieri's "self-reflexive affective intensities"),[19] but that moment may itself arrive only for readers who value being startled in this way, readers trained (mostly in the classroom) by professionals whose own reading practices, as John Guillory points out, are the product of highly specific disciplinary constraints.[20] The emotional intelligence attributed to criticism today thus recalls an old paradox of "aesthetic judgment": although aesthetic experience must be singular and therefore nonprescriptive, it is also the result of careful, disciplined preparation. Kant acknowledged that the sublime, for all its disruptive power, requires more cultural preparation than the beautiful, though he tried to dismiss any implication that the sublime is "therefore first generated by culture and so to speak introduced into society merely as a matter of convention."[21] Professional criticism also disseminates techniques for generating and recognizing surprise, but for those who take the time to master its sophisticated protocols, it may also run the risk of routinizing wonder, *producing* estrangement in forms that in fact would surprise no one. When we read the title given by a poet to a recent volume of essays, *Feeling as a Foreign Language: The Good Strangeness of Poetry,* we can't help but worry that this "strangeness" might be too "good" to be true, and that the *unheimlich* has been domesticated to the point where defamiliarization has itself become all too programmatic.[22]

Given the slippage between mechanism and feeling, the promise of emotional intelligence depends on the idea that the double life of emotion involves a productive tension: *within* emotion there must be a built-in critical capacity to detect the rub of innovation against convention. If it is to inform agency meaningfully, emotion must be able to perform a kind of autocriticism, either because an unpredictable emotion can unsettle the assumptions governing a more comfortable one, or because—within a single, self-conflicted emotion—familiar elements can give way to a beneficial disturbance. "Emotional regimes" can be altered, Reddy proposes, not because they succumb to rational analysis from above, but because they succumb to the experimental pressure of other emotions.[23] One version of this idea—not Blake's—recurs often among those cognitive theorists for whom the autocritical potential of emotion serves to reinforce the idea of an Enlightenment subject still more or less capable of self-governance and self-transformation. Although emotions can become entangled in habitual beliefs and practices, they also "evaluate, assess, or appraise" and can therefore outsmart their own passive tendency to repeat.[24] Writes Nussbaum, "Indeed, a great advantage of a cognitive/

evaluative view of emotion is that it shows us where societies and individuals have the freedom to make improvements. If we recognize the element of evaluation *in the emotions,* we also see that they can themselves be *evaluated*—and in some ways altered, if they fail to survive criticism . . . [T]hey are intelligent pieces of human normative activity, of the sort that can in principle, within certain limits, be changed by more intelligent human activity."[25] For Nussbaum, self-adjusting emotions set the subject on a path of progressive development; their dynamic intelligence provides the agency necessary to make Enlightenment go. We see something similar in Jerome Neu's recent essay, "Emotions and Freedom," where the interplay of active and passive emotions becomes the testing ground for subjects who learn to distinguish contingency from necessity and thereby incrementally increase their sphere of freedom, in an experimental practice akin to Foucault's "ontology of the self." Neu happens to quote Blake in support of his thesis: "A Tear is an Intellectual Thing."[26] Not surprisingly, emotions this intelligent have prompted an inevitable backlash. Recent critics of the cognitive theory have reminded us of the importance of autonomic "primitive emotions" (the "fear circuit," for instance), returning with modifications to the physiological emphasis of the James-Lange thesis. Even they, however, accept that more "discriminating" emotions modify the primitive ones in a process that maintains the progressive benefits of judgment and agency.[27] The new subject of emotion, in other words, is still built on the old Enlightenment model, only better, we're told, this time able to perform the progressive work that Reason, as it turns out, could not manage alone. The tendency to counterpose emotion to inadequate Enlightenment dualisms, only to then assimilate it into the instrumental resources of an enlightened subject, is a strategy Blake himself would have recognized and resisted—though, as we will see, he has his own version of autocritical emotion.[28]

As my preliminary choice of examples indicates, one of my claims is that our current investment in emotional intelligence can be traced through a series of overlapping circles that starts with studies of Romanticism, widens to the disciplinary practices of literary criticism, and ultimately includes a broad cultural tendency to emphasize the transformative agency of emotion, particularly as it informs acts of reading and interpretation. Another claim is that the question of emotional intelligence—and especially its capacity for autocriticism—was already being taken up by Blake. If, as we saw in the previous chapter, Blake sought to transfer the claims of political action to the critical reader's feeling of agency, he also understood that feeling must be able to turn upon itself, that the uncritical emotions that underwrite the norms of social and political life must be subject to the critical emotions mobilized by reading—and, perhaps even more importantly, that one must be able to differentiate between critical and uncritical emotions.

Both the promise and the problems of emotional intelligence shape Blake's work. To pursue this idea, we will examine a poem that has received surprisingly little attention given its prominent position as the last entry in most versions of Blake's *Songs of Innocence*: "On Anothers Sorrow." Perhaps, to borrow McGann's term, we have tended to "pre-read" this song, seeing it only in terms of the innocence it concludes and the experience it anticipates. "On Another's Sorrow" is a poem about a single emotion—compassion—but because it is a critique of emotional intelligence that nevertheless retains a faith in emotional intelligence, it also provides a template for reading the other passions that preoccupy Blake's work. The poem helps explain why "pity," like so many of Blake's other emotion terms (especially "wrath," but even those that would seem unequivocally positive, such as "joy"), is alternately an object of suspicion and desire. In short, it helps us understand how a passion works *in* Blake—while also indicating the stakes of our own passion *for* Blake.

"Behold Pitying"

Before pausing at length with "On Anothers Sorrow," I want briefly to sketch a broader approach to "pity" in Blake. Because Blake could be blunt in his social analysis—claiming, for instance, that "pity" has "become a trade . . . / That men get rich by" (*America* 11:10–11, E 55), or that "Pity would be no more, / If we did not make somebody Poor" ("The Human Abstract" 1–2, E 27)—it would be easy but misleading to conclude that he aims merely to demystify compassion, as if to demonstrate that the social manipulation of emotion may be brought to the light of critical understanding and corrected. Although Blake supplies pity with a complicated history of construction, naming, and gendering, especially in *The Book of Urizen,* prompting us to expose its apparent spontaneity to genealogical analysis, he does not cynically discredit the feeling as if it amounted to nothing more than a ruse society performs on its members in order to tie them to a particular distribution of privileges. And yet, simply to undertake a critique of compassion—then or now—lays one open to the charge of destructive cynicism. Lauren Berlant, the editor of a recent volume on the topic, finds herself on the defensive from the outset: "Some readers might feel that to think about compassion as a social and aesthetic technology of belonging and not an organic emotion is to demean its authenticity and its centrality to social life . . . But scholarly critique and investigation do not necessarily or even usually entail nullifying the value of an affirmative phrase or relation of affinity. It is more likely that a project of critique seeks not to destroy its object but to explain the dynamics of its optimism and exclusions."[29]

We can start with a scene in which Blake dramatizes Berlant's fears precisely.

The Bard's Song in *Milton* presents a critique of sentimental poetry in allegorical form, narrating the disastrous effects of Satan (Hayley) "Driving the Harrow in Pitys paths" (12:28, E 106). The swift, negative reaction to the Bard's criticism suggests the danger of questioning an emotion understood to be organic, necessary, and affirmative. Compassion is so revered that *any* critique of it will offend certain readers: "many condemn'd the high tone'd Song / Saying Pity and Love are too venerable for the imputation / Of Guilt" (13:47–49, E 107). Thus the audience's response reduces the debate over compassion to a stark choice: either one shelters the emotion from critique or risks losing it altogether to suspicion. Blake charts another path. That Milton himself is "mov'd" to his "unexampled deed" (2:21, E 96) by the very song others consider an assault on the foundation of benevolent feeling suggests that the critique of an emotion does not necessarily entail the cold, analytical evacuation of emotion. Milton acts on the compassion newly aroused in him by a critique of compassion; the redemptive action of this brief epic begins with critical feeling.

If it is wrong to confuse Blake's critique of emotion with an opposition to emotion altogether, it is equally mistaken to suppose that Blake's approach is simply a matter of sifting the good pity (spontaneous and benevolent) from the bad (calculating and hypocritical), though again, there is evidence for such an argument. In *The Book of Urizen*, "pity" first appears (along with "compassion") in Urizen's catalogue of founding principles: "Laws of peace, of love, of unity: / Of pity, compassion, forgiveness" (4:34–35, E 72). Given that Urizen is responsible for instituting the "Self-closd" (3:3, E 70) subject, the private individual as isolated, bounded unit, the inclusion of pity among these laws suggests that it serves the needs of a social order founded on self-interest and self-preservation. At the same time, by echoing Gnostic parodies of Genesis and of a self-asserting, imposter god, *The Book of Urizen* leaves open the possibility that Urizen has appropriated pity and in the process displaced a prior, more authentic form of emotional energy. That Blake's representations of pity often take diametrically opposite forms might lead us to conclude that his work amounts to a giant taxonomy of pre- and postlapsarian feeling. If (bad) "pity divides the soul" (*Urizen* 13:53, E 77; *Milton* 8:19, E 102), then (good) "Pity must join together those whom wrath has torn in sunder" (*Jerusalem* 7:62, E 150). Reading "pity" would be a matter of sorting cases.[30] Nothing, however, could be further from the demands placed on the reader by Blake's work, where each occurrence of "pity" is ghosted by its others, making it impossible to disentangle authentic from programmatic expressions of the emotion. We can state the case even more emphatically: to experience "pity" *is* to be caught up in that mesh. Because Albion's "machines are woven with his life," there is no inherently vital experience of emotion that one can oppose to mechanical versions, something Jerusalem (the character) indicates in a speech that places her visions of pity and love in apposition with the mills of delusion: "I am deluded by the turning mills. / And by these visions of pity & love" (60:63–64, E 211).

Consider two brief examples from opposite ends of Blake's career. Early on, in a highly formulaic manuscript fragment not included in *Poetical Sketches*, Blake describes "Sympathy" as an automatic (even automatonic) response at once deeply embodied in the intimacy of blood and nerves *and* expropriated in the type of personification that Wordsworth would soon deplore as the worst kind of artifice: "Woe cried the muse tears Started at the Sound. Grief perch't upon my brow and thought Embracd Her. What does this mean I cried . . . why. Grief dost thou accost me. The Muse then Struck her Deepest string & Sympathy Came forth. She Spred her awful Wings. & gave me up. my Nerves with trembling Curdle all my blood. & ev'ry piece of flesh doth Cry out Woe" (E 448). As the speaker's flesh echoes the call of the Muse ("Woe cried the muse . . . & ev'ry piece of flesh doth Cry out Woe"), Blake slyly recalls the repetition and tedium of lyric emotion he describes in another poem, "To the Muses," one of his published sketches: "The languid strings do scarcely move! / The sound is forc'd, the notes are few!" (E 417).[31] Even at this earliest moment, it would be impossible to tell whether the "Sympathy" brought forth by music in this fragment is meant to reanimate or merely impersonate the muses' dead mechanisms. After all, the speaker finds himself ventriloquized by a stale language that would have been familiar to readers almost a century earlier, as in this sermon from 1708: "We are all Counterparts one of another: The Instruments *tun'd* Unison: the doleful Cry of one in extreme Distress, makes the Strings to tremble at our very Hearts."[32]

Late in his career, midway through the first chapter of *Jerusalem,* just before he surveys Golgonooza for the first time, Blake describes a vision of Zion in London, with Paddington "Becoming a building of pity and compassion." Reminiscent of George Herbert's "The Church-floore," the materials of this redemptive architecture consist of human feelings and virtues ("The stones are pity, and the bricks, well wrought affections"), all bound by "The mortar & cement of the work, *tears of honesty*" (emphasis added).[33] Free from deceptive manipulation, from Urizen's "hypocritical pity,"[34] these honest tears should hold the structure together and bind the community in sympathy ("Pity must join together"), but when they are examined with unflinching honesty, with teary eyes wide open, so to speak, they also signify "tears" in the social fabric woven by sympathy ("pity divides the soul"). That is, they also represent the persistence of a divisive self-interest so deeply conditioned that it remains embedded even in the ego's feelings of selflessness. The same "tears" join and rend. Another emotion term, similarly riven, resounds through the passage like a musical accent:

The stones are pity, and the bricks, well *wrought* affections . . .

And the screws & iron braces, are well *wrought* blandishments . . .

The curtains, woven tears & sighs, *wrought* into lovely forms

For comfort . . .   (12:30–40, E 155–156, emphasis added)

At one and the same moment, "wrought" describes a state of excessive, unmeasured emotion (to be worked up in passion), and a piece of artifice, a product of techne, the end result of having been worked over.[35]

If the undecidability of emotion in Blake is enacted, not resolved, by reading, then what exactly does he expect us to do with "pity"? Perhaps we can take our cue from a single, isolated proof of the frontispiece to *Jerusalem* (figure II I.2), a variant that incorporates across its top, among other additions, seven lines that Blake never included in any printing of the book. As these lines descend they begin to separate onto either side of the arched, gothic doorway Los enters, and, for reasons unknown, Blake deleted almost all of the left half of the final line. Restoring the deleted original in brackets, Erdman conjectures that the line should read: "O [Albion behold Pitying] behold the Vision of Albion" (E 809).[36] For the moment, let's assume the phrase is addressed to the reader rather than to Albion (it allows for both possibilities) and that its simplest form can be reduced to a two-word imperative: "behold Pitying." Is "Pitying" then an object of perception, something the reader must submit to scrutiny, as if from a distance—or is it adverbial, invoking the interior emotion that ought to accompany the act of reading, infusing perception with feeling? Should the reader observe pitying (as an object, studying it like a cultural critic) or observe *while* pitying? Although we cannot know with certainty whether Erdman's rendition of the deleted phrase is correct, it seems to concentrate the strange exigency of autocritical emotion that I believe is central to Blake: one must feel and critique feeling simultaneously—or, to turn the phrase around, one must critique feeling and continue to feel *something* nonetheless.[37] The reader must uphold both ends of a difficult injunction: feeling must come neither before critique (as the unreflective, compulsive experience that criticism should analyze and overcome) nor after critique (as a supplement that would humanize the science of criticism), but as a crucial component *of* critique itself.

Perhaps it is useful to think of Blake's representation of emotion in terms of the "internal distantiation" Louis Althusser identified as the peculiar work "authentic art" performs on the ideology that conditions it, or in terms of what Fredric Jameson describes as the "essential movement of all dialectical criticism": "to reconcile the inner and the outer, the intrinsic and the extrinsic, the existential and the historical, to allow us to feel our way within a single determinate form or moment of history at the same time that we stand outside of it, in judgment on it as well."[38]

Figure II I.2 Jerusalem: The Emanation of the Giant Albion, frontispiece, single proof. © *Fitzwilliam Museum, Cambridge*, The Keynes Family Trust, on deposit at The Fitzwilliam Museum, Cambridge

Blake anticipates such ideas in *Jerusalem* when Los opens his furnaces (his mode of aesthetic production) for viewing, and his spectre "saw from the ou[t]side what he before saw & felt from within" (8:25, E 151). History on the inside (what it feels like to be a historical subject) becomes partially available to Los's perception, providing a glimpse not just of what one sees and feels but *how*—as if the dual aspect of experience (inside/outside, subjective/objective, personal/historical) could itself be witnessed. Writes Althusser,

I believe that the peculiarity of art is to "make us see" . . . , "make us perceive," "make us feel" something which *alludes* to reality . . . What art makes us *see*, and therefore gives to us in the form of *'seeing,' 'perceiving,'* and *'feeling'* (which is not the form of *knowing*), is the *ideology* from which it is born, in which it bathes, from which it detaches itself as art, and to which it *alludes* . . . Balzac and Solzhenitsyn give us a 'view' of the ideology to which their work alludes and with which it is constantly fed, a view which presupposes a *retreat*, an *internal distantiation* from the very ideology from which their novels emerged. They make us 'perceive' (but not know) in some sense *from the inside*, by an *internal distance*, the very ideology in which they are held.[39]

But rather than accepting that art (seeing, perceiving, and feeling) and science (knowing) are "quite different ways" of presenting the same object, and rather than accepting that art presents nonconceptual versions of what critical science can (must) do better, Blake's work suggests that the peculiar agency of criticism involves a kind of knowledge accessed by and indistinguishable from affect.

In Blake, then, criticism works in and on feeling. A poem's critical labor cannot be detached from its affective performance. The poem not only solicits the very emotion it makes the object of critique (inviting the reader to feel compassion, for instance—to behold pitying *while* pitying), but it also solicits a countervailing affect, an agitation specific to the act of critical thought. Criticism is the friction between affective registers, the jostling of one feeling by another, in which the reader of a poem on pity, say, experiences compassion and something more or less. Let's call this friction "adverse emotion," to remind us of cogs turning wheels by means of contrary forces.[40] Articulate and inarticulate at the same time, the adverse emotion of a pity poem gestures not toward abstract knowledge but toward feeling otherwise, toward an enlarged capacity for social relationship that pity, as it exists in its normative form, neutralizes as well as obscures. There is a moment, again in *Jerusalem*, that can help illustrate this possibility. In this scene, Blake's eternals discuss the nature of antinomian collective life, "as they labour'd at the furrow" (55:48, E 205). Because their conversation is indistinguishable from their agricultural labors and from the poet's verse labors (*versus*: furrow), it prepares the ground for the future. Its agency turns on an implicit critique of compassion, which the eternals claim would be unnecessary in a world without social suffering. "It is better to prevent misery than to release from misery" (55:49, E 205), they say, in a line resembling the ones we have already quoted from "The Human Abstract": "Pity would be no more, / If we did not make somebody Poor." Blake concludes this part of the conversation by telling us, "They Plow'd in tears"; at the end of the conversation's next round, he adds, "So cried they at the Plow" (55:54, 67, E 205), where "cried" might refer either to emphatic speech or inarticulate weeping. As they plow in tears, these eternals enact an autocritical structure of feeling. They act with feeling (plowing while crying), but they also act upon feeling (plowing tears into the ground), turning "tears" into an object of their critical action, problematizing them, as Foucault would say, by stepping back from what they do habitually in order to make the habitual an object of reflection. Given Blake's recurring association between the farmer's plow and the engraver's burin, this work of/on feeling would also have to include engraving, transforming an emotional state by representing it, displaying the infinite that was hid, its capacity to be otherwise. To plow in tears is to engrave "tears," to plow these marks into this copper plate, so that readers may eventually traverse the lines of poetry as so many furrows in a textual field. Like the eternals, these readers may begin to see from the outside what they feel at the same time within. If one could feel and critique feeling simultaneously, if one could experience pity rubbing against the critical feeling of reading pity—if one could experience the enmeshed cogs of this "adverse emotion"—then one's current tears might become the seeds of an affect as yet unimaginable. That is the form I believe the promise of emotional intelligence takes in Blake's work.

Let's conclude this introduction by returning to Milton, the epic hero moved to redeem his errors by another Bard's critique of emotion. How should we describe the emotional state of a character who, before he reaches Blake's left foot, enters the world of heroic action by falling through the heart? "Thus Milton fell thro Albions heart, travelling outside of Humanity" (20:41, E 114). Milton falls *into* the heart, into the fallen medium of emotion, but he also falls *through* the heart toward something else. Paradoxically, the heart supplies Milton with the agency he needs to experience the heart as a vortex, a transitional portal between old and new affects. The heart provides the autocritical means to pass beyond itself, not toward a knowledge that overcomes the passions but toward a feeling beyond (existing) feeling, or—to borrow the Derridean phrase "x without x"[41]—toward a feeling without feeling. Blake understood that emotion could serve an instrumental function in his culture, even when it presented itself as spontaneous benevolence. But he was too much a creature of the first age of sensibility—too much a part of the momentum that would lead the young Marx and Engels to declare in the Preface to *The German Ideology*, "Let us revolt against the rule of thoughts"[42]—to believe that merely rational analysis could solve the social problems he grouped together as "mind forg'd manacles." If the answer to ideology was criticism, that answer came to Blake by way of falling through the emotions, not abandoning them.

CHAPTER THREE

"On Anothers Sorrow"

We have *brave* as well as *tender* emotions. The latter, if they reach
the level of an affect, are good for nothing at all; the tendency toward
them is called *oversensitivity*. A sympathetic pain that will not let
itself be consoled . . . proves and constitutes a tenderhearted but at
the same time weak soul.

—Immanuel Kant, *Critique of Judgment*

Suffering remains foreign to knowledge; though knowledge can
subordinate it conceptually and provide means for its amelioration,
knowledge can scarcely express it through its own means of experience without becoming irrational.

—Theodor Adorno, *Aesthetic Theory*

God . . . plants [suffering] in the soul as something irreducible, a foreign body, impossible to digest, and constrains one to think about it.
The thought of suffering is not of a discursive kind. The mind comes
slap up against physical suffering, affliction, like a fly against a pane
of glass, without being able to make the slightest progress or discover
anything new, and yet unable to prevent itself from returning to the
attack . . . Suffering has no significance.

—Simone Weil, *Notebooks*

Grief/Relief

Anyone who has known distress knows the relationship between need and speed.
"If you're gonna help me, help me now," sang pop star Joan Armatrading; "Another
ten minutes will be too late." Whenever it can, relief must answer grief immediately,
for delay adds to suffering by prolonging it. Eighteenth-century ideas of sympathy
included a double ideal of immediacy, first in the nearly (but never fully) telepathic
bond of identification between sufferer and observer, then in the observer's auto-

matic, nearly simultaneous desire to assist. The following passages from Adam Smith's *Theory of Moral Sentiments,* the sixth and final edition of which was finished in the same year Blake first printed *Songs of Innocence,* illustrate these two moments:

> Upon some occasions sympathy may seem to arise merely from the view of a certain emotion in another person. The passions, upon some occasions, may seem to be transfused from one man to another, *instantaneously,* and antecedent to any knowledge of what excited them in the person principally concerned. Grief and joy, for example, strongly expressed in the look and gestures of any one, *at once* affect the spectator with some degree of a like painful or agreeable emotion. (emphasis added)

> The plaintive voice of misery, when heard at a distance, will not allow us to be indifferent about the person from whom it comes. *As soon as* it strikes our ear, it interests us in his fortune, and, if continued, forces us almost involuntarily to fly to his assistance. (emphasis added)[1]

There are many passages in *Theory of Moral Sentiments* (even most, perhaps) that contradict this idea of a zero-time sympathy, and Smith spends almost his entire treatise elaborating the slower roles played by judgment and mediation in defending vulnerable observers against being overwhelmed by invasive feelings. But his work begins with the assumption that human nature is inherently sympathetic because sympathy comes so quickly and thoroughly. The first couplets of "On Anothers Sorrow" rehearse both of Smith's arguments about the immediacy and the sequence of sympathy:

> Can I see anothers woe,
> And not be in sorrow too.
> Can I see anothers grief,
> And not seek for kind relief.   (1–4, E 17)

For the sympathetic I, to "see" is first to "be" (identification) and then to "seek" (take action), in rapid, irresistible sequence. With its simple diction and rhythm, with its mostly tuneful rhymes, with so little visual distraction in the plate (figure 3.1), this poem can be read so quickly that the (nearly nonexistent) time of reading about sympathy mimes the immediacy of experiencing sympathy. Perhaps the poem has received so little critical attention because it requires so little interpretation of its reader. Beginning with the rhetorical questions that organize the first half of the poem, the speaker calls not for reading but for assent. "Can I see anothers woe, / And not be in sorrow too"? Of course not. Blake critics have given or withheld this response, finding the speaker either credible or naïve, but few have found the poem interesting.[2]

We might start to complicate this song by remembering Paul de Man's lesson about the underlying complexity of rhetorical questions: the tension between

Figure 3.1 "On Anothers Sorrow," *Songs of Innocence and of Experience*, copy L, plate 28, 1789–1794. Yale Center for British Art, Paul Mellon Collection

rhetoric and grammar generates an irresolvable confusion, contradicting the no-tion that a question might automatically contain its own answer, as if it were not a question at all. In de Man's famous example from popular culture, Archie Bunker responds to his wife's question about how to lace his bowling shoes by shooting back a question in turn: "What's the difference?" He means to say, "Don't bother me with something that makes no difference"; however, the question that would dismiss in advance all possible responses but one cannot prevent itself from being misread. Edith takes the question literally and answers accordingly. Thus "[r]he-toric radically suspends logic and opens up vertiginous possibilities of referential aberration."[3] Put another way, the rhetorical question opens the time of reading upon which it was meant to foreclose. The rhetorical questions in "On Anothers Sorrow" compound this problem of rhetoric and time. Not only can one take the first stanza's questions literally—as genuine questions open to "yes," "no," and every shade of "it depends"—but it is also impossible to know exactly what these questions are asking. Reading takes the time that sympathy, in principle, does not, and from one angle, the poem is as much about reading as it is about sympathy. Again taken literally, but in a different way, the second couplet ("Can I see anothers grief / And not seek for kind relief") could be glossed as follows:

Can I *read* "anothers grief" [these printed words]

And not *anticipate* "kind relief"

[words sure to follow at the end of the very next line, to complete the couplet]

In eighteenth-century poetry, "relief" often followed "grief," offering the rhyming poet a ready supply of "kind relief" indeed. The pairing goes back at least as far as Spenser, where it already includes the important notion that articulating suffering, forming it into words for another, is a necessary step toward relieving it.

Fair sir, I hope good hap hath brought

You to inquire the secrets of my *grief,*

Or that your wisdom will direct my thought,

Or that your prowess can me yield *relief:*

Then hear the story sad, which I shall tell you *brief.*[4]

By the time Una agrees to share her sorrows with Arthur, the word "grief" has been spoken five times between them, accruing enough verbal momentum to ini-tiate its own relief. In his *Dictionary,* Johnson illustrated the fourth definition of "relief" ("that which frees from pain or sorrow") by quoting from Dryden's *Aeneid*: "Nor dar'd I to presume, that press'd with grief / My flight should urge you to this dire relief." The *OED* prefers Cowper's "Truth," a hymn published in 1781, which reverses the order of the rhyme but expresses a sentiment very close to the mani-fest content of Blake's poem: "The soul, reposing on assured relief, / Feels herself

happy amidst all her grief." "Relief" appears only seven times in all of Cowper's poetry, six times as a rhyme word, four times joined with "grief." A cursory glance at
the Pope concordance tells the same story: fifteen uses, twelve of those in rhymes,
seven in the predictable pairing. Half a century later, Wordsworth would make the
same rhyme central to the Intimations Ode: "To me alone there came a thought of
grief: / A timely utterance gave that thought relief."[5] Whether or not relief follows
grief irresistibly in fact—an open question, even to Cowper—one can safely bet it
will do so in sentimental literature.[6] By itself, this regularity need not imply that
compassion amounts to little more than a scripted recital, though it raises the possibility. It does indicate, however, that the response to suffering is bound up with
the representation of suffering, and that sympathy—its objects and its quality—is
conditioned at least in part by what and how one reads about sympathy.

"Relief" itself is a complicated, layered word in this poem, and "kind relief" an
even more complicated notion. More than most, Blake would have understood that
"relief" raises questions about representation. Starting with a pun on reinscrip-
tion—the "re-leaving" of the grief/relief rhyme on page after page (leaf after leaf)
coming from Blake's printing press, which in turn mimics the reiterations on page
after page descending from poetic tradition—the word bears special relevance to
the production methods Blake used for his *Songs*. Although the term would not
become part of the professional engraver's lexicon until later in the nineteenth
century (with "relief plates," "relief prints," "relief processes"), it was always associated with the production of images, first describing the raised surfaces carved
in stones and impressed upon metal coins, and later the three-dimensional effects
that clear and distinct figures could achieve in mimetic drawing and painting.
Although the word appears rarely in his own writing, Blake was familiar with
its application to both sculpture and drawing. In the Descriptive Catalogue, he
refers to monuments "carved as basso relievos" (E 531), which he claimed to have
seen in visions, while the Public Address defends the older, linear style of English
engraving—"Drawing on Copper"—against the European shading effects then in
vogue: "I do not shrink from the Comparison in Either Relief or Strength of Colour
with either Rembrandt or Rubens" (E 579). More important than either of these
technical meanings, however, is the idea that, in processes of representation, relief
indicates a raised figure, an image literally brought to the surface, "lifted" (Old
French *relever*) from an indistinct background. Johnson defined the relevant Italian
term "Relievo" simply as "The *prominence* of a figure or picture," and the 1796 *En-
cyclopaedia Britannica* provided this definition of "Relief, in painting": "the degree
of boldness with which the figures seem, at a due distance, *to stand out* from the
ground of the painting" (16:60, my emphasis). In general, relief encompasses all
the techniques for sharpening the appearance of particular figures in a medium,

for differentiating what gets seen from what does not. It invokes the interplay of political and aesthetic possibilities Jacques Rancière calls "the distribution of the sensible."[7] By making certain images stand out, relief rescues them from obscurity and recommends them to our attention.

In "On Anothers Sorrow" the word is intimately self-reflexive, bearing reference to the relief process that—by "melting apparent surfaces away, and displaying the infinite which was hid" (*Marriage* 14, E 39)—lifted the word materially from the empty background of a copper plate and ultimately brought it to our notice in print. With a self-consciousness, moreover, that makes it stand out from the repertoire of homogenous, sentimental rhymes it reproduces, the word also makes evident the mutual work of sympathy and representation. Representation is implicated at every moment of sympathy: before, during, and after. At the far end of the sequence, to seek for kind relief after experiencing sympathy is, in one sense of the phrase, to respond to suffering by seeking to represent it and make it public. This representation of suffering may be an act of kindness (and not an evasion or a displacement, to name only two alternatives) *if* the representation does justice to the suffering and, by making it known to those who can help, enables its relief.[8] Central to this poem and to the entire volume of *Songs* it concludes are familiar questions about whether sorrow can be represented and whether the attempt to do so achieves the desired effect. Does "relief" (representation of suffering) bring "relief" (alleviation of suffering)? If so, for whom? But even *before* the observer begins to consider whether representation forms an appropriate response to suffering, images already bear upon the experience of sympathy, at its point of origin. We can only attempt to relieve the grief we have seen and recognized in the first place. If representation is the cultural mechanism for making suffering visible, it is a selective mechanism, a "programme for perception," as Pierre Bourdieu would say.[9] It foregrounds objects discriminately, ignoring one as it recognizes another. In the world of sympathy, relief is not consistently kind.

What shape, then, must suffering take in order to become a conspicuous figure that catches our eye? "That ours is an age of the picture is more than a cliché," write the editors introducing a volume of interdisciplinary essays on *Social Suffering*. Although the media have changed and multiplied, to the point where literature no longer competes as prominently in the field of representation, their account of the socially constructed relation between grief and relief is one Blake would have understood, not least because of its emphasis on the role played by visual imagination in the practices of compassion: "Experience, including experiences of social suffering, has been *mediatized* . . . How we 'picture' social suffering becomes that experience, for the observers and even for the sufferers/perpetrators. What we represent and how we represent it prefigure what we will, or will not, do to intervene. What is not pictured is not real. Much of routinized misery is invisible; much that is made visible is not ordinary or routine. The very act of picturing distorts social experience in the popular media and in the professions under the impress of ideology and political economy."[10] Long before television, sentimental culture recognized that abstract sorrow moves us only weakly: strong sympathy requires a *scene* of suffering. "Who can contemplate such a scene unmoved?" asks a typical caption to a typical illustration in a typical conduct book of 1822.[11] The question echoes those asked by the speaker at the beginning of "On Anothers Sorrow"— "Can I see . . . And not be"? "Can I see . . . And not seek"? "Can I see . . . And not feel"? If sensibility always takes place in "an age of the picture," then these questions should lead us to wonder why, in this of all poems, Blake's plate provides no spectacle of grief whatsoever, despite the opportunity afforded by the mixed media, an opportunity he did not hesitate to exploit elsewhere in the *Songs*. As we have seen, Smith argued that "Grief . . . strongly expressed in the look and gestures of any one, at once affect[s] the spectator," but Blake, in a poem that seems to express the same sentiment, pictures the sorrow of no one. In the plate's mostly ornamental decoration, we can identify a few birds amid foliage, a piper, and—barely visible toward the upper left, sketched in a few meager lines—a figure with arms lifted, apparently in prayer, but "On Anothers Sorrow" refuses to throw into bold relief the suffering of even a single figure. If forced to respond literally to the poem's first question—"Can I *see* anothers woe"?—a reader of this page would have to answer "no." The same poem that identifies Jesus as the ideal practitioner of unlimited sympathy ("he who smiles on all") and embraces the incarnation as the ultimate act of kindness ("He becomes an infant small") is also one of Blake's most aniconic, withholding the kind relief of the graven image it invites us to expect.

These, then, are some of the initial questions raised by "relief," but what about "*kind* relief"? As a qualifier, "kind" means benevolent, of course, but as a substantive that also signifies general "class," "type," or "sort," sometimes even "race," the word carries connotations of classification and belonging, the propriety of shared origins and the proprietary nature of social groups—that is, membership. We have already seen one (merely formal) version of the kinship between "grief" and "relief," which belong to the same family of words that rhyme. Another (social) version of the relationship suggests that for sympathy to begin there must first be an underlying feeling of kinship—call it "kindness"—between the one who grieves and the one who would relieve. As far back as Aristotle, philosophers have argued that we tend to respond to sufferers with whom we readily identify; a crucial feature of compassion is the belief that their sorrows could have been ours, had circumstances so dictated.[12] "Each may be tomorrow what the one whom he helps is today," writes Rousseau.[13] The closer the sorrow the more compelling the picture imagination can form. To play once again upon the element of kinship in kindness: we respond most fully to sorrows that are *familiar*, to suffering we are predisposed to recognize because it occurs to someone sufficiently like us, or in an environment sufficiently local, or in a representational medium with which we are sufficiently comfortable. In short, the visual imagination of sympathy is parochial; it tends to see the grief previewed by its bias. For Nussbaum, this remains the one argument against compassion that even its most loyal defenders, herself included, struggle to answer. "[C]ompassion remains narrow and unreliable. It takes in only what the person has been able to see or imagine, and its psychology is limited by the limitations of the sensory imagination" (361). Because sympathy reinforces the kindness of local attachments only, "it is very likely to present an unbalanced picture of the world" (360).[14]

Nussbaum contends that prejudicial sympathy can be corrected, at least to some extent, by education, but the question of how far the horizon of sympathy may extend remains an open one. Grounding the emotion first in sensory experience and then in social pragmatism, Adam Smith implied that sympathy weakens as it extends outward, ultimately reaching only as far as a nation's borders, or only to the farthest possible reach of one's own influence on one's own kind.[15] Beyond that sphere, any attempt to reduce the suffering of others would be ludicrous and self-defeating. Watching Smith try to map the boundaries of affect provides one of the clearest indications that sympathy, as he constructs it, is as much about managing potentially excessive emotions as it is a spontaneous expression of one's capacity to identify with others. On either side of compassion lie the dangers of a quantitative and a qualitative sublime: too many others capable of provoking too strong a response. Lauren Berlant puts the problem this way: "When we are taught, from the time we are taught anything, to measure the scale of pain and attachment, to feel *appropriately* compassionate, we are being trained in stinginess, in not caring."[16] Three quarters of a century before Smith wrote *Moral Sentiments*, the Anglican preacher William Clagett could articulate the dilemma of sympathy with remarkable clarity. How can we reconcile our natural disposition to universal benevolence, endowed by God, with the actual limits of our ability to do good? How, in other words, can we settle the difference between a generosity unlimited in principle and a practice that, for our own self-protection, if nothing else, must necessarily be finite? "I observed before, that we have so limited a Power, that we cannot be actually beneficent to All, and therefore must choose our Objects with discretion. There are several good Works which many do not need from us, and we cannot perform them for All that do. And therefore Charity must be guided by Judgment in determining upon whom to let fall the effects of our readiness to do good to All." To help teach his audience how to be properly stingy with their sympathy, Clagett's sermon offers a set of ready preferences: put family before others, acquaintances before strangers, countrymen before foreigners, and above all, Christians before anyone else. ("It is very fit and just that we should *love them* more than others; For they are really better than other men are.") Yet Clagett also recognizes that the moral calculus can be muddied by circumstance. What if the magnitude of a stranger's suffering gives him greater claim on our sympathy? In the end, when faced with such moral dilemmas, one must trust that prudence and judgment will be sufficient to guide the appropriate choice: "as to this matter, when all is said that can be said, the prudence of every honest Man will be requisit to apply general Rules to particular Cases."[17]

According to Smith, Nature herself has installed the discretionary mechanism: "when she loaded us with our own sorrows, [Nature] thought that they were enough, and therefore did not command us to take any further share in those of others, than what was necessary to prompt us to relieve them" (58). Why bother to search for sorrows that exceed one's practical powers, sorrows one cannot possibly hope to relieve? Smith had no patience for those "who are perpetually reproaching us with our happiness" because somewhere someone must be miserable (160). The "whining and melancholy moralists" he ridiculed would become a fixture of future literary production. One thinks of the maniac in Shelley's "Julian and Maddalo" ("*Me*—who am as a nerve o'er which do creep / The else unfelt oppressions of this earth") or the man with the hammer in Chekhov's "Gooseberries": "Behind the door of every contented, happy man there ought to be someone standing with a little hammer and continually reminding him with a knock that there are unhappy people."[18] But Smith categorically rejected the idea of an exponentially enlarged sympathy: "Commiseration for those miseries which we never saw, which we never heard of, but which we may be assured are at all times infesting such numbers of our fellow-creatures, ought, they think, to damp the pleasures of the fortunate, and to render a certain melancholy dejection habitual to all men" (161). Such "extreme sympathy with misfortunes" is "altogether absurd and unreasonable" because it is (a) manufactured ("artificial," not based on anyone's direct experience); (b) "unattainable" (beyond the limits of possible experience); (c) "perfectly useless," serving "no other purpose than to render miserable the person who possessed it" (161).

In her reading of this passage, Julie Ellison has proposed that Smith cannot shut down the possibility of "extreme sympathy" he himself introduces here, for the "person overimplicated in others" in fact fulfills the logic of Smith's system, only to excess.[19] To draw the line of caring at the national (or any other) border—to say that on this side of a threshold there can be sympathy but on the other, none—only highlights the artifice of imagined communities, raising the question of scope that Smith claims we are entitled by nature to ignore. What sympathy, then, *do* we owe to "miseries which we never saw, which we never heard of," to sufferers "with whom we have no acquaintance or connexion," whose particular sorrows have not been raised from the background of general misery into the relief of clear, distinct, and accessible pictures, whose grief, if we are aware of it at all, we have no idea how to relieve because it takes place in settings so remote from our own (Smith names China and the moon as examples)? Any single figure Blake might have chosen to represent on the plate of "On Anothers Sorrow" could only serve to repeat the arbitrary and selective nature of sympathy, which pictures one suffering figure in order to avoid having to picture all. It is a trap Blake chose not to enter. By emptying his visual field of representative figures, by leaving the "other" of his title unspecified, Blake was not merely demonstrating that the speaker's programmatic optimism depends upon the neglect of actual suffering; he was also *unlimiting* sympathy. What would it mean to identify with a grief that the prejudicial imagination, collective or individual, had not preselected in advance? "Extreme sympathy," beyond the perceptual conventions of sensibility, would first have to overcome the eye's comfort with the "scene" of suffering. Thus a poem that begins "Can I see . . . Can I see . . . Can I see . . ." (ll. 1, 3, 5) quickly abandons its insistent visuality and turns abruptly to an auditory emphasis instead. Unlike the seeing "I" who models sentimental conventions, Jesus, the poem's figure for sympathy without limits, only listens. Matching and displacing the trio of questions that begins the poem, the fourth stanza asks, "Can he [Jesus] . . . Hear . . . Hear . . . Hear" (ll. 13–16)? In this poem, as we will later discuss in detail, sympathetic response begins not with the eye but with the ear.

Nussbaum raises another complaint about compassion, one she believes is more easily answered than its narrowness and visuality: it is susceptible to self-indulgence. The charge will move us closer to understanding the alienation of sympathy Blake's poem is effecting: "[W]e should be on our guard lest the invitation to weep over the distress of others should motivate self-indulgent and self-congratulatory behavior, rather than real helpfulness. People can all-too-easily feel they have done something morally good because they have had an experience of compassion—without having to take any of the steps to change the world that might involve them in real difficulty and sacrifice . . . At the worst, the experience of tragic contemplation can even involve an aestheticizing of the person's plight that has a most unwholesome moral character" (399). The last criticism bears hard on the poetry of social suffering, which—as Wordsworth critics are sometimes quick to point out—always risks the danger of building its aesthetic pleasures, to say nothing of a career, "On Anothers Sorrow." Nussbaum's recommendation—that the best remedy for feel-good sympathy is always to keep "real helpfulness" in mind—recalls De Quincey's complaint about "The Ruined Cottage": that Wordsworth's peddler would have served poor Margaret better had he supplemented his good will with a guinea.[20] Others in the first age of sensibility also recognized the irony that sympathy, the imaginative capacity to "put [oneself] in the place of another and of many others,"[21] was not incompatible with exquisite self-absorption. As Frances Burney described it, "wayward Sensibility" is a "delicate, but irregular power, which now impels to all that is most disinterested for others, [and] now forgets all mankind, to watch the pulsations of its own fancies."[22]

For our purposes here, the solution Nussbaum proposes to the problem of self-indulgence in sympathy is useful primarily because it shows us a path Blake did not follow. Nussbaum worries that "people are frequently too weak to keep their attention fixed on a course of action, and that a momentary experience is frequently much easier for them than a sustained commitment" (399). The remedy for a momentary, do-nothing feeling is action (do something), and intelligent sympathy should serve as the means to a measurable end—seeking kind relief. Blake's worry is rather the opposite. Within the conventions of sympathy, attention has become so fixed on pursuing the right course of action that sympathetic agents have become unreceptive to the kind of "momentary experience"—as subtle as a beating artery—in which, as Blake puts it in *Milton*, a "Poets Work is Done."[23] Sympathy should pay more, not less, attention to the tiny events of the pulses. In "On Anothers Sorrow," the problem with compassion is not its complacency but its can-do attitude, its confidence (shared by Nussbaum) that one can indeed recognize sorrow and know what to do about it. When Nussbaum laments the detachment of compassion from self-sacrifice and then argues that genuine sympathy should motivate one *"to take . . . the steps* to change the world," she invokes a common understanding that values sympathy for its role as an engine of narrative action—for moving along a story that begins with grief and ends with relief. The idea is as old as Burke's *Enquiry*, which argues that the misery we share with others promotes the contrary pleasure of remedial action (prompting us "to relieve ourselves in relieving those who suffer").[24] John Hunter, the famous London surgeon satirized by Blake in *An Island in the Moon*, perhaps even his acquaintance, similarly folds sympathy into instrumental action: "One of its chief uses is to excite an active interest in favour of the distressed, the mind of the spectators taking on nearly the same action with that of the sufferers, and disposing them to give relief or consolation."[25] If we could not relieve suffering by means of our actions, Kant argued, sympathy would serve only to multiply the world's misery.[26] These assumptions about the proper action sequence of sympathy make Blake's rendition of the emotion look utterly strange by comparison. The hero of "On Anothers Sorrow," who knows something about self-sacrifice, takes no forward step at all, neither to change the world nor to do anything else. Instead, "He doth sit by us and moan" (his sitting, like his hearing, is mentioned three times). Blake's Jesus suspends words and action, the two necessary elements of narrative. If "On Anothers Sorrow" forms no picture of suffering, it also tells no story. It represents the apotheosis of a sympathy that is perversely, adamantly passive.

Dysfunctional Jesus, or Emotion without Narrative

The second couplet of "On Anothers Sorrow" outlines in miniature a self-contained story. The movement from grief to relief, with sympathy intervening, traces the beginning, middle, and end that Aristotle considered necessary for any plot to be complete. In Blake's era, scenes of sympathy not only take narrative form, but their internal action pivots on the ability of characters to tell and assess stories. One character *earns* another's sympathy when he (or more likely, she) tells a persuasive tale of suffering. Against the background of deep moral convention supplied by this narrative structure, "On Anothers Sorrow" points toward a sympathy not so much deviant as derelict—a sympathy without plot, without character, without eloquence. Against the expectations raised by its title, then, the poem becomes an affective performance nesting an emotion that is not narratable within and against an emotion defined by its narrative function. Reading becomes the experience of friction between these registers, or the autocritical experience we earlier called "adverse emotion."

In the normative accounts of compassion that extend from Aristotle to Adam Smith, and from Smith to Martha Nussbaum, sympathy involves not one narrative only but the intersection of two: the story of distress that accounts for the sufferer's current misfortune and the story of the observer who recognizes grief and strives to relieve it. We should remember, however, that Smith's *Theory of Moral Sentiments* entertains (even if it immediately qualifies) the idea of an instantaneous sympathy that, flying from sufferer to observer, would preempt the narrative arrangement and management of emotion. Smith pathologizes this dangerous immediacy, including among his earliest cautionary examples a description of overly sensitive "Persons of delicate fibres" who "are apt to feel an itching or uneasy sensation" simply by "looking on the sores and ulcers which are exposed by beggars in the streets" (12). Ordinarily, he explains, these unnarrated griefs provoke only a proto-compassion, an inclination to sympathize that fully realizes itself only when given a story to work with:

> Even our sympathy with the grief or joy of another [emotions which, in the passage I quoted earlier, "at once affect the spectator"], before we are informed of the cause of either, is always extremely imperfect. General lamentations, which express nothing but the anguish of the sufferer, create rather a curiosity to inquire into his situation, along with some disposition to sympathize with him, than any actual sympathy that

is very sensible. The first question which we ask is, What has befallen you? Till this be answered, though we are uneasy both from the vague idea of his misfortune, and still more from torturing ourselves with conjectures about what it may be, yet our fellow-feeling is not very considerable. (14–15)

One can already observe Smith narrowing the range of sympathy, protecting against invasive excess by limiting response to *articulated* sorrows; emotional intelligence responds best to those emotions that others make intelligible for us. Suzie Park has identified the scene of "compulsory narration" as a set-piece of sentimental literature, where suffering characters are required to answer the question invariably put to them: "What has befallen you?" The main purpose of such scenes is to enforce cultural expectations that persons should be as interesting as characters in novels, defined by a deep interiority they are able to indicate to others on demand, as ready-made information.[27] For sympathy to occur, the distressed person must be able to justify her circumstances and so prove herself worthy of the observer's inclination to sympathize. Indeed, verbal justification is already a step toward winning sympathy, for the ability to manage emotion through narration (to tell one's story) is itself a sign of good character, while unintelligible outbursts—though initially affecting—can indicate a failure of self-control that, according to Smith, tends to interest another only briefly. The successful narrative of sympathy thus requires two persons of good character: the sufferer who narrates grief and serves as its first-person protagonist and the observer who receives the narrated grief, responds to it, and acts upon it appropriately. In Smith's dual sense of the term, both characters must be "accountable," that is, morally responsible and thus capable of fulfilling the proper narrative role: "A moral being is an accountable being. An accountable being, as the word expresses, is a being that must give an account of its actions to some other, and that consequently must regulate them according to the good-liking of this other" (130). The sufferer's story must earn the sympathy of the observer, of course, but the actions undertaken by the sympathetic observer must also form a story, one that would earn the respect of a third party's dispassionate judgment. The observer must act as if the judgment he exercises will be judged in turn. Like the sufferer, he answers to the question of his self-command—first before God, then before other men, who serve as God's surrogates, and finally before his own internalization of the standard of judgment they represent (the "internal spectator" who ultimately guarantees that sympathy will be "sensible").[28]

In order for Smith's moral economy to function, judgment must operate everywhere at once. Charged with maintaining an improbable equilibrium between identification with suffering and detachment from it, judgment is prophylactic, protecting the sympathetic self from being inundated by external sorrows and thus securing a boundary between self and others. We have already seen how Smith attempts to limit sympathy spatially by enclosing it within a social geography more or less local. Now we see that judgment also provides for emotional management in time, defining character as that core of personal identity which should remain more or less inviolable, more or less itself, across any sequence of social encounters, no matter how many, how unpredictable, or how overpowering they may be. Whatever self-sacrifice it may entail, sympathy also mobilizes a project of self-preservation; it foregrounds the judgments and actions of an "I" whose composure, integrity, and consistency shape time into a continuous, legible narrative. In principle, the "I" who sees grief and the "I" who acts to relieve it are identical, "self-clos'd." In this sense, sympathy is all about managing the survival of the "I," securing its extension into the future, and one of the earliest indications of Blake's departure from convention is the quick disappearance of the first person pronoun that grammatically dominates the poem's opening. After the fifth line of "On Anothers Sorrow," the "I" is gone for good.

Consider Nussbaum's account of the close association between compassion and altruism. Despite her interest in describing a subject more accepting of vulnerability than allowed for by Smith's program of "self-command," which clings too closely to its roots in ancient stoic philosophy, Nussbaum's own understanding indicates the persistence of self-preservation in the story of sympathy. In her account, we recall, willing acts of self-sacrifice are necessary to fulfill compassion's potential and to prevent it from lapsing into self-indulgence, a point she elaborates on in a discussion of altruism.

> Compassion is frequently linked to beneficent action. Given my analysis, it is easy to see how this link might be thought to occur. If one believes that the misfortunes of others are serious, and that they have not brought misfortune on themselves, and, in addition, that they are themselves important parts of one's own scheme of ends and goals, then the conjunction of these beliefs is very likely to lead to action addressing the suffering. It may not do so, if there is no available course of action that suggests itself. But if there is, it will be difficult to believe that the compassionate person really does have all three judgments, if she does not do something to address the victims' vulnerability. (335)

Momentarily setting aside the possibility that no course of action may be available, we see that compassion describes a threshold of emotional intelligence that, once certain conditions have been met, should trigger action irresistibly. If one did not act in such circumstances—if, say, one were to take the sorrow of another sitting down, as Blake's Jesus does—one could hardly claim to have experienced compassion as Nussbaum describes it. For her, compassion involves a balancing act surely as impressive as anything Smith's sympathy managed to accomplish. Even as it expresses a powerful sense of urgency, compassion also avoids the impulsiveness that philosophy has traditionally considered a principal danger of strong emotion. Nussbaum's action-oriented subject is by no means "force[d] almost involuntarily to fly to [another's] assistance," as if in a vise-grip of sympathetic immediacy. Instead, compassion cultivates sound judgment within a space of deliberation, allowing it to exemplify one of Nussbaum's largest arguments about emotions in general—that they perform (rather than disrupt or overwhelm) acts of critical thinking. Emotions forestall blind, undesirable impulses, though without resulting in the opposite extreme of inertia. Yes, they "are closely connected with *action*; few facts about them are more obvious," she writes. "And yet it would be a mistake to identify them with *desires* for particular types of action," for "not all emotions suggest a definite course to follow" (135). The advantage of emotional intelligence, then, is that it points toward action, while also allowing time for inquiry and experiment before deciding on the best plan of action available.

In the specific case of compassion, deliberation means determining whether the other's sorrow satisfies three conditions required by the observer's judgment, conditions Nussbaum specifies in the passage above: the grief must be serious; the sufferer must not be at fault; the observer must feel he has a stake in the other's sorrow (a feeling that can be expanded, Nussbaum believes, by liberal education). After the recognition of grief, there must be deliberation; after deliberation, the effort to relieve—or not, depending upon the judgment called for by the situation. Such is the narrative of sympathy. "Can I see anothers grief / And not seek for kind relief"? Yes, if in between seeing and seeking I learn that the sufferer grieves for the loss of a trivial object, especially if I learn that the sufferer is herself responsible for the loss. Like all of the emotions as Nussbaum explains them, compassion is neither compulsive nor paralytic; it is the intelligent agency that motivates responsible action, taking its time but not taking forever, moving along a story line which has at its center a person who balances kindness and principled consistency (another way of saying "self-command"). Emotion occupies the "middle" of compassion's tale, as Aristotle used the term in the *Poetics*: "that which itself naturally follows something else [grief], and has something else [relief] after it" (10). The sympathetic person who carries into future encounters the ability to assess circumstances and to act upon them without being overwhelmed by them has "character."

Against these criteria, one could say of "On Anothers Sorrow" only that it features the double negative of inaction without judgment. The poem auditions a series of potential sympathizers (first the "I," then a father, then a mother), until it arrives at the figure of Jesus, who occupies a strangely empty center where the promise of character used to be. The hero of the greatest story ever told won't act the part scripted by sympathy's narrative or by any other narrative. "He becomes a man of woe," but he won't become a "person," if—as stories of sympathy imply— that word means a "moral being" who is "accountable," judging the stories of others while hoping in turn that his own responsive actions, if narrated, would also meet with approval. How does one account for someone who seems to have forgotten all about "real helpfulness" and who does nothing but "sit by . . . and moan"? (Imagine what De Quincey would advise *him*.) Not only does Jesus sit "by us," he sits by any- one, indiscriminately, by any sentient being, exhibiting an unprincipled sympathy detached from the kind of preliminary appraisal that, for Smith and Nussbaum, places compassion among the intelligent (or "sensible") emotions. In their story of sympathy, the observer listens to the sufferer's tale in order to assess the propriety of sorrow: "When we blame in another man the excesses . . . of grief, . . . we say . . . his misfortune is not so dreadful . . . as to justify so violent a passion. We should have indulged, we say; perhaps, have approved of the violence of his emotion, had the cause been in any respect proportioned to it" (23). Even apart from the content of the judgment, the measured and measuring language of what "we say" already indicts the emotional violence and disproportion of the other simply by articulat- ing them in a way that the overwrought other could not. Blake's Jesus, on the other hand, responds to the "sighs" of grief, not its "size" (Aristotle's term for proportion, for measuring the seriousness of sorrow).[29] The poem emphasizes that no sorrow is too trivial to fall beneath the threshold of sympathy's notice, which attends even to "the wren with sorrows small," "the small birds grief & care," and "the woes that infants bear." Devoid of curiosity, Jesus neglects to ask the first question that is supposed to occur to any sympathetic observer: "What has befallen you?" With its disarming simplicity, the poem thus exhibits no interest at all in the narratabil- ity that entangles grief in a calculus of blame and approval. Unlike his muscular counterpart in Michelangelo's Last Judgment fresco, say, Blake's Jesus holds no one accountable, asks no questions, *says* nothing, indeed *does* nothing to relieve the sorrows he makes himself adjacent to—all with a passivity so immoderate it startles. Within a poem that upon first reading seems little more than a rehearsal of pious conventions, we encounter a Jesus who seems less and less recognizable.

Nowhere is this estrangement better evident than in the suspended temporality Jesus occupies, a topic we will return to in chapter 4. Above, we described emo- tion as the "middle" of compassion's tale, preceded by grief and followed by relief, or responsible action. In "On Anothers Sorrow," however, sympathy distends the middle, and Blake invites us to imagine the indefinite postponement of any sequel. Through the dilatory figure of Jesus, the poem embodies a sympathy willing to wait out any sorrow, unwilling, that is, to enter into the compromised narratives of relief that serve (in part, if not primarily) the observer's need to get on with the story, any story, and so avoid being rendered inactive and futureless, disabled by an excessive attachment to sorrow. Preoccupied by the present (as designated by an unvarying present tense), the poem describes no past at all (sorrows are simply there, without causes) and only a vague future ("Till our grief is fled and gone"). Perhaps distant in time, that endpoint remains disconnected from any imaginable narrative that would join this present grief to that griefless future, as cause might lead progressively to effect. Without any available course of action to get from here to there, Jesus sits with the sufferer, even if their sitting together should last forever. He utterly lacks the survival skills of ordinary sympathy, the social bargain made by moral agents who give as much of themselves to others as they can without jeopardizing their own prospects, joining the immediate need of another to their own need for continuous movement into a secure future. Already in two of Johnson's definitions of "relief," one can observe a built-in negotiation over the extent of one's obligation to grief: either "relief" is (1) the "*Alleviation* of calamity; *mitigation* of pain or sorrow" or (2) "That which *frees* from pain or sorrow" (emphasis added). Blake's Jesus would "destroy" grief, and until that is possible he does nothing rather than something palliative, eschewing a course of action which might accommodate suffering by degrees and so normalize it. For Smith and Nussbaum, it is paramount that the observer retain a capacity for uninterrupted action; psychic health depends upon an unshaken belief in agency, a confidence that one can act (or choose not to act) on another's sorrow. Those we can't relieve should not concern us, argues Smith, because concern is interlocked with effort, and both of these responses should be directed only toward those we can actually help. As we have seen, Burke and Kant share the same faith in the link between sympathy and responsible action. For Nussbaum, compassion prompts us to relieve those who deserve sympathy; if no means of assistance present themselves, the impasse challenges us to invent new ones. Either way, the story must go on, propelled forward by the efforts and emotions of a character whose worst fear is to find himself idled by demands in excess of his know-how. The sympathetic character must understand the meaning of "enough," as Wordsworth's traveling philosopher, Armytage, instructs the speaker of "The Ruined Cottage," in a classic statement of the continuous forward motion built into the narrative structure of sympathy, when properly managed:

"My Friend, enough to sorrow have you given,
The purposes of wisdom ask no more;
Be wise and chearful, and no longer read
The forms of things with an unworthy eye.
She [Margaret] sleeps in the calm earth, and peace is here.

I well remember that those very plumes,
Those weeds, and the high spear-grass on that wall,
By mist and silent rain-drops silver'd o'er,
As once I passed did to my heart convey
So still an image of tranquillity,
So calm and still, and looked so beautiful
Amid the uneasy thoughts which filled my mind,
That what we feel of sorrow and despair
From ruin and from change, and all the grief
The passing shews of being leave behind,
Appeared an idle dream that could not live
Where meditation was. I turned away
And walked along my road in happiness."[30]

Having told Margaret's story well, and having transformed a halting melancholia into the progressive work of mourning, Armytage enables his listener and Wordsworth's reader (both of whom now read with a worthy eye) to join him in the one act that matters most: moving on. "Together casting then a farewell look / Upon those silent walls, we left the shade / And ere the stars were visible attained / A rustic inn, our evening resting-place" (ll. 535–538). Without ever casting a farewell look on suffering, Blake's Jesus sits by; he never feels compelled to move on. It is as if he has undone the social training that lets one turn away, that teaches us how to think of sympathy—for the living or the dead—as a finite experience that must eventually give way to subsequent experience, like a book or a poem we can put aside when we have finished reading. Without moving his poem's central figure toward any closure, Blake leaves his reader with the kind of uneasy, open-ended question that Wordsworth's reader is supposed to have put to rest: Just how much time *should* one spend "On Anothers Sorrow"?

It is important to remember that Armytage's final words in "The Ruined Cottage"—"I turned away / And walked along my road in happiness"—describe him not only keeping busy but getting on with business, in every sense of the word. He is, after all, a peddler, and the road that carries him perpetually into the future is also his workplace. Philip Fisher notes that modern economies depend upon "a stable world of effort" (34), and effort is supported by an "idea of the prudential self, which weighs the near and long-term future, balances the full range of desires and obligations, and integrates the many inclinations into the actions of any one moment" (44). It is against the idea of this always goal-oriented, economic self and the "emotions" sustaining it that Fisher develops his theory of premodern "passions," an opposition he sums up in the following aphorism: "Emotions sustain daily life; the passions break it off" (45). In terms of this dichotomy, the kind of stoic sympathy Armytage peddles aspires to become an emotion that (sustaining daily life) transcends the disability of passion. By facing suffering but avoiding disturbance, this sympathy promotes "the smooth unfolding of the predictable future . . . on which our shared world of everyday work and economic life depends" (33). In Armytage, Wordsworth describes a self so steady in his efforts, so persistently himself, that one can foresee no future condition—no matter how extreme or how opposite—that would prevent him from circulating through a landscape that is also an economy:

> I roved o'er many a hill and many a dale
> With this my weary load, in heat and cold,
> Through many a wood, and many an open ground,
> In sunshine or in shade, in wet or fair,
> Now blithe, now drooping, as it might befal   (289–293)

This "I" works, through weather, through moods, through the sorrows of others, through any of the surprise encounters along the road that might interrupt its progress, maintaining a momentum in stark contrast with the tragic immobilization of Margaret. Unable to adjust to the changing economic conditions that destroy her family, Margaret experiences a grief so profound that "she would sit / The idle length of half a sabbath day" (450–451), with sorrow "Fast rooted at her heart" (490). She cannot go on. Neglectful of all domestic obligations, she experiences a premodern passion in a modern world that couples its sympathy with impatience. "Vehement passions," suggests Fisher, are so "all-engrossing," so self-absorbing, that they displace concern for anything outside the immediacy of their feeling. Fisher names three, the second of which bears directly on Margaret's situation: "Falling in love, mourning for the death of a loved one, and being enraged by anger to the point of seeking vengeance" (33). In a certain sense, then, "On Anothers Sorrow" proposes an outrageous question: what if sympathy, defined ideally by its selflessness, were so absorbing that it too belonged among the passions? Moreover, what if it were immune to the gradual waning of affect that eventually returns even the most vehement passion to the temporality of everyday, economic, prudential life, a diminution over time encouraged by every modern institution (psychotherapy and the Family Leave Act come to mind) that would say, sooner or later, in the gentlest of tones: "Enough to sorrow have you given"? By joining vehement sympathy with voluntary immobilization, by making himself the exact opposite of "The busy bee [who] has no time for sorrow" (*Marriage* 7, E 36), Jesus asks the observer of suffering to consider a work stoppage of impossible duration. His compassion takes on the qualities of an anarchist general strike, which is to say he won't return to work after some merely local adjustment in suffering but only when suffering itself is "fled and gone."[31]

The entanglement within sympathy of emotion (self-preserving) and passion (self-suspending)—to continue with Fisher's distinction for another moment—contributes to the tension Blake explores in a relevant proverb of Hell: "The most sublime act is to set another before you" (*Marriage* 7, E 36). The proverb turns upon an obvious ambiguity: Another what? Act or person? If one could imagine both possibilities inserted into the proverb simultaneously, superimposed as it were, one would form a pretty accurate picture of the well-meaning prudential self. This person maximizes a reasonable sympathy, seeking out continual acts of compassion by always setting another person before him, yet he never jeopardizes the steadiness of his own linear agency. Perpetual action, even when that action is undertaken to relieve the suffering of others, sustains the subject (the "you" here) across time. Pursuing one benevolent intervention after another, in a rush to kindness, this enactive-compulsive figure points to a stubborn problem in Blake. The restless energy he valued as a creative, disruptive force historically overlaps with the industrious energies and perpetual desires indispensable to capitalist innovation and consumption. Never stop moving forward or working. Cast a farewell glance, then don't look back again. "Drive your cart and plow over the bones of the dead" (*Marriage* 7, E 35). At the same time, however, Blake's proverb also recommends a sympathy so exorbitant that it cannot be reconciled with any particular plan of action, let alone with an ethos of inexhaustible activity. If you were literally to set another [person] before you, in front of you, then the road, previously *your* road, would become a shared impasse, and you would have undone your role as a self-determining actor. This moment's charged inertia would resemble the encounter Ann Smock describes in Blanchot, when you come face to face with another and "all of a sudden you have at your disposal none of the human ways of being close and distant."[32] You would find yourself arrested by sympathy, by an encounter that could not be turned into the occasion of another act along the subject's path of self-confirmation. The most sublime act, then, is to keep the other *always* before you, to forgo the temptation to say "enough" and to turn away. By giving priority to the other (setting her *before* you), you would also have to forgo the assumption of privilege implied spatially by acting *on* another's sorrow. You would find yourself in the same kind of Levinasian prepositional relation that describes Jesus in Blake's song: *beside* the sufferer, *near* or *by*, but not above.[33] You would thus find yourself involved in a wholly unfamiliar grammar—a language with beings but without subjects, just as the implied beings who encounter each other in Blake's proverb each occupy object positions (one of a verb, the other of a preposition) in a sentence about action but without any explicit actor. Finally, you would find yourself at risk in a new social relation, without ready egress into a subsequent narrative moment. Embedded within a hyperfunctional and therapeutic sympathy, the proverb suggests, lies a dysfunctional sympathy with no next step into "real helpfulness," a radical sympathy that calls for a response no "character" could perform—a response that "lies athwart modernity" because it resembles nothing so much as incompetence.34 The most sublime act is to put oneself in a position that disables every conceivable action.

In an experiment of some significance to theorists of emotional intelligence, psychologist M. E. P. Seligman, a founder and hero of the new "positive psychology" movement, has shown that optimism and confidence are important components of successful agency.35 When Seligman placed dogs in a "shuttle box," they quickly learned to avoid an electric shock by jumping across a barrier from one side of the box to another. Other dogs conditioned to feel impotent by receiving repeated, unavoidable shocks would not jump the barrier even when they were later given the freedom to do so. For Nussbaum, experiments like Seligman's demonstrate "that emotional health requires the belief that one's own voluntary actions will make a significant difference to one's most important goals and projects" (5). Who would deny the good sense of an argument that says belief in agency is a prerequisite of agency? Still, I cannot help but wish that, instead of exhibiting the emotional health management necessary to avoid a series of incidental shocks, Seligman's dogs had set loftier goals and somehow plotted their escape from the box altogether. The deeply limited agency enabled by their canine confidence recalls the question of structure and agency raised by Foucault, which I quoted earlier, in chapter 2: "[I]f we limit ourselves to this type of always partial and local inquiry or test, do we not run the risk of letting ourselves be determined by more general structures of which we may well not be conscious, and over which we may have no control?"36 Now imagine that the shuttle box is a general social and economic structure that includes social suffering as one of its manifestations and that seeking kind relief is the agency emotional intelligence exercises in order to overcome local pain—that is, to jump a barrier and avoid a shock. In poems such as "The Human Abstract" and *The Book of Urizen,* Blake, unlike Adam Smith, made clear his understanding that "pity" is not a spontaneous manifestation of some original human nature but rather a performance structured by social hierarchy, by an arrangement of privileges that "pity" both answers and serves. Like the gender conventions that attribute higher cognitive powers to men and embodied feelings to women, pity's appearance already indicates a late stage in the history of social divisions Blake called The Fall. Even today, debate over the competing merits of an institutional safety net and the privatization of compassion takes place on a common ground in certain ways unchanged from Blake's era. Neither of these "relief" agendas (public or private) seriously challenges the structural inequalities responsible for the effects of social suffering, effects they would rather "mitigate" or "alleviate" than "destroy." Relief would be no more (no longer necessary) if we did not make somebody poor. In this context, it would take an extravagant act of imagination, perhaps an impossible one, to see another's grief and *not* seek for kind relief, to refrain from the seductive optimism of a personal (or governmental) agency that promises a reassuring vista of continuous, consecutive actions, all leaping the obstacles of incidental suffering within a box the overall confinement of which one would rather ignore. To echo the language of cognitive theorists of emotion: to "destroy" grief seems to rank highly among Jesus' "most important goals and projects"—it is important to his sense of "flourishing"—but that outcome would require an agency wholly unlike the kind illustrated by Seligman's dogs.[37]

Brief Interlude: "Pity" and "Transactions in the Construction of Pain"

We are now in a position to recognize the poignancy of a well-known print Blake executed in 1795, which he gave the title *Pity* (figure 3.2). Gathering up pity in order to broadcast to the world the injustice of suffering, an angel is already casting a farewell look at the motionless, prostrate victim beneath her (him?), a victim who—in the precise moment Blake captures—is just about to be left behind. Although pity represents the kinship newly formed between them, the observer and the sufferer occupy altogether different temporal planes, their difference rendered by, among other things, the streaming hair of the one and the pooling hair of the other.[38] Complicating matters, Blake puts the viewer of the picture in an awkward position: she can immobilize herself in front of the picture indefinitely, keeping the sufferer before her; or she can gather her pity and move on—to the next picture in a gallery, to a subsequent action inspired by her pity, or to an entirely unrelated experience. Whatever the sequel, it would propel her into the future along an axis exaggerated in the picture by the blind, speeding horses that carry pity but stop for no one. The observer of suffering—even when she is inspired to altruism—has a future that may overleap the event and the victim of suffering.

Since Tatham first identified the source, Blake scholars have agreed that *Pity* illustrates lines from *Macbeth*:

> And pity, like a naked new-born babe,
> Striding the blast, or heaven's cherubin, hors'd
> Upon the sightless couriers of the air,
> Shall blow the horrid deed in every eye,
> That tears shall drown the wind.　　　　　　　(I.vii.21–25)[39]

Figure 3.2 Pity, c. 1795, color print finished in ink and watercolor on paper. Tate Gallery London

The passage conveys something of the same tension between momentum and arrest that threatens to pull apart Blake's picture. Pity strides the blast (the wind that blows it into the future and disseminates its knowledge), but pity also hopes to provoke tears that will drown the wind and make the rush of time pause for sympathy. Whether actions "were done quickly" (I.vii.2) or "cree[p] in . . . petty pace from day to day" (V.v.20), *Macbeth* describes a world where actions never stop, moving time forward irrevocably and remorselessly, producing effects regardless of intentions. Even the sympathy for silent, neglected suffering, and the outrage that makes one want to "blow the horrid deed in every eye," moves the observer and his agency forward, whether or not they meet the needs of another which motivated response in the first place.

For that reason, Veena Das has recommended that anthropologists dealing with trauma learn to resist casting themselves in the "heroic" role of "empowering women to speak and [giving] voice to the voiceless."[40] Having studied the massive and undocumented atrocities experienced by women following the partition of India and Pakistan, she does not find it easy to relinquish the activist longings that feed the anthropologist's self-image. Nevertheless, she tries to describe the forfeited agency—the waiting and listening (the besideness)—that a noninstrumental relation to another's pain would entail if it were possible, and thus she provides one of our best glosses on the phantasmatic passivity of "On Anothers Sorrow":

> I cannot locate your pain in the same way as I locate mine. The best I can do is let it happen to me. Now it seems to me that anthropological knowledge is precisely about letting the knowledge of the other happen to me . . . My own fantasy of anthropology as a body of writing is that which is able to receive this pain. Thus while I may never claim the pain of the other, nor appropriate it for some other purpose (nation building, revolution, scientific experiment), that I can lend my body (of writing) to this pain is what a grammatical investigation reveals.[41]

Here Das has incorporated Stanley Cavell's response to an earlier version of her argument—especially his idea that one cannot "quest" after knowledge of others: "their separateness . . . is something that finds me."[42] If we were to trace this notion of the need to relax cognitive activity, slowing one's quest after knowledge, which even when pursued with noble intentions overleaps the suffering it would record and redress, it would lead us back to the eighteenth-century emphasis on receptive passivity in aesthetic experience. Schiller's *Letters*, for instance, which he published in the same year Blake printed *Pity*, locates this necessary passivity in the "sensuous" (but not in the more aggressive "formal") drive: "How can we, however laudable our precepts, how can we be just, kindly, and human towards others, if we lack the power of receiving into ourselves, faithfully and truly, natures unlike ours . . . ?"[43] What Schiller describes as the problem of "impatient anticipations," or "seeking nothing in [an object] but what we have put into [it]," Das describes by way of a parable from Wittgenstein: in pursuit of knowledge, you dig until you hit bedrock, but then you must turn over the spade. For Das, anthropology, the science of others, is the digging that must become waiting when its instrumental activities fail. "But in this gesture of waiting," she adds, "I allow the knowledge of the other to mark me" ("Wittgenstein," 193). One could say of sympathy just what Das says of anthropology here, for pity becomes something else the moment one suspends the effort to scoop it up in one's arms.

The Long O of Sorrow

> To Sorrow,
> I bade good-morrow,
> And thought to leave her far away behind.
>
> —John Keats, Endymion, IV. 173–175[44]

Full little weenest thou what sorrows are.

> —*For Children: The Gates of Paradise*,
> inscription from Edmund Spenser

The penultimate stanza of "On Anothers Sorrow" upsets the dictum that sorrows must be articulate and intelligible to merit sympathy. Compare, for instance, Adam Smith's observation that "We are disgusted with that clamorous grief, which, without any delicacy, calls upon our compassion with *sighs and tears* and importunate lamentations" (29, emphasis added):

> Think not. thou canst sigh a sigh,
> And thy maker is not by.
> Think not, thou canst weep a tear,
> And thy maker is not near.   (ll. 29–32)

Blake's unorthodox punctuation (following the Blake Trust transcription) allows one to read at least the first of these lines and possibly the third as imperatives preferring sighs and tears to the type of verbal intelligence they preclude: Don't think, when you can sigh or weep instead. The breathy redundancy in these lines ("sigh a sigh," "weep a tear") recalls the earlier image of Jesus "Weeping tear on infants tear" (stanza five), which in turn recalls "An infant groan an infant fear" (stanza three), repetitions that insist upon the *wordless* state of *infancy* (Latin *infans*, "without speech"). In a poem generally structured by repetition, these single-line redundancies correspond to a shift in attitude, from depicting a father who *sees* his distressed child to a mother who prefigures Jesus because she "sit[s] and *hear*[s]" her troubled infant. The poem moves us, in other words, away from the legible and toward the auditory, the excessive, and the inarticulate.

If Blake had in mind Smith's version of a similarly attentive mother—"What are the pangs of a mother, when she hears the moanings of her infant that during the agony of disease cannot express what it feels?" (15)—he wrote her into his poem to point in quite another direction. Maternal sympathy is the second of three crucial examples Smith provides (compassion for the insane and for the dead are the others) to affirm the cognitive basis of sympathy, which depends more on the observer's judgment than on the sufferer's immediate experience. In each of these cases, the observer projects onto suffering a meaning, concept, or image the sufferer cannot himself supply because he lacks sufficient powers of reflection (or in the case of the dead, any). The infant "feels only the uneasiness of the present instant"; it is the mother's understanding that places sorrow's immediacy within a horizon of possible futures: "In her idea of what it suffers, she joins, to its real helplessness, her own consciousness of that helplessness, and her own terrors for the unknown consequences of its disorder; and out of all these, forms, for her own sorrow, the most complete image of misery and distress" (15). For the infant: wordlessness, thoughtlessness, and the punctuated affect of a futureless present tense. For the mother: feeling joined with idea, formed into image, and placed into the narrative time of possible sequences. As Blake's poem modulates from an "infant groan" to an "infant fear" (from immediacy to anticipation), one can still hear a lingering hint of this kind of cognitive projection, but when Jesus enters the scene, even forward-looking "fear" drops out of the poem's vocabulary. If the "woes," "griefs," and "sorrows" that Jesus hears possess any cognitive content beyond their auditory immediacy, we never hear about it. Instead, the poem offers up a correspondence between suffering and irreducible aurality, a correspondence that is sensory but, as Adorno puts it, "foreign to knowledge." "Weeping tear on infants tear," Jesus undergoes an ascesis of linguistic meaning, concept, and image parallel to the becoming-infant of the incarnation itself. He abdicates his divine title (the Word) and concedes to a passion he recognizes but does not translate into speech. Somehow "On Anothers Sorrow" asks us to "read" its printed sighs and tears not only with the eye but with an open, unguarded ear. The reader follows the parallel tracks of "a falling tear"—the visual one "I see" first in line 5 ("Can I see a falling tear"?) and then in lines 20, 22, and 31 but also the auditory "tear" that drops through a third of the poem's eighteen rhymes, forming a fluid sound path that includes pairs (fear/share or care/bear) more tightly linked by the "ear" than by the eye.

As with many of the *Songs of Innocence*, "On Anothers Sorrow" features an abundance of vowel play. *Weeping* tears becomes *wiping* them away. "[S]miles on **all**" (what Jesus does) compresses into the next line's "sorrows **small**," joining impossible breadth to improbable focus. Within stanza two alone, the *falling* tear becomes the sorrow I *feel* before it finally pools in the sorrow with which the father is *fill'*d. Most important, however, is the sound of *o* in "sorrow." To begin with, the meter and masculine rhyme scheme preclude Blake from placing the last word of his title in a rhyme position as other poets have done (think of Keats), thus preventing him from aligning the poem's subject, the sharing of sorrow, with the analogous formal pleasures of consonance and correspondence. Adam Smith seems to have had something like this analogy in mind when, responding to an objection by Hume, he revised a footnote in *Moral Sentiments* to take notice of the power of harmony. Why, Hume asked, should sympathy be agreeable even when it involves the sharing of disagreeable feelings? Smith responded, "Two sounds, I suppose, may, each of them taken singly, be austere, and yet, if they are perfect concords, the perception of their harmony and coincidence may be agreeable" (56). Sorrow rhymed, like sorrow shared, would be sorrow harmonized and relieved.

The word occurs five times in Blake's song, always near but never at the end of a line, and it is almost always followed by a word that invokes shared feeling while at the same time preventing "sorrow" itself from participating in the resolution of rhyme: "sorrow too," "sorrows share," "sorrow fill'd," "sorrows small," "sorrow too." Moreover, in a poem that trades regularly in the easy pleasures of chiming, predictable harmony, the sound left by "sorrow" reverberates through all but one of Blake's occasional but deeply unsettling off-rhymes. The long, open *o* generates dissonance where the first rhyme should occur ("Can I see anothers woe / And not be in sorrow too"); it recurs in stanza seven ("He becomes a man of woe / He doth feel the sorrow too"); and it undermines the movement toward closure that the final rhyme—concluding poem and volume—might be thought to promise ("Till our grief is fled & gone / He doth sit by us and moan"). Gone/Moan repeats the short/long value pattern of the *o*s in "sorrow," and it matters, to my ear at least, that the poem leaves us with an echo of sorrow, extended indefinitely. Imagine the effect of reversing the last two lines, a possibility allowed for by rhyme and syntax:

He doth sit by us and moan
Till our grief is fled & gone.

Poem, moan, and grief would all end decisively with the word "gone," indulging the fantasy that sympathy had achieved its work of kind relief, reversing even the vowel sequence of "sorrow." Instead, Blake leaves us with the disturbance of an *o* so long and so inassimilable to comfort that its moan could endure forever, without period (a possibility Blake's absent punctuation actively suggests).[45]

Within the poem's discourse of sympathy, then, sound traces a fault line between eye and ear, content and nonsense, kinship and dissonance, closure and duration—all versions of the tension between a sympathy that works (by moving on) and another that doesn't. Sorrow cannot easily be made to disappear into the good light of meaningfulness; it leaves an impression on the ear with no clear referent, performing a kind of cognitive evacuation analogous, visually, to the absence of suffering figures in the plate and also, perhaps, to the graphic emptiness of the *o*'s own alphabetic figure. Too aggressive an approach to sorrow—to understand it, to make it speak, to act upon it—misses it, which is probably why the poem's most persistent verbs (hearing and sitting) occur almost always together, as a redundant passivity. Theorists of emotional intelligence are sometimes too eager to make us believe that taking emotion seriously requires us to understand it in terms of its propositional content, a point central to some forms of psychoanalysis, for instance, where emotions without meaning are simply emotions not yet understood. Emotions must always be telling us something. Although the disavowal of Cartesian dualism has led emotion advocates to gesture inclusively toward a whole spectrum of nonverbal activity, extending emotional intelligence even to animals, often the result is to widen the sphere of meaningfulness (modeled on language, if not linguistic per se) rather than to acknowledge any boundaries where intelligibility might falter.[46] Two times in "On Anothers Sorrow," at the beginning of lines 23 and 33, the *o* of "sorrow," "woe," and "moan" unmoors itself from words altogether, even from neighboring consonants. Every reader of lyric poetry knows this sentimental routine. (Poe claimed to have settled on the long *o* of "nevermore" even before deciding on his poem's subject matter; he knew he wanted the effect of forceful, sonorous rhymes, "and these considerations inevitably led [him] to the long *o* as the most sonorous vowel").[47] And yet the *o* that fulfills convention also hollows it, leaving an estrangement in excess of the bare mechanism it has exposed (as Poe also understood). How odd it would be to ask what this sound means (Smith's "What has befallen you?" would overshoot it), for it invokes nothing, *literally,* that is, "no thing" which might get caught in the crosshairs where words and concepts intersect. Holding the place of absence where diction ("the expression of meaning in words") used to be, the *o* is what's left of a sorrow assimilated into the conventions of sympathy, but not completely.

There are relevant *o*-events in Blake's other songs as well. The first two words of "The Sick Rose" ("O Rose") perform in miniature a drama of containment by naming that the speaker enacts upon the other's desire (E 23). When "The Little Black Boy" (E 9) exclaims, "And I am black, but O! my soul is white," the sound of sorrow cuts across the prevailing racial, religious, and visual vocabularies that make little sense of his singular condition. A placeholder left where substantive accounts of identity fail (on either side: "I am" / "my soul is"), this inarticulate "O" competes with the round figure of the sun rising above it in the illumination (figure 3.3). The sun signals a transition from ear to eye. As a figure for the dawn of progress and enlightenment, it promises to dispel darkness and dissonance in a movement the speaker wants to understand, under the tutelage of his mother, as a stage in his own maturation. In order to make sense of suffering, the mother tries to anchor her son's experience in a knowable, well-lighted world. She first identifies an image she can point to empirically and name ("pointing to the east [she] began to say / Look on the rising sun"), which she then turns into the moral center of a redemptive grief/relief narrative ("Look on the rising sun: there God does live"). Even the gentlest of educations brings intransigent sound ("but O!") into the eye's domain, subordinating sorrow to meaningfulness. The rising sun of the illustration is itself, of course, also an eye, a single, ascending eye that oversees the text beneath it on the plate. Simply to read the words of this poem is tantamount to laboring "Under a cruel eye outworn."

This last phrase appears in another song, this time from *Experience,* "The

School Boy" (E 31). Without literally separating an auditory from a visual "O," as in "The Little Black Boy," this poem manages to reproduce the same perceptual tensions. The second stanza begins,

> But to go to school in a summer morn,
> O! it drives all joy away;
> Under a cruel eye outworn,
> The little ones spend the day,
> In sighing and dismay.

Directly underneath the "O," the line "Under a cruel eye outworn" prompts us to see the letter above it as a figure for the instructor's watchful eye, which in turn becomes the antecedent subject that "drives all joy away." Education of this kind involves a steadily increasing visual discipline; to acquire literacy one must adopt a pleasureless eye: "Nor in my book can I [eye] take delight" (13). Even as it charts this process, however, the unattached "O" continues to sound, conveying a residue of distress that remains when "joy" wears away, while also retaining some memory of the auditory but nonverbal pleasures of summertime (birdsong, music) described in the first stanza:

> I love to rise in a summer morn,
> When the birds sing on every tree;
> The distant huntsman winds his horn,
> And the sky-lark sings with me.
> O! what sweet company.

Thus the poem's entire education narrative could be condensed into the three single syllables that, in sequence, begin lines 5–7:

> O! what sweet company.
>
> But to go to school in a summer morn,
> O! it drives all joy away.

In shorthand, "O! But O!" tells the story of lost innocence that occurs when sound is taught meaning and is pressed into the service of vigilant insight. It forms the briefest possible tale of piping become reading.

According to Joseph Viscomi, Blake's production methods required him to print "The School Boy" together with "On Anothers Sorrow" and "Spring."[48] Perhaps we can imagine these three poems forming their own "O! But O!" sequence, with "On Anothers Sorrow" looking back to the "Merry voice / Infant noise" (E 15) of "Spring" and forward to "The School Boy," which ends "When the blasts of winter appear" (E 31). If that were the case, then "On Anothers Sorrow" would position the acqui-

Figure 3.3 "The Little Black Boy," *Songs of Innocence and of Experience*, copy L, plate 8, 1789–1794. Yale Center for British Art, Paul Mellon Collection

sition of sympathy as an important point along the temporal axis of a sentimental education. The passage from wordlessness to verbal mastery would include the moment when one learned to believe one could understand the sound of sorrow. At the same time, however, "On Anothers Sorrow" is at best an embarrassing relay between know-nothing innocence and the trained know-how of experience. It allows for only an incomplete *bildung*, since even its round formulations cannot fully assimilate the persistent unease of sound, which continues to weep and sigh and moan "without any delicacy," leaving reminders and remainders of the *infant* sorrows (and joys), unspeakable affects, that mortify even the most articulate linguistic performances from within. Once again it is worth recalling Kevis Goodman's study of the eighteenth-century georgic revival, for Goodman has alerted us to the pathways by which "cognitive noise" enters into convention-laden poems that cannot prevent themselves from conveying the unexpected historical effects their well-turned forms are typically designed to tune out: "historical presentness is often 'turned up' by georgic as *unpleasurable* feeling: as sensory discomfort, as disturbance in affect and related phenomena that we variously term perceptive, sensorial, or affective—I refer to the noise of living . . . rather than to shapely, staged, or well-defined emotions."[49] Goodman makes excellent use of Raymond Williams's late interviews in the *New Left Review,* where he elaborated on his concept of "structures of feeling" as "all that is not fully articulated, all that comes through as disturbance, tension, blockage, emotional trouble" (7). Cognitive noise, one might say, is the sound poems make despite the stories they wish to tell, for the verbal medium that would "shield" them is also an "aperture" through which unfamiliar and often averse emotions—the sorrows we don't want to know—make themselves felt. Every articulate voice bears the potential disruption of its own noise. Blake reminds us of this fault line within diction even in a poem of such childlike transparency as "Spring." The faulty rhyme I quoted above turns on a dissonance that linguists recognize as the difference between voiced and unvoiced consonants: "Merry voi**ce** / Infant noi**se**." "Sorrow" is also a noisy word, voiced and unvoiced, not technically, but in the difference between its sounding and its reading. For that reason, it will never fully rhyme with understanding, and its moaning will always rub against its meaning.

The most painful sorrows are also possibilities not yet found by language, which is why we want to believe their sounds have a future unaccountable to knowledge or narrative: they follow their own "complex path, a dissonant and polyphonic drive." The quoted phrase is Fred Moten's, the preceding paraphrase mine. It recaps my understanding of an essay called "Black Mo'nin'," where Moten describes (performs really) how *sound* matters in the visual medium of a Civil Rights–era photograph of Emmett Till, murdered and disfigured. Toward the end of his essay, Moten likens this sound path, unbearable but also open and therefore potentially affirmative, to "the Music, which is, as Mingus says, not just beautiful, but *terribly beautiful*." He does not even have to mention that Mingus contributed to sorrow his own version of "Moanin'," or that, before Yeats, one source of "terrible beauty" is Blake's own description of Ireland: "Beautiful but terrible struggling to take a form of beauty" (*Jerusalem* 74:53, E 230).[50]

Toward an Auditory Imagination

Interlude on Kenzaburo Oe's *Rouse Up O Young Men of the New Age*

When the young men of the new age arrive, what will their imaginations *sound* like? Taking his novel's title from the Preface to *Milton* and including, among many citations of Blake, an important reference to "On Anothers Sorrow," Kenzaburo Oe teaches us to ask precisely this improbable question and thus to prepare for the arrival of the new through the ear rather than the eye. Like much of Oe's fiction, *Rouse Up O Young Men of the New Age* (1986; English translation 2002) is skewed autobiography, but here the author's career-long fascination with Blake becomes an explicit and dominant concern of his narrator double. The novel begins with a crisis: K's mentally disabled son—whom he has always called "Eeyore," after the A. A. Milne character—is on the verge of adulthood and exhibiting signs of aggression and sexual frustration. In order to prepare him for the world of experience, K decides to equip his son with a collection of core, practical definitions, a guidebook of accessible meaning culled from his own experience as mediated by his understanding of Blake. Not only does this unlikely project fail (predictably K abandons it), it undergoes a reversal when K and Eeyore collaborate on a children's operetta based on *Gulliver's Travels,* to be performed by a school for students with serious disabilities. After the production, for which K writes the libretto and Eeyore composes the music, K sits in the audience and thinks: "Until now, it had been my goal to provide definitions of things and people for Eeyore's sake; but at this moment it was Eeyore, presenting me with a stanza from Blake's *Milton* as a lucid vision, who was creating a definition for his father:

> *Then first I saw him in the Zenith as a falling star,*
> *Descending perpendicular, swift as the swallow or swift;*
> *And on my left foot falling on the tarsus, enter'd there."*[1]

K sees his son as if for the first time, as if he were an astrological sign of the end time—just as Blake received the Milton he thought he knew as a suddenly unfamiliar guest entering and altering his world.

But the reversal of roles here leaves a question unanswered: Eeyore creates a definition for K, but a definition *of what?* One possibility, cued by the quotation from *Milton,* is the word "foot." After all, the chapter that ends with Eeyore still sitting inside the stage set's giant papier-mâché foot (Gulliver's) began with the son's sympathetic attachment to his father's gout-ridden foot. The reversal of definitions thus seems to pivot on access to another through the mediation of the "foot," the lowest and therefore least likely of body parts to provide such access. This improbable idea in turn calls for a fundamental reconsideration of another word important to the chapter—"imagination." What K receives from Eeyore—though I would argue that Oe keeps its occurrence just beneath the threshold of the narrator's recognition—is neither a "lucid vision" nor a definition: he receives instead the event of *auditory* imagination.

"Imagination" has been at stake throughout the chapter that culminates in the operetta. A writer himself, K thinks it important to define "imagination" for Eeyore, but his reflections on the word lead him to wonder (despairingly) whether his son possesses any degree of this faculty at all, especially as Gaston Bachelard describes it in the text that forms the basis of K's understanding. "Even today," writes Bachelard in *Air and Dreams,* "Imagination is considered to be the ability to form images. But it is rather the ability to deform images presented by perception, the ability to liberate us from basic images, the ability in particular to change images. If there is no changing of images, no unexpected merging of images, there is no imagination and the act of imagining does not occur" (127).[2] This familiar idea—reminiscent of Coleridge's definition of the secondary imagination and Blake's own critique of empiricism in the Natural Religion tracts—presents imagination as an engine of transformation. Without its active agency, change cannot occur, and perception becomes only the compulsory repetition of givens (thus K's despair for his son). K seems unaware, however, of the irony involved in his own act of citation. He transmits his source definition unimaginatively, without alteration, and in the process of quotation repeats the narrow visual bias he inherits from Bachelard's revisionary account. These three sentences about the need to deform and change images, about the need to be liberated from basic images, cannot liberate themselves from the burdensome word "image" (which, along with variants, appears nine times). In this limited, insistent definition, the visual is the only perceptual medium that counts.

The eye's self-perpetuating regime and its inability to imagine otherwise constrain the narrator right from the novel's beginning, where they underlie K's crucial misreading of "On Anothers Sorrow," a poem he mistakes for an unproblematic representation of sympathetic immediacy and shared sorrow. Like the operetta scene, the first chapter ends epiphanically, with K discovering what he takes to be an overwhelming insight into "grief," assisted by Blake's text. Only now does he enter into the suffering evident in his son's eyes, which he earlier misunderstood as an expression of Eeyore's newly awakened animal desires:

> Writing this now it is hard to imagine how as a father I could have failed to see that massive grief in the desolation of my son's eyes. And I can't help feeling that, healing the rift with my son, I became aware of his grief through the agency of a Blake poem, "On Another's Sorrow," which includes this stanza:
>
> *Can I see a falling tear,*
> *And not feel my sorrows share,*
> *Can a father see his child,*
> *Weep, nor be with sorrow fill'd.*
>
> One of the "Songs of Innocence," the poem concludes with the following verse:
>
> *O! he gives to us his joy,*
> *That our grief he may destroy*
> *Till our grief is fled & gone*
> *He doth sit by us and moan.*   (25–26)

K presents these stanzas as if they confirmed one another and formed a unitary representation of sympathy, missing altogether the later stanza's auditory departure from the earlier one's visuality. Referring to the convergence of three memories (of a colleague's sorrow, of the Blake poem, of his son's eyes), all of which involve *reading* another's *eyes*, K concludes the chapter by adding: "I was able to read the grief in my son's eyes even more directly, as though it were in my own experience, because I was equipped with a definition of grief that had appeared for just an instant in Mr. H's eyes that day at the bar in the New Delhi airport" (26). K believes he has corrected a failure of imagination, a misinterpretation, but he has in fact substituted a new error for an old one. Like "On Anothers Sorrow," *Rouse Up* begins with an apparent affirmation of imagination and sympathy (imagination *as* sympathy) that it will eventually supersede, not least by breaking the closed circuit of visuality that prevents other imaginings from being heard. Much later in the novel we learn that the lust and grief K thought he saw in Eeyore's eyes were in fact a projection of his own self-loathing based on his experiences as a young father of a severely disabled infant (experiences hauntingly detailed in *A Personal Matter*). The "eye" that would receive the suffering of others is little more than an extension of the egoistic "I," finding mirrors in everything it reads.

In "The School Boy"—a poem that provides the first half of the English title for another of Oe's novels, *Nip the Buds, Shoot the Kids*—we saw how the disciplinary figure of the eye displaces the wayward pleasures of the ear ("O! It drives all joy away"). The student who once rose to the sound of birds in summer ("the skylark sings with me") now labors under the "cruel eye" of his teacher. Although it is never mentioned in *Rouse Up*, the poem can help us understand how Blake's poetry works in and on this novel, saturating it, reverberating through it—at times directly, but not always so. In a scene of instruction that may or may not deliberately invoke "The School Boy," K describes Eeyore's early love of birdsong, the first manifestation of his developing musical gifts, which K studies intently for signs of imaginative activity. Even as a preschooler, Eeyore's first sustained use of words involved identifying bird calls his father recorded for him: " 'Thrush—it's dusky thrush,' or 'Titlark, it's titlark, it's flycatcher, nightingale, it's nightingale . . .' " (130). Part cognitive scientist, part pedagogue, K observes the pleasure his son takes in these moments of rudimentary communication ("the same pleasure he took in eating"), but sees no evidence of imagination at work, precisely because Eeyore cannot translate his auditory activity into visualization:

> There was no possibility that Eeyore was picturing the shape of the bird from the sound of its voice on the tape. His vision was impaired in a way that could be corrected only by a complex configuration of prism and lens. In those days before he was wearing glasses, he couldn't possibly have resolved the shape or figure of a bird; even so, I went to the trouble of pointing to photographs of birds on record-album jackets and repeating for him, "This is a magpie; this is a starling." But it seemed never to occur to him to look at the photographs on his own as he listened to the tape.
>
> In short, the bird as object did not exist. (130–131)

No images, no imagination. If, however, we are attuned to the Blakean intertext, a different possibility emerges: the ear hears more than the eye understands. Many of the same birds K mentions here also appear in Blake, often in association with moments of perceptual possibility—call it "imagination"—that "Satans watch-fiends cannot find." The thrush, the nightingale, and the lark, for instance, all participate in *Milton*'s "Song of Spring," a bird chorus so extravagant it could rival anything composed by Olivier Messiaen:

> Thou hearest the Nightingale begin the Song of Spring;
> The Lark sitting upon his earthy bed: just as the morn
> Appears; listens silent; then springing from the waving Corn-field! loud
> He leads the Choir of Day! trill, trill, trill, trill,
> Mounting upon the wings of light into the Great Expanse:

Reecchoing against the lovely blue & shining heavenly Shell:

His little throat labours with inspiration; every feather

On throat & breast & wings vibrates with the effluence Divine

All Nature listens silent to him & the awful Sun

Stands still upon the Mountain looking on this little Bird

With eyes of soft humility, & wonder love & awe.

Then loud from their green covert all the Birds begin their Song

The Thrush, the Linnet & the Goldfinch, Robin & the Wren

Awake the Sun from his sweet reverie upon the Mountain:

The Nightingale again assays his song, & thro the day,

And thro the night warbles luxuriant; every Bird of Song

Attending his loud harmony with admiration & love.

This is a Vision of the lamentation of Beulah over Ololon!   (31:28–45, E 130–131)

Thomas Vogler writes of this passage: "The striking emphasis on attentiveness to the sounds of the Nightingale and the Lark on plate 31, reinforced by the anagrammatic emphasis on the repeated phrase 'listens silent,' calls our attention to the issue of hearing in *MIL/TON* and to what is at stake in how we hear the Lark's 'trill, trill, trill, trill' when in Book II the 'high ton'd Song' of the 'loud voic'd Bard' gives way to 'this little bird,' whose trill, though not 'words,' may concern our 'eternal salvation.'"[3] The ear, not the eye, opens onto salvation, the birdsong, not the referential word. We don't have to sentimentalize Eeyore's nonvisual and minimally linguistic interiority, and thus risk making *his* alterity serve *our* desire for a nonsymbolic space, to realize that his unaccountability tests the limits of a visual imagination and reveals its tendency to foreclose on other possibilities of identification and sympathy.

This "deafness of established forms" (to borrow a phrase from Lyotard) appears with poignant clarity in one other scene from the novel that bears mentioning.[4] In one of K's most vivid dreams, he and his son emerge from tunnels of isolation into a landscape of fantastic, mutual access. Now Eeyore appears to K fully revealed, a naked, exuberant youth whose ideal image has been superimposed onto the figure of Blake's "Albion rose." At the same time, K realizes that his own "spiritual essence" must be symbolically apparent to Eeyore, taking the form of a Wren:

Presently, I become aware that to my son in my dream, I, too, appear as a symbol manifesting a certain spiritual essence. I notice that I have assumed the form of the birds whose voices were the only sounds he took pleasure in hearing as an infant. "Wren" is the spiritual essence my life conveys. If I could see its shape, invisible to me, the meaning of my life, having been born into the universe to labor, sorrow, learn, and forget, would be revealed. With the quiet beating of wren's wings I fly toward my son's gleaming head, trying to see my own form reflected in his eyes. (93)

To see oneself through the eyes of the other would fulfill the dream of a fully achieved, mutually sympathetic imagination, but K routes his desire through a visual circuit that guarantees its frustration: "a dark whirlpool drew me down." Neglecting the ear, quieting the beating of his Wren-wings as he approaches his son (compare Blake's Lark-wings, every feather of which "vibrates with the effluence Divine"), K flies after meaning, essence, and revelation, only to miss the luxuriant sound of an unseen agency, of an imagination independent of images, of a "Song of Spring":

Then loud from their green covert all the Birds begin their Song
The Thrush, the Linnet & the Goldfinch, Robin & *the Wren*
Awake the Sun from his sweet reverie upon the Mountain.

In order to apprehend himself as his son apprehends him, in order to approach himself through the medium of Eeyore's imagination, K would have to pass through the ear rather than the eye, listening without looking.

There are several things we can now say as we return to the role reversal at the end of the operetta, where Eeyore does not so much supply his own definition of "imagination" as indicate the limited reach of his father's. It makes sense that Eeyore, after serving as prompter throughout the performance, won't come out from hiding within the papier-mâché foot, despite the audience's call for his appearance. For whatever reason, he prefers not to be seen. It also makes sense that K, moved by the event to join the audience in song, continues to describe his experience in visual terms he will never quite be able to relinquish. Eeyore, we remember, presents him with "a lucid vision," and the passage K chooses from *Milton* to gloss this moment, a text about receiving the other, also features a visual emphasis:

Then first I saw him in the Zenith as a falling star,
Descending perpendicular, swift as the swallow or swift;
And on my left foot falling on the tarsus, enter'd there.

In Blake, however, a "lucid vision" sometimes consists almost entirely of sound. The birdsong of spring, for instance, is called "a Vision of the lamentation of Beulah over Ololon!" Visual images, even in a composite art form such as Blake's, do not preclude the possibility of sounds uncoupling themselves to follow their own path. Thus the massive foot dominating the scene on Oe's stage also opens onto the rhythmic *foot* of poetry, the auditory vehicle of patterned language, a musical element picked up immediately by the bird presence in the quotation from

Milton—"swift as the swallow or swift." The repetition of "swift" (and of the *sw* sound generally) introduces a soundtrack irrelevant to the image, an independent aural vector enhanced by a pleasurable but largely meaningless wordplay that has little to do with visualizing a bird in rapid descent. And because the operetta is based on *Gulliver's Travels,* this spiral paronomasia now expands to include an echo of Jonathan *Swift* in Blake's wordplay. Later in *Milton,* Blake will double this word again when he refers to "Times swiftness / Which is the swiftest of all things" (24:72–73, E 121), suggesting not only that the new, when it comes, comes suddenly but also that sound detached from established meaning becomes an experimental medium (the "swift-test of all things"), a medium in which disjointed "things" open onto new dimensions of themselves or get reimagined. Even if K can't quite hear this sound path, Oe allows it to work on his ear and ours. It follows the course of its own strange historicity, which must now include the wholly improbable event of *Milton*—the strangest of English Romantic poems—resounding through a modern novel, its translated feet falling on Japanese ears in a way no one could have anticipated. Whether or not this event heralds a new age remains to be heard.

CHAPTER FOUR

Strange Pulse

This is how the human comes into being, again and again, as that
which we have yet to know.

—Judith Butler, *Precarious Life*

[W]ayward Sensibility [is a] delicate, but irregular power, which now
impels to all that is most disinterested for others, [and] now forgets
all mankind, to watch the pulsations of its own fancies.

—Frances Burney, *Camilla*

Even among eighteenth-century advocates of sensibility, the danger of self-indulgence was a common theme. The sorrows of others, they complained, were
too often an excuse for "[n]ursing" the pleasures of sympathy "in some delicious
solitude," as Coleridge remarked.[1] Blake also had little patience for negligent self-
absorption, but his answer to the problem was rather different from the one implied by Frances Burney. If sensibility is to overcome its self-ease, and thus open
itself onto the possibility of different social relations, it must do so by paying more,
not less, attention to the pulses. According to Blake, poetry accomplishes its work
in the tiniest event of affect: "the Poets Work is Done . . . / Within a Moment: a
Pulsation of the Artery" (*Milton* 29:1–3, E 127). Even more: "all the Great / Events
of Time start forth & are concievd in such a Period" (29:1–2, E 127). Blake's astonishing statement challenges us to rethink three elements that converge in an
event both singular and continuous: poetic labor, the experience of time, and the
feeling of the blood as it moves through the body. Why *these* three things converge—and why pulsation becomes Blake's figure for the work of poetry—is the
question I want to address first in this chapter. If these considerations will lead us
away from "On Anothers Sorrow" and into a broader account of feeling in Blake's
critical aesthetics, they do so only to return in the end to the problem of sympathy.

Only by passing through the heart—following the lead of Milton at the start of his epic journey—can we grasp the deviant relationship between time and feeling that structures the work of emotion in Blake's poetry. At the heart of sensibility, Blake suggests, lies an experience of embodied time that—when attended to minutely—can hardly result in self-ease, for the agitation of the pulse, at once slight, vital, and strange, does not reinforce one's sense of self but alienates it. The subject of pulsation no longer knows what it would mean to feel or act naturally, for the same pulsations that support life also interrupt the familiar ways of being human. In this sense, Blake's pulses serve the task of cultural critique as Judith Butler has recently described it: "to return us to the human where we do not expect to find it, in its frailty and at the limits of its capacity to make sense."[2]

From Plots to Pulsations

Blake develops the question of pulsation most fully in the great passage on time toward the end of the first part of *Milton*, from which I have quoted the lines on the poet's work above. Before we turn to that passage, however, we can frame our inquiry by returning to the question of narratability raised by "On Anothers Sorrow," where the passivity and impossible duration of Jesus' sympathy pose a problem for narrative representation. Here we can ask the question more broadly: Are there scenes of emotion too short or too long to be plotted?

In his foundational discussion of narrative in the *Poetics*, Aristotle likened well-crafted plots to beautiful objects and natural organisms: their size must be just right for their purpose. To illustrate his point he conjured two ludicrous counterexamples: a form so "very small" it would pass by in "an imperceptible instant of time" and one so "very large" it would stretch "a thousand miles long." For good plots a certain length is necessary, and Aristotle defined proper "magnitude" as the time it takes a spectator to grasp the *peripeteia* of a fully developed, self-contained action sequence, either "a change from misfortune to good fortune [from grief to relief, say], or from good fortune to misfortune."[3] These norms regarding narrative length can help us grasp the bad timing of Blake's Jesus (and, as we will see in a moment, the bad timing of pulsation). For if Blake's Jesus sometimes occupies the excessive passivity we see in "On Anothers Sorrow," elsewhere he becomes a figure of impetuous energy, the kind of antinomian rebel made famous, for instance, in *The Marriage of Heaven & Hell*'s lawbreaker who "acted from impulse not from rules" (23–24, E 43). One Jesus waits without limits, in a state of inaction with no foreseeable end; the other acts so impatiently that the moment from which his action springs occurs "in an imperceptible instant of time," much too quickly, as

Aristotle notes, to be narratable. One waits so long that he postpones the possibility of story indefinitely; the other's impulse has already passed by before any story can claim it.

In the example from *The Marriage of Heaven & Hell,* Blake's printed text can point toward this vanishing instant of action but cannot narrate it. Even while the "Memorable Fancy" that tells of an encounter between devil and angel moves along a narrative arc toward conclusion, the text itself disintegrates internally into smaller and smaller units. As described by the devil, Jesus can only exhibit his volatility negatively, by violating the rules that would contain it. Just so, Blake's printed text first breaks up the word "commandment" by double-hyphenating it ("I tell you, no virtue / can exist without breaking these ten comand- / -ments").[4] It then carries its fracturing energies into the word "impulse" itself, the last syllable of which carries over from plate 23 to plate 24 in a way no transcription can effectively render because it cannot reproduce the effect, at once disruptive and quickly forgotten, of turning a page, and in a way no description can effectively render because, like this one, it takes too long to represent a stutter lasting only an instant. A faithful, though still inadequate transcription would look something like this, where the vertical line represents the break between pages:

-pulse. not from rules.

Jesus was all virtue, and acted from im-
-pulse|

Blake follows the eighteenth-century convention of placing a catchword at the bottom of one page to anticipate the start of another, thus helping the printer assemble pages in proper order and assuring the text never skips a beat, but here, the catchword itself becomes the occasion, barely noticeable, of a palpitation (figure 4.1). "Pulse" detaches itself from any of the continuous linguistic units that would subsume it (from the word "impulse," from the printed line above it, from the sentence across pages, from the parable that forms the whole of this "Memorable Fancy"), mimicking in sound and meaning the cardiac rhythm that expands and contracts an artery, just as this repeated, beating syllable ("-pulse / -pulse.") closes one page and opens another. Within linguistic performances, this pulsation seems to say, events occur that are too small to notice—just as the attention-grabbing spectacle of breaking the ten commandments (in which Blake's Jesus is preceded biblically by Moses and followed cinematically by Charlton Heston) is underwritten by a much less traceable impulse, itself the result of a pulse so exceedingly common and quick and small as to elude representation, except by tricks that would suggest it obliquely. These tricks become crude when magnified by analysis but escape attention altogether when not. The poet's work is indeed done in a moment: a pulsation of the artery.

In these representations of Jesus, then, Blake is exploring alternative ways of being in time. Confounding ordinary distinctions between activity and passivity, his Jesus cannot be represented by the narrative time of self-contained characters performing recognizable action sequences. He is at once too quick and too slow to be plotted, too patient and too impulsive.[5] "On Anothers Sorrow" and *The Marriage of Heaven & Hell* are necessary counterparts; one Jesus plays systole to the other's diastole. In fact, the Jesus of Blake's song already displays these reciprocal tendencies. His hyperbolic sympathy is itself an impulsive passivity—ungoverned by principle, heedless in its attachments, formed without judgment or deliberation and therefore instantaneous but also unacted upon, inconsequential (literally without sequel), opening a space of desistance unimaginably extensive. If we ordinarily think of impulse as a "[s]udden or involuntary inclination or tendency to act" (*OED*), one of the threats posed by passion (in the Kantian sense) to responsible, premeditated action, Blake provides the unthinkable: a figure swept by emotion into inaction. His Jesus shares the "HURRY UP / HOLD BACK" tendency Ann Smock has taught us to see in the strange subjectivities and temporalities explored by Herman Melville and Maurice Blanchot: "rushing to procrastinate"; "seized by a veritable outburst of patience"; a "lack of restraint . . . entangled with sheer inertia."[6]

As we have seen, the sympathy that characterizes this improbable figure is at once too large and too small for the kind of interactions (the grief/relief stories) that existing social relations can script, prompting the song's speaker to ask, in a voice both incredulous and adulatory, "Can he who smiles on *all* / Hear the wren with sorrows *small*"? Such extremes of magnitude, unamenable to narrative solutions, present a problem Blake never grew weary of exploring. If, for instance, one set out to invent a single literary work capable of simultaneously inhabiting both of the margins Aristotle considered outside the bounds of plot, a single work at once too vast (with interminable novelistic length, except nothing happens) and too exceedingly small (because its actions fall beneath the threshold of ordinary perception, taking place at a level of such minute particularity), and if, moreover, one were determined to cast Jesus in the starring role, one could hardly do better than invent *Jerusalem*, that giant form in which "Every word and every letter is studied and put into its fit place" (E 146). On a miniature scale, "On Anothers Sorrow" anticipates the nonnarrative experiment of *Jerusalem*. The expansion and contraction its sympathy performs (all/small) returns in the "Visionary forms dramatic" of the redeemed Eternals, whose conversation pulsates "according to the Expansion or Contraction, the Translucence or / Opakeness of Nervous fibres" (98:28, 36–37, E 257–258). Even more, the song's impulsive inaction prefigures the relation between present and future imagined by *Jerusalem*, a poem in which the break from the past simply happens—on plate 94 perhaps[7]—unwilled, with-

greatest men best, those who envy or calumniate
great men hate God, for there is no other God.
The Angel hearing this became almost blue
but mastering himself he grew yellow, & at last
white pink & smiling, and then replied,
Thou Idolater, is not God One? & is not he
visible in Jesus Christ? and has not Jesus Christ
given his sanction to the law of ten commandments
and are not all other men fools, sinners, & nothings?
The Devil answerd: bray a fool in a mortar with
wheat yet shall not his folly be beaten out of him;
if Jesus Christ is the greatest man, you ought to
love him in the greatest degree; now hear how he
has given his sanction to the law of ten commandments: did he not mock at the sabbath, and so
mock the sabbaths God? murder those who were
murderd because of him? turn away the law from
the woman taken in adultery? steal the labor of
others to support him? bear false witness when
he omitted making a defence before Pilate? covet
when he prayd for his disciples, and when he bid
them shake off the dust of their feet against such
as refused to lodge them? I tell you, no virtue
can exist without breaking these ten commandments. Jesus was all virtue, and acted from im-
-pulse

Figure 4.1 (left) The Marriage of Heaven and Hell, copy D, plate 23. Lessing J. Rosenwald Collection, Library of Congress. Copyright © 2011 the William Blake Archive. Used with permission. *(right) The Marriage of Heaven and Hell,* copy D, plate 24. Lessing J. Rosenwald Collection, Library of Congress. Copyright © 2011 the William Blake Archive. Used with permission.

out cause or warning, when (suddenly, for no obvious reason) "our grief is fled & gone." And the song anticipates this improbable temporality not because it maps out any steps that would lead from suffering to redemption, as a liberal reformer might reasonably do, but because it withdraws from the idea that the future can be attained only by the kinds of actions we can imagine in narrative form.[8]

The central text for juxtaposing or superimposing the exceedingly small and the

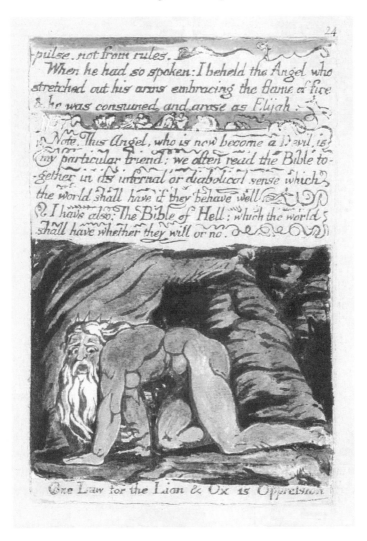

vast, the momentary now and an expansive forever, without the usual transitions provided by narrative scale, is the passage on time in *Milton*. It is here that Blake introduces pulsation as a figure for poetic labor and thus raises a series of questions about the time and space of aesthetic agency. Although the primary figure in these lines is the pulse, we can start by thinking of the passage as an elaborate pun on the word "period."

> But others of the Sons of Los build Moments & Minutes & Hours
> And Days & Months & Years & Ages & Periods; wondrous buildings
> And every Moment has a Couch of gold for soft repose,
> (A Moment equals a pulsation of the artery)

And between every two Moments stands a Daughter of Beulah
To feed the Sleepers on their Couches with maternal care.
And every Minute has an azure Tent with silken Veils.
And every Hour has a bright golden Gate carved with skill.
And every Day & Night, has Walls of brass & Gates of adamant,
Shining like precious stones & ornamented with appropriate signs:
And every Month, a silver paved Terrace builded high:
And every Year, invulnerable Barriers with high Towers.
And every Age is Moated deep with Bridges of silver & gold.
And every Seven Ages is Incircled with a Flaming Fire.
Now Seven Ages is amounting to Two Hundred Years
Each has its Guard. each Moment Minute Hour Day Month & Year.
All are the work of Fairy hands of the Four Elements
The Guard are Angels of Providence on duty evermore
Every Time less than a pulsation of the artery
Is equal in its period & value to Six Thousand Years.
For in this Period the Poets Work is Done: and all the Great
Events of Time start forth & are concievd in such a Period
Within a Moment: a Pulsation of the Artery.   (28:44–63; 29:1–3, E 126–127)

When the ever-expanding measures of time ("Moments & Minutes," "Months & Years") reach their outer limit and collapse in "Periods," the word designates two things at once: temporal units so vast and complex they strain the credibility of narrative to account for them (think of the literary historian's suspicion of periodization, resulting in our current need for ever longer centuries) but also units so small as to form single, unattached points, dense instants, the visual analogy of which would be the punctuation marks that ordinarily end written sentences but, as we have seen in Blake, can appear anywhere, unexpectedly ("-pulse / -pulse." is one example; "Think not." another). Expanding and contracting, the period not only imitates the rhythmic pulse featured in the passage, it also helps clarify the mathematically illogical notion that "Every Time less than a pulsation of the artery / Is equal *in its period & value* to Six Thousand Years." The exceedingly small and the vast share the quality of being before and beyond narratable time. They share what Blake calls "eternity." As if joined abruptly by an equal sign, the instant and the era stand in a relation that cannot be represented by a progressive cause and effect sequence; that is, they cannot be thought of as a beginning and an ending on either side of a building narrative middle. Earlier it was Jesus who occupied eternity; now we're told it is the poet who conceives and completes his labor outside narratable time. To be sure, Blake's identification of divine and poetic agency recurs throughout his later prophecies, but here the further identification of agency with the pulses, with the rhythmic, affective work of an embodied sensibility, raises fundamental questions. What kind of subject inhabits the time of pulsation? If the labor performed by this pulsating subject lies outside ordinary causality and therefore cannot be narrated, what kind of labor does this subject perform? And finally, what would it feel like to labor in a moment that can contract almost to the point of disappearance or expand beyond measure but cannot serve as part of a developmental, narrative progression?

All of these questions presuppose that Blake is indeed divesting poetic labor from a story of progressive development, and it might seem counterintuitive, at first, to read this particular passage from *Milton* in these particular terms. After all, the passage seems to consist of nothing but man-made progressions, enabled by the Sons of Los; Blake's temporal units and the architectural spaces that correspond to them expand continuously, sequentially. These times and spaces *build,* from a moment into seven ages, from a couch beneath a sky-like tent into the "high Towers" of an epic city—a New Jerusalem walled, moated, and "incircled with a flaming fire." Indeed, it would be hard to argue with Wai Chee Dimock's reading of this passage:

> For Blake, as for Heidegger, time is a built environment. There is nothing natural about it; it is not given but made. This *unnatural* status of time is what enables human beings to dwell in it, to be sheltered by its walls, tents, couches, and to leave their mark there, a labor-intensive signature, crafted brick by brick, the most gorgeous to come from human hands. Unnatural time is something that takes the entire history of the species to emerge, now housing those human "vegetables" lying there on their couches. Only this built environment can save human beings from biology. Only this built environment can offer significant duration to a species doomed by numerical finitude.[9]

Far from detaching itself from developmental narrative, the whole passage seems to exemplify the grand narrative most often told about Blake's work and rendered eloquently here by Dimock: Nature is humanized by labor, transformed into an enormous redemptive art form, resulting in a sheltering environment "not given but made."[10] Here we have *poesis* (making) on the grandest possible scale, and what poetry seems to make happen is the triumph of a fully human form.

While this passage generally aligns with an epic framework, it also possesses an undeniable ghost-town quality, a strange emptiness exacerbated by the conspicuous absence of specific acts of labor. To read these lines is to watch buildings arise as fully achieved architectural spaces but to see no builders, no Sons of Los, in action. Only the Daughters of Beulah work this scene, and their labor serves solely to nourish sleepers we never see awaken, sleepers who—unlike Blake's chimney sweepers—never seem to rise with their bags and their brushes to work. The only labor depicted—feeding sleepers on couches—is a labor devoted to sustaining rest, as if the city that springs up around these sleepers were a giant castle of indolence, a space walled round to protect a fragile dream of inaction. When the units of time and their manufactured spaces do begin to arise, they correspond to one another only by verbs of possession ("every Day and Night, *has* Walls") or by passive constructions ("every Age *is Moated* deep with Bridges") or without any verbs at all ("every Month, a silver paved Terrace"). Although they are artifacts, these times and spaces elide the labor that went into them. One by one, the "wondrous buildings" of time materialize fully formed, "brick by brick," perhaps, but not by the work of "human hands," as Dimock puts it—rather by "the work of Fairy hands of the Four Elements." It is as if time had become magically, materially auto-poetic, with a capacity for innovation and self-organization that discredits, on the one hand, any idea of nature as a realm of blind "vegetable" passivity but also, on the other, any privileging of willful human ambition. Clearly, a narrative template that imagines humanity saving itself from biology and nature by installing a constructed environment, saving itself from the given by means of its own self-determining energies, does not quite fit the passage's countervailing tendency to empty itself of all deliberate activity. Even Dimock's emphasis on time as a "nonbiological clock" is difficult to square with Blake's own emphasis on pulsating arteries. In response to her proposal that "biology is both preserved and stretched beyond its limits," one wonders how a temporality with "nothing natural about it" can also "preserve" biology.

The *Milton* passage could not be stranger. If it imagines time in terms of the kind of monumental teleology we expect from high Romantic historiography ("something that takes the entire history of the species to emerge," according to Dimock), its grandeur rests upon the sublimity of small, bodily repetitions—that is, upon pulsations without end and without transcendence. Blake presents history in terms of a pulse, not a plot. And if the passage invites us to consider the history of a world humanized by labor, it also leaves us quite unable to determine what it means to labor and what it means to be human. Even as he transforms time into a built environment, Blake hollows out agency to the point where it becomes unrecognizable. Strangest of all, Blake gives us a world in which end-time architectural spaces entail not the elimination of primitive autonomic rhythms (still beating) but the disappearance of an identifiable human subject. Rather than imagining that humanity would achieve its fullest expression by transforming the given into the made, at the end of a long process of turning nature into culture, Blake instead imagines a redeemed world where the given (the biological body) and the made (the architectural) coincide, but without any need for a familiar human agent to transform one into the other. In this redeemed world, "man" has either been left behind or is still to come; that is, the conceptual place formerly occupied by the "human" as laboring subject has been momentarily evacuated. In this sense, Blake's vision of these end-time architectural spaces may remind us of Alexandre Kojève welcoming the "disappearance of Man at the end of History," for what will have disappeared by that moment is neither the body nor the world but an erroneous idea of "Man" as the self-willing agent who commands his own destiny by dominating nature:

> The disappearance of Man at the end of History . . . is not a cosmic catastrophe: the natural World remains what it has been from all eternity. And therefore it is not a biological catastrophe either: Man remains alive as animal in *harmony* with Nature or given Being. What disappears is Man properly so-called—that is, Action negating the given, and Error, or in general, the Subject *opposed* to the Object. In point of fact, the end of human Time or History—that is, the definitive annihilation of Man properly so-called or of the free and historical Individual—means quite simply the cessation of Action in the full sense of the term.[11]

In *Milton*'s vision of the end-time world, the being once called "Man," who used to consist of "Action negating the given," now sleeps instead. And in place of "Action in the strong sense of the term," Blake gives us the strange dream-work of poesis and pulsation. Turning from Kojève's language to Blake's own, perhaps we can grasp these changes by reconsidering a well-known proverb of Hell: "Where man is not nature is barren" (*Marriage* 10, E 38). Not only does this proverb invite us to imagine a space from which man has disappeared, it also, like the passage on time in *Milton,* performs the double function of supporting a teleological human-ism while also allowing for its estrangement. If a first reading of the proverb sug-gests that nature becomes fertile only under man's transformative labor, a second allows for nearly the opposite conclusion: if the concept of "man" as productive agent were to disappear, then the correlative concept of "nature" as a raw given, as a resource that exists only to be developed, would likewise become inoperative or "barren." Like the pulsation passage in *Milton,* this proverb lies suspended be-tween two competing versions of apocalyptic redemption: one in which the given becomes fully human, the other without "man" altogether.

In *Milton,* this tendency to estrange the human is driven by the most ordinary, ongoing event of biology: the heartbeat. With every opening and closing of the arteries, the narrative time normally occupied by individual subjects slips further out of joint. Rather than leading us into a temporality that would shelter us, a world made home, each pulsation tends toward dispossession, rendering us strangers in our own bodies, homeless. To repeat Judith Butler's words, the pulses "return us to the human where we do not expect to find it, in its frailty and at the limits of its capacity to make sense." What is it, then, that fits the pulses for this task of self-alienation? In what follows, I want to emphasize two features. First, the pulsations that open and close the build-up of time in *Milton* are not *willed*, they *happen*. Troubling any easy distinctions between "the given" and "the made" or "the passive" and "the active," their eventfulness puts them at odds with the productive agency necessary for a story of voluntary labor and heroic will. Second, pulsations involve affects that require a body but not a human subject. Although Dimock invokes the word four times in her commentary, Blake's pulsations are not exactly (or exclusively) "human"; they belong to a realm of somatic function that human beings share widely with other animals (*zoa*). If Burney understood that fixation on one's own pulsations amounts to a form of narcissistic enchantment, Blake suggests that diverting attention to the pulses might instead enable an act of "self-annihilation," breaking the egoistic spell cast by consciousness, the spell Nietzsche described (we recall) as a barrier to knowing: "What do human beings really know about themselves? . . . Does nature not remain silent about almost everything, even about our bodies, banishing and enclosing us within a proud, illusory consciousness, far away from the twists and turns of the bowels, the rapid flow of the blood stream and the complicated tremblings of the nerve-fibres?"[12] Rather than presupposing an account of subjectivity, an anthropomorphism they can do without, the quick current of Blake's pulsations passes along a shifting, moment-to-moment border—between the productive and the involuntary, between the human and the not human. In the work of poesis, "All the great events of time start forth" from this embodied indeterminacy, when we suddenly find ourselves surprised by our own strange pulse.

Vigorous Inactivity: "Futurity is in this moment"

Driving the blood through the body, pulsation might be considered the engine of animal vitality and thus the source of the body's labor power. In *Milton*, however, Blake associates the moment of pulsation with rest, with a *cessation* of labor: "A Moment equals a pulsation of the artery" (28:47, E 126), and "every Moment has a Couch of gold for soft repose" (28:46, E 126). We have encountered this "couch / Of gold" before (15:12–13, E 109), in our discussion of Samson's strength and "Albion rose." There we observed Blake taking up Milton's interest in elusive moments of active passivity ("vigorous most / When most unactive deem'd" [*Samson Agonistes*, 1704–1705]), which he then incorporated into his own fantastical portrait of Milton, asleep on a couch while at the same time engaged in the epic labor of redeeming the world. Milton sleeps and works simultaneously, a paradox Blake extends further by also representing his poet-hero as a sleepwalker. Attended by "the Seven Angels of the Presence," the sleeping Milton receives active perceptions of his own dormant state: "they gave him still perceptions of his Sleeping Body; / Which now arose and walk'd . . . tho walking as one walks / In sleep" (15:3–7, E 109). Milton receives the divine gift of having his darkness made visible: he finds himself aware of somatic functions ordinarily opaque to consciousness, and thus he observes the mobilization of a body that can run (or at least walk) on its own, with a soft agency independent of his intellect or will. The experience is not alarming. Somnambulance does not turn Milton into an automaton of the sort described by Hannah Arendt ("Unthinking men are like sleepwalkers"), a person in need of arousal because sleeping and thinking are mutually exclusive states that can only follow one another alternately (again Arendt: "[Thinking] rouses you from sleep").[13] For Arendt, the sleepwalker looks active but isn't; he represents the actual passivity beneath the illusion of voluntary action, which mostly proceeds automatically because such action is ruled by mental habit. People are generally *inactive* (unthinking) right when they think themselves most vigorous and self-assertive. Blake gives us an exact reversal of this idea. In this strange, difficult scene, Milton's moving, somatic body does not undermine agency so much as expand its range of possibility, by confusing the very opposition between sleep and effort, rest and motion, motor force and relaxation of the will. Rather than awakening to action like a strong man after slumber, Milton sleeps on, discovering the hidden cooperation between his work as a poet and his slumber's apparent passivity. The sleepwalker moves in a temporality enabled only by loosening the self's grasp on knowledge, action, and purpose, a temporality one can only let happen, not force. To return to our starting point, this is the very same temporality Blake associates with pulsation. Thus the "couch / Of gold" from which Milton rises in order to sleepwalk returns thirteen plates later in the passage on time to describe the arterial rhythm that, neither active nor passive, underpins every great event of time: "And every Moment has a Couch of gold for soft repose, / (A Moment equals a pulsation of the artery)."

We are accustomed, of course, to think of Blake in terms of giant mythic figures performing monumental acts of world-building imaginative labor. It comes as no surprise to find Geoffrey Hartman contrasting Blake's brash, emancipatory confidence with the gentleness he prefers in Wordsworth, whose poetry is characterized by a "consciousness of unselfconsciousness," a "sensitivity to the minimal, to that which, precisely, is *not* eventful."[14] According to this view, Blake's model of relentless, prophetic energy would call for conspicuous pulsations of the kind Samuel Johnson defined, following the Latin *pulsare* (to drive, beat, or strike): "The act of beating or moving with quick strokes against anything opposing." If this definition calls to mind the explosive force Blake associated with Los's hammer, leading us to supply the event of pulsation with a subject (man), an opposing object (nature), and a mode of agency (art), it can, however, also point us toward a more nuanced understanding of the term, one closer to accommodating the contrary tendencies Blake loaded into the word, for pulsation can also describe an action without designated agents or clear predication. Although on occasion one may command pulsation violently—like a blacksmith—one is *always* subject to uneventful pulsations, and in these moments it would be hard to say whether the subject acts or is acted upon. Who (or what) acts when a pulse beats? Linnaeus understood the botanical name *anemone pulsatilla* to mean "the beating of the flower by the wind," and Erasmus Darwin explained that this same flower, featured on the title page of *The Book of Thel,* cannot survive unless the wind opens its petals to allow for pollination.[15] Like the pulsatilla, animal being (zoa) is also moved rhythmically, acted upon without effort, though its beating comes not from the wind outside but from the internal, self-moving impulse of blood and muscle fiber. The most important proponent of this proto-vitalist theory, William Harvey, whose 1628 treatise *Exercitatio anatomica de motu cordis et sanguinis in animalibus* (*On The Movement of the Heart and Blood in Animals*) profoundly influenced all subsequent studies, speculated that blood preexists the body in embryogenesis, supplying life with a principle of autogenerative motion. From its first appearance, a single, unincorporated point of blood pulsates, and from this *punctum sanguineum palpitans* vitality begins. Having removed the shell from a chicken egg five days old and suspended the contents in water, Harvey observed the origins of life in a "red or white point" of blood that would later develop into a "vesicle or auricle": "In the middle of this small cloud the throbbing point of blood was so tiny that it disappeared from view on its contraction, to reappear as a red point during its relaxation, and thus between being visible and invisible, or so to speak between existing and not existing, it gave a representation of the heart beat and of the beginning of life."[16] Emerging and vanishing almost like the "periods" that alternately expand or contract, appear or don't, to punctuate Blake's text ("pulse / pulse."), this primary, moving point *precedes* the organism: "life begins with that throbbing" (37). But Harvey also recognized that pulsation *survives* the organism, citing animal experiments in which he observed heart fibers continuing to beat even after death, even after the heart had been removed from the body. Pulsation thus describes a primary, autonomous rhythm before and beyond integrated life. If in one sense it is the origin and end of the individual creature's organic, developmental narrative—the first and last movements that frame its biography, as it were—in another sense it involves a motion in excess of individual biological forms. The subject of pulsation realizes a force that precedes and survives its own story, a force no volition can command.[17]

It is worth staying with Harvey for a moment, for his account of pulsation also describes the blood's vital rhythm as an interplay of activity and passivity too complex to be reduced to a simple binary system, with action either "on" or "off." All life, like that first pre-embryonic point within the chicken's egg, contracts and expands: "alternating between movement and rest, moving at one time and devoid of movement at another" (26). However, this oscillation—of "expulsion" and "reception" (29)—happens almost too quickly for empirical observation. In his laboratory study of live animals, Harvey at first found it difficult to discern systole from diastole: "This was because of the rapidity of the movement, which in many animals remained visible for but the wink of an eye or the length of a lightning flash, so that I thought I was seeing now systole from this side and diastole from that side; now the opposite; the movements now diverse, and now inextricably mixed" (23). This inability to differentiate clearly between activity and passivity, and the tendency to mistake one for the other, was in fact a regular problem in the history of physiology that Harvey inherited. Prior to his discovery of circulation, established medical opinion held that the heart's dilation, and not its contraction, was responsible for moving the blood through the body. Early anatomists assumed that the heart, modeled on the lungs, "breathed in" the blood like a swelling bellows rather than expelling it forcibly through contraction; that is, they mistook the heart's passive phase (its "relaxation and collapse" [29]) for its primary action. It was up to Harvey to demonstrate the counterintuitive notion that "expansion . . . occurs only passively and not autonomously" (as science historian Thomas Fuchs puts it).[18] To make matters even more complicated, Harvey explained that systole and diastole reverse themselves in heart and arteries: when the one contracts the other dilates, and vice versa, but synchronously, in a single, simultaneous event. Later, in his magnum opus *De Generatione Animalium* (*On Animal Reproduction,* 1651), Harvey would argue that the heart's muscle tissue possesses an innate sensibility or receptivity (*sensu*) that leads it to contract when stimulated by the blood. The blood moves (stimulates) the heart, which in turn moves (pumps) the blood: "the contraction or activity of the heart becomes the passivity of the blood while the activity of the blood becomes the relaxation and passivity of the heart" (Fuchs 71). All animal life consists of the reciprocity embodied by this rhythm, which Fuchs describes as "a harmonious interaction of rest and movement" (73). For Harvey, in other words, pulsations not only precede and survive individual life forms, they make it impossible to isolate active and passive functions. At the level of primary rhythmic vitality, receptive passivity is built into the very nature of activity. Every moment of pulsation, by definition, includes "a couch of gold for soft repose."

Blake may have been familiar with Harvey through his influence on contemporary medical and anatomical texts, some of which were published by Joseph Johnson and included Blake's engravings.[19] Harvey's idea of the heart's active and passive mechanics remained crucial throughout the next centuries, although his theory of the blood's originary vitality remained controversial, going in and out of fashion. We will return to the mechanics of the heart, but here I want to emphasize that the active passivity (or passive activity) of pulsation, whether or not it is derived directly from Harvey, provides Blake with a favorite figure for poesis precisely because it allows him to distinguish the work of poetry from other, predominantly instrumental, forms of labor. The moment of pulsation—the moment when "The Poets Work is Done"—remains foreign to the kind of heroic self-empowering agent whose motto, as both Arendt and Derrida put it, can be reduced to the two-word phrase, "I can."[20] Because the pulses belong to a body but not to a sovereign subject in command of his actions, their unaccountable labor occurs in a moment "Satans watchfiends cannot find."

One of the best glosses on this moment of poetic labor occurs in Night the Ninth of *The Four Zoas*, in a crucial speech by Urizen. This speech is easily overshadowed by the spectacular apocalyptic labor Urizen undertakes soon after: "Then Urizen arose & took his Sickle in his hand / . . . And went forth & began to reap & all his joyful sons / Reapd the wide Universe & bound in Sheaves a wondrous harvest" (132:2–7, E 400). Centered on a single monumental laborer performing cosmic feats of labor, Night the Ninth would seem an unlikely text to pair with the passage on time, pulsation, and creative inaction we have been considering in *Milton*. Even more, the speech I want to emphasize makes no mention of the pulses, and though it does feature a monumental built environment, its hellish modern cityscape forms a direct contrast to the pristine, crafted architecture we looked at in *Milton*. What directly links these two passages, however, and thus invites us to consider them together, is the emphasis both place on the generative nature of the present moment, the dense instant which (like a period, like a pulsation of the artery) makes innovation possible only by dislodging time from an end-oriented narrative of labor and by allowing for the unexpected effects of passivity. Without this prior, easily neglected moment of passivity, Urizen's subsequent labors could not take place. Paradoxically, Urizen can only enter into his heroic, messianic role by first renouncing the heroic ethos of "strong action" and choosing to inhabit the time and space of receptive passivity instead. In *Milton* we learn that "all the Great / Events of Time start forth & are concievd . . . / Within a Moment: a Pulsation of the Artery." In Night the Ninth of *The Four Zoas,* in his pivotal speech, Urizen also discovers that if there is to be any "futurity" at all, it can only happen "in this moment."[21]

The speech in which Urizen announces his conversion to passivity is *literally* pivotal; he initiates a *return* to paradise by *turning himself around*—not in space but in time. Throughout the course of fallen history, we learn, Urizen's error has been to turn his back on the present moment, facing forward on a timeline always aimed at future achievement (teleology, acquisition, the afterlife). That is, he faces a future he is determined to make happen, by willing it into existence. Now returning, facing away from economic progress and moral improvement, he suddenly discovers in the idle present an altogether different "futurity": "for lo futurity is in this moment." That is, he suddenly perceives a mundane potentiality (a "lo[w] futurity") that his former teleological ambitions overshot.

> O that I had never drank the wine nor eat the bread
> Of dark mortality nor cast my view into futurity, nor **turnd**
> **My back** darkning the present clouding with a cloud
> And building arches high & cities turrets & towers & domes
> Whose smoke destroyd the pleasant gardens & whose running Kennels
> Chokd the bright rivers burdning with my Ships the angry deep
> Thro Chaos seeking for delight & in spaces remote
> Seeking the Eternal which is always present to the wise
> Seeking for pleasure which unsought falls round the infants path
> And on the fleeces of mild flocks who neither care nor labour
> But I the labourer of ages whose unwearied hands
> Are thus deformd with hardness with the sword & with the spear
> And with the Chisel & the mallet I whose labours vast
> Order the nations separating family by family
> Alone enjoy not I alone in misery supreme
> Ungratified give all my joy unto this Luvah & Vala
> Then Go O dark futurity I will cast thee forth from these
> Heavens of my brain nor will I look upon futurity more
> I cast futurity away & **turn my back** upon that void
> Which I have made for lo futurity is in this moment
>
> (121:3–22, E 390, emphasis added)

Prior to this moment, Urizen was nothing but the industrious master builder we typically see in Blake's representations of him: a "labourer of ages whose unwearied hands / Are thus deformed," hardened into instruments by his uninterrupted drive to shape the world according to the "view" he "cast . . . into futurity."

No one would have confused his active and his passive phases; until now he had no passive phases. His chisel and mallet never stopped working. Urizen's story gives giant form to the teleological narrative of production that organizes the entire late eighteenth-century, modernizing economy—starting, as Saree Makdisi has shown, with the atomistic subject formed for industrial labor ("I the labourer of ages," "I alone in misery supreme") and the divisive social units that bind modern labor to an impoverished collective life ("I whose labours vast / Order the nations separating family by family").[22] The figure for his collective, relentless, *imperialist* striving is the always forward-moving ship, which enables modern trade and conquest on a global scale. Its verb (like the verb for overeager sympathy in "On Anothers Sorrow") is "seeking," a word we can gloss with Adorno and Horkheimer's blunt analysis of modernity: "What human beings seek to learn from nature is how to use it to dominate wholly both it and human beings. Nothing else counts."[23] At the same time, however, Urizen's ships fail to acquire the pleasures they seek, for instrumental agency cannot make joy happen; joy only arrives "unsought."[24] If "there is a moment Satans watchfiends cannot find," it is because this moment does not exist for those who seek it as an object of pursuit; it occurs only as a slackening in the taut fabric of motivated activity, a gap in time through which anyone fortunate enough to fall lands softly on a "couch of gold." When the reformed Urizen alludes to the Gospel of Matthew in his speech ("Behold the fowls of the air: for they sow not, neither do they reap . . . Consider the lilies of the field, how they grow: they toil not, neither do they spin" [6:26–28]), he momentarily sounds as if he were preparing to write Keats's "Ode on Indolence." Or to mime Hartman on Wordsworth, he has learned to appreciate a "sensitivity to the minimal, to that which, precisely, is *not* eventful."[25]

But as I have already indicated, this description of Urizen is not quite sufficient either, for only a few lines later, his "ha[n]d [is] on the Plow" (124:25, E 393). At the very moment when the text would represent apocalyptic change—something Blake would undertake again on this scale only toward the end of *Jerusalem*—*The Four Zoas* presents its readers with a challenge. How can we reconcile Urizen's renunciation of instrumental labor with the epic magnification of labor that immediately follows his speech, including the glorification of those apocalyptic instruments necessary for the final harvest and vintage: plow, harrow, sickle, millstone, and wine press? Urizen is no infant or mild lamb who "neither care[s] nor labor[s]"; unlike Matthew's fowl, he sows and reaps in cosmic proportions:

> The limbs of Urizen shone with ardor. He laid his ha[n]d on the Plow
> Thro dismal darkness drave the Plow of ages over Cities
> And all their Villages over Mountains & all their Vallies

Over the graves & caverns of the dead Over the Planets
And over the void Spaces over Sun & moon & star & constellation

(124:25–29, E 393–394)

Just as Blake asks us to consider extremes of impulse and patience in his representations of Jesus, here, in this representation of another messianic figure, he
asks us to hold together, at one and the same time, impossible extremes of vigor
and indolence. Rather than simply rejecting one for the other, then, as if they were
mutually exclusive options, this apocalyptic plowman takes on the much more
difficult task of displacing the opposition between them. In the figure of Urizen,
Night the Ninth calls on us to imagine an unthinkable labor, a labor *coincident*
with passivity, a labor like the pulsation at the center of vitality, in which force
and relaxation, agency and involuntariness, happen all at once, one within the
other. Not "Rest before Labour" (the initial motto of *The Four Zoas* [2, E 300]), as
if in narrative sequence, but rest (the moment's "Couch of gold") *within* labor, at
its core. By turning his back on all courses of action oriented toward futurity, by
no longer seeking to capitalize on the present moment, by choosing instead to
make nothing happen, Urizen's labor *allows* futurity to happen. He allows time to
pulsate, to be "vibrated by the reflexes of the future," as a much later poet would
say.[26] This is the "work" of poesis, and the cosmic plow he employs stands in for
the engraver's burin, the instrument of choice for the poet-agent who chooses to
divest himself of instrumental powers. The irony of course is that any labor *seeking*
futurity forecloses upon innovation, for it colonizes the future in advance, producing it as a predetermined outcome of one's own developmental, narrative scheme.
Rather than casting the future as if he were some monumental sculptor, molding
it to fit his own anticipatory vision, Urizen learns to "cast futurity away." And because he no longer shapes the future with his "unwearied hands . . . deformd with
hardness," he allows other times and spaces to arise, such as those auto-generative
architectural spaces produced in *Milton* by the "Fairy Hands of the Four Elements."

In Night the Ninth, then, we see a convergence of all the features that will allow Blake to identify the moment of poetic labor with pulsation: its freedom from
end-oriented plot lines; its occurrence as momentary affect, ordinary ("low") and
startling ("lo!"); its interchange of activity and passivity; its opening onto the possibility of the new and unexpected, in a future that cannot be anticipated because it
cannot be conceived or manufactured by an already existing subject. Blake locates
apocalyptic consequences in the repetition of the smallest possible unwilled event,
and in so doing, he assigns to poesis a task modern art will never stop undertaking: to achieve agency under erasure, to create by means of a labor both redemptive and involuntary (redemptive *because* involuntary, since it is the fallen will the

modern artist wishes to overcome).[27] And already in Night the Ninth we can see Blake bumping up against a difficulty Adorno would later identify as a perennial feature of experimental art: How can artists enable an innovative passivity if any strategic *effort* they undertake reintroduces the very will they are trying to avoid? The possibility of innovation depends on successfully negotiating this impasse. The artist cannot simply "make it new" (as Pound would enjoin), as if the old will could bring something genuinely new into existence by sheer determination.[28] Even experiments in "self-annihilation" aimed at suspending the will and allowing the new to happen, as if on its own initiative, remain suspect, for they too must be set in motion voluntarily. To pick a mundane example: one can randomly drop colored shapes onto paper rather than arrange them strategically, but only if one first strategically chooses randomness over arrangement. "[I]t is clear," writes Adorno, "that insofar as experimental procedures . . . are in spite of everything undertaken subjectively, the belief is chimerical that through them art will divest itself of its subjectivity and become the illusionless thing in itself which to date art has only feigned."[29] This dilemma leads to the modernist art games Adorno associates with "velleity." Given that the will cannot be eliminated entirely, is it possible to will so slightly that one's effort would not prevent the new from arriving? Adorno has in mind the automatic writing of the surrealists and other experiments designed to foster unexpected consequences in the artwork (dropping colored shapes, say).[30] In this light we can also remember Blake's claim to have written under the influence of spirits, against his will, and we might even think of Night the Ninth's Urizen—who attempts to trigger the apocalypse with his passive labor—as a giant figure of velleity, a mythopoeic forerunner of André Breton. The question now is whether Urizen, despite his best effort to go passive, tries too hard. Is his effort to initiate a poesis that lets happen rather than makes happen yet another way of falling into the trap of "seeking" the "unsought"? Adorno, for one, remains skeptical of such undertakings. "[T]he work that is ostensibly not the result of making," he writes, "is of course all the more fabricated" (26). Rather than opening onto the new, "Velleity binds the new to the ever-same" (22).[31] If modern art requires a weak messianism to be genuinely transformative, Urizen's messianism may never be weak enough.

And yet, according to Adorno, there is another entry into vigorous inactivity that might avoid this inevitable disenchantment: an entry *through criticism*. Although we must wait until chapter 5 to take up this possibility more fully, we can finish here by noting a few places where Adorno suggests that critical engagement might succeed where aesthetic experiments in velleity do not. Critical engagement turns the original problem upside down: rather than adopting a passive stance that only masks the underlying operation of the will, critical analysis willfully exercises the intellect in order to experience a latent, unpredictable passivity. The critic's act of concentration makes no pretense of avoiding volition, yet it can bring the will to a limit where interpretation opens onto a receptive passivity. Consider, for instance, Adorno's account of the experience of natural beauty, which he distinguishes from naïve fantasies of a Zen-like "wise passiveness." "Pure immediacy does not suffice for aesthetic experience. Along with the involuntary it requires volition, concentrating consciousness; the contradiction is ineluctable. All beauty reveals itself to persistent analysis, which in turn enriches the element of in-voluntariness; indeed, analysis would be vain if the involuntary did not reside hidden within it" (69). Voluntary contraction (of focus) results dialectically in an expansion of involuntary response; activity and passivity are two parts of a shared rhythm. "Persistent analysis" does not illuminate the object by mastering it intellectually, as a subject might master an object, but arrives instead at a point where both subject and analysis become vulnerable, losing control of themselves. Paradoxically, this passive state can be accessed only while the will is being exercised. It is Adorno's "Couch of gold," his generative moment of rest within intellectual labor. Adorno suggests something similar when he discusses our response to art. If artworks can act on us and *move* us, producing the famous *Ershütterung* or "feeling of being overwhelmed," their agency occurs only as our critical exertion acts on them: "Under patient contemplation artworks begin to move" (79). Adorno sometimes calls this dialectical moment in analysis "second reflection": the artwork reacts upon us when our intellectual effort meets the provocative friction of an unexpected opacity, a "darkness" that he says "must be interpreted, not replaced by the clarity of meaning" (27). *Must be interpreted*: although one cannot make darkness *knowable* (replacing it, as Satan's watchfiends would like to do, with the clarity of meaning), one can make darkness *visible* by interpreting it. This darkness only emerges in the first place because it is structurally bound to the interpreter's careful act of attention; you cannot have one without the other. Unlike the critic who undertakes to explicate the artwork, the responsible interpreter brings forth a darkness he discovers only inadvertently, as a moment within analysis but beyond its control, a moment of "second reflection" accessible to affective response but not to conceptualization. In the intellectual feeling brought on by interpretation, activity and passivity cross over one another, trading places.[32]

If the active passivity Adorno locates as a possibility in modern criticism seems to have taken us far from Blake, perhaps we can take up his challenge to *read darkness* by revisiting the image of Milton sleepwalking, where this section began. As we have seen, Milton's internal darkness becomes visible to him when he is made strangely self-aware of his sleeping, moving body. In turn, this impossible state, which requires the poet to be conscious and unconscious all at once, becomes

available to the reader as a particular kind of image. Joining with the "Seven Angels of the Presence," Milton himself becomes an eighth angel, a messianic agent.
Rather than likening his transfiguration to that of Jesus in the Gospels, whose
clothes shined "white as snow" when he joined with Moses and Elias (Mark 9:2–4),
Blake describes the transformed Milton as a visible darkness: "his Sleeping body
. . . / . . . now arose, and walk'd with them in Eden, as an Eighth / Image *Divine, tho'*
darken'd" (15:4–6, E 109, emphasis added). For Blake and Adorno, futurity might
lie in *this* moment, if only a reader could interpret (without explicating, without
clarifying) a poet's moving darkness.

The Half-Life of Emotion: "Outside of the Gates of the Human Heart"

Let's return to our touchstone from *Milton* and point it now in another direction.
The poet's work is done in a moment, a pulsation of the artery. We have been
emphasizing the strangeness of Blake's statement, but in some ways, it would be
hard to find a proposal more sentimental: follow the heart. In the age of sensibility,
the idea that vital feelings perform an ongoing, wordless alternative to abstraction
went without saying. When Keats argued in 1818 that "axioms in philosophy are
not axioms until they are proved upon our pulses,"[33] implying that most axioms
couldn't stand up to the body's test, he neglected to mention just how axiomatic
proof by pulsation had become. Thirty years earlier, Blake defended his criticisms
of Johann Kaspar Lavater, whom he admired, by asserting their origin in innocent,
heartfelt impulse: "For I write from the warmth of my heart. & cannot resist the
impulse I feel to rectify what I think false in a book I love so much. & approve so
generally" (E 600). On the title page of the volume, he printed his name under
Lavater's and enclosed both within the outline of a heart. It is significant that even
in these early annotations Blake describes criticism as a joint effort of analysis
and affect, but his hackneyed language indicates just how trite and mechanical
the discourse of criticism could become, supporting one set of conventions (affective) to contest another (logical). Why should one trust the pulses, then, if they
can slip so automatically into readymade forms, beating without any friction? If
its assumption-disrupting work—its *critical* work—were itself a cliché, wouldn't
pulsation always be at risk of confirming established expectations? Nothing could
be more predictable than the surprise of authenticity promised by impulse. In
Sense and Sensibility, Austen used this very principle to create Marianne Dashwood.

The same heart and arteries Blake turns to in order to defamiliarize the human being could (and commonly did) serve the opposite function. Rather than
dispossessing the self, the pulses (along with the feelings thought to be anchored

in them) could provide a reassuring, all-too-automatic proof of a robust, inherent humanity. For this reason, in a passage from *Jerusalem* we consider toward the end of this section, Blake has Los build Golgonooza, the city of art, "Outside of the Gates of the Human Heart" (53:16, E 203). The poet who would work within the self-alienating moment of pulsation must also work *outside the human heart*; that is, he must remove himself from a moral economy that identifies the heart with a set of established assumptions about human nature. This expropriation of oneself is no easy task, for the moral economy masks its constitution by grounding its social emotions in the body, making it virtually impossible for any individual to distinguish emotions such as sympathy from the heartbeat's immediate, self-evident vitality. Nothing could feel more natural than to feel human *in this way*. "Can I see anothers grief / And not seek for kind relief"? Not if I have a heart; not if I am human. The poet's critical task, then, is to dislodge the heart from this spontaneous experience of familiar humanity, and the project of self-estrangement begins by recognizing that heartfelt experience is as much a product of convention as a manifestation of inherent human nature. The very emotions that seem to spring directly from the heart are indeed embodied personally but are only half alive, for their origin is both mechanical and vital. If as Butler says the goal of cultural critique is to return us to the human where we do not expect to find it, then another side of the same project must be to uncover the mechanical in those experiences that feel most immediately vital and human. *Critical* feeling is not the sudden eruption of liberating impulse but the discovery of the machine within emotion; it is the uneasy awareness that, within emotion, the *unnatural* is always scraping against, even as it props up, the comfortably human. Rather than centering and unifying human life, as it can readily seem to do, the heart illustrates the real difficulty of distinguishing liveliness from mechanism, and to get at this unsettling of categories we can begin by returning to the account of circulation Blake's era inherited from Harvey.

There are times in *De Motu Cordis* when Harvey describes the heart as a secondary construction ("a sort of hearth and home") built to house a primary living energy ("innate fire"): the heart, he writes, is the "site and source of warmth, a sort of hearth and home to contain and preserve the natural kindling materials and the beginnings of innate fire" (88). At other times, however, his tropes shift, and the heart takes on the qualities of a primary, autonomous being ("like some inner animal"), which in turn generates the organic body (the outer animal) necessary to contain and preserve *its* inner life. In this latter case the heart creates the secondary structures that shelter it, and the body becomes "*its* dwelling-place": "With its special organs designed for movement the heart, like some inner animal, was in place earlier. Then, with the heart created first, Nature wished the animal as a whole to be created, nourished, preserved and perfected by that organ, to be in effect its work and its dwelling-place" (108). For the next two hundred years, such arguments for the heart's autonomy would reverberate in vitalistic accounts of circulation. These arguments emphasized that formation of the heart precedes formation of the brain in embryogenesis and that the heartbeat continues to function independently of the nervous system once the creature is fully formed. By the middle of the eighteenth century, the continuation of the heart's auto-rhythm even after death was commonly understood to indicate an innate, involuntary life principle, one that could persist even when the heart was removed from its "dwelling place," the body. Julien Offray de La Mettrie relished a macabre passage in Bacon describing "a man convicted of treason whose heart was torn out while he was still alive, and thrown into the flames; this muscle first leapt vertically to a height of one and a half feet, but then, losing force, it leapt less high each time, for seven or eight minutes."[34] This is hardly the familiar and reassuring "natural piety" Wordsworth had in mind when he wrote "My Heart Leaps Up." Starting with Harvey, the heart's autonomous vitality could make the organ seem like a strange creature never fully assimilated into the body it produces, an alien animal presence at the center of the animal body. At other times, however, the heart's secondary nature could take on nearly opposite properties, making it seem more like a domesticating structure, a "hearth and home" built precisely to organize and contain that feral vitality. Harvey makes it difficult to know whether the heart is more like a wild animal or an animal shelter, a way to organize life or a wayward presence with a life of its own.

Given the heart's place in Harvey's system, this slippage is almost inevitable, for the heart stands midway between the original, autonomous vitality he associates with the blood and the body's achieved organic unity. It is midway temporally, in terms of embryogenesis, in that the heart develops after the blood but before the organism as a whole, but it is midway also in terms of a conceptual contradiction regarding the nature of the heart, a contradiction identified by Fuchs. Sometimes the heartbeat appears to be an extension of the blood's own primary pulse (an "impulse amplifier"), while at other times it serves the secondary function of disciplining and regulating the pulse mechanically. Is the heartbeat akin to the blood's pulsation, continuing and magnifying that first sign of life, or does it work *against* the blood's natural tendency, as a counterpoint to its pulsation? According to Harvey, blood is not inert, but a "mass with a will of its own" (quoted in Fuchs 48). It is like an even deeper, more primitive "inner animal." Harvey believed that the blood possesses an innate "centripetal tendency"; it directs itself always toward the body's center, with an impulsive drive that the heart must resist by expelling the blood outward "against its will." If the heart did not act as this counterforce it would be impossible to nourish the whole body of a large, complex organism.[35]

This dual aspect of the heart—on one side, an embodiment of the lifeblood's original autonomy; on the other, a "mechanical system of pump and pipes" (Fuchs 9) regulating blood flow—lends itself to the competing accounts of circulation that would alternately guide the next two centuries of physiology. Such is the argument of Fuchs's masterwork, *The Mechanization of the Heart: Harvey and Descartes.* Although proponents on either side of the controversy sought to displace vitalism with mechanism or mechanism with vitalism, they in fact continuously demonstrate the inherence of each paradigm within the other. Mechanistic explanations (especially after Descartes) would dominate until around 1750 and return to dominance a century later, but "whatever thought-style is dominant at a given time shows itself in many ways to be influenced and modified by its predecessor" (7). Harvey himself supplied the circulatory system with both its machine metaphor ("with one wheel moving another, all seem to be moving at once" [39]) *and* its vital impulse. Most importantly, however, he brought to representations of the heart the impossibility of distinguishing clearly between mechanism and vitality, generating an indeterminacy that plays itself out at every level of his system.[36] In his subsequent treatise on muscle movement, *De Motu Locali Animalium,* Harvey would define "Mechanics" as "whatever controls that through which nature is overcome, and helps with the difficulties [that arise] when something unnatural is useful."[37] On these terms, the heart is both natural and unnatural. Like the double-valve one-way water pump that provided a key model for Harvey's discovery of circulation, the heart is a mechanism opposed to nature, opposing the innate force of the blood as the water pump opposes gravity, but it is itself a mechanism that grows out of nature.[38] In his writings, vitalism and mechanism trade places with an irresolution that would continue to inflect all further discourse on the heart. In 1748, toward the end of *L'Homme Machine,* La Mettrie could proclaim with typical materialist drama, "Let us then conclude boldly that man is a machine" (39), but the evidence he cites, including experiments from Harvey, serves primarily to demonstrate that "matter moves by itself" (33), that there is an "innate force in our bodies" (28). These principles soon became the basis for a resurgent vitalism and eventually led the London surgeon John Hunter, Blake's famous neighbor and the most important theorist of blood in the period, to declare that "blood [is] alive in itself."[39]

In his *Treatise on the blood, inflammation, and gun-shot wounds* (originally published in 1794), Hunter argued that coagulation demonstrates the blood's inherent power of self-organization; our concern is less the controversial theory itself than its influence on his description of the heart, for it leads him into a representation every bit as polarized as Harvey's. Hunter believed that the greatest obstacle to accepting his theory was the mind's resistance to conceiving of a "living fluid" (71). Because we are accustomed to associating life with "solids" (organic bodies,

masses, organs) it is almost impossible, he argued, to grasp the idea that the shapeless blood is also independently alive. Thus Hunter's first step in breaking down
this barrier was to demonstrate, through experiment, that the blood shares the
same living principle found in all the body's solids. Although this living principle
is nonempirical and therefore not directly knowable, it makes itself evident in the
three powers of self-preservation, receptiveness to external impressions, and "consequent reciprocal action," all of which, he argued, can be observed in the blood.[40]
At its most fundamental level, then, Hunter's account affirms the continuity between the heart and the blood. Although one is a solid and the other a fluid, they
both share in the same fundamental principle of vitality.

At the same time, however, Hunter is so determined to make his case for the
blood that the heart diminishes by comparison. The heart is alive, of course, but
secondary, purely instrumental, a biological machine engineered for a single
purpose. Unlike the blood, the heart is not even absolutely necessary, for some
animals manage their circulation without one. As we have seen in Harvey, blood
comes first in the developmental process, and crucial to Hunter's account is the
idea that all living solids were originally fluid before being organized into form.[41]
Thus the life principle preexists any particular organic form it can take, and the
blood, in its fluid state, lies closer to this earlier, pre-differentiated vitality. Hunter
notes that blood remains essentially the same across species despite the great variety of animal forms; if the heart can do one thing only, the blood—like a source
of pure morphological potentiality—is capable of producing all kinds of variety.
Finally, the blood retains an echo of the original generative power in its ability to
coagulate, thereby repeating the process of forming solids from fluids. It may be
true, as Coleridge says, that "a living body is of necessity an organized one,"[42] but
Hunter insists that life precedes organization and that the blood—like the "living
fluids" of Blake's printing house in hell (*Marriage* 15, E 40)—shares in that first,
generative indeterminacy. One must never confuse life itself with mere organization (what Coleridge calls "organic form"): "[O]rganization may arise out of living
parts and produce action, but . . . life can never rise out of, or depend on organization. An organ is a peculiar conformation of matter, (let that matter be what it
may) to answer some purpose, the operation of which is mechanical; but, mere
organization can do nothing, even in mechanics, it must still have something corresponding to a living principle; namely, some power" (72). The heart, then, is not
the source of life itself but a secondary organic form—"a peculiar conformation
of matter" organized from solid parts that were themselves generated from the
primary fluid, the blood. It is undeniably important but not nearly as interesting
as the blood. After spending most of his theoretical introduction on the "General Principles of the Blood," after arriving at the conclusion that, ultimately, "life

is a property we do not understand" (84), Hunter can turn briefly to the heart, which he describes without drama or enigma as a fine piece of living machinery quickly grasped and appreciated: "The heart may be considered as a truly mechanical engine; for although muscles are the powers in an animal, yet these powers are themselves often converted into a machine, of which the heart is a strong instance; for from the disposition of its muscular fibres, tendons, ligaments and valves, it is adapted to mechanical purposes; which make it a complete organ or machine in itself" (128). The heart's only real mystery is the regularity of its pulse, a rhythm Hunter declares independent of the brain's influence (140) and therefore a link back to the earliest, autonomous life force, prior to formation of the nervous system. The heartbeat is a sign of the elusive living principle that abides within the body's mechanical organization—a mysterious vitality Wordsworth claimed he could occasionally glimpse in the lively movements of his wife, Mary Hutchinson: "And now I see with eye serene / The very pulse of the machine."[43]

This undecidability at the "heart" of man—at once alive and mechanical—bears widely and significantly on Blake's engagement with the social, biological, and linguistic mechanics of the feelings. When Milton entered the world by falling through Albion's heart, he fell into an opening no discourse could properly close. Despite Coleridge's assertion to the contrary, there is no sustainable distinction between mechanic and organic form: every heart has its pump, every living passion its mechanism, every feeling a figure drawn from the mill of convention. Albion's "machines," we recall, "are woven with his life" (*Jerusalem* 40:25, E 188). Although this line speaks to the newly alienated work conditions of the early nineteenth century ("laboring at the mill with slaves"), it penetrates much more deeply, to the interior weave of life and machine that characterizes a modern subjectivity shaped from the start to function within an increasingly mechanized world. The great achievement of Makdisi's study is its insight into Blake's systematic representation of modern subject formation, which Blake everywhere figures as a kind of industrial embryogenesis. According to Makdisi, even the *organs* of individual, embodied life are, from the start in Blake, shaped by and for the disciplinary *organization* of production they serve. Focusing on the bounded and divided forms ("self-closd") that emerge from and displace a previous state of undifferentiated energy, as if they were "solids" emerging from "living fluids," Makdisi persuasively maps Blake's central myth—the Fall—onto the historical narrative of a modern work force painfully wrenched from premodernity, with individual subjects taking the form of living machines that early nineteenth-century social theorists described equally well in organic or mechanical terms, often interchangeably. The horror of the Fall—and the basis of Blake's critique of modernity as Makdisi powerfully describes it—is that life cannot be opposed to machine because mechanization precedes, organizes, and constitutes the very forms of modern life.[44] In such conditions, vitality itself is unnatural; it is an experience modern living-machines have been made to feel. The pulse is by no means a reliable indicator of authentic life.

Although Makdisi does not place his argument in this context, a similar idea has long influenced studies of Romanticism generally and deconstructive readings of Romantic lyric specifically. Barbara Johnson, Adela Pinch, and most recently Sara Guyer, for instance, have all emphasized the slippage in the Preface to *Lyrical Ballads* between the living passions Wordsworth attributes to authentic poetry and the personifications he famously rejects as "a mechanical device of style." Wordsworth hoped that a new poetics would avoid the dead mechanisms of lyric convention and so return the reader to "the company of flesh and blood,"[45] to a human poetry as self-substantiating as the organic body. As Guyer has shown, however, "flesh and blood" is itself a phrase haunted by contradictory meanings and thus unable to perform the stabilizing function Wordsworth asks of it. If the phrase summons connotations of "living substance" or "animal life" as a counterpoint to convention and abstraction, it does so only by equating life with "bodily mechanism, a circulation machine." And if it positions immediacy and embodiment against the encroachment of figurative language, the phrase also turns out to be among the oldest of figures, a synecdoche going back at least to the New Testament, substituting part ("the body—animal") for whole ("human life"). Weaving together any number of polarities—the figurative and the nonfigurative; the passionate and the conventional; the human and the nonhuman—"flesh and blood" reopens the irresolution between authenticity and inauthenticity it was introduced to close.[46] A similar slippage appears at the climax of *Milton* when Blake's poet hero announces the ultimate goal of his mission: to put off the "false Body" of the "Not Human":

> This is a false Body: an Incrustation over my Immortal
> Spirit; a Selfhood, which must be put off & annihilated alway
> To cleanse the Face of my Spirit by Self-examination.   (40:35–37, E 142)
>
> To bathe in the Waters of Life; to wash off the Not Human
> I come in Self-annihilation & the grandeur of Inspiration.   (41:1–2, E 142)

In Wordsworth's "flesh and blood" figuration survives any effort to purge "mechanical devices" from the truly human. Similarly, when Milton claims to cleanse his spirit of all false bodies and incrustations, that spirit remains entangled with figure: it still shows a "face." Rather than defending human life as if it were either real bodily substance or pure, unformed energy ("Immortal / Spirit"), Milton defends a prosopopoeia, another surface beneath the exteriorities he would remove.[47]

As figures for human being, Milton's "face," the poet's "pulsation of an artery,"

Wordsworth's "flesh and blood," and even Harvey's heart (half animal, half mechanism), all belong to the category Johnson has called "figures of half-aliveness," a term that also provides an apt description of what adverse emotion feels like in Blake: at once substantive and spectral, intimate and impersonal, animated and artificial.[48] Whenever literary texts make their readers aware of these "half-alive" emotions, it is tempting to consider such moments in terms of paranoid, gothic discovery. To their horror, the living discover that the experience they have all along mistaken for self-authenticating vitality is instead the byproduct of a mechanical function: of the biological machine, the social machine, or the linguistic machine. Rei Terada, for instance, describes one such scene in her conclusion to *Feeling in Theory*, "Night of the Human Subject," where the best representative of a unified, fully functional human subject turns out to be the zombie automaton of classic horror films. Blake's work is full of such gothic moments, with selfhoods revealing their possession by inauthentic specters: the long night of Enitharmon is a night of living machines who pass themselves off as human forms. But in Blake (and in Terada, for that matter), the discovery that one is only "half-alive" is never a matter of gothic undoing only, for the *loss* of liveliness and immediacy (and the shock entailed by that loss) is also the *origin* of critical disturbance. The awkwardness of feeling not quite human is the beginning of feeling otherwise. True, Blake posits no alternative to feeling "half-alive," no emotional plenitude or "spontaneous overflow of powerful feeling"—not even enthusiasm—that could serve as a counterweight to the heart's irresolution of vitality and mechanism, for the heart *is* that irresolution. No warm, real life exists apart from or prior to historical, cultural, and linguistic organization, no self-substantiating testimony of feeling. But when the alien or mechanical rubs within and against the natural, the critical reader experiences an estrangement necessary to turn vitality into a question—necessary, that is, to ask whether vitality *ought* to be the measure of emotional and poetic value, whether it can indeed automatically confirm and substantiate human nature. If we are to take Makdisi's argument seriously, as I do, and understand the individual subject's experience of its own immediate vitality as itself an indication of the Fall, then the critical disturbance that results from feeling the mechanization of one's own emotion serves to point experience past its own historically conditioned self-evidence. To feel the heart's mechanism, to experience the strangely mechanical underpinnings of one's emotion, is to take a half-step outside of one's received human nature.[49] It is, as Blake puts it, an invitation to move outside of the gates of the human heart.

We have now reached a point where we can return to the problem of sympathy as represented in "On Anothers Sorrow," for at this juncture one is struck by how seamlessly this song joins together emotional spontaneity (representing sympathy as an irresistible effusion, a hardwired response a human subject cannot help but feel) and the rote performance of a received vocabulary, a too-familiar syntax. Everything in the poem proceeds *automatically*, in both senses of that term: impulsively, naturally, and without need for deliberation, as if an inherent human nature were directly manifesting itself; mechanically, formulaically, and with conspicuous regularity, as if the speaker were conforming to an inherited, predetermined program. Alive, on the one hand; half-alive, on the other. The person who inhabits the speaking voice of "On Anothers Sorrow" experiences the automatic nature of sympathy in both ways. He becomes a personification produced (and half emptied) by the poem's sentimental performance, the mechanization of which rises to the surface in many of the poem's formal features (its inevitable rhymes and rhetorical questions, for instance) and takes thematic shape in the hydraulic flow of its recycled sympathetic tears, from child to father and back again, from infant to Jesus and back again: "weeping tear on infants tear." The poem's speaker embodies—proves upon the pulses, we might say—the axiom announced by Richardson in *Clarissa*: "I ever honoured a man that could weep for the distresses of *others*; and ever shall."[50] In this way the poem mimes, makes available for critical disturbance, the interfusion of received convention and affective immediacy that sentimental subjects had for a century experienced as a spontaneous expression of their humanity. "On Anothers Sorrow" demonstrates just how strange it feels to be a living axiom.

By way of contrast, compare a familiar scene of sympathy from Laurence Sterne's *A Sentimental Journey*, the one where Yorick comforts mad, abandoned Maria by the roadside:

> . . . the tears trickled down her cheeks.
>
> I sat down close by her; and Maria let me wipe them away as they fell with my handkerchief.—I then steep'd it in my own—and then in hers—and then in mine—and then I wiped hers again—and as I did it, I felt such undescribable emotions within me, as I am sure could not be accounted for from any combinations of matter and motion.
>
> I am positive I have a soul; nor can all the books with which materialists have pester'd the world ever convince me of the contrary.[51]

Sterne's sentimental scene shares many stock-in-trade elements with Blake's: falling tears, sitting by, wiping tears away. And like "On Anothers Sorrow," this scene foregrounds the automatic nature of its sympathy—first through the tears reciprocated by spectator and sufferer, but most conspicuously through the back-and-forth motion of Yorick's handkerchief, which transforms Sterne's narrative language into a rhythmic infrastructure of moving, repeatable parts (that is, into a mechanical pulse): "and then . . . and then . . . and then." According to Yorick, there is nothing strange about this automatic motion. Rather than emptying his sympathy or turning it into a question, he presents this automation as evidence of a fundamental human nature ("a soul") and thus as an answer to the mechanistic theories of French materialists like La Mettrie. The scene with Maria completes an argument Yorick has been advancing since the opening pages of the novel, where, exhilarated by his journey from Dover to Calais, he presents the self-evidence of his heightened physical state as living proof of his spirit: "I felt every vessel in my frame dilate—the arteries beat all chearily together, and every power which sustained life, perform'd it with so little friction that . . . with all her materialism, [France] could scarce have called me a machine" (4). Given Sterne's notoriously elusive irony, it is hard to know just how seriously to take these arguments. Here, the reader may well experience the friction or unease that Yorick claims has all but disappeared from the matter and motion of his body, which now functions so harmoniously it seems nearly incorporeal. As Nietzsche once commented, "The reader who demands to know . . . whether [Sterne] is making a serious or a laughing face, must be given up for lost," and Yorick, after all, is flush with French wine when he enlists his warm arteries as an ally against French materialism.[52] Far more subtle but perhaps even more suspicious is Yorick's later claim that his sympathy for Maria lies outside of linguistic production ("such *undescribable* emotions") and his implication that, by contrast, the theories of his adversaries amount to little more than a vast echo chamber of empty words ("all the books with which materialists have pester'd the world"). In defense of an essential human nature, Yorick puts his body up against a mere body of writing, but in so doing he echoes, *on his side,* arguments so familiar as to be nearly ubiquitous themselves, arguments such as this one put forth by an anonymous writer more than a decade earlier: "Moral weeping is the sign of so noble a passion, that it may be questioned whether those are properly men, who never weep upon any occasion . . . What can be more nobly human than to have a tender sentimental feeling of our own and other's [*sic*] misfortunes?"[53] Yorick, in other words, elides the fact that sympathy-advocating respondents to materialism had been pestering the world with *their* books for nearly as long as their antagonists. Eventually it becomes apparent that Yorick's answer to the materialist charge of being a mere body-machine takes refuge in a competing machine, a machine of repeated words, phrases, idioms, and concepts, a whole reiterative discourse on sympathy already old by the time of *A Sentimental Journey* and—thanks to the popularity of Sterne's novel—exhausted even further by the time of "On Anothers Sorrow."

In a 1934 article, R. S. Crane exhaustively reviewed the sermons and tracts written by Latitudinarian clergymen between 1660 and 1720 to show just how extensively they prepared the way for the next generation's discourse on sensibility. As Crane explains, even before Shaftesbury began to extol the virtues of sympathy and enthusiasm, these Anglican preachers devoted themselves "to picturing the heart of man as 'naturally' good in the sense that when left to its own native impulses it tends invariably to humane and sociable feelings" (220). Often they pursued this argument to rebut "Mechanick Philosophers" they associated with their nemesis, Thomas Hobbes.[54] What La Mettrie was to Sterne in 1768, Hobbes was to his predecessor Samuel Parker, Arch-deacon of Canterbury, in 1681: chief proponent of the error "[t]hat humane Nature is a meer Machine, and that all the contrivances of the minds of Men are nothing but the mechanical Results of Matter and Motion" (Parker, Preface, iii). Like so many others, and like Yorick in his scene with Maria, Parker set out to demonstrate that "if there be any Mechanism (as no doubt there is) it is Divine Mechanism" (Preface, xxiv). The most remarkable feature of the texts surveyed by Crane, however, at least in light of our discussion, is the way they explicitly and recurrently collapse together the terms Yorick wishes to keep not only separate but opposed: sympathy and mechanism. In this Anglican tradition, the latter term signifies emotions that require no learning and no deliberation because they spring *automatically* from an original mechanism installed in human nature by God:

> [A]s for the generality of Men their hearts are so tender and their natural affections so humane, that they cannot but pity and commiserate the afflicted with **a kind of fatal and mechanical Sympathy**; their groans force tears and sighs from the unafflicted, and 'tis a pain to them not to be able to relieve their miseries.   (Samuel Parker, 1681)

> Nature has endu'd us with the tenderest Passions: We are all Counterparts one of another: The Instruments *tun'd* Unison: the doleful Cry of one in extreme Distress, makes the Strings to tremble at our very Hearts . . . [This is] the Voice of Nature, ***charity of the Machine***, and Formation..   (Knightly Chetwood, 1708)

> God has implanted in our very Frame and Make, a compassionate Sense of the Sufferings and Misfortunes of other People, which disposes us to contribute to their Relief; so that when we see any of our Fellow-Creatures in Circumstances of Distress, **we are naturally, I had almost said, mechanically** inclined to be helpful to them..   (Richard Fiddes, 1720)[55]

> [original italics; my emphasis in bold]

These preachers would not have hesitated to praise Yorick by calling him "a machine," for they understood the mutual inherence of vitality and mechanism to be a sign of divine providence rather than a sign of its absence. In this early phase especially, they were determined to reclaim the word "machine" from materialists like Hobbes. Even more important, though, than the semantic blurring of the natural and the mechanical in the matter of emotion is how these sermons and treatises ventriloquize an established discourse on sympathy that, with modifications and variations, would remain more or less intact straight into the Romantic period. Whether or not these texts express a living principle of human nature, they most certainly spring from a readymade vocabulary; they practically write themselves. With the opening question of Blake's poem in mind, "Can I see anothers grief / And not seek for kind relief," one cannot but be struck by the sheer monotony of precursor texts in which words like "grief," "kind," "relief," and "another" appear with all the reassembled regularity of refrigerator magnets. Already in 1686, William Clagett could write: "*Man* only of all Creatures under Heaven, God has given this quality, to be affected with the **Grief** and with the Joy of those of his own **kind**; and to feel the Evils which others feel, that we may be universally disposed to help and **relieve** one **another**."[56] Throughout the century the language on sympathy recycles itself just as predictably as the back-and-forth movement of Yorick's tear-absorbing handkerchief and with just as much efficiency as the water pump system Harvey likened to the circulation of blood by the heart. Whatever else it might be, sympathy was a vast, self-perpetuating machine for inadvertent plagiarists, a technical apparatus only ever "half-alive," and—Yorick's claim to a soul notwithstanding—almost a better argument for materialism than against it.[57]

Blake inherited this apparatus and knew it intimately. He understood its capacity both to animate the feelings and to reiterate them mechanically, endlessly. He himself contributed "On Anothers Sorrow" to its massive, growing repertoire. At times, in mythic form, Blake's late poetry seems to reflect on the collective cultural labor of producing sympathy, as well as on the ambivalence he must have felt by participating in its century-long construction. The same plate in *Milton* that describes the uncanny work of time and ends by equating the pulsation of an artery with the duration of six thousand years begins with a team of pity artists building "the beautiful House" of sentimental forms:

> Some Sons of Los surround the Passions with porches of iron & silver
> Creating form & beauty around the dark regions of sorrow,
> Giving to airy nothing a name and a habitation
> Delightful! with bounds to the Infinite putting off the Indefinite
> Into most holy forms of Thought: (such is the power of inspiration)
> They labour incessant; with many tears & afflictions:
> Creating the beautiful House for the piteous sufferer.   (28:1–7, E 125)

By no means is Blake exclusively (or even obviously) critical of this process. The heart-work he describes here gives form to sufferings that have yet to find an idiom;

like the feeling of damage Lyotard called "the differend," these sorrows clamor for recognition but have no medium in which to make themselves known.[58] Two plates earlier, Blake describes the plight of defenseless souls born into the fallen world without access to representation: their "piteous Passions & Desires" have "neither lineament nor form" but are "like to watry clouds" (26:26–27, E 123). It is the task of Los's Sons to "clothe them & feed & provide houses & fields" (26:30, E 123), a labor of sympathy so obviously noble and worthy it might seem immune to criticism. But in the later passage we begin to realize that these laborers are almost too good at what they do, creating forms for "piteous" sufferers almost too "beautiful," too satisfying, too habitable. Yes, these forms put off what is "indefinite" in sorrow by establishing limits ("surround," "around," and "bounds" are all key words in these lines), but they are made of "iron" as well as "silver": they not only "delight," they shackle. And *whom*, exactly, do they delight? If a socially responsible art form can provide some measure of relief to those whose suffering has gone unrepresented, it can also provide pleasure to those who take in the sad spectacle at a distance, those sympathetic readers, in other words, who across the latter half of the eighteenth century demonstrated an insatiable appetite for figures like Sterne's mad Maria. Of course these Sons of Los must "labour incessant"; no matter "how many tears and afflictions" they translate into textual form, there will never be enough to meet the market demand. They labor on the front lines of their era's pity industry.

As Blake recognized, the danger of building so beautiful a house for suffering is that it might lead sentimental subjects to take up permanent residence. By the end of the eighteenth century, sentimental discourse had laid such a durable and attractive foundation that sympathy could seem no more subject to challenge than human nature itself. Thus the sentimental labor of the Sons of Los stands in striking contrast to the more radical sympathy explored in "On Anothers Sorrow," where Blake's Jesus aims to destroy grief, not house it. Rather than building sorrow and pity a comfortable home, the artist (like Jesus) must point to a time when "Pity would be no more." Despite the strong gravitational pull of sentimental discourse, it would be better, were it possible, to write not from the heart but outside it. Rather than making himself at home with his human feelings, the artist must find ways to inhabit the counterintuitive, to feel half-alive. In *Jerusalem*, when Blake describes Los building Golgonooza "Outside of the Gates of the Human Heart" (53:16, E 203), his protagonist's location at first seems to be the result of exile, a sign of his fall from paradise. The "roots of Albions Tree" have entered into his soul (53:4, E 202). His children have become "Inclos[ed]," their "Giant forms condensing into Nations & Peoples & Tongues" (53:7–8, E 202); that is, they have become exiles in the biblical, imperial state known as Babylon, with its "peoples, and multitudes, and nations, and tongues" (Revelation 17:15). Los works "on the banks of the Thames" like another Ezekiel on the banks of the Euphrates, building Golgonooza "In fears / . . . in rage & in fury" (53:15, 17–18, E 203). Every detail leads us to believe that Los labors outside his true home, his native Zion, far from the life-affirming feelings of a lost original condition. Every detail, in other words, seems to suggest that he builds Golgonooza in order to reverse the Fall, to pass back through the gates (of paradise), past the guardian cherub with his flaming sword, to reclaim the territory of his Edenic Human Heart. The allure of such a reading is manifest but seriously misguided. Blake's fallen artist does not suffer exile from the heart as a punishment; he undertakes exile as a tactical and necessary departure from a dwelling where he has been made to feel too much at home, too fully at ease. Turning away from the human heart, and away from the "beautiful House" the heart creates for suffering, Golgonooza turns instead toward a more alienated structure of feeling. Like Milton in Blake's shorter epic, Los has a future only if he can "f[a]ll thro Albions heart" and "trave[l] outside of Humanity" (*Milton* 20:41, E 114).

Although the description of Los building Golgonooza occurs only a few lines into the first plate of Chapter 3, almost at the center of *Jerusalem*, the word "heart" has already become troubled, appearing three times in this chapter, each time with a different qualifier: first as "the Natural Heart," then as "the Human Heart," and finally as "the Animal Heart." Blake uses the first two interchangeably, and, given his antipathy to the "natural," the collapse of distinction between these terms tells us how undesirable it would be to return to the human heart. The idea of an inherent human nature is a false paradise. Blake's argument is with the Deists, whom he addresses in the introduction to Chapter 3. Like their precursors the Latitudinarians—who understood sympathy to be the sign of inherent, God-given benevolence, "implanted in the Nature and Constitution of humane Bodies" (Parker 54)—the Deists also preach "Natural Morality or Natural Religion" (52, E 200). Blake expands the category of Deist to include anyone ("Voltaire! Rousseau!" [52, E 201]) who believes that a universal human nature is acquired at birth, anyone who claims to know "the Virtues of the Human Heart" (52, E 201) and dictates moral law to others on that basis. Man is not born with an authentic human heart, naturally disposed to sympathy; he is born into a culture, in Blake's case, a culture deeply penetrated by the discourses and practices of sympathy. In his address to the Deists, Blake puts the argument this way: "Man is born a Spectre . . . & must continually be changed into his direct Contrary" (52, E 200). It is this need to transform the received self, to become unfamiliar, that the Deists and other advocates of an essential human nature disable in advance. Deism, as Blake understands it, secures the status quo by identifying things as they are with the immutable laws of Nature, or, again as Blake puts it, "Deism, is the Worship of the God of this World by the means of what you call Natural Religion and Natural Philosophy, and of Natural Morality or Self-Righteousness, the Selfish Virtues of the Natural Heart" (52, E 201). The last thing Los or anyone else should want is a Natural Heart (or a human one; again, in this address, Blake uses the terms interchangeably).

Is it possible to pass beyond the natural heart and thus "travel outside of humanity"? The fallen artist begins the process of critical engagement by repeating the word "Natural" so often, so mechanically, that it becomes an irritant; he also introduces grating counterintuitive phrases ("the Selfish Virtues of the Natural Heart"). Both are favorite strategies of Blake's; rather than oiling the machine, they turn language into so much grit in the mill. But what about the third term in the sequence leading up to Los's work on Golgonooza: "the *Animal* Heart"? Like the others, it would seem to associate the heart with the (fallen) state of Nature, but "the Animal" does something more here. It introduces a category confusion that "the Human" tends to elide, at least in the discourse of those Blake called Deists. Because it has nothing to do with reason, "the Animal" applies equally well to spontaneous vitality and bodily mechanism. Descartes used it in the latter sense, treating the animal as a living machine. It would be impossible, he argued in one of his thought experiments, to distinguish between a living animal and an ingeniously contrived replica or automaton. Moreover, he added, this confusion could never pertain to human beings, who speak and reason and could therefore be tested.[59] By adding "the Animal" to his sequence, Blake revives the indeterminacy Descartes dismissed. In matters of the heart, how can one tell the human from the animal, or either one from something made, a machine? In *Jerusalem*, "the Animal Heart" occurs in a description of Los's workshop, his space of production in the fallen world, the instruments of which turn out to be indistinguishable from the labor power of his animal body: "The Bellows are the Animal Lungs. the hammers, the Animal Heart / The Furnaces, the Stomach for Digestion" (53:12–13, E 202). This heart involves a continuum between vitality and artificial construction; it is both organ and artifact, a corporeal instrument within a system of mechanical organization. Only half-alive, it is nonetheless an engine of aesthetic production. Because this heart is not entirely one thing (vital) or another (mechanical), because it is not self-evidently human but strangely "animal," it does not return us to human nature where we expect to find it, to the all too easily moralized body of the natural philosophers; it gives us a human nature already beside itself, in the process of becoming something else.

The pulse hammered out by such a heart must be a strange one indeed. If it cannot easily be assimilated into the tendency of natural philosophers to humanize heart and blood, this pulse also resists, even as it acknowledges, the vitalist temptation to posit animal blood as a source of wild, unaccountable feelings contrapuntal to instrumental conscious control (a temptation irresistible in much of our own contemporary affect theory). Blake's pulse ultimately stakes its innovative potential on the feeling of friction instead, the disturbance that occurs when the human, the natural, and the animal lock gears and grind uncomfortably against one another. If the interlacing of the human and the mechanical extends so deeply (all the way down, as Blake reluctantly intuited), then the unknowable architecture of Golgonooza—if it is to arise at all—can only be built upon an inorganic rhythm.

Wordsworth's Pulsation Machine, or the Half-Life of Mary Hutchinson

Interlude on "She was a Phantom of delight"

She was a Phantom of delight
When first she gleam'd upon my sight;
A lovely Apparition, sent
To be a moment's ornament;
Her eyes as stars of Twilight fair;
Like Twilight's, too, her dusky hair;
But all things else about her drawn
From May-time and the chearful Dawn;
A dancing Shape, an Image gay,
To haunt, to startle, and way-lay.

I saw her upon nearer view,
A Spirit, yet a Woman too!
Her household motions light and free,
And steps of virgin liberty;
A countenance in which did meet
Sweet records, promises as sweet;
A Creature not too bright or good
For human nature's daily food;
For transient sorrows, simple wiles,
Praise, blame, love, kisses, tears, and smiles.

And now I see with eye serene
The very pulse of the machine;

A Being breathing thoughtful breath;
A Traveller betwixt life and death;
The reason firm, the temperate will,
Endurance, foresight, strength and skill;
A perfect Woman; nobly plann'd,
To warn, to comfort, and command;
And yet a Spirit still, and bright
With something of an angel light.

The germ of this poem was four lines composed as part of the verses on the Highland Girl. Though beginning in this way, it was written from my heart as is sufficiently obvious.

—William Wordsworth to Isabella Fenwick

Any machine moving in rhythm has a pulse. Take Mary Hutchinson. Composed in honor of his "dear wife," as Wordsworth told Isabella Fenwick, "She was a Phantom of delight" is a lyric so sentimental one might wish he had written it from any organ but the heart.[1] The poem describes Mary as the manifest ideal of natural supernaturalism, joining high and low, this world and beyond. It also testifies to the idea that wonder can persist even in an institution as durable and day-to-day as marriage, for becoming a wife never seems to have cost Mary her radiant "virgin liberty" (14). Wordsworth liked this idea enough to incorporate it directly into a late revision of *The Prelude*. The same chiasmus that structures the earlier lyric in 1807—"A Spirit, yet a Woman too!" (12); "A perfect Woman . . . / And yet a Spirit still" (27–29)—enters into lines on Mary he added to Book XIV sometime between 1816 and 1819: "an inmate of the heart, / And yet a Spirit" (269–270).[2] It was important to Wordsworth that Mary retain this otherworldliness even in ordinary domesticity, that (like some conjugal version of Heisenberg's uncertainty principle) she remain a "Phantom" never quite captured by any system of binary categories one might employ to locate and identify her. Thus, even if Mary is an "inmate of the heart," her husband's heart, she somehow remains in perpetual motion, always at liberty, "Her household motions light and free" (13). And because she is a figure of uncorrupted freedom, she in turn allows her poet husband to experience the surprising, unsettling joy of the spirit world, without ever having to leave the safety of his own home. Wordsworth finds himself "haunt[ed], . . . startle[d], and way-la[id]" (10) by a wife familiar to him from childhood, indeed his cousin. That the ideal, elusive freedom he sees in Mary is a needy construction hardly needs stating; that it is the stuff of lyric convention is evident in its transferable, generalized nature. When this phantom "first . . . gleam'd upon [his] sight" (2), she was someone else. Wordsworth originally devised the idea for his portrait of the High-land Girl, whose foreign, primitive vitality ("The freedom of a Mountaineer" [31]) makes her a cliché of the Romantic Celtic revival.[3] In short, "She was a Phantom of delight" is an anxious poem. It tries to retain the effect of phantoms and delight in a sentimental era where the "good strangeness of poetry" occurs too regularly, too automatically, to carry much force.[4] The problem the poem addresses, then, is not just whether there is any wonder left in the ordinary—the burden Wordsworth asks Mary to bear—but whether, in poems written from the heart, extraordinary emotion is even possible.

Into this context Wordsworth introduces a pulsation, perhaps the pulsation of an artery. The final stanza begins,

> And now I see with eye serene
> The very pulse of the machine;
> A Being breathing thoughtful breath;
> A Traveller betwixt life and death.   (21–24)

"Machine" is the poem's only surprising word. At least it is the only word most editors feel compelled to gloss, typically to assure modern readers that it refers to the living creature, the organic body, and not some "mechanical device."[5] If that is the case—if "pulse of the machine" invokes the corporeal, systemic rhythms of circulation and respiration—then the phrase represents one side of a polarity Mary ultimately transcends (the embodied "Woman," as opposed to "something of an angel" [30]). Against the tendency to over-idealize her, or to turn her into an abstraction, the pulse machine grounds her in the kind of spontaneous, physical pleasures "Tintern Abbey" calls the "glad animal movements" (75).[6] Mary's pulse keeps us "in the company of flesh and blood" (Preface to *Lyrical Ballads*, 161). But in fact, the poem no more favors the animal body than it does the spirit, for it represents Mary in constant motion between the two. Against the tendency to embody her fully, to make her too earthy, the very next line elevates her animal breath into "*thoughtful* breath." Mary's authentic, indefinite "Being" makes her a mysterious "Traveller"—"betwixt life and death" (24) but also between any imaginable opposi-tions. At the center of domesticity one encounters the *unheimlich*, a dislocated be-ing whose "heart and home, / Is with infinitude, and only there" (*Prelude* VI [1850], 606–607). Mary, then, is a figure for what lies outside or beyond figuration, and the ability to appreciate her phantom human nature is a sign that the poet—and through the poem, the reader—shares in her freedom.

As we have seen, it is not easy to separate the organic body from mechanical or-ganization, especially when it comes to pulsations. Mary shuttles not only between animal and angelic being but also between vital and mechanistic functions. Within the next hundred years, the discourse of pulsations would be everywhere—in organic or inorganic bodies (Emerson: "life pulsates in rock or tree"); in intellectual, affective, and physiological life; in the circulation of blood and the circuitry of electric currents; in any machine that performs a rhythmic function (my favorite: the "pulsator," manufactured by the dairy industry to simulate the intermittent sucking action of a calf, in use as early as 1907).[7] Here, even this early on, we should not be misled by the poem's absence of explicit reference to a "mechanical device"; "pulse of the machine" may refer equally well to Mary's living body *and* the poem's own "mechanical device[s] of style," which generate Mary and her motion to and fro as so many ghosts in a machine. Mary's pulse is the poem's pulse, a rhythm built not only on the regular counterpoint of stressed and unstressed syllables but also (thematically) on an internal frame of identity and difference. Only because everything in this poem comes in binary pairs can Mary move back and forth between the poles, as in the typical, chiasmic exchange between person and nature structuring the first stanza (eyes-Twilight / Twilight-hair):

> Her eyes as stars of Twilight fair;
> Like Twilight's too, her dusky hair.   (5–6)

Nothing in this poem is fixed in place because everything is itself and something else "too" ("two"). There are two "twilights" (each an intermediate, "between light") and two corresponding facial features (eyes and hair). The second twilight resembles Mary's "dusky hair" but will soon give way contrapuntally to "the chearful Dawn" (8). Two (animal) eyes are also two (heavenly) stars. Mary may be an elusive, phantom traveler, but in these lines we see right through to the linguistic infrastructure, the motion generator, that produces her ghostly effects. We might think of this poem as if it were a strange film that allows its audience to see two things at once: the convincing illusion of an embodied figure in motion and, frame by frame, the very medium in which that figure's vitality and freedom are being mechanically produced. Reading "She was a Phantom of delight," we watch a medium becoming vaguely human; we see how a mechanism can take on the emerging silhouette of a face, a shape apparent in the only physical features emphasized by the poem: eyes, hair, a "countenance," and—given the attention to eating, breathing, smiling, kissing, and speaking—a mouth. The reader sees prosopopoeia as it happens, in plain sight.

It is significant, then, that the poem begins and ends with the mechanics of perception. Like everything else in the poem, vision oscillates rhythmically between two possibilities:

She was a Phantom of delight
When first she gleam'd upon my sight;
A lovely Apparition, sent
To be a moment's ornament.   (1–4)

A perfect Woman . . .
And yet a Spirit still, and bright
With something of an angel light.   (27–30)

From one view, Mary is a sensory appearance of the spirit, of human life in excess of mere embodiment, a symbol in Coleridge's sense of the word: the "translucence of the Eternal through and in the Temporal."[8] She appears, but she has been sent from elsewhere, by an unfigured agency beyond appearance. At the same time, she is a purely optical phenomenon, a flat, momentary, and ornamental "apparition," a "gleam" in the eye—a "phantom" only of the light. Her appearance impresses itself upon the retina not as "an angel light" but as an angled light, reflected in a random, passing moment. This second possibility reduces perception to an interplay of surfaces, and its thin vision lies very close to the depthlessness, the "*material* vision," Paul de Man describes as the basis of the "flat, third-person world" in Kant's Third Critique.[9] De Man focuses on a passage in the Analytic of the Sublime where Kant likens the absence of concepts in aesthetic experience to the photomechanical vision he sees represented in poetry: "one must see . . . as poets do, as the eye seems to perceive," without the intrusion of thought or purpose or any sense of one's own subjectivity. Writes de Man, "[T]he eye, left to itself, entirely ignores understanding; it only notices appearance."[10] Perhaps this is what it would mean to "see with eye serene" (21), to see untroubled by any desire to transform a medium of perception into an indication of human nature. With an eye made quiet by the materiality of the medium, one might just see a pulse of light moving across an optical and textual surface, in a mechanical process devoid of subjects.[11] Mary would still be a "dancing Shape" (9), but (with neither visual nor emotional depth) she would be dancing in Andy Warhol's diamond dust shoes.[12]

As Mary goes, so goes the emotion-response of the poet (and in turn, the reader). Rather than being haunted, startled, and waylaid by a sudden glimpse into human freedom, one would be hard pressed, in response to this flat apparition, to feel anything at all. Again de Man: "The dynamics of the sublime mark the moment when . . . no pathos, anxiety, or sympathy is conceivable; it is, indeed, the moment of a-pathos, or apathy, as the complete loss of the symbolic."[13] And yet, emotion will not disappear so gently into that good, flat light. As Rei Terada has recently taught us, even de Man's "Alpine *apatheia*" retains a residual affective charge. Apatheia cannot empty itself of feeling altogether for it cannot escape "the paradoxical thrill of affectlessness," a thrill that originates in the stoic's very desire for "intellectual freedom from emotion."[14] T. S. Eliot had a similar insight when he called poetry "an escape from emotion" and "personality" but recognized that "only those who have personality and emotions know what it means to want to escape from these things"[15] in the first place. If de Man's theory of the sublime proved helpful in demystifying Wordsworth's sentimental attachment to an idea of freedom, it turns out that de Man is just as attached as Wordsworth is, though one tries to liberate himself by depleting emotion and the other by heightening it to a point where he hopes its excess will surprise him. Both would like to startle their readers into experiencing freedom, and both find the condition they value entangled with its exact opposite. Wordsworth's pulse is really a machine; de Man's machinery has a pulse. Wordsworth's poem can no more avoid a critique of emotion than a de Manian critique can escape the persistence of emotion.

This realization is not a matter of catching de Man at his own sport, of demystifying the demystifiers as if in a game one can win. Rather, it speaks to the intricate and unresolved relation between emotion and criticism that occurs whenever one reads critically. To read "She was a Phantom of delight" is to find oneself positioned at the intersection of emotion and critique, vitality and mechanism. It is to feel strangely half-alive, partially detached from a human nature one cannot trust, but feeling something nonetheless.

CHAPTER FIVE

Criticism and the Work of Emotion

I conclude with what I said at the beginning: to have the sense of
creative activity is the great happiness and proof of being alive, and it
is not denied to criticism to have it . . . And at some epochs no other
creation is possible.

—Matthew Arnold, "The Function of Criticism at the Present Time"

Reading the local particularities of events in form, we discover the
most complex measures of human art—the terms of its durable
social, political, and psychological interest. We also feel the charge of
an historically persistent, forever various, aesthetic vitality.

—Susan Wolfson, *Formal Charges: The Shaping of
Poetry in British Romanticism*

The Vitality of Criticism: Preliminaries

Distant from one another by more than a century, Matthew Arnold and Susan
Wolfson both conclude a defense of criticism by appealing to the self-evidence of
vitality. This turn to life-feeling places them in a shared history, a history of criticism at once formalist and humanist—and justifying itself in terms of an intellectual agency palpable enough to be felt. For Arnold, criticism is neither as creative
nor as active as literature, the gold standard for cultural production, but criticism
matters, especially at times when creative activity seems blocked and culture at
an impasse. Against the numbing forces of sameness and repetition—which for
Arnold in 1864 included the party propaganda that had turned the British constitution into "a colossal machine for the manufacture of Philistines"—criticism
matters because it keeps the possibility of agency and innovation alive.[1] Critics
know this because they feel it, sense it. Emotion and criticism support one another;
standing firm against deterministic constraints, they stand together for the possibility of living or acting more freely. (Here Arnold's idea of "happiness" anticipates

Adorno's: "Happiness in artworks would be the feeling they instill of standing firm."[2]) The "man of insight and conscience" (51), as Arnold calls the critic, never feels so free as when engaged in reading. Then the responsive, interpretive faculties rouse into action, rubbing against the mechanical self's tendency to conform. In the friction generated by critical thought lies vitality, convincing the critic that one can scarce call *him* a machine.

The idea that freedom depends on the capacity to think critically receives its classic modern statement in Kant's "What Is Enlightenment?" For all of the objections this essay has provoked (recall Foucault) one can hardly imagine a defense of the liberal arts today without some version of its argument (again recall Foucault). The idea that *authentic* critical thinking depends on the evidence of emotion is more complicated and controversial, notwithstanding the new scholarly admiration of emotion I have invoked throughout this book. Unable to shake off suspicion, social critics (including Blake) continue to worry that sentiment can be a source of manipulation, not freedom, that because feelings are bound up not only with innovation but also with superstition, prejudice, and ideology ("a well known capacity to fortify opinion, to inflame cognition," as Wimsatt and Beardsley once put it),[3] they serve purposes that remain hidden to those who are subject to them. In the modern discourse on criticism, feelings are sometimes the very constraint criticism is supposed to overcome. Arnold may trust the feeling of vitality, for instance, but that does not mean he trusts the feelings generally. Criticism instead requires the disinterestedness he borrowed directly from Kant; it involves detachment and objectivity, the power of *ideas* to resist the conspiracy of monological language and party politics, which together act on the ready complicity of prejudicial feeling with a coercive force Arnold likens to a locomotive: "That is what I call living by ideas: when one side of a question has long had your earnest support, when all your feelings are engaged, when you hear all round you no language but one, when your party talks this language like a steam-engine and can imagine no other,—still to be able to think, still to be irresistibly carried, if so it be, by the current of thought to the opposite side of the question" (35). Arnold's example of critical independence is Edmund Burke, whose *Thoughts on French Affairs* involved a reassessment of the revolution at the height of the partisan controversy Burke himself played such a crucial role in initiating. In this celebration of the mind's inherent power to change direction, thinking appears to run counter to feeling, as if they came from sources as antithetical as "the world of ideas" and "the world of practice" (33). But Arnold in fact opposes one feeling to another, the feeling of going against to the feeling of going along. Worried as he is about the latter ("It is true that the critic has many temptations to go with the stream, to make one of the party of movement" [43]), he cannot do without the former, for the feeling of going against, of thinking for oneself, is the great proof of being alive. Ideas cannot affirm this freedom by themselves alone; they need a living body, a texture and a temperature, to substantiate them.[4]

To see why this is so, perhaps all we need do is contrast the famous conclusion of "What Is Enlightenment?" In those final sentences Kant triumphantly asserts that thought will extend its freedom incrementally and irresistibly, but his confidence soars without substantiation: "Thus once the germ on which nature has lavished most care—man's inclination and vocation to *think freely*—has developed within this hard shell [of repressive law], it gradually reacts upon the mentality of the people, who thus gradually become increasingly able to *act freely*. Eventually, it even influences the principles of governments, which find that they can themselves profit by treating man, who is *more than a machine,* in a manner appropriate to his dignity" (original emphasis).[5] How does one know one thinks freely? (Foucault raises this question forcefully.) How does one know one is more than the machine described by La Mettrie and denied by Sterne? What evidence is there that thought *gradually* becomes act and act *eventually* alters the world by enlarging the sphere of freedom? (Arnold, we remember, understood that the "very subtle and indirect action" of criticism "condemns [it] to a slow and obscure work" [41].) The critic cannot supply the evidence that would demonstrate these things but nevertheless feels them to be so. Even the critic who makes a career of interrogating emotion can hardly do without the notion that his critical feelings substantiate his freedom. When Kant wished to demonstrate "the disposition and capacity of the human race to be the cause of its own advance toward the better"[6]—when he wished, in other words, to demonstrate the inherent capacity of collective self-determination—even he turned to critical feeling for corroboration, in this case, the feelings exhibited by enthusiasts for the French Revolution who had no intention of participating in the event. The great proof that man is "more than a machine" lies not in the enlightened mind or in the responsive heart (as Sterne proposed) but in the vitality of thought where a free mind and a feeling heart converge. That convergence represents an ideal enshrined for Arnold by the word "criticism."

Needless to say, few critics today would align themselves with Kant and Arnold, who themselves have long been favorite targets of critique. It would be a mistake, however, to dismiss criticism's appeal to the evidence of feeling as the product of a worn-out, humanist reflex periodically revived by projects such as Wolfson's. We remain invested in the affective textures of criticism—in the "*sense* of creative activity" it affords—even if we have problematized the concept of freedom and turned to other affects in order to imagine its possibility. Let's start over, then, with a different set of quotations, this time a sampler of posthumanist heartbeats and pulsations.

> **Antonio Negri**: It is the innovation brought about by *kairòs* that produces the world . . . (Every instant of life, of that which has been or that which will be, is a creative act.) Innovation . . . is always singular and determinate; considered from the point of view of this being and of its intensity there is no first and no last, no past and no future. Consequently, there is no 'becoming' . . . When we use the erroneous name 'becoming', we lose the sense of temporality, **of its living pulsation**: not transformation (i.e. becoming) . . . but . . . the emergence of differences.

> **Eve Kosofsky Sedgwick**: For if, as I've shown, a paranoid reading practice is closely tied to a notion of the inevitable, there are other features of queer reading that can attune it exquisitely **to a heartbeat of contingency**.

> **Jacques Derrida**: This heteronomy . . . opens autonomy on to itself, it is a figure of its **heartbeat** . . . *In sum, a decision is unconscious*—insane as that may seem, it involves the unconscious and nevertheless remains responsible. And we are hereby unfolding the classic concept of decision. It is this act of the act that we are attempting here to think: "passive," delivered over to the other, suspended over **the other's heartbeat** . . . Where I am helpless, where I decide what I cannot fail to decide, freely, necessarily, **receiving my very life from the heartbeat of the other. We say not only heart but** heartbeat: that which, *from one instant to another* . . . will *perhaps* **receive in a rhythmic pulsation** what is called blood, which in turn will receive the force needed to arrive.

> **Isobel Armstrong** (on Gilles Deleuze): **The heartbeat itself**, one assumes, possesses a kind of Heraclitean metrics, always different in a new space and time, **generating a unique pulse with every movement of the blood through the valves of the heart.**

> **Steven Shaviro** (on Alfred North Whitehead): Such a building-up of intensity through contrast is the basic principle of Whitehead's aesthetics, applying to all entities in the universe. At the low end of the scale, even the most rudimentary **"pulses of emotion"** (like the vibrations of subatomic particles) exhibit a "primitive provision of width for contrast." And at the highest end, even God is basically an aesthete . . . "God's purpose in the creative advance is the evocation of intensities."[7]

No doubt it is unfair to wrench these elusive quotations from their challenging, original contexts, but their juxtaposition allows us to see some features they hold in common, features we have already observed in Blake: an interest in alternative temporalities, centered on the moment's innovative potential; an interest in anonymous, alternative subjectivities; an interest in the transformative potential these strange times and beings might entail; a vocabulary of materialist affects, of alternative, inorganic pulses. Point by point, but especially in their radical particularity, these affects are meant to counteract the integrity of a self-contained Arnoldian subject. Thus Derrida insists on the heartbeat rather than the heart. What matters is the small disruption a single, unassimilated pulse can generate, not the whole organ or larger biological system a cooperative pulse might support.

With these quotations, we are very far from Arnold's understanding of vitality, though perhaps not as far as we might think. As in the old, the new criticism still summons the feeling of going against—or, more precisely, the feeling that it is possible to go against—even when history seems emptied of dynamism (in need of the innovative moment) and genuinely transformative agency seems blocked. Heightened feeling provides a foretaste of altered conditions, a reassurance that some current configuration of determining forces is neither absolute nor permanent. Even the least sentimental criticism harbors this minor enthusiasm, working to defamiliarize the conditioned self, testing constraints in order to alter the inherited practices that constitute the subject in the first place. Arnold called the subject's tendency to remain inert, to prevent itself from becoming otherwise, "self-satisfaction" (39). Blake called the countertendency of critical force, "self-annihilation." Today, however, it is Arnold's liberal ideal of a nonconforming, sovereign individual that represents the "self-satisfaction" criticism often strives to overcome. The vitality Arnold opposed to the machine as the affective sign of the subject's healthy autonomy has now itself become the very trademark of the machine, the ideological embodiment of a programmatic humanism. In order for criticism to perform its estrangement function now, it needs stronger, stranger emotions, less comfortable indications of our potential to experience the unknown and thereby supersede ourselves. If for Arnold "vitality" was once the great proof of critical freedom, alien heartbeats and pulses now serve that function. How does one know one is something other than the liberal subject written into being by Kant and Arnold? How does one know one can't be reduced to the "man" inscribed by a mechanical humanism? Critics know this when their thoughts are surprised by "the heartbeat of the other."

I do not wish to argue that poststructuralist theorists have taken to repeating the humanism they renounce. A different problem concerns me. If modern criticism has always depended on the resistance of deviant feelings to substantiate the possibility of going against, then criticism also quickly runs into trouble, for critical feelings *can never be strange enough* to perform their estrangement function convincingly. The moment that defamiliarization becomes axiomatic—and that moment might be traced back to Kant's account of reflective judgment in the Third Critique—defamiliarization also begins to seem like an impossible task. It is as if the very desire for the strange and the unpredictable—for agitations irreducible to concepts and therefore detectable only as affect—makes their occurrence predictable and their authenticity doubtful. No matter how unintegrated or unnarratable the pulse of critical feeling is supposed to have become, it can make itself neither minimal enough nor disturbing enough to escape the anticipation of a poststructuralist rhetoric that values nothing so much as estrangement. What could be more familiar right now than the "sense of creative activity" that is supposed to accompany ever more minutely attentive acts of defamiliarization? Like the leopards in Kafka's parable, which keep breaking into the temple and defiling its sacred objects, poststructuralist feeling has repeated its transgression so often that "finally it can be calculated in advance, and it becomes a part of the ceremony."[8]

In the previous chapter, we saw how an eighteenth-century discourse on sympathy continuously affirmed itself through reiteration and familiarity. The poststructuralist passages I just quoted may not share the mechanical consistency of Latitudinarian sermons, but they echo sufficiently to make any critic wary, as Arnold puts it, of the "temptations to go with the stream, to make one of the party of movement." The evidence of feeling does not always make it easy to know whether one goes along or against. It is the function of criticism at the present time—or at any time—to make that distinction, but given the intimacy between criticism and feeling that has been with us since Romanticism, we face a prospect of dizzying uncertainty. The feelings that would provide us with the best evidence of critical agency, of the very possibility of thinking otherwise, may themselves be ritual conventions subject to suspicion. Where do these *critical* feelings come from? What purposes do *they* serve? To what corporate body does *their* vitality belong?

We will return to the question of emotion and suspicion, but first, in order to indicate the state of intimacy between emotion and contemporary criticism, I want to consider two recent books published in the same year (1997): Derrida's *Politics of Friendship* and Wolfson's *Formal Charges*. These books have so little in common it might be surprising to learn they share an interest in Blake. A survey of emotion in contemporary criticism would be neither possible nor desirable, but by demonstrating the similar affective investments of Wolfson's return to aesthetic humanism and Derrida's ethical leap "beyond man and humanism,"[9] I at least hope to make more plausible my assertion of a broad interdependence between emotion and criticism. Focusing on Derrida and Wolfson has another advantage; it shows the extent to which affective agency is now linked to *reading* as a privileged site of transformative activity. Recent studies have described emotion as the subject's means of expanding its cognitive horizons. Grounded in the resources of the body, emotion directs attention to aspects of experience not yet distilled by higher concepts and cognitive norms. Even when circumstances suggest no clear path for agency, and the subject seems reduced to a state of unfreedom, emotion remains a way of paying attention otherwise, of maintaining an opening onto new, unrecognized possibilities. Standing at the intersection of blockage, responsiveness, and breakthrough, the subject of emotion, I want to argue, is closely aligned with the subject of reading. We see this not only in Wolfson and Derrida but also in some of Blake's best recent critics, who tend to describe his work as an encounter with ideological impasse that suddenly gives way—to an opening onto the new experienced as the agency of reading.

In this context we will return once more to *William Blake and the Impossible History of the 1790s*. Saree Makdisi draws his title from the following passage in the *Descriptive Catalogue*: "Historians . . . being weakly organized themselves, cannot see either miracle or prodigy; all is to them a dull round of probabilities and possibilities; but the history of all times and places, is nothing else but improbabilities and impossibilities; what we should say, was impossible if we did not see it always before our eyes" (E 543). Makdisi is exactly right to call these lines "astonishing,"[10] for their counterintuitive thrust is meant to induce the wonder latent in every historical moment. But this opening of history onto wonder, I would argue, is modeled in the first place by reading, in fact by the reading of these very lines at this very moment. What we first see—right "before our eyes"—are Blake's words. For Descartes, we recall, wonder "is the first of all the passions": "When the first encounter with some object surprises us, and we judge it to be new, or very different from what we knew in the past or what we supposed it was going to be, this makes us wonder and be astonished at it."[11] For Blake, *reading* works wonders. The text becomes the medium of surprise encounter, the site where impossible history erupts unpredictably and is experienced by the reader affectively. According to Makdisi, Blake's radical affect, his "faith based on joy" (xiii), baffles and eludes today's secular critics, and sometimes even embarrasses them with its unrestrained enthusiasm. To the contrary, faith-based affect may be the one thing that, for all their diversity, Blake critics share in common. It may also be the very thing that allows Blake criticism (and Makdisi's exuberant version in particular) to tell us something about the current practice of criticism generally. What should really astonish us about Blake's idea of transformation through reading is our abiding receptiveness to its appeal, which continues to elicit our enthusiasm. For Blake and his critics, there is something in the power of reading akin to magic, something that can only be experienced as emotion.

If "magic" seems like a deliberately provocative word, anticipating a predictable disenchantment, I have a somewhat different purpose in mind. Toward the end of this chapter—when we return to the questions of emotion and agency, on the one hand, and emotion and suspicion, on the other—we must consider one last theory of emotion, Jean-Paul Sartre's *The Emotions: Outline of a Theory*, a small pamphlet

(Sartre calls it an *esquisse*) that defines emotion as magical action. Whatever its limitations as an account of emotion, Sartre's theory remains relevant as an account of reading, criticism, and the feelings they involve—feelings at once indispensable to a sense of intellectual agency but nearly impossible to trust.

"The Chances of Deception," in Two Scenes

Let's conclude these preliminaries by considering two scenes that challenge their readers to confront the problematic interdependence of emotion and criticism, a challenge persistent ever since the Enlightenment discovered its need for the emotions. The first scene occurs in Henry Mackenzie's sentimental novel *The Man of Feeling* (1771). Harley has befriended a young prostitute in distress, reviving her when she faints from hunger and promising to visit her the next morning. When the time comes to fulfill his pledge, he begins to doubt the girl's sincerity, having had his eager feelings manipulated by a variety of con artists in the past. The chapter describing this crisis begins as a characteristic impasse between impulse and judgment. How can one tell whether another person's apparent suffering deserves our instinctive sympathy or our cautious skepticism? Here is the first paragraph in full:

> The last night's rallery of his companions was recalled to his remembrance when he awoke, and the colder homilies of prudence began to suggest some things which were nowise favourable for a performance of his promise to the unfortunate female he had met with before. He rose uncertain of his purpose; but the torpor of such considerations was seldom prevalent over the warmth of his nature. He walked some turns backwards and forwards in his room; he recalled the lanquid form of the fainting wretch to his mind; he wept at the recollection of her tears. "Though I am the vilest of beings, I have not forgotten every virtue; gratitude, I hope, I shall still have left."—He took a larger stride—"Powers of mercy that surround me!" cried he, "do ye not smile upon deeds like these? to calculate the chances of deception is too tedious a business for the life of man!"—The clock struck ten!—When he was got down stairs, he found that he had forgot the note of her lodgings; he gnawed his lips at the delay; he was fairly on the pavement, when he recollected having left his purse; he did but just prevent himself from articulating an imprecation. He rushed a second time up into his chamber. "What a wretch I am," said he; "ere this time perhaps—" 'Twas a perhaps not to be born:—two vibrations of a pendulum would have served him to lock his bureau; —but they could not be spared.[12]

Should he stay or should he go? At stake is not so much the worthiness of the prostitute as the trustworthiness of Harley's feelings for her. Are they a reliable basis for action? Harley finally sides with feeling, recognizing that "the chances of deception" can be calculated ad infinitum, and that the only way to act at all—to break the back-and-forth impasse represented first by his pacing, then by his movement up and down the stairs between his apartment and the street, and finally even by the pendulum vibrations that would turn every passing moment into a site of tedious indecision—is to risk the agency of emotion. Here we have an example of what Derrida calls the madness of decision, mad because the actual moment of decision must occur outside any rational process of deliberation.[13] If it didn't, one would still be deliberating, taking into account further evidence. Harley is thus the opposite of Arnold's Burke, who despite having all his feelings engaged in one direction is carried irresistibly to the other side by thought. Harley's feelings carry him irresistibly against thought's skepticism. Burke lives with ideas; for Harley, the "life of man," to have any life at all, must be a life of feeling.

If the passage were about Harley's feelings only, we could end our reading now and shelve *The Man of Feeling* alongside other companion pieces from the age of sensibility. What makes this scene remarkable, however, is that doubt survives the agency of emotion, just as the narration of Harley's uncertain deliberations *follows* the resolution already announced by the chapter's title: "HE KEEPS HIS APPOINT-MENT." That Harley keeps returning to his apartment suggests that he's still calculating the chances of deception even after deciding in favor of emotion against calculation. The bureau he leaves unlocked at the end of this sequence represents a victory of generosity over self-interest, but it also suggests he has made himself unnecessarily vulnerable. Rather than deciding against any further delay, he would have benefited from delaying just another moment. In fact, while Harley is already rushing out the door, the reader who follows his course of action is still pausing, inserting further moments for deliberation, still trying to determine whether Harley has indeed done the right thing. In other words, the impasse broken in the passage by Harley's affective agency remains an impasse still to be broken by the reader, who continues to calculate the chances of deception while also recognizing that any critical judgment for or against Harley would finally have to depend on exactly the kind of decisive feeling that created the reader's ambivalence in the first place. No evidence, in this scene or beyond, can resolve this conflict. Almost immediately afterward, the prostitute's sad tale of seduction and abandonment vindicates Harley's feelings—*for Harley*—but the story she tells is too generic to persuade the reader and resolve *his* impasse. As such stories are wont to do, the prostitute's even includes a cautionary tale about the power of popular romance novels to exploit their readers, pre-seducing them by playing on their vulnerable feelings. This warning could apply just as easily to any reader naively inclined to identify with Harley's feelings as to the maiden turned prostitute whose bad reading habits marked the beginning of her decline. Mackenzie has created a perfect scene to dramatize the critical reader's dilemma. The reader can exercise agency only by relying on the emotions he is systematically led to distrust, which is why *The Man of Feeling* is at one and the same time, at every moment of its swinging pendulum, a text of sensibility and irony. Should the reader go with or against the emotions? The novel's only answer is "yes."

Forward now to a very different scene, though one still wrestling with the chances of deception, with the question of whether criticism can trust its emotions. Here is the final paragraph of the introduction to Rei Terada's *Feeling in Theory*:

> This book coincides with a surge in the academic study of feeling. I am glad of this interesting development and glad to be part of it. I would not seem to have read my own words, however, if I didn't also wonder where the attraction to emotion comes from and why it comes just now. The texts discussed below suggest that historically, the idea of emotion has been activated to reinforce notions of subjectivity that could use the help. They also suggest that people deploy emotion in epistemologically defensive ways. Criticism's newfound thematization of emotion may be no exception; rising feeling may acknowledge and ward off antinomies in institutional life and thought, much as Rilke's *Duino Elegies*, de Man finds, "constantly appeal to the reader's emotion" just where they give up on classical reference. Conversation about emotion often attempts to supply a sense of substantiality and purpose where there is and sometimes should be none. The discussion of critical emotions can always be ideological in this way. Respect for the power of emotion should encourage scholars to inquire closely into their assumptions about their own. Of course, this does not mean there is anything unreal about the emotionality of experience, or that we ever could or should trade our emotions for the empty lucidity of a neutral world.[14]

In this quiet, introspective drama, Terada suggests several reasons to question the appeal of and to emotion in contemporary academic culture, all centering on emotion's ideological power to create the mirage of a unified, satisfying subjectivity. By now we are familiar with her main argument. The emotions that would, as Harley puts it, constitute "the life of man"—giving life support to a mere concept, a "notion of subjectivity that could use the help"—in fact unravel the idea of "man," for "emotion requires the death of the subject" (4). Harley and Terada stand at opposite ends of a humanist to post-humanist spectrum. And yet, in the end, like Harley in a way, Terada also sides with emotion against the "tedious business" (she calls it "the empty lucidity") of "a neutral world." Close inquiry into our cultural and professional assumptions about emotion (calculating the chances of deception) may demystify our illusions but it cannot (and should not) make emotion go away.

Doubt survived Harley's decision to go with his feelings; here emotion survives the skepticism Terada encourages. It survives, but in a different form, in the cognitive difficulty that criticism experiences as it sheds its humanist enchantment.

Terada's account, then, bears resemblance to the practice of autocritical emotion we discovered in our reading of Blake. The real strangeness of emotion's subjectlessness rubs critically against the ideological fullness and familiarity of identity-affirming experience. This half-alive emotion survives the death of the subject and possesses its own kind of vitality—not to be confused with "the life of man," to be sure, but not reducible to "the empty lucidity of a neutral world" either. The emotion that survives in and as criticism still carries an unsettling electric charge. We sense this not only as a logical outcome of Terada's arguments, which continually demonstrate how discourses on emotion break against the contradictions they cannot resolve, but also in her tone. Her cool, spare thoughtfulness (*never* sentimental) nonetheless allows itself the rebellious pleasure of going against, the kind of pleasure that comes from astonishing the reader with a simple but counterintuitive declaration: "emotion requires the death of the subject." The elegant abrasion of Terada's prose makes her world anything but neutral, her lucidity anything but empty. One would scarce call *her* a machine. In this criticism, in other words, we are still discovering the edges of our agency through feeling. As it did for Arnold, emotion still provides the evidence criticism needs to affirm its transgressions, its "sense of creative activity," especially in an epoch of impasse when constraints upon agency have become so formidable that the very idea of its exercise can seem wishful.

The passages I quoted earlier from Negri and Derrida, Sedgwick and Armstrong, suggest that poststructuralist affect does more than resist the attractions of a dubious humanism. It exercises attractions of its own, perhaps reinforcing notions that could use some help themselves. No doubt Terada would urge us to apply the same close inquiry to her conclusions about poststructuralist emotion that she herself applies to the humanist tradition. Where does *its* attraction come from and why does *it* come just now? No doubt the elusive, unrecognizable emotions recommended by poststructuralist criticism will have to yield to stranger emotions yet, themselves subject in turn to further skeptical inquiry, in a critical pursuit of freedom that is both substantiated and rendered dubious by the feelings it generates. Terada's reflection on critical emotion is as intellectually honest as is possible, but it gets us no further than we got with *The Man of Feeling*. Should the reader go with or against the emotions? Again the answer can only be "yes."

"Activist Formalism": Wolfson and Derrida

In her introduction to *Reading for Form*, a special issue of *MLQ* coedited with Marshall Brown, Susan Wolfson announces a new formalism in which attention to literary form—on the part of authors and readers alike—would itself constitute a kind of political practice. The journal's wide-ranging essays all passionately defend the political relevance of a return to close reading, and the various historical fields they cover dramatically expand upon Wolfson's own impressive defense of Romantic formalism published three years earlier as *Formal Charges: The Shaping of Poetry in British Romanticism*. There she sums up her "deepest claim" as follows: "language shaped by poetic form is not simply conscriptable as information for other frameworks of analysis; the forms themselves demand a specific kind of critical attention."[15] By attending to the specificity of literary language, readers participate in a text's resistance to cultural generalization. No one's words should be conscripted, least of all "as information."

If for Wolfson this idea of "activist formalism" begins with Romanticism,[16] then Romanticism begins with Blake's earliest, prerevolutionary writing. *Poetical Sketches* is the first text Wolfson puts to the test of sustained scrutiny in *Formal Charges*. Blake's small, first volume anticipates all the bigger things to come: the linguistic experiments of his later, difficult verse; the theory and practice of Romanticism in general; even the critical movement for which Wolfson supplies the manifesto two centuries later. "Blake's formalist practices," we learn, "are actions that call readers to a critical awareness of the work of form, not only in poetic but also in cognitive, social, and historical practices" (32). If one were to rewrite that sentence, substituting "Wolfson's formalist practices" for "Blake's," one would not need to alter another word. Blake stands at the origin of the "activist formalism" Wolfson sees herself helping to revive.

Derrida also regards Blake as an opportunity to rethink the political in terms of readerly agency, but Blake's place in *Politics of Friendship* is more difficult to determine. Rather than entering at the beginning of this book, he appears in passing, invoked only by a single entry from the poet's notebook, a couplet on friendship addressed bitterly to Hayley: "Thy Friendship oft has made my heart to ake / Do be my Enemy for Friendships sake" (E 506). Derrida introduces his reading of these lines abruptly, only two pages from the end of Chapter 3 (which otherwise makes no mention of Blake), and he drops them just as quickly. Thus Blake seems to play a rather modest part in *Politics of Friendship,* of interest largely because this cameo appearance represents, to my knowledge, Derrida's first print reference to the poet. Still, this barely present Blake resonates widely in *Politics of Friendship* and beyond. The couplet discussed at the end of Chapter 3 also serves as an epigraph to Chapter 2, and so Blake opens and closes a two-chapter sequence in which Derrida introduces two concepts crucial to his own "activist formalism": the "new type of address" he calls "teleiopoesis," and the revolutionary reading practice he calls "passive" or "unconscious decision."[17] I will return to these concepts shortly, but to complete this positioning of Blake in *Politics of Friendship,* we should note that the poet does not quite receive the final word of Chapter 3. After calling on us to listen for "the incessant return of [Blake's] ghosts" (73), the chapter closes by citing relevant passages from *Jerusalem* on Los's specter. In turn, these quotations are themselves followed by a footnote on "[s]pectral affinities" that ends by naming "Marx" (74). If Blake is a ghostly figure presiding over a pair of chapters within *Politics of Friendship,* he also provides a relay back to the text Derrida published one year earlier, *Specters of Marx.* In this way Derrida aligns Blake with the future-oriented, messianic demand for justice he considers the genuinely revolutionary event of the Marxist inheritance—and precisely the event activated by deconstructive reading practices.

In content and style, even in length, Wolfson's and Derrida's readings of Blake bear no more resemblance than one would expect from such differently motivated projects. More interesting than their predictable differences, however, is a conviction they share, one that might explain their affinity with Blake in the first place. For Wolfson and Derrida both, the agency of reading is bound up with the affect of reading, and it is through this linkage that interpretation, as they understand that term, becomes a politically relevant event with legitimate claim to changing the world.

Wolfson

We can begin by unpacking Wolfson's evocative title—*Formal Charges*—a title fully charged, loaded to capacity. Among other shades of meaning, "charges" primarily suggests three things: accusation; task or responsibility; and accumulated force or energy, with a literal reference to electricity and a figurative one to aesthetic stimulation. Given "the demonizing of aesthetic form" that is supposed to have accompanied the rise of historicism and cultural studies,[18] formalism, we are told, has stood professional trial for a generation now, its attention to literary form accused of inattention to the world, abdication of political responsibility, and "patent retreat from social reference, inflection, or application" (7). The lesser charge against formalism is negligence and escapism; the greater, "complicit[y] with reactionary ideologies" (1). Careful readings take time—both in the long-term preparation of critical skills and in the unfolding of any particular analysis—and such indulgence will always seem to take time away from political responsibility in a world where suffering and injustice demand urgent response. The time spent reading (and re-reading) "On Anothers Sorrow," say, could have been better spent relieving another's sorrow. On page one of *Formal Charges,* Wolfson cites Wordsworth's anxiety concerning the errors of judgment that inevitably befall a reader who has not bestowed "much time" on poetry, including "the time one spends with any one poem." But even as the Preface to *Lyrical Ballads* urges readers to slow themselves in order to acquire the powers of formalist agency, Wordsworth confesses to a second anxiety: the "shame" he feels when he weighs the apparently "feeble effort" of poetic agency against the "magnitude of general evil" it is supposed to "counteract."[19] In *Politics of Friendship,* we find Derrida similarly on the defensive, at pains to explain why slow and excessively subtle readings of philosophical texts are not the merely formalist exercises his politically impatient detractors take them to be. Sentences I quoted earlier in our discussion of Blake's Samson bear repeating here, for they indicate Derrida's own familiarity with the charge against formalism: "[A] reading may perhaps seem too philological, micrological, *readerly*—complacent, too, with the time it allows itself when matters are urgent . . . [T]he political and historical urgency of what is befalling us should, one will say, tolerate less patience, fewer detours and less bibliographic discretion. Less esoteric rarity. This is no longer the time to take one's time, as a number of our well-intentioned contemporaries must no doubt think" (78–79).

Wolfson's first defense against such well-intentioned charges is to release form from traditional spatial vocabularies that would seal it in a vacuum of timeless autonomy, returning it instead to a lively rhetoric of agency, energy, and historicity. Form is not a matter of inert structure but of "action," "performance," "event." It is not a substantive but a verb that "informs," "reforms," and "transforms." Because its specificity can rub against the cultural abstractions it sometimes passively inhabits but just as often contests, form is already charged with a critical agency, which it becomes the close reader's responsibility to activate. A catalogue of Blake's formal actions indicates their rebellious dynamism: they violate, refuse, and strain against, even defy; they aggravate, challenge, and compel the reader's involvement (36). The close reader becomes the text's accomplice in transgression, discovering and participating in a capacity for criticism without which cultures could do little more than mechanically repeat the same dull round of their inheritance, enforcing a "social determinism" (229) and extreme pessimism that Wolfson associates with the sociological theory of Pierre Bourdieu. Thus Wolfson concludes her introduction to *Reading for Form* by deploring the "erosion of reading ability" as if that loss were tantamount to an erosion of the progressive agenda. "Whether the textual object is literary, nonliterary, aural, visual, or broadly social, the ability to read is essential for discovering forms that are not known and judged in advance."[20] Without form to "bite back" against generalization (as Ellen Rooney puts it), the new and the other would have no entry point into experience.[21] Hardly apolitical or escapist, responsible formalism becomes the precondition for bringing change into the world, thus answering the injunction (another meaning of "charge") conveyed best by Marx's eleventh thesis on Feuerbach: that one not only interpret but change the world.

Similar arguments abound in the recent theoretical return to aesthetics, for instance in Robert Kaufman's call for a "left Kantian[ism]" that would reread the Third Critique through the lens of Adorno.[22] In a series of remarkable essays, including one on Blake in *Reading for Form*, Kaufman has argued that

> [t]he aesthetic . . . serves as a mold or frame for the construction of conceptual thought in general; it also serves as the formal and imaginative engine for new, experimental (because previously nonexistent) concepts: concepts that may bring obscured aspects of substantive social reality to light, or at least may provide the formal ability to do so. Lyric experiment thus constructs and makes available the intellectual-emotional apparatus for accessing, and to that extent the social material of, the new. This constructivist theory and practice see that experiment in lyric—lyric *as* experiment—helps make new areas of the modern fitfully available to perception in the first place.[23]

The convergence that Kaufman refers to as "the *intellectual-emotional* apparatus for accessing . . . the new," Isobel Armstrong (who also draws regularly on Blake) simply calls "thought/affect."[24] The new formalist's attention to heightened affect brings us back, then, to the third and last meaning of "charge," the feeling of dynamism or live-wire energy that draws its language from the science of amps, watts, and volts. This is the feeling Wolfson invokes when she describes "the performative charge" of Blake's *Poetical Sketches*, "energized by opposing attitudes toward form" (31). What is the function of *this* rhetoric in articulating an overlooked relation between formalism and politics? Gone is an outdated notion of aesthetic response: the "balanced poise," "[t]he equilibrium of opposed impulses" or homeostatic pleasure that once told I. A. Richards "all is right here and now in the nervous system."[25] Operating under a different understanding of cognitive health, the new formalist comes to literature, perhaps especially to Blake, looking to have composure startled and the nervous system mobilized, readied for action. Corresponding to the text's resistance to cultural generalization is the reader's own energetic feeling of exemption from predetermined categories. "[A] flagrantly emancipatory, unapologetically radical aesthetic," writes Armstrong, must be "[i]nteractive, sensuous, [and] *epistemologically charged*" (emphasis added).[26]

Wolfson is less extravagant but equally unapologetic. Here is the last paragraph of *Formal Charges*, in full:

> I want to conclude this book, however, by urging attention to form not only defensively, in terms of its potential agency within and against the cultural regimes that Bourdieu describes, but also affirmatively. That the formal actions of Romantic-era poetry can have such agency and that its performances can penetrate wider social and political formations has been a central argument in my chapters. But formal actions also involve a kind of density and intricacy that, I'm convinced, can neither be encompassed by theories of a totalizing cultural form nor be dismissed for a failure to address them. Reading the local particularities of events in form, we discover the most complex measures of human art—the terms of its durable social, political, and psychological interest. We also feel the charge of an historically persistent, forever various, aesthetic vitality. (232)

"Vitality" is an odd, conspicuously *Arnoldian* word on which to land, especially given Wolfson's previous emphasis on poetry's self-conscious artifice and construction, as well as her determination to uncouple form from a mystifying organicism. But the word's very incongruity may help to advance the most important aspect of aesthetic "charge": the exhilarating feeling of anonymous life that neither "vitality" nor any other available term will ever get just right. The universalism of Wolfson's conclusion—her appeal to "human art," as well as her movement from "I'm convinced" to "we discover" and finally to "we also feel the charge"—boldly recalls classical aesthetics, where the capacity to feel that which cannot be conceived underlies the claim to universality. For Kant, the aesthetic vitality he sometimes calls the subject's feeling of pleasure or pain, sometimes simply its life feeling, becomes universal by virtue of its freedom not only from idiosyncratic preferences (merely individual taste) but also from the concepts that culturally and contingently mediate judgments of understanding. The universality of the aesthetic, Kant writes, "cannot originate from concepts."[27] Whatever the springs of vitality are, then, they elude any particular apparatus for recognizing and assimilating experience too quickly, for making experience an object of systematic knowledge. In Wolfson's conclusion, good form (active, dense, intricate, local, particular, above all, *alive*) cannot ultimately be encompassed by the bad (totalizing and abstractly theoretical), and it is the feeling of unscripted life that allows her to generalize her conviction in good faith. "I'm convinced," she says.

We might sum up the three "charges" of *Formal Charges* as follows:

1. Formalism has been accused of detaching itself from political relevance or of serving a conservative agenda.
2. Formalism can be (though is not always) a responsible agent of transformation, performing a task without which progressive politics would be impossible.
3. We believe this is so because we feel our freedom enhanced and energized by the excitement of aesthetic response.

In this defense, charged affect is not merely the result or supplement of agency, but the index of agency as it happens. It persuades us, right here and now in the nervous system, that we are already actively resisting as we read. According to this view, the very pleasure we take in taking our time, in reading closely, is not the guilty or irresponsible pleasure of self-absorption but the sign of our activism taking root in the world.

Derrida

Almost from the moment his work became mandatory reading in American universities, Derrida was defending deconstruction against the charge of formalism in terms of responsibility. The word "responsibility" recurs often in his later writing and always with at least two meanings—ethical or political *obligation* and a capacity for aesthetic *response,* a "response ability" exercised in acts of interpretation.[28] Together, these two responsibilities gather up the continuous project of Derrida's last decades, which was to rethink politics in terms of a radical ethics and to rethink ethics in terms of a radically responsive subject, what Simon Critchley calls a "preconscious subject defined in terms of sensibility."[29] As obligation, to put matters all too hastily, Derridean responsibility is one part Levinas, one part Benjamin. From Levinas, it involves a responsibility to the other-than-oneself, to the absolute singularity of other persons that cannot be calculated by the application of any moral principle. It is in this sense that Derrida's invented terms for friendship and love, "amiance" and "lovence," express a utopian relation of affection and respect between unknowable singularities. From Benjamin, responsibility owes itself to a messianic justice in excess of any possible law, an ultimately unknowable justice always still to come. The challenge of responsibility so conceived is that its object *must not* be conceived; it describes an openness—a "hospitality to the impossible" (Derrida 68)—upon which determinative judgments programmatically foreclose. A reasonable but aesthetically unresponsive subject (the so-called "classic, free, and wilful subject," the subject Derrida later names "I can"[30]) is a "subject to whom nothing can happen" (68). Therefore, it is a subject without real agency, unable to make anything *new* happen. Reversing the charge that deconstruction is incompatible with political decision making, Derrida suggests that, without the "ordeal of the undecidable" to unsettle judgments and open onto the inconceivable,[31] decision making would be nothing more than calculation, comprising a program of known quantities and predictable results. It would "repeat, repeat and repeat again, with neither consciousness nor memory of its compulsive droning" (81).

Derrida developed his ideas on responsibility against the backdrop of an early 1990s post–cold war triumphalism, represented in shorthand by the title of Francis Fukuyama's *The End of History and the Last Man* (1992). At the time, Fukuyama had become a cause célèbre among neoconservatives because of the case he made, based on a dubious reading of Hegel, for the inevitable and then permanent success of global capitalism and liberal, democratic government. Fukuyama, whom Derrida addresses directly in *Specters of Marx*, sought to create the impression of an era essentially beyond change, of a present world-horizon secure from future turbulence because it was no longer possible to imagine a serious rival to capitalism. In this context of seeming permanence, Fredric Jameson exaggerated only slightly when he lamented, "It seems to be easier for us today to imagine the thoroughgoing deterioration of the earth and of nature than the breakdown of late capitalism."[32] *The Seeds of Time* and *Specters of Marx* are contemporaries in date and spirit, each seeking to revive an idea of radical agency at a time when fundamental political transformation had begun to seem unthinkable. In such circumstances of perceived inevitability, Derrida argues, "in order for change to occur . . . a certain non-knowledge is necessary" (31). Responsible agency begins whenever a subject receptive to the singularity of persons and events experiences a heightened affect unencompassed by the routines of knowing. Just before he mentions Blake in *Politics of Friendship,* Derrida names this coincidence of agency and affect "passive" or "unconscious decision." To be more than the effect of a program, to open onto "a freedom that would no longer be the power of a subject,"[33] a genuine decision must first spring from the subject's preconscious and unwilled sensibility. For something, anything, to happen, the event must first "surprise . . . the very subjectivity of the subject, affecting it wherever the subject is exposed, sensitive, receptive, vulnerable and fundamentally passive, before and beyond any decision" (68). It is this aesthetic "opening" of oneself, "trembling, on to the 'perhaps' " (70), that Derrida calls "lovence" and that one experiences as a kind of arrhythmia, as the singular pulsation of an irregular heartbeat.

This idea of an affective threshold onto future possibility is good news for close readers everywhere, for the events that would startle us into reconceiving both agency and political responsibility are textual events, events of minute, readerly attention. Certain writings (Derrida calls them teleiopoetic—a sentence from Nietzsche or Blake, for example, or the entire corpus of Marx) propel themselves into the future through events of reader responsibility, made possible not by the unchanging continuity of their intellectual content but by the rupture of the text's performative charge. These writings fly like arrows past their immediate, known audience toward an unimagined community they cannot foresee but will have helped bring into existence nonetheless. They arrive, Derrida explains, with all the "force of a teleiopoetic propulsion" (42), addressing us wherever our subjectivity is "exposed, sensitive, receptive, vulnerable and fundamentally passive."[34] We cannot tell whether they come from friend or enemy, with affection or hostility, for they unsettle the very categories that would allow for such distinctions in advance. (We can think of Blake's *Milton*, entering the future through Albion's heart, overcoming misinterpretation and resistance, as a personification of teleiopoesis avant la lettre.) *Politics of Friendship* takes off from one such sentence, a "performative contradiction" (27) attributed to Aristotle: "O my friends, there is no friend" (26). Blake's notebook couplet to Hayley is another, which perhaps explains why Blake presides over a chapter sequence dedicated primarily to a reading of Nietzsche. In Derrida's later writing, even the word "democracy" becomes teleiopoetic, vibrating undecidedly between notions of self-sovereignty ("the faculty of decision and self-determination") and play ("the license to play with various possibilities").[35] Teleiopoetic texts carry the future as contingent, unpredictable potential. They call for a reading that will radically alter their own nature—"What other thinker," writes Derrida of Marx, "has ever called for the *transformation* to come of his own theses?"[36]—but in such a way that the reader to be incorporated into the performance is also transformed. In the event of reading, the unknowable future breaks in upon the present and makes its components—text, reader, and world—waver with a possibility previously concealed by their seeming ontology and stability. Teleiopoesis is both a "messianic structure" (37) and a structure of feeling.

To illustrate how teleiopoesis might work in practice, we can consider a single relevant passage from *Specters of Marx*. In this passage, Derrida explicitly sets out to answer the call of Marx's famous thesis on Feuerbach, which he recasts as an "injunction not just to decipher but to act and to make the deciphering [the interpretation] into a transformation that 'changes the world'" (brackets in the original).[37] In this rendition, Derrida responds to Marx's impatience with interpretation by charging interpretation with the task of making itself consequential. But even as Derrida assumes this responsibility, one can still hear the old charge haunting formalism, perhaps the very charge Marx intended: that readers and interpreters make nothing happen. The question becomes how to read Marx responsibly, so as to make something happen, for "[t]here will be no future without this [responsibility]."[38] Taking on the character of an event—Derrida calls it a "political gesture"—the passage implodes within *Specters* parenthetically, insisting we respond to the uncompromising passion for justice that turns Marx's writings into an ongoing performative event irreducible to their propositional content.

"Why insist," Derrida begins, "on imminence, on urgency and injunction, on all that which in them does not wait?" Of immediate concern is that intellectuals have begun to defuse Marx by making him a topic of scholarship. "[O]ne already hears whispered: 'Marx, you see, was despite everything [read "communism"] a philosopher like any other,'" to be treated "calmly, objectively, without bias: according to the academic rules, in the University, in the library, in colloquia!"

> What risks happening is that one will try to play Marx off against Marxism so as to neutralize, or at any rate muffle the political imperative in the untroubled exegesis of a classified work. One can sense a coming fashion or stylishness in this regard in the culture and more precisely in the university. And what is there to worry about here? Why fear what may also become a cushioning operation? The recent stereotype would be destined, whether one wishes it or not, to depoliticize profoundly the *Marxist reference,* to do its best, by putting on a tolerant face, to neutralize a potential force, first of all by enervating a *corpus,* by silencing in it the revolt [the *return* is acceptable provided that the *revolt,* which initially inspired uprising, indignation, insurrection, revolutionary élan,[39] does not come back].

To neutralize a potential force, to enervate a corpus, to silence revolt—each of these figures for the depoliticization of Marx resonates within an intricate web of metaphors, developing the passage into a performance of teleiopoetic excess that would overwhelm the disinterested philosophical judgment it parodies. A careful reading, for instance, would want to follow the passage's vulgar body language. The enervated corpus Derrida conjures here returns a moment later, first as a dead body ("Marx is dead"), then as a decaying body ("now that Marxism seems to be in rapid decomposition"), and finally as a vanished body, leaving only the trace of a "ghost that goes on speaking." Worthy of a scene from *Frankenstein,* the encrypted narrative of a weakened, immobilized body subject to death and decay but also able to be revived by galvanization participates in the deliberately revolting discourse that makes *Specters* as much gothic melodrama as philosophy. One would also want to attend to the passage's tonal extravagance. To counteract the muffling or silencing of revolt, the reader must be alert to the play of sound, the drama of vocal dynamics. "Marxists have fallen silent." On the subject of Marx's political injunction, scholars likewise maintain "a silence." Nominating him instead for "our great canon of Western political philosophy," they thin their nearly disembodied voices to whispers. All the while Derrida clamors in his "apocalyptic tone,"[40] insisting that we *hear* (even "in colloquia!") the urgency that hermeneutics would lull us into forgetting, for whatever agency the corpus of Marx still bears is a matter of tone.

Most importantly, Derrida collapses any distinction between the formal action of Marx's writings and the reader's affective, even somatic response, making it impossible to locate revolt in one or the other exclusively. The revolt that the academic establishment would silence is two things at once: the call to revolt within Marx's message and the uprising against cognitive priority that occurs whenever a reader hears, feels, and responds. The enervated corpus is both the neglected materiality of Marx's writings (irreducible to philosophical judgment) and the body of the reader whose creaturely sensibility or "response ability" has been so weakened it may no longer be moved.[41] The potential force that is neutralized is both the power of the text's performance to make events happen and the reader's feeling of dynamism when activating that potential. Neutralization conveniently returns us to Wolfson's language of "formal charges." The word appears four times, lastly in Derrida's plea that we "do everything we can so as to avoid the neutralizing anaesthesia of a new theoreticism." Here Derrida warns scholars against trading their emotion for "the empty lucidity of a neutral world," to borrow Terada's relevant phrasing. By choosing not to take sides, by avoiding political commitment altogether, these neutral readers invite the old charge against formalism of detachment. Yet Derrida's critique of neutralization goes even further, suggesting that the simple *neutrality* feigned by philosophers masks a more aggressive, strategic effort to *neutralize* Marx, to render inoperative the threat he continues to represent. Deliberately or not, these philosophers collaborate in affirming the "end of history." They prevent Marx from having a future, suspending him in "conventions that neutralize the pure eventfulness of the event."[42]

But "neutralize" can also mean "to make void of electricity; to render electrically inert." By referring this process to the numbed body, "neutralizing anaesthesia" describes a reading practice ("a new theoreticism") that would so deaden sensibility as to make it incapable of responding to or conducting the text's charge. Presumably, its opposite would be a mobilizing aesthesia, in which the affective charge elicited by reading Marx would indicate an agency already starting to exercise itself. In the new an-aesthetic scholarship, Derrida tells us, "the *return* [to Marx] is acceptable provided that the *revolt* . . . does not come back." But for those responsive to the formal work of language, revolt will be irrepressible. As Derrida discusses elsewhere, "volte" means "turn."[43] Re*volt* (*la révolte*) is always already at work in any re*turn* (*le retour*) to Marx, waiting—like a unit of electromagnetic force, another meaning of "volt"—to be activated by anyone responsive to the singular event of the wordplay. To attend to that almost indiscernible "volt," to make oneself susceptible to its disruptive and demanding charge, to overcome the cultural and cognitive mechanisms that conspire to neutralize it—that, in miniature, is what Derrida means when he urges us to read in the spirit of Marx and to turn our formalism into an activism that might transform the world.

"Impossible History": Makdisi and the Reader's Enthusiasm

In sum, the new, the unfamiliar, and the unforeseeable depart from or break in upon the present, the familiar, and the predictable, thus agitating the subject who experiences an opening onto the future in a form he feels but cannot easily recognize. The event presents itself as unusual emotion, a charged affect within the subject that feels as if it came from elsewhere. And the model for this experience is reading. This pattern, more or less shared by Wolfson and Derrida, echoes among others who have recently defended aesthetic experience as the prerequisite of significant change, whether personal, political, or historical. Not everyone would agree with the deconstructive premises of Thomas Docherty's *Aesthetic Democracy*, but his rhetoric of "the event" and of the innovation made possible by reading is typical of this trend. "[W]ith the unpredictability of the simplest outcome, we enter the realm of the event. This entry into the event is precisely the entry into youthful experience [i.e., wonder]; and more precisely still, it is the entry into play. Our critical task is to rehabilitate such experience . . . [T]he event arises through the defamiliarising contact with the unknown. Another word for this is *reading* or any such related aesthetic activity" (original emphasis).[44] Both plainspoken and blatantly romantic, Docherty, like Blake, would restore the Golden Age (of youth, of historical innocence lost to enlightenment)—and he would do so by teaching us how to read. Defined by its "defamiliarising contact with the unknown" reading becomes the occasion of a new enthusiasm, or at least, as Kant might say, it borders closely on enthusiasm.[45]

In one of the last books published before his death, Derrida included a frank confession of enthusiasm that is as instructive as it is surprisingly intimate, for even as his testimonial speaks broadly to the catalytic role of feeling in philosophy, it can also help us frame an approach to Blake criticism in particular. *Rogues* appeared in the same year Makdisi published his account of Blake as a poet of "impossible history" (2003), and the two works share something of a kindred spirit, for in *Rogues* Derrida was renewing his own commitment to a politics of the impossible, to a "democracy to come" detached from the sovereign subject and the existing democratic states that an individualist model of sovereignty supports. While pursuing this political argument, Derrida abruptly and personally begins to testify to the feeling of the impossible as it occurs to him—as if risking the embarrassment of confession were the only way to convey the insistent materiality of his experience. Neither utopian nor wishful, he suggests, this event is impossible but actual, its emphatic reality measured by the involuntary recipient's enthusiasm:

> This im-possible is not privative. It is not inaccessible, and it is not what I can in-definitely defer: it announces itself; it precedes me, swoops down upon and seizes me *here and now* in a nonvirtualizable way, in actuality and not potentiality. It comes upon me from on high, in the form of an injunction that does not simply wait on the horizon, that I do not see coming, that never leaves me in peace and never lets me put it off until later. Such an urgency cannot be *idealized* any more than the other as other can. This im-possible is thus not a (regulative) *idea* or *ideal*. It is what is most undeniably *real*. And sensible. Like the other. Like the irreducible and nonappropri-able *différance* of the other.[46]

Like the inspired poet described by Socrates in the *Ion,* who cannot create unless touched by a "divine power,"[47] or the religious enthusiast Samuel Johnson scorned when he defined "enthusiasm" as "a vain confidence of divine favour or communi-cation," Derrida succumbs to an indefinite agent (an "it") that agitates him "from on high." But this agitation also remains stubbornly materialist, transforming his embodiment rather than transcending it in mystical fashion.

As idiosyncratic as this scene of enthusiasm may seem, it can guide us in three ways as we return specifically to Blake criticism:

1. According to Derrida, *feeling* substantiates the subject's freedom from the merely possible. The impossible and the future it opens onto are not just "undeniably *real*" and "sensible"; they are undeniably real *because* they are sensible. If they did not occur first as embodied feeling, one might suspect them of being theoretical abstractions or mystifications, much as Johnson suspected that all modern assertions of divine revelation are in fact ground-less pretensions. As we saw earlier in chapter 1, Lyotard ratified the "impos-sible phrase" of the Kantian sublime in much the same way, identifying it as "an eloquent silence, . . . a feeling that is always an agitation."[48]

2. The sensibility that receives the impossible and makes it real must partici-pate in two domains simultaneously; it must straddle the line between the possible and the impossible, forming—within the subject—a border zone between two orders of experience that would otherwise have no point of con-tact. Without sensibility to receive the future, the impossible would fall like an unobserved tree in an unobserved forest; there would be no way to hear its sound. Or, changing figures, it wouldn't arrive at all, passing continu-ously by like a teleiopoetic arrow with no ground for landing. In short, sen-sibility makes the impossible possible in experience, providing the ground for its reception or emergence.

3. We are now close to a longstanding predicament of Blake criticism. As in Derrida's account, the Blakean subject must also stand at the intersection between worlds (fallen and apocalyptic, possible and impossible, single vision and fourfold being), but the subject only exists at all because it is the product of the ideological conditions that precede it and bring it into being in the first place. Subjectivity is itself a manifestation, perhaps the primary manifestation, of the Fall. This problem has special bearing on the redemptive agency attributed to affect, for sensibility is an attribute of a subject who possesses attributes only because he is fallen. How, then, can the apocalyptic arise from the fallen, or the impossible from the merely possible, when the subject's future depends upon the receptive powers of a sensibility that the subject's own origin renders problematic at best, dubious at worst?

In slightly different terms, this is the problem Nicholas Williams addresses so powerfully in *Ideology and Utopia in the Poetry of William Blake*. Williams is exactly right to start out from "an odd feature" he identifies in Blake's poetry—"the exhilarating newness of his conceptions" exists right alongside "a crushing, almost debilitating pessimism."[49] How can utopia ("exhilarating newness") emerge from existing ideological conditions without becoming an extension or repetition of those conditions in another form? Williams eventually answers this question by developing a redemptive model of reading based on Ernst Bloch's theory of "concrete utopia," but it's not clear that he ever fully overcomes the "crushing pessimism" he initially describes. The problem stems from the fact that Blake grasps the constraints of Urizenic ideology almost too well, leading him into a trap Jameson has called "a 'winner loses' logic." Jameson associates this phrase with the early Foucault, but his elaboration of a cultural criticism too acute for its own good touches closely on Blake as well. "[T]he more powerful the vision of some increasingly total system or logic . . . the more powerless the reader comes to feel. Insofar as the theorist wins, therefore, by constructing an increasingly closed and terrifying machine, to that very degree he loses, since the critical capacity of his work is thereby paralyzed, and the impulses of negation and revolt, not to speak of those of social transformation, are increasingly perceived as vain and trivial in the face of the model itself."[50] As many critics besides Williams have observed, the special power of Blake's social analysis lies in its comprehensiveness, in his identification of the seamless ideological links among disparate institutions (social, political, economic, religious, educational, and so on—where the open-endedness of the *and so on* indicates the indefinite extent of the network). Blake's vision, writes Williams, is of a "chain which links all segments of society in a fallen whole and which ultimately binds consciousness itself."[51] Subjectivity is itself an epiphenomenon of this worldwide web. Given this idea of a total system, in which even the critic is a product of the system he would critique ("Mannheim's paradox"),[52] one begins to understand Williams's emphasis on *exhilaration,* for without "the *exhilarating* newness of [Blake's] conceptions" to confirm poetic agency by means of immediate, unscripted feeling, one might be tempted to explain the apparent innovation of these conceptions as a standard deviation allowed for by the Urizenic system. Because agency (critical or otherwise) cannot be logically deduced or empirically demonstrated—that is, because agency always runs the risk of being only apparent, reducible by analysis to some prior determination or cause—charged affect must work to persuade the reader that the new isn't simply a return of the old in disguise and that "impossible history" isn't simply the latest edition of what's possible. Without the exemption provided by feeling, the Urizenic subject might have no exit.

A more extreme version of the same problem structures Makdisi's massive study. While Makdisi remains faithful to Blake's enthusiasm, absorbing it into the very rhythms of his prose, he follows the logic of Blake's social criticism to conclusions even more pessimistic than Williams's. As we have seen, Makdisi traces Blake's critique of modernity to the formation of the unitary subject, which takes its shape in order to meet the emerging needs of industrial capitalism. His argument leans heavily on the idea that Blake rejected the individualist ethos of the new bourgeois republicans, recognizing that this ethos served primarily to advance the ideological interests of an economic class in the process of empowering itself. Already in the 1790s, at the advent of modernity, Blake could see the need for an impossible history—for a democracy-to-come detached from "the supposed freedom of the sovereign individual" (6). In terms of political theory, Makdisi's Blake mirrors Derrida rather closely. Ironically, however, Makdisi's argument bumps up against the very power of the social analysis he attributes to Blake. If, for instance, Blake recognized that "[t]he individual human subject . . . is a product like any other, an assemblage, a machine: a making machine, a consuming machine, *a desiring machine,* a living machine" (12, emphasis added), then it becomes difficult to understand how Blake can chart a path of redemption by locating "the foundation of both his aesthetics and his politics, as well as his sense of being, *in desire*" (7, emphasis added). Such an argument assumes that one can distinguish between mechanical and authentic desires while also describing the subject that must make this distinction as itself a product like any other, a desiring machine. Throughout his book, Makdisi describes a modern subject so thoroughly sealed by the processes of its social construction that one cannot imagine how an alternative to such construction would arise, or why the idea of an alternative wouldn't be one more illusion that a finite desiring machine is capable of producing.

A single, extended paragraph at the book's center can foreground this predicament for us. Here Makdisi argues that, in Blake, "the organism making these choices [political and economic] is seen as a product of the system" and that its "autonomy and freedom" are actually the result of "a closed circuit of production and consumption, producer and consumer, organism and organ, all generated by the same continuous process as parts subservient to the requirements of a larger whole composed by them." He continues, "If the logic of the reified object is extended to the logic of the reified subject, it becomes difficult to imagine a realm within this process which might avoid or evade the laws of the commodity and hence the rule of necessity; in other words, it becomes difficult or impossible to imagine genuine freedom within such a social system." Thus "Blake is, in effect, arguing that *there can be no escape* from the determination of the social field and its rule of necessity" (emphasis added). Despite this conclusion, Makdisi proceeds to assert, just a few sentences later, that "[w]hat [Blake] proposes *instead* is a kind of freedom—into the infinite—that is ultimately incompatible with the unitary subject and with bourgeois society" (emphasis added, 144–145). Where would this *instead* come from? How can a fallen poet, whose own subjectivity is a condition from which *there can be no escape,* propose an alternative to his subjectivity? How does genuine desire come to a subject systematically incapable of it—even worse, a subject with a history of self-deception, consistently mistaking his own constraints for freedom? Given an ideological regime as totalizing and as formidable as this one appears to be, redemptive agency could only arrive from elsewhere. In this world, it would take a messianic *Stranger from Paradise* to make the impossible possible.

To be fair, Makdisi's Blake is not quite the Romantic hero embraced by the title of Bentley's recent biography.[53] In his view, Blake's understanding of the modern subject's socioeconomic construction derives not from some prelapsarian insight but from the specific material conditions of his labor, from the fact that nineteenth-century engraving had become an early laboratory for mass commodity production. Makdisi is also careful to historicize the poet's challenge to the ideological impasse of modernity. When Blake introduces his alternative vision of a communal "power to create the world" (267), of a collective agency entirely at odds with the individualist "I can," he draws upon radical elements of premodernity (seventeenth-century antinomianism), remnants that themselves anticipate certain strands of postmodern thought (Marxian and deconstructive materialism). But Makdisi's argument goes much further. It is not enough for Blake to *propose* an alternative to the false freedoms of the modern subject; he must provide the time and place of its enactment, the occasion for a "freedom into the infinite" here and now, for an "impossible history" right before our eyes. The real hero of Makdisi's story, I would argue, is reading—and the enlarged vitality or "sense of being" it enables. According to Makdisi, Blake's poetry requires us to experience reading as "unlearning" or "unthinking," as a reversal of the social and cultural processes (especially education) that have constituted the modern unitary subject as such. This decentering event releases the reader from his bourgeois inscription and allows him to enter into "the creative political potential of the multitude" (296), thus joining the ranks of others marginalized by modernity: the children, the poor, and the illiterate (whom Blake believed would be his most receptive audience), as well as the dangerous plebeian radicals of the 1790s (who Makdisi believes were Blake's closest conceptual allies). We will return to this idea in the next section. What matters for the moment is that, for Makdisi, reading becomes a revolutionary act.[54] To read Blake—not like a scholar silencing his revolt, but as he asks to be read, with spirit—is to become an outsider to one's culture, a transgressor of modernity.[55]

In every sense of the word, then, *enthusiasm* is Makdisi's touchstone. It describes his explicit object of study: the historically specific content—religious, vulgar, and dynamic—that alienated Blake's visionary poetry from the developing liberalism it challenged. It describes the critic's own feeling for this object of study, his unqualified admiration for Blake's work. But enthusiasm can also name the state of inspired affect to be achieved by Blake's readers—an emotional intensity Makdisi helps along by turning his own discourse into an engine of the vital energies it mimes, with forward-driving clauses geared to transmit conviction. Makdisi's exuberant prose would persuade the reader that "freedom into the infinite" is not merely another conceptual possibility but a material urgency happening now, embodied in the reader's very excitement. The reader's enthusiasm thus occupies a crucial opening between worlds that would otherwise remain strictly Manichean, with the false freedoms we know on one side and the infinite freedom we desire on the other, but with no plausible way across the divide. Blake's "open text"—a poetry without borders, activated only by a reader "tracing and retracing different interpretive paths" (164)—empowers an open subject without borders, turning the reader's aesthetic play into "a profoundly political activity" (69).[56] No longer a fixed conceptual content, textual meaning becomes a multidirectional electric current, located "in the very logic animating [the work], the kinds of connections it allows us to make, the freedom of thought and of energy it enables" (164). Because the open text pulsates like a living nervous system, expanding and contracting, charged by an "array of perpetually open channels" or a "network of continually firing synapses" (168), we discover a neat chiasmus between text and reader: the text takes on the reader's sensibility (*his* "continually firing synapses") while the reader takes on the text's limitlessness. Together they join in a freedom that (to recall

Derrida) is both "impossible" and "undeniably real" because it is "sensible." And Makdisi does not stop here. The dynamic sensibility activated by reading becomes the basis of the future communal relations entered into by these newly unenclosed subjects, who now experience themselves in Deleuzean fashion as "ever-changing bundles of relations and affects," maintaining an "infinite desire to keep making connections and forming new lines of affect" (291). These dynamic, materialist subjects—who, like Blake's *Jerusalem,* are persons, texts, and communities all at once—remain always in motion, always "striving." Their antinomian life consists of an "infinitely prolific number of re-makings, re-imaginations, re-becomings, the joyous life of pure potential, of endless striving, of *élan vital*" (318).

Enthusiasm is excessive by definition. The embarrassment it may cause others the enthusiast considers an honor, a necessary affront to the safe conformity of established taste. It would be misleading, however, to suggest that Makdisi's whole-hearted embrace of enthusiasm actually succeeds in challenging rather than reinforcing critical decorum. Instead, I would argue, *William Blake and the Impossible History of the 1790s* enlarges to giant proportions some of criticism's rather ordinary affects; it is as if the quieter, unnoticed enthusiasms happening all the time were suddenly made to pass under the lens of a very large magnifying glass. Makdisi's "*élan vital*" exaggerates features we see elsewhere, different by degree, not kind. It bears family resemblance to the "revolutionary élan" Derrida locates in Marx, inaccessible to scholars who read without feeling; to "the charge of . . . aesthetic vitality" that, according to Wolfson, affirms the formalist's activism; and even to Arnold's "sense of creative activity," which, at certain historical moments, belongs only to criticism, providing our only access to "the great happiness and proof of being alive." In all of these examples, despite their wide differences, we observe a set of common elements: first of all, an anxiety of freedom curtailed, especially at the level of the subject itself, a fear that the current horizon of experience forms the only possible horizon and that consequently nothing new will happen; next, a turn to reading as the indispensable event of transformation; and finally, the work of affect, which tells the reader that genuine freedom is not hypothetical but real and sensible, something being enacted here and now. These are the features of criticism's abiding enthusiasm.

When Makdisi writes that "[t]he freedom to imagine is the power to create the world" (267) and that "the antinomian tradition empowers *us* not because it allows us to read, but because through reading it allows *us* to create" (317, emphasis added), we begin to understand the full transhistorical reach of his enthusiasm. Of course, he does not expect *us,* today's critics, to reincarnate either a heroic Romanticism or an earlier seventeenth-century millenarianism, but he does remain confident that enthusiasm has traction still. He assumes we remain receptive to the idea that reading and aesthetic response bear the potential of transformative agency, that they stand—like Los in the frontispiece to *Jerusalem*—at the pivot point between possible and impossible histories, with one foot planted in the world as it is and the other already stepping into a world to be recreated otherwise. By exaggerating the impasse of ideology on the one hand, and the reader's freedom on the other, Makdisi foregrounds the promise of empowerment carried by the many varieties of critical enthusiasm. He also suggests that, even for modern readers, despite all their disenchantments, reading has not yet lost its magic.

Impasse and Magic

Against all this, I will contend that the university and its once central disciplines of humanistic criticism ought to be a site of fantasy, in the genuine sense of that term—not Disneyland, which would not know magic if it suddenly appeared in a puff of smoke; but fantasy, as in imagining the impossible, the unforeseeable. The activity of criticism ought to be a site for the exploration of the unpredictable and of the unspoken.

—Thomas Docherty, *Aesthetic Democracy*

It is my sense that academic literary critics have attempted to repoliti-
cize literary study without fully understanding the relation between disciplines of study in the university and the political domain. This defect of understanding is nowhere more evident than when we attempt to determine what are the actual effects in the world of what we do, either as teachers or as scholars. We have as yet no credible way to assess these effects, and in the absence of such determinable measures, we tend to indulge in what I will call a political fantasy, the fantasy of transforming the world to a degree vastly greater than can reasonably be expected of perhaps any disciplinary practice. Despite the manifest appeal of this fantasy, there is a reality against which it must always come to grief. However much we may hope to produce specifically political effects, or to "change the world" in a specified political sense, any and every effect we have in the world must be achieved through a practice of reading. The limits of this reading practice constitute the limits of disciplinary power.

—John Guillory, "The Ethical Practice of Modernity:
The Example of Reading"

At present, we can conceive of what an emotion is. It is a transformation of the world. When the paths traced out become too difficult, or
when we see no path, we can no longer live in so urgent and difficult
a world. All the ways are barred. However, we must act. So we try to
change the world, that is, to live as if the connection between things
and their potentialities were not ruled by deterministic processes, but
by magic. Let it be clearly understood that this is not a game; we are
driven against a wall, and we throw ourselves into this new attitude
with all the strength we can muster. Let it also be understood that
this attempt is not conscious of being such, for it would then be the
object of reflection. Before anything else, it is the seizure of new connections and new exigencies.

—Jean-Paul Sartre, *The Emotions: Outline of a Theory*

Should criticism calculate the chances of its self-deception or cultivate the transformative potential of fantasy? Leaving Sartre aside for a moment, we can imagine
Docherty and Guillory in dialogue.[57] Answering Guillory's charge of indulging
in "political fantasy," Docherty might object that Guillory's pragmatism and empiricism leave no room for impossibilities. By emphasizing measurable results,
reasonable expectations, "actual effects in the world," and "specifically political
effects," Guillory misunderstands the nature of the event that criticism should
strive to enable. With no specific political goal in mind, and no expectations or
guarantees in advance, the aesthetic event would unlink itself from the determinism and instrumentalism governing existing political practices. The critic indulges
in fantasy only in that he prefers the chance of the unpredictable to the circuit of already known quantities and programs. By releasing the reader from the obligation
of having to "change the world" in some already "specified political sense," and
by promoting open-ended "passion" rather than some particular, compromised
path of "action," the event allows for the world to change in ways that are currently
inconceivable.[58]

   In turn, while acknowledging the virtues of a criticism free from specific political aims, Guillory might nevertheless point out the manifest appeal of *this* fantasy,
for the indeterminate event Docherty values must still "be achieved through a
practice of reading," and "[t]he limits of this reading practice constitute the limits
of disciplinary power." Even though Docherty identifies critical activity with a specific institutional setting (the university), he tends to generalize the power of reading to produce indeterminate effects, thus forgetting the "enormous gap between
reading as it is practiced within and without the academy" (31). This gap includes
the "large amounts of time and resources" (31) required for academic reading, an

investment made possible only by the support (and constraint) of an education system that participates in the division of labor and contributes to social stratification.[59] Given the circumscribed nature of this disciplinary practice, it is indeed a fantasy to imagine that critical reading might leap the gap and exercise some widespread influence on anything one might be ambitious enough to call "the world." "Impossible history," Guillory might say, is now a specialist's affair, a passion of professional readers and the students they train. The impossible is a fantasy in the ordinary sense of the term, neglecting the real economic, social, and labor-specific conditions that make theorization of the impossible possible.

With tongue in cheek, then, let's rephrase our question about fantasy and deception, this time borrowing language from the Preface to *Prometheus Unbound*. Would one rather be damned with Guillory's sociological disenchantment of reading or go to the heaven of *Aesthetic Democracy* on the wings of Docherty's deconstructive utopianism? Of course, it may be the other way around—damned with Docherty, uplifted by Guillory. When Shelley declared he "had rather be damned with Plato and Lord Bacon, than go to Heaven with Paley and Malthus," he included both idealism (Plato) and empiricism (Bacon) on his side, for he believed that the meaningful difference lay not between these two interpretations of the world but between those interpreters who have "a passion for reforming the world" and those who don't.[60] Redrawing the lines in this way, one can imagine Docherty and Guillory joining forces. When Guillory undertakes to deflate the academic critic's exaggerated agency, it's not because he is uninterested in transforming the world; it's because he believes the critic's self-deception stands in the way of the real work of transformation that a properly sociological critique can perform. Although he is much more cautious than Docherty, Guillory also sets about removing obstacles and enabling blocked, unimagined possibilities. Anyone who has been surprised by the sudden appeal to "an aestheticism unbound" in the inspired closing sentences of *Cultural Capital* knows just how strong Guillory's passion for reforming the world can be. Although at present this unbound prospect may be nothing more than a critical fantasy—Guillory calls it "a thought experiment" in the last words of his book—it's clear he would rather take his chances with Shelley than compile evidence of the world's stubborn immunity to transformation.[61]

Throughout these pages, my own emphasis has been on the role of passion in criticism's practice and self-conception. In much recent criticism, as I have been arguing, passion is not merely an underlying desire motivating an external end ("reforming the world"); it is understood to be the precondition of that end, the present-time indication of an enhanced intellectual agency effective now. Critical passion does not simply express what Foucault calls "our impatience for liberty"[62]; it is considered a sign of freedom already at work in a world already being transformed. It is akin to the passion (bordering on enthusiasm) Kant observed in the nonparticipant spectators of the French Revolution, whose feelings meant more to the historical extension of freedom than all the actions then taking place in Paris. And by no means is critical passion limited to high-voltage displays of enthusiasm or near enthusiasm; it can take many forms. It may be thematized or not. It may involve the imperceptible influence of long, slow time or the sudden rupture of a moment. It may announce itself as activism or passivity—or as a displacement of that opposition altogether. It can beat with a lively human pulse or with a strange, posthuman half-life. In all these cases and others, the passion is not incidental but vital to the experience of change as it is taking place, or of the potential for change as it becomes active. It supplies the evidence of change when no other evidence presents itself. Even the least sentimental criticism has tended to harbor this minor enthusiasm, holding fast to the idea that affect in criticism indexes agency as it happens, even in the least promising of situations. We can say of the passion in criticism, then, what Sartre says when defining emotion in general—in itself "it is a transformation of the world."

Of course, Sartre stirs trouble by adding one small phrase to his definition of emotion: a transformation "by magic." For Sartre, as in the epigraph at the start of this section, emotion arises when we must act in a world that affords us few or no desirable means of action. Immediately, one thinks of the political impasse that accompanied the rise of Romanticism, first following the Terror, then after Waterloo; or one thinks of the end-of-history impasse described by Jameson and Derrida at the close of another century almost two hundred years later. Sartre first published his theory of emotion in 1939, during another moment of geopolitical despair, but in his account he avoids explicitly political statements, limiting himself instead to the kind of mundane psychic activities that might occur under any historical circumstances. Since we cannot objectively alter a world that remains implacable, he argues, our emotions transform the world subjectively. They substitute a new world magically free from necessity, thus allowing us room to maneuver. Sartre's examples are unremarkable. A man faints in order to make the object of his fear disappear. Of course, the threatening object "disappears" only in the subjective world evacuated by the man's emotion. A girl finds it too painful to confess her symptoms to her doctor. When she breaks down in tears, her emotion substitutes a magical world in which she is no longer obligated to speak, turning her doctor into a comforter rather than an inquisitor, although the condition that brought her to the doctor in the first place remains unaddressed. Sartrean emotion, we could say, is the everyday, unreflective expression of Satan's desperate hubris in *Paradise Lost*: "The mind is its own place, and in it self / Can make a Heav'n of Hell, a Hell of Heav'n" (I. 254–255).[63] Protesting against necessity, there is a radical imagination subtly at work in the most ordinary but difficult situations, generating by means of emotion a world of subjective qualities and syntheses that Sartre likens to the world of dreams and madness (80). Emotion reconstitutes the world, working, as Isobel Armstrong writes of the radical aesthetic impulse, "to make what we know already *look* different," though emotion performs this work on its own, without our deliberate guidance.⁶⁴ But Sartre also makes clear that the "magical action" (62) of emotion "is not *effective*"; it alters appearances "without modifying [the world] in its actual structure" (60). Emotion promotes the fantasy that the world can be transformed by redescription and, even further, that we can live in our redescribed world. It is escapist by nature.

Whatever one thinks of Sartre's account generally (and it has not fared well among philosophers of emotion), it allows us to articulate a worst-case scenario for critical emotions specifically: that they insert feelings of agency into a world that remains structurally unchanged by those feelings. As we saw when we considered Jameson's "winner loses logic," critics with a passion for reforming the world are often also the ones most likely to describe a world systematically resistant to transformation, making it appear that "all the ways are barred." Impasse and the passion for reform escalate together. Sartre himself describes a subject caught in a world "ruled by deterministic processes," a Urizenic starry mill that he compares to "the moving plates of the coin-making machines on which the ball-bearings are made to roll . . . The ball-bearings must travel across a determined route, taking determined paths and without falling into the holes" (58). The analogy of the coin-making machine is not coincidental, implying something more than a rigid, encompassing world limited to already mapped-out options, which we sense instinctively in difficult circumstances. The image suggests a total system of unfreedom or (as Jameson puts it) "an increasingly closed and terrifying machine" in which the subject's paths of enactment are all determined by preexisting economic structures. It envisions a subject not only constrained by this machine but—even worse—constituted by it, minted. And it is at this point of paranoia and impasse that critical emotion begins its work, transforming by magic a world it cannot transform otherwise. The moment of magical action as Sartre describes it thus resembles the passage we highlighted in Makdisi, where he imagines Blake "arguing that there can be no escape from the determination of the social field" *and* then proposing the alternative of infinite desire nonetheless. It also resembles the moment in *Cultural Capital* when, just before he imagines "an aestheticism unbound," Guillory states, "If there is no way out of the game of culture, then, even when cultural capital is the only kind of capital, there may be another kind of game, with less dire consequences for the losers, an *aesthetic* game."⁶⁵ Sartre tells us that emotion creates the illusion of a way out even when we sense there isn't really one, a feeling of agency even when we have no access to agency in fact. If we were to apply this theory to criticism, then Sartre would indeed one-up Guillory's sociological demystification of the critic's world-transforming fantasy, for if Guillory explains the disjunction between the critic's political self-image and the institutional reality, Sartre explains the affective mechanism that allows the fantasy to take hold anyway and to feel substantial, despite the absence of supporting evidence. According to Sartre, emotion is effective because it needs no corroboration. It bears the evidence of its seriousness in the body; its physiological immediacy is a necessary component of belief. "[W]e *throw* ourselves into this new attitude with all the strength we can muster." Ratified by the dynamism of rising skin temperatures and changing heart rates, of vasoconstriction or expansion, magical action feels as palpable as any other action—undeniably real because sensible.[66] As Sartre puts it, emotion sets up "a magical world by using the body as a means of incantation" (70). Unable to change our situation, we instead perceive the world as if it had adjusted itself to the altered contours of our embodied feeling.

There is more to Sartre's theory of emotion, and I will return to another aspect of it momentarily. Here, however, I want to continue calculating the chances of deception, as if we were conducting a thought experiment of our own, for the tools Sartre and Guillory provide will take our disenchantment of critical emotion as far as it can go. There are reasons not to trust the emotions central to our work, starting with our desire that criticism should do more than identify systems of unfreedom, that it should, by the force of its own activity, exert a counterthrust to such systems. We badly want our acts of criticism to matter, not only to justify the time (the lives) we have given to them, but also to turn our passion for reading—a passion every critic has cultivated and wishes to share—into a more widely meaningful event. When I say "we," I mean the teachers, scholars, and students who, in all honesty, are the only possible audience for a book like the one you are now reading, whatever hope any of us may secretly harbor that our work will teleiopoetically find some future audience or some future resonance we cannot currently anticipate. Our emotions—as we experience them, as we consider them theoretically—underwrite our sense of purpose, warding off through the incantations of embodied thought our anxiety of inconsequence, our worry that our labors exercise little influence beyond the narrow sphere of our professional or institutional life. We need to consider the possibility that our enthusiasm for reading amounts to a kind of Sartrean magic. This fantasy may be most apparent when criticism openly thematizes the significance of feeling, but it would also be at work in the ordinary affective textures of academic life: in the pleasurable excitement stirred by close reading, in the bafflement that arises from welcoming cognitive difficulty, in the surging estrangement one feels when reading seems to open a portal between the familiar and the new. It is in such moments, when "we throw ourselves into this new attitude with all the strength we can muster," when we feel the Arnoldian "sense of creative activity," that we are most likely to forget that this work of emotion is also work in a less elevated sense, that it is a product of specialized, professional labor that has as much to do with long histories of preparation, supportive institutional contexts, and elaborate disciplinary protocols as it does with the specific nature and potentiality of emotion per se. Fantasy, then, would involve crediting emotion with transformative power—or, more modestly, with opening onto the chance of transformation—while forgetting the specific world that conditions the academic reader's experience of emotion in the first place. Substituting the immediate world of critical feeling for the contextual world that enables it, substituting the "impossible history" discovered by reading for the actual history of reading that made it possible, we occupy a space (a phenomenological space, Sartre would say) where our own vitality takes on magical qualities, making one world disappear as another arises in its place. This magic lies so close to the way we experience our work that we might not recognize it even if it suddenly materialized in a puff of smoke.

It would not be difficult to translate these anxieties into our reading of the three critical thinkers who have primarily occupied us in this chapter: Wolfson, Derrida, and Makdisi. The sense of resistance and innovation supplied by critical reading can also be understood to fulfill the expectations of a professional community. Guillory writes that a *"disciplinary* activity . . . is governed by conventions of interpretation and protocols of research developed over many decades. These techniques take years to acquire; otherwise we would not award higher degrees to those who succeed in mastering them" (31). Thus the vitality Wolfson describes as the close reader's immediate experience of resistance to social conscription is, from another angle, the feeling that signifies membership in a group distinguished by its acquisition of a particular skill set. Alan Liu has described the critical skills needed by "knowledge workers" to compete in a market-driven information culture, but I am also adapting an older, well-known argument from Pierre Bourdieu, Guillory's forerunner in the sociological critique of culture.[67] Wolfson directly challenges Bourdieu's pessimism, objecting to his tendency to describe culture in terms of a deterministic machine every bit as terrifying as Sartre's coin-making device. Bourdieu leaves "no space," she writes, "for symbolic productions to do other than serve and conserve its regime—no space, that is, for any work of resistance or critique, or nonculpable pleasure" (229). At the same time, however, she neglects a more serious implication of Bourdieu's argument: that critical discrimination (close reading) demonstrates an acquired cultural competence and thus functions as a kind of cultural capital itself, securing status and membership at the very moment of its pretense to resistance and activism. Bourdieu raises this very contradiction when he turns to a critique of Derrida toward the end of *Distinction: A Social Critique of the Judgment of Taste*. The "ritual transgressions" of Derrida's scrupulously close readings, he contends, are "in fact circumscribed by the interests linked to membership in the philosophical field." Derrida's work manages to "combine the profits of transgression with the profits of membership."[68] In such circumstances, the charged affect to which criticism turns for evidence of the reader's agency will always risk looking like a justification of professional interests in terms of political or ethical relevance.

Nowhere is this risk more evident than in Makdisi's reading of Blake, specifically in his idea that Blake's enthusiasm requires us to put our education in reverse and "unlearn" the acquired reading habits that are so deeply intermeshed with our modern, bourgeois subjectivity. As many readers have noted (and just as often complained), Blake's manifest difficulty after the *Songs* threatens to limit his audience almost entirely to an elite corps of advanced, dedicated students.[69] According to Makdisi, however, the truth is rather the opposite: our education *prevents* us from reading him. Blake's text is open, not hermetic; it requires "a revolutionary model of reading" incompatible with the exclusionary effects of training.

> Blake offered a series of "open" texts, suggestive of a kind of reading that would open out from the text rather than trying to seduce the reader into its hidden confines—a revolutionary model of reading better suited to the uninitiated and the uneducated, and hence to "the people," than to the servants of power . . . [We] need to devise a new approach to Blake's work, one that would involve "unlearning" whatever it is that makes us "learned," or taking seriously Blake's implicit suggestion that our very "learning" is what stands in the way of our reading his work with all the freshness of a child, whose "rouzing" faculties are uninhibited by paradigms of reading and by literary, aesthetic, and political conventions, and perhaps even by the regulations of "state trickery" itself. (162–163)

This theme emerges early and recurs often: "Clearly, Blake was not interested in trying to conform to the tastes and standards of a learned and refined audience, a fact which undoubtedly contributed to his decline into poverty and obscurity, as well as his inaccessibility to educated audiences ever since" (26). I have addressed Blake's complicated relation to bourgeois values and aspirations elsewhere in this book; here I want to focus briefly on a telling, if somewhat obvious, performative contradiction in Makdisi's language. What happens when a critic mobilizes all the instruments of contemporary scholarship to recommend "unlearning" to his university press audience?

William Blake and the Impossible History of the 1790s is a crucial, even thrilling work of scholarship, one that has made good on the back-cover prediction that it "will redefine the possibilities *within Blake studies* for the next generation and beyond" (emphasis added).[70] It is not, however, an example of "unlearning." Indeed, Makdisi's particular magic is to make learning *feel like* unlearning, to transform, by sheer force of his own enthusiasm, an academic reading practice into something that feels like a "revolutionary reading model"—rough and tumble, populist, and volatile. Yet the dynamism that would perform this work, that would result in the "perpetually firing synapses" Makdisi recommends, itself depends on an academic foundation Makdisi would have us forget. For if Blake's demanding intertextuality calls for a process of "ongoing rereading," for a reader who can move experimentally across "the wide virtual network of traces among different plates, different copies, different illuminated books" (164, 166), generating new linkages with each singular reading, then this reader must have at his disposal at least two resources that separate him from the uninitiated, uneducated, or childlike reader Makdisi aligns with the potentiality of "the people": the (compensated) time to read slowly, to contextualize, and to reread compulsively; and the archival support (electronic images, facsimiles, photo-reproductions, to say nothing of the financing necessary to visit widely dispersed originals) without which Blake's infinite network of signs lies dormant. In the *"élan vital"* of reading, when the faculties are most fully "rouzed" into action, it is easy for the critic to forget that "[t]he limits of [his] reading practice constitute the limits of disciplinary power."

In the worst-case scenario we are tracing, then, the fantasy of agency supported by Makdisi's enthusiasm for Blake would illustrate a general tendency of critical emotion to compensate for the gap between theories and practices of reading. That is, emotion allows the critic to mistake a contextually narrow experience of intellectual arousal for a more widely consequential exercise of freedom. This tendency of criticism to rely more or less explicitly on enthusiasm is not limited to Blake studies, though it has indeed been prevalent there; it is widespread. Consider the parallel case of Brian Massumi's *Parables for the Virtual: Movement, Affect, Sensation,* a broadly influential book published in the same year as Makdisi's. These two works share a vocabulary of "virtual" energies, as well as a materialist's passion for Spinoza and Deleuze. Massumi's most important contribution to the recent surge in affect studies lies in his distinction between affect and emotion: in his account, "emotion" names a determinate content belonging to a clearly defined subject while "affect" indexes a dynamic, modal intensity always operating beneath the threshold awareness of fixed, conscious identity. From the start, however, his entire undertaking is motivated by a desire to reintroduce agency into studies of ideology and subject position that—again following a kind of "winner loses logic"—have resulted inadvertently in "gridlock." When Massumi laments the effect of aligning spatial concepts of ideology with airtight, immutable systems, his terms recall the immobilizing machine-worlds described by Blake, Sartre, and Jameson: "Where has the potential for change gone? How does a body perform its way out of a definitional framework that is not only responsible for its very 'construction,' but seems to prescript every possible signifying and countersignifying move as a selection from a repertoire of possible permutations on a limited set of predetermined terms? How can the grid itself change?"[71] In this model of the social field, the subject of ideology cannot be anything other than a ball-bearing rolling through a complicated maze of predetermined paths—unless (and Massumi's language already anticipates this solution) its own moving body is somehow able to outperform structural, definitional constraint. Against the gridlock of subject formation, it becomes the task of affect—of "[t]he slightness of ongoing qualitative change," "[f]elt and unforeseen" (1), of "the charge of indeterminacy carried by a body" in motion (5)—to introduce a feeling of ongoing difference that makes transformation not only possible but inevitable. For Massumi, the transformative energies of affect—always at work everywhere, if only one had eyes to see—turn even the critic's own practice into an engine of change. Urging us to adopt "*affirmative* methods," he offers this advice to the critic: "If you don't enjoy concepts and writing and don't feel that when you write you are adding something to the world, if only the enjoyment itself, and that by adding that ounce of positive experience to the world you are affirming it, celebrating its potential, tending its growth, in however small a way, however really abstractly—well, just hang it up" (12–13). *Feeling* that the critic adds to the world, and tends its growth, and celebrates its potential—while piling on clauses as evidence—makes it so. One could hardly imagine a better example of Sartre's definition of emotion as in itself "a transformation of the world" or of his idea that emotion (here "affect") conjures "a magical world by using the body as a means of incantation."

If Makdisi's faith in reading ("tracing and retracing different interpretive paths" [164]) and Massumi's faith in "movement as qualitative transformation" (3) are representative of a general confidence in the transformative work of feeling, then perhaps there is no vitality that criticism should trust completely, no feeling of intellectual vigor ("mental fight") that might not be compensating for and masking the actual limits of our institutionally conditioned agency. To rearrange the lines from *Samson Agonistes*, perhaps we are most inactive when we deem ourselves most vigorous. If so, then de Man was probably right to warn us against being "too easily satisfied with one's own satisfaction,"[72] though we should also extend his warning to the various forms of *dissatisfaction* we have recently managed to mobilize so effectively. Having learned to distrust the pleasures of harmony and to prefer the romance of discomfort instead, our enthusiasm has turned to aesthetic disturbance—to "ugly emotions"—to signal access to the new, the unknown, and the impossible.[73] The stranger the emotion, the more disturbing it should be; the more disturbing, the more trustworthy. This is the special appeal of what we have been calling autocritical emotion—that a more authentic emotion might disturb and displace a pleasing and misleading one. Sartre, however, warns that the credibility of emotion plays upon its power to disturb mind and body: "*in order to believe in magical behavior it is necessary to be highly disturbed*" (75, original emphasis). Disturbance and defamiliarization are the vital components of an embodied, animated fantasy; they translate freedom into sensibility, while the world as is remains intact.[74]

At this point one might sensibly decide, like Harley in *The Man of Feeling*, that calculating the chances of deception is indeed too tedious a business for the critical reader. Yes, feeling is potentially manipulative; it may promise one thing and do another. It is also inescapable. The critic has little choice but to take a chance with feelings there will never be sufficient reason to trust. Alternatively, like de Man in *Aesthetic Ideology*, say, one could continue to disenchant feeling forever, even while recognizing that feeling will survive disenchantment one way or another. In fact, criticism must occupy the roles of Harley *and* de Man, not alternately but simultaneously. This is the dual, difficult task Blake asks of his reader: to feel and critique feeling at once—to "behold Pitying."

Rather than stop here, however, I want to return once more to Sartre. Despite his unsparing identification of emotion with escapism—a linkage he goes so far as to call a "degradation of consciousness" (77)—Sartre differentiates between two types of magic in a way that may help us further navigate the impasse of fantasy and disenchantment. In his essay's surprising final pages, Sartre introduces a new way to distinguish among emotions. There are emotions that emanate *from us* and others that happen *to us*, with the latter pointing to sources outside our own subjectivity. It is possible, of course, that Sartre's conceptual schema may itself involve a trick of emotional ventriloquism. That is, the emotions that seem to happen to us (as if from external agents) may in fact emanate from us, conjured by our own powerful desire to get outside ourselves. Still, if we have taken the disenchantment of critical emotion as far as we can, then perhaps we should also explore the opportunity Sartre provides, as another kind of thought experiment. If we have no choice but to go with and against the emotions, Sartre at least provides a principle to guide us in this paradoxical labor. Let's test this principle.

In order to introduce its new, late-arriving taxonomy of emotion, Sartre's essay turns to an example of horror at once conventional and unexpected: "[S]uddenly," he writes, "a grinning face appears flattened against the window pane; I feel invaded by terror" [*un visage grimaçant apparaît soudain et se colle á la vitre de la fenêtre;*

je me sens envahi de terreur] (82). Sartre invokes this face in order to illustrate "certain abrupt reactions of horror and admiration" (82) unaccounted for by the theory of emotion he has spent his entire essay elaborating. And it is significant that his example of horror should take the form of a face. Throughout the essay, Sartre describes the ordinary work performed by emotion as a kind of prosopopoeia (*prosopon*, face), though he does not use that term. Emotion magically animates a mechanical, material world that is otherwise dead to our interests; it gives that hard world a face. *This* face at the window, however, neither answers to our needs nor indicates a world magically succumbing to our powers of redescription. Suddenly, an inhuman world *faces us*, exposing the limits of our anthropomorphic powers and bringing us "*face to face*" (87) with an otherness that, in actuality, we understand has neither subjectivity nor face.[75] If this terrifying apparition draws on the archetypal scene of horror in *Frankenstein* where the creature appears with "ghastly grin" "at the casement" outside Victor's remote Scottish laboratory,[76] then Sartre also departs significantly from his gothic source. Here we experience the figure as magical not because it has been conjured by human powers, as Victor conjured his creature by animating a body composed of dead parts, but because it follows no recognizable rules or laws. Rather than emphasizing the facial expression of deep emotion (the "ghastly grin" that, in *Frankenstein*, gives the creature a human interiority like our own, no matter how distorted by circumstance), Sartre draws our attention to the flatness of the face pressed against the windowpane. This face is not a figure for personal, inner turmoil but for depthless sur*face*. It indicates a world suddenly strange and lacking in ordinary spatial orientation; its action is not so much psychological as adhesive (*se coller*, to cling together; *coller*, to paste or glue), joining exteriorities in an all-surface world that no longer allows for any reassuring distance between people and things, subjects and objects. Flattened against the window, this face is also flattened directly *against the perceiver*, for in the unitary, depthless field of horror, events collapse into simultaneity and objects touch one another immediately, without having to pass through a Newtonian mechanics of time and space. Here, where distinctions between interior and exterior have vanished, neither emotional transformations nor rational constructions can serve the viewer's needs. He can neither faint nor run away. There is no "away," for events no longer occur step-by-step over distances.[77] Here, even "doors, locks, walls, and arms [instruments that might modify other instruments in a world where mechanics prevail] are not recourses against . . . menaces" (89).

Traditionally, Sartre's critics have complained that he reduces emotion to intentional action, to something people do in and to the world to accomplish a specific purpose, even if they do not typically recognize they are doing this. Thus Sartre anticipates the cognitive theory of emotion, privileging beliefs over physiology, and yet he goes too far, describing emotions that are too purposive and (in a sense) always voluntary.⁷⁸ This objection has merit only if one ignores his essay's final pages. For starting with that mocking, flattened face, Sartre begins to distinguish between two kinds of emotion and thus between two kinds of magic, depending on whether the emotion originates in the subject or the object. Emotion involves either a transformation of the material world by the subject or of the subject by the material world. One kind of magical agency belongs to us; the other does not. Sartre refers to this other agency as "a reciprocal action": "We have seen that, in emotion, consciousness is degraded and abruptly transforms the determined world in which we live into a magical world. But there is a reciprocal action: this world itself sometimes reveals itself to consciousness as magical instead of determined, as we expected of it. Indeed, we need not believe that the magical is an ephemeral quality which we impose upon the world as our moods dictate. Here is an existential structure of the world which is magical" (83). Sartre goes on to describe this reciprocal action in terms of horror and wonder: "The abrupt passage from a rational apprehension of the world to a perception of the same world as magical, if it is motivated by the object itself and if it is accompanied by a disagreeable element, is horror; if it is accompanied by an agreeable element it will be wonder . . . Thus, there are two forms of emotion, according to whether it is we who constitute the magic of the world to replace a deterministic activity which cannot be realized, or whether it is the world itself which abruptly reveals itself as being magical" (85). Arnold considered it the aim of criticism to see the object as it really is. In this other magical world, the object shows itself with a vengeance, and without any regard for how criticism conceives of its mission.

In Sartre's account, both magical worlds stand opposite an "instrumental world," the realm of cause and effect or means and ends that we have already glimpsed in his example of the "coin-making machine." "The world can appear . . . as a complex of instruments so organized that if one wished to produce a determined effect it would be necessary to act upon the determined elements of the complex. In this case, each instrument refers to other instruments and to the totality of instruments; there is no absolute action or radical change that one can immediately introduce into this world. It is necessary to modify a particular instrument and this by means of another instrument which refers to other instruments and so on to infinity" (89–90). Consciousness can operate in this infinitely instrumental world in two ways: rationally or emotionally. Ordinarily, we adopt the appropriate, available mechanism to achieve a particular end. We pursue our goals by working the machine and becoming one of its parts. But when the instrumental world frustrates desires that can find no means of enactment, emotion transforms the machine, creating a substitute world that magically accommodates our need for the impossible. With these alternatives, we find ourselves back with Guillory and Docherty, one proposing a politics of "actual effects" and "determinable measures" to be achieved only by fully and honestly grasping the social machine in which one must operate, the other proposing fantasy as a way to reimagine the rules governing politics, to retool the machine, as it were. According to Sartre, however, these different ways for consciousness to "be-in-the-World" (89) mask underlying similarities. Both involve the subject's effort or will; both attempt to exercise agency within and against an overdetermined, mechanistic world. Thus both dispositions are instruments at the subject's disposal, although one (the rational) is limited by the field of operation to which it submits, the other (the emotional) by its ultimate ineffectiveness. And yet, according to Sartre, there is another magic altogether, one that has nothing to do with our agency, effective or wishful. This magic occurs when the build up of "rational superstructures" caves in (though not by means of anything we have done) and consciousness abruptly plunges "into the magical." The world, it turns out, is *already* magical, *not* instrumental as we expected—though it is not magical in any way we can desire or imagine or enable or make use of. When emotion becomes receptive to this originary and utterly indifferent magic, it manifests a "magical attitude" that Sartre calls "one of the great attitudes which are essential" to consciousness (90–91).

Sartre's essay thus performs a rather remarkable turnabout. Just when you think emotion is a matter of what subjects do, how they exercise magical agency when all practical means of action are blocked and thus entangle themselves in questions of escapism and efficacy, it turns out that emotion can actually disclose a noninstrumental world, different and indifferent, answering neither to our desires nor to natural, deterministic laws. In effect, Sartre is describing two kinds of indeterminacy, both of which are at work in the world, both of which are manifested as emotion. Here, perhaps, is where his account has something to say to criticism, something to say about how we read. There is an indeterminacy we want and an indeterminacy that happens. We project or impose the first when we observe no other way to create time and space for agency in a world too difficult and overdetermined. This indeterminacy serves our needs by magically transforming the world, opening it to our powers of reinterpretation. The second indeterminacy—if it exits at all—has nothing to do with our mental structures and acts, rational or emotional, except occasionally and abruptly to reveal itself, like a grinning face suddenly flattened at our window. Sartre might say: do not entirely trust emotions that seem to enhance agency or freedom or promise to transform the world in even the most attenuated or indirect manner. Trust them no more than one would trust the instrumental agencies that have promised, since the Enlightenment, to transform the world. Trust only those emotions that do nothing—nothing, that is, but reveal there is a world that does not act as object to our subject. Following these principles would seriously disable any fantasy of coordinating aesthetics and politics, just as it would challenge any belief that critical emotion is the precondition of a future agency to come. At the same time, however, it would continue to allow for an element of experience irreducible to instrumentality, a small, flat window that only emotion might access.

Still, Sartre offers no way to differentiate among these types of magic in practice. The emotions on either side go by the same names and arise with the same set of physiological indicators. How then could one ever tell the indeterminacy we want to discover, introduced into the world by our "impatience for liberty," from the indeterminacy that happens regardless of what we want? Would one "magical attitude" *feel* stronger or stranger or flatter than the other? Distinguishing vitality from its proxies remains, as it did for Blake, the critic's task and dilemma.

Blake Again, or Reading without Empowerment

In Blake's literary world, the transition from impasse to magic is mediated by reading. But what kind of magic does reading involve? And what kind of world would Blake's magical world be? One no longer measured by a compass or determined by instruments, to be sure. But would it be a world our emotions have magically transformed, a home built for desires, or an alien world with a magic of its own, transforming the emotions because it does *not* correspond to what we want?

On Plate 54 of *Jerusalem* there is a schematic image that a modern reader might be tempted to call Blake's "emoticon" if its flat, stony disk bore closer resemblance to a face (figure 5.1):

Reason

Pity   Wrath

This World

Desire

It would not be difficult to map this figure onto the problematic of impasse and magic. A world determined entirely by rational laws, like Sartre's world of infinite instruments, would be a world of impasse; its complicated wheels would allow no other way through, requiring the subject who would act to become a cog in the machine. A world transformed to accommodate infinite desire would be a world of magic, at least according to Sartre's first definition of magic. The world in between—pictured above as "a Globe rolling thro Voidness" (*Milton* 29:16, E 127)—is the space where reason and desire, impasse and magic, negotiate their opposition.

Figure 5.1 Jerusalem, copy E, plate 54, 1804–1820, detail. Yale Center for British Art, Paul Mellon Collection

For Blake "*This* World" is the planetary sphere of the emotions. Here desire rises from below, expressing its resistance to the fallen world through emotions such as pity and wrath. Under the influence of desire, these emotions become agents of transformation, though this is by no means a simple process. Emotions are themselves complex, ambiguous phenomena—part impasse, part magic. In Blake's world, pity and wrath are shadowed by spectrous doubles, inauthentic proxies that serve the instrumental function of *blocking* desire's ascent. The cartography of emotion is thus reminiscent of Blake's division of humanity into three classes or regions: emotion can either be an instrument of the tyrannical "elect" above or it can belong to the rebellious energies of the "reprobate" below, but for the most part it comprises the fraught middle ground in which the "redeemed" must struggle to realize their freedom. Trying to distinguish between emotions that serve "Reason" and reinforce the instrumental world as it is from emotions that welcome "Desire" and its transformative potential is the great task of autocritical emotion in Blake, the task that allows his lifelong project of mental fight to represent the modern critical task in general.

The pivotal role of emotion in shaping Blake's world suggests that we should modify the emphasis his readers have traditionally placed on perception. The *affect* altering alters all. What we have not as yet taken into account, however, is the possibility Sartre raises that "this world" might not change "as our moods dictate," appearing overdetermined by "Reason" at one moment and open to messianic "Desire" the next, but instead might work on our emotions with its own "reciprocal action," in a way that has nothing to do with the vertical axis of our rationalizations and desires. Does Blake consider any emotion or any magic that, rather than empowering the reader to transform the world, would allow for "this world"—this other, alien, indifferent world—to act upon the reader?

Not directly. Blake's magical world is nowhere better evident than in the celebrated final sequence of the first book of *Milton,* in the plates that conclude: "Such is the World of Los the labour of six thousand years. / Thus Nature is a Vision of the

Science of the Elohim" (29:64–65, E 128). This sequence describes a fully creative universe in which nature is sustained by ongoing vision rather than by physics, for "every Natural Effect has a Spiritual Cause, and Not / A Natural: for a Natural Cause only seems" (26:44–45, E 124). In this world free from mechanical instruments, "every Generated Body" is internally "a garden of delight," "a building of magnificence, / Built by the Sons of Los" (26:31–33, E 123). Here one also finds the extended passage on time and pulsation we looked at earlier, lines that participate in the sequence's general transfiguration of Newtonian categories. Although it is not immediately evident that this is the case, this magical world is an effect of reading and emotion. It arises in response to the teleiopoetic arrival of Milton, who enters the world (as we recall) "thro Albions heart" (20:41, E 114) and resuscitates the supine giant by agitating his dormant sensibility. "Now Albions sleeping Humanity began to turn upon his Couch; / Feeling the electric flame of Miltons awful precipitate descent" (20:25–26, E 114). Albion is moved by Milton, turning only when he receives the poet's formal charge.[79] The lines immediately following these introduce an interrogative phrase ("Seest thou") that will eventually become the refrain for describing the magical world. Just as Albion begins to stir, Blake writes,

> Seest thou the little winged fly, smaller than a grain of sand?
> It has a heart like thee; a brain open to heaven & hell,
> Withinside wondrous & expansive; its gates are not clos'd,
> I hope thine are not.   (20:27–30, E 114)

Several plates later, the same language returns as a declarative, "*Thou seest* the Constellations in the deep & wondrous Night," and then a few lines later, "*Thou seest* the gorgeous clothed Flies that dance & sport in summer," and finally, "*thou seest* the Trees on mountains" (25:66; 26:2, 7, E 123). The recurrence of the fly as an object of enhanced perception seals the link between the two passages. Apparently, a change in affect ("feeling the electric flame of Milton's awful precipitate descent") allows for a change in perception; the one leads directly to the other. Moreover, Blake makes no distinction between (redeemed) perception and (perceptive) reading. Because the lines directly address a reader, the "thou" who *sees* "the gorgeous clothed Flies" is also, at the very same moment, *reading* these words. By the end of Book the First, as a result of the reader's affective agency, the entire world looks different. Time has become "the work of Fairy hands of the Four Elements" (28:60, E 127) and "The Sky is an immortal Tent built by the Sons of Los" (29:4, E 127). We recall Sartre. "At present, we can conceive of what an emotion is. It is a transformation of the world." "All [emotions] are tantamount to setting up a magical world by using the body as a means of incantation." All we need add is that the emotions

Figure 5.2 *Milton a Poem*, copy C, Bentley 16, Erdman 17 [19], c. 1804–1811, detail. *Rare Books Division, The New York Public Library, Astor, Lenox and Tilden Foundations*

performing this world-transforming work originate in a moment of reading, in the precise moment when a poet finds his way into a reader's fallen heart.

The transformative agency of reading does not come easily in *Milton*; it advances one foot at a time, meeting resistance every step of the way. Milton faces one obstacle after another on his journey through the world of Urizenic instruments. He is always up against a wall, as if "all the ways are barred." For the most part, these barriers take the form of the bad readers he encounters. While Urizen acts deliberately to stop Milton from advancing, freezing the "dark rocks between" his "footsteps," "infixing deep the feet in marble beds" (19:1–2, E 112), others serve Urizen inadvertently, misreading the eschatological signs of Milton's descent into the heart. No one is more complicitous in this regard than Los, whose errors Blake represents pictorially with surprising literalism (figure 5.2):

> Los heard in terror Enitharmons words: in fibrous strength
> His limbs shot forth like roots of trees against the forward path
> Of Milton's journey.   (17:34–36, E 111)

In his fallen ("generated") state, Los has become indistinguishable from the vegetative world around him. In these lines, the "limbs" blocking Milton's forward motion spring from either human or botanical agency; it makes no difference whether they are arms or branches. But Blake also turns this hybrid, naturalized figure upside down, describing "limbs . . . like roots." The subject whose misreading would block messianic redemption is an inverted subject, with roots in air. If this image anticipates the analogy Marx and Engels would soon propose between the distortions of ideology and the camera obscura—"men and their circumstances appear upside-down"[80]—Blake himself may have in mind a surreal, vivid scene from the Gospel of Mark. There, when Jesus' first attempt to heal a blind man succeeds only partially, the man (momentarily suspended between darkness and clarity) announces: "I see men as trees, walking" (8:24). These tree-people resemble Los; although their roots have become feet, they remain caught between nature and freedom, between an ideology not yet left behind and a free mobility not yet fully achieved. In *Milton* successful completion of this transition turns on the ability to read better, in a way more receptive to Albion's stirring heart and Milton's electric flame, and the reader's empowerment manifests itself in the sudden appearance of a world no longer comprised of blocked paths. As the reader moves through *Milton*, he encounters a world increasingly (magically) open to his mobility. Milton enters the world not only through Albion's heart, of course, but also through Blake's left foot, linking motion and emotion, and Los becomes an empowered and empowering agent when he straps on Blake's sandal, joining forces with Blake and Milton. This sandal is itself a vehicle of magical action: as it moves through space, it makes "this Vegetable World" appear to be "formd immortal of precious stones & gold" (21:12–13, E 115). Before long, even the sky has been mobilized. It too follows the lead of human feet: if a man should "move his dwelling-place, his heavens also move" (29:12, E 127). By the magnificent ending of Book the First, *everything* is moving. The heart, the feet, the world are one.

In *Milton,* in other words, a change in reading—which itself begins as a change in affect—stands between the instrumental and the magical worlds. The extent to which Blake indulges in a fantasy of intellectual empowerment, underwritten by emotion, becomes apparent when Los declares his newly recovered prophetic omnipotence: "Time & Space obey my will" (22:17, E 117). The magical world is something he and his sons make happen. No longer a giant mechanism, nature has become a giant prosopopoeia, the human effect of a human cause, without which it would be barren. There is little question as to whether Blake's magical world precedes or follows the change in emotion—or, to adopt Sartre's language, little question as to "whether it is we who constitute the magic of the world to re-place a deterministic activity which cannot be realized, or whether it is the world itself which abruptly reveals itself as being magical" (85). Whatever freedoms are revealed by the magical world at the end of the first book of *Milton* are freedoms our feelings have put there.

If the emotions—no matter how unfamiliar they may appear—eventually feed into a narrative of empowerment, we have reached the limit of Blake's work in and on feeling. Even his exploration of active passivity may, in the end, put passivity in the service of agency. This does not mean, however, that Blake's work simply marches forward. In his halting moments, when his hesitant text neither advances nor comes to a standstill, perhaps we can glimpse an opening onto a different magical world, one that Blake, caught between his suspicion of the fallen will and his investment in the promise of renewed agency, could not realize directly. Let's conclude with one such moment—the moment in *Milton* just before the "Constellations" arise to present our first view of the magical world, "deep & wondrous." In what amounts to his final speech in the book, Los issues one last set of instructions. Because the end time is near, and "The Great Vintage & Harvest is now upon Earth" (25:17, E 121), his sons must do two things:

> Go forth Reapers with rejoicing. you sowed in tears
> But the time of your refreshing cometh, only a little moment
> Still abstain from pleasure & rest, in the labours of eternity
> And you shall Reap the whole Earth, from Pole to Pole! from Sea to Sea.
>
> . . . .
>
> . . . Break not
> Forth in your wrath lest you are also vegetated by Tirzah
> Wait till the Judgement is past, till the Creation is consumed
> And then rush forward with me into the glorious spiritual
> Vegetation; the Supper of the Lamb & his Bride.   (25:44–47; 57–61, E 122)

These lines are fraught with Blake's usual wordplay. "Sow[ing] in tears," for instance, may conjure the image of a farmer planting tears instead of seeds or planting seeds while weeping, but the phrase also invokes the impossible labor of an unimaginable weaver, *sewing* tears into fabric. What kind of labor is Blake calling for? That this is a problem not only for Los's sons but also for the reader appears in the treacherous enjambment between lines 60 and 61 that Blake all but dares the reader to negotiate successfully. This impossible crossing between lines, between worlds, recalls the long history of failed revolutionary transitions and unfulfilled apocalyptic promises, the very same history Arnold would soon see epitomized in the "grand error" of the French Revolution: "quitting the intellectual sphere and rushing furiously into the political sphere."[81] At this critical moment in *Milton*, poised on the verge of apocalyptic change, what would it mean to "rush forward . . . into the glorious spiritual / *Vegetation*"? Suspended between these lines, the reader rushes across a phrase he resists completing, for it is impossible to know whether "Vegetation" negates the "glorious spiritual" expectations that precede it, resulting in yet another disappointment, or whether, having crossed the divide, "Vegetation" will now mean something else altogether, wholly transformed by the prehistory of "glorious spiritual" struggle one will have passed through to reach it. The stakes in negotiating this textual impasse could not be higher. (Our spiritual or vegetable life depends on it.) Should the reader rush too quickly, prompted by eagerness and wrath to "Break . . . / Forth" prematurely, he risks being "vegetated by Tirzah"—that is, he risks becoming a tree-person yet again. To illustrate this danger, Blake posi-

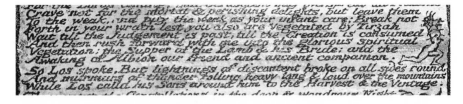

Figure 5.3 Milton a Poem, copy C, Bentley 25, Erdman 25 [27], c. 1804–1811, detail. Rare Books Division, The New York Public Library, Astor, Lenox and Tilden Foundations

tions a small hybrid figure just to the right of these lines: human from the torso down, a prickly bush above (figure 5.3). If this is the fate that awaits Los's disobedient sons, who indeed break out in discontent immediately after his warning,[82] it also signals the fate of the bad reader. For this figure—who breaks forth from the text in a left-to-right movement mirroring the direction of our eyes, sprinting with us into the transitional space of enjambment—appears to be vegetating in midair.

But what would it mean to be a good reader of this passage? Los demands two things of his listeners that, while not exactly contradictory, are not easily synchronized either. They must continue working, and then rest later ("Still abstain from pleasure & rest"). But they must also "Wait . . . And then rush forward." If one could successfully negotiate the transition between worlds, between lines, would the apocalyptic event result from one's working or one's waiting? Is this event something one should make happen (without waiting) or let happen (without rushing)? Just for a moment, suspended on the brink of the magical world, this enjambment stalls, asking the reader not to cross over into a world his own affective agency will transform but to slow the momentum of his enthusiasm. Rather than "hurrying the Will in Pursuit of [its] Object" (one definition of enthusiasm),[83] Blake opens a space irreducible to activity or passivity, where the impassioned work of reading must also accommodate the slow time of waiting. Would the feeling of urgent but suspended agency required by such a space disclose an altogether other world, of the kind Sartre suggests is sometimes sensed by emotion? Rather than allowing us to reimagine "the Constellations in the deep & wondrous Night," perhaps this feeling would receive the constellations just as they show themselves—whatever they are—flattened against the surface of our windowpane. But how could we know the answer to this question when we have hardly begun to notice those emotions in Blake that, rather than transforming the world, transform the reader's desire for empowerment?

Acknowledgments

A book as long in the making as this one accrues significant debt. Many people have contributed to its development—some by generously reading early drafts, others by the gift of their own critical writing, still others by their friendship. Indeed, many have contributed in all of these ways. I thank the following colleagues here at Berkeley and beyond: Mitch Breitwieser, Marshall Brown, Ian Duncan, Morris Eaves, Denise Gigante, Geoffrey Galt Harpham, Noah Heringman, Steve Justice, Rob Kaufman, Colleen Lye, Saree Makdisi, Bill Musgrave, Thomas Pfau, Joanna Picciotto, Kent Puckett, Steve Sarratore, Sue Schweik, Richard Sha, Ann Smock, Janet Sorensen, James Turner, and Joe Wittreich. This book also benefited from lively conversations with more students than I can name, though I do want to thank participants in the remarkable Blake seminars of 2005 and 2008, as well as a few former students who directly influenced this project and made thinking about it much more pleasurable: Amy Campion, Julie Carr, Amanda Jo Goldstein, Lily Gurton-Wachter, and Suzie Park. I also want to recognize two research assistants, Richard Lee and Corinna Burrell, for their diligence in helping me prepare the final manuscript for press.

My deepest gratitude, however, goes to four colleagues, dear friends all, without whose encouragement, engagement, and sheer intellectual radiance this book would have remained unwritten. Anne-Lise François, Kevis Goodman, and Celeste Langan have made the last ten years feel like a golden age for the study of Romantic poetry at Berkeley. Whatever value this book may possess is a reflection of that flourishing. During the same period, Janet Adelman pored over my drafts—and poured her brilliant, prodding commentary into them—delighting in Blake's provocations and never giving up on this project. Janet died in April 2010; how I wish I could return her generosity by giving her the gift of a book she helped to enable.

Research on this book received crucial fellowship and sabbatical support on several occasions from the College of Letters and Science at the University of California at Berkeley. Publication has been ably shepherded by Matt McAdam, Humanities Editor at the Johns Hopkins University Press, who recruited a sensitive and insightful (and still anonymous) reader for the manuscript. Julia Ridley Smith improved my prose with her scrupulous copyediting. Parts of the book appeared first in article form. An early version of chapter 1 was published as "Blake's Agitation" in *South Atlantic Quarterly* 95.3 (Summer 1996): 753–796. The title stuck. Parts of the introduction and chapter 5 appeared as "William Blake and the Future of Enthusiasm" in *Nineteenth-Century Literature* 63 (March 2009): 439–460. I thank both journals for their permission to reuse material from these essays.

I also wish to thank my family: my parents, Arnold and Gladys Goldsmith; my sisters, Marsha Goldsmith Kamin and Janet Sarratore; and my sons, Sam and Joel. All of them heard about this project for far too long and offered nothing but kindness, patience, and genuine interest in return. Before my father became ill and passed away, he worked through long portions of the manuscript, sometimes finding himself baffled by Blake, at other times by my approach to Blake, but always taking pleasure in my best insights. To reread *his* work on Henry James, Bernard Malamud, or the Golem of Prague is to discover a standard of clarity and vigor to which I will always aspire. Finally, this book is dedicated to Cathy: my partner in all things, my closest friend, my love.

This book is very much the product of a time and place. That may be true of all books, but there is at least one way in which circumstance plays an unusually significant role in this instance. The time of this book's writing coincides with a steady decline in public funding for the University of California and a rapid collapse of state support in recent years. Every day in the Berkeley English Department I feel the influence—the inspiration, rather—of an extraordinary gathering of minds committed to the study of literature. That crucible of thought informs every word of *Blake's Agitation*; it is the book's condition of possibility. As I commit these last words to print, I, like many others today, wonder how long work of this kind will remain possible—work achieved in a public setting, supported by public funds, in service of the public good.

Appendix

Blake's Variations on "cracked across"

From David V. Erdman, ed., *The Complete Poetry and Prose of William Blake* (1988)

America: A Prophecy (1793), *cancelled plate b*
    So still the terrors rent . . .
          . . . so the dark house was rent
    The valley mov'd beneath; its shining pillars split in twain,
    And its roofs **crack across** down falling on th'Angelic seats.   (20–24, E 58)

The Book of Urizen (1794), *plate 23*
    Grodna rent the deep earth howling
    Amaz'd! his heavens immense **cracks**
    Like the ground parch'd with heat . . .   (15–17, E 81)

The Book of Los (1795), *plate 4*
    1: The Immortal stood frozen amidst
    The vast rock of eternity; times
    And times; a night of vast durance:
    Impatient, stifled, stiffend, hardned.

    2: Till impatience no longer could bear
    The hard bondage, rent: rent, the vast solid
    With a crash from immense to immense

    3: **Crack'd across** into numberless fragments
    The Prophetic wrath, strug'ling for vent
    Hurls apart, stamping furious to dust
    And crumbling with bursting sobs; heaves
    The black marble on high into fragments

4: Hurl'd apart on all sides, as a falling

Rock: the innumerable fragments away

Fell asunder; and horrible vacuum

Beneath him & on all sides round.

5: Falling, falling! Los fell & fell

Sunk precipitant heavy down down

Times on times, night on night, day on day . . .   (11–29, E 92)

The Four Zoas (c. 1797–1805), *Night the Third*

[Ahania] Continued falling. Loud the Crash continud loud & Hoarse

From the Crash roared a flame of blue sulphureous fire from the flame

A dolorous groan that.struck with dumbness all confusion

Swallowing up the horrible din in agony on agony

Thro the Confusion like a **crack across** from immense to immense

Loud strong a universal groan* of death louder

Than all the wracking elements   (p. 44; ll. 6–11, E 329)

Night the Ninth

Los his vegetable hands

Outstretchd his right hand branching out in fibrous Strength

Siezd the Sun. His left hand like dark roots coverd the Moon

And tore them down **cracking** the heavens **across** from immense to immense

Then fell the fires of Eternity with loud & shrill

Sound of Loud Trumpet thundering along from heaven to heaven

A mighty sound articulate Awake ye dead & come

To judgment from the four winds Awake & Come away

Folding like scrolls of the Enormous volume of Heaven & Earth

With thunderous noise & dreadful shakings rocking to and fro

The heavens are shaken & the Earth removed from its place . . .

(p. 117; ll. 6–16, E 386–387)

*["Noise call you it or universal groan" (*Samson Agonistes*, 1511)]

Notes

Introduction

1. "A Vision of the Last Judgment," in *The Complete Poetry and Prose of William Blake*, ed. David V. Erdman, newly rev. ed., (New York: Anchor Books, 1988), 560. Unless otherwise noted, all further citations of Blake are from this edition. Wherever appropriate, Blake citations include a short title, followed by plate and line numbers, followed by the page number in Erdman—for example, *Urizen* 23:2–7, E 81.

2. Fredric Jameson, *Marxism and Form: Twentieth-Century Dialectical Theories of Literature* (Princeton: Princeton UP, 1971), 307. Further citations are to this text.

3. See *The Political Unconscious: Narrative as a Socially Symbolic Act* (Ithaca: Cornell UP, 1981), 102, and *Postmodernism, or the Cultural Logic of Late Capitalism* (Durham: Duke UP, 1991), 10. Jameson's interest in the emotions goes back to his first book, *Sartre: The Origins of a Style* (New York: Columbia UP, 1984 [1961]), based on his doctoral dissertation. There he notes that "Sartre has spoken of the way emotion, to strengthen itself, to ratify the merely mental reaction with the solidity of the flesh, fills itself out with physical concomitants, such as blushing, trembling, cold sweat" (94). We will return to Jameson's reading of Sartre in chapter 5, when we directly take up Sartre's *The Emotions: Outline of a Theory*.

4. The distinction between determinism and historical necessity occurs in a discussion of Georgi Plekhanov. After stating that "[i]t is perhaps more a question of a feeling than of a concept," Jameson continues, "and I am tempted to say that the feeling of necessity or historical inevitability is simply the emotion characteristic of historical understanding as such, that feeling which accompanies the mental process by which, through that movement of specification or rectification which we have described, we now as for the first time suddenly comprehend a historical event, which is to say that we understand for the first time how it had to happen *that way and no other*" (original emphasis, *Marxism and Form*, 360–361). Most important for our topic is how feeling *verifies* a concept (historical necessity) that, without such affective verification, would have trouble distinguishing itself from other, rival abstractions. Jameson has replaced the innate moral sense of eighteenth-century theories of sympathy with another version of sensibility, this time in the form of a subjective (and reliable) historical sense.

5. Jameson, *Postmodernism*, 43.

6. The modern, anti-affective tradition summed up in William K. Wimsatt Jr. and Monroe C. Beardsley's 1949 classic "The Affective Fallacy" is itself testimony to the power of

emotion-based criticism, which was (and is) sufficiently forceful and persistent to provoke a sustained counteroffensive. Rather than attempting to eliminate emotion, the anti-affective tradition generally tries to control its influence by separating art's reliable and universal emotions from the raw, biased, and relativistic emotions of ordinary experience. Maneuvering in this way, Wimsatt and Beardsley modify Eliot's remarks on the difference between "art emotion" and "personal emotions" in "Tradition and the Individual Talent," but they also anticipate the cognitive theory of emotion, which posits that emotions are not the blind, chaotic forces they sometimes appear to be but cognitive judgments with decipherable, propositional content. In Wimsatt and Beardsley's discussion of emotion, the salient distinction is not between body and mind but between good judgments (universally valid) and bad (idiosyncratic). See Eliot, "Tradition and the Individual Talent," in *The Sacred Wood* (New York: Methuen, 1920; repr., 1972), 57; and Wimsatt and Beardsley, "The Affective Fallacy," in Wimsatt, *The Verbal Icon: Studies in the Meaning of Poetry* (Lexington: U of Kentucky P, 1954), 21–39. Paul de Man takes his suspicion of emotion much further than his new critical forebears, though he shares their idea that literary language, when adhered to rigorously, will act as a corrective to the ideological distortions introduced by feelings. Moreover, as Rei Terada has demonstrated, de Man's programmatic efforts to eliminate emotion from criticism cannot escape generating affects of their own. We will return to Terada's reading of de Man later in this chapter and at various points throughout this book.

7. Joanna Picciotto describes how early modern secularization transformed rather than jettisoned the mystical incorporation promised by the Church: "The *corpus mysticum* became a public: a body whose members were united by their shared participation in the labor of knowledge production—a labor that could confer on each of its agents the character of a 'public person.'" No doubt Blake would agree with her (Milton-inflected) assertion that "a fully restored England would be a paradisal state in which every inhabitant participated in the innocent labor of truth production" (*Labors of Innocence in Early Modern England* [Cambridge, MA: Harvard UP, 2010], 3, 28). For Picciotto's claim that the experimentalist tradition survived the Restoration, allowing the "culture of the losers" to continue to exert its influence into the eighteenth century, see 23–24.

8. John Guillory, "The Ethical Practice of Modernity: The Example of Reading," in *The Turn to Ethics,* ed. Marjorie Garber, Beatrice Hanssen, and Rebecca L. Walkowitz (New York: Routledge, 2000), 31.

9. Matthew Arnold, "The Function of Criticism at the Present Time" (1864), in *"Culture and Anarchy" and Other Writings,* ed. Stefan Collini (Cambridge: Cambridge UP, 1993), 41.

10. Jacques Derrida, *Politics of Friendship,* trans. George Collins (London: Verso, 1997), 61 ff.

11. Samuel Johnson, entry for "Enthusiasm," *A Dictionary of the English Language* (London: W. Strahan, 1755).

12. Thompson, *Witness Against the Beast: William Blake and the Moral Law* (New York: New Press, 1993), 46. The recent books I refer to here are Jon Mee, *Romanticism, Enthusiasm and Regulation: Poetics and the Policing of Culture in the Romantic Period* (Oxford: Oxford UP, 2003), and Saree Makdisi, *William Blake and the Impossible History of the 1790s* (Chicago: U of Chicago P, 2003), both of which are cited parenthetically hereafter.

13. As far as I know, Susie I. Tucker was the first to use this term in her still indispensable *Enthusiasm: A Study in Semantic Change* (Cambridge: Cambridge UP, 1972), 3, but in fact it has become commonplace. See, e.g., Jan Goldstein's "Enthusiasm or Imagination?

Eighteenth-Century Smear Words in Comparative National Context," in *Enthusiasm and Enlightenment in Europe, 1650–1850*, ed. Lawrence E. Klein and Anthony J. La Vopa (San Marino, CA: Huntington Library, 1998), 29–49. Mee's *Romanticism, Enthusiasm and Regulation* provides the best recent account of the complex ways in which Enlightenment culture came to associate "enthusiasm" with religious fanaticism, delirium, and error as it tried to define itself against the religious and political excesses of the seventeenth century. Also see Clement Hawes, *Mania and Literary Style: The Rhetoric of Enthusiasm from the Ranters to Christopher Smart* (Cambridge: Cambridge UP, 1996) and two important essays by J. G. A. Pocock: "Edmund Burke and the Redefinition of Enthusiasm: The Context as Counter-Revolution," in *The Transformation of Political Culture 1789–1848*, vol. 3 of *The French Revolution and the Creation of Modern Political Culture*, ed. François Furet and Mona Ozouf (Oxford: Pergamon, 1989), 19–43, and "Enthusiasm: The Antiself of Enlightenment," in *Enthusiasm and Enlightenment in Europe, 1650–1850*, 7–28.

14. I am borrowing from the title of Mee's earlier book on Blake, *Dangerous Enthusiasm: William Blake and the Culture of Radicalism in the 1790s* (Oxford: Clarendon, 1992).

15. Norman Vincent Peale, *Enthusiasm Makes the Difference* (New York: Simon and Schuster, 2003, first published 1967).

16. "The Greeks represent Chronos or Time as a very Aged Man this is Fable but the Real Vision of Time is in Eternal Youth" ("A Vision of the Last Judgment," 563).

17. Hazard Adams, "Post-Essick Prophecy," *Studies in Romanticism* 21 (Fall 1982): 402–403.

18. "An Essay on Criticism," l. 676, p. 55, in *Poetry and Prose of Alexander Pope*, ed. Aubrey Williams (Boston: Houghton Mifflin, 1969). Pope famously describes Longinus as "An ardent *Judge* . . . / Whose *own Example* strengthens all his Laws, / And *Is himself* that great *Sublime* he draws" (ll. 677–80, p. 56).

19. In 1947, Edith Sitwell writes of *Fearful Symmetry*, "To say it is a magnificent, extraordinary book is to praise it as it should be praised, but in doing so one gives little idea of the huge scope of the book and of its fiery understanding" (*Spectator* 179 [Oct. 10, 1947]: 466). In the same year, Alfred C. Ames testifies, "Frye conducts his ambitious study with unflagging energy, great enthusiasm, and immense erudition . . . [Blake's] vision . . . is vouchsafed only to 'the man with an opened center.' The careful and sympathetic reader of *Fearful Symmetry* will have great openings" (*Poetry* 71 [Nov. 1947]: 102–103).

20. Laura Quinney, *William Blake on Self and Soul* (Cambridge, MA: Harvard UP, 2009), xi, xiv. With its emphasis on occult sources (Gnostic and Neoplatonic) rather than seventeenth-century antinomian texts, and with its emphasis on psychological rather than social or political conflict, Quinney's important study departs significantly from the dominant historicist trends in Blake criticism. Yet despite these differences, her book continues to feature the link between emotion and agency prominently. Quinney's topic is the soul's resistance to the empirical self thrust upon it, and this resistance to unfortunate subjectivity begins with the work of emotion: "the soul feels, and thus comes to know, its discomfiture in the material world through the anguishing emotion of 'homesickness' " (15). Negative affect prompts the soul to seek transcendence by escaping or transforming the worldly self that binds it.

21. To put this another way: in critical practice, the *pre*modern enthusiasm excavated by scholarship serves as the ground of a *counter*modern enthusiasm, a set of oppositional hopes and desires already evident in Blake and persistent ever after. Blake entangled these two enthusiasms from the moment he drew on the dissenting cultures (religious and political)

that *preceded* modernization in order to formulate his critical stand *against* nascent modernization. A similar entanglement of premodernity and countermodernity recurs today, but with a difference, for Blake scholarship carries the additional (and often tacit) burden of its *late* modernity. By reading Blake with enthusiasm, critics seek to revive and sustain a countermodernity whose historical origins, receding ever further into the past, can no longer be separated from our own interest in reconstructing them. The premodern practices that survived into Blake's era in active but diminished form now survive only archaeologically.

22. Burke, "How WORDS influence the passions," in *A Philosophical Enquiry into the Origin of our Ideas of the Sublime and Beautiful* (Oxford: Oxford UP, 1990), 160.

23. Makdisi's title, *William Blake and the Impossible History of the 1790s*, quotes from Blake's "Descriptive Catalogue": To historians, "all is . . . a dull round of probabilities and possibilities; but the history of all times and places, is nothing else but improbabilities and impossibilities; what we should say, was impossible if we did not see it always before our eyes" (E 543).

24. "We believe that feelings are immutable, but every sentiment, particularly the noblest and most disinterested, has a history" (Michel Foucault, "Nietzsche, Genealogy, History," trans. Donald F. Bouchard and Sherry Simon, in *The Foucault Reader*, ed. Paul Rabinow [New York: Pantheon, 1984 (1971)], 87).

25. Rei Terada, *Feeling in Theory: Emotion after the "Death of the Subject"* (Cambridge, MA: Harvard UP, 2001), 14.

26. In an important recent essay ("The Turn to Affect: A Critique," *Critical Inquiry* 37.3 [Spring 2011]: 434–472), Ruth Leys finds herself asking the same question Terada asked ten years earlier: "Why are so many scholars today in the humanities and social sciences fascinated by the idea of affect" (435)? Leys's focus is on the currently dominant anti-intentionalist paradigm of the emotions, which views affect as "a matter of autonomic responses that are held to occur below the threshold of consciousness and cognition and to be rooted in the body" (443). Although she does not dwell on the relationship between emotion and agency in such studies, her examination of the ways in which contemporary affect theorists appropriate and misread neuroscientific evidence suggests that their desire to locate an embodied, materialist source of agency apart from instrumental reason indeed drives (and misleads) their scholarship. Such theorists hold that, for better and for worse, "action and behavior are . . . determined by affective dispositions that are independent of consciousness and the mind's control" (443)—for worse, because such affective dispositions are subject to subliminal, ideological manipulation; for better, because they carry a "potential for ethical creativity and transformation that 'technologies of the self' designed to work on our embodied being can help bring about" (436). It is precisely the latter possibility (of tapping into an innovative, materialist agency outside the conscious control of a socially constructed subject) that forms the desideratum of much contemporary affect theory. For a more direct treatment of this wish-fulfilling tendency in contemporary affect theory, see Constantia Papoulias and Felicity Callard, "Biology's Gift: Interrogating the Turn to Affect," *Body and Society* 16.1 (2010): 29–56. Papoulias and Callard contend that many affect theorists selectively sift the new biology for scientific evidence of the "gift" they would like embodied experience to provide: "a certain kind of agency that is not reducible to the social structures within which subjects are positioned" (34), an agency that therefore bears "emancipatory potential" (35).

27. See Martha Nussbaum, *Upheavals of Thought: The Intelligence of Emotions* (Cambridge: Cambridge UP, 2001); William Reddy, *The Navigation of Feeling: A Framework for*

the *History of Emotions* (Cambridge: Cambridge UP, 2001); Brian Massumi, *Parables for the Virtual: Movement, Affect, Sensation* (Durham: Duke UP, 2002); Philip Fisher, *The Vehement Passions* (Princeton: Princeton UP, 2002); Eve Kosofsky Sedgwick, *Touching Feeling: Affect, Pedagogy, Performativity* (Durham: Duke UP, 2003); Charles Altieri, *The Particulars of Rapture: An Aesthetics of the Affects* (Ithaca: Cornell UP, 2003); Sianne Ngai, *Ugly Feelings* (Cambridge, MA: Harvard UP, 2005); Denise Riley, *Impersonal Passion: Language as Affect* (Durham: Duke UP, 2005); Thomas Pfau, *Romantic Moods: Paranoia, Trauma, and Melancholy, 1790–1840* (Baltimore: Johns Hopkins UP, 2005); Jenefer Robinson, *Deeper Than Reason: Emotion and its Role in Literature, Music, and Art* (Oxford: Clarendon, 2005); Daniel M. Gross, *The Secret History of Emotion: From Aristotle's "Rhetoric" to Modern Brain Science* (Chicago: U of Chicago P, 2006). For an overview of "the recent upsurge in interest in affect" (1159) that concentrates on scholarship relevant to Romanticism, see Mary Favret's incisive survey, "The Study of Affect and Romanticism," *Literature Compass* 6.6 (2009): 1159–1166.

28. Nicholas Williams, "Blake Dead or Alive," *Nineteenth Century Literature* 63.4 (Mar. 2009): 498.

29. Having referred twice now to Marx's eleventh thesis on Feuerbach, I should comment directly on its relevance. According to Antonio Negri, Marx's thesis does not oppose philosophy (interpreting the world) to action (changing the world); it calls upon philosophers to develop materialist practices of interpretation that themselves act *as* transformations: "It is possible to transform the world *at the same time* as it is interpreted" (my emphasis, *Time for Revolution*, trans. Matteo Mandarini [New York: Continuum, 2003], 158). Derrida makes virtually the same point with his revisionary paraphrase of Marx's thesis, calling it an "injunction not just to decipher but to act and to make the deciphering [the interpretation] into a transformation that 'changes the world' " (*Specters of Marx: The State of the Debt, the Work of Mourning, and the New International*, trans. Peggy Kamuf [London: Routledge, 1994], 32). Regardless of whether Marx would approve of these modifications, my interest lies in the frequency with which critical intellectuals turn to affect to substantiate, in the body, their claim that interpretation has indeed become active and transformative—not least in *Time for Revolution* and *Specters of Marx*.

30. A. R. Damasio, *Descartes' Error: Emotion, Reason, and the Human Brain* (New York: Putnam, 1994).

31. James Chandler, "Blake and the Syntax of Sentiment: An Essay on 'Blaking' Understanding," in *Blake, Nation and Empire*, ed. Steve Clark and David Worrall (Basingstoke: Palgrave, 2006), 104. Further citations are to this text. The other essays on Blake's relation to sentimentalism are by Jon Mee, "Bloody Blake: Nation and Circulation," 63–82, and Susan Matthews, "Blake, Hayley and the History of Sexuality," 83–101.

32. "Adverse emotion" will become a leading concept in the second half of this book, when we consider Blake's engagement with eighteenth-century models of sympathy as a primary example of his critical work in and on the emotions. Chandler approaches this idea closely when he draws on language from *Jerusalem* (13:12–14, E 156) to describe how critical emotions exert reverse pressure in Blake's mechanical system of cogs and wheels. For my account of "adverse emotion," see the introduction to Part Two, "A Passion for Blake," where the same passage from *Jerusalem* serves as an epigraph.

33. See Kevis Goodman, *Georgic Modernity and British Romanticism: Poetry and the Mediation of History* (Cambridge: Cambridge UP, 2004), and Mary A. Favret, *War at a Distance: Romanticism and the Making of Modern Wartime* (Princeton: Princeton UP, 2010). For Good-

man's illuminating discussion of Williams's "structures of feeling," see *Georgic Modernity,* 5–7, which anticipates Pfau's own adaptation of this important concept (*Romantic Moods,* 68). For Favret's understanding of the term (as mediated by Goodman), see 57–59. Also rewarding in this vein is Miranda Burgess's discussion of the close relation between Romantic "transport" and the pervasive but unfathomable dynamics of transportation that allowed for the global circulation of affects, goods, and people in the period. Although she does not employ Williams's terminology, Burgess's treatment of anxiety in the period "upholds Pfau's argument for 'mood' " (257) ("Transport: Mobility, Anxiety, and the Romantic Poetics of Feeling," *Studies in Romanticism* 49 [Summer 2010]: 229–260).

34. Although he borrows the term "openness" from Hölderlin (*das Offene*), Pfau's use of the "unpresentable" will inevitably recall Lyotard's interpretation of the Kantian sublime. Returning to an "unknown, perhaps unpresentable 'openness,' " literature exercises the reverse grammar of the sublime, which, as Lyotard describes it, places the question mark *before* the question itself, holding onto the unformed event of agitated uncertainty before the mind begins to shape experience by formulating its questions. "That it happens 'precedes,' so to speak, the question pertaining to what happens . . . The event happens as a question mark 'before' happening as a question" (Jean-François Lyotard, "The Sublime and the Avant-Garde" [originally published 1984], in *The Lyotard Reader,* ed. Andrew Benjamin [Cambridge: Basil Blackwell, 1989], 197).

35. "In such instances, the georgic mode can act as a shield against the possibility of sensory over-extension that shadows both the technologies of the new science and the territorial growth of nation and empire, but it is also an *aperture,* disclosing the pressures it might seek to cover" (Goodman, *Georgic Modernity,* 12).

36. In the 1790s, as Pfau describes that decade, the reliability of one's own immediate experience becomes a problem for the critique of ideology. For how could one ever be confident in the testimony of experience if (and here I am quoting Pfau's expert rendition of the axiom underlying the decade's suspicious hermeneutics) *"the experience of the real hinges on one's constant preparedness to distrust the reality of experience and to expose the latter as so many ideological frames conspiring against our genuine access to the real"* (*Romantic Moods,* 20, original emphasis)? In these circumstances, "mood" too may be just another (though better disguised) veil separating subjective experience from the real.

37. Adela Pinch, *Strange Fits of Passion: Epistemologies of Emotion, Hume to Austen* (Stanford: Stanford UP, 1996), 15; Riley, *Impersonal Passion*; Terada, *Feeling in Theory,* 3. Seeking to overturn a longstanding humanist tradition that "casts emotion as proof of the human subject," Terada argues that emotion has always been "poststructuralist" and indeed "requires the death of the subject" (*Feeling in Theory,* 4).

38. By the time of *On the Aesthetic Education of Man, in a Series of Letters,* Friedrich Schiller was already noting how ordinary discourse expresses the anonymity involved in certain emotional states: "For this condition of self-loss under the dominion of feeling linguistic usage has the very appropriate expression: to be beside oneself, i.e., to be outside one's own Self" (ed. and trans. Elizabeth M. Wilkinson and L. A. Willoughby [Oxford: Clarendon, 1967], 79).

39. Favret, "The Study of Affect and Romanticism," 1162.

40. Jacques Khalip, *Anonymous Life: Romanticism and Dispossession* (Stanford: Stanford UP, 2009), 1. Further citations are to this text. Although *Anonymous Life* focuses on the younger Romantics, it resonates with readings of Blake that emphasize "the unhappiness

of the subject within its own subjectivity" (Quinney, *William Blake on Self and Soul*, 11). Quinney's account of the soul's Gnostic determination to unlimit the personal self shares in Khalip's understanding of Romanticism as a movement generally committed to undoing identity, but her Bloomian emphasis on an internal and transcendental quest is often incompatible with the terms of Khalip's study.

41. Susan J. Wolfson, *Formal Charges: The Shaping of Poetry in British Romanticism* (Stanford: Stanford UP, 1997), 232.

42. The idea that emotion decenters and redistributes attention recurs throughout Reddy's *The Navigation of Feeling*. Given that the mind can attend to "only a tiny fraction of [the data] available" (15) to it through the senses and memory, unexpected emotions "reflect a monitoring process that makes up, in part, for the narrow focus of consciousness at any given moment" (25). Ronald De Souza states a similar idea in these terms: "More subtly, [emotions] influence decisions not so much by 'motivating' as by orienting attention toward this or that among the plethora of considerations that might be thought relevant at any particular juncture" ("Emotions: What I Know, What I'd Like To Think I Know, and What I'd Like To Think," in *Thinking about Feeling: Contemporary Philosophers on Emotions*, ed. Robert C. Solomon [Oxford: Oxford UP, 2004], 65).

43. René Descartes, *The Passions of the Soul*, trans. Stephen Voss (Indianapolis: Hackett, 1989), 52.

44. Fisher, *The Vehement Passions*, 1.

45. Ngai, *Ugly Feelings*, 14.

46. Samuel Taylor Coleridge, *Biographia Literaria*, ed. James Engell and W. Jackson Bate, 2 vols., in vol. 7 of *The Collected Works of Samuel Taylor Coleridge*, Bollingen Series (Princeton: Princeton UP, 1983), II:7; Percy Bysshe Shelley, "Defence of Poetry," in *Shelley's Poetry and Prose*, ed. Donald H. Reiman and Neil Fraistat (New York: Norton, 2002), 533.

47. I am referring to the titles of Nussbaum's *Upheavals of Thought* and a volume edited by Brian Massumi, *A Shock to Thought: Expression after Deleuze and Guattari* (London: Routledge, 2002).

48. Fisher, *The Vehement Passions*, 43–45; Massumi, *Parables for the Virtual*, 34, 28; Terada, *Feeling in Theory*, 3–4; Goodman, *Georgic Modernity*, 9–10. Massumi's definitions of "affect" and "emotion" have been especially influential. See, e.g., Eric Shouse's brief explication of Massumi's terms in "Feeling, Emotion, Affect," which starts from the following definitions: "Feelings are *personal* and *biographical*, emotions are *social*, and affects are *prepersonal*." "The power of affect," he concludes, "lies in the fact that it is unformed and unstructured" (*M/C Journal* 8.6 (2005), http://journal.media-culture.org.au/0512/03-shouse.php).

49. The arbitrariness and at best heuristic value of the standard terminology has become the object of endless complaint among literary and cultural theorists of emotion, as well as among some philosophers. William James was unsparing on the topic: "The merely descriptive literature of the subject, from Descartes downwards, is one of the most tedious parts of psychology. And not only is it tedious, but you feel that its subdivisions are to a great extent either fictitious or unimportant, and that its pretences to accuracy are a sham" (*Psychology: The Briefer Course*, ed. Gordon Allport [New York: Harper, 1961], 241). Amelie Oksenberg Rorty offers a similarly grim assessment in her essay, "Enough Already with 'Theories of the Emotions.'" Rorty stages a series of questions—"Is greed a motive, an emotion, a character trait? Is joy a mood? A feeling? . . . Is love a passion, an emotion, a sentiment?"—in order to argue that "any sensible person would refuse to answer" such questions, the emptiness of

which can only serve to indicate "how subtle, how complex the 'emotions' are" (in Solomon, *Thinking about Feeling*, 269). Throughout this book I use "emotion," "affect," and "feeling" almost interchangeably, not because I ignore distinctions among the intellectual or physiological aspects of these experiences, but because I wish to emphasize the mutual shading of mind and body that renders any firm distinction among terms insupportable.

50. Altieri carries this preference for disturbance into the very issue of terminology, usefully distinguishing between "adjectival" and "adverbial" treatments of affect. The former treats emotions as relatively uniform and easily categorized states, which subjects enter into: thus we say, the *sad* subject, the *angry* subject, the *jealous* subject, and so forth. Alternatively, the adverbial method treats emotions as complex, qualitative actions that require more dynamic description than simple naming allows. Altieri warns "that we cannot even name most of the emotions that matter to us. Many compelling affective states do not have names or are experienced as efforts to move among names to some more appropriate predicate" (*The Particulars of Rapture*, 11).

51. Martha Nussbaum, "Emotions as Judgments of Value and Importance," in *What Is an Emotion?* ed. Robert C. Solomon (Oxford: Oxford UP, 2003), 281. The "cognitive theory" of the emotions argues that "emotions are more like judgments or thoughts than perceptions," as Jesse Prinze puts it in "Embodied Emotions," in Solomon, *Thinking about Feeling*, 44. On the dominance of the "cognitive theory" in studies of emotion, Robert Solomon writes: "The cognitive theory has become the touchstone of all philosophical theorizing about emotion, for or against. It used to be the battering ram (in its various guises) against the primitivist theories of [William] James and his successors. Now it is the target of neurologically based 'precognitivist' theories of emotion." Solomon schematizes the backlash against the cognitive theory as the pitting of a new slogan ("Emotion precedes cognition") against an old one (Emotions are judgments) ("Emotions, Thoughts, and Feelings," also in *Thinking about Feeling*, 78). For an implicit defense of the cognitive theory against the recently ascendant "anti-intentionalist paradigm" (469) favored by many cultural theorists and social scientists (though not philosophers), see Leys, "The Turn to Affect: A Critique," 434–472.

52. Altieri, *The Particulars of Rapture*, 31 and 12.

53. Sharon Cameron, *Impersonality* (Chicago: U of Chicago P, 2007), 7. Further citations are to this text.

54. Paul de Man, "Kant's Materialism," in *Aesthetic Ideology*, ed. Andrzej Warminski (Minneapolis: U of Minnesota P, 1996), 127.

55. See Chap. 2, "Pathos (Allegories of Emotion)," of Terada, *Feeling in Theory*, 48–89.

56. Terada quotes from Keats's "Drear-Nighted December" in *Feeling in Theory*, 14.

57. This phrase appears at line 1691 of *Samson Agonistes*, a text that will play a central role in chapter 2. See *The Riverside Milton*, ed. Roy Flannagan (Boston: Houghton Mifflin, 1998), 842.

58. As Ian Balfour aptly puts it, the corporate subject formed by this reception renders "the singularity of the proper name . . . at best a convenient fiction" (*The Rhetoric of Romantic Prophecy* [Stanford: Stanford UP, 2002], 157). "One of the spectacular features of Blake's poem," he observes, "is the striking series of incorporations that occur when one figure after another—Milton, Blake, the Bard, Los—are folded into one another" (157).

59. Nicholas Williams astutely reads this scene as a reflection on the problem of representing motion. Drawing on Maurice Merleau-Ponty's distinction between logical and nonthetic perspectives and Brian Massumi's account of a "subject who cannot feel himself move

and see himself move at the same time," Williams explains why Blake can retrospectively name the moving object he claims he did not recognize at the time.

> The oddness of Blake's retrospective report on the falling object—"I knew not that it was Milton"—itself reflects the representational bind of depicting motion . . . [T]he first-person perspective here fractures between a perspective that can see motion but "knew not" the thing in motion and one that ends motion in order to know it. By thematizing this problem, however, Blake points to the unavailable Living Form that could conceivably represent motion—or, rather, he points to the living experience of motion that representation stubbornly excludes . . . Only when "periods of Space & Time" have allowed the thetic consciousness to catch up with its "earthly lineaments" will the experience of motion be resolved into a propertied, known, and, for all purposes, stationary object. ("Blake Dead or Alive," 496–497)

60. See Balfour's useful comments on these lines: "Blake's inability to recognize Milton for who he is 'until periods of Space & Time reveal the secrets of Eternity' is one crucial instance of a pervasive deferral of knowledge or at least of a pervasive uncertainty about whether or not (something like) the Apocalypse has arrived" (*The Rhetoric of Romantic Prophecy*, 165).

61. "Nether" also has a long history of erotic connotation, as when Chaucer's bawdy Miller relates how Absolon was tricked into kissing Alisoun's "nether yë" (*The Miller's Tale*, in *The Riverside Chaucer*, ed. Larry D. Benson [Boston: Houghton Mifflin, 1987], l. 3852, p. 77). By placing the term in such close proximity to "member," Blake is reclaiming its eroticism from Milton, who has Sin describe her hideous embodiment in terms of the deformity of her "nether regions": "All my nether shape thus grew transformed" (*Paradise Lost*, II.784, in *The Riverside Milton*, 404).

62. Wai Chee Dimock, "Nonbiological Clock: Literary History against Newtonian Mechanics," *SAQ* 102.1 (Winter 2003): 163. Dimock goes on to empty this foot of all substance, claiming, "It has become a cipher, an entry point to dimensions of space and time not computable by any biological clock" (163). She also asserts that literary history becomes Blake's escape from biological finitude: "As a biological individual Blake is completely under the thumb of Newton. His days are numbered. Only literary history can give him days that are not: days that stretch backward and forward, weaving in and out of other days, an indeterminate fabric" (164).

63. Georges Bataille sheds some light on Blake's symbolic inversion when he discusses "Man's secret horror of his foot" in "The Big Toe," in *Visions of Excess: Selected Writings, 1927–1939*, ed. and trans. Alan Stoekl (Minneapolis: U of Minnesota P, 1985), 21. Of this bias against the foot, Bataille writes: "with their feet in mud but their heads more or less in light, men obstinately imagine a tide that will permanently elevate them, never to return, into pure space. Human life entails, in fact, the rage of seeing oneself as a back and forth movement from refuse to the ideal, and from the ideal to refuse—a rage that is easily directed against an organ as *base* as the foot" (20–21).

64. Kenzaburo Oe underscores this tactic in his novel *Rouse Up O Young Men of the New Age!* when the narrator turns to *Milton* to explain his mentally disabled son's "unreasoning love for, or at least extraordinary interest in, his father's feet." Rather than approaching his father directly, the child "seeks a handhold at the 'margins' of his father's body," for "the head, face, chest, and other parts which constitute the body's center appear to be connected

directly to the individual's, in this case to my own, consciousness, but the feet are at a distance, beyond the reach of consciousness." For Oe's narrator, the arrival of Milton's spirit "at Blake's core by entering through the tarsus" indicates the pathway of an alternative sympathy, one that passes through the "nether" rather than the upper "Regions of the Imagination," and one that, rather than requiring the face-to-face recognition of securely established subjects, enables them to be moved indirectly without precisely knowing by what or by whom (*Rouse Up O Young Men of the New Age!*, trans. John Nathan [New York: Grove, 2002], 122–123). Oe titles this chapter "The Soul Descends as a Falling Star, to the Bone at My Heel."

65. Richard C. Sha, *Perverse Romanticism: Aesthetics and Sexuality in Britain, 1750–1832* (Baltimore: Johns Hopkins UP, 2009), 206.

66. Friedrich Nietzsche, "On Truth and Lying in a Non-Moral Sense," trans. Ronald Speirs, in *Nietzsche: The Birth of Tragedy and Other Writings*, ed. Raymond Geuss and Ronald Speirs (Cambridge: Cambridge UP, 1999 [written 1873]), 142.

67. Nietzsche, "On Truth and Lying in a Non-Moral Sense," 142.

68. Blake, "There is No Natural Religion," sequence [b], E 3.

69. Gertrude Stein, *The Making of Americans: Being a History of a Family's Progress* (Normal, IL: Dalkey Archive Press, 1995 [1925]), 294. See Ngai's valuable discussion of this term in *Ugly Feelings*, esp. 283–284.

70. Williams, "Blake Dead or Alive," 488. Along these lines, Denise Gigante's "Blake's Living Form: *Jerusalem*," in *Life: Organic Form and Romanticism* (New Haven: Yale UP, 2009), reads *Jerusalem* as a "poetics of epigenesis on an epic scale" (108). Gigante wants to emphasize what critics until recently have tended to ignore: Blake's "deployment of the specific properties of living matter, namely generation (the production of new living forms) and vegetation (the growth of living forms), which figure at the core of his visionary system" (108–109). In *Perverse Romanticism*, Richard Sha argues that "transcendence in Blake goes through as opposed to above the body." Sha situates Blake within his era's medical discourse to show that, though aware of "what can go wrong with the body," Blake also "knew what could go right" (208). Also see Noel Jackson, *Science and Sensation in Romantic Poetry* (Cambridge: Cambridge UP, 2008). Jackson places Blake's narratives of body formation within a "history of the senses" (65), emphasizing Blake's awareness of the dialectical relation between bodily and historical development, such that "historical time . . . emerge[s] coevally with that of the body" (92).

71. This quotation and the next are both from William James, "What Is an Emotion?" in *Mind* 9 (1884): 191–192.

72. Voltaire, *Philosophical Dictionary*, trans. Peter Gay, 2 vols. (New York: Basic Books, 1962), 1:251.

73. By calling James a radical empiricist I am borrowing from the title of his *Essays in Radical Empiricism* (Lincoln: U of Nebraska P, 1996).

74. Those who wish to discredit the James-Lange thesis (which posits that emotions do not precede physiological changes but are identical to those changes) sometimes assert that the body's mechanisms are insufficiently subtle and varied to account for the nuances of emotion. They may (or may not) have current science on their side, but they are not good readers of James. For James, the sensible body is a source of affections "almost infinitely numerous and subtle," and *"every change that occurs must be felt"* ("What Is an Emotion?" 193, my emphasis). Drawing on Walter B. Cannon's early critique of James, Jerome Neu has argued that visceral responses are simply too similar across emotional states to account for

their differences. If one were to ground these differences in a deeper level of bodily response, Neu continues, then one must have recourse to some nonsensical idea of "unfelt feelings": "If one starts appealing to physiological changes too subtle actually to be felt, then the differences in emotions are reduced to differences in unfelt feelings, and it becomes mysterious how we manage to make the emotional discriminations we do in fact make" (*A Tear is an Intellectual Thing: The Meanings of Emotion* [Oxford: Oxford UP, 2000], 19). James, however, describes a nether region of embodied experience that can be felt without being translated into cognitive or discursive judgment. In this way, Blake lies closer to James than to Neu (despite that Neu borrows the intellectual tear in his book's title from Blake's *Jerusalem* [52, E 202]).

75. De Man, a materialist of another sort, once remarked on the trouble he had driving a car after reading in a newspaper that "for every 100 metres one drives one has at least thirty-six decisions to make" ("Aesthetic Formalization: Kleist's *Über das Marionettentheater*," in *The Rhetoric of Romanticism* [New York: Columbia UP, 1984], 277). Imagine, then, the challenge of continuing on as a subject after becoming aware of the host of hidden events routinely driving one's personality. Writes Tristanne Connolly: "[T]he body is as alien as it is commonplace, as unfathomable as it is known: think of how many involuntary movements, such as heartbeat, are essential to its regular functioning, and how unexpectedly and inexorably disease and death can overtake the body" (*William Blake and the Body* [Basingstoke: Palgrave, 2002], vii).

76. In a series of experiments from the early 1880s, the Italian physiologist Angelo Mosso (1846–1910) developed new laboratory instruments to study the otherwise undetectable physiological changes accompanying states of emotion. When a subject inserted his arm into Mosso's plethysmograph—a sealed, water-filled glass tube connected to a graphing device—the apparatus measured the subject's blood flow, tracing the slightest dilation and contraction of the vessels by recording the limb's volumetric changes. See Otniel E. Dror, "The Scientific Image of Emotion: Experience and Technologies of Inscription," *Configurations* 7.3 (1999): 358 and figure 3.

77. William James, *Psychology: The Briefer Course*, 29. James explains, "There is not a conjunction or a preposition, and hardly an adverbial phrase, syntactic form, or inflection of voice, in human speech, that does not express some shading or other of relation which we at some moment actually feel to exist between the larger objects of our thought" (29). Were one to apply this description of linguistic affectivity, like an analytical lens, to James's account of the bodily interior quoted above, scrutinizing each of its *ands, ifs,* and *buts,* one would quickly realize that James is not transparently surveying his subject but attempting to induce in his reader some of the same affective changes he attributes to the viscera in general.

78. The minute particular, such an important aspect of Blake's aesthetic discourse, is kin to Kant's reflective judgment, in which the mind does not subsume particularity under a concept but instead experiences it as a feeling with no available predicate or concept: "only the particular is given, for which the universal is [yet] to be found" (*Critique of the Power of Judgment*, ed. and trans. Paul Guyer and Eric Matthews [Cambridge: Cambridge UP, 2000], 67). Blakean particularization also bears resemblance to what Adorno, modifying Kant, calls "second reflection." Rather than opposing determinative and reflective judgment, as Kant does, Adorno suggests that the former will inevitably arrive at its limits and give way to the latter, as a succession of phases in a single process. Active and focused contemplation of an artwork (first reflection) will increase knowledge but will also make the intellect aware of a

dark content it is incapable of illuminating (second reflection). "As reflection increases in scope and power, content itself becomes ever more opaque" (*Aesthetic Theory*, ed. and trans. Robert Hullot-Kentor [Minneapolis: U of Minnesota P, 1997], 27). We will return to Adorno's second reflection in chapter 4.

79. Joanna Picciotto, *Labors of Innocence in Early Modern England*, 5–6. Further citations are to this text.

80. Noting that the text of the poem's last plate consists of a single, unpunctuated line ("To go forth to the Great Harvest & Vintage of the Nations"), Frye describes *Milton*'s conclusion in musical terms as "an expectant dominant seventh," there to remind us that *Milton* "is the prelude to a longer poem [*Jerusalem*] on the theme it announces" (*Fearful Symmetry: A Study of William Blake* [Princeton: Princeton UP, 1947], 355). Others, like Quinney, hear anxiety in the poem's lack of resolution: "*Milton* stutters, ending on a liminal note. The poem takes us to the verge of apocalypse and stops there, unwilling to cross the border into Utopia" (*William Blake on Self and Soul*, 152). My own sense is that Blake is trying to prolong the period of incompletion, as if one could stretch the time of enjambment that carries over from plate 49 to 50 and thereby always go forth, without having to arrive. I am reminded of Mallarmé's reverie "The Demon of Analogy," in which the speaker inexplicably finds himself intoning the enjambed phrase, "The Penultimate / Is Dead": "I said it with a silence after 'Penultimate,' in which I felt a painful pleasure: 'The Penultimate,' then the taut forgotten string, stretched over the *nul* sound, which broke, no doubt, and I added, in the manner of a funeral oration, 'Is dead'" (trans. Barbara Johnson, in *Divagations* [Cambridge, MA: Harvard UP, 2007], 17–18). The nonending of *Milton* is like a refusal to complete (and thus kill) the penultimate.

81. Given the broad and dynamic materialism that informs the term "emotion," even the two early sciences most often dismissed as mechanistic, physics and chemistry, become relevant to the study of Romantic era emotion, for they are also "the two disciplines that had the most to say about movement" (1). Examining "The Motion Behind Romantic Emotion," Richard Sha has demonstrated how eighteenth-century discourses on force (matter in motion) humanized the material world by infusing it with affective vitality but also troubled the "human" by identifying emotion with strictly mechanical movements. Sha suggests that echoes of this "vital mechanicity" can be heard today in discourses that turn to emotion in order to salvage agency of some kind, with or without subjects: "It seems that we are still harnessing the elasticity of force either to grant ourselves agency at the expense of a mechanistic materiality, or to emphasize the vitality of matter in hopes that the mechanical automaticity of our emotions will not disallow the possibility of choice or will" ("The Motion Behind Romantic Emotion: Towards a Chemistry and Physics of Feeling"; manuscript quoted by permission of the author).

82. Milton, *Paradise Regain'd*, I. 91–93, in *The Riverside Milton*, 724.

83. Milton, *Paradise Regain'd*, IV. 197, in *The Riverside Milton*, 769.

84. "Modern man," writes Foucault, "is not the man who goes off to discover himself, his secrets and his hidden truth; he is the man who tries to invent himself" ("What Is Enlightenment?" in Rabinow, *The Foucault Reader*, 42). Here Foucault is explicating Baudelaire, but the statement lies very close to the program he calls a "critical ontology of ourselves" (47).

85. See the useful notes to these lines provided by Robert N. Essick and Joseph Viscomi in the Blake Trust / Princeton edition of *Milton a Poem* (Princeton: Princeton UP, 1993),

188–189. Essick and Viscomi point out that Hillel is linked to "heylel," Hebrew for the morning star, and thus to "Lucifer."

86. Hillel's call for a life of self-critique belongs to the history of Enlightenment as Foucault redefines it: "[I]t has to be conceived as an attitude, an ethos, a philosophical life in which the critique of what we are is at one and the same time the historical analysis of the limits that are imposed on us and an experiment with the possibility of going beyond them" ("What Is Enlightenment?" 50). Quinney has also usefully linked Hillel's instructions to Foucault: "It is not a question of returning to, or recalling, a lost self. You must altogether remake yourself or, more pointedly, remake your self. Despite Blake's quarrel with Stoicism, his prescription resembles the Stoic injunction to self-transformation, as Foucault analyzes it in *The Hermeneutics of the Subject*: the goal is to 'become again what we should have been but never were' "; see *William Blake on Self and Soul*, 23.

87. See Jacob Bronowski, *William Blake: A Man without a Mask*, originally published in 1944, reissued as *William Blake and the Age of Revolution* (London: Routledge and Kegan Paul, 1972); Mark Schorer, *William Blake: The Politics of Vision* (New York: Henry Holt, 1946); and David V. Erdman, *Blake: Prophet against Empire: A Poet's Interpretation of the History of His Own Times* (Princeton: Princeton UP, 1954).

88. Milton, *Samson Agonistes*, 1704–1705, in *The Riverside Milton*, 843.

89. Sartre, *The Emotions: Outline of a Theory*, trans. Bernard Frechtman (New York: Philosophical Library, 1948), 58–60.

90. See the first three parts of Joseph Viscomi's *Blake and the Idea of the Book* (Princeton: Princeton UP, 1993): "Invention," "Execution," and "Production," 1–149. For a brief summary of Blake's production methods, see Viscomi, "Illuminated Printing," in *The Cambridge Companion to William Blake*, ed. Morris Eaves (Cambridge: Cambridge UP, 2003), 37–62.

91. Samuel Taylor Coleridge, *Biographia Literaria*, I:146–147. Further citations are to this text.

92. Kant, "An Answer to the Question: 'What Is Enlightenment?' " in *Kant: Political Writings*, trans. H. B. Nisbet, ed. Hans Reiss (Cambridge: Cambridge UP, 1991 [1784]), 54.

93. See Mee, *Romanticism, Enthusiasm, and Regulation*, 167 ff.

94. Of course, it is possible that Blake played this role for Coleridge too. Less than a year after publishing the *Biographia*, Coleridge commented on a copy of *Songs of Innocence and Of Experience*, borrowed from Charles Augustus Tulk, in terms vaguely echoing those used to describe Boehme: "He is a man of Genius—and I apprehend, a Swedenborgian—certainly, a mystic *emphatically*" (letter to H. F. Cary, Feb. 6, 1818, in *Blake Records*, ed. G. E. Bentley Jr. [New Haven: Yale UP, 2004], 336).

95. Frye, *Fearful Symmetry*, 374.

Chapter 1 · Blake's Agitation

1. Unless otherwise noted, all dictionary references in this chapter refer to the *Oxford English Dictionary* (*OED*).

2. Likening the aesthetic state she calls "animatedness" to "agitation," Sianne Ngai observes a slippage between affective turbulence and political agency similar to the one I am describing: "In its association with movement and activity, animatedness bears a semantic proximity to 'agitation,' a term which is likewise used in the philosophical discourse to des-

ignate a feeling prior to its articulation into a more complex passion, but that also underlies the contemporary meaning of the political agitator or activist" (*Ugly Feelings* [Cambridge, MA: Harvard UP, 2005], 31).

3. Samuel Johnson, entry for "agitation," *A Dictionary of the English Language* (London: W. Strahan, 1755).

4. Immanuel Kant, "Announcement of the Near Conclusion of a Treaty for Eternal Peace in Philosophy," in *Raising the Tone of Philosophy: Late Essays by Immanuel Kant, Transformative Critique by Jacques Derrida*, ed. and trans. Peter Fenves (Baltimore: Johns Hopkins UP, 1993), 83.

5. Blake, letter to Reverend Dr. John Trussler, Aug. 23, 1799, E 702.

6. The *OED* also quotes Robert Boyle, who described bringing water to a boil as "agitating water into froth" (*The origine of formes and qualities, according to the corpuscular philosophy*, 1667). The image of a watery surface whipped into turbulence underlies one of the two instances in which Blake himself employs the word "agitation." On the penultimate page of "Night the Ninth" of *The Four Zoas*, Blake describes "the stormy seas" that "Eddying fierce rejoice in the fierce agitation of the wheels / Of Dark Urthona" (138:5–7, E 406). In the other instance (*Jerusalem* 88:8, E 246), "agitation" also describes an intensification of elemental movement building toward an apocalyptic climax, this time in terms of earthquake.

7. William Blake, *Jerusalem*, ed. Morton Paley (Princeton: Princeton UP, 1991), 130.

8. Regarding a similarly loud passage in *The Four Zoas*, Robert Essick suggests that Blake "may be our noisiest poet" (*William Blake and the Language of Adam* [Oxford: Oxford UP, 1989], 173).

9. Calling paranoia "a situation of extreme interpretive agitation and urgency" (80–81), Pfau suggests that "no other writer's oeuvre is more richly informed by paranoid and conspiratorial figures than William Blake's" (98). As depicted in the frontispiece to *Jerusalem*, Los is one of these figures (*Romantic Moods: Paranoia, Trauma, and Melancholy, 1790–1840* [Baltimore: Johns Hopkins UP, 2005]). The frontispiece also anticipates the process of subject formation Althusser called "interpellation." Pausing at the threshold to turn his head, perhaps in answer to a voice from behind ("Hey, you there!"), Los remains trapped within the fallen subject-form he seems determined to leave behind. In Althusser's hypothetical scene, the individual hailed by a policeman "turn[s] around" and by means of "this mere one-hundred-and-eighty-degree physical conversion . . . becomes a subject" (Louis Althusser, "Ideology and Ideological State Apparatuses," in *Lenin and Philosophy*, trans. Ben Brewster [New York: Monthly Review Press, 1971], 174).

10. Jean-François Lyotard, "The Sign of History," trans. Geoff Bennington, in *The Lyotard Reader*, ed. Andrew Benjamin (Oxford: Blackwell, 1989), 394.

11. Lyotard refers to the informal grouping of Kant's "historical-political texts" as a "fourth Critique" (*The Differend: Phrases in Dispute*, trans. Georges Van Den Abbeele [Minneapolis: U of Minnesota P, 1988], xiii). For a contrary view, see Hannah Arendt's claim that these essays "certainly do not constitute a 'Fourth Critique,'" since the real kernel of Kant's political philosophy is to be found in the Third Critique on aesthetic judgment (*Lectures on Kant's Political Philosophy*, ed. Ronald Beiner [Chicago: U of Chicago P, 1982], 7–9).

12. Immanuel Kant, *The Conflict of the Faculties*, trans. and ed. Mary J. Gregor (Lincoln: U of Nebraska P: 1979 [1798]), 165.

13. Jean-François Lyotard, "Judiciousness in Dispute, or Kant after Marx," trans. Cecile Lindsay, in *The Lyotard Reader*, 327–328.

14. Lyotard, "The Sign of History," 394.

15. "There is a Moment in each Day that Satan cannot find / Nor can his Watch Fiends find it" (*Milton* 35 [39]: 42–43, E 136). To identify this moment with the sublime is useful theoretically but askew to Blake's own use of the term. Blake did not privilege the "sublime" to the same extent as his contemporaries, in part because common usage made it synonymous with obscurity and thus incompatible with his commitment to line drawing. Thus he could write in the Reynolds annotations, "Obscurity is Neither the Source of the Sublime nor of any Thing Else" (E 658), and in *Jerusalem*, he could describe Jerusalem herself as "A sublime ornament not obscuring the outlines of beauty" (86:15–16, E 244). For a full account of Blake's engagement with the period's aesthetics of sublimity, see Vincent Arthur De Luca, *Words of Eternity: Blake and the Poetics of the Sublime* (Princeton: Princeton UP, 1991).

16. Jerome Christensen, *Lord Byron's Strength* (Baltimore: Johns Hopkins UP, 1993), 181.

17. Kant, "Announcement," 84, 87.

18. Ibid., 88. Elsewhere, Kant argues that the British monarch must be considered an absolute monarch because his power to declare war exceeds any formal limitations placed upon him by the constitution. "What is an *absolute* monarch? He is one at whose command, if he says, 'war is necessary,' a state of war immediately exists. What is a *limited* monarch, on the other hand? He who must first consult the people as to whether war is or is not to be . . . Now the British monarch has conducted wars aplenty without seeking the consent for them. Therefore this king is an absolute monarch who ought not to be one, of course, according to the constitution" (*Conflict of the Faculties*, 163).

19. Nelson Hilton considers this a representative pun in Blake's "polysemous and multidimensional practice," summarizing Blake's point as "to worship is to warship" (*Literal Imagination: Blake's Vision of Words* [Berkeley and Los Angeles: U of California P, 1983]), 17–18. Morris Eaves, however, reminds me that Blake's *o* and *a* are often indistinguishable, leaving "warshipped" an uncertain reading.

20. Blake uses the word "bonify" three times in three lines, including: "They flee over the rocks bonifying: Horses: Oxen: feel the knife. / And while the Sons of Albion by severe War & Judgment, bonify" (58:9–10, E 207). For Napoleon as Old Boney, see Alan Liu, *Wordsworth: The Sense of History* (Stanford: Stanford UP, 1989), esp. 437–440.

21. Lyotard, "Judiciousness in Dispute," 331.

22. Ibid.

23. Ibid., 357.

24. Resisting the violence of generalization per se, Blake predates (just as Lyotard echoes) Walter Benjamin, who argues in "Critique of Violence" that general law "contradicts the nature of justice": "For ends that for one situation are just, universally acceptable, and valid, are so for no other situation, no matter how similar it may be in other respects" (trans. Edmund Jephcott, in *Reflections*, ed. Peter Demetz [New York: Schocken Books, 1978 (1921)], 294). Pfau also notes Blake's anticipation of Benjamin in this regard; see *Romantic Moods*, 100. In Blake's antinomian discourse, Mosaic law is inherently violent and must be rejected: "No Individual can keep these Laws, for they are death / To every energy of man, and forbid the springs of life" (31:11–12, E 177).

25. Lyotard, "Judiciousness in Dispute," 333.

26. In a passage in *Jerusalem* closely echoing this one in *Milton*, Los views "all that has existed in the space of six thousand years: / Permanent, & not lost not lost nor vanishd, & every little act, / Word, work, & wish, that has existed, all remaining still . . . / For every thing

exists & not one sigh nor smile nor tear, / One hair nor particle of dust, not one can pass away" (13:59–14:1, E 157–158).

27. As we saw in the introduction, Frye and Makdisi both emphasize the intellectual vigor and mobility required of Blake's readers, the former in terms of "allusive agility," the latter in terms of continuous "striving." We will return to this aspect of Makdisi in chapter 5.

28. Paul de Man, "Phenomenality and Materiality in Kant," in *Aesthetic Ideology*, ed. Andrzej Warminski (Minneapolis: U of Minnesota P, 1996), 90.

29. Frances Ferguson, *Solitude and the Sublime: Romanticism and the Aesthetics of Individuation* (New York: Routledge, 1992), 14.

30. Martin Jay, " 'The Aesthetic Ideology' as Ideology: Or What Does It Mean to Aestheticize Politics?" in *Force Fields* (New York: Routledge, 1993), 81. For another critique of the politics of extreme particularism, see Alan Liu, "Local Transcendence: Cultural Criticism, Postmodernism, and the Romanticism of Detail," *Representations* 32 (1990): 75–113.

31. This theme recurs often in the annotations to Reynolds and elsewhere in *Jerusalem*: "Art & Science cannot exist but in minutely organized Particulars" (55:62, E 205).

32. Barrell charged Blake studies generally with a symptomatic misreading of Blake as a champion of liberalism, targeting Eaves specifically: "Blake becomes a founding father of the liberal individualism which has been the prevailing ideology of 'Blake Studies,' and which can understand the public only as an invasion of private space" (John Barrell, *The Political Theory of Painting from Reynolds to Hazlitt* [New Haven: Yale UP, 1986], 224). Eaves responds: "It is exceedingly difficult if not perverse to erase the celebration of individual expression from Blake's work . . . So surely does he seem to share the 'fundamentally individualistic bias' of Protestantism, which Christopher Hill and many others have connected with the 'insistence that each believer should look inward to his own heart,' that it seems finally impossible to save Blake from the house of romanticism that individualizes and internalizes Christian discourse with increasing emphasis on psychology, the creative imagination, and the connection of art ('vision') with that mental faculty, pestering old metaphors of divinity in the process" (Morris Eaves, *The Counter-Arts Conspiracy: Art and Industry in the Age of Blake* [Ithaca: Cornell UP, 1992], 151).

33. John Milton, *A soveraigne salve to cure the blind* (London: Printed by T. P. and M. S., 1643), 33. Quoted in *OED* entry for "agitate."

34. Immanuel Kant, *Perpetual Peace*, trans. and ed. Lewis White Beck (Indianapolis: Bobbs-Merrill, 1957 [1795]), 14.

35. Jürgen Habermas, "The Model Case of British Development," in *The Structural Transformation of the Public Sphere*, trans. Thomas Burger (Cambridge: Cambridge UP, 1989), 57–67; quotation (of German historian K. Kluxen) from p. 60.

36. Thomas Sheridan, *A Course of Lectures on Elocution* (London, 1762); Hugh Blair, *Lectures on Rhetoric and Belles Lettres* (Philadelphia, 1784); James Burgh, *The Art of Speaking* (Danbury, 1795). See Jay Fliegelman, *Declaring Independence: Jefferson, Natural Language, and the Culture of Performance* (Stanford: Stanford UP, 1993), esp. 28–35. Cited parenthetically hereafter.

37. Edmund Burke, *A Philosophical Enquiry into Our Ideas of the Sublime and Beautiful* (Oxford: Oxford UP, 1990 [1757]), 160.

38. Emphasizing his marginal status in the Joseph Johnson circle of liberal intellectuals and reformers, Jon Mee has argued that Blake's "vulgar enthusiasm functioned as the mark of unrespectability which excluded him" from the bourgeois public sphere he inhabited

peripherally and aspired to enter more fully (*Dangerous Enthusiasm: William Blake and the Culture of Radicalism in the 1790s* [Oxford: Clarendon, 1992], 224). Taking this idea a radical step further, Makdisi contends that Blake rejected the model of subjectivity presented by his social superiors just as forcefully as they rejected him. According to Makdisi, Blake's antinomianism put him fundamentally at odds with the rationalist self-discipline enshrined by bourgeois republicans like Tom Paine and John Thelwall, who argued that the "sovereign individual" earned the right "to exercise choice in politics and commerce" because of his "ability to regulate, control, [and] police" himself (*William Blake and the Impossible History of the 1790s*, 4).

39. Michael Warner, *The Letters of the Republic: Publication and the Public Sphere in Eighteenth-Century America* (Cambridge: Cambridge UP, 1990), 7–9. Modifying Habermas, Warner argues that national identity in prerevolutionary America developed through a print medium (a "Republic of Letters") in which power, freed from embodiment in special persons, was supposed to be constituted instead by a general discourse belonging to the public at large (the people). As we will see, Blake's experience of Enlightenment print culture is hardly one of simple antagonism, and even his attitude toward its commercial function is mixed and complex. Late in his career especially, after his own prospects had declined, Blake often ranted against commerce: "Commerce cannot endure Individual Merit its insatiable Maw must be fed by What all can do Equally," he exclaimed in the Public Address (E 573). In "The Laocoön," he added: "Where any view of Money exists Art cannot be carried on, but War only" (E 275). Views like these would put him directly at odds with liberals such as Kant, who claimed that "the spirit of commerce . . . is incompatible with war" (*Perpetual Peace*, 32) and believed that upward mobility through "talents, industry, and good fortune" (*Conflict of the Faculties*, 76) made capitalist society dynamic and inclusive, at least potentially. For Kant, "liveliest competition" (*Perpetual Peace*, 32) was an antidote to tyranny, whether it took place in the intellectual or economic marketplace. If this failure to distinguish between intellectual and commercial values seems anathema to Blake, we should remember that only two years prior to Kant's remarks in *Perpetual Peace*—in 1793, the peak year of the radical 1790s— Blake, too, was pitching his own talents, industry, and products in the commercial art world, claiming in a Prospectus that he would print his illuminated books on demand ("No Subscriptions . . . are asked") and "offer them to sale at a fair price" (E 693). As Eaves points out, despite its "inflated language," this Prospectus is pretty typical of late eighteenth-century advertising. Blake "anticipates that his new invention will provide the commercial platform for the display of individual talents and skills that will issue in marketable products," resulting in "a bourgeois independence . . . free from economic dependence on others" ("National Arts and Disruptive Technologies in Blake's Prospectus of 1793," in *Blake, Nation, and Empire*, ed. Steve Clark and David Worrall [Basingstoke: Palgrave, 2006], 126). Eaves's essay delivers on the editors' promise in *Blake, Nation, and Empire* to supplement the image of Blake as radical artisan with another view of him as a "small businessman, autodidact, an ambitious entrepreneur whose attitude to both nation and empire is ambiguous but far from uniformly hostile" (Clark and Worrall, introduction, 4).

40. Given the importance of the figure of the Bard in Blake's own work and in contemporary scholarship, it is curious that he chooses the word "Orator" here instead. For a useful survey of Blake's interest in the Bard, see Mee's chapter, "'Northern Antiquities': Bards, Druids, and Ancient Liberties," in *Dangerous Enthusiasm*, 75–120.

41. Blake's only other use of the word appears in a bit of notebook doggerel: "I asked my Dear Friend Orator Prig / Whats the first part of Oratory he said a great wig" (E 514).

42. On Blake's "radical social imagination," see James Swearingen, "William Blake's Figural Politics," *English Literary History* 59 (1992): 125–144, esp. 137. Against the idea that *Jerusalem* seems increasingly otherworldly and remote from practical politics, Swearingen argues, "Blake envisions a process of perpetual constituting that needs no legitimating principle because it locates the origin of power in the pluralism of 'Mental Warfare'" (127). Swearingen emphasizes the utopian potential of the public sphere in a way akin to Habermas, who claims that, at least in its formative stage, the bourgeois public sphere was "more than ideology": "If ideologies are not only manifestations of the socially necessary consciousness in its essential falsity, if there is an aspect to them that can lay claim to truth inasmuch as it transcends the status quo in utopian fashion, even if only for the purposes of justification, then ideology only exists at all from this period on" (*Structural Transformation of the Public Sphere,* 88).

43. Discussing the intersection between private and public discourses conveyed by eighteenth-century usage of "conversation," Clifford Siskin writes, "*Conversation* became a crucial term . . . for describing not just the private individual exchanges, nor the public ones generated out of their multiplicity, but the flow *across* those newly reconstituted fields" (*The Work of Writing: Literature and Social Change in Britain, 1700–1830* [Baltimore: Johns Hopkins UP, 1998], 164).

44. According to Mitchell, the 1790s was marked by "the battle lines between the conservative oral tradition and the radical faith in the demotic power of printing" (54). Under the influence of the English free press tradition, "Blake never forsook the 'republic of letters' for the tranquility of the oral tradition . . . Blake continued, in short, to think of writing as a 'wond'rous art' when many of his contemporaries were blaming it for all the evils attendant on modernity" (W. J. T. Mitchell, "Visible Language: Blake's Wond'rous Art of Writing," in *Romanticism and Contemporary Criticism,* ed. Morris Eaves and Michael Fischer [Ithaca: Cornell UP, 1986], 55).

45. Briskly surveying the ideal of print "conversation" from eighteenth-century antecedents to current models of academic discourse, David Simpson emphasizes the abiding appeal of its fantasy: "We voice ourselves into presence" (65), trying to achieve "the mitigation of alienation and the experience of identity" (64). "The facsimile of speech and intimate contact" may be, as it always was, "nothing less than a compensation for a deepening sense of alienation and social diversification" (49), but even modern critics who see through the ruse of a printed conversation poem repeat the pattern with new variations, for we "do not yet have a solution to the problems [such poems were] designed to make us forget" (62). See "Anecdotes and Conversations: The Method of Postmodernity," in *The Academic Postmodern and the Rule of Literature: A Report on Half-Knowledge* (Chicago: U of Chicago P, 1995), 41–71.

46. The Erdman edition collates the eight extant copies of *Jerusalem* as well as several unique plates. The Princeton/Paley edition reproduces Copy E, and while the transcription of plate 98, line 35, reads "every Word & Every Character" (just as it does in Erdman), the photograph of plate 98 clearly shows "every Word & every Character."

47. The one exception here could be Paine, whom Blake might have known through the Johnson circle. Even in this case, however, there is little evidence of actual friendship and none to support the story that Blake saved Paine's life by helping him flee to Paris in 1792. Erdman reviews the pertinent anecdotes and the historical record, concluding that, beyond

a few specific, verifiable instances, "we do not know whether any of the English Jacobins were aware of Blake except as a minor engraver occasionally employed by Johnson." See David Erdman, *Prophet against Empire: A Poet's Interpretation of the History of His Own Times* (Princeton: Princeton UP, 1954), 139–141.

48. Benedict Anderson, *Imagined Communities: Reflections on the Origin and Spread of Nationalism* (London: Verso, 1991 [1983]), 6.

49. Albion's "fibres" are pathways of communication, but they are also what John Brewer has called "the sinews of power." (See *The Sinews of Power: War, Money and the English State, 1688–1783* [London: Routledge, 1989].) Across the eighteenth century, the developing network of roads enabled the print culture of a debating public, but it also allowed for two other things as well: the circulation of commodities through a national marketplace and the centralization of government, which secured its administrative power by more efficiently collecting taxes from the provinces and disseminating its rulings among them. At times, Blake represents this century-long concentration of power at home and extension abroad as the growth of an asphyxiating "mighty Polypus":

> And Hand & Hyle rooted into Jerusalem by a fibre
> Of strong revenge & Skofield Vegetated by Reubens Gate
> In every Nation of the Earth till the Twelve Sons of Albion
> Enrooted into every Nation: a mighty Polypus growing
> From Albion over the whole Earth: such is my awful vision (15:1–5, E 158–159)

Against these enrooting forces, we see Los "forming an Ax of gold" and his sons "cutting the Fibres" (15:22–23, E 159). Despite this vision of an apocalyptic struggle between forces of domination and freedom, an intractable problem remains: the routes (or "roots") of domestic and colonial trade are identical to those along which ideas and information pass. Even with "an Ax of gold," one could not surgically remove the economic function from an imaginative or intellectual public sphere, as if it were a cancerous growth invading an originally healthy body. Commerce and debate share the same infrastructure and grow together, a point Anderson underscores by noting that printed matter was "the first modern-style mass-produced industrial commodity" and by referring to print culture as "print-capitalism" (*Imagined Communities*, 34–36).

50. Eaves, *Counter-Arts Conspiracy*, 149, 151. If at one time Barrell was the main opponent of Eaves's understanding of Blake, that role has since been taken up by Makdisi, who strenuously objects to Eaves's idea of art as a form of individual "self-expression" and his emphasis on Blake's "middle-class self-construction." While it is true that Eaves reaches "a kind of dead end" in what he calls "the baffling union of individualism and communalism at the heart of [Blake's] thinking," I can't agree with Makdisi that this contradiction is merely "apparent," more the product of Eaves's own formulation of the problem than of anything truly central to Blake. On the contrary, this quarrel arises from Makdisi's own vision of a unified Blake whose antinomianism is uncompromising, invariable, and consistent—i.e., a Blake without contradictions (see *William Blake and the Impossible History of the 1790s*, 171–174). No one has described Blake's antinomianism better or more fully than Makdisi, and his account gets Blake exactly right, but only by half. In chapter 2, we will continue to explore how Blake held together his irreconcilable tendencies, and how this agitated union of contrary elements becomes a regular feature of modern critical engagement.

51. Friedrich Schiller, *On the Aesthetic Education of Man, In a Series of Letters*, ed. and

trans. Elizabeth M. Wilkinson and L. A. Willoughby (Oxford: Oxford UP, 1967 [1795]), 89. Schiller also argues that "if man is ever to solve that problem of politics in practice, he will have to approach it through the problem of the aesthetic, because it is only through Beauty that man makes his way to Freedom" (9). In *The Philosophical Discourse of Modernity*, trans. Frederick Lawrence (Cambridge, MA: MIT Press, 1989), Habermas assimilates Schiller into his own set of concerns: "Art is supposed to become effective in place of religion as the unifying power, because it is understood to be a 'form of communication' that enters into the intersubjective relationships between people. Schiller conceives of art as a communicative reason that will be realized in the 'aesthetic state' of the future" (45).

52. Laura Quinney, *William Blake on Self and Soul* (Cambridge, MA: Harvard UP, 2009), 150–151.

53. Sharon Cameron, *Impersonality: Seven Essays* (Chicago: U of Chicago P, 2007), 7. See my discussion of Cameron in the introduction.

54. Schiller, *On the Aesthetic Education of Man*, 95.

55. The speaking and listening of Blake's public conversation thus resemble not only Schiller's two drives but also the first two imperatives of Kant's *sensus communis*: "1. To think for oneself; 2. To think in the position of everyone else" (*Critique of the Power of Judgment*, trans. Paul Guyer and Eric Matthews [Cambridge: Cambridge UP, 2000 (1790)], 174).

56. Fenves, *Raising the Tone of Philosophy*, 105–106.

57. See Thomas Paine, *The Age of Reason, Being an Investigation of True and Fabulous Theology* (New York: Prometheus Books, 1984 [1795]), where Paine makes virtually the same argument against revelation as Kant, only substituting "hearsay" for "opinion": "No one will deny or dispute the power of the Almighty to make such a communication, if he pleases. But admitting, for the sake of a case, that something has been revealed to a certain person, and not revealed to any other person, it is revelation to that person only. When he tells it to a second person, a second to a third, a third to a fourth, and so on, it ceases to be a revelation to all those persons. It is revelation to the first person only, and *hearsay* to every other person, and consequently they are not obliged to believe it" (9–10).

58. Others have similarly argued that we need a more nuanced approach than a strict opposition between Habermas and Lyotard allows. See Emilia Steuerman, for instance, who contends that Lyotard's postmodernism is "a *radicalization* that in no way challenges the modernity project as such" and that Lyotard in fact "answers Habermas' plea for the development of modernity as a yet unfinished project" ("Habermas vs Lyotard: Modernity vs postmodernity?" in *Judging Lyotard*, ed. Andrew Benjamin [New York: Routledge, 1992], 100).

59. Habermas, *Structural Transformation of the Public Sphere*, 102.

60. Kant, *Conflict of the Faculties*, 59.

61. Kant, *Perpetual Peace*, 47.

62. Contrasting Kant and Schiller on this basis, de Man believed that just such an identity between the individual and the state was the ultimate ideological purpose of Schiller's aesthetic education. See "Kant and Schiller," in *The Aesthetic Ideology*, 129–162. In "The Subversive Kant: The Vocabulary of 'Public' and 'Publicity,'" *Political Theory* 14 (4), John Christian Laursen demonstrates how Kant deliberately and provocatively departed from common German usage in his employment of the term "public." From 1600 the word steadily narrowed until by the mid-seventeenth century it almost exclusively referred to things having to do with the state. Against this tendency, Kant restored earlier associations of *publicus*—refer-

ring, first, to the community, and second, to that which is out in the open, outside one's own house (German *öffentlich*). See 584–588.

63. Immanuel Kant, "An Answer to the Question: 'What Is Enlightenment?'" ed. and trans. H. B. Nisbet, in *Kant: Political Writings* (Cambridge: Cambridge UP, 1991 [1784]), 55.

64. Kant, *Perpetual Peace*, 30.

65. Recognizing the same ambiguity at work in Kant's proposal for academic freedom, Derrida suggests that in *The Conflict of the Faculties* "Kant defines a university that is as much a safeguard for the most totalitarian of social forms as a place for the most intransigently liberal resistance to any abuse of power, resistance that can be judged in turns as most rigorous or most impotent." See "Mochlos; or, the Conflict of the Faculties," in *Logomachia: The Conflict of the Faculties*, ed. Richard Rand (Lincoln: U of Nebraska P, 1992), 18.

66. Kant, *Perpetual Peace*, 30.

67. Jon Mee, *Romanticism, Enthusiasm, and Regulation: Poetics and the Policing of Culture in the Romantic Period* (Oxford: Oxford UP, 2003), 293.

68. Makdisi, *William Blake and the Impossible History of the 1790s*, 3, 26. On Habermas's "lack of attention to the plebeian public sphere," see Craig Calhoun's introduction to *Habermas and the Public Sphere*, ed. Craig Calhoun (Cambridge, MA: MIT Press, 1992), 37–39, and Habermas's response to this charge in the same volume, "Further Reflections on the Public Sphere," trans. Thomas Burgher, 425–427.

69. "One complaint only was she ever known to make during her husband's life, and that gently,—'Mr. Blake was so little with her, though in the body they were never separated; for he was incessantly away in Paradise.'" Alexander Gilchrist attributes this report to Seymour Kirkip; see Alexander Gilchrist and Anne Burrows Gilchrist, *Life of William Blake*, new and enlarged ed. (London: Macmillan, 1880), 410.

70. Frederick Tatham, *Life of Blake* (ca. 1832), in *Blake Records*, 2nd ed., ed. G. E. Bentley Jr. (New Haven: Yale UP, 2004), 673.

71. J. T. Smith, from *Nollekens and His Times* (1828), in *Blake Records*, 609.

72. Tatham, *Life of Blake*, 673.

73. Immanuel Kant, "What Is Orientation in Thinking?" in *Kant's Political Writings*, 247.

74. "In regard to enlightenment, therefore, thinking for oneself seemed to coincide with thinking aloud and the use of reason with its public use" (Habermas, *Structural Transformation of the Public Sphere*, 104).

75. The possibilities, in brief: The political environment may well have been too repressive, but Blake could equally well have been too cautious, afraid to test the forces of repression. He may have refused to enter the marketplace of mass print commodities, or willing enough, may have been stigmatized by a respectable, middle-class culture that considered his dissenting enthusiasm vulgar and unworthy of general interest. These possibilities remain unresolved.

76. David Erdman, *Prophet against Empire*, 138.

77. See, e.g., Warner, *Letters of the Republic*, 34 ff.; Habermas, *Structural Transformation of the Public Sphere*, 42–43; and Jon Klancher, *The Making of English Reading Audiences* (Madison: U of Wisconsin P, 1987), 21 ff.

78. Clifford Siskin and William Warner, "This Is Enlightenment: An Invitation in the Form of an Argument," in *This Is Enlightenment*, ed. Clifford Siskin and William Warner (Chicago: U of Chicago P, 2010), 13. Siskin discusses the development of these author-readers and their contribution to the rising popularity of the novel in *The Work of Writing*, 163–170.

79. Habermas, *Structural Transformation of the Public Sphere*, 2; Warner, *Letters of the Republic*, 52.

80. Warner, *Letters of the Republic*, 65–67.

81. Although his topic is the growth of book reading, which does not take off proportionately until the Romantic period, William St Clair notes "the astonishingly rapid growth of periodical publications, journals and newspapers" (14) across the long eighteenth century, a trend he documents in tabular form in Appendix 8: Periodicals, 572–577, in *The Reading Nation in the Romantic Period* (Cambridge: Cambridge UP, 2004).

82. Klancher, *The Making of English Reading Audiences*, 23.

83. With access to an information world and a public discourse of debate that would have been unimaginable a century earlier, Blake, who spent all but three years of his life in London and never left England, was a citizen of the world in his own quirky, antinomian way. Given the circulation of print through even a small Sussex town like Felpham, it is not without a certain mundane logic that the visionary climax of *Milton* depicts the descent of cosmic forces upon Blake's own rural cottage. The author of *Jerusalem* was right to claim, "In my Exchanges every Land / Shall walk," although it's not clear what he meant by adding, "& mine in every Land" (27:85–86, E 183).

84. Frederick Tatham, letter of June 8, 1864, cited in *Blake Records*, 2nd ed., ed. G. E. Bentley, 57.

85. H. J. Jackson, *Romantic Readers: The Evidence of Marginalia* (New Haven: Yale UP, 2005), 170. Also see Jason Allen Snart, *The Torn Book: UnReading Blake's Marginalia* (Selinsgrove, PA: Susquehanna UP, 2006), and Hazard Adams, *Blake's Margins: An Interpretive Study of the Annotations* (Jefferson, NC: McFarland and Company, 2009).

86. Makdisi, *William Blake and the Impossible History of the 1790s*, 67–68.

87. Kant, *Conflict of the Faculties*, 153.

88. See Lyotard, "The Sign of History," in *The Lyotard Reader*, 393–411, which overlaps considerably with a chapter of the same title in *The Differend*, 151–181; Habermas, "Taking Aim at the Heart of the Present," in *Foucault: A Critical Reader*, ed. David Couzens Hoy (Oxford: Blackwell, 1986), 103–108; Arendt, *Lectures on Kant's Political Philosophy*, esp. 45–65; Michel Foucault, "The Art of Telling the Truth," in *Critique and Power: Recasting the Foucault/Habermas Debate*, ed. Michael Kelly (Cambridge, MA: MIT Press, 1994), 139–148; and Slavoj Žižek, *Violence* (New York: Picador, 2008), 51–53.

89. Habermas, "Taking Aim at the Heart of the Present," 105.

90. Arendt shares this view as well. For Kant, she writes, "the importance of the occurrence is . . . exclusively in the eye of the beholder, in the opinion of the onlookers *who proclaim their attitude in public*" (*Lectures on Kant's Political Philosophy*, 46 [emphasis added]).

91. Kant, *Conflict of the Faculties*, 157.

92. Lyotard, *The Differend*, 170.

93. Lyotard, "Judiciousness in Dispute," 327.

94. Lyotard, "The Sign of History," 399–400.

95. Although Kant's spectators "exist only in the plural," as Arendt puts it, the size and nature of their community is left undefined, leaving open the possibility that Kant may have had a small intellectual elite in mind, fit though few. Arendt emphasizes the spectator's "disinterestedness, his nonparticipation, his noninvolvement," which allows him to "discover a meaning in the course taken by events, a meaning that the actors ignored." Exercising independent, rational judgments, her spectators most closely resemble philosophers (*Lectures on*

Kant's Political Philosophy, 63, 54). Lyotard, on the other hand, enlarges and volatilizes Kant's public, identifying it with the vast, anonymous, and amorphous response made possible by mass media. Emphasizing the "episodic outbursts" of mass feeling precipitated by modern events, Lyotard sees Kant as the first to understand that "the meaning of history . . . does not only show itself in the great deeds and misdeeds of the agents or actors who become famous in history, but also in the feeling of the obscure and distant spectators who see and hear them and who, in the sound and fury of the *res gestae,* distinguish between what is just and what is not." Accordingly, Kant is locating historical agency in the unpredictable possibilities of popular culture, whether he realizes it or not.

96. Kant, *Critique of the Power of Judgment,* 144.

97. Kant, *Conflict of the Faculties,* 155.

98. Lyotard, *The Differend,* 166.

99. Ibid., 165.

100. Ibid., 167.

101. In "A Vision of the Last Judgment," the same text that equates paradise with conversation, Blake disqualifies revolution in a way similar to Kant. At first glance, Blake seems to be retreating from politics altogether; in fact, he is explaining why revolution is incompatible with politics. If a revolution claims to embody true principles of justice and thus to fulfill history, it puts an end to conversation and shuts down historical dynamism. Genuine politics belong only to those who can sustain critical debate and thus continuously propel history forward. Blake describes this contrast as the difference between those who insist on living in paradise and those who continue to debate the nature of paradise and thereby come as close as is humanly possible to living in one: "Many Persons such as Paine & Voltaire <with <some of> the Ancient Greeks> say we will not Converse concerning Good & Evil we will live in Paradise & Liberty You may do so in Spirit but not in the <Mortal> Body as you pretend till after the Last Judgment . . . You cannot have Liberty in this World without <what you call> Moral Virtue & you cannot have Moral Virtue without the Slavery of that half of the Human Race who hate <what you call> Moral Virtue" (E 564).

102. Lyotard, *The Differend,* 167.

103. Joanna Picciotto, *Labors of Innocence in Early Modern England* (Cambridge, MA: Harvard UP, 2010), 411. See my discussion of this phrase in the introduction.

104. Arendt, *Lectures on Kant's Political Philosophy,* 65.

105. Reflecting on the French Revolution, Matthew Arnold also argues in favor of criticism over politics. "Ideas cannot be too much prized in and for themselves, cannot be too much lived with; but to transport them abruptly into the world of politics and practice; violently to revolutionize this world to their bidding,—that is quite another thing." Arnold concludes that the "grand error of the French Revolution" lay in "quitting the intellectual sphere and rushing furiously into the political sphere" ("The Function of Criticism at the Present Time," in *Culture and Anarchy and other writings,* ed. Stefan Collini [Cambridge: Cambridge UP, 1993 (1864)], 32–33).

106. In the *Critique of the Power of Judgment* (154–157), Kant addresses a similar set of issues with a threefold vocabulary of *enthusiasm, nobility,* and *fanaticism (scwhärmerei).* Here "enthusiasm" occupies a middle ground, sharing in the intellectual and moral ideals of "nobility" but at risk of falling prey to the delusions of "fanaticism" whenever its aesthetic urgency is translated into action.

107. In a footnote to *The Conflict of the Faculties,* Kant declares that "revolution . . . is

always unjust" (157). In *Perpetual Peace*, he takes up the question "Is rebellion a legitimate means for a people to employ in throwing off the yoke of an alleged tyrant?" His answer: "it is in the highest degree illegitimate for subjects to seek their rights in this way. If they fail in the struggle and are then subjected to severest punishment, they cannot complain any more than the tyrant could if they had succeeded" (48).

108. Kant, *Conflict of the Faculties*, 165.

109. Lyotard, "Judiciousness in Dispute," 357.

Chapter 2 · Blake's Virtue

1. Peter Ackroyd, *Blake: A Biography* (New York: Ballantine, 1995), 160. Cited parenthetically hereafter. Blake's notebook passage can be found in David V. Erdman, *The Complete Poetry and Prose of William Blake* (New York: Anchor Books, 1988), 580.

2. Alexander Gilchrist, *The Life of William Blake*, "*Pictor Ignotus*", 2 vols. (London: Macmillan, 1863), 1:94. Cited parenthetically hereafter.

3. Jon Mee, *Dangerous Enthusiasm: William Blake and the Culture of Radicalism in the 1790s* (Oxford: Clarendon Press, 1992), 1. Cited parenthetically hereafter.

4. Laura Quinney, *William Blake on Self and Soul* (Cambridge, MA: Harvard UP, 2009), xi.

5. The differences I am sketching for heuristic purposes between Blake's biographers and critics diminish somewhat after the 1940s. Jacob Bronowski, an early champion of the political Blake, first published his biography in 1944 under the title *William Blake: A Man without a Mask*. When the book was reissued as *William Blake and the Age of Revolution* (London: Routledge and Kegan Paul) in 1972, he added a new introduction, explaining the changes that made this new title timely: "When I wrote my book in 1942, Blake was regarded as an untaught and remote mystic whose poems lay quite outside his times and our tradition. I showed, in his life and in his writings, that his inspiration was both more robust and more universal than this, and that his vision never missed the meaning of the tremendous years through which he lived. Since my book was first printed, this more ample view of Blake has begun to enter the textbooks" (17). Starting with Blake's contemporaries, however, and running virtually uninterrupted through the first half of the twentieth century, biographers persistently downplayed Blake's politics. By acknowledging the advances that began with Bronowski, Mark Schorer, and Erdman but returning nevertheless to the trend that preceded them, Ackroyd updates and boldly validates an older, longstanding, and more conservative biographical tradition.

6. Saree Makdisi, *Romantic Imperialism: Universal Empire and the Culture of Modernity* (Cambridge: Cambridge UP, 1998), 163. Acknowledgement of this nonparticipation mostly disappears from Makdisi's fuller treatment of Blake's antinomian radicalism in *William Blake and the Impossible History of the 1790s* (Chicago: U of Chicago P, 2003).

7. Besides the works by Mee, Makdisi, and Thompson discussed elsewhere in this book, I should mention two other important historicist treatments of Blake and his world: David Worrall's *Radical Culture: Discourse, Resistance and Surveillance, 1790–1820* (Detroit: Wayne State UP, 1992); and Iain McCalman's *Radical Underworld: Prophets, Revolutionaries, and Pornographers in London, 1795–1840* (Oxford: Clarendon, 1993). Worrall's essay, "Blake and 1790s Plebeian Radical Culture," in *Blake in the Nineties*, ed. Steve Clark and David Worrall (New York: St. Martin's Press, 1999), is typical of the historicist tendency to radicalize Blake

by association. Worrall amasses wide and impressive archival evidence of the existence of "an emergent, assertive, innovative and long-lasting artisan public sphere" (208–209) contemporary with Blake. Time and again he demonstrates that writings thematically and stylistically similar to Blake's drew the attention of repressive authorities. The difficulty arrives in finding just the right terms to describe Blake's relation to this plebeian public sphere, which he echoed freely without ever joining. Sliding between stronger and weaker terms of relationship, Worrall writes of Blake assimilating (194), echoing (195), engaging (195), paralleling (200), reflecting (202), and absorbing (209) the radical culture with which his work is adjacent (197), symbiotic (199), integral (200), and in proximity (207). Eventually, cumulative proximity becomes sufficient for Worrall to assert, "It has not particularly been the concern of this essay to argue that Blake was a radical, although we may guess that he was" (207).

On the other hand, when I speak of Blake's "formalist" critics, I am using the term in both a specific and a general sense. Specifically, I refer to the "new formalists" who defend literary and aesthetic form against the "demonization" they believe it has suffered through the ascendancy of historicism and cultural studies. Among the new formalists prominently featuring Blake have been Susan Wolfson, *Formal Charges: The Shaping of Poetry in British Romanticism* (Stanford, 1997) and Robert Kaufman, "Everybody Hates Kant: Blakean Formalism and the Symmetries of Laura Moriarty," in *Reading for Form,* ed. Susan Wolfson and Marshall Brown, *MLQ,* special issue, 61.1 (March 2000). See my discussion, esp. of Wolfson's work, in chapter 5 of this book. But I also wish to extend the term more broadly to include critics of Blake who, even when they reject a narrow, internal formalism in favor of the historically informed critical action performed by Blake's texts, nevertheless privilege textual dynamics and the hypothetical reader response such strategies are supposed to provoke, because Blake's difficult poetry "rouzes the faculties to act" (E 702). In this way, "formalism" includes many critics who are self-consciously anti-formalist, going as far back as Jerome McGann's claim that Blake's "poetry is a form of action rather than a form of representation" (*Towards a Literature of Knowledge* [Chicago: U of Chicago P, 1989], ix).

8. Wolfson, intro. to *Reading for Form,* 2.

9. Makdisi, *Romantic Imperialism,* 159.

10. *The Cambridge Companion to William Blake,* ed. Morris Eaves (Cambridge: Cambridge UP, 2003). The consecutive chapters are by Makdisi (110–132) and Mee (133–149), respectively.

11. Nicholas Williams's *Ideology and Utopia in the Poetry of William Blake* (Cambridge: Cambridge UP, 1998) provides an example of this merger at its best. Drawing on Ernst Bloch's concept of "concrete utopia," Williams describes Blake's project as an attempt "to retain the particulars of history while bringing them to utopian perfection" (31). Historicism allows us to grasp with specificity the concrete in Blake; formalism describes his mode of utopian action. In Williams's account, the concrete turns utopian in moments of transformative reading, that is, when the formal operations of Blake's text provoke a reader to perceive the concrete differently.

12. Steve Clark and David Worrall, intro. to *Blake, Nation and Empire* (Basingstoke: Palgrave Macmillan, 2006), 5. One of Clark and Worrall's main objectives is to challenge the predominant assumption of Blake's oppositional attitude and his automatic location within a 1790s radical culture. Thus the essays in this volume supplement the "now familiar" account of "radical subcultures"—an account to which these author-editors contributed in two previous volumes—by looking at Blake's participation in "the public spheres of genteel

sentimentalism and bourgeois nationalism" (5). The Blake that emerges "is as much bourgeois patriot as artisan rebel, as much mainstream sentimentalist as isolated mystic" (6). One could quibble with any of these labels, but the aim of acknowledging a more complex, even contradictory Blake, without cancelling the radical stance so central to his work, is no doubt a valuable one.

13. David Erdman, *Prophet Against Empire: A Poet's Interpretation of the History of His Own Times* (Princeton: Princeton UP, 1954), 6. Cited parenthetically hereafter.

14. Morton Paley, *William Blake* (Oxford: Phaidon, 1978), 36.

15. For the evidence supporting these generally accepted dates, see Robert N. Essick, *William Blake, Printmaker* (Princeton: Princeton UP, 1980), 70–73, 178–183, and *The Separate Plates of William Blake: A Catalogue* (Princeton: Princeton UP, 1983), 27–29; Martin Butlin, *The Paintings and Drawings of William Blake,* 2 vols. (New Haven: Yale UP, 1981), 27; Joseph Viscomi, *Blake and the Idea of the Book* (Princeton: Princeton UP, 1993), 302.

16. As Ian Haywood points out, the fact that no Catholics were killed quickly led to speculation that the Gordon Riots had deeper, political motives. Haywood also contends that representations of the riots formed a lasting image of "the spectacular mob," which haunted British response to the French Revolution a decade later (*Bloody Romanticism: Spectacular Violence and the Politics of Representation, 1776–1832* [Basingstoke: Palgrave Macmillan, 2006], 184–185).

17. So confident, for instance, was Ronald Paulson that "Albion rose" is an "image of revolution" that he referred (in a footnote) to the few available dissenting opinions as "counter-interpretations" (*Representations of Revolution* [New Haven: Yale UP, 1983], 89). Today, the image automatically raises the question of politics, as on the cover of Williams's book, where it serves to introduce the theme of "revolutionary consciousness faced with seemingly intractable fallenness" (*Ideology and Utopia in the Poetry of William Blake,* 31). For further political readings of "Albion rose," see Mee, who likens the image to "the sun of liberty" symbolism found in Paine and Spence (*Dangerous Enthusiasm,* 136), and Makdisi, who argues in *Romantic Imperialism* that Blake's labor-oriented inscription turns "Albion rose" into the emblem of a redemptive, internationalist apocalypse: "undertaken not only by the workers of a nascent industrial Britain, but by the slaves and the others bound into this Urizenic system throught [sic] the conduits of the Universal Empire" (165). In *William Blake and the Impossible History of the 1790s,* Makdisi endorses the linkage of "Albion rose," the Gordon Riots, and *America* advocated by Erdman and Essick (Makdisi 35–38).

18. Edward Gibbon, letter to Dorothea Gibbon, June 8, 1780, in *The Letters of Edward Gibbon,* ed. J. E. Norton, 3 vols. (London: Cassell, 1956), 2:243.

19. Mark Schorer, *William Blake: The Politics of Vision* (New York: Henry Holt, 1946), 157. Cited parenthetically hereafter.

20. Stanley Gardner, *The Tyger, the Lamb, and the Terrible Desert: "Songs of Innocence and of Experience" in Its Times and Circumstance* (London: Cygnus Arts, 1998), 25. Cited parenthetically hereafter.

21. Aileen Ward explains why we cannot depend on the reliability of Gilchrist's sources for this or any other episode: "Gilchrist's account of Blake's life up to his sixties was based largely on Blake's own recollections of his earlier years as recited to his youthful admirers long afterward, which they recalled in confused fragments thirty years later" ("William Blake and His Circle," in *The Cambridge Companion to William Blake,* 20).

22. Not only does G. E. Bentley quote Gilchrist's account without comment, but he also

retains some of his Victorian predecessor's moral indignation, calling Blake "a horrified witness of these outrages" and referring to his "anguished recollection of the scene" (*The Stranger from Paradise: A Biography of William Blake* [New Haven: Yale UP, 2001], 56–57).

23. See G. E. Bentley Jr., *Blake Records* (New Haven: Yale UP, 2004), 21. Cited parenthetically hereafter.

24. Ackroyd notes, for instance, that "George Cumberland wrote an ode in praise of the radical agitator Horne Tooke, and himself became the object of attention from government spies" (*Blake*, 72).

25. "The Speech of Counselor Rose in Defense of Blake the Artist" is reprinted in Bentley's *Blake Records*, 179–183.

26. In this dedication, Blake refers to himself "Bowing before my Sov'reign's Feet" (E 480).

27. Quoted by Mee in *Romanticism, Enthusiasm, and Regulation: Poetics and the Policing of Culture in the Romantic Period* (Oxford: Oxford UP, 2003), 100.

28. See Erdman, *Prophet Against Empire*, 379; and Ackroyd, *Blake*, 251.

29. Annotations to Reynolds, E 636. The exact passage reads, "I [*was*] <am> hid."

30. Worrall notes that Blake was prosecuted under English Common Law, not under the statutes typically invoked in such cases, including the Seditious Meetings Act (1795), the Traitorous Correspondence Act (1793), and the Seduction from Duty and Allegiance Act (1797). *Radical Culture: Discourse, Resistance and Surveillance, 1790–1820*, 68. Since each of these laws targets group activity, the absence of such charges is further evidence that Blake did not participate in collective political activities.

31. Another interesting contrast comes by way of Blake's contemporary, Thomas Evans, an ultraradical member of the London Corresponding Society and later a Spencean activist. According to McCalman, it is difficult to find direct evidence of Evans's activities, since his radical career "was not conducive to leaving any strong traces"; his "potentially treasonous activities" required a "habitual deviousness and caution" (*Radical Underworld*, 7, 13). And yet, despite these obstacles, McCalman is able to construct his vivid account of Evans's political life from the abundance of information contained in the reports of government spies and informers. We can specify Evans's role at the scene of radical activity because he drew the attention of others. Blake drew no such attention.

32. See Gardner, *The Tyger, the Lamb, and the Terrible Desart*, 24; Ackroyd, *Blake*, 74–75; and Aileen Ward, "Romantic Castles and Real Prisons: Wordsworth, Blake, and Revolution," *Wordsworth Circle* 30.1 (1999): 9, for renditions of these often repeated arguments. Considering the Gordon Riots to be "the crucial experience of [Blake's] youth," Ward states the majority opinion: "[I]t seems clear that he joined and remained with the march of his own free will, if in fact he was not present from the start" (9).

33. William Keach, *Arbitrary Power: Romanticism, Language, Politics* (Princeton: Princeton UP, 2004), 130, 132. Cited parenthetically hereafter.

34. Departing from the mainstream of commentary, Makdisi and Steve Clark emphasize Blake's voluntary participation in the violence, but for opposite reasons. Makdisi argues that Blake's antinomian enthusiasm made him sympathetic to urban crowds willing to use physical force in a revolutionary cause, thus distancing him from the cautious, individualist, and nonviolent stance of bourgeois reformers. Clark decouples enthusiasm from radical politics altogether and instead aligns it with an ugly and persistent anti-Catholic bias Blake supposedly shared with fellow reactionary Protestants. Overstating his case that *Jerusalem*

should be considered "anti-papal propaganda" (171), Clark cannot resist revisiting the Gordon Riots as the earliest possible evidence of what he considers a longstanding prejudice in Blake, even while acknowledging that evidence of Blake's participation is hardly reliable. If we accept that the riots "were clearly primarily if not exclusively directed against Catholics," and if we posit Blake's voluntary participation in them, then we must also "at least entertain the hypothesis of [his] religious sectarianism" ("*Jerusalem* as Imperial Prophecy," in *Blake, Nation and Empire*, quotation on 170, 167–185). In *William Blake and the Impossible History of the 1790s*, Makdisi acknowledges the ambiguity of Blake's role as "either a participant or an observer" (35), but he uses the Gordon Riots as a primary example of the "fierce rushing"—the "collective action of a crowd of angry citizens surging through city streets" (34)—that he sees Blake celebrating in *America*, in sharp contrast to the liberal model of revolution that dominated middle-class discourse of the 1790s. If Blake approved of the multitude "assuming an agency of its own, of taking matters into its own hands, of learning, writing, speaking, acting, and rushing" (49), then that approval began with his warm appreciation of events such as the Gordon Riots.

35. Ackroyd, *Blake*, 260.

36. For questions of dating, see note 15 above.

37. Along with Blake's representations of Orc, one should also consider lines spoken by Lord Audley in Blake's early drama, "King Edward the Third":

> . . . the bright morn
> Smiles on our army, and the gallant sun
> Springs from the hills like a young hero
> Into the battle, shaking his golden locks
> Exultingly; this is a promising day. (Scene iii, ll. 1–5; E 427)

Similar imagery persists many years later in Blake's description of a redeemed Urizen rising "in naked majesty / In radiant Youth," in Night the Ninth of *The Four Zoas* (121:31–32, E 391).

38. See David Erdman's "Dating Blake's Script: The "g" Hypothesis," *Blake Newsletter* 3 (1969): 11, where he recommends a later date for "Albion rose," 1800–1803, based on a stylistic change in Blake's engraving of the lower case "g."

39. John Milton, *Samson Agonistes*, in *The Riverside Milton*, ed. Roy Flannagan (Boston: Houghton Mifflin, 1998), l. 41, p. 803. Cited parenthetically hereafter, by line number only.

40. Christopher Hill, *Milton and the English Revolution* (New York: Viking, 1977), 441–442. Cited parenthetically hereafter.

41. Bentley, *Blake Records*, 160, emphasis added.

42. Contesting those who have "configured" Blake "as a soft liberal" (19), Makdisi argues that Blake opposed the incoming liberal hegemony as vehemently as he opposed an outdated feudalism, and that he clearly stood on the side of urban radicals against respectable reformers who insisted on renouncing all violence. See Chap. 2 of *William Blake and the Impossible History of the 1790s*, 16–77, esp. 45–54. In *How Milton Works* (Cambridge, MA: Harvard UP, 2001), Fish warns against "a criticism that would make Milton into the Romantic liberal some of his readers want him to be" (14), rather than the antinomian who knows only one injunction: "do God's will" (5), even if God's will demands violence. Fish continues his case for antinomianism—Milton's and Samson's both—in " 'There Is Nothing He Cannot Ask': Milton, Liberalism, and Terrorism," in *Milton in the Age of Fish: Essays on Authorship, Text, and Terrorism*, ed. Michael Lieb and Albert C. Labriola (Pittsburgh: Duquesne UP, 2006).

Responding to an imagined liberal interlocutor who believes it the responsibility of civil law to protect against religious violence, Fish writes: "Samson, or perhaps the more reflective Milton, might reply that there are worse things than death and that the destruction of cities or civilizations informed by the spirit of Sodom and Gomorrah is a necessary prelude to the building of a better, purer world" (261).

43. Respectively, Michael Lieb, " 'Our Living Dread': The God of *Samson Agonistes*," in *Milton Studies* 33, ed. Albert C. Labriola and Michael Lieb (Pittsburgh: U of Pittsburgh P, 1997), 4; and Michael Lieb, "Returning the Gorgon Medusa's Gaze," in Lieb and Labriola, *Milton in the Age of Fish*, 242. Feisal G. Mohamed has also argued against the predominant tendency of Milton scholars to downplay the poet's attraction to violence. According to Mohamed, even Fish underplays Milton's commitment to Samson's militancy by overemphasizing the mitigating role of textual ambiguity: "If Fish is to be faulted, it is not for being too strenuous in asserting that *Samson Agonistes* is a work that looks favorably on Samson's final action but rather for not being strenuous enough in doing so" ("Confronting Religious Violence: Milton's *Samson Agonistes*," *PMLA* 120 [March 2005]: 329).

44. The key texts in the debate on Samson and terrorism are Stanley Fish's "The Temptation of Understanding," in *How Milton Works*, 391–431, and John Carey's response to that essay, published just before the first anniversary of the 9/11 attack: "A Work in Praise of Terrorism?" *TLS*, Sept. 6, 2002, 15–16. The *New York Times* covered the controversy in an article called "Is Reading Milton Unsafe at Any Speed?" (Dec. 28, 2002). Among many entries on the topic, see three essays (including Fish's last response to Carey) in Lieb and Labriola, *Milton in the Age of Fish*: David Loewenstein, "*Samson Agonistes* and the Culture of Religious Terror," 203–228; Lieb, "Returning the Gorgon Medusa's Gaze: Terror and Annihilation in Milton," 229–242; and Fish, " 'There Is Nothing He Cannot Ask': Milton, Liberalism, and Terrorism," 243–264.

45. Also relevant is Frank Lentricchia and Jody McAuliffe's discussion of "avant-garde artistic movements," which for two centuries have "presented themselves as revolutionary and sought to shake up—and even overturn—the order of the West." Although Blake goes unmentioned in this context, they do contend that "disturbing events of violence and terror—including the events of September 11—are in many ways governed by a logic that grows out of romantic tradition, as life imitates art with a vengeance and real terrorists take their inspirations from books" (*Crimes of Art and Terror* [Chicago: U of Chicago P, 2003], 3).

46. Samuel Johnson, *Milton*, vol. 1 of *The Lives of the Poets*, 4 vols., ed. Roger Lonsdale (Oxford: Oxford UP, 2006), 276.

47. Andrew Marvell, "On Mr. Milton's *Paradise Lost*," in *The Poems and Letters of Andrew Marvell*, 2 vols., ed. H. M. Margoliouth (Oxford: Clarendon Press, 1927), 1:131. After likening Milton to Samson, Marvell then dismisses the association as inappropriate. Others have found that identification harder to resist. Observing that Samson "talks of patience, and mouths threats of revenge in the name of God," Kenneth Burke called *Samson Agonistes* "a wonder-working spell by a cantankerous old fighter-priest who would slay the enemy in effigy" (*A Rhetoric of Motives* [Berkeley and Los Angeles: U of California P, 1969 (1950)], 3, 5).

48. Erdman, *Prophet Against Empire*, 384.

49. Joseph Wittreich, *Interpreting Samson Agonistes* (Princeton: Princeton UP, 1986), xxii. As early as *Angel of Apocalypse: Blake's Idea of Milton* (Madison: U of Wisconsin P, 1975), Wittreich was already contending that *Samson Agonistes* provided Blake with a cautionary lesson about the temptations of revolutionary violence. This argument became the basis

of an extended series of explorations, first in *Interpreting Samson Agonistes*, then in *Shifting Contexts: Reinterpreting Samson Agonistes* (Pittsburgh: Duquesne UP, 2002), and most recently in *Why Milton Matters: A New Preface to His Writings* (New York: Palgrave, 2006), where Wittreich champions the continuing relevance of Milton's critique of violence in a post–9/11 world. In *Interpreting Samson Agonistes*, Wittreich explains his resistance to the tendency among readers to identify Milton with his dramatic hero: "It is conceivable that Milton wrote his poem simply accepting that identity with Samson and, through him, urging another, this time successful, revolution; it is equally conceivable that, divorcing himself from Samson, Milton composed this poem as a retrospective repudiation of the cause he once championed" (xxi). Wittreich's object is to defend the plausibility of the latter position while explaining why the former has garnered considerable support. Most importantly, he demonstrates that in *Samson Agonistes* Milton never passively reflects his culture's understanding of the Samson legend but reflects upon it comprehensively and *critically*.

50. Wittreich, *Angel of Apocalypse*, 57.

51. Essick, *William Blake, Printmaker*, 182. See Blake's letter to Hayley, Oct. 23, 1804 (E 756).

52. The same tendency to detach the biographical subject from his world receives exaggerated treatment in both the title of Bentley's *The Stranger from Paradise: A Biography of William Blake* and its cover design, which features Thomas Phillips's 1807 portrait of a well-lit, self-contained Blake materializing out of black, empty space.

53. Celeste Langan, *Romantic Vagrancy: Wordsworth and the Simulation of Freedom* (Cambridge: Cambridge UP, 1995), 142; William Wordsworth, *The Fourteen-Book Prelude*, ed. W. J. B. Owen (Ithaca: Cornell UP), VI. 606, p. 130.

54. Langan, *Romantic Vagrancy*, 162, 167.

55. Blake, "A Vision of the Last Judgment" (E 556), quoted in Ackroyd, *Blake*, 279.

56. Wordsworth, *The Fourteen-Book Prelude*, I. 6–8, p. 27.

57. The persistent influence of high Romantic concepts is also evident in Ackroyd's untroubled use of the word "genius." *Blake* begins and ends with autochthonous genius: it begins in "the true soil of [Blake's] genius" (23) and ends by opposing his "true genius" to the "world which distrusted and despised him" (369).

58. Mee, *Romanticism, Enthusiasm, and Regulation*, 257.

59. Jacques Derrida, "Structure, Sign and Play in the Discourse of the Human Sciences," in *Writing and Difference*, trans. Alan Bass (Chicago: U of Chicago P, 1978), 285. Also see Claude Lévi-Strauss, *The Savage Mind* (Chicago: U of Chicago P, 1966), 16–22.

60. McCalman, *Radical Underworld*, x.

61. Makdisi, *William Blake and the Impossible History of the 1790s*, 20; Mee, *Dangerous Enthusiasm*, 1. For Mee's introduction of "bricolage" to explain Blake's characteristic strategies as an artist and writer, see 3–10.

62. The phrase is Steve Clark's, from *"Jerusalem* as Imperial Prophecy," 181, but it is characteristic of many of the essays in *Blake, Nation and Empire*.

63. See Gardner, *The Tyger, the Lamb, and the Terrible Desart*, 127; and Worrall, *Radical Culture*, 21. Makdisi points out that a splinter group of the London Corresponding Society met in Lambeth, "close to where Blake was at the same time composing his prophecies." There they practiced military drills, perhaps anticipating an urban insurrection (*William Blake and the Impossible History of the 1790s*, 47).

64. Robyn Hamlyn and Michael Phillips, *William Blake* (New York: Harry N. Abrams, 2000), 100.

65. Bentley describes the new arrangement: "In Hercules Buildings they had not merely space but unaccustomed elegance as well. There were many roomy cupboards in which Catherine could store the silverware and china which they were accumulating. The walls were panelled to a height of three feet, and there were Georgian hob grates and marble mantelpieces . . . The front of the house on the north was dark in winter, but it faced across the lane to open fields and the river. The stairwell led down to the back door which faced south to a long garden with a privy at the bottom among the poplar trees. Blake's studio was the back parlour, a sunny panelled room facing south over the garden" (*The Stranger from Paradise*, 122–123). For extended description of No. 13 Hercules Buildings and its Lambeth surroundings, see Michael Phillips, *William Blake*, 100–102, 144–145. In a section titled "Lambeth and the Terror" (152–154), Phillips also details the local forms of intimidation that followed upon conservative reaction to the September massacres and subsequent events in France.

66. Sharon Marcus, *Apartment Stories: City and Home in Nineteenth-Century Paris and London* (Berkeley and Los Angeles: U of California P, 1999), 94–97. Cited parenthetically hereafter.

67. Adcock's engraving of No. 13 Hercules Buildings was one of many such illustrations he produced for a book on *Famous Houses and Literary Shrines of London*, by A. St. John Adcock (London: J. M. Dent and Sons, 1912).

68. Morris Eaves, *The Counter-Arts Conspiracy: Art and Industry in the Age of Blake* (Ithaca: Cornell UP, 1992), 175. Cited parenthetically hereafter.

69. Bentley explains why this story is generally considered apocryphal in *Blake Records*, xxvi-xxvii.

70. Emphasis added. Quoted in G. E. Bentley Jr., "Blake's Engravings and his Friendship with Flaxman," in *Studies in Bibliography*, vol. 12 (Charlottesville: U of Virginia P, 1959), 171.

71. Bentley, *Blake Records*, 745–746.

72. Quoted in Ackroyd, *Blake*, 218.

73. Jane Austen, *Sense and Sensibility* (Oxford: Oxford UP, 1990 [1811]), 219.

74. For "the idealization of cottage life" (30) that begins in this period and quickly escalates with the Victorians, see George H. Ford, "Felicitous Space: The Cottage Controversy," in *Nature and the Victorian Imagination*, ed. U. C. Knoepflmacher and G. B. Tennyson (Berkeley and Los Angeles: U of California P, 1977), 29–48. Ford notes that George Sand divided all people "into two types—those whose ideal dwelling-place is a palace and those whose ideal is a cottage. Most representative Victorians [like Blake, we might add] would have opted for the cottage" (30).

75. As I have indicated throughout, Makdisi makes the strongest possible, and indeed persuasive, case for Blake's comprehensive radicalism. No one understands the depth and reach of Blake's antinomianism better, and for that reason *William Blake and the Impossible History of the 1790s* is a landmark study. Makdisi's political arguments falter, however, when they insist on Blake's unvarying, uncompromising consistency. Drawing up clear ideological antagonisms—between plebeian radicals and bourgeois reformers, between artisans aspiring to respectability and others committed to enthusiasm and activism—Makdisi makes the best possible case for placing Blake "firmly on one side of this divide," a phrase he likes well enough to repeat. Speaking of *America*'s "affirmation . . . of the insurrectionary politics of

the multitude," for instance, he writes, "The prophecy cracks open the discourse of liberty along the latter's fault lines and contradictions, between reform and revolution, between polite and plebeian, between the respectable and disrespectable; and it locates itself and the striving for the infinite firmly on one side of this divide" (52–53). The challenge, as I see it, is rather to straddle the divide in a way that accounts for Blake's constitutive contradictions, starting with the coexistence of his antinomianism and his nonparticipation, his fiery aesthetic practices and persistent detachment.

76. According to Eaves, Pye argued that the entrepreneurial spirit had turned English engravers "into businesslike artisans historically allied with commerce instead of dangerous radicals or financial prima donnas" (69). Testifying before the Committee on Arts and Manufactures in 1836, Pye promoted his long crusade to win official recognition for engravers from the Royal Academy. At about the same time, Place, a tailor and labor archivist, rewrote the history of 1790s labor activism from the perspective of his later "respectability and self-improvement," exaggerating the tendencies of moderation and marginalizing the radical element of such groups as the London Corresponding Society. Emphasizing "the march of mind" that accompanied worker education and self-improvement, he associated economic prosperity with "a transformation in popular manners and morals" (McCalman, *Radical Underworld*, 181; also see 8–13). McCalman is primarily interested in recovering the ultra-radical, Spencean practices Place disparaged, but E. P. Thompson describes Place in terms that, apart from the emphasis on organization, suggest aspects of Blake's own self-construction. His is "the policy of those self-respecting tradesmen or artisans who preferred to build bridges towards the middle class than to try to bridge the gulf between themselves and the tumultuous poor. As such, it represents a withdrawal from the agitation among 'members unlimited,' while at the same time embodying the strengths of self-education and painstaking organization" (Thompson, *The Making of the English Working Class* [New York: Penguin, 1968 (1963)], 153).

77. Frederick Tatham, *Life of Blake* (c. 1832), in *Blake Records*, 677.

78. Writes Bentley, "Tatham's vigorous but naive piety both colours his views and repeatedly leads him from his subject. Further, Tatham's facts are not uniformly reliable" (*Blake Records*, 661).

79. The phrase is Makdisi's; see *William Blake and the Impossible History of the 1790s*, 52.

80. Bentley, *Blake Records*, 14.

81. McCalman, *Radical Underworld*, 43.

82. "Workers' militant identity would seem to go in the opposite direction from collective professional identity . . . The militant worker population was situated within the poorest of the world of organic professional collectivities." Jacques Rancière is writing of French worker movements in the 1840s, but his findings coincide closely with McCalman's work on late eighteenth- and early nineteenth-century English artisans ("The Myth of the Artisan: Critical Reflections on a Category of Social History," *International Labor and Working Class History* 24 [Fall 1983]: 4).

83. Because Blake owned his own printing press and worked from home, with the assistance of Catherine, it may seem appropriate to associate him with a vanishing cottage industry economy rather than with the strict division of public and private spheres promulgated by the domestic ideology of the nineteenth century. When they could no longer afford separate rooms for separate tasks, the Blakes are supposed to have cooked and eaten in the same room on South Molton Street where they made prints for a living. Despite this

arrangement, Blake's early biographers had no trouble assimilating him into a version of domestic ideology, replacing the clear division of work and home with another emphasizing a distinction between imaginative and merely professional activities. In their eyes, Blake divided his day just as if he left home for work. "It was wonderful that he could thus, month after month, and year after year, lay down his graver after it had won him his daily wages, and retire from the battle for bread, to disport his fancy amid scenes of more than earthly splendour, and creatures pure as unfallen dew" (Allan Cunningham, "William Blake" [1830], in *Blake Records*, 635–636). Here is a character worthy of Dickens.

84. Mee, *Dangerous Enthusiasm*, 222.

85. Henry Crabb Robinson, "William Blake: Artist, Poet, and Religious Mystic" (1811), and Benjamin Heath Malkin, *A Father's Memoirs of His Child* (1806), both in *Blake Records*, 598 and 565, respectively.

86. Ward, "William Blake and His Circle," 19.

87. Samuel Johnson, *The Rambler* No. 139, in *The Yale Edition of Works of Samuel Johnson*, ed. W. J. Bate and Albrecht B. Strauss, 23 vols. (New Haven: Yale UP, 1969 [1751]), 4:376.

88. The centrality of waking and sleeping in the Samson story may derive from an ancient association between Samson and a sun god. Although Northrop Frye cautions against simply reducing the Samson cycle to a "solar myth," he summarizes well the reasons behind this theory: "We may notice that Samson's name resembles early Semitic words for the sun, and that his story tells of a supernaturally powerful hero associated with the burning of crops, who eventually falls into a dark prison-house in the west. That the story shows structural or narrative analogies to the kind of story that might be suggested by the passage of the sun across the sky is true, and no storyteller worth his keep would try to eliminate such analogies" (*The Great Code: The Bible and Literature* [New York: Harcourt Brace Jovanovich, 1983], 35). Also see *Fearful Symmetry* (Princeton: Princeton UP, 1969 [1947]), where Frye suggests that "the echo of *Samson Agonistes*" in the inscription to "Albion rose" "indicates the unifying of Orc, Samson and Albion in [Blake's] mind" (363). By etymological convention, Samson was often linked to the sun in biblical exegesis; commentators saw in his Hebrew name *Shemshon* an echo of *shemesh*, Hebrew for "sun." See Leslie Tannenbaum, *Biblical Tradition in Blake's Early Prophecies: The Great Code of Art* (Princeton: Princeton UP, 1982), 266.

89. Fish, *How Milton Works*, 470.

90. Johnson, *The Rambler* No. 140, 378. Johnson believed the phoenix an "incongruous" image for Samson, "contrary to reason and nature," "the grossest error."

91. Milton's reference to *"Herculean Samson"* (*Paradise Lost*, in *The Riverside Milton*, ed. Roy Flannagan, IX. 1060) draws upon a conventional association between the two strong men that began with the earliest patristic exegesis. See Michael Lieb, *The Sinews of Ulysses: Form and Convention in Milton's Works* (Pittsburgh: Duquesne UP, 1989), 113.

92. Before 9/11 made terrorism an inevitable focus of interpretation, readings of *Samson Agonistes* generally fell into three camps: (1) those who believe Milton commemorates Samson's violence as a heroic act inspired by faith and coincident with divine purpose; (2) those who find Samson's violence repugnant whether or not Milton believed it to be divinely sanctioned; (3) those who believe Milton views Samson critically, employing him as a negative example in order to move readers away from violence and toward an ideal of individual or intellectual transformation. Proponents of the first view would include Christopher Hill in *Milton and the English Revolution* (1977), Michael Lieb in *The Sinews of Ulysses* (1989), and Jackie DiSalvo in "'The Lord's Battells': *Samson Agonistes* and the Puritan Revolution," *Mil-*

ton Studies 4 (1972): 39–62. The second position, as we have seen, was Samuel Johnson's. It is given a powerful, modern statement in Irene Samuel's "*Samson Agonistes* as Tragedy," in *Calm of Mind*, ed. J. A. Wittreich (Cleveland: Case Western Reserve UP, 1971), 235–257. Two important book-length studies putting forth variations on the third position are Mary Ann Radzinowicz's *Toward Samson Agonistes* (Princeton: Princeton UP, 1978) and Wittreich's *Interpreting Samson Agonistes* (Princeton: Princeton UP, 1986). The latter is especially important to this chapter: first, because it develops an argument about Milton's wariness of Samson and revolution that Wittreich earlier presented in relation to Blake's "Albion rose" (*Angel of Apocalypse*, 48–74); second, because it shows how Milton's incorporation of contemporary attitudes toward violent revolution in *Samson Agonistes* does not amount to an uncritical identification with those attitudes. The drama pivots upon a crucial ambiguity: "[I]s *Samson Agonistes* written to engender, or to repudiate, a state of mind that would confront the existing order in an attitude of war, urging sympathizers to strike when the iron is hot and to impose justice rather than wait upon its eventual implementation" (12)? As I will argue in this section, Milton exploits this ambiguity to install reading or interpretation as that activity which mediates between waiting for justice and imposing it directly.

93. Victoria Kahn, "Political Theology and Reason of State in *Samson Agonistes*," *South Atlantic Quarterly* 95.4 (Fall 1996): 1086–1087, 1084.

94. See David Loewenstein's comments in "*Samson Agonistes* and the Culture of Religious Terror," in *Milton in the Age of Fish*, 215 and 227. Loewenstein aims to contextualize the meanings of holy terror available to Milton and thus to dissociate *Samson Agonistes* from anachronistic comparisons to modern terrorism.

95. According to Fish, the essential danger of antinomianism, as Milton understood it, is that "people who believe themselves to be acting in response to God's will may, in fact, be acting in response to the urgings of their own will, and may therefore clothe their commission of sin in the robe of self-righteousness." " 'There Is Nothing He Cannot Ask': Milton, Liberalism, and Terrorism," in *Milton in the Age of Fish*, 254–255. Fish's citation and discussion of *A Treatise of Civil Power* also occur in these pages.

96. This absence is especially conspicuous in a work such as Stephen C. Behrendt's *The Moment of Explosion: Blake and the Illustration of Milton* (Lincoln: U of Nebraska P, 1983), which makes no mention of *Samson Agonistes*.

97. In *The Paintings and Drawings of William Blake*, Martin Butlin catalogues two paintings on the Samson theme that have been lost: *Samson Pulling down the Temple*, which Butlin dates 1799–1800, and *Samson and the Philistines* (1:320–321, 344).

98. *William Blake's Designs for Edward Young's Night Thoughts*, ed. David V. Erdman, John E. Grant, Edward J. Rose, and Michael J. Tolley (Oxford: Clarendon, 1980), Night IX, 119. Further citations, by night and page number, are to this text.

99. Kevis Goodman, *Georgic Modernity and British Romanticism: Poetry and the Mediation of History* (Cambridge: Cambridge UP, 2004), 6–10.

100. *King Lear*, III.ii.1–8, in *The Riverside Shakespeare*, 2nd ed., ed. G. Blakemore Evans (Boston: Houghton Mifflin, 1997), 1322.

101. D. W. Dörrbecker makes this point in his edition of *America: a Prophecy*, in William Blake, *The Continental Prophecies* (Princeton: Princeton UP, 1995), 137. Like Dörrbecker, I am using copy H of *America* as my reference text throughout this chapter. *America*'s canceled plate b can also be found in Erdman, *Complete Poetry and Prose of William Blake*, 58.

102. In Roberto Bolaño's novel *2666* a character attempts to describe the deafening vio-

lence of World War II carpet bombing, settling on the word "noise" despite its inadequacy: "Impossible as it seems, the noise grows louder. Call it noise, why not. One might call it a din, a roar, a clamor, a hammering, a great shriek, a bellow of the gods, but *noise* is a simple word that serves just as well to describe what has no name" (trans. Natasha Wimmer [New York: Picador, 2009], 794–795).

103. Carey, "A Work in Praise of Terrorism?" 16.

104. Tannenbaum, *Biblical Tradition in Blake's Early Prophecies*, 263–264.

105. See notes 49 and 92 above.

106. Mary Ann Radzinowicz, *Toward Samson Agonistes*, 7. For a reading of the kind Radzinowicz is parodying, see Barbara K. Lewalski, "*Samson Agonistes* and the 'Tragedy' of the Apocalypse," *PMLA* 85 (1970): 1050–1062.

107. Roland Barthes, *The Pleasure of the Text*, trans. Richard Miller (New York: Hill and Wang, 1973), 36.

108. Reference is to the page and line numbers of Blake's *Four Zoas* manuscript, as reproduced in Erdman, *Complete Poetry and Prose of William Blake*, 300–407.

109. Percy Bysshe Shelley, *The Cenci*, V.iii.74–75, in *Shelley's Poetry and Prose*, ed. Donald H. Reiman and Neil Fraistat (New York: Norton, 2002), 197.

110. Repeated with slight variation on 119:21–23, E 388.

111. Did Milton himself draw this phrase and image from *The Odyssey*? In the final book of Homer's epic, when the shades of the suitors slain by Odysseus arrive in Hades and are greeted there by Agamemnon, the ghost of Amphimedon explains,

> our bodies lie untended even now,
> strewn in Odysseus' palace. They know nothing yet,
> the kin in our houses who might wash our wounds
> of clotted gore and lay us out and mourn us.
> These are the solemn honors owed the dead. (XXIV: 206–210)

So Robert Fagles translates a passage with clear parallels in *Samson Agonistes*: in both texts, heaps of bloody corpses await a ritual washing to honor the dead (*The Odyssey* [New York: Penguin, 1996], 474). Of course it is possible that Fagles introduced this phrasing under Milton's influence. Even more likely, however, is that Fagles completed a Miltonic echo that had already entered into English translations of *The Odyssey* through Pope: "Our mangled bodies now deform'd with gore, / Cold and neglected, spread the marble floor. / No friend to bathe our wounds!" (Alexander Pope, trans., *The Odyssey of Homer*, Books XIII–XXIV, ed. Maynard Mack et al. [London: Methuen, 1967], XXIV: 214–216, p. 358). Long before he undertook his own translation of Homer, Fagles was on the editing team that published this modern edition of Pope's *Odyssey*.

112. Richard Watson, Lord Bishop of Llandaff, *An Apology for the Bible, in a Series of Letters, Addressed to Thomas Paine, Author of a Book Entitled "The Age of Reason"* (reprinted at Lichfield: T. Collier, 1797), 5. Further citations are to this text.

113. Fish, *How Milton Works*, 426. In "'There Is Nothing He Cannot Ask': Milton, Liberalism, and Terrorism," Fish continues to defend this position by insisting that, for Milton, only inward persuasion matters: "Milton would have us proceed by looking to the spirit within which an act is performed—to its intentional structure—rather than to what may or may not occur in its wake" (*Milton in the Age of Fish*, 250).

114. Carey, "A Work in Praise of Terrorism?" 16.

115. John Locke, *An Essay Concerning Human Understanding*, ed. Peter H. Nidditch (Oxford: Clarendon Press, 1975 [1700]), 703–704.

116. In *On Revolution* (New York: Viking, 1965), Hannah Arendt takes Watson's argument a step further, while also using the French Revolution as her exemplary case. From the brutal aggression of Jacobin virtue, we learn "that absolute goodness is hardly any less dangerous than absolute evil" (77). As Arendt further suggests in a remarkable reading of "Billy Budd," this collapse of moral distinction in violence is also the lesson taught by Melville's story of a malignant agitator abruptly killed by an innocent young sailor: "It is as though [Melville] said: Let us suppose that from now on the foundation stone of our political life will be that Abel slew Cain. Don't you see that from this deed of violence the same chain of wrongdoing will follow, only that now mankind will not even have the consolation that the violence it must call crime is indeed characteristic of evil men only?" (83).

117. In his recent discussion of these lines, Fish suggests that Milton lies closer to Watson's reasoning than to Blake's on the question of whether idolaters are themselves responsible for the violence against them. "The key phrase is 'drunk with idolatry' . . . Hence, [the Philistines] deserve what they get and have, in the strongest sense, brought it on themselves. Indeed, because they are spiritually dead to the living God, they are in effect already dead; they are barely human beings, for the spirit of God does not live within them" ("There Is Nothing He Cannot Ask," 246).

118. Walter Benjamin, "Critique of Violence," originally pub. 1921, trans. Edmond Jephcott, *Reflections* (New York: Schocken, 1978), 298–299. Benjamin writes: "Those who base a condemnation of all violent killing . . . on the commandment [Thou shalt not kill] are therefore mistaken. It exists not as a criterion of judgment, but as a guideline for the actions of those persons or communities who have to wrestle with it in solitude and, in exceptional cases, to take on themselves the responsibility of ignoring it. Thus it was understood by Judaism, which expressly rejected the condemnation of killing in self-defense" (298).

119. Fish, "There Is Nothing He Cannot Ask," 261. See note 42 above.

120. Benjamin, "Critique of Violence," 300. Sharing similar views of violence, *Samson Agonistes* and "Critique of Violence" form pre- and anti-modern bookends of a theological resistance to Enlightenment. In Benjamin's essay, which Beatrice Hanssen calls a "decidedly antimodern gesture" (*Critique of Violence: Between Poststructuralism and Critical Theory* [Routledge: London, 2000], 20), the messianic rupture of history arrives in the form of a "divine violence" that would forfeit its claim to legitimacy were it enacted in the service of any rational, identifiable end: "it is never reason that decides on . . . the justness of ends, but . . . God" (Benjamin, "Critique of Violence," 294). Although the human agent of divine violence possesses clear knowledge of the injustice he opposes, he must not prematurely define the form of justice-to-come, even as he acts to create the conditions of its possibility. He must enact violence without applying it to specific instrumental purposes. Thus, in a related essay, Benjamin describes the agent he calls the "destructive character" in terms reminiscent of the antinomian potential Milton invests in Samson: "No vision inspires the destructive character. He has few needs, and the least of them is to know what will replace what has been destroyed. First of all, for a moment at least, empty space, the place where the thing stood or the victim lived. Someone is sure to be found who needs this space without its being filled" ("The Destructive Character," in *Reflections*, 301–302). Like Milton's before him, Benjamin's "theological foundationalism" (Hanssen, *Critique*, 23) encourages the reader to acknowledge the possibility of divine violence ("someone is sure to be found"), even as it provides no

method for distinguishing between true and false prophets, between those agents who have genuinely emptied themselves of misguided human objectives and those who wage holy war in order to realize a particular historical motive. Whatever their intentions, the agents of divine violence always risk substituting their own finite and instrumental will for God's.

121. Emphasizing Samson's traditional association with the sun, Tannenbaum argues that "Samson, with open eyes, represents the apocalyptic new sun of inner vision that causes all previous suns to expire. Here Blake interprets Samson's death as symbolizing the role of the true deliverer" (*Biblical Tradition in Blake's Early Prophecies*, 268). Wittreich takes the opposite view: "Samson the liberator, instead of releasing mankind from bondage, unleashes destruction; instead of being an awakener and a redeemer, he is a destroyer and a perverter" (*Angel of Apocalypse*, 52).

122. Blake shared Young's disdain for superficial "virtue" and "morality" of this kind. In *Jerusalem*, for instance, Los lectures Albion: "I have no time for seeming; and little arts of compliment, / In morality and virtue: in self-glorying and pride" (42:27–28, E 189).

123. Anonymous, *Grubb Street Journal*, 1735, cited in Susie I. Tucker, *Enthusiasm: A Study in Semantic Change* (Cambridge: Cambridge UP, 1972), 18.

124. Recall Christopher Hill's characterization of *Samson Agonistes* as Milton's "call of hope to the [politically] defeated," urging "potential Samsons . . . enslaved at the mill" to "be ready to act when the time comes . . . Milton believed that the war against Antichrist continued, and that it was the duty of God's people to hit back when they could" (*Milton and the English Revolution*, 441–442).

125. Jacques Derrida, *Politics of Friendship*, trans. George Collins (London: Verso, 1997), 78–79. "The one thing that is unacceptable these days," Derrida states elsewhere, "is intellectuals taking their time" ("The Deconstruction of Actuality: An Interview with Jacques Derrida," *Radical Philosophy* 68 (Autumn 1994): 30).

126. For Kahn, Milton's dramatization of "contradiction, equivocation, ambivalence" in *Samson Agonistes* is not meant to paralyze decision and action in the potentially infinite delay of interpretation but instead conveys the difficult cognitive experience that must precede decision and action ("Political Theology and Reason of State in *Samson Agonistes*," 1068). Thus *Samson Agonistes* is no set piece of new critical ambiguity, displacing the need to act with homeostatic aesthetic tension. Still committed to social action, even as he recognizes its inherently tragic dimension, Milton "is not a liberal thinker" (1089). Nevertheless, the question raised by Milton, picked up by Blake, and later echoed by Derrida (who supplies an important voice in Kahn's essay), is not whether reading is a prelude to or an evasion of political action but whether critical reading is itself already a politically significant act. And if that is the case—if, as Derrida argues in *Specters of Marx*, to interpret the world *is* to change it—then it becomes increasingly difficult to distinguish between categories such as social activist and "liberal thinker" in the first place. *Samson Agonistes* renews Milton's revolutionary commitments *and* points to a new liberal quietism. Therein lies Milton's profound influence on Blake.

127. William Michael Rossetti's description of Blake's lost tempura *Samson Pulling Down the Temple* is also relevant: "Samson occupies almost the entire composition. The only other figure is a boy crouched in the corner, horror-struck at his impending fate" ("Annotated Catalogue of Blake's Pictures and Drawings," in Gilchrist, *Life of William Blake, "Pictor Ignotus"* [London: Macmillan, 1863], 2:224). In *Why Milton Matters*, 190–191, Wittreich observes the ethical dilemmas posed in the biblical narrative by the presence of the boy who leads Sam-

son to the pillars, a difficulty Milton heightens by emphasizing the boy's unawareness of the imminent catastrophe ("He unsuspitious led him") but also eases somewhat by describing him simply as a "guide" of unidentified age (*Samson Agonistes*, ll. 1630–1635).

128. See W. J. T. Mitchell's still definitive account of Blake's iconography of the senses in "Blake's Pictorial Style," Chap. 2 of *Blake's Composite Art: A Study of the Illuminated Poetry* (Princeton: Princeton UP, 1978), 58–69.

129. Butlin, *The Paintings and Drawings of William Blake*, 1:252.

130. Mee notes that the *Night Thoughts* illustrations generally make "little distinction between spiritual and corporeal forms," and that this "incongruous mixing of the senses with spiritual matter" was typical of the visionary enthusiasm Blake's critics (like Robert Hunt) condemned as vulgar and absurd. " 'As portentous as the written wall': Blake's Illustrations to *Night Thoughts*," in *Prophetic Character: Essays on William Blake in Honor of John. E. Grant*, ed. Alexander S. Gourlay (West Cornwall, CT: Locust Hill Press, 2002), 181, 186. When one adds the subtle but forceful attack on monarchy that Mee also finds woven into Blake's images, the Samson figure, which Mee does not discuss, could easily be considered a direct embodiment of radical spiritual strength in robust, muscular form. Nevertheless, Blake's image troubles such an interpretation even as it invites it, subjecting agent and object to the materialist force of gravity that governs both.

131. Blake incorporated another echo of Newton's compass in *Samson Subdued* (see figure 2.4), this time in the form of Dalila's scissors.

132. *Simone Weil's "The Iliad or the Poem of Force": A Critical Edition*, trans. and ed. James Holoka (New York: Peter Lang, [1939] 2003), 45. If one were to substitute Israelites and Philistines for Greeks and Trojans, Weil's commentary on Homer's deluded warriors could often serve as a gloss on *Samson Agonistes*. For instance: "As pitilessly as force annihilates, equally without pity it intoxicates those who possess or believe they possess it. People in the *Iliad* are not segregated into conquered, slaves, suppliants on one side and conquerors and masters on the other; every human being may at any moment be compelled to submit to force" (51).

133. Blake, *The Early Illuminated Books*, ed. Morris Eaves, Robert N. Essick, and Joseph Viscomi (Princeton: The Blake Trust / Princeton UP, 1993), 115.

134. The slogan "Urgent: Slow Down" provides a heading in Nicholas Royle's *Jacques Derrida* (New York: Routledge, 2003), 4. Royle explains the paradox as follows: although the "guiding dictum for approaching Derrida" is to "slow down," "this does not mean, even for a moment, that Derrida advocates quietism, inactivity, a studied *laissez faire*. As [Derrida] has put it: 'It is necessary to defer, to take one's distance, to tarry; but also to rush in precipitately' " (4–5). Here Royle quotes from "The Deconstruction of Actuality: An Interview with Jacques Derrida," in *Radical Philosophy* 68 (Autumn 1994): 31.

135. Joanna Picciotto, *Labors of Innocence in Early Modern England* (Harvard: Harvard UP, 2010), 439. In Picciotto's reading, "[*Paradise Lost*] everywhere calls attention to the constructed nature of the perceptual experiences it records. Rather than representing completed images or perceptions, the poem recreates the conditions of viewing, engaging the reader's conscious effort to complete the task of perception" (438). In this way the poem becomes "a literary counterpart to experimentalist observation" (439).

136. Jon Mee, *Romanticism, Enthusiasm, and Regulation*, 61. That "[e]nthusiasm was taken to avoid reflection and meditation" (11) is an ongoing theme of Mee's survey of seventeenth- and eighteenth-century attitudes toward enthusiasm. J. G. A. Pocock has shown

how enthusiasm eventually came to signify "any system that presents the mind as of the same substance, spiritual or material, as the universe that it interprets, so that the mind becomes the universe thinking and obtains an authority derived from its identity with its subject matter" ("Enthusiasm: The Antiself of Enlightenment," *Huntington Library Quarterly* 60.1/2 (1997): 14.

137. Fish, *How Milton Works*, 455. What J. Hillis Miller has claimed of narrative in general is certainly true of *Samson Agonistes*: "What the good reader confronts in the end is not the moral law brought into the open at last in a clear example, but the unreadability of the text" (Miller, *The Ethics of Reading* [New York: Columbia UP, 1987], 33).

138. Picciotto, *Labors of Innocence in Early Modern England*, 503.

139. Simone Weil's description of the Homeric warrior's illusory power again provides a useful gloss on Samson: "He who possesses force moves in a frictionless environment; nothing in the human matter around him puts an interval for reflection between impulse and action. Where reflection has no place, there is neither justice nor forethought: hence the ruthless and mindless behavior of warriors" (*Simone Weil's "The Iliad or the Poem of Force,"* 53). Setting Samson within the mediation of a textual environment, Milton and Blake restore the friction the warrior would ignore, cultivating an interval between impulse and action that allows for the reader's, if not the hero's, reflection.

140. As it appears in biblical narrative, the term "judge" is notoriously difficult to define. Although it often indicates temporary, charismatic leadership in response to a specific military crisis, it also occasionally includes a regular judicial function, as is the case with Deborah (Judg. 4:5) and Samuel (1 Sam. 7:15–17). Samson's birth story and nazaritic career anticipate Samuel's, inviting a comparison between judges that reflects poorly on the former figure. For biblical authors trying to explain why an Israelite monarchy became necessary, Samson's impulsive violence provides a spectacular example of the general moral and social deterioration among the tribes.

141. Unless otherwise indicated, citations in this paragraph are from Sigmund Freud, "Negation," in *The Standard Edition of the Complete Psychological Works of Sigmund Freud*, trans. James Strachey, 24 vols. (London: Hogarth Press, 1961), 19:235–239.

142. Sigmund Freud, *The Ego and the Id*, in *The Standard Edition*, 19:55.

143. Benjamin Libet, "Unconscious Cerebral Initiative and the Role of Conscious Will in Voluntary Action," *Behavioral and Brain Sciences* 8 (1985): 536–539. Cited parenthetically hereafter.

144. Ibid.

145. In *Organs without Bodies: On Deleuze and Consequences* (New York: Routledge, 2004), Slavoj Žižek raises serious questions about the metaphysics of Libet's hypothesis (namely, why wouldn't the veto function of consciousness itself be subject either to blind neuronal impulses or to the influence of other unconscious processes, or both?). He nevertheless smuggles the hypothesis virtually intact into his approving discussion of "the Kantian 'incorporation thesis' ": "We subjects are passively affected by pathological objects and motivations; but, in a reflexive way, we ourselves have the minimal power to accept (or reject) being affected in this way . . . I retroactively determine the causes allowed to determine me" (112). Many of the responses published alongside Libet's original article raise objections similar to Žižek's. Charles C. Wood, for instance, complains that the conscious decision to veto or trigger must itself be based on preceding brain activity: "To assume otherwise is to assume that conscious intention arises full-blown, out of nothing, instantaneously" ("Unconscious

cerebral initiative," 557). For a different critique of Libet's conclusions and their influence on contemporary affect theorists, especially Massumi, see Ruth Leys, "The Turn to Affect: A Critique," *Critical Inquiry* 37.3 (Spring 2011): 452–458. According to Leys, Massumi and other modern Spinozists have reinstated a rigid mind-body dualism despite their self-proclaimed materialism, relying on Libet for experimental evidence that "intentionality has no place in the initiation of [bodily] movements and that therefore it must be the brain which does all the thinking and feeling and moving for us" (457). The extent to which affect theorists tend to ignore significant objections to Libet's findings indicates how determined they are to claim clinical support for their belief in the body's priority to and autonomy from the mind.

146. Gordon Teskey, *Delirious Milton* (Cambridge, MA: Harvard UP, 2006), 168.

147. Derrida, *Politics of Friendship*, 15. Derrida discusses the "passive decision" on 68–69. In Simon Critchley's useful explanation, the passive decision "is not something taken by a subject, but rather the subject (insofar as one can still employ this word post-deconstructively) is *taken by the decision* that is made without its volition" (*Ethics Politics Subjectivity* [London: Verso, 1999], 263).

148. Derrida, *Politics of Friendship*, 15.

149. Edmund Ludlow, *A Voyce from the Watch Tower Part 5 (only): 1660–1662*, ed. Blair Worden (London: Royal Historical Society, 1978), 309–310.

150. Teskey, *Delirious Milton*, 167.

151. Libet, "Unconscious cerebral initiative," 539.

152. "*In sum, a decision is unconscious*—insane as that may seem, it involves the unconscious and nevertheless remains responsible" (Derrida, *Politics of Friendship*, 69, original emphasis).

153. Michel Foucault, "What Is Enlightenment?" trans. Catherine Porter, in *The Foucault Reader*, ed. Paul Rabinow (New York: Pantheon, 1984), 47.

154. Derrida, *Politics of Friendship*, 297.

155. Michel Foucault, "Polemics, Politics, and Problematizations: An Interview with Michel Foucault," trans. Lydia Davis, in *The Foucault Reader*, 388.

156. Foucault, "What Is Enlightenment?" 50.

157. Rather than provide yet another interpretation, let me simply point out that these icons have become the subject of contradictory readings, signs of either Blake's identification with or dissociation from the design's central figure. Believing that the picture "portrays a false apocalypse," Wittreich decodes the iconic worm by reference to a passage in *The Four Zoas* Night VII, in which Orc is caught in a Samson-like bind: "Like a worm I rise . . . unbound / From wrath Now When I rage my fetters bind me more" (80: 29–30, E 356) (*Angel of Apocalypse*, 57). Essick, however, sees a far more positive representation of authentic liberation and thus refers to *Jerusalem*: "Let the Human Organs be kept in their perfect Integrity / At will Contracting into Worms, or Expanding into Gods" (55: 36–37, E 205) (*William Blake, Printmaker*, 183). One reading associates Albion with the worm and thus leads us to temper our enthusiasm for him; the other contrasts Albion with the worm and strengthens our identification with his liberating gesture. Both are valid and together they characterize a reading process that, once started, may hesitate in the realm of "experimental action" forever.

158. Erdman, *Prophet Against Empire*, 6.

159. Matthew Arnold, "The Function of Criticism at the Present Time," in *Culture and Anarchy and Other Writings*, ed. Stefan Collini (Cambridge: Cambridge UP, [1864] 1993, 41.

160. Radzinowicz describes Milton's understanding of catharsis in a way compatible with the idea of active passivity I have proposed in this chapter. Because Milton sustains the passions that tragedy is supposed to temper, the "calm of mind" achieved at the end of *Samson Agonistes* "accommodates . . . an aspect of renewed energy for the future . . . The tragic experience is forward looking"; its object is "[t]o change men and make it possible for them to think the new and the true" (*Toward Samson Agonistes*, 363).

161. Kenzaburo Oe, *Somersault*, trans. Philip Gabriel (New York: Grove, 2003), 307. *Somersault* is not as unlikely a reference point as it at first might seem. Oe is an avid reader of Blake, and (through Blake) *Somersault* can be considered his distant variation on *Samson Agonistes*. The novel recounts the history of a Japanese church loosely modeled on Aum Shinrikyo, the cult responsible for the sarin gas attacks on the Tokyo subway in 1995. Poised between apocalyptic inspiration and terrorist violence, Oe's fictional church finds itself heir to the same problems regarding action and inaction that Blake himself inherited from Milton. Thus when Oe's would-be prophet, Patron, prays for a divine command from "the *other side*" that would authorize an act of sacred violence, he replays the predicament of Samson at the pillars, who "stood, as one who pray'd, / Or some great matter in his mind revolv'd" (ll. 1637–1638). And when his interpreter, Guide, reworks the content of his vision "into ordinary language," telling their followers "neither to take action nor to desist," he translates the noise of history into paradoxical terms that both Milton and Blake would have understood. Finally, the problem of action here is also a problem of timing, of knowing when to begin, for the verb repeated and negated in Oe's text (*kaishi se ye . . . kaishi suru na mo*) literally means "to begin": "You must begin, but also you must not begin." My thanks to Shelby Oxenford for this literal translation.

162. Kant, *Conflict of the Faculties*, 153.

163. Michel Foucault, "The Art of Telling the Truth," trans. Alan Sheridan, in *Critique and Power: Recasting the Foucault/Habermas Debate*, ed. Michael Kelly (Cambridge, MA: MIT Press, 1994), 146.

164. Foucault, "The Art of Telling the Truth," 147.

165. Foucault, "What Is Enlightenment?" 47.

166. Hill, *Milton and the English Revolution*, 441.

167. See Wittreich, *Angel of Apocalypse*, 229–236. Other attempts to credit Hayley's influence on Blake include Philip Cox, "Blake, Hayley and Milton: A Reassessment," *English Studies* 75 (1994): 430–441, and Cato Marks, "Writings of the Left Hand: William Blake Forges a New Political Aesthetic," *Huntington Library Quarterly* 74 (Mar 2011): 43–70. Although Marks shares Wittreich's sense of Hayley's importance, he objects to the claim that Hayley's theory of epic poetry taught Blake to internalize political goals and privilege the poetic transformation of consciousness. "In fact," Marks writes, "Hayley explicitly attacks poetry that is disengaged from political activity . . . Hayley's poem is a politically charged manifesto" (48). "[C]austic criticism of Hayley aside," he concludes, "the transmission of ideas about Milton and epic poetry during the interlude in Felpham marks a crucial stage in the development of Blake's perception of the poet as a public, political figure" (50).

168. *Angel of Apocalypse*, 230–231.

169. Hill, *Milton and the English Revolution*, 445.

170. William Hayley, *The Life of Milton, In Three Parts*, 2nd ed. (London: Printed for T. Cadell, Junior and W. Davies, 1796), 137, x. Cited parenthetically hereafter.

171. Byron, *English Bards and Scotch Reviewers*, in *The Poetical Works of Byron* (Boston: Houghton Mifflin Company, 1975), 246, l. 314.

172. Gibbon died the same year *Life of Milton* was published. A friend of Hayley's, he considered it ill advised to call attention to Milton's prose in the early 1790s. See Hayley's comment to this effect in the dedication to the second edition, vii. In fact, Hayley was unable to publish his discussion of Milton's politics in its entirety until the revolutionary panic of 1793–1795 began to subside. See Wittreich's account of the book's publication history in his introduction to *Life of Milton*, 2nd ed. (Gainesville, FL: Scholars' Facsimiles and Reprints, 1970), viii–x.

173. Dustin Griffin quotes from the anonymous editor of a 1791 reprint of Milton's *A Readie and Easie Way to Establish a Commonwealth*, in *Regaining Paradise: Milton and the Eighteenth Century* (Cambridge: Cambridge UP, 1986), 17.

174. As Griffin has demonstrated, Hayley's main strategies in defending Milton—assimilating him to the principles of the Glorious Revolution and urging liberal tolerance of his misguided but sincere passion for liberty—were common in eighteenth-century writings on Milton. Both tactics are already evident, for instance, in Thomas Newton's 1749 edition of *Paradise Lost*. See *Regaining Paradise*, 11–21.

175. In his letters, Hayley variously referred to his new friend as "warmhearted indefatigable Blake," "our good enthusiastic Blake," and the like (*The Letters of William Blake*, ed. Geoffrey Keynes [Oxford: Clarendon Press, 1980], 36, 39). When he presented Blake with a copy of *The Triumphs of Temper* previously owned by his deceased son, he drafted a dedication addressing his new friend as "visionary Blake, / Sublimely fanciful & kindly mild" (G. E. Bentley Jr., "Blake's Engravings and his Friendship with Flaxman," *Studies in Bibliography* 12 [1959]: 171).

176. Georges Bataille, *Literature and Evil*, trans. Alastair Hamilton (New York: Marion Boyers, 1985 [1957]), 79.

177. Blake's unctuous proposal indicates that he and Phillips considered Hayley's name recognition crucial to the magazine's success, but it is hard to imagine him inviting Hayley's assistance in this particular project if he considered his politics objectionable. Phillips, who intended to finance the project, had previously been jailed for distributing *Rights of Man*. To the extent that this incident is representative, Blake's politics seem capacious enough to have included radical and liberal partners alike.

178. Philip Cox astutely observes the various strategies by which Hayley's "apolitical compromise" (436) attempts "to celebrate [Milton's] imaginative liberty and at the same time control, or 'guide,' the poet" (435). However, Cox falls into the traditional trap of exaggerating Hayley's conservativism in order to exaggerate Blake's radical rejection of it. Thus, after finding Hayley's embrace of rural retirement irreconcilable with Milton's ethos of political engagement, Cox goes on to align Blake with Milton, arguing that *Milton* expresses Blake's own "final rejection of retirement at Felpham in favour of *a return to radical action* within the city" (436, my emphasis). Such an approach can explain neither the attraction that originally drew Blake into rural retirement nor the oblique, largely private forms of "radical action" (such as "Albion rose") he took up when he returned to London ("Blake, Hayley and Milton: A Reassessment").

179. Foucault, "The Art of Telling the Truth," 147.

180. Johnson, *Milton*, in *The Lives of the Poets*, 1:276.

181. Here I am following J. H. Bernard's translation of *Critique of Judgment* (New York: Hafner Press, 1951), 112.

182. Lyotard, "The Sign of History," in *The Lyotard Reader,* ed. Andrew Benjamin (Oxford: Basil Blackwell, 1989), 403–404.

183. Here I am invoking the title of Jon Mee's *Dangerous Enthusiasm: William Blake and the Culture of Radicalism in the 1790s.*

184. "The same calmness, and even greater self-possession, may be affirmed of Milton, as far as his poems, and poetic character are concerned. He reserved his anger, for the enemies of religion, freedom, and his country" (Samuel Taylor Coleridge, *Biographia Literaria,* ed. James Engell and W. Jackson Bate, 2 vols., in *The Collected Works of Samuel Taylor Coleridge,* 16 vols., Bollingen Series (Princeton: Princeton UP, 1983), vol. 7, 1:36–37. By removing Milton's anger from his poetry, Coleridge can enlist Milton to refute Horace's complaint against the irritability of poets. Just before introducing the examples of Chaucer, Shakespeare, Spenser, and Milton, Coleridge contrasts the "self-sufficing power of absolute *Genius*" with "men of *commanding* genius": "While the former rest content between thought and reality, as it were in an intermundium of which their own living spirit supplies the *substance,* and their imagination the ever-varying *form*; the latter must impress their preconceptions on the world without" (31–32). For analysis of Coleridge's complex attitude toward anger and his attempt to separate "poetic, creative rage from rage-as-anger" (60), see Andrew M. Stauffer, *Anger, Revolution, and Romanticism* (Cambridge: Cambridge UP, 2005), 54–63.

185. Mee, *Romanticism, Enthusiasm, and Regulation,* 18. Mee quotes from Shaftesbury's *Characteristics of Men, Manners, Opinions, Times,* but it is hard not to recall the combustible matter of *Samson Agonistes* in this context. Although Mee does not mention Hayley, his account of a broad eighteenth-century tendency to regulate enthusiasm by channeling it into literary expression provides exactly the right context for understanding Hayley's *Life of Milton.*

186. Immanuel Kant, *Conflict of the Faculties,* trans. Mary J. Gregor (Lincoln: U of Nebraska P, 1979 [1798]), 155, 157.

187. Arnold, "The Function of Criticism at the Present Time," 32–33.

188. Ibid., 32.

189. Kant, *Conflict of the Faculties,* 153.

190. "Ideas cannot be too much prized in and for themselves, cannot be too much lived with; but to transport them abruptly into the world of politics and practice, violently to revolutionise this world to their bidding—that is quite another thing" (Arnold, "The Function of Criticism at the Present Time," 32–33).

191. Arnold, "The Function of Criticism at the Present Time," 41–42.

192. Johnson, *Milton*, in *Lives of the Poets*, 1:248.

193. Milton, *The Second Defence of the English People,* in *The Riverside Milton,* 1098–1099.

194. *The Letters of William Blake,* 37.

195. Johnson, *Milton*, in *Lives of the Poets*, 1:248.

196. Algernon Charles Swinburne, *William Blake: A Critical Essay* (London: John Camden Hotten, 1868), 17–18.

197. Makdisi, *Romantic Imperialism,* 160.

198. William Hogarth, *The Analysis of Beauty with Rejected Passages from the Manuscript Drafts and Autobiographical Notes,* ed. Joseph Burke (Oxford: Clarendon Press, 1955), 227.

199. *The Letters of William Blake*, 36.

200. Jürgen Habermas, "Taking Aim at the Heart of the Present: On Foucault's Lecture on Kant's *What Is Enlightenment?*" in *Critique and Power: Recasting the Foucault/Habermas Debate*, 149–150.

201. Foucault, "What Is Enlightenment?" 50. Imagining Hayley imagining Foucault is a fanciful way to raise the question of Foucault's liberalism. Richard Rorty, for instance, sees Foucault as a liberal-despite-himself, describing him in terms that echo my own account of Blake in this chapter. Consider the following sentences from his "Moral Identity and Private Autonomy: The Case of Foucault," in *Essays on Heidegger and Others* (Cambridge: Cambridge UP, 1991):

> "[W]hether he wanted to be or not, [Foucault] was, among other things, a useful citizen of a democratic country." (198)
>
> "Just as Kierkegaard's knight of faith looks like a bank clerk, and in public acts like one, so the Romantic intellectual can be, for public purposes, your ordinary bourgeois liberal." (194)
>
> "Romantic intellectuals, religious mystics, sexual fetishists, and others whose private self has nothing much to do with their public self, are under the same moral obligations as all the rest of us." (197).

Perhaps it shouldn't surprise us that, for Rorty, the Romantic intellectual's creed of private and radical self-invention, which need not interfere with an obligatory performance of public virtue, is "summed up" by Blake's line from *Jerusalem* (10:20, E 153): "I must Create a System, or be enslav'd by another Mans" (E 153).

With characteristic indignation, Christopher Norris declares Rorty "absurdly wide of the mark" (38), but it is worth noting that he can rescue Foucault only by detaching the Foucault he rejects (private and aesthetic) from the one he approves (public and engaged). "In short: there is a near-schizophrenic splitting of roles between (1) Foucault the 'public' intellectual, thinking and writing on behalf of those subjects oppressed by the discourses of instituted power/knowledge, and (2) Foucault the avowed aesthete, avatar of Nietzsche and Baudelaire, who espouses an ethos of private self-fashioning and an attitude of sovereign disdain toward the principles and values of enlightened critique" (*The Truth about Postmodernism* [Oxford: Blackwell, 1993], 70). Although Norris pathologizes a schizophrenia that Rorty would normalize ("I wish that [Foucault] had been more comfortable with that self-description than he was" [198]), they equally share a desire to bar aesthetics from public discourse, Norris by eliminating it altogether, Rorty by privatizing it. Neither is willing to recognize, as Habermas does, the unresolved entanglement of critical and aesthetic judgments involved in Foucault's stubborn *enthusiasm*. Positioned at the frontier between public and private, and thus displacing any easy distinction between them, such enthusiasm poses a double risk that pleases neither the self-professed liberal nor the self-professed radical. On one hand, it risks collapsing politics into merely subjective judgments and individual acts of self-fashioning (as Norris fears), but on the other, it preserves a revolutionary affect that may spill over, at any time, into public discourse and risky political action (as Rorty fears).

Part II · Introduction

1. Douglas Barnett and Hilary Horn Ratner, "Introduction: The Organization and Integration of Cognition and Emotion in Development," *Journal of Experimental Child Psychology* 67 (1997): 312.

2. A. R. Damasio, *Descartes' Error: Emotion, Reason, and the Human Brain* (New York: Putnam, 1994). For "emotional intelligence," I am thinking primarily of the subtitle of Martha Nussbaum's magisterial study *Upheavals of Thought: The Intelligence of Emotions* (Cambridge: Cambridge UP, 2001). Also see Robert C. Solomon's "Emotions, Thoughts, and Feelings: Emotions as Engagements with the World," in *Thinking about Feeling: Contemporary Philosophers on Emotions,* ed. Robert C. Solomon (Oxford: Oxford UP, 2004). Solomon points out that recent modifications of the "cognitive theory" of emotions in fact testify to the theory's staying power: "the idea that emotions . . . display a kind of intelligence [has] become mainstream, even popular" (76).

3. Francisco J. Varela, Evan Thompson, and Eleanor Rosch, *The Embodied Mind: Cognitive Science and Human Experience* (Cambridge, MA: MIT Press, 1993).

4. In fact, the sentences are Antonio Negri's; see *Time for Revolution,* trans. Matteo Mandarini (New York: Continuum, 2003), 205.

5. Eve Kosofsky Sedgwick, *Touching Feeling: Affect, Pedagogy, Performativity* (Durham: Duke UP, 2003), 2. Cited parenthetically hereafter.

6. William M. Reddy, *The Navigation of Feeling: A Framework for the History of Emotions* (Cambridge: Cambridge UP, 2001), 122–123.

7. Philip Fisher, *The Vehement Passions* (Princeton: Princeton UP, 2002), 60. Cited parenthetically hereafter.

8. Rei Terada, *Feeling in Theory: Emotion after the "Death of the Subject"* (Cambridge, MA: Harvard UP, 2001), 4, 22. Cited parenthetically hereafter.

9. "In wonder we notice against the background of a lawful and familiar world something that strikes us by its novelty and by the pleasure that this surprising new fact brings to us. Each of us has at every stage of our lives a distinct but provisional horizon line separating the familiar from the unknown and the unknowable. Any one experience of wonder informs us about the momentary location of this horizon line" (Fisher, *The Vehement Passions,* 1). See my discussion of this passage in the introduction to this book.

10. Amelie Oksenberg Rorty suggests that "the rich variety of words for emotions in contemporary Anglo-American folk speech" indicates a corresponding variety of "theoretical implications: *passion* suggests fervor; *feeling* connotes sensation, *affect* implies a change, *sentiment* indicates a cognitive attitude, *emotion* (*ex-motu*) suggests a motivational charge." Given the complexity of emotions, she also suggests that it defies common sense to believe that such terminological distinctions refer to elements that can actually be separated in experience ("Enough Already with 'Theories of the Emotions,'" in Solomon, *Thinking about Feeling,* 269–270). Charles Altieri approaches the problem of complexity by recognizing category differences (feelings, moods, emotions, and passions) but designating one overarching term to convey the whole gray-scale spectrum: "I use the term 'affect' as my umbrella term so that one discourse can engage the entire range of states that are bounded on one side by pure sensation and on the other by thoughts that have no visible or tangible impact on bodily states" ("Towards an Expressivist Theory of the Affects," *Soundings: An Interdisciplinary Journal* 86 [Spring-Summer 2003]: 72).

11. The idea that affect empowers rather than opposes the mind's agency runs counter to a long-standing dualism that represents bodies and feelings as threats to reason—a notion that led figures such as Wollstonecraft and Coleridge to equate virtuous self-governance with the disciplining of emotion. In a notoriously ascetic passage from *A Vindication of the Rights of Woman* (New York: Norton, 1982 [1792]), Wollstonecraft urges husbands and wives "not to indulge those emotions which disturb the order of society" (30). A few years later, Coleridge urged readers to join him in a similar project of self-control: "Let us exert over our own hearts a virtuous despotism, and lead our own Passions in triumph, and then we shall want neither Monarch nor General" (*Lectures 1795 on Politics and Religion*, ed. Lewis Patton and Peter Mann, in *Collected Works of Samuel Taylor Coleridge*, ed. Kathleen Coburn and Bart Winer, 16 vols. [Princeton: Princeton UP, 1971], 1:229). Equating the highest aesthetic standards with emotional control, Sir Joshua Reynolds told artists that "to preserve the most perfect beauty *in its most perfect state*, you cannot express the passions, all of which produce distortion and deformity," to which Blake of course responded, "What Nonsense" (E 653).

12. Fisher, *The Vehement Passions*, 1–2.

13. Paul de Man, "The Return to Philology," in *The Resistance to Theory* (Minneapolis: U of Minnesota P, 1986), 23.

14. Virtually every aspect of the modernist judgment against sensibility can already be found in Coleridge's *Aids to Reflection* (1825). Sensibility is *"passive,"* not active ("apart from choice and Reflection"); it is a matter of embodied particularity, not universal judgment ("for the greater part a quality of the nerves, and a result of individual bodily temperament"); it is "effeminate." "Can any thing *manly*, I say, proceed from those, who for Law and Light would substitute shapeless feelings, sentiments, impulses . . . ?" *Aids to Reflection*, ed. John Beer, in *The Collected Works*, 9:57–65.

15. Jerome McGann, *The Poetics of Sensibility: A Revolution in Literary Style* (Oxford: Clarendon Press, 1996), 1–6.

16. Geoffrey Hartman, "The Sympathy Paradox: Poetry, Feeling, and Modern Cultural Morality," in *The Fateful Question of Culture* (New York: Columbia UP, 1997), 145. The advantage of Hartman's sober position—recognizing that culture and emotion are always mutually constitutive—is that it avoids endowing emotion with a talismanic, Archimedean sublimity it will always fail to live up to. For Hartman, emotions perform their work within culture, quietly or not at all.

17. Adela Pinch, *Strange Fits of Passion: Epistemologies of Emotion, Hume to Austen* (Stanford: Stanford UP, 1996), 48.

18. Barbara Johnson, "Strange Fits: Poe and Wordsworth on the Nature of Poetic Language," in *A World of Difference* (Baltimore: Johns Hopkins UP, 1987), 95.

19. Altieri, "Towards an Expressivist Theory of the Affects," 71.

20. John Guillory argues that by ignoring the "enormous gap between reading as it is practiced within and without the academy," "we tend to indulge in what I will call a political fantasy, the fantasy of transforming the world to a degree vastly greater than can reasonably be expected of perhaps any disciplinary practice" ("The Ethical Practice of Modernity: The Example of Reading," in *The Turn to Ethics*, ed. Marjorie Garber, Beatrice Hanssen, and Rebecca L. Walkowitz [New York: Routledge, 2000], 31). We will return to Guillory's argument and its implications for reading Blake in chapter 5.

21. Immanuel Kant, *Critique of the Power of Judgment*, ed. Paul Guyer, trans. Paul Guyer and Eric Matthews (Cambridge: Cambridge UP, 2000 [1790]), 149.

22. Alice Fulton, *Feeling as a Foreign Language: The Good Strangeness of Poetry* (Saint Paul, MN: Graywolf Press, 1999). Fulton sings the praises of poetry's "eccentricity"—"a positive value, capable of injecting the foreign into the dully familiar" (4).

23. See Reddy, *The Navigation of Feeling*, 118–122.

24. Jesse Prinz, "Embodied Emotions," in Solomon, *Thinking about Feeling*, 44.

25. Nussbaum, *Upheavals of Thought*, 172–173. Cited parenthetically hereafter.

26. Neu, "Emotions and Freedom," in Solomon, *Thinking about Feeling*, 178. In fact, Neu has used this line from *Jerusalem* on several occasions, first as the title of an important article in *Representations* (1987) and later as the title for a collection of essays (including the earlier article), *A Tear Is an Intellectual Thing* (New York: Oxford UP, 2000). In "Emotions and Freedom," Neu's treatment of "Activity and Passivity in Emotional Life" (a section heading) sounds similar to the critical project Foucault proposed in answer to the question, "What Is Enlightenment?": "One often-neglected aspect of freedom depends on a recognition of those constraints that are given—that is, an acknowledgement of the necessities of our nature . . . Of course, when we mistake social impositions for the necessities of nature, we turn contingencies into constraints. We can be shackled by our own failures to appreciate the difference . . . One of the great values of the imagination, as of historical and cross-cultural study, is to open us to possibilities that may not be obvious to us in our immediate circumstances. Literary and personal explorations—as well as philosophical ones—can help us to discover real limitations and to overcome illusory ones. Of course, one of the ways to discover limitations is to test them, to try to overcome them" (175–176). Neu is a faithful cognitivist ("Why do we cry? My short answer is: because we think" [*A Tear Is an Intellectual Thing*, 14]). As such he sometimes treats emotion as if it is primarily an internal modification of Enlightenment, retaining the hope, "the Spinozist hope, that understanding can make us free" (163). Elsewhere, however, Neu recognizes that a program of converting passive into active, more thoughtful emotions occurs at too great a cost, making it difficult to see how aesthetic and sexual feelings could survive such a conversion. Neu comes closest to my own idea when he briefly suggests that Blake's understanding of imagination may avoid this problem because it does not seem to rely on opposing active to passive emotions.

27. Jenefer Robinson's *Deeper than Reason: Emotion and its Role in Literature, Music, and Art* (Oxford: Clarendon Press, 2005) is typical here. Following the laboratory work of Joseph Ledoux, Robinson proposes that emotion is indeed based on a set of in-built affective appraisal mechanisms (galvanic skin response, for instance) that operate too quickly and automatically for awareness but also that this "quick and dirty processing system" is soon followed by "a slower, more discriminating" one, which can "assess the appropriateness of the prior automatic response, and presumably attempt to modify and control both the initial appraisal and the organism's subsequent responses" (50–52). Affective appraisal first, cognitive-emotional assessment quickly after. It is fascinating that arguments of this sort, aiming to defend the priority of hardwired physiology to cognition, end up doing nearly the opposite, extending a kind of unconscious cognition all the way down, such that the animal body itself turns out to be an information processor in each of its material aspects. Too much depends, in my view, on a semantic distinction between *appraisals* and *judgments* or *evaluations*. Robinson, for instance, claims that "*affective appraisals*" require "no cognitive intervention" (52), as higher processing certainly does, but because they provide rapid assessment of an organism's wellbeing in relation to its environment, she also suggests that these embodied responses can be thought of as "special kinds of information-processing devices" (43).

Given that the difference here involves the degree of complexity and self-awareness, and not the kind of activity (since both higher and lower responses evaluate information), Robinson has to confess that "whether these fast emotional appraisals are cognitive or not depends on how you define 'cognition'" (45). That is, even though she insists that affective appraisals are "non-cognitive," her model of emotional process invites us to think of such appraisals as *differently* cognitive. As Ronald De Sousa complains, if any "transmission of information" makes a process cognitive, then "it is difficult to see what ground is left for noncognitivism to occupy" ("Emotions: What I Know," in Solomon, *Thinking about Feeling*, 61–62). Rather than restoring a body prior to cognition, Robinson's "affective appraisals" present us with a body always making judgments, with some deep-level cognition always "on."

28. Nussbaum's approach to autocritical emotion raises another problem. If one emotion can be subjected to the criticism of another, and that emotion to the criticism of a third, and so on, then how can one reconcile the progressive vision of emotional reform with the prospect it opens of infinite, potentially paralytic self-mistrust? As we will see in the account of compassion she derives from Adam Smith, Nussbaum depends upon the role played by judgment within emotion, but judgment requires the detachment of an internal spectator, a capacity to self-monitor emotional response. Given that detachment can never recede to a point where it might produce credible judgments and overcome self-suspicion, one is tempted to join Mackenzie's protagonist Harley and declare, with an exclamation point that announces a renewed faith in emotion, however blind: "to calculate the chances of deception is too tedious a business for the life of man!" (Henry Mackenzie, *The Man of Feeling* [Oxford: Oxford UP, 1987 (1771)], 41).

29. Lauren Berlant, "Introduction: Compassion (and Withholding)," in *Compassion: The Culture and Politics of an Emotion*, ed. Lauren Berlant (New York: Routledge, 2004), 5.

30. See Tristanne J. Connolly, for instance, who distinguishes sympathy—which retains a healthy sense of identity—from pity, which indulges in an invasive fantasy of entering into another's experience. "True sympathy relies on being truly oneself, while 'pity', or trying to put oneself in another's place, which is impossible, 'divides the soul' (BU 12: 53)" (*William Blake and the Body* [London: Palgrave, 2002], 69).

31. The weariness of "To the Muses" closely resembles the "fatigue" Thomas Pfau associates with Romantic melancholy: "the deep-structural fatigue of a culture that has grown oppressively familiar with itself and hence begins to despair over the apparent inefficacy of its generic and rhetorical means" (*Romantic Moods: Paranoia, Trauma, and Melancholy, 1790–1840* [Baltimore: Johns Hopkins UP, 2005], 23).

32. Knightly Chetwood, *A Sermon Preach'd before the Lord Mayor, April 5, 1708*. Quoted in R. S. Crane, "Suggestions Toward a Genealogy of the 'Man of Feeling,'" *ELH* 1.3 (1934): 225.

33. "But the sweet cement, which in one sure band / Ties the whole frame, is *Love* / And *Charitie*" ("The Church-floore," in *The English Poems of George Herbert*, ed. C. A. Patrides [Totowa, NJ: Rowman and Littlefield, 1977], 84).

34. I'm quoting W. J. T. Mitchell, *Blake's Composite Art* (Princeton: Princeton UP, 1978), 133, but the distinction between types of pity on the basis of sincerity and hypocrisy is a commonplace of Blake criticism. See S. Foster Damon's *A Blake Dictionary* (New York: Dutton, 1971), 327.

35. "Wrought" is thus a word every bit as contradictory as the "fit" that has received so much attention in readings of Wordsworth's "Strange Fits of Passion," which provides the title for the studies of poetry and feeling by Barbara Johnson and Adela Pinch cited earlier.

As for "wrought," Laurence Sterne plays upon the word's doubleness in his sermon on "The Prodigal Son": "lessons of wisdom have never such power over us, as when they are wrought into the heart, through the ground-work of a story which engages the passions: Is it that we are like iron, and must first be heated before we can be wrought upon?" *The Sermons of Laurence Sterne,* ed. Melvyn New, in *The Florida Edition of the Works of Laurence Sterne* (Gainesville: UP of Florida, 1996), 4:186.

36. Also see Geoffrey Keynes's discussion of this proof in *Blake Studies* (New York: Haskell House, 1971), 111 ff.

37. Blake may have found precedent for his equivocal treatment of "pitying" (substantive and adverbial) in John Gabriel Stedman's *Narrative of a Five Years' Expedition against the Revolted Negroes of Surinam,* a text he illustrated. Describing the misery of his disease-ridden post at Devils Harwar, Stedman resorted to quoting lines from James Thomson's "Summer" in *The Seasons:* "You Gallant Vernon Saw / The miserable Scene: you Pitying Saw," (ed. Richard and Sally Price [Baltimore: Johns Hopkins UP, 1988 (1796)], 152).

38. Fredric Jameson, *Marxism and Form* (Princeton: Princeton UP, 1971), 330–331.

39. Louis Althusser, "A Letter on Art in Reply to André Daspre," in *Lenin and Philosophy,* trans. Ben Brewster (New York: Monthly Review Press, 1971), 222–223.

40. For a compatible understanding of "adverse emotion" in Blake, and in Blake's engagement with sentimentalism specifically, see James Chandler's "Blake and the Syntax of Sentiment: An Essay on 'Blaking' Understanding," in *Blake, Nation and Empire,* ed. Steve Clark and David Worrall (Basingstoke: Palgrave, 2006), 102–118. Also recall my reading of Chandler's essay in the introduction to this book.

41. Jacques Derrida often uses this formulation. For late examples, see *Rogues: Two Essays on Reason* (Stanford: Stanford UP, 2005): "an essence without essence" (32); "a concept without concept" (32); "force *without* force" (86); and especially "messianicity without messianism" (88, 110, 153).

42. Karl Marx and Frederick Engels, *The German Ideology,* trans. and ed. C. J. Arthur (New York: International Publishers, 1970), 37.

Chapter 3 · "On Anothers Sorrow"

1. Adam Smith, *The Theory of Moral Sentiments,* ed. Knud Haakonssen (Cambridge: Cambridge UP, 2002), 13, 44–45. Cited parenthetically hereafter.

2. In his commentary, Andrew Lincoln notes, "The song reveals not only the emotional appeal of this state of the soul, but also the limitations" (*Songs of Innocence and of Experience,* ed. Andrew Lincoln, in *Blake's Illuminated Books,* vol. 2, ed. David Bindman [Princeton: Princeton UP, 1991], 170). See also Edward Larrissy's remarks on how the speaker's insistence discredits his assertions, in *William Blake* (Oxford: Blackwell, 1985), 61–62.

3. Paul de Man, "Semiology and Rhetoric," in *Textual Strategies: Perspectives in Post-Structuralist Criticism,* ed. Josué V. Harari (Ithaca: Cornell UP, 1979), 128–129.

4. The Faerie Queene, I.vii.42, in *Books I and II of The Faerie Queene,* ed. Robert Kellogg and Oliver Steele (New York: Odyssey Press, 1965), 161.

5. Wordsworth, "Ode" ["Intimations of Immortality"], 22–23, in *Poems in Two Volumes, and Other Poems, 1800–1807,* ed. Jared Curtis (Ithaca: Cornell UP, 1983), 272.

6. Nelson Hilton points out that Blake's song may be answering Cowper's acknowledgement of maternal neglect: "Can a woman's tender care / Cease towards the child she

bare? / Yes, she may forgetful be." See "What has *Songs* to do with Hymns?" in *Blake in the Nineties*, ed. Steve Clark and David Worrall (New York: Palgrave Macmillan, 1999), 106.

7. Jacques Rancière, *The Politics of Aesthetics*, trans. Gabriel Rockhill (New York: Continuum, 2004), 12. For Rancière, politics and aesthetics, at a primary level, can be thought of as the communal, heterogeneous practices involved in "the parcelling out of the visible and the invisible" (19), either in service of preserving or altering existing regimes of experience. "This primary aesthetics," he suggests, should be "understood in a Kantian sense—reexamined perhaps by Foucault—as the system of *a priori* forms determining what presents itself to sense experience. It is a delimitation of spaces and times, of the visible and the invisible, of speech and noise, that simultaneously determines the place and the stakes of politics as a form of experience. Politics revolves around what is seen and what can be said about it, around who has the ability to see and the talent to speak, around the properties of spaces and the possibilities of time" (13).

8. According to Anne-Lise François, the idea that representation might relieve suffering underlies "the new historicist project of exposing hidden violences and rescuing silenced voices," a project "often weighted with a Benjaminian redemptive cast and a sometimes naïve, self-important faith in the moral efficacy of representation" (*Open Secrets: The Literature of Uncounted Experience* [Stanford: Stanford UP, 2008], 30–31).

9. "In a sense, one can say that the capacity to see (*voir*) is a function of the knowledge (*savoir*), or concepts, that is, the words, that are available to name visible things, and which are, as it were, programmes for perception" (Pierre Bourdieu, *Distinction: A Social Critique of the Judgement of Taste*, trans. Richard Nice [Cambridge, Ma: Harvard UP, 1984], 2).

10. Arthur Kleinman, Veena Das, and Margaret Lock, eds., *Social Suffering* (Berkeley and Los Angeles: U of California P, 1997), xii–xiii.

11. Reproduced by G. F. Barker-Benfield in "Sensibility," in *An Oxford Companion to the Romantic Age: British Culture, 1776–1832*, ed. Iain McCalman (Oxford: Oxford UP, 1999), 103.

12. In the *Poetics*, Aristotle makes identification a precondition of catharsis. Of "pity or terror," he writes, "the former is [felt] for a person undeserving of his misfortune, and the latter for a person like [ourselves]" (*Poetics I: with the Tractatus Coislinianus, A Hypothetical Reconstruction of Poetics II, and The Fragments of the On Poets*, trans. Richard Janko [Indianapolis: Hackett, 1987], 16). Cited parenthetically hereafter.

13. Rousseau, *Émile*, trans. Alan Bloom (New York: Basic Books, 1979), 224. Martha Nussbaum quotes this passage in her discussion of compassion (*Upheavals of Thought: The Intelligence of Emotions* (Cambridge: Cambridge UP, 2001), 315).

14. In *Aids to Reflection*, Coleridge issues a similar complaint against sympathetic sensibility, suggesting further that local acts of relief might be motivated by the observer's desire to reduce disturbance and maintain a comfort zone: "How many are there whose sensibility prompts them to remove those evils alone, which by hideous spectacle or clamorous outcry are present to their senses and disturb their selfish enjoyments." Coleridge adds, "Sensibility is not necessarily Benevolence" (*Aids to Reflection*, ed. John Beer, *The Collected Works of Samuel Taylor Coleridge*, vol. 9 [Princeton: Princeton UP, 1993], 58–59).

15. "The state or sovereignty in which we have been born and educated, and under the protection of which we continue to live, is, in ordinary cases, the greatest society upon whose happiness or misery, our good or bad conduct can have much influence. It is accordingly, by nature, most strongly recommended to us" (*Theory of Moral Sentiments*, 268).

16. Berlant, "Introduction: Compassion (and Withholding)," in *Compassion: The Culture and Politics of an Emotion*, ed. Lauren Berlant (New York: Routledge, 2004), 10.

17. William Clagett, *Of the Humanity and Charity of Christians, A Sermon Preached at the Suffolk Feast in St. Michael Cornhill, London, Nov. 30, 1686* (Printed by J. D. for J. Robinson and Thomas Newborough, 1687), 15–17.

18. "Julian and Maddalo," 449–450, in *Shelley's Poetry and Prose*, ed. Donald H. Reiman and Neil Fraistat (New York: Norton, 2002), 131; *The Portable Chekhov*, ed. Avrahm Yarmolinsky (New York: Viking Penguin, 1947), 381. The speaker of Alice Fulton's "Fair Use" is another literary figure burdened by sympathetic overload. Emphasizing a word Fulton also uses for her book's title—*Felt*—this poem's primary trope signifies both the vulnerability of individual feelings to the pressure of others and the "meshed . . . fabric of entanglement" that results. "Felt"

is formed by pressing
fibers till they can't be wrenched apart,
nothing is separate, the entire planet
being an unexpected example . . .
There is no size
limitation. It
expands equally in all directions as more
fibers are pressed in.

In the unlimited and painful sympathy ("Synthesis is blistering") that this speaker wears like a badge of honor, Smith would have recognized pathology (*Felt* [New York: Norton, 2001], 17–18).

19. Julie Ellison, *Cato's Tears and the Making of Anglo-American Emotion* (Chicago: U of Chicago P, 1999), 11.

20. "Pray, amongst your other experiments, did you ever try the effect of a guinea?" Thomas De Quincey, "On Wordsworth's Poetry," in *Works*, vol. 15 of 21, ed. Frederick Burwick (London: Pickering and Chatto, 2003), 15:231.

21. Shelley, "Defence of Poetry," in *Shelley's Poetry and Prose*, 517.

22. Fanny Burney, *Camilla* (Oxford: Oxford UP, 2009), 680.

23. "[T]he Poets Work is Done . . . / Within a Moment: a Pulsation of the Artery" (29:1–3, E 127). Blake's representation of the pulse and its role in the work of emotion is the subject of our next chapter.

24. Edmund Burke, *A Philosophical Enquiry into the Origin of our Ideas of the Sublime and Beautiful* (Oxford: Oxford UP, 1990), 43. Burke's comments on "The effects of *Sympathy* in the distresses of others" follow his discussion of the age-old problem of the pleasures of tragedy. Rather than distinguishing between real and represented suffering, however, Burke argues that there must be pleasure in both kinds of sympathy. Without the "delight" that draws us toward real misery we would find it too easy to shun suffering, pass it by. For Burke, the pleasure of sympathy derives from its association with action; it first prompts us to approach grief, then to relieve it. "[P]ity is a passion accompanied with pleasure . . . Whenever we are formed by nature to any active purpose, the passion which animates us to it, is attended with delight, or a pleasure of some kind, let the subject matter be what it will" (42).

25. Quoted by Hermione de Almeida in *Romantic Medicine and John Keats* (New York:

Oxford UP, 1991), 35. For Blake's familiarity with Hunter, and his parody of him as "Jack Tearguts" in *An Island in the Moon,* see George H. Gilpin's "William Blake and the World's Body of Science," *Studies in Romanticism* 43.1 (Spring 2004): esp. 38–40.

26. "[W]hen another suffers, and although I cannot help him, I let myself be infected by his pain (through my imagination), then two of us suffer, though the trouble really (in nature) affects only *one*" (Immanuel Kant, *The Metaphysics of Morals,* trans. and ed. Mary Gregor [Cambridge: Cambridge UP, 1996], 205). In the same section, Kant distinguishes between sympathy as the moral duty of a "rational being" and sympathy as the merely natural response mechanism of an "animal endowed with reason" (204). Sympathy only rises to the level of moral duty when a free agent decides it can and should act upon the feelings prompted by nature.

27. In a chapter on compulsory narration in *Caleb Williams* that I am relying on here, Suzie Park describes the importance of the demand for narrative in Adam Smith's account of sympathy: "By 1789, then, demanding what has 'befallen' another becomes the individual's most reliable means of achieving Smith's ideal equilibrium between sympathetic identification and rational distance. As the glue holding together the social order, sympathy allows individuals to enter imaginatively into one another's situation. Since we could be overwhelmed by any and every call for feeling, entering into situations without discrimination, judgment of narratives needs to provide a check on runaway sympathy. The demand for narrative upfront seems to be the best way of explaining how we minister our own checks on potentially harmful impulses to feel indiscriminately and excessively. Thus we open the floodgates of fellow-feeling only *if* the right narrative 'situation' is delivered or found out quickly enough" ("Compulsory Narration and the Politics of Wasted Feeling," Ph.D. diss., University of California Berkeley, 2004).

28. In his account of Smith's theory of sympathy, Thomas Pfau also recognizes the mutually reinforcing work of verbalization and judgment: "As an obliquely juridical faculty charged with evaluating . . . sympathy operates primarily as a discursive, often narrowly lexical, principle" (*Romantic Moods: Paranoia, Trauma, and Melancholy, 1790–1840* [Baltimore: Johns Hopkins UP, 2005], 4). James Chandler's treatment of Smith in "Blake and the Syntax of Sentiment" is also relevant in this regard. See my discussion of this important essay in the introduction to this book.

29. "In fact, internal to our emotional response itself is the judgment that what is at issue is indeed serious—has 'size,' as Aristotle puts it" (Nussbaum, *Upheavals of Thought,* 307).

30. "The Ruined Cottage," ll. 508–525, Manuscript D, in William Wordsworth, *"The Ruined Cottage" and "The Pedlar,"* ed. James Butler (Ithaca: Cornell UP, 1979), 73–75. Further citations are to this edition.

31. I am thinking of Walter Benjamin's distinction, adapted from Georges Sorel, between the political general strike, which seeks to reform the power ratios of the state, and the anarchist general strike, which seeks to undo the state altogether. Benjamin considers the former "violent" because it aims, by means of specific strategic goals, to redistribute power, but he considers the latter "nonviolent" because it involves no attempt to envision and install new power relations. "While the first form of interruption of work is violent since it causes only an external modification of labor conditions, the second, as a pure means, is nonviolent. For it takes place not in readiness to resume work following external concessions and this or that modification to working conditions, but in the determination to resume only a wholly

transformed work, no longer enforced by the state, an upheaval that this kind of strike not so much causes as consummates" ("Critique of Violence," in *Reflections,* ed. Peter Demetz [New York: Schocken, 1978], 291–292). Blake's Jesus also anticipates another modern political practice, the sit-in. In Berkeley I recently saw a hand-painted sign suspended high in the upper branches of a redwood tree, with this cleverly inverted message: "Don't just do something, sit there!"

32. "[Y]ou have no means of approaching him, no access to him whatsoever. You cannot touch him. You cannot be touched by him or even reached, but neither have you any means of backing off, of getting away" (Ann Smock, *What Is There To Say?* [Lincoln: U of Nebraska P, 2003], 46).

33. Jesus "sit[s] beside the nest" (17), "sit[s] the cradle near" (19), and "doth sit by us and moan" (36). Each preposition expressing proximity without privilege occurs alongside the suspension of will Blake associates with sitting. In relation to the value of "besideness," consider Sedgwick's discussion of why she prefers *beside* to *beneath, behind,* and *beyond,* the reigning prepositions of current critical discourse: "*Beside* is an interesting preposition . . . because there's nothing very dualistic about it . . . *Beside* permits a spacious agnosticism about several of the linear logics that enforce dualistic thinking: noncontradiction or the law of the excluded middle, cause versus effect, subject versus object" (*Touching Feeling: Affect, Pedagogy, Performativity* [Durham: Duke UP, 2003], 8).

34. In an essay on recent commemorations of the Irish potato famine, David Lloyd aligns therapeutic models of mourning with colonialist ideologies of development that require self-disciplining subjects to master loss and ensure continuous productivity into the future. "[T]herapeutic modernity," he writes, would "have us lose our loss in order to become good subjects." Its message: "[I]f we could leave our dead and their sufferings behind and overcome our melancholy, we could shake off at last the burden of the past and enter modernity as fully formed subjects." Against this ideology, Lloyd prefers the melancholic grieving that colonial ethnographers historically interpreted as signs of Irish incompetence: emotional excess, inappropriate swings between joy and sorrow, failures of self-control, etc. For those who would resist conscription into modernity, Lloyd argues, "it is crucial to discern in those 'melancholy survivals' complex forms of *living on* that preserve not simply belated and dysfunctional practices but potentialities for producing and reproducing a life that lies athwart modernity" ("The Memory of Hunger," in *Loss: The Politics of Mourning,* ed. David L. Eng and David Kazanjian [Berkeley and Los Angeles: U of California P, 2003], 217–220). Like Lloyd's, many of the essays in *Loss* attempt to "depathologize" melancholy, in order to trace how, as Judith Butler puts it in the volume's conclusion, "the irrecoverable becomes, paradoxically, the condition of a new political agency" (467).

35. M. E. P. Seligman, *Helplessness: On Depression, Development, and Death* (New York: W. H. Freeman, 1975). Nussbaum discusses Seligman's experiments and their importance to the cognitive-evaluative approach to emotions on pp. 100–106 of *Upheavals of Thought.* Seligman's clinical studies of optimism and pessimism, as described in such books as *Authentic Happiness: Using the New Positive Psychology to Realize Your Potential for Lasting Fulfillment* (New York: Free Press, 2002) and *Learned Optimism: How to Change Your Mind and Your Life* (New York: Vintage, 2006), have been central to the recent development of "happiness studies" in the field of psychology.

36. Michel Foucault, "What Is Enlightenment?" in *The Foucault Reader,* ed. Paul Rabinow (New York: Pantheon, 1984), 47.

37. Consider Slavoj Žižek's polemical conclusion to *Violence* (New York: Picador, 2008): "Better to do nothing than to engage in localised acts the function of which is to make the system run more smoothly . . . The threat today is not passivity, but pseudoactivity, the urge to 'be active,' to 'participate,' to mask the nothingness of what goes on. People intervene all the time, 'do something'; academics participate in meaningless debates, and so on. The truly difficult thing is to step back, to withdraw" (216–217).

38. The question of kinship in sympathy is also raised and tested by the resemblance between the observer and the sufferer in the print. Blake leaves open the possibility that the observer has taken on the identity of the sufferer, granting pity a potential for complete identification. At the same time, the fact that the observer's intent gaze is not returned by the sufferer suggests the wishful nature of such identification, while the separate spatial and temporal planes occupied by the figures suggests the unbridged gap between them.

39. William Shakespeare, *Macbeth*, in *The Riverside Shakespeare* (Boston: Houghton Mifflin, 1997), 1365. Further citations are to this edition.

40. Veena Das, "Language and Body: Transactions in the Construction of Pain," in Kleinman, Das, and Lock, *Social Suffering*, 88.

41. Veena Das, "Wittgenstein and Anthropology," *Annual Review of Anthropology* 27 (1998): 192.

42. Stanley Cavell, "Comments on Veena Das's Essay 'Language and Body: Transactions in the Construction of Pain,'" in Kleinman, Das, and Lock, *Social Suffering*, 98.

43. Friedrich Schiller, *On the Aesthetic Education of Man: In a Series of Letters*, ed. and trans. Elizabeth M. Wilkinson and L. A. Willoughby (Oxford: Clarendon, 1967), 89.

44. Thanks to Celeste Langan for reminding me of this passage.

45. The couplet of Shakespeare's Sonnet 71, a poem also about grief and relief, employs the same rhyme but inverts it. The speaker urges the reader/lover not to mourn forever, to set a reasonable limit on grief, and finally, to forget and move on:

Lest the wise world should look into your moan,
And mock you with me after I am gone.

Ironically, each time the speaker calls for the reader to forget grief he insinuates a continuing memory of his loss, an effect conveyed, as Sara Guyer has shown, by the poem's extraordinary use of enjambment: "if you read this line, remember not / The hand that writ it." Sonnet 71 makes it impossible to differentiate between the finality and survival of loss; its "gone" remains haunted by its "moan." See Guyer's remarkable reading of Paul Celan's translation, which turns this sonnet into a performance of holocaust memory and survival (*Romanticism after Auschwitz* [Stanford: Stanford UP, 2007], 160–186).

46. Jenefer Robinson's *Deeper than Reason* provides an instructive example. Although she grounds emotion in "affective appraisals" that are supposed to precede propositional cognition, thus restoring the primacy of the body to emotion, she nevertheless proceeds to describe the content of these "quick and dirty" responses in terms of linguistic propositions, only less complex. Robinson acknowledges the problem: "Given that an affective appraisal is by definition not describable in propositional or linguistic terms, it is difficult to know how to describe these appraisals in ordinary language" (62). Her decision to render noncognitive evaluations in bold print to convey the difference between intellectual reasoning and their "fast, automatic, 'hot' evaluation" (64) only exacerbates the problem: "An emotional response of fear, for example, is evoked by an affective appraisal: **This is a *threat*.** Disgust

is evoked by an affective appraisal, **This is *nauseating***. Anger is evoked by an affective appraisal, **This *wrongs* me (or mine)** or **This is an *offence***" (68). Affective appraisals aren't nonlinguistic; they're just short, and they shout (*Deeper than Reason: Emotion and its Role in Literature, Music, and Art* [Oxford: Clarendon, 2005]).

47. Edgar Allan Poe, "The Philosophy of Composition," in *Literary Theory and Criticism*, ed. Leonard Cassuto (New York: Dover, 1999), 104.

48. Joseph Viscomi, *Blake and the Idea of the Book* (Princeton: Princeton UP, 1993), 115.

49. Kevis Goodman, *Georgic Modernity and British Romanticism: Poetry and the Mediation of History* (Cambridge: Cambridge UP, 2004), 3–4. Cited parenthetically hereafter.

50. Fred Moten, "Black Mo'nin'," in Eng and Kazanjian, *Loss*, 73. Charles Mingus's "Moanin'" first appeared on *Blues & Roots* (Atlantic Records) in 1960.

Interlude · Toward an Auditory Imagination

1. Kenzaburo Oe, *Rouse Up O Young Men of the New Age*, trans. John Nathan (New York: Grove, 2002), 156. Cited parenthetically hereafter.

2. Oe is quoting from Eiji Usami's translation of the opening passage of *L'air et les songes: essai sur l'imagination du movement* (Paris: Librairie Jose Corti, 1943). In the full citation used by Oe, Bachelard goes on immediately to support his idea of the active imagination by referring to Blake's *Milton* (32:32, E 132): "[T]here is no imagination and the act of imagination does not occur . . . If a present image does not recall an absent one, change images, liberating us from, in particular, basic images. As Blake proclaims, 'The Imagination is not a State: it is the Human Existence itself' " (*Rouse Up*, 127).

3. Thomas Vogler, "Re: Naming *MIL/TON*," in *Unnam'd Forms: Blake and Textuality*, ed. Nelson Hilton and Thomas A. Vogler (Berkeley and Los Angeles: U of California P, 1986), 145–146.

4. Jean-François Lyotard, "The Sign of History," trans. Geoff Bennington, in *The Lyotard Reader*, ed. Andrew Benjamin (Oxford: Blackwell, 1989), 394.

Chapter 4 · Strange Pulse

1. Samuel Taylor Coleridge, "Reflections on Having Left a Place of Retirement," l. 58, in *Samuel Taylor Coleridge: The Major Works*, ed. H. J. Jackson (Oxford: Oxford UP, 1985), 31.

2. Judith Butler, *Precarious Life: The Powers of Mourning and Violence* (London: Verso, 2004), 151.

3. Aristotle, *Poetics I: With the Tractatus Coislinianus, A Hypothetical Reconstruction of Poetics II, and the Fragments of the On Poets*, trans. Richard Janko (Indianapolis: Hackett, 1987), 10–11.

4. The slashes here do not indicate verse lineation (the passage is in prose) but the line endings of Blake's printed text. See the photographic reproductions and transcriptions in William Blake, *The Early Illuminated Books*, ed. Morris Eaves, Robert N. Essick, and Joseph Viscomi (Princeton: Princeton UP and The William Blake Trust, 1993), 184–187.

5. Sianne Ngai has explored a similar paradox in the mixed temporalities and affects of avant-garde works after Stein, works that simultaneously induce "astonishment and boredom": "Sudden in onset, brief in duration, and disappearing quickly, astonishment involves high levels and steep gradients of neural firing; whereas boredom, slow or gradual in onset

and long in duration, involves low and continuous levels of neural firing. Yet even as the temporalities of shock and boredom are inarguably antithetical, both are responses that confront us with the limitations of our capacity for responding in general." In much the same way, Blake's Jesus alternately shocks with sudden gestures (shattering the Ten Commandments) and outlasts all limits of boredom (sitting and waiting indefinitely), occupying temporalities that preclude the ordinary range of emotional response associated with meaningful action. These extreme states, especially in tandem, serve as a provocation. As Ngai states, "The shocking and the boring prompt us to look for new strategies of affective engagement and to extend the circumstances under which engagement becomes possible" (*Ugly Feelings* [Cambridge: Harvard, 2005], 261–262).

6. Ann Smock, *What Is There to Say?* (Lincoln: U of Nebraska P, 2003), 23–25. Among the many pleasures of reading Smock's book is tracing the vocabulary she invents to describe the impossible but necessary task of allowing otherness to speak. *What Is There To Say?* offers a compendium of phrases for the alternative temporality of impossible speech. Such speech, like the sympathy of Blake's Jesus, confounds the measured tempo of ordinary practices, joining hesitancy and impetuousness. Thus: "without even thinking, precipitously you . . . hesitate, delaying impatiently"; or "speech, in the uneasy indifference of too fast and too slow, too soon and too late—maintains a wavering, undecided movement between what you cannot possibly do and what you can't help doing" (48).

7. "Time was Finished!" *Jerusalem* 94:18, E 254.

8. We have neither time nor space to read the line I have singled out (somewhat artificially) as the apocalyptic turning point of *Jerusalem* ("Time was Finished!"), but it is worth pointing out that in this passage the future arrives in/as a moment of somatic rhythm—in this case, breathing:

> Albion lays cold on his Rock: storms & snows beat round him. (94:1, E 254)
> . . . deep heaves the Ocean black thundering
> Around the wormy Garments of Albion: then pausing in deathlike silence
> Time was Finished! The Breath Divine Breathed over Albion (94:17–18, E 254)

If these lines represent the before and after of apocalypse—of death and resurrection, of chaos and Genesis-like creation—they also take the mundane, ongoing form of inhalation and exhalation, the expansion and contraction of the lungs. The divine breath breathing over Albion here is the breath exhaled by speech itself, following the silence of a pause for inhalation. Blake's enjambment suggests that "silence" does not necessarily signify death (it is "death*like*") and that the end of time is poised between the time it takes to pause for breath and the time it takes to say, "Time was Finished!"

9. Wai Chee Dimock, "Nonbiological Clock: Literary History against Newtonian Mechanics," *South Atlantic Quarterly* 102.1 (Winter 2003): 166–167. For reasons we will see momentarily, Ian Balfour comes closer to the mark in his brief description of this passage: "The double figuration of this moment is paradoxical: On the one hand, it is identified with the pulsation of an artery, an entirely instinctual and natural action; on the other hand, poetic labor is imaged as the construction of building blocks, as if involved, say, in reconstructing some version of the temple of Jerusalem . . . In any event, the figuration constructs the poetic moment as both temporal and timeless, organic and inorganic, narrative and architectonic" (*The Rhetoric of Romantic Prophecy* [Stanford: Stanford UP, 2002], 162).

10. See esp. Northrop Frye's comments on labor as the realization of dream and as the

transformation of nature into human form in his grand and condensed essay, "Blake's Treat-ment of the Archetype," in *English Institute Essays: 1950*, ed. Alan S. Downer (New York: Columbia UP, 1951), 172 ff.

11. Alexandre Kojève, *Introduction to the Reading of Hegel: Lectures on the Phenomenology of Spirit*, trans. James H. Nichols, ed. Alan Bloom (Ithaca: Cornell UP, 1980), 158–159.

12. Friedrich Nietzsche, "On Truth and Lying in a Non-Moral Sense," trans. Ronald Speirs, in *Nietzsche: The Birth of Tragedy and Other Writings*, ed. Raymond Geuss and Ronald Speirs (Cambridge: Cambridge UP, 1999), 142.

13. Hannah Arendt, *The Life of the Mind* (New York: Harcourt, 1971). See pages 178 and 191.

14. Geoffrey Hartman, "The Sympathy Paradox: Poetry, Feeling, and Modern Cultural Morality," in *The Fateful Question of Culture* (New York: Columbia UP, 1997), 148, 150. For the contrast between Blake and Wordsworth, see 142–143. Although Blake openly contested Wordsworth's "natural piety," his notion of pulsation bears surprising resemblance to Word-sworth's "wise passiveness." The distance between the two poets is not as great as Hartman suggests. Consider the recent (Hartman-inflected) work of Anne-Lise François on Word-sworthian modes of "recessive action." François considers it a mistake to think of Word-sworth clinging to nature as a mystified, already lost origin. Rather, we should understand nature as his "spatial trope for 'down' or idle time, a name for habitual experiences chiefly defined by their capacity to be repeated, and for states of mind in which the cognitive and acquisitive faculties are suspended and yet a surprising continuity with dimly perceived modes of being is discovered" ("'O Happy Living Things': Frankenfoods and the Bounds of Wordsworthian Natural Piety," *diacritics* 33.2 (Summer 2003): 57. These words could double as an account of Blake's pulsations and Milton's somnambulance. Throughout this section, I am generally indebted to the "Theory of Recessive Action" François proposes in *Open Secrets: The Literature of Uncounted Experience* (Stanford: Stanford UP, 2008), where she outlines an attitude of countermodernity evident in literary works "that define themselves against the many figures we have for action" (xv), thereby exempting themselves from the "spirit of discontent" that has often aligned Western modernity with a war on "the given." "[A]ttending to unobserved, not-for-profit experience," these works display a "propensity for narrative waste—or readiness not to make event *x* a cause for subsequent event *y*" (21). That is, they share an interest in the nonnarrative modes of passive agency I am tracing in Blake.

15. The *OED* cites this phrase from Linnaeus to illustrate its definition of "pulsatilla." Erasmus Darwin describes the "sad ANEMONE" in *The Botanic Garden, Part II, containing The Loves of the Plants. A Poem. with Philosophical Notes*, 3rd ed. (London: J. Johnson, 1791; repr., Bristol: Thoemmes Continuum, 2004), 1:317–346. Darwin's note cites Pliny as saying, "this flower never opens its petals but when the wind blows" (33).

16. William Harvey, *Movement of the Heart and Blood in Animals: An Anatomical Essay*, trans. Kenneth J. Franklin (Springfield, IL: Charles C. Thomas, 1957), 38. Cited parentheti-cally hereafter.

17. With a somewhat different emphasis, Neil Hertz observes a similar dynamic in *George Eliot's Pulse* (Stanford: Stanford UP, 2003). According to Hertz, "pulse" is one of Eliot's key-words, "a small, replicable unit of vitality, and as such a sign of life," referring alternately to the living subject's agency or vulnerability (13). This ambiguous pulse in turn reflects the author's paradoxical relation to language: "at once the dangerously chancy producer of writ-ing and the target of its unrelenting force" (19).

18. Thomas Fuchs, *The Mechanization of the Heart: Harvey and Descartes,* trans. Marjorie Grene (Rochester: U of Rochester P, 2001), 46. Cited parenthetically hereafter. Associating expansion with passivity, Harvey's account of the heart adds an interesting twist to our understanding of Blake's iconography. As W. J. T. Mitchell has demonstrated, Blake's core images alternate between negative figures of contraction ("Ancient of Days") and positive ones of expansion ("Albion rose"), figures Mitchell likens to "systole" and "diastole" (*Blake's Composite Art: A Study of the Illuminated Poetry* [Princeton: Princeton UP, 1978]), 53). Mapping Harvey's pulsations onto Mitchell's account would quickly complicate matters, involving us in a paradoxical rhetoric of expansive passivity.

19. David Worrall notes Blake's medical textbook commissions in his commentary on *The Urizen Books,* ed. David Worrall (Princeton: Princeton UP, 1995), 136. Also see F. B. Curtis's review of Blake's likely acquaintance with anatomy in "William Blake and Eighteenth-Century Medicine," *Blake Studies* 8.2 (1979): 187–199, and Carmen S. Kreiter's discussion of similarities between Blake and Harvey in "Evolution and William Blake," *Studies in Romanticism* 4.2 (Winter 1965): 110–118. For further evidence of Blake's interest in medical discourse, see Tristanne J. Connolly, *William Blake and the Body* (New York: Palgrave, 2002); George H. Gilpin, "William Blake and the World's Body of Science," *Studies in Romanticism* 43.1 (Spring 2004): 37–40; and Richard C. Sha, *Perverse Romanticism: Aesthetics and Sexuality in Britain, 1750–1832* (Baltimore: Johns Hopkins UP, 2009), which pays special attention to John Hunter's theory of the blood (217–220), discussed below. Finally, Jon Mee has recently described how cardiovascular circulation became the primary figure for circulation and exchange in the eighteenth century (social, political, and economic) and how Blake, perhaps under the influence of John Brown's *Elements of Medicine* (1788), contested the regulative norms of smooth, systematic circulation by emphasizing the inherent energy and vitalist stimulation involved in moving blood through the body. Blake's new interest in the blood first becomes apparent in *The Book of Urizen,* where "the excitability of the physiological being" (79) becomes a primary figure for life's resistance to Urizenic abstraction and systematization ("Bloody Blake: Nation and Circulation," in Steve Clark and David Worrall, eds., *Blake, Nation and Empire* [Basingstoke: Palgrave, 2006], 63–82.)

20. See Jacques Derrida, *Rogues: Two Essays on Reason* (Stanford: Stanford UP, 2005), 10–11, 42–45; see Arendt, *Life of the Mind,* 2:162.

21. Invoking Walter Benjamin, Noel Jackson describes well the adherence of bodily and historical temporalities in Blake—and the danger that seemingly linear, developmental histories in fact consist of empty repetition: "Both temporal and corporeal units . . . are characterized by a principle of repetition without difference closely identified with the deathly monotony of history as homogeneous, empty time." In these circumstances, poetry's role is "to impose a breach in the [temporal] continuum" (*Science and Sensation in Romantic Poetry* [Cambridge: Cambridge UP, 2008], 97–98). By turning around within the linear history he has been forging, Urizen allows for such a breach—one that would transform the empty repetition of pulsation into repetition with a difference.

22. Saree Makdisi develops this important argument throughout *William Blake and the Impossible History of the 1790s* (Chicago: U of Chicago P, 2003), but see esp. Chap. 3, "Laboring at the Mill with Slaves," 78–154. Significantly, Makdisi likens Blake's idea of time to that of Benjamin, noting that prophecy shifts attention to the moment and "away from what had already been identified in Blake's age as the relentless march of progress" (156). We will return to Makdisi later. Here I wish only to add that Makdisi's celebration of Blakean

"striving" and his powerful insight into Blake's critique of progress are sometimes difficult to reconcile. Energy and modernity are not as clearly antithetical as he occasionally suggests.

23. Max Horkheimer and Theodor W. Adorno, *Dialectic of Enlightenment*, ed. Gunzelin Schmid Noerr, trans. Edmund Jephcott (Stanford: Stanford UP, 2002), 2.

24. The case François makes for a literature of "recessive action" is again relevant: "the novels and poems in question locate fulfillment not in narrative fruition but in grace, understood both as a simplicity or slightness of formal means and as a freedom from work, including both the work of self-concealment and self-presentation" (xvi). By defending the inconsequence implied by these texts, *Open Secrets* "contests the normative bias in favor of the demonstrable, dramatic development and realization of human powers characteristic of, but not limited to, the capitalist investment in value and work and the Enlightenment allegiance to rationalism and unbounded progress" (xvi). It would be hard to find better language for the conversion Urizen undergoes in Night the Ninth.

25. Or to add one more voice to this chorus: "It is not man's lapse into luxurious indolence that is to be feared, but the savage spread of the social under the mask of universal nature, the collective as a blind fury of activity . . . Perhaps the true society will grow tired of development and, out of freedom, leave possibilities unused, instead of storming under a confused compulsion to the conquest of strange stars" (Theodor W. Adorno, "*Sur L'Eau*," from *Minima Moralia: Reflections on a Damaged Life*, trans. E. F. N. Jephcott (1974; repr., London: Verso, 2005), 156.

26. André Breton: "The work of art is valuable only in so far as it is vibrated by the reflexes of the future." Quoted by Walter Benjamin in a footnote to "The Work of Art in the Age of Mechanical Reproduction," trans. Harry Zohn, in *Illuminations*, ed. Hannah Arendt (1936; repr., New York: Schocken, 1969), 249.

27. The idea of a redemptive but involuntary labor lies at the inception of modern aesthetic discourse. Immanuel Kant's "purposiveness without a purpose" conveys a similar paradox, as does Friedrich Schiller's notion that "play" can activate opposing drives without canceling them—"within the purview of feeling, intensifying passivity to the utmost . . . within the purview of reason, intensifying activity to the utmost" (*On the Aesthetic Education of Man*, trans. and ed. Elizabeth M. Wilkinson and L. A. Willoughby [Oxford: Clarendon, 1967], 87).

28. Blake often characterizes Los in terms of self-defeating determination, self-defeating because his determination to break the hold of the fallen self through acts of aesthetic production only entangle him further. Pound's famous dictum forms the title of an essay collection, *Make It New* (London: Faber and Faber, 1934).

29. Theodor W. Adorno, *Aesthetic Theory*, trans. Robert Hullot-Kentor (Minneapolis: U of Minnesota P, 1997), 24. Cited parenthetically hereafter.

30. Adorno writes of "solutions that the imagining ear or eye does not immediately encompass or know in full detail" (24).

31. "Velleity binds the new to the ever-same, and this establishes the inner communication of the modern and myth. The new wants nonidentity, yet intention reduces it to identity; modern art constantly works at the Münchhausean trick of carrying out the identification of the nonidentical" (22–23).

32. I can think of no better recent example of second reflection (as I have been describing it here) than T. J. Clark's *The Sight of Death: An Experiment in Art Writing*. Clark invokes the shifting, resistant, and inexhaustible materiality of two paintings by Nicolas Poussin

by patiently submitting them to daily and microscopic empirical analysis. "I know there is something excessive," states one of Clark's entries, "and maybe ludicrous, to entering this closely into someone else's imagined world. But these diary entries are partly meant as an argument in favor of such entry. They are meant as an apology for (a glorification of) painting's stasis and smallness and meticulousness—for the way a painter like Poussin does not know when to stop" ([New Haven: Yale UP, 2006], 42–43).

33. John Keats, letter to John Hamilton Reynolds, May 3, 1818, in *Selected Poems and Letters by John Keats*, ed. Douglas Bush (Boston: Houghton Mifflin, 1959), 273. Keats's insistence that philosophy prove itself in the body provides another example of his interest, as Alan Richardson puts it, in "the interconnectedness among psychological and physiological functions, conscious and unconscious mental activity, the head and the heart, the viscera and the 'powers of mind'" (*British Romanticism and the Science of the Mind* [Cambridge: Cambridge UP, 2001], 130–131).

34. Julien Offray de La Mettrie, *Machine Man and Other Writings*, 1747, trans. and ed. Ann Thomson (Cambridge: Cambridge UP, 1996), 27. Cited parenthetically hereafter.

35. Harvey remained conflicted across his career on the question of whether life force is a property of the heart or of the blood itself. According to John Rogers, however, Harvey's emphasis changed under the influence of the new vitalism popular in the 1640s and 1650s, leading him to devalue the role of the heart and privilege the blood's spirited vitality instead. Rogers identifies this shift with the changing political vocabularies of the period. Although Harvey remained an unreformed Royalist throughout his life, his discourse on circulation modulated away from a model centered on the agency of the heart to one emphasizing the dispersed, generalized agency of the blood, an emphasis more easily adapted to republican ideologies. "Harvey, whose father and four of whose brothers were successful merchants," writes Rogers, "was, perhaps like many Royalist capitalists in this period, in the discursively awkward position of propounding both a decentralized economy and a centralized political state" (*The Matter of Revolution* [Ithaca: Cornell UP, 1996], 27; see "William Harvey and the Revolution of Blood," 16–27).

36. Fuchs believes that the historical dialectic between vitalism and mechanism is ultimately grounded in the nature of the heart itself, which "stands between the voluntary ('animal') and the vegetative ('natural') movements that remain wholly in the unconscious." The heart therefore "acts as *equilibriating organ* between various polar influences"; it "not only moves itself" but also "perceives . . . influences," "just as much reacting to the blood stream as it is regulating and driving it" (*Mechanization*, 228).

37. Quoted by Fuchs, *Mechanization*, 51.

38. Harvey refers to the water pump in a lecture from 1616, the notes to which weren't discovered until almost the end of the nineteenth century: "It is plain from the structure of the heart that the blood is passed continuously through the lungs to the aorta as by two clacks of a water bellows to raise water. It is shown by application of a ligature that the passage of the blood is from the arteries into the veins. Whence it follows that the movement of the blood is constantly in a circle, and is brought about by the beat of the heart" (quoted by William F. Hamilton and Dickinson W. Richards in "The Output of the Heart," in *Circulation of the Blood: Men and Ideas*, ed. Alfred P. Fishman and Dickinson W. Richards [Oxford: Oxford UP, 1964], 74). Hamilton and Dickinson note that the water pump was developed for mining purposes over a century before Harvey's discovery and was commonly used in ships and mines during Harvey's era.

39. John Hunter, *A Treatise on the blood, inflammation, and gun-shot wounds*, vol. 1 (Philadelphia: Thomas Bradford, 1796), 79. In the middle of the eighteenth century, between Harvey and Hunter, Albert von Haller demonstrated the heartbeat's independence from the central nervous system, sparking a return to vitalistic theories. Joseph Johnson published Thomas Henry's *Memoirs of Albert de Haller* in 1783. For the most recent review of the evidence connecting Blake and Hunter (and Hunter's brother, William, also an important surgeon), see George H. Gilpin, "William Blake and the World's Body of Science," *Studies in Romanticism* 43.1 (Spring 2004): 37–40.

40. The living principle "is, as it were, diffused through the whole solids and fluids, making a necessary constituent part of them, and forming with them a perfect whole; giving to both the power of preservation, the susceptibility of impression; and, from their construction, giving them consequent reciprocal action." It is because of this continuity that "the blood, and the body, are capable of affecting, and being affected, by each other" (Hunter, *Treatise*, 82–83).

41. See p. 10, but also p. 15, where Hunter identifies this principle with the genesis of organic forms from the blood: "[A]ll the solid parts of the body are formed from the blood." Sha notes that this idea of "blood as an especially flexible form of materiality," providing "the basic building materials for the body," would have supported Blake's own sense of "the dynamic materiality of the body" and may have influenced his representation of the globule in *The Book of Urizen* and elsewhere (*Perverse Romanticism*, 217–220).

42. Samuel Taylor Coleridge, "Shakespeare's Judgment equal to his Genius," in *Notes and Lectures upon Shakespeare and Some of the Old Poets and Dramatists*, vol. 1, ed. Mrs. H. N. Coleridge (London: William Pickering, 1849; repr. Elibron Classics, Adamant Media, 2005), 65.

43. William Wordsworth, "She was a Phantom of delight," ll. 21–22, in *Poems, in Two Volumes, and Other Poems, 1800–1807*, ed. Jared Curtis (Ithaca: Cornell UP, 1983), 75. Hunter uses a phrase similar to Wordsworth's when he refers to "the blood in the machine" (15). See my discussion of Wordsworth's lyric in the interlude following this chapter.

44. "The individual human subject . . . is a product like any other, an assemblage, a machine: a making machine, a consuming machine, a desiring machine, a living machine" (Makdisi, *William Blake and the Impossible History of the 1790s*, 12). For Makdisi's idea that Blake enlists the myth of the Fall to represent the emergence of modern "organ-ization," see the beginning of Chap. 3, 79 ff. In a section of this chapter called, "Automation and Panopticon," 115–133, Makdisi explores the "conceptual slippage between the mechanical and the organic" (128) shared by early industrial theorists and Blake's critique of this developing discourse.

45. "[Personifications] are, indeed, a figure of speech occasionally prompted by passion, and I have made use of them as such; but I have endeavoured utterly to reject them as a mechanical device of style, or as a family language which Writers in metre seem to lay claim to by prescription. I have wished to keep my Reader in the company of flesh and blood, persuaded that by doing so I shall interest him" (Wordsworth, "Preface of 1800, With a Collation of the Enlarged Preface of 1802," in William Wordsworth and Samuel Taylor Coleridge, *Lyrical Ballads, 1798*, ed. W. J. B. Owen [Oxford: Oxford UP, 1969], 161). For deconstructive readings of these lines, see Barbara Johnson, "Strange Fits: Poe and Wordsworth on the Nature of Poetic Language," in *A World of Difference* (Baltimore: Johns Hopkins UP, 1987), 89–99; Adela Pinch, *Strange Fits of Passion* (Stanford: Stanford UP, 1996), 49; and Sara Guyer, *Ro-*

manticism after Auschwitz (Stanford: Stanford UP, 2007), Chap. 2, "Naked Language, Naked Life: Wordsworth's Rhetoric of Survival," 46–70.

46. Guyer, *Romanticism after Auschwitz*, 53–56.

47. In making this argument, I am adapting Guyer's haunting account of prosopopoeia in *Romanticism after Auschwitz*, where she describes the "survival" of rhetorical figures despite the life and death of human subjects. Further support for her account can be found in *Jerusalem*, when Los laments the beautiful worldly appearance generated by the Daughters of Albion and urges Albion's sons to separate themselves (though gently) from this superficial, feminine realm. In other words, Blake again asks his readers to put off the "Not Human":

> As a beautiful Veil so these Females shall fold & unfold
> According to their will the outside surface of the Earth
> An outside shadowy Surface superadded to the real Surface;
> Which is unchangeable for ever & ever Amen: so be it!
> Separate Albions Sons gently from their Emanations . . . (83:45–49, E 242)

Although this passage seems to dichotomize appearance and reality, it in fact upends any surface/depth model dependent on the idea of an unfigured human essence beneath the weave of appearance, for the reality underlying shadowy illusion is itself another surface ("the real Surface"). The difference between "the natural" and "the human," then, is a difference not between appearance and reality but between competing surfaces. Figure survives.

48. Johnson, "Strange Fits," 97. Focusing on racial performance, Sianne Ngai has made a similar argument about "animatedness," a term she applies to media as various as 19th century abolitionist writings and late twentieth-century, stop-motion animated television. The "concept of animatedness," she writes, "returns us to the connection between the emotive and the mechanistic," specifically by blending "the spontaneous with the formulaic, the unpremeditated with the predetermined, and the 'liberating release' of psychic impulses with 'the set of learned, more or less rote conventions (*automatisms*) contained within [a system or traditional medium]'" (*Ugly Feelings* [Cambridge, MA: Harvard UP, 2005], 100).

49. Rei Terada interprets an anecdote from Derrida in a way that can help further explain what I mean by "feeling half-alive." Derrida recalls being "strangely moved" by a conversation between his son and Paul de Man, in which the two discussed the support mechanism—a small piece of wood—installed inside the body of a string instrument to allow for communication between the sounding boards. The French word for this piece of wood, this bit of artifice within an empty interior, is *l'âme* (or "soul"). Writes Terada: "There is nothing in interiority but a 'small and fragile piece of wood,' or, perhaps, the small and fragile '*word* "soul."'" But in Derrida's anecdote that 'nothing' is what generates emotion—Derrida's emotion, in this case, of being 'strangely moved and unsettled.' Derrida is moved, not in spite of the fact that the soul is a piece of wood, but because it is; the very absence of depth compels emotion. Far from being impossible without the subject, emotion is our recognition of the subject's 'death'" (151). If one were to substitute "heart" for "soul" here, one would come pretty close to what it means in Blake to experience "feelings half-alive." One could even say that *pulsation* "is our recognition of the subject's 'death.'" (*Feeling in Theory: Emotion after the "Death of the Subject"* [Cambridge, MA: Harvard UP, 2001]).

50. Samuel Richardson, *Clarissa: or, The History of a Young Lady*, ed. Angus Ross (New York: Penguin, 1985), 1224.

51. Laurence Sterne, *A Sentimental Journey and Other Writings*, ed. Ian Jack and Tim Parnell (Oxford: Oxford UP, 2003), 95. Cited parenthetically hereafter.

52. Friedrich Nietzsche, *Human, All Too Human, A Book for Free Spirits*, trans. R. J. Hollingdale (Cambridge: Cambridge UP, 1986), 238–239.

53. Quoted in R. S. Crane, "Suggestions Toward a Genealogy of the 'Man of Feeling,'" *ELH* 1.3 (Dec. 1934): 206.

54. Samuel Parker, *A Demonstration of the Divine Authority of the Law of Nature, And of the Christian Religion* (London: M. Flesher, for R. Royston and R. Chiswell, 1681), xvi. Cited parenthetically hereafter.

55. Quoted in Crane, "Suggestions," 224–225.

56. Quoted in ibid., 212.

57. It would take another essay altogether to develop the point fully, but it is worth noting here that another common term in sympathy's self-perpetuating rhetoric is "bowels." During the long reign of sympathy discourse, "bowels" could refer specifically to the intestines but also generally to any of the body's internal organs. This general usage made it a synonym of "heart" and a favorite term to describe "the seat of the tender and sympathetic emotions," pity and compassion especially (*OED*). Like the heart, then, the bowels were a place where the social emotions could be experienced directly in the body. In a sermon from 1700, Z. Isham writes that "Nature it self moves our Bowels to Compassion" (quoted in Crane, "Suggestions," 225), and Samuel Parker puts it this way: "The Divine Providence has implanted in the Nature and Constitution of humane Bodies a principle of Love and Tenderness, and the bowels of Men are soft and apt to receive impressions from the complaints and calamities of their Brethren" (*A Demonstration of the Divine Authority of the Law of Nature*, 54–55). Blake directly mimes this kind of language on the last plate of the first chapter of *Jerusalem*: "And there was heard a great lamenting in Beulah: all the Regions / Of Beulah were moved as the tender bowels are moved" (25:1–2, E 170), but he calls into question the idea of an automatic, embodied sympathy by coupling these lines with one of his most disturbing images: Albion being *disemboweled* by Vala, Tirzah, and Rahab. Blake's humor is dark and grotesque; at the very moment when Beulah's tender bowels are moved, Albion's bowels are being *removed*. Of course, it is also possible to read this image in reverse, that is, to see it as a scene in which Albion, rather than having his bowels removed, is having them installed, "implanted," as Parker puts it, "in the Nature and Constitution of [his] humane" body. If so, the female figures weave his organic life into his body, providing another example of how Albion's "machines are woven with his life." Thus his immediate, inner feelings, the ones tied directly to his viscera, have external sources. Either way, whether the scene depicts embowelment or disembowelment, Blake wants us to see that the seemingly spontaneous, interior movements of the body cannot supply evidence for the authenticity of emotion.

58. "The differend is the unstable state and instant of language wherein something which must be able to be put into phrases cannot yet be . . . This state is signaled by what one ordinarily calls a feeling: 'One cannot find the words,' etc. A lot of searching must be done to find new rules for forming and linking phrases that are able to express the differend disclosed by the feeling . . . What is at stake in a literature, in a philosophy, in a politics perhaps, is to bear witness to differends by finding idioms for them" (Jean-François Lyotard, *The Differend*, trans. Georges Van Den Abbeele [Minneapolis: U of Minnesota P, 1988], 13).

59. Descartes compares humans, animals, and "automata or moving machines" in Part V of *Discourse on the Method for Guiding One's Reason and Searching for Truth in the Sciences*, in *Discourse on Method and Related Writings*, trans. Desmond M. Clarke (London: Penguin, 1999). "[I]f there were such machines with the organs and shape of a monkey or of some other non-rational animal, we would have no way of discovering that they are not the same as these animals. But if there were machines that resembled our bodies and if they imitated our actions as much as is morally possible, we would always have two very certain means of recognizing that, none the less, they are not genuinely human. The first is that they would never be able to use speech . . . The second means is that, even if they did many things as well as or, possibly, better than any one of us, they would infallibly fail in others. Thus one would discover they did not act on the basis of knowledge, but merely as a result of the disposition of their organs" (40–41).

Interlude · Wordsworth's Pulsation Machine

1. "She was a Phantom of delight," in *Poems, in Two Volumes, and Other Poems, 1800–1807*, ed. Jared Curtis (Ithaca: Cornell UP, 1983), 74–75. For Wordsworth's comments on the poem to Isabella Fenwick and Justice Coleridge, see the annotations on 404.

2. William Wordsworth, *The Fourteen-Book Prelude*, ed. W. J. B. Owen (Ithaca: Cornell UP, 1985), 266.

3. "To a Highland Girl," in *Poems, in Two Volumes*, 193.

4. Alice Fulton, *Feeling as a Foreign Language: The Good Strangeness of Poetry* (Saint Paul, MN: Graywolf, 1999).

5. For example, see the note by Michelle Turner Sharp in the Mark Van Doren edition of *Selected Poetry of William Wordsworth* (New York: Modern Library, 2002): "human creature; here, Mary. The word does not carry the connotation of mechanical or machinelike" (732).

6. William Wordsworth, "Lines written a few miles above Tintern Abbey," in *Lyrical Ballads 1798*, ed. W. J. B. Owen, 2nd ed. (Oxford: Oxford UP, 1969), 114. Cited parenthetically hereafter.

7. All of these possibilities, and more, are represented in the *OED* entries on "pulsation" and its cognates. For Emerson's phrase, see "Saadi," in *Ralph Waldo Emerson: Collected Poems and Translations*, ed. Harold Bloom and Paul Kane (New York: Library of America, 1994), 102.

8. Samuel Taylor Coleridge, "The Statesman's Manual," in *Lay Sermons*, ed. R. J. White, *The Collected Works of Samuel Taylor Coleridge*, vol. 6 (Princeton: Princeton UP, 1972), 30.

9. Paul de Man, "Phenomenality and Materiality in Kant," in *Aesthetic Ideology*, ed. Andrzej Warminski (Minneapolis: U of Minnesota P, 1996), 82.

10. De Man, "Kant's Materialism," in *Aesthetic Ideology*, 126–127.

11. De Man's comments in *Allegories of Reading: Figural Language in Rousseau, Nietzsche, Rilke, and Proust* (New Haven: Yale UP, 1979) are also relevant here: "The text as body, with all its implications of substitutive tropes ultimately always retraceable to metaphor, is displaced by the text as machine and, in the process, it suffers the loss of the illusion of meaning" (298).

12. Andy Warhol's "Diamond Dust Shoes, 1980" appears on the cover of Fredric Jameson's *Postmodernism or, The Cultural Logic of Late Capitalism* (Durham: Duke UP, 1991),

where, in contrast to Vincent Van Gogh's "A Pair of Boots," it famously serves as Jameson's first example of postmodernism, with its "new . . . flatness or depthlessness, a new kind of superficiality" and its "waning of affect" (9–10).

13. De Man, "Kant's Materialism," 127.

14. Rei Terada, *Feeling in Theory* (Cambridge, MA: Harvard UP, 2001), 49, 52.

15. T. S. Eliot, "Tradition and the Individual Talent," in *The Sacred Wood* (1920; repr., London: Methuen, 1980), 58.

Chapter 5 · *Criticism and the Work of Emotion*

1. Matthew Arnold, "The Function of Criticism at the Present Time," in *Culture and Anarchy and other writings*, ed. Stefan Collini (Cambridge: Cambridge UP, 1993), 42. Cited parenthetically hereafter.

2. Theodor Adorno, *Aesthetic Theory*, trans. Robert Hullot-Kentor (Minneapolis: U of Minnesota P, 1997), 15.

3. William K. Wimsatt Jr. and Monroe C. Beardsley, "The Affective Fallacy," in Wimsatt, *The Verbal Icon: Studies in the Meaning of Poetry* (Lexington: U of Kentucky P, 1954), 26.

4. So powerful and persistent is Arnold's notion of an oppositional vitality in criticism that a strong semblance makes its way into the work of one of his most strenuous twentieth-century opponents. Describing the need for criticism even within the most committed partisan causes, Edward Said might as well be echoing Arnold's description of Edmund Burke: "I take criticism so seriously as to believe that, even in the very midst of a battle in which one is unmistakably on one side against another, there should be criticism, because there must be critical consciousness if there are to be issues, problems, values, even lives to be fought for." Said adds that "criticism must think of itself as life-enhancing and constitutively opposed to every form of tyranny, domination, and abuse" ("Secular Criticism," in *The World, the Text, and the Critic* [Cambridge, MA: Harvard UP, 1983], 28–29).

5. Immanuel Kant, "An Answer to the Question: 'What Is Enlightenment?' " in *Kant: Political Writings*, ed. Hans Reiss, trans. H. B. Nisbet (Cambridge: Cambridge UP, 1970), 59–60.

6. Immanuel Kant, *The Conflict of the Faculties*, trans. and ed. Mary J. Gregor (Lincoln: U of Nebraska P, 1979), 151.

7. Antonio Negri, *Time for Revolution*, trans. Matteo Mandarini (New York: Continuum, 2003), 165; Eve Kosofsky Sedgwick, *Touching Feeling* (Durham: Duke UP, 2003), 147; Jacques Derrida, *Politics of Friendship*, trans. George Collins (London: Verso, 1997), 69; Isobel Armstrong, *The Radical Aesthetic* (Oxford: Blackwell, 2000), 62; Steven Shaviro, "Pulses of Emotion," in *Without Criteria: Kant, Whitehead, Deleuze, and Aesthetics* (Cambridge, MA: MIT Press, 2009), 68.

8. Franz Kafka, *The Complete Stories and Parables*, ed. Nahum N. Glatzer (New York: Quality Paperback, 1983), 472.

9. Jacques Derrida, "Structure, Sign, and Play in the Discourse of the Human Sciences," in *Writing and Difference*, trans. Alan Bass (Chicago: U of Chicago P, 1978), 292.

10. Saree Makdisi, *William Blake and the Impossible History of the 1790s* (Chicago: U of Chicago P, 2003), 1. Cited parenthetically hereafter.

11. René Descartes, *The Passions of the Soul*, trans. Stephen H. Voss (Indianapolis: Hackett Publishing, 1989), 52.

12. Henry Mackenzie, *The Man of Feeling* (Oxford: Oxford UP, 1987), 40–41.

13. See Jacques Derrida, *Politics of Friendship*, trans. George Collins (London: Verso, 1997), 68–69.

14. Rei Terada, *Feeling in Theory: Emotion after the "Death of the Subject"* (Cambridge, MA: Harvard UP), 14–15. Cited parenthetically hereafter.

15. Susan Wolfson, *Formal Charges: The Shaping of Poetry in British Romanticism* (Stanford: Stanford UP, 1997), 30. Cited parenthetically hereafter. For an astute survey of recent criticism in this area, see Marjorie Levinson's "What Is New Formalism?" *PMLA* 122.2 (Mar. 2007): 558–569. Levinson usefully distinguishes between two types of formalist criticism: an "activist formalism" that sets out to restore the dynamic engagement of form characteristic of the earliest (and most complex) new historicism, and a "backlash" or "normative formalism" that defends the autonomy of art against historicist practice and emphasizes the cognitive or affective work of aesthetic forms (559).

16. Susan Wolfson, "Reading for Form," in *Reading for Form*, ed. Susan J. Wolfson and Marshall Brown, *MLQ*, special issue, 61.1 (Mar. 2000): 2.

17. Derrida, *Politics of Friendship*, 61, 68–69. Cited parenthetically hereafter.

18. Wolfson, "Reading for Form," 15.

19. Preface (1802), in *Lyrical Ballads 1798*, 2nd ed., ed. W. J. B. Owen (Oxford: Oxford UP, 1969), 160.

20. Wolfson, "Reading for Form," 16.

21. Rooney, "Form and Contentment," in Wolfson and Brown, *Reading for Form*, 38.

22. Robert Kaufman, "Red Kant, or The Persistence of the Third *Critique* in Adorno and Jameson," *Critical Inquiry* 26 (Summer 2000): 709.

23. Robert Kaufman, "Everybody Hates Kant: Blakean Formalism and the Symmetries of Laura Moriarty," in Wolfson and Brown, *Reading for Form*, 148.

24. Armstrong, *Radical Aesthetic*, 59. Armstrong puts more emphasis on aesthetic play than on aesthetic construction, but like Kaufman she understands aesthetic experience to be a precondition of new thought and therefore of the possibility of political change. "[O]ur play is . . . the transformation of categories, which constitutes a change in the structure of thought itself: it is not only an aspect of knowledge but the prerequisite of political change" (40–41). "The aesthetic is not the political, but it may make the political possible" (43). Immediately following this sentence, Armstrong turns to a reading of Blake's "Infant Joy" to illustrate her point.

25. I. A. Richards, *Principles of Literary Criticism* (New York: Harcourt Brace Jovanovich, 1925), 248, 251, 246, respectively.

26. Armstrong, *Radical Aesthetic*, 30, 37. Describing Adorno's famous *Ershütterung*, Robert Kaufman provides another example of our current emphasis on the ethical and political value of charged agitation: "Adorno conceives *Ershütterung* as that which, by dint of aura's dynamic of charged distance, can break down the hardening of subjectivity—can break down through this *shaking*, in other words, 'the subject's petrification in his or her own subjectivity' and hence can allow the subject to 'catch . . . the slightest glimpse beyond that prison that it [the 'I'] itself is,' thus permitting 'the "I,"' once 'shaken,' to perceiv[e] its own limitedness and finitude' and so to experience the critical possibility of thinking otherness" ("Aura, Still," *October* 99 [Winter 2002]: 49).

27. Immanuel Kant, *Critique of the Power of Judgment*, trans. Paul Guyer (1790; repr., Cambridge: Cambridge UP, 2000), 97.

28. The crucial text on responsibility is *The Gift of Death* (Chicago: U of Chicago P, 1995), but the topic recurs almost everywhere in Derrida's writing. See, e.g., "Mochlos; or, The Conflict of the Faculties," which begins with a reflection on "university responsibility": "Are we responsible? For what and to whom?" (in *Logomachia: The Conflict of the Faculties*, ed. Richard Rand [Lincoln: U of Nebraska P, 1992], 3). Derrida originally presented this lecture in 1987.

29. Simon Critchley, *Ethics, Politics, Subjectivity* (London: Verso, 1999), 62.

30. Jacques Derrida, *Rogues: Two Essays on Reason*, trans. Pascale-Anne Brault and Michael Naas (Stanford: Stanford UP, 2005), 45.

31. Jacques Derrida, *Specters of Marx*, trans. Peggy Kamuf (New York: Routledge, 1994), 87. Also see Derrida, *Politics of Friendship*, 15.

32. Fredric Jameson, *The Seeds of Time* (New York: Columbia UP, 1994), xii.

33. Derrida, *Rogues*, 152.

34. Here is Derrida describing the formal action of a particular sentence in Nietzsche: "And here again, the shudder of the sentence, the shudder of an arrow of which it is still not known where and how far it will go, the vibration of a shaft of writing which, alone, promises and calls for a reading, a preponderance to come of the interpretive decision. We do not know exactly what is quivering here, but we perceive, in flight, at least a figure of the vibration" (*Politics of Friendship*, 31). It would be difficult not to think of Blake's "Bow of burning gold" and "Arrows of desire" (*Milton* 1, E 95).

35. Derrida, *Rogues*, 25. "We are undeniably the heirs or legatees, the delegates, of this word, and we are saying 'we' here as the very legatees or delegates of this word that has been sent to us, addressed to us for centuries, and that we are always sending or putting off until later" (9).

36. Derrida, *Specters of Marx*, 13.

37. Ibid., 31–32. Unless noted otherwise, all further citations of *Specters* are to these pages.

38. Derrida, *Specters of Marx*, 13.

39. Peggy Kamuf translates "*l'élan révolutionnaire*" as "revolutionary momentum." I have restored the original in order to maintain Derrida's careful balance, in this sentence, between specific historical event (*l'insurrection*, for instance) and spirited, subjective response—what we might call "enthusiasm." See Derrida, *Spectres de Marx* (Paris: Editions Galilée, 1993), 61.

40. See Jacques Derrida, "Of an Apocalyptic Tone Recently Adopted in Philosophy," *Oxford Literary Review* 6.2 (1984): 3–37.

41. With "creaturely," I mean to invoke Levinas's reading of Derrida: "This critique of Being in its eternal presence of ideality allows, for the first time in the history of the West, the thought of the *Being of the creature*." Levinas goes on to add parenthetically, "Derrida will probably deny it" ("Wholly Otherwise," in *Re-reading Levinas*, ed. Robert Bernasconi and Simon Critchley [Bloomington: Indiana UP, 1991], 6).

42. The last phrase comes from *Rogues* (84), another text concerned with "The Neutralization of the Event" (118), as one chapter heading puts it. See esp. p. 143, where Derrida argues that any horizon of concepts ("horizontal ideality") that allows us to recognize or foresee events as they happen neutralizes the future. This horizon "will have neutralized in advance the event, along with everything that, in any historicity worthy of this name, requires the eventfulness of the event."

43. See Derrida, *Rogues*, 1, 7, 37.

44. Thomas Docherty, *Aesthetic Democracy* (Stanford: Stanford UP, 2006), 69.

45. Docherty's "event" recalls Blake's idea of "impossible history," which erupts both unpredictably and all the time, even as it eludes the weakened perception of historians who see only the "dull round of probabilities and possibilities." The "event" also recalls Blake's interest in the renovative moment "Satans watch fiends cannot find," when "All the Great Events of Time Start Forth." All of *Milton*, it has been suggested, is about enabling that one impossible, eventful moment—and enabling it *while one reads*. In *Milton*, Ian Balfour writes, the "moment of descent and self-sacrifice is in some sense the only real action of the poem," and "it may be that all of *Milton* can be thought of as the allegory of one such impossible act" (*The Rhetoric of Romantic Prophecy* (Stanford: Stanford UP, 2002), 163, 140).

46. Derrida, *Rogues*, 84.

47. Plato, "Ion," in *Two Comic Dialogues: Ion and Hippias Major*, trans. Paul Woodruff (Indianapolis: Hackett, 1983), 25.

48. Jean-François Lyotard, "Judiciousness in Dispute, or Kant after Marx," trans. Cecile Lindsay, in *The Lyotard Reader*, ed. Andrew Benjamin (Oxford: Blackwell, 1989), 328.

49. Nicholas Williams, *Ideology and Utopia in the Poetry of William Blake* (Cambridge: Cambridge UP, 1998), 2.

50. Fredric Jameson, *Postmodernism, or The Cultural Logic of Late Capitalism* (Durham: Duke UP, 1991), 5–6.

51. Williams, *Ideology*, 19.

52. Williams explains "Mannheim's paradox" (named after the work of Karl Mannheim in the 1930s) in terms of "[t]he curious position of the ideology critic, whose own critique is itself subject to the charge of ideology" (9). According to Williams, Blake's notion of "mind-forg'd manacles" is conceptually "the equivalent of Mannheim's paradox" (19). In this context, Thomas Pfau's reading of Blake's "paranoid and conspiratorial figures" (98) within the pervasive paranoia of the 1790s is also relevant. According to Pfau's general characterization, the paranoiac recognized something closely akin to Mannheim's paradox and Jameson's "'winner loses' logic": "that the very transformation he had sought to defend against by indicting it as someone else's as yet unconsummated design has already succeeded and, consequently, has also shaped his anxious outlook on it, perhaps even made him an unwilling co-conspirator in it . . . The paranoid subject gradually comes to recognize its own suspicious intelligence as the unwitting instrument for bringing about an outcome that it had sought to preempt by its contestation of established values" (*Romantic Moods: Paranoia, Trauma, and Melancholy, 1790–1840* [Baltimore: Johns Hopkins UP, 2005], 83–84).

53. G. E. Bentley Jr., *The Stranger from Paradise: A Biography of William Blake* (New Haven: Yale UP, 2001).

54. Although few have pursued it with Makdisi's passion, the transformative power of reading is one of the most persistent themes of Blake criticism. For Nicholas Williams, too, reading becomes the means of revolutionary transformation, the one act necessary to effect a transition from ideology to utopia. Drawing on Ernst Bloch's concept of "concrete utopia," Williams argues that utopia need not negate material or historical reality but can rather fulfill it, realizing its existing but latent potentiality. "The problem of a utopia, then, as it is expressed in Blake, is not that of an escape from history, but instead the strategic problem of history's culmination, how to retain the particulars of history while bringing them to utopian perfection. This is the problem of a revolutionary consciousness faced with seemingly intractable fallenness, the utopian problematic of change" (*Ideology*, 31). In each of Williams's thoughtful engagements with Blake's poetry, this strategic problem is over-

come by the agency of reading. To mention just one example, when Williams discusses the troubling return to a language of "net[s] and trap[s]" (94) in Oothoon's last, ecstatic speech in *Visions of the Daughters of Albion*, he raises a necessary question: Doesn't this repetition suggest that utopian freedoms have failed to emerge, and that the realm of ideology extends itself right through to the poem's end? Not so, writes Williams, for Blake requires us "to adopt a new way of reading," one that emphasizes the "difference in the image between its ideological and its utopian reflection" (93). In other words, reading allows us to bring out the utopian latency within the ideological reality, to see that even "nets and traps" have the potential to be otherwise. "It is not a question of abandoning the ideological world, but of teasing utopian significations out of ideological forms" (96). In practice, concrete utopia is the byproduct of reading.

55. "In this sense," writes Makdisi, "Blake rejects systems of knowledge whose decipherment and interpretation require training, preparation, and rational examination, require the aid of . . . scholarly weaponry" (*William Blake and the Impossible History of the 1790s*, 317). Just as Derrida claims that one should not read Marx as a scholar (to do so is to miss his ghosts), Makdisi claims one cannot read Blake as a scholar without missing his most important aspect, his enthusiasm.

56. "That Blake seeks to undermine the sovereignty of the text, and indeed sovereignty as such, . . . can in this context no longer amount simply to a certain playfulness with words, but must also be recognized as a profoundly political activity" (Makdisi, *William Blake and the Impossible History of the 1790s*, 69). Furthermore, "Far more than most literary and artistic work, Blake reminds us of the extent to which all texts are open and virtual; and hence, far more than most, it frees us from the determinism of those texts that pretend to be closed and definite" (169).

57. Docherty, *Aesthetic Democracy*, xvii; John Guillory, "The Ethical Practice of Modernity: The Example of Reading," in *The Turn to Ethics*, ed. Marjorie Garber, Beatrice Hanssen, and Rebecca L. Walkowitz (New York: Routledge, 2000), 30–31; Jean-Paul Sartre, *The Emotions: Outline of a Theory*, trans. Bernard Frechtman (New York: The Philosophical Library, 1948), 58–59. Further citations to these texts appear parenthetically.

58. Drawing upon *Either/Or*, Docherty argues that "action is to be replaced by passion, that passionate commitment to ambiguity as such, that [Kierkegaard] identifies as 'the passion of the possible'" (*Aesthetic Democracy*, 86). An authentic and democratic culture, he asserts, requires the kind of urgent "critical consciousness" that allows one "to inhabit potentiality in this unsettling way" (xviii). Criticism aims "to make culture happen, to bring about the event that reveals the extraordinary by making us step out of that which is ordinary for us" (xvii). This announcement of objectives appears just after the passage on fantasy I quoted as an epigraph above.

59. Guillory contrasts reading practices in terms of what he calls "professional" and "lay" reading. Schematically, professional reading is compensated labor, a disciplinary activity, a vigilant activity, emphasizing reflection over pleasure, and a communal practice engaged with other professional readers. Lay reading is a leisure activity, an activity with its own set of conventions, an activity emphasizing pleasure, and a solitary practice. See 31–33.

60. Preface to *Prometheus Unbound*, in *Shelley's Poetry and Prose*, ed. Donald H. Reiman and Neil Fraistat (New York: Norton, 2002), 208–209.

61. John Guillory, *Cultural Capital: The Problem of Literary Canon Formation* (Chicago: U of Chicago P, 1993), 340.

62. Michel Foucault, "What Is Enlightenment?" trans. Catherine Porter, in *The Foucault Reader,* ed. Paul Rabinow (New York: Pantheon, 1984), 50.

63. John Milton, *Paradise Lost,* in *The Riverside Milton,* ed. Roy Flannagan (Boston: Houghton Mifflin, 1998), 362.

64. Armstrong, *Radical Aesthetic,* 57.

65. Guillory, *Cultural Capital,* 340.

66. "Ratify" is a verb Fredric Jameson uses to describe the work of emotion in Sartre: "Sartre has spoken of the way emotion, to strengthen itself, to ratify the merely mental reaction with the solidity of the flesh, fills itself out with physical concomitants, such as blushing, trembling, cold sweat: these are the moments of 'seriousness' in real emotion" (94). Jameson recognizes, in other words, that Sartrean emotion serves to substantiate and embody experiences that might otherwise remain merely phenomenological, unrealized anywhere but in the mind. It remains unclear, however, whether Jameson sees this kind of emotional "transformation" as a wish-fulfilling fantasy or as a participation in actual, historical dynamism, for his own analysis of Sartre renders it either way at different times. Thus Sartrean emotion is "a kind of second-best intoxication" that compensates for the "stubborn perseverance" of a seemingly immutable world (92)—an embodied fantasia that erupts when change outside one's own body seems impossible—but it is also a nearly apocalyptic experience that tears away false appearances of stability to reveal a rupturing historical turbulence beneath: "the revelation of the historical nature of something thought of as permanent and changeless" (*Sartre: The Origins of a Style* [1961; repr., New York: Columbia UP, 1984], 95). Already in his first book, based on his doctoral dissertation, Jameson understands the strong appeal of the emotions as an index of change. While their very appeal renders the emotions suspect, he is not ready to give them up, especially when faced with the anxiety of blocked history: "a massive appearance of permanence [that] restricts not only the development of individual destinies but even the mobility of ideas and the spontaneity of our language" (92).

67. Alan Liu, *The Laws of Cool: Knowledge Work and the Culture of Information* (Chicago: U of Chicago P, 2004).

68. Pierre Bourdieu, *Distinction: A Social Critique of the Judgement of Taste,* trans. Richard Nice (Cambridge: Harvard UP, 1984), 495–497.

69. See, e.g., Tristanne J. Connolly: "the need to learn the associations of Blake's cryptic, invented mythology . . . does keep Blake's later works secret from most who have not proceeded to the cloister of postgraduate study" (*William Blake and the Body* [Basingstoke: Palgrave, 2002]), 12–13).

70. This back-cover prediction comes courtesy of Jon Mee.

71. Brian Massumi, *Parables for the Virtual: Movement, Affect, Sensation* (Durham: Duke UP, 2002), 3. Further citations appear parenthetically.

72. Paul de Man, "Sign and Symbol in Hegel's *Aesthetics,*" in *Aesthetic Ideology,* ed. Andrzej Warminski (Minneapolis: U of Minnesota P, 1996), 92.

73. Consider Sianne Ngai's brilliant recent work, *Ugly Feelings* (Cambridge, MA: Harvard UP, 2005). In one sense, Ngai's discussion of emotions involved in situations of "suspended" or "restricted agency" would seem a useful counterpoint to any association between emotion and agency. "Ugly" emotions arise precisely when, for one reason or another, we *cannot* act; they hang about us as reminders that we cannot transform the world. At the same time, however, Ngai credits these emotions with a critical or diagnostic function. Despite their appearance of passivity, they act as readings or "interpretations" of the very

"predicaments" that disable agency, providing crucial information about "general state[s] of obstructed agency" that lie beyond our current powers of articulation or conceptualization. These unpleasant emotions, in other words, provide critical access to situational constraints we may not otherwise perceive. "[P]art of this book's agenda," Ngai writes, is "to recuperate several of these negative affects for their *critical* productivity" (1–3). To the extent that *ugly* feelings get rehabilitated as *critical* feelings (productive forms of critical engagement)—and to the extent that aversion, even in situations of suspension and constraint, opens onto the possibility of future agency, acting as a prelude to empowerment—these useful, recuperated feelings hardly seem ugly at all. One irony of Ngai's argument is that, taken to its logical conclusion, it leaves us altogether without ugly feelings.

74. Even de Man came to realize that absence of feeling is in fact no alternative to the danger of deception in feeling, for apatheia is not an emotional vacuum but another affective state. In certain conditions, moreover, apatheia is a *desirable* state, arousing admiration in others and providing a satisfying moral distinction for those who seem to have achieved it. One thinks of Wordsworth's "Old Man Traveling." For these reasons, in the revisions of his late essays on Kantian aesthetics, de Man downplays the apatheia that at first appealed so powerfully to him, discrediting this condition *because* it appeals so powerfully, and finally identifying it as one more vehicle of "[m]oral nobility . . . the best ego booster available" ("Phenomenality and Materiality in Kant," in *Aesthetic Ideology*, 84–85). Over the course of revising his understanding of the Kantian sublime (a topic first addressed in his lecture on "Kant's Materialism"), de Man seems to have discovered that apatheia is yet another emotional state masquerading as the absence of emotion.

75. Reading the famous "roots" passage in *Nausea*, Jameson describes Sartre's effort to turn prosopopoeia and anthropomorphism against themselves. In this case the lingering, exaggerated prosopopoeia calls attention to its own rhetorical inadequacy, to the paradox that access to things "mute, stubborn, inaccessible" comes only by "render[ing them] in the language of that which absolutely they are not," "through a process of humanization." Rather than pretending to represent radical otherness transparently, as if that were possible, "the extreme humanization of things is the one formulation of them which will not falsify them: we know that they are not human, that they are the absolutely non-human, and the terms are sufficiently exaggerated for us to make no mistake about it." Thus when Sartre provides the alien world with a face in *The Emotions* or when he writes (in Bernard Frechtman's shrewd translation), "In order that an object may in reality appear *terrible*, it must realize itself as an immediate or magical presence *face to face* with consciousness" (87), he is not humanizing the alien but demonstrating the limits of language. Writing on the anthropomorphism in *Nausea*, Jameson comes very close to observing the horror effect of the face flattened against the windowpane in Sartre's *The Emotions*: "behind this terrifying suddenly human *mask*, the inhuman being of things makes its presence felt" (emphasis added; *Sartre: The Origins of a Style*, 108–109). For another reading of Sartre's face at the window, see the conclusion to Terada's *Feeling in Theory*, 152–157.

76. Mary Shelley, *Frankenstein*, 2nd ed., ed. D. L. Macdonald and Kathleen Scherf (Peterborough, Ontario: Broadview, 1999), 190–191.

77. "In horror," writes Sartre, "we suddenly perceive the upsetting of the deterministic barriers. That face which appears at the pane—we do not first take it as belonging to a man who might open the door and with a few steps come right up to us. On the contrary, he is given, passive as he is, as acting at a distance. He is in immediate connection, on the other

side of the window, with our body; we live and undergo his signification, and it is with our own flesh that we establish it. But at the same time it obtrudes itself; it denies the distance and enters into us." No longer an instrument in a world of instruments, the window does not have to be opened or broken or entered in order for this face to touch or affect us. Even our bodily response, our experience of horror, "is no longer *ours*; it is the expression of the face, the movements of the body of the other person which come to form a synthetic whole with the disturbance of our organism" (*The Emotions: Outline of a Theory,* 85–86).

78. According to Robert C. Solomon, Sartre understands emotions as "voluntary ways in which we alter our consciousness of events and things to give us a more pleasing view of the world . . . [O]ur emotions are strategies we employ to avoid action, to avoid responsibility, to 'flee from freedom,' in the language of *Being and Nothingness*" (Solomon, *What Is an Emotion?* 2nd ed. (Oxford: Oxford UP, 2003), 191–192. According to Jerome Neu, Sartre "believes *all* emotions are actions," though "not, to be sure, . . . ordinary intentional action." "This is a reversal of ordinary assumptions as radical as [William] James's. We usually regard emotions as rooted in the body and thus as at least partly passive, as the word *passions* might itself suggest—things that sweep over us without our will or consent." Sartre, however, "gives us a sense of being more responsible for our lives than we might like to believe," representing emotion not only as action but "as chosen" (Neu, *A Tear Is an Intellectual Thing: The Meanings of Emotion* [Oxford: Oxford UP, 2000], 26–27).

79. Richard Sha provocatively links "the electric flame of Milton's awful precipitate descent" to John Birch's experiments with "medical electricity." Birch treated Blake's wife Catherine for swelling in her legs. See *Perverse Romanticism: Aesthetics and Sexuality in Britain, 1750–1832* (Baltimore: Johns Hopkins UP, 2009), 216–217.

80. "Consciousness can never be anything else than conscious existence, and the existence of men is their actual life-process. If in all ideology men and their circumstances appear upside-down as in a *camera obscura,* this phenomenon arises just as much from their historical life-process as the inversion of objects on the retina does from their physical life-process" (Karl Marx and Frederick Engels, *The German Ideology,* ed. C. J. Arthur [New York: International Publishers, 1970], 47). Blake uses the image of roots in air elsewhere, most prominently in the speech of the "nameless shadowy female" (1:1, E 60) early in *Europe*: "My roots are brandish'd in the heavens. my fruits in earth beneath / Surge, foam, and labour into life, first born & first consum'd! / Consumed and consuming!" (1:8–10, E 60). Here inversion is the symptom of a perspective rooted in an ideology of cyclical generation.

81. "This was the grand error of the French Revolution; and its movement of ideas, by quitting the intellectual sphere and rushing furiously into the political one, ran, indeed, a prodigious and memorable course, but produced no such intellectual fruit as the movement of ideas of the Renascence" (Arnold, "The Function of Criticism at the Present Time," 33).

82. "So Los spoke. But lightnings of discontent broke on all sides round / And murmurs of thunder rolling heavy long & loud over the mountains" (25:63–64, E 122).

83. Susie Tucker quotes this definition from the *Grub Street Journal* in 1735: "*Enthusiasm* is any exorbitant monstrous Appetite of the Human Mind, hurrying the Will in Pursuit of an Object without the Concurrency or against the Light of Reason and Common Sense" (*Enthusiasm: A Study in Semantic Change* [Cambridge: Cambridge UP, 1972], 18).

Index